SOCIAL AND CULTURAL DYNAMICS

SOCIAL & CULTURAL DYNAMICS

A Study of Change in Major Systems of Art, Truth, Ethics, Law and Social Relationships

Revised and abridged in one volume by the author

PITIRIM SOROKIN

extending horizons books — Porter Sargent Publisher — Boston

Second Printing, November 1970

Library of Congress Catalog Number 57-14120
ISBN 0-87558-029-7

FOREWORD

Some twenty years have passed since the original publication of *Social and Cultural Dynamics* in four volumes. During this period, numerous popularizations of the work have appeared in the form of articles, doctoral theses, chapters in texts on sociological theories, and books like my own *Crisis of Our Age* (so far translated into eight languages), F. R. Cowell's *History, Civilization and Culture: An Introduction to the Historical and Social Philosophy of P. A. Sorokin*, Winston C. P. Fan's *Introduction to P. A. Sorokin's Theories* (in Chinese), Jacques J. Maquet's *Sociologie de la Connaissance* (*The Sociology of Knowledge* in American edition), Johanne Gjermoe's *P. A. Sorokin's Social and Historical Philosophy* (in Norwegian), among others. However admirable these popularizations, they in no way suffice as an authentic abridged version of the *Dynamics*. None of these works reproduces verbatim the text, the order of chapters of *Dynamics*; neither do they outline all of the important theories developed in it.

During these twenty years I have been urged by several scholars and readers to prepare a one-volume abridgement of this work which, by cutting out all the secondary paragraphs, pages and chapters of the original text, would reproduce verbatim all its important parts in exactly the same order and phrasing in which they were originally given in the four volumes. In the friendly opinion of these scholars and readers such an abridgement would make the *Dynamics* accessible to a large circle of scholars and intelligent readers who would otherwise have neither the time to study nor the means to purchase the bulky four-volume edition. When *Extending Horizons Books* of Boston in February, 1957, and the *Instituto de Estudios Politicos* of Madrid offered to bring out such an edition respectively in English and Spanish, I accepted and this one-volume edition upon which I immediately set to work, is the result of my abridgement.

The condensation of *Dynamics* to one-fourth of its original size is effected by cutting out: (1) all the paragraphs and pages of secondary importance; (2) practically all the numerous foot-notes; (3) references and extensive bibliography; (4) all the appendixes and the sources on which the statistical tables and their respective conclusions are based ; and, finally, (5) the first eleven chapters of the fourth volume. Of these omitted parts, the numbers: 2, 3, 4, 5 are cut out not because they are unimportant, but for the reason that they are not urgently necessary for comprehension of the basic conceptual framework of the *Dynamics*, and because they can easily be found by any probing researcher in the unabridged edition of the work. So much for explanation of what is omitted and reproduced in this abridged edition.

Now a few words about what is added to, and changed from the original text of the work. Besides a basic bibliography, a few short paragraphs are added to bring the development of main trends and fluctuations up to date. While the quantitative evidence and qualitative analysis of *Dynamics* (published in 1937–41) does not go beyond the years 1925–30, added paragraphs outline briefly what, if any, important changes have occurred during this recent period, also which of the old trends have continued, and whether several forecastings of the *Dynamics* have come to pass. In this way, the analysis of the Western sociocultural world is brought up to date.

As to the changes in the original text of the work, practically no change is made because none is needed. Since the original publication historical events have been unfolding according to its diagnosis and prognosis, and its main forecastings have been coming to pass during the last twenty years. There is no need for correction of any of its significant propositions, since up to this moment, the historical processes have been proceeding as outlined.

In accordance with these prognoses, three basic processes of the last few decades have consisted in: (a) an epochal shift of the creative center of mankind from Europe to the larger area of the Pacific-Atlantic ; (b) in a progressive disintegration of Sensate culture, society, and man; and (c) in an emergence and slow growth of the first seedlings of the new — Idealistic or Ideational — sociocultural order.

We all know that up to roughly the fourteenth century the creative leadership of mankind was carried on by the peoples and nations of Asia and Africa. While our forefathers in the West had still a most primitive way of life and culture, in Africa and Asia the great civilizations — the Egyptian, the Babylonic, the Iranic, the Summerian, the Hittite, the Hindu, the Chinese, the Mediterranean (the Creto-Mycenaean, the Graeco-Roman, the Arabic) and others — emerged, grew, and fluctuated in their repeated blossoming and decay for millennia. The Western, Euro-American, peoples were the latest in taking the creative leadership of mankind. They have carried this torch only during the last five or six centuries. During this short period they discharged their creative mission brilliantly, especially in the fields of science, technology, Sensate fine arts, politics, and economics. At the present time, however, the European monopolistic leadership can be considered as about ended. The unfolding of the history of mankind is already being staged on the much larger scenery of Asiatic-African-American-European cosmopolitan theater. And the stars of the next acts of the great historical drama are going to be: besides Europe, the Americas, Russia, and renascent great cultures of India, China, Japan, Indonesia, and Islamic world. This epochal shift is already under way and is rapidly moving from day to day. It has manifested itself in the dissolution of the great European empires like the British and the French, in the decreasing political and cultural influence of Europe in the international relationships, in the shift of creativity from several European nations to other continents: the Anglo-Saxon to the United States, Canada, and Australia; the Spanish and Portuguese to the Latin America; in the creative growth of the Asiatic Russia in comparison with its European part, and so on. A still stronger manifestation of this shift is the unquestionable renaissance of the great cultures of Asia and Africa: the Indian, the Chinese, the Japanese, the Indonesian, the Arabic, and others. This renaissance lies at the basis of a successful liberation of these nations from Colonial servitude. It has shown itself in a rapid growth of their political and social independence, and of their influence in international affairs; in their rapid scientific and technological development, in the successful diffusion of their religious, philosophical, ethical, artistic and cultural values in the Western world; as also many other phenomena mark the shift of the creative leadership of mankind from the monopolistic domination of Europe to the Americas, Asia, and Africa. Such is the first basic sociocultural process of the last few decades.

The other two processes: a continued decay of Sensate sociocultural system of the West and an emergence and growth of a new — Idealistic or Ideational — sociocultural order are possibly still more important for the present and the future of mankind. Both these trends increasingly manifest themselves in all compartments of Western culture and society: in the dynamic changes in science, philosophy, religion, fine arts, ethics, law, politics, and economics, in remodeling of our social institutions, in revaluation of our system of values, and in the transformation of our mentality and overt behavior. Our whole social, cultural, and personal way of life is in the state of a tragic and epochal transition from the dying Sensate culture of our magnificent yesterday to the coming new culture of the creative tomorrow. We are living, thinking, and acting at the darkest hour of this transitory night with its nightmares, gigantic destruction, and heartrending horrors. If mankind can avoid the irretrievable catastrophe of greater world wars, the dawn of a new magnificent order in the human universe is waiting to greet the coming generations.

PITIRIM A. SOROKIN,
Harvard University, 1957

PUBLISHER'S NOTE: For those who wish to refer to the original four-volume edition, the following concordance:

Vol. I, pp. 1–224 *of the present edition*
II, pp. 226–434
III, pp. 436–628
IV, pp. 630–704

TABLE OF CONTENTS

PLATES, FIGURES AND TABLES

For technical reasons, it has been necessary in this abridged edition to retain the numbering of the plates, figures, and tables of the original four-volume edition.

PLATES

FIGURES from Volume II

FIGURES from Volume III

TABLES

TABLES from Volume I

TABLES from Volume II

TABLES from Volume III

PART ONE

INTRODUCTORY

I

FORMS AND PROBLEMS OF CULTURE INTEGRATION AND METHODS OF THEIR STUDY

I. Culture Integration and Culture Unity — a Dark Problem

Is every culture an integrated whole, where no essential part is incidental but each is organically connected with the rest? Or is it a mere spatial congeries of cultural objects, values, traits, which have drifted fortuitously together and are united only by their spatial adjacency, just by the fact that they are thrown together, and by nothing more? If it is the first, then what is the principle of integration, the axis around which all the essential characteristics are centered and which explains why these characteristics are what they are and why they live and pulsate as they do? If the second, then how did it happen that in a given area one kind of conglomeration of cultural objects and values took place, while in another area a different kind occurred?

For the moment it is unimportant how we define human culture. *In the broadest sense it may mean the sum total of everything which is created or modified by the conscious or unconscious activity of two or more individuals interacting with one another or conditioning one another's behavior.* According to this definition, not only science, philosophy, religion, art, technics, and all the physical paraphernalia of an advanced civilization are cultural phenomena; but the trace of a footstep on the sand left by a savage and seen by Robinson Crusoe, a heap of refuse and broken trees left by an exploring party in a virgin forest, the bones and shells and ashes left by some prehistoric tribe in the ground excavated by an archeologist — these and millions of other human creations and modifications are all a part of culture.

II. Various Meanings of Culture Integration

Many of us are familiar with the fine living rooms of some of our well-to-do friends. I have in mind just such a room. It is spacious and is filled with exquisite furniture and rare art objects. There are a few pieces of antique New England furniture. The ceremonial costume of a Russian priest ("riza") is fastened on one of the walls. Side by side with it there is a picture of a famous Japanese school of painting. Then there are two works by a French Impressionist, and one by a prominent cubistic painter. There are also an Italian Primitive, two genuine statues of

Buddha imported from Siam, two Chinese vases of the T'ang period, and several other treasures of different times and countries. On the floors antique Oriental rugs lie near a hooked rug of old New England. The living room is a "culture area." Now the question arises: Is the culture represented by the living room an integrated whole, or is it a mere spatial conglomeration of various things (each valuable separately), and is this adjacency the only bond which unites them into a single cultural complex?

Let us assume for a moment that spatial adjacency is the only bond of union. Shall we then style an array of this sort by the term "integrated culture"? Or shall we refuse the term to such accumulations?

Whether or not we grant the term is of little importance. What is important is that there do exist cultural conglomerations where the parts are bound together by different and additional ties.

Let us turn, for further instances, to "immaterial" culture. Suppose we take, on the one hand, August Comte's *System of Positive Philosophy* and, on the other, one of the recent elementary texts in social problems. Putting aside the question as to whether or not this or that theory expounded in these works is true, throughout all the volumes of Comte there runs a unity of fundamental principles which binds all the chapters logically. Without Comte's law of the three states connected with his classification of sciences and principles of positive knowledge the chapters lose their chief meaning. The work is inwardly integrated by the logic of its main principles. In the text on social problems, however, usually one chapter treats of poverty, the next of crime, the third of fascism or communism, the next of case method, the next of religion, another of the city and the farmer. Something may be said on ecology; ecology is perhaps followed by a chapter on the negro and race problems; then all this farrago is further enriched by pages on the family and birth control, the League of Nations, and countless other subjects. When one tries to find out what unites all these topics, one often finds only the binding of the book. They are connected neither logically nor functionally. The book has become a dumping place for a miscellaneous heap of topics, theories, ideas, and facts; their only connection is that of spatial adjacency.

Enough of illustration. It has already sufficiently shown that there are various forms of integration which differ from one another fundamentally. Now we can attempt to order them and to reduce their multiplicity to the simpler form of a few fundamental classes with an indication of the basis of integration in each class.

III. Classification of the Main Forms of the Integration of Culture Elements

All the numerous interrelations of the various elements of culture can be reduced to four basic types: (1) *Spatial or Mechanical Adjacency*, ranging from a loose and accidental concurrence of two or more cultural objects to a mechanical union of the elements into one structural unity (say, glued or cemented or sewn or tied together); (2) *Association Due to an External Factor;* (3) *Causal or Functional Integration;* (4) *Internal or Logico-meaningful Unity.*

A. *Spatial or Mechanical Adjacency* (*Congeries*). This means any conglomeration of cultural elements (objects, traits, values, ideas) in a given area of social and physical space, with spatial or mechanical concurrence as the only bond of union. A dump in which are fragments of a great variety of objects — pieces of paper, broken bottles, empty cans, fragments of clothing, discarded spoons, wire, garbage, furniture, ashes, coal, tools — offers an example of such a combination. All these objects just drifted or were thrown together, and this is the only bond that unites them. An untidy attic, with its miscellaneous array of many articles, is yet another example. The same thing can be said of the cases of the spatial conglomeration of various architectural styles and of the logically unrelated discussions of various social problems within the limits of one book. Two pieces of paper (say, a page from Plato's *Republic* and the advertisement of an automobile company) glued together into one meaningless mechanical unity; a piece of wood nailed to a remnant of a shoe without any meaning or function as an instrument for anything; an Ionic or Corinthian column attached to a flat-roofed garage without architectural, aesthetic, or structural significance — these and hundreds of similar combinations are examples of the spatial and purely mechanical congeries of various cultural objects and values. As a matter of fact, what anthropologists call a culture area is often nothing more than a spatial adjacency of the traits and complexes of the area in question.

B. *Indirect Association through a Common External Factor.* A somewhat greater unification occurs in such cases where two or more culture elements, spatially adjacent but with no functional or logical connection, are also related to one another through the association of each with a common factor external to both or all of them. In the northern part of Vologda province in North Russia, for example, the following culture elements exist together: *vodka* as a beverage, skis used by the peasants in the winter time, houses built out of heavy timber, large stoves for heating, felt winter boots, the gathering together during the winter evenings of the boys and girls in each of their houses in turn, the performance of plays, singing, and love making. None of these elements requires the others either logically or functionally. *Vodka* as such does not require skis or felt boots; felt boots do not require a large stove or specific forms of winter-evening entertainment. But all of these traits are perceptibly connected with the climatic conditions of the area with its cold and its long winters. Each trait, through its connection with the climatic factor, is likewise affiliated indirectly with the other traits. As a result we have a unification of heterogeneous culture elements, not only spatially but also through their connection with one common external factor. That is the unification talked of by many sociological and anthropological integrators.

C. *Causal or Functional Integration.* By this is meant a combination of cultural elements in which they compose one causal (functional) unity. Usually, where the elements are "material," functional unity is superimposed upon spatial adjacency and external association, but not every spatially adjacent or externally related combination will be a functionally integrated unity. The parts of an automobile spread over the floor of a factory or packed into one box before being assembled into one functional whole, the finished automobile, are a mere spatial array. When they are assembled into one whole, their combination becomes functional and operates so that every important part depends upon the others. The same can be said of the house in contradistinction to the sum of the materials of which it is built: stone, cement, bricks, timber, paint, nails, and so on. Dumped together in one yard these elements form a mere heap of contiguous parts. When the house is built, it is a structural and functional unity.

Similarly, causal or functional unity is likewise of a far higher degree of integration than that of a number of elements spatially adjacent but also related through a common external factor. In a functional array as a rule the parts are related to one another directly, or, if indirectly, by several internal "centers" which are closer to them in essential nature than would be the case in a purely external integration. Not every cell of an organism or bolt in a car is adjacent or directly related to all the other cells or parts. But all the cells are directly connected through the nervous system, the blood circulation, and the organs, just as the bolts or other parts are united through the whole frame of the car, the electric system, and so on. And these unifying factors are all internal to the system itself.

But the simple cases we have been considering are far from exhausting the problems of the functional integration of cultural elements. The field is infinitely larger and more important. In order to make this clear, a few diagnostic criteria of the functional relationship between the parts of a cultural configuration should be pointed out. Simply stated, they consist chiefly of the *tangible, noticeable, testifiable,*[20] *direct interdependence (mutual or one-sided) of the variables or parts upon one another and upon the whole system.* If variation A is always followed by B (under the same conditions and in a large enough number of cases so that mere chance is eliminated), we say that they are functionally related. *This means that any cultural synthesis is to be regarded as functional, when, on the one hand, the elimination of one of its important elements perceptibly influences the rest of the synthesis in its functions* (*and usually in its structure*); *and when, on the other hand, the separate element, being transposed to a quite different combination, either cannot exist in it or has to undergo a profound modification to become a part of it.* Such is the symptomatic barometer of internal integration, a barometer which simply applies the principle of causality or functionalism to each case in question.

One can now see the profound difference between mere spatial adjacency, between external unification, and the deeper synthesis of functional unity. A bolt or spring taken from an unassembled pile of automobile parts does not modify the pile essentially; removed from an assembled car, it may completely impede the performance of the car. Moreover, the bolt or spring itself does not change in significance when removed from a miscellaneous heap, but if it be detached from a machine in which it performs an essential function, it loses that function entirely.

Let us now pass on to more complex examples. Can we take, say, the stock-market system of Wall Street from the modern capitalistic type of economic organization and transpose it, say, to the society of the Trobriands? The answer is that as soon as this is done, the capitalist system of economy here fails to function normally for lack of the stock market, while among the Trobriands, Wall Street does not have any chance to exist or survive generally in the form which it has in the United States. This means that the stock market is essentially a functional part of the American economic system. Suppose we should take the parliamentary regime in its English form, together with the principles of contractual relations and of the equality of all citizens before the law, and the other democratic tenets of Victorian England, and transplant them in the Hindu caste society. The results would be similar; the democratic politico-juridical complex can hardly be grafted on the caste-society tree and yet retain the same form which it had; it would either die or be changed enormously. On the other hand, the rest of the Victorian democratic sociopolitical system could hardly function as it did without the aid of the transplanted parts of the complex. As a matter of fact, even in Continental European societies, where the configuration of cultural elements differs from that of England, though by less than does the Hindu, the parliamentary system has never functioned in the way in which it does in England. One has only to glance at the history of parliamentarism in Germany, Austria, Russia, or Italy to perceive the difference.

In brief, in any culture area there are always present in the totality of the traits, patterns, objects, and values of which it consists, complexes which represent a functional integration.

There is no need to stress the fact that *the degree of functional unity or functional interdependence is everywhere not the same:* it fluctuates from unity to unity; in some cases it is exceedingly close, in others looser, until finally it imperceptibly passes into either a mere external unity or even a mere spatial adjacency.

In sociology and the social sciences there is a multitude of theories that attempt to describe and interpret culture generally along the lines of functional unity. All the theories that take some specific variable internal to a culture (whether it be modes of production, technique and invention, religion, morals, art and science, philosophy and forms of government) and try to "explain" all or the majority of the other characteristics of the culture in question as a "function" or "superstructure" or "effect" of this variable: all such theories, as I have already suggested, assume the existence of a causal-functional integration between the parts. In other words, their promulgators appear to be partisans of the view of the functional unity of all culture elements.

In view of the virtual unanimity of opinion it is unnecessary to insist upon the existence of the causal-functional sort of integration as a form *sui generis*. But the application of the theory is to be somewhat moderated. We have seen and shall see that not all the components of any culture are linked together causally, but only a part of them. In any culture there are also spatial and external unities where no causal association in the narrow sense can be found. And in many cultural complexes there are "logico-meaningful" unities, different from the causal-functional. Therefore it is fallacious to assume, as many causalists do, that every conglomeration of cultural objects is a functional unity and that there must be a functional connection between all of the components.

D. *Logico-meaningful Integration of Culture.* Having beclouded the true nature of functional integration by being unable to distinguish its elements from those of spatial adjacency and external association in highly heterogeneous conglomerations of cultural elements, many integrators have also failed to see that above functional integration proper there is an additional form of association quite different from it, and more different still from the spatial and external types of unification. For lack of a better term, I style this the Logico-meaningful Integration of Culture. This is integration in its supreme form. In what does it consist? What are its qualities? Suppose we have before us the scattered pages of a great poem, or of Kant's *Critique of Pure Reason*, or fragments of the statue of Venus of Milo, or the scattered pages of the score of Beethoven's *Third Symphony*. If we know the proper patterns of meaning and value, we can put these pages or parts together into a significant unity in which each page or fragment takes its proper place, acquires a meaning, and in which all together give the supremely integrated effect that was intended. I say "supremely integrated" because in such instances each part, when set in its designated position, is no longer noticeable as a part, but all the parts together form, as it were, a seamless garment. Their unification is far closer than that of mere functional association. The connection is similar in nature to that between the premises, "All human beings are mortal," and "Socrates is a human being," and the conclusion, "Ergo, Socrates is mortal." Is this connection functional? Hardly, unless we broaden the meaning of functional to such an extent that it loses distinct meaning altogether.

What must be used are the *logical* laws of identity, contradiction, consistency; and it is these laws of logic which must be employed to discover whether any synthesis is or is not *logico-meaningful.* Side by side with such logical laws, in the narrow sense, the broader principles of "keeping," of internal consistency, must also be used to determine the existence of this higher unity, or the lack of it. These are the principles expressed in the terms "consistent style," "consistent and harmonious whole," in contradistinction to "inconsistent mingling of styles," "hodgepodge," "clashing" patterns or forms, and they apply especially to the examination of artistic creation. Many such superlative unities cannot be described in analytical verbal terms; they are just felt as such, but this in no way makes their unity questionable. One cannot prove by mere words — no matter what they are — the inner consistency and supreme integration of the Cathedral of Chartres, or the Gregorian chant, or the musical compositions of Bach or Mozart or Beethoven, or the tragedies of Shakespeare, or the sculpture of Phidias, or the pictures of Dürer or Raphael or Rembrandt, or many other logico-meaningful unities. But not being completely describable in terms of language, their supreme unity is felt by competent persons as certainly as if they could be analyzed with mathematical or logical exactness. All such unities are covered here by the term logico-meaningful, though many are not logical unities in the formal sense of the word logic.

A few concrete illustrations will make still clearer the nature of this sort of integration. Suppose we find side by side in some cultural conglomeration a highly developed ascetic-monastic life and a materialistic-Sensate philosophy. At once we feel that the two are inconsistent; they do not belong together; they do not make any sense; their combination is not integrated in a logico-meaningful unity. This conclusion will remain valid no matter how frequently such a coexistence of these two variables is found. Asceticism and a purely idealistic philosophy of life, on the contrary, do belong to each other logically. If we find together in a given cultural area the strictest caste system and the equalitarian ideology shared by all castes, it once again becomes evident that we are faced with inconsistency. These opposing elements, though they may form a spatial or some other form of congeries, cannot be integrated in a logico-meaningful unity.

IV. Logico-meaningful Integration and the Method of Its Study

A. The causal-functional and the logico-meaningful methods of integration both act as the *means of ordering into comprehensible systems the infinitely numerous and complex phenomena of the sociocultural world.* What we style the sociocultural world consists of endless millions of individual objects, events, processes, fragments, having an infinite number of forms, properties, and relationships. With a proper modification we can say of it what is said of the whole universe: "The universe is infinite: unbounded in space and time and infinitely complex. In its infinite complexity it cannot be known and understood through direct sensory perception."

The same is true of the sociocultural universe. To our perception it also is given as a complicated and inexhaustible chaos of infinitely numerous, diverse, and seemingly unrelated fragments. In fact, none of us perceives directly the culture of any area as something whole which is bound compactly and comprehensively in a book, or packed in a box, or depicted upon a single canvas.

One way of ordering the chaos of the whole universe as well as of the cultural world is furnished by the causal-functional or probablistic formulas of integration. They give us the *patterns of uniformity* that are to be found in the relationships of a vast number of individual components of this infinite chaos. By means of these formulas we can reduce the chaos to a series of comprehensive systems, in which we are more easily oriented and which permit us to distinguish more important from less important aspects. Causal-functional formulas like the Newtonian Law of Gravitation sum up briefly a prodigious number of separate relationships. They are like a beam of light that cuts across chaotic darkness through all its unlimited depths. This, with proper reservations, can be said of any causal formula. It achieves its purpose by establishing a *uniformity* of relationship between the variables under scrutiny. Through it a vast concurrence of fragmentary events, forms, objects, and relationships becomes a comprehensive whole. When the formula shows that the variables A and B — depression and birth rate, modes of production and ideological forms, isolation and suicide, urbanization and crime — are more or less uniformly associated with each other in the sense that B normally follows A or changes with A, this *uniformity* binds the variables together, introduces a readily understood causal order into disorder.

Different in nature, but similar in function, is the role of the *logico-meaningful method of ordering chaos.* Here, however, the ordering element is not uniformity of relationship between the fragmentary variables, but *identity of meaning* or *logical coalescence.* Hidden behind the empirically different, seemingly unrelated fragments of the cultural complex lies an identity of meaning, which brings them together into consistent *styles,* typical *forms,* and significant *patterns.* If, therefore, *uniformity of relationship is the common denominator of causally united phenomena, in the logico-meaningful union it is identity of central meaning or idea.*

The procedure involved in arranging the scattered pages of a treatise or putting into a comprehensible unity the individually meaningless fragments of a jigsaw puzzle is, as we have seen, a concrete example of such a logically meaningful ordering. Of course, if the sociocultural conglomeration — the scattered pages or the fragments of the puzzle — do not belong together, the procedure is impossible. But this means only that where there is no factual logical unity in the cultural conglomeration one cannot find it; and if one tries to impose it upon the mass, one commits an error similar to that of finding or imposing a causal relationship where it does not exist.

We thus see that the ordering natures of the causal and of the logico-meaningful principle are different, but that their cognitive functions are similar: both serve the same purpose, each in its own way; both sum up in their formulas large accumulations of events, objects, relationships; both connect into a unity chaotic masses of fragments. Both are necessary for a study of the sociocultural phenomena, each in its own field.

B. The causal method, especially in the natural sciences, obtains its formulas mainly through breaking up the complex phenomena into their simpler units; and the more general the formula, the further the reduction of complex to simple, until ultimate simplicity — the atom, electron, proton — is reached. Studying the relationships between these simplest and therefore universal units and discovering the nature of their uniformity, the causal method offers *eo ipso* formulas of uniformity which are also universal in their application.

In the logico-meaningful method of formulating the unifying principles, such a procedure is impossible. Despite the endless efforts of a legion of social scientists, simple social atoms or units have not been found, and cannot be found, so far as the logically integrated part of culture is concerned. One cannot indicate what is the cultural atom in literature, painting, music, science, philosophy, architecture, or in any other similar compartment of culture. Instead, however, the logico-meaningful method has its own common denominator of all relevant phenomena: *it is the identity (or similarity) of central meaning, idea, or mental bias that permeates all the logically related fragments.* Because of this all the fragments in question are identical or similar in their significance, all of them have the same common denominator, which binds them together, conditions their relationship, makes them a unity.

C. The functional or causal or probablistic connection of separate units is almost always inferential and external; it rarely gives us an internal comprehension of the connection. Through experimental or observational or statistical manipulations we find that two variables, A and B, seem always to go together: they either coexist, or follow each other, or vary together. But why they do so — why, for instance, the force of gravitation is in direct ratio to the mass and in inverse ratio to the square of the distance; why the volume of gas varies in inverse ratio to the pressure; why oxygen and hydrogen in certain conditions turn into H_2O — we do not know. All we know is that within the limits of our perception they have usually done so, and that they will probably continue to do so in the future. Beyond this externally observed connection, we do not have any intimate understanding of such associations.

Different is the feeling we have in regard to logically integrated unities. The properly trained mind apprehends, feels, perceives, senses, and understands the supreme unity of Euclid's or Lobachevski's geometry of perfect mathematical deduction; of Platonic metaphysics; of Phidias's Athena; of a suite or concerto by Bach; of a Shakespeare drama; of the architecture of the Parthenon or the Cathedral of Chartres. Such a mind comprehends their sublime unity internally, intimately; often feels it immediately and directly, senses it without any experimental or statistical manipulations and without indirect reasoning. It is given to such a mind axiomatically, so to speak, as the supreme certainty to which no inference can add anything.

D. The primary difference between the causal and logico-meaningful connection leads to a further derivative difference between them. The essentially external nature of the causal association in many cases precludes our grasping the relationship between discrete variables in time or space. If variables A and B are not met with regularly, nor coexist, nor follow each other in immediate sequence, nor vary uniformly, such variables cannot be declared to be connected causally. Even if theoretically such a causal chain exists between them (as is possible from the standpoint of "singularistic causality"), it cannot be discovered and understood and, therefore, for the observer is practically nonexistent. Considerably different is the situation in regard to logico-meaningful connection. Theoretically (and not infrequently in fact) this sort of association is comprehensible even when the interrelated fragments are met with at quite different periods, and in quite different places, and only once or a few times. Conversely, the mere fact of our regular observation of the variables A and B in causal association does not necessarily force us to recognize that they are logically and meaningfully integrated.

If one meets only once and only in one culture (say, the Egyptian) a belief in the hereafter, funeral rites, and the practice of mummifying the body, this one case is sufficient to establish the logical connection between these three elements. Or if one finds only once the association of a dominant philosophical materialism, the naturalistic style of painting, and the economic and mechanistic interpretation of history, this case is sufficient to make clear that they belong logically together, though on the basis of one case we cannot say anything of their causal connection. Contrariwise, a scientist could prove, on the basis of a large number of "cases," that the variables A and B — say, the number of yellow leather shoes in use and the divorce rate — always vary together. And yet such an exceptionless causal association in no way forces us to conclude that the elements are united also logically and meaningfully. A competent person could listen as many times as you like to a musical composition where jazz and crooning are interspersed with bars from Tschaikovsky, Stravinsky, or Wagner. Any number of repetitions of these bars would not oblige him in any way to declare that such musical compositions are logical and consistent unities. Suppose we find a large number of houses in the classical style upon which is superimposed a Gothic tower. This does not prevent our declaring such houses architectural "hash." For the same reason we would declare illogical the conclusion, "Socrates is immortal," from the premises which should establish his mortality; or the answer, "Six," to the question, "How much do two and two make?" There certainly must be *causes* for such illogicality; but no matter how frequent such answers are or how many people make them, they still remain illogical. This shows once again that the causal and logical forms of connection are governed by entirely different principles.

Now it frequently happens in fact, as will be shown in the subsequent parts of this work, that the presence of the logical connection between variables is accompanied by their causal cohesion. It thus comes about that the discovery of a logico-meaningful relationship is often one of the best heuristic symptoms of a probable causal link as well. But not every causal association is followed necessarily by a logical connection. All the causal-functional connections in the field of the natural sciences, for example, and many in the field of human culture are free from additional logical bonds. And this throws light on the mixture of different architectural forms, opposing musical styles, disparate premises and conclusions which were cited above as examples of alogical, nonlogical, and illogical combinations which might yet be causally explicable.

E. Causal-functional or probablistic connections vary so in *degree of intensity* that we not only have cases in which we can be fairly certain of the causal nature of the association, but also others in which we are not certain whether the association is really causal or merely incidental (*post hoc propter hoc* and the like). Similarly, the closeness of logico-meaningful integration also varies from the sublime unity to one barely perceptible and merging into the lower grades of association. The greatest values in all the important compartments of culture represent, as a rule, the logico-meaningful synthesis in its most intense form. A mere heaping-up of various bits of information, on the contrary, hardly ever has acquired the distinction of being considered a great scientific or philosophical contribution; nor has a mere hodgepodge of various styles made great music, painting, or poetry

F. Causal integration, being external and inferential, exists supposedly in the inorganic, organic, and superorganic worlds. The logico-meaningful unities can be looked for only in the field of the phenomena that involve human thought and imagination; that is, in the field of human culture, and there only in that part which is a result of the activity of the human mind, whether this activity is scientific, religious, artistic, philosophical, moral, or technical. *Meaningful and logical integration by definition can only exist where there is mind and meaning.*

G. As a corollary to this statement it is to be pointed out that, since the highest values and complexes of values in any great culture belong to the class of the logico-meaningful unities, *this level gives it its sociocultural* and *logico-meaningful individuality; its specific style; its physiognomy and personality.* When we talk of the Greek culture of the fifth century B.C. as something peculiar and distinct, what we in fact mean first and most of all is the totality of the specific logico-meaningful systems created by their great men of genius — such men as Phidias, Praxiteles, Aeschylus, Pindar, Sophocles, Polygnotus, Socrates, and later, Plato. And this is true of any other culture or cultural period so far as its highest form of individuality is concerned.

H. Causal relationships and the formulas which describe their uniformities vary widely in the *extent of their applicability.* Some have a very limited range of pertinence; others are relevant to an infinitely great number of cases. Newton's Law of Gravitation is more general, covers a much larger class of phenomena, than Kepler's laws.

In a similar fashion the logico-meaningful principles of integration in the cultural world vary in range of applicability, beginning with the narrow principle which describes the coalescence of a few components of infrequent occurrence and in a limited cultural scheme — as, for example, the concurrence of images of anchor, dove, and olive branch in the frescoes of the Catacombs with the peculiar contents of the early Christian funeral prayer — and ending with the principle that explains and fits together millions of cultural fragments of wide distribution in space and time. The hedonistic or utilitarian principle may give sense and unity to many scattered phenomena in a large cultural conglomeration, which includes such elements as large-scale kidnaping, "get-rich-quick" schemes, emphasis on the *useful* in arts and science, "wine, women, and song" morality, and the philosophy of pragmatism with its utilitarian tenet to the effect that if the belief in God is useful, God exists; if not, God does not exist. But there may be a still broader principle in which that of utilitarianism itself becomes only one of the small subordinate fragments. In this sense we may speak of a long gradation of logico-meaningful formulas from the very limited to the most general.

I. From everything that has thus far been said, it follows that the investigation of each type of culture integration requires its own special procedure and brings about its characteristic results. *A study of any purely spatial and mechanical congeries cannot give anything but a mere descriptive catalogue of the parts.* Since these are not united causally, no formula of causal uniformity, no causal or functional generalization, can be made for them.

In a study of cultural syntheses the parts of which are united causally or functionally, the causal-functional method with its more or less general causal formulas provides the proper procedure.

Finally, in the study of logico-meaningful relationships, the proper method is neither a mere concrete description nor a causal formula, but the appropriate unification of the fragments into a whole according to their logical significance or their logical cobelonging.

The essence of the logico-meaningful method of cognition is, as has already been mentioned, in the finding of the central principle (the "reason") *which permeates all the components, gives sense and significance to each of them, and in this way makes cosmos of a chaos of unintegrated fragments.* If in a given concurrence of cultural elements such unity exists, and if it is correctly discovered and the unifying principle accurately formulated, the formula is as important in its field from the cognitive standpoint as any causal formula in a case of causal coalescence. As what follows in later chapters of this work will be a systematic realization of these statements, it is unnecessary to try to present extensive proof here. For the purposes of clarification a few examples will suffice. Suppose, of two given cultural complexes, we find one through which, among countless other elements, runs the predominant thought that the true or *ultimate reality is supersensory*, that the reality detected by our organs of perception is illusory. Suppose, further, that in the second culture the current of thought is just the opposite: that the only reality is that of our organs of sensory perception. We now begin a series of logical deductions which runs something like this: If each of the two cultures is logically integrated to a substantial degree, we shall find the following characteristic details representing the dominant current in it. (I have intentionally enumerated variables taken from the different compartments of culture.)

First Culture	*Second Culture*
Dominance of	Dominance of
Rationalism, Mysticism	Empiricism
Idealism	Materialism
Eternalism	Temporalism
Indeterminism	Determinism
Realism	Nominalism
Sociological Universalism	Sociological Singularism
The Conception of Corporation or Juridical Personality as a Primary Reality	The Conception of Corporation or Juridical Personality as an Expedient Fiction
Ethics of Absolute Principles	Ethics of Happiness (Hedonism, Utilitarianism, Eudaemonism)
Few Discoveries in the Natural Sciences and Few Inventions	Many Discoveries and Inventions
Static Character of Social Life with a Slow Rate of Change	Dynamic Character of Social Life with a Rapid Rate of Change
Ideational Style of Painting	Visual Style of Painting
"Scripture" as the Main Form of Literature	Secular Realism and Naturalism in Literature, with Sensualism and even Sexualism
Pure or Diluted Theocracy	Pure or Diluted Secular Power
"Expiation" as the Basic Principle of Punishment and of Criminal Law	"Adjustment," Re-education Mixed with Extermination of the "Unadjusted" and "Socially Dangerous" Persons

We shall find these variables because each of them is connected logically with the dominant attitude toward the nature of ultimate reality. All the traits of the first culture follow logically from the principle that reality is supersensory; all the traits of the second culture follow from the belief that reality is sensory.

Thus, the distinguishing of one variable of a culture enables us to construct logically a large network of connections with many of its other variables; to forecast what will be the nature of each of these variables *if the culture is logically integrated;* and, in this way, to comprehend quickly the enormous diversity of its traits, qualities, quantities, in one united and all-embracing system.

Now, when the two sets of deductions have been made and the series of expected patterns formulated, there remains the second step, namely, the application of the proper set of formulas to a specific culture in order to find out whether or not it is logically integrated. If we discover that this culture does contain the appropriate body of traits and variables, by one stroke we obtain several important cognitive results: (1) a highly intimate and certain understanding of many of the important aspects of the culture; (2) an insight into the nature and workings of most of its significant components; (3) a knowledge of the spectrum of its dominant mentality; (4) a comprehensive grasp of the very complex network of relationships between many of its traits which otherwise would escape us; and (5) an answer to the question as to whether or not, and to what extent and in what parts, the culture is indeed logically integrated.

Such, in brief, are the nature and the possible results of the logico-meaningful method of study.

J. If the fruitfulness of this method depends upon the discovery of the unifying principle that permeates a large or small portion of the components of a given cultural synthesis, the questions now arise: *How can such a principle be discovered? What are the guarantees that it is an adequate principle and not the mere phantasy of a "speculative" mind superimposed upon a reality in which it does not actually occur? If different investigators offer quite different principles, how can it be ascertained which of them is valid, which not, or which is more valid than the others?*

The first question is almost superfluous. As is true also of scientific or causal investigation, the principle may be suggested by observation, statistical study, meditation, logical analysis, even by dreaming and by what is called mere "chance," or "intuition." All of these ways, alone or in various combinations, have been operative in the first stages of most scientific discovery.

More important is the question: *How can it be ascertained that a given principle of logical integration is valid?* The criteria of validity are virtually the same as for any scientific law. First of all, the principle must by nature be logical; and second, it must stand successfully the test of the "relevant facts," that is, it must fit and represent them.

Here the comparative value of the principles is decided by the same criteria as those used in the natural sciences. *Of several rival theories, that theory is best which describes the field of the phenomena in question most accurately and embraces in its description the largest number of phenomena.* For these reasons the Copernican system is better than the Ptolemaic, Newton's laws than Kepler's. Similarly, in the realm of sociocultural phenomena, where several different principles of integration may be formulated, some may be more correct and more broadly applicable than others. Some, for example, may fit only a limited set of phenomena, while others will apply to several sets. But one will stand forth as giving the most satisfactory meaning to the larger part of the elements. And this is the theory we must choose.

These remarks clarify sufficiently the nature of the logico-meaningful form of integration, the situations in which it is relevant, and the methods of its application.

It is hardly necessary to add that the method is not new: it has been used, and used effectively, by the great social thinkers of the remote, as well as the more recent, past.

V. Some Results of the Preceding Analysis

If it is valid that there are at least four different types of cultural integration — spatial, external, functional, and logical — each with the properties described, then one may draw a definite series of conclusions.

A. All the cultural conglomerations can be ranged theoretically upon a scale beginning with those which are a mere spatial congeries, that is, are unintegrated in the proper sense of the word, and ending with those which are completely integrated logically.

B. If spatial adjacency and, in part, external unification are present in nearly every cultural complex, the same cannot be said of the functional and logical forms of synthesis. It is probable that at least some of the elements are bound either functionally or logically; but what they are, and how great a part of the whole they compose depends upon the culture and the period, and must be found by special study. No generalization equally applicable to all cultures is possible here.

C. If propositions A and B are valid, then the following theories widely accepted are fallacious:

(1) That every culture is an integrated unity (unless, of course, by integration is meant a mere spatial congeries, a meaning which in its turn not only destroys the significance of the term, but also leads to other errors and illogicalities).

(2) That any change in any component of a given cultural configuration functionally or logically affects all the other components and therefore the whole of the given culture.

D. The nature of the change of a spatial congeries differs from that of functionally or logically unified systems. In the congeries the change would mean mainly a mechanical addition or subtraction of elements, or their rearrangement chiefly through external forces. In the unified cultural systems the change would mean a transformation of the system as a whole or in its greater part.

Change in spatial congeries is almost always accidental. It does not have any inner logic and is the result of the interplay of various external factors.

Somewhat similar is the situation in a cultural congeries. A force external to the heap may dump into it some additional elements or carry away some of the objects which were there; it may change their mechanical order. The congeries remains passive through all these changes, does not have initiative, preferences, attraction and repulsion.

The difference between the merely spatial accumulation and the genuinely integrated system is so profound that the nature and methods of their change are also profoundly different.

E. So far as the logically and functionally integrated systems are concerned, because they are real systems, they possess several fundamental traits and give rise to a number of important considerations which are usually neglected.

(1) Any functional or logical system as a unity has a certain degree of autonomy and inherent self-regulation in its functioning and change ("equilibrium" of the imitators of mechanics). Any system, whether it be a mechanism like an automobile, an organism like even the paramecium, or a cultural system, has a certain degree of independence of, or immunity to, external conditions. In some cases this freedom may be large, in others narrow, but it is possessed to some extent by every system which pretends to integration.

(2) The autonomy of any system means further the existence of some margin of choice or selection on its part with regard to the infinitely great number of varying external agents and objects which may influence it. It will ingest some of these and not others. It has an affinity for some and a repulsion for others.

(3) Autonomy means further still that the functions, change, and destiny of the system are determined not only and not so much by the external circumstances (except in the case of catastrophic accidents), but by the nature of the system itself and by the relationship between its parts.

A cultural system has its own logic of function, change, and destiny, which is a result not only (and regularly not so much) of the external conditions, but of its own nature. This does not deny the influence of the external circumstances; neither does it deny the possibility of occurrence of the most decisive, catastrophic accidents caused by an external force; but it stresses what seems to have been forgotten for the last few decades, namely, that one of the most important "determinators" of the functioning and course of any system lies within the system itself, is inherent in it. In this sense any inwardly integrated system is an autonomous self-regulating, self-directing, or, if one prefers, "equilibrated" unity. Its life course is set down in its essentials when the system is born. This is one of the specific aspects of the larger principle which may be called "immanent self-regulation and self-direction."

(4) If this is true, then it is incorrect to "explain" any true system as the mere plaything of external conditions and reduce the explanation of the change in the system to this or that external factor.

(5) Reliance upon one element of an integrated combination as a main factor in explaining changes within the combination, as many

investigators in the field have done, is a serious error in procedure. The partisans of the economic interpretation of history make the economic factor the source of change in all the compartments of culture; partisans of religion, of race, of heredity, and of other factors, make each of these respectively the chief source. But, in the meantime, if a given culture is a unity in which economic, religious, populational, and other compartments are but single elements, its change can be explained through such a main factor procedure with as little accuracy as, for instance, the change of the human organism as it passes from childhood to puberty could be explained through increase in stature or some other such "factor."

At a certain point of its history (slightly accelerated or retarded by the external circumstances) the cultural system must undergo its inwardly ordained change. When this begins, all the main compartments of the culture change. It is therefore equally futile to argue that the transformation of one factor causes another, or all the others, to change, or vice versa.

From these conclusions it is apparent that the investigators of cultural phenomena who have sought to explain the transformations of an integrated system by means of a factor which is merely a symptom or result have failed to recognize the true nature of change in such a system. In addition if their main factor is dependent on something external and accidental, they are also guilty of failing to discriminate between a genuine integration of cultural elements and a mere spatial congeries.

2

IDEATIONAL, SENSATE, IDEALISTIC, AND MIXED SYSTEMS OF CULTURE

I. Internal and External Aspects of Culture and Methods of Reading Them

The elements of thought and meaning which lie at the base of any logically integrated system of culture may be considered under two aspects: the *internal* and the *external.* The first belongs to the realm of inner experience, either in its unorganized form of unintegrated images, ideas, volitions, feelings, and emotions; or in its organized form of systems of thought woven out of these elements of the inner experience. This is the realm of mind, value, meaning. For the sake of brevity we shall refer to it by the term "mentality of culture" (or "culture mentality"). The second is composed of inorganic and organic phenomena: objects, events, and processes, which incarnate, or incorporate, or realize, or externalize, the internal experience. These external phenomena belong to a system of culture only as they are the manifestations of its internal aspect. Beyond this they cease to be a part of integrated culture. This means that for the investigator of an integrated system of culture the internal aspect is paramount. It determines which of the externally existing phenomena — and in what sense and to what extent — become a part of the system. In other words, it controls the external aspect of the culture.

Deprived of its inner meaning, the Venus of Milo becomes a mere piece of marble identical in its physicochemical qualities with the same variety of marble in the state of nature. A Beethoven symphony turns into a mere combination of sounds, or even into a vibration of air waves of certain lengths to be studied by the laws of physics. Aristotle's *Metaphysics* becomes a material paper object — a book similar to millions of other books. Deprived of this internal aspect, many phenomena fundamentally different in their cultural nature become similar. The action of a surgeon plunging his knife into the body of his patient and that of a murderer knifing his victim become indistinguishable, on account of the likeness of their external forms.

Several questions now arise: Can we grasp the internal aspect of a given culture adequately? Since it is somewhat elusive, and often inferential — in the sense that in order to grasp it, one has to "read" it in external vehicles which differ from the internal meaning — how can we be sure that our reading is correct, that we do not superimpose on a given configuration of external cultural phenomena meanings which are not there?

The answer to the above questions depends upon what is meant by the true, or *real*, mentality incorporated in a given complex of external vehicles. Out of several possible kinds of real meanings the following may be mentioned.

The term *real* meaning can refer to the state of mind of the person or group of persons creating or using given external vehicles — for instance, the meanings which Beethoven had in mind in the composition of his music, or which Dante kept before him in writing the *Divine Comedy*, or which are intended by any other creator or modifier of a complex containing cultural value. Here we have the *psychological* interpretation of what is the *real* meaning of a given phenomenon. According to this point of view the correct reading of the internal aspect of culture is that which regards it *exactly in the same way as it was regarded by its creators or modifiers.*

But can this be done with any certainty? Can the reading of the creators, the modifiers, of any individual or group be correctly restored and restated? In many cases, yes. And for a simple reason: the meaning or purpose is often clearly and explicitly announced by the creator. We can grasp the essential meaning of Aristotle's *Politics* or Dante's *Divine Comedy* or Newton's *Principia* or Lincoln's "Gettysburg Address" because it is there in their works, expressed explicitly.

The character of the cultural objects in themselves — inscriptions, letters, chronicles, books, memoirs, and other "evidences" — often furnishes a sufficient basis for the restoration of the original meanings intended by the creators. If this were not so, the whole science of history would have to be discarded because such a psychological reading of culture is one of the main procedures of history.

This, then, is one way of reading the real mentality of cultural phenomena. It will be used to some extent in the present work.

It is not, however, the only form of reading possible. There may also be a *sociologico-phenomenological* reading of the inner aspect of cultural phenomena. This form of interpretation is perhaps more important for my purposes, and for sociologists in general, than that which is purely psychological.

What are the essentials of the sociologico-phenomenological reading?

First there is a causal-functional reading of culture which aims to discover the *causal-functional relationships* between the component parts of a cultural value or complex. Many persons may not be aware of the real causes of their actions and that there is a causal relationship between their activities and those of their contemporaries; they may not be aware of the causal connection between many of the variables in their cultural scheme; yet such causal relationships may exist. It is the privilege of the scientist to discover and to demonstrate their existence. As soon as this is done, the details of a cultural configuration, independently of any psychological meaning which may be given to them, become at once comprehensible as the elements of a causally bound unity. In other words, *the first form of the sociologico-phenomenological interpretation of the mentality of cultural phenomena is the causal-functional reading.* Theoretically at least it may be quite independent of the psychological reading. The significance of the relationship between density of population and crime, business cycles and the mortality rate, modes of production and forms of property, religion and the divorce rate, are examples of the sort of phenomena to which the causal reading may be applied.

A second form of the sociologico-phenomenological interpretation of the internal aspect of culture is the *logical reading.* We may know nothing about the psychological meaning of cultural values or about their causal relationships; yet in regard to many cultural complexes we can legitimately put the following questions and expect to find satisfactory answers: Are the elements of a given culture logically united, or are they logically contradictory? Do they make a comprehensible and consistent system, or do they not? If they do, what is the nature of the system? Are there unifying principles that permeate all the components of a given configuration, or not? These and similar problems may arise and be answered regardless of any psychological reading of the cultural configuration in question. In many cases the psychological interpretation helps to discover the logical meaning; often they go together; sometimes we cannot say anything about the psychological meaning; sometimes it clashes with the logical reading. Whatever the situation is, the logical reading stands upon its own feet, theoretically independent of the psychological significance.

The necessity for the logical interpretation follows also from the limitations of the psychological reading. The point is, in other words, that most of the cultural phenomena represent the results of the activities of many individuals and groups, whose purposes and meanings may be different from one another, often opposite. They all mix together, partly reinforcing, partly inhibiting, partly modifying one another, to such an extent that there is little likelihood of our distinguishing one from another. Whether we take the Parthenon or one of the great Christian cathedrals or a set of mores or laws or beliefs or any other cultural creations, they all are the manifestations of the activities, efforts, aims, volitions, ideas, feelings, of large masses of individuals and combinations of groups. It would be next to impossible to decipher or separate what in these complex cultural values manifests the aims and meanings of each of the participants in their creation, or what is the "psychological reading" of each.

The assumption of the present work is that any cultural complex may be logically interpreted, an assumption made by any scientific study.

One special aspect of this assumption deserves, however, to be mentioned specifically. It is as follows: Euclid's and Lobachevski's systems of geometry are both logically unimpeachable; both follow the canons of the same mathematical logic in the most perfect way; yet their theorems and deductions differ. How are we to explain such a discrepancy? The answer is simple. Both are logically correct, both follow the same canons of mathematical logic, *but they start with different major premises:* one with the axiom that the straight line is the shortest distance between two points, the other with a different assumption. *This discrepancy at the roots of each system leads to a whole series of differences in subsequent deductions, despite the identity of the logico-mathematical canon being applied in both cases.* The major premise of each system once accepted, each is logically valid within its own limits. This principle is particularly important in the field of the logical readings of culture.

We may sum up this discussion with the statement that a proper logical reading of cultural phenomena requires: first, the application of the canon of deductive and inductive logic; second, the realization of the possibility that the major premises of various cultures may differ; third, the assumption of an impartial position in regard to the validity or invalidity of the major premises. If the investigator grasps the characteristic premises of a culture accurately, his main task then is to show to what extent the culture is integrated from the standpoint of these premises, judged by the inflexible canons of logical validity. If he succeeds in solving this problem, his main task is ended. In defining the major premises of a given culture, he illuminates its soul, body, and its socio-cultural physiognomy; by indicating the extent and the character of its logical integration, he answers the question as to its integration or nonintegration.

In the logical interpretation of culture complexes this rigorously scientific and impartial attitude is preserved throughout the present work. *The canon of logical norms remains the same in the study of all the different cultures, but the logicality or nonlogicality of each is judged always from the standpoint of its major premises (if it has any).*

A further point in regard to method suggests itself. *If the nature of the major premises of a culture plays such an important part in the qualification of its logical integration, it follows that the key principle by which the character of an integrated culture may be understood should be sought, first of all, in these premises.* In any chain of logical judgments, whether in regard to culture or otherwise, the entire series of deductions, and especially the conclusion, are conditioned by the statement with which the chain begins. Thus in the syllogism, "All human beings are mortal; Socrates is human; therefore Socrates is mortal," the choice of Socrates, the statement that he is human, and the conclusion as to his mortality, all were controlled in advance by the original premise, which therefore embodies the key by which the nature of the entire unity, *i.e.*, the syllogism, is characterized. Thus, if we wish to discover the key to such a unity aside from the logic by which it is shaped, we must turn, not to second premise or conclusion, but to the major premise itself. A similar method must be employed in dealing with a logically integrated culture unity. It is for this reason that in the subsequent pages, which are devoted to preliminary classification of the main types of integrated culture, I shall follow the rule of arranging the types of culture not upon the basis of their secondary characteristics but according to their major premises.

II. Ideational, Sensate, and Mixed Systems of Integrated Culture. Preliminary Definitions

Many systems of logically integrated culture are conceivable, each with a different set of major premises but consistent within itself. Not all those, however, are likely to be found in those cultural complexes which have been in actual existence; and still fewer will serve as fruitful instruments for ordering the chaos of the cultural worlds which we can perceive into a limited number of completely comprehensible unities.

We can begin by distinguishing two profoundly different types of the integrated culture. Each has its own mentality; its own system of truth and knowledge; its own philosophy and *Weltanschauung;* its own type of religion and standards of "holiness"; its own system of right and wrong; its own forms of art and literature; its own mores, laws, code of conduct; its own predominant forms of social relationships; its own economic and political organization; and, finally, its own type of *human personality*, with a peculiar mentality and conduct. The values which correspond to one another throughout these cultures are irreconcilably at variance in their nature; but within each culture all the values fit closely together, belong to one another logically, often functionally.

Of these two systems one may be termed *Ideational* culture, the other *Sensate.* And as these names characterize the cultures as a whole, so do they indicate the nature of each of the component parts.

The probability is that neither the Ideational nor the Sensate type has ever existed in its pure form; but all integrated cultures have in fact been composed of divers combinations of these two pure logico-meaningful forms. In some the first type predominates; in others, the second; in still others both mingle in equal proportions and on an equal basis. Accordingly, some cultures have been nearer to the Ideational, others to the Sensate type; and some have contained a balanced synthesis of both pure types. This last I term the *Idealistic* type of culture. (It should not be confused with the Ideational.)

Let us now turn to a closer scrutiny of the culture types we have named. *What specifically is meant by the Ideational, the Sensate, the Idealistic, and other intermediary categories? What are their major characteristics? How are these characteristics combined and how do they operate to give united or integrated systems of culture? And, finally, why should these types of culture be regarded as fundamental and capable of providing the best possible means of understanding how the millions of fragments of the perceptual sociocultural world have been integrated into ordered systems?* Such are the problems with which we shall start our study.

Since the character of any culture is determined by its internal aspect — by its *mentality*, as we agreed to call it — the portraiture of the Ideational, Sensate, and Mixed types of culture begins properly with the delineation of the major premises of their mentality. As a starting point let us assume that these major premises concern the following four items: (1) *the nature of reality;* (2) *the nature of the needs and ends to be satisfied;* (3) *the extent to which these needs and ends are to be satisfied;* (4) *the methods of satisfaction.*

A. *The Nature of Reality.* The same complex of material objects which compose one's milieu is not perceived and interpreted identically by various human individuals. Without entering here into the psychological, biological, and other reasons for this, let us simply state the fact that the heterogeneity of individual experiences, together with other factors, leads to a multiplicity of the modes of perception of the same phenomenon by different persons. On one extreme is a mentality for which reality is that which can be perceived by the organs of sense; it does not see anything beyond the sensate being of the milieu (cosmic and social). Those who possess this sort of mentality try to adapt themselves to those conditions which appear to the sense organs, or more exactly to the exterior receptors of the nervous system. On the other extreme are persons who perceive and apprehend the same sensate phenomena in a very different way. For them they are mere appearance, a dream, or an illusion. True reality is not to be found here; it is something beyond, hidden by the appearance, different from this material and sensate veil which conceals it. Such persons do not try to adapt themselves to what now seems superficial, illusory, unreal. They strive to adapt themselves to the true reality which is beyond appearances. Whether it be styled God, Nirvana, Brahma, Om, Self, Tao, Eternal Spirit, *l'élan vital*, Unnamed, the City of God, Ultimate Reality, *Ding für und an sich*, or what not, is of little importance. What is important is that such mentality exists; that here the ultimate or true reality is usually considered supersensate, immaterial, spiritual.

It is evident that the mentality which accepts the milieu in its sensate and material reality will stress the satisfaction of the sensual bodily needs. Those who see it as a mere appearance will seek the satisfaction mainly of spiritual needs through an interaction with the ultimate reality. Those who occupy an intermediate position will be sensitive to needs partly sensate and partly spiritual.

B. *The Nature of the Needs and Ends to Be Satisfied.* Needs may be viewed as purely *carnal* or *sensual*, like hunger and thirst, sex, shelter, and comforts of the body generally; as purely *spiritual*, like salvation of one's soul, the performance of sacred duty, service to God, categoric moral obligations, and other spiritual demands which exist for their own sake, regardless of any social approval or disapproval; or as *mixed* or *carnal-spiritual*, like the striving for superiority in scientific, artistic, moral, social, and other creative achievements, partly for their own sake and partly for the sake of human fame, glory, popularity, money, physical security and comfort, and other "earthly values" of an empirical character.

C. *The Extent to Which These Needs and Ends Are to Be Satisfied.* Each need may be regarded as requiring satisfaction to a different extent or on a different level, from the widest and most luxurious maximum to the narrowest and poorest minimum. One's need for food may range from a small amount of coarse bread and water, barely sufficient to maintain the physiological expenditures of the body, to the most extravagant gluttony, where all means are employed not only to supply luxurious and fine foods but also to stimulate the satiated appetite by various devices. The same is to be said of clothing, shelter, sex, self-protection, recreation, and amusement. This also holds true for the purely spiritual and for the mixed or carnal-spiritual needs.

D. *The Methods of Satisfaction of Needs.* These may be, or appear to be, different with various individuals. We can divide them roughly into three main classes:

(1) Modification of one's milieu in that manner which will yield the means of satisfying a given need: for instance, one suffering from cold can start a furnace, build a fire, put on a warm fur coat, etc.

(2) Modification of self, one's body and mind, and their parts — organs, wishes, convictions, or the whole personality — in such a way as to become virtually free from a given need, or to sublimate it through this "readjustment of self." In the above illustration of suffering from cold one can train oneself to become less sensitive to cold or to endure it within considerably broad limits. The same can be said of other needs.

(3) Modification partly of milieu and partly of self. In the case of cold, to return to our example, we often resort to both methods — we may light a fire, but also engage in vigorous physical activity to warm ourselves.

I. IDEATIONAL CULTURE

In the terms of the above four items its major premises are these: (1) Reality is perceived as nonsensate and nonmaterial, everlasting Being (*Sein*); (2) the needs and ends are mainly spiritual; (3) the extent of their satisfaction is the largest, and the level, highest; (4) the method of their fulfillment or realization is self-imposed minimization or elimination of most of the physical needs, and to the greatest possible extent. These major premises are common to all branches of the Ideational culture mentality. But, on the basis of variations under (4), it is possible to distinguish two fundamental subclasses of the Ideational culture mentality and the related culture system:

A. *Ascetic Ideationalism.* This seeks the consummation of the needs and ends through an excessive elimination and minimization of the carnal needs, supplemented by a complete detachment from the sensate world and even from oneself, viewing both as mere illusion, nonreal, nonexisting. The whole sensate milieu, and even the individual "self," are dissolved in the supersensate, ultimate reality.

B. *Active Ideationalism.* Identical with general Ideationalism in its major premises, it seeks the realization of the needs and ends, not only through minimization of the carnal needs of individuals, but also through the transformation of the sensate world, and especially of the sociocultural world, in such a way as to reform it along the lines of the spiritual reality and of the ends chosen as the main value. Its bearers do not "flee from the world of illusion" and do not entirely dissolve it and their own souls in the ultimate réality, but strive to bring it nearer to God, to save not only their own souls but the souls of all other human beings. The great spiritual reformers, like the early Christian Apostles and such popes as Gregory the Great and Leo the Great, may serve as examples of the Active Ideational mentality.

II. SENSATE CULTURE

The Sensate mentality views reality as only that which is presented to the sense organs. It does not seek or believe in any supersensory reality; at the most, in its diluted form, it assumes an agnostic attitude toward the entire world beyond the senses. The Sensate reality is thought of as a Becoming, Process, Change, Flux, Evolution, Progress, Transformation. Its needs and aims are mainly physical, and maximum satisfaction is sought of these needs. The method of realizing them is not that of a modification within the human individuals composing the culture, but of a modification or exploitation of the external world. In brief, the Sensate culture is the opposite of the Ideational in its major premises.

These traits are common to all varieties of the Sensate culture mentality. But on the basis of the variation in the fourth item (*i.e.*, method of adjustment) it is possible to distinguish three main varieties of this type.

A. *Active Sensate Culture Mentality* (Active "Epicureans"). Sharing with other forms of Sensate mentality all the above four premises, it seeks the consummation of its needs and ends mainly through the most "efficient" modification, adjustment, readjustment, reconstruction, of the external milieu. The transformation of the inorganic, organic (technology, medicine, and the applied disciplines), and the sociocultural world, viewed mainly externally, is the method of this variety. The great executives of history, the great conquerors, builders of empire, are its incarnation.

B. *Passive Sensate Mentality* (Passive "Epicureans"). This is characterized by the attempt to fulfill physical needs and aims, neither through the inner modification of "self," nor through efficient reconstruction of the external world, but through a parasitic exploitation and utilization of the external reality as it is, viewed as the mere means for enjoying sensual pleasures. "Life is short"; "*Carpe diem*"; "Wine, women, and song"; "Eat, drink, and be merry" — these are the mottoes of this mentality.

C. *Cynical Sensate Mentality* (Cynical "Epicureans"). The civilization dominated by this type of mentality, in seeking to achieve the satisfaction of its needs, uses a specific technique of donning and doffing those Ideational masks which promise the greatest returns in physical profit. This mentality is exemplified by all the Tartufes of the world, those who are accustomed to change their psychosocial "colors" and to readjust their values in order to run along with the stream.

III. THE MIXED TYPES OF MENTALITY AND CULTURE

All the other culture mentalities represent in their major premises a mixture of the Ideational and Sensate forms in various combinations and proportions. With one conspicuous exception they are, therefore, eclectic, self-contradictory, poorly integrated logically.

A. *Idealistic Culture Mentality*. This is the only form of the Mixed class which is — or at least appears to be — logically integrated. Quantitatively it represents a more or less balanced unification of Ideational and Sensate, with, however, a predominance of the Ideational elements. Qualitatively it synthesizes the premises of both types into one inwardly consistent and harmonious unity. For it reality is many-sided, with the aspects of everlasting Being and ever-changing Becoming of the spiritual and the material. Its needs and ends are both spiritual and material, with the material, however, subordinated to the spiritual. The methods of their realization involve both the modification of self and the transformation of the external sensate world: in other words, it gives *suum cuique* to the Ideational and the Sensate.

B. *Pseudo-Ideational Culture Mentality.* Another specific form of the Mixed type is the unintegrated, Pseudo-Ideational mentality. One might style it "subcultural" if the term culture were used to designate only a logically integrated system.

The nature of reality is not clearly defined, but is felt largely as Sensate. Here needs and ends are predominantly of a physical nature. They are only moderately satisfied, and the method of satisfaction is neither an active modification of the milieu to any appreciable degree, nor a free modification of self, nor a search for pleasure, nor successful hypocrisy. It is a dull and passive endurance of blows and privations, coming from the outside, as long as these can be borne physically. This minimization of spiritual and carnal needs is not freely sought, it is imposed by some external agency (*vis absoluta*). It is the result of helplessness to resist. The oppressive power is so overwhelming that, after several unsuccessful attempts to oppose it, there remains to those oppressed no energy to try to free themselves and to adapt themselves physically and spiritually to a better order. Given an opportunity, a Pseudo-Ideationalist may easily plunge into Passive, Cynical, or even Active "Epicureanism." The life processes of slaves under dire and cruel conditions, of many prisoners, of subjects under the cruel regime of their rulers, of some primitive people who live in a condition of misery and privation, of groups stricken by a great catastrophe bringing with it utter ruin, of sensate persons stricken by an incurable malady — these offer examples of this type of mentality.

It is obvious that an examination of the characteristics of the Ideational and Sensate culture types is a different problem from that of how these mentalities and their characteristics are distributed in various actual culture complexes and in the actual behavior of individuals and groups. Our investigation thus falls into two parts or has two aspects: (1) the elucidation of the meaning and content of each culture type, as these follow from the major premises; and (2) the discovery of the actual distribution of the characteristics of all types in time and space.

In concrete social reality none of the types which are designated above is often found in pure form, unmixed with others, either in an individual or in a group or culture. On the other hand, these types and their characteristics are not distributed identically among individuals, groups, or cultures. In some the Ascetic Ideational, in some the Active Ideational, in some the Passive or Active Sensate, in some the Idealistic, predominates. A close examination of the life history of an individual or group would reveal the major current of the flow of its culture patterns.

Each of the seven forms described above and the combination of elements of which it is composed are associated, logically and functionally, with several additional characteristics.

(1) Since the Ascetic Ideational mentality strives toward the ultimate, supersensory reality, lasting, eternal, unchangeable, and not toward the everchanging and ephemeral Sensate reality, it associates itself either with indifference to, and a detachment from, the physical environment ("What is the use of trying to adapt oneself to that which is merely illusory!"), or a reluctance to change it ("Only fools try to write on waves."), or with a contempt for it. Hence ataraxia, self-sufficiency, apathy, imperturbability, indifference, Nirvana, and insensibility to temporal existence, to its pains and pleasures, sorrows and joys, life and death, are traits common to all shades of such a mentality — from the Hindu, Buddhist, Taoist, Sufist, Jainist, Zoroastrian, Greek, Roman Ascetic "Primitive" Ideationalism, Cynicism, Skepticism, and, in part at least, Stoicism, to Ascetic Christianity, and to all other varieties of the Ascetic Ideational culture mentalities.

(2) The above attitude leads logically either to a repression of bodily needs, or to a detached indifference to them as if nonexistent.

(3) The attention is turned to the principle of Being, views reality as everlasting and unchangeable Being (*Sein*), in contradistinction to ever-changing Becoming (*Werden*);[13] the ultimate reality remains eternally the same, unchangeable even in its manifold modifications. Only illusions and appearances change. Empirically viewed this mentality is thus static in its essence: static in its philosophy, in its *Weltanschauung*, in its choice of values and behavior. *Time*, in the sense of "before and after," "past, present, and future," "long and short," measured by empirical units, either does not play any role in such a mentality, or it becomes identical with the eternal, ultimate reality and, as such, is "punctuated" only by the changes in the distance of the Ascetic Ideational mind from total engulfment by, or union with, this everlasting Being.

Quite contrary are the standpoint and satellites of the Active Sensate mentality. It sees only the empirical reality. Full of appetites and vigor, it wants to change the surrounding sensate environment to meet its needs. The empirical reality is ever changing, is ever in a flux; consequently, the adaptive activities must also vary incessantly.

Therefore, this mentality is inseparable from a dynamic, evolutionary, progressive principle. From the earlier representatives of this mentality, from Heraclitus and Lucretius to the modern Evolutionists, devotees of Transformation, Progress, Dynamism, Movement, Mobility, Revolution, Incessant Change, and Adjustment, the dynamic principle has regularly been an integral part of the theories and practices of the followers of the Active Sensate mentality. Here the time category plays a most conspicuous part, and Time perspective is an indispensable trait of a mentality which is historical par excellence.

Likewise, in their practical activity, when it is integrated consistently with the Active Sensate mentality, the eternal panacea of such theorists is "readjustment"; *readjustment by all means, at all times, at all cost.*

Active Ideationalism and the Idealistic mentalities occupy an intermediate position between the two extreme standpoints. Active Ideationalism, side by side with the philosophy of Being and Eternal Value, or Eternalism, admits some, though subordinated, Becoming; some interest in the affairs of this world; some empirical activities; and some temporal values, subordinate to, and, as it were, a shadowy reflection of, the Eternal. Similar is the position of the Idealistic mentality, but it puts more emphasis on Becoming, on the empirical, temporal aspects of things and values.

Passive Sensate mentality is imbued with a still more pointed, extreme philosophy of Becoming ("The past is no more; the future may never be; the present is all that we can be certain of."), with its *Carpe diem*, with decisive preference for the values of the given moment rather than any lasting, future values.

Cynical Sensate mentality is somewhat similar to the Passive Sensate. But, being obliged to exert themselves to get what Passive "Epicureans" receive as gifts, the devotees of this type of mentality have to resort to hypocrisy as their technique, and in this lies their principal difference from Passive "Epicureans."

Finally, an enslaved Pseudo-Ideationalist is here, as in other points, a creature of the circumstances rather than their master.

(4) The Ascetic Ideational mentality facilitates *man's control of himself*, especially of his bodily senses, of his emotions, feelings, wishes, lusts. The Active Sensate mentality leads to *man's control of the external world*, so far as its material and sensate aspects are concerned (since any externality is apprehended mainly as a material and sensate phenomenon or process). The reasons for this are evident and follow directly from the nature of each mentality. Historically, the character of the first type has been frequently demonstrated by the almost miraculous repression of vital needs in the asceticism of Hindus, Buddhists, Taoists, Christians, Jainists, Sufists, not to mention the numberless ascetics affiliated with smaller sects. On the other hand, full-blooded, energetic "Epicureans" always have been the main transformers of the external milieu, whether it involved pioneering in the wilderness, or the organization of business empires, metropolitan centers, political or other organizations.

As to the other forms of mentality, the Active Ideational and the Idealistic, each of these types logically combines in itself satellites of both opposite sorts. Each implies the development of self-control, as well as control of environments. The first is stressed more in the Active Ideational, the second in the Idealistic mentality, though in neither is there stress to such an extent as in each of the extreme types of Sensate and Ideational.

The Passive Sensate mentality does not imply either of these controls; it seeks only an uninhibited satisfaction of individual lusts from the given milieu.

(5) The Ascetic Ideational mentality is mainly of an "introvert" nature (directed upon self and its analysis and modification). The Active Sensate mentality and its adaptational activities by definition are of an "extrovert" nature (pointed toward the transformation of the sensate milieu).

(6) The Ascetic Ideational mentality, on the one hand, opens wide the mental eyes and ears to grasp, register, and understand the essence of Soul, Mind, Ultimate Reality, God, the Devil, Good, Evil, Salvation, Eternal Value, Consciousness, Conscience, Justice, and so on. One is plunged into this intangible realm. However, an Active Sensate mentality, on the contrary, dissolves the inner life and inner world into external. In contrast to Ideationalists, "Epicureans" view the whole inner life, its processes, and all spiritual and immaterial phenomena, as either ignorant delusion or aberration or a peculiar by-product ("function," "effect," "resultant") of purely physiological processes in the nervous system or in any other part of the body.

An Ideationalist spiritualizes the external, even the inorganic, world; an "Epicurean" mechanizes and materializes even the spiritual, immaterial self.

The position of the Active Ideational and Idealistic mentalities in this respect is intermediary. Both imply internal and external worlds, the Active Ideationalist paying more attention to internal and immaterial reality than the Idealist. The Passive Sensate mentality implies a generally narrow tendency to view everything in terms of sensual pleasure and its opposite. With such a view much of the content of reality is missed.

(7) Each of the types of adaptation discussed implies logically a different conception of self, or the "ego," and its relationship to other forces and agencies. The Ascetic Ideational mentality tends to dissolve the self in the universe of impersonal and immaterial reality.

The Active Sensate mentality implies a corporeal conception of self which makes it inseparable from the body; a skeptical or irreligious or disrespectful attitude toward nonmaterial forces and agencies; individual pride and self-reliance and a care of the body and its well-being, because it is looked upon as identical with self and personality.

(8) The above being true, it is logically inevitable that the Ascetic Ideational mentality will require and stimulate *cognition of inner, psychical, and mental processes* (not, however, in terms of physiology or chemistry) from the most elementary psychological processes of sensation, perception, recollection, representation, thinking, emotions, wishes, volitions, etc., to the most sublime and subtle experiences of ecstasy, trance, mysticism, suggestion, and hypnosis, and others like "reunion with the absolute," "revelation," "divine inspiration," etc.; from the simplest ideas about immaterial phenomena to the most difficult conceptions of ultimate reality, the human soul, immortality, God, truth, justice, value, and others which are the concern of the humanitarian sciences, *i.e.*, ethical systems, religions, law, aesthetics, philosophy, and education. Since an Ideationalist is, so to speak, everlastingly brooding over such matters, since the knowledge and the understanding of them are essential for him in his attempt to modify, control, or dissolve his inner self, it is obvious that all this should lead to an increase of the Ideationalist's direct experience in these fields of immaterial phenomena. Hence it will not be surprising later when we discover inductively that the periods of predominance of Ideational mentality always have led to a domination, in human knowledge, of theological, ethical, and other systems of thought which deal with these immaterial and sublime problems. On the other hand, such cultures and periods have regularly been marked by a stagnation and regress of the natural sciences and other disciplines dealing with the external, sensate, material phenomena.

For the same reasons, the Active Sensate mentality is naturally associated with, logically requires, and stimulates man's knowledge of the external, material world. Thus, in a society or culture which at a given period is predominantly Sensate we must expect a successful development of natural sciences and a blossoming of man's knowledge of the material, external world and of the technical inventions for its control.

(9) For similar reasons the whole intellectual, moral, and psychosocial *Gestalt* of the Ideational mentality is profoundly different from the Active Sensate.

(*a*) *Ideational truth and its criteria cannot be identical with Sensate.* What is truth or science for one is often prejudice, ignorance, error, heresy, blasphemy, for the other.

(i) Ideational mentality implies the acceptance of the validity of the inner experience — divine inspiration, mystical union, revelation, pure meditation, ecstasy, trance — as the ultimate basis and source of truth. The Sensate mentality implies the validity of perception, rests entirely, or mainly, on man's external sense organs.

(ii) The Ideational wisdom, knowledge, mentality, seems to be marked by idealism, spiritualism, quietism, religiosity, organicism, mysticism, indeterminism, qualitativism. The Sensate mentality, knowledge, science, is characterized by materialism, empiricism, mechanisticism, determinism, quantitativism.

(iii) An Ideationalist is prone to interpret the whole external world according to the patterns and traits of his inner experience. As a result, he spiritualizes the material world, even in its inorganic part; he dissolves it in the inner experience.

An "Epicurean," on the contrary, materializes and externalizes the inner experience.

(*b*) Similarly, and for similar reasons, *the moral, social, and other values should be different in these mentalities.* Since an Ideationalist is indifferent to the external world and is centered at the inner, always "immaterial," or supersensate world, and since his ideal is to repress his sensual and material needs as much as possible, the external values of material character which can give but a transient satisfaction of sensual needs have no, or little, value for him. He seeks to be independent of them and self-sufficient. He wants to live in the eternal, imperishable world. His values are of an inner and immaterial character. The reverse is the situation for the Sensate mentality. Its criteria of value are the fitness of a given external object, of the way of handling it, and of specific forms of extrovert activity to satisfy mainly sensual needs. He does not want to seek imperishable, everlasting values. Such values are nonvalues to him, being almost useless for the satisfaction of his manifold needs. Life is short, and in this short life the sensual needs are transient — a good meal has its value only when one has an appetite and can enjoy it. Love and sex again are of value only when they can be enjoyed; for an old or impotent man they are of no value at all. Therefore, why miss a chance when it comes and can be enjoyed, why seek for something eternally lasting, since such a thing either does not exist, or, if it exists at all, provides a much smaller measure of enjoyment than the incessant series of pleasures which follow from the satisfaction of all wishes at the moment of their greatest intensity?

In regard to *all values*, as has been pointed out, an Ideationalist places more emphasis on the long-time, permanent values than on those that are immediate, transient, short-lived. His standpoint gravitates to the philosophy of Being, everlasting, unchangeable, enduring.

After these considerations, the following typical traits implied in Ideational and Sensate mentalities will be comprehensible.

(*c*) In the field of moral values *the Ideational mentality tends to be associated with the values which are absolute, eternal, and everlasting.* Ideational moral systems, whatever their secondary traits, are marked first, by indifference to, or contempt of, or a low evaluation of, the external empirical world and its material values. ("My kingdom is not of this world.")

The Sensate mentality implies and is associated with an opposite type of moral code. It chooses and emphasizes predominantly the sensate, empirical, material values. *Eudaemonism, hedonism, utilitarianism, sensualism; the morals of "Carpe diem," of "Wine, women, and song"* — these are forms established by the Sensate mentality. Man should seek pleasure and avoid pain; utility is positive, disutility is negative. The maximum pleasure for the greatest number of beings, this is in essence the motto of Sensate moralists.

The second characteristic of the moral systems of a Sensate culture type is that they are never absolute, but are always relativistic, varying "according to circumstances and situations." They can be modified, have no sacred, unalterable, eternal imperatives.

The third quality of the Sensate code is that it has little to do with any transcendental or supersensory values, and either mocks at such values, ignores them, or mentions them only to repudiate them and to bolster up its own principles.

(*d*) Logically, *aesthetic value*, art, likewise cannot be identical in the Ideational and Sensate culture mentalities. They should be as profoundly different as are the other values. So far as the *style* of art is concerned — whether it be in painting, sculpture, music, literature, drama, architecture — in the Ideational mentality it is symbolic, its physical exemplars being merely the visible signs of the invisible world and inner values. But in the Sensate culture art must be sensate in form; "naturalistic," in the sense that its intention is to reproduce objects in a shape which imitates closely that in which they appear to our organs of sense. As to the *subjects* and the *aims* and *purposes* of art, they show analogous divergences in the two culture types. In general, Sensate art deals with those materials which serve and help to increase the sensate happiness of man; Ideational is the handmaid of religion, absolutistic ethics, eternal values.

(*e*) The same difference appears in regard to *social and practical values*. A regime professing Sensate ideals will approve anything that increases the sum total of Sensate enjoyment; and that leads to man's control over nature and over other men, as the means of satisfying ever-expanding needs. Of a special importance in such a state of society is the search for material objects which under the circumstances are particularly efficient in bringing satisfaction. As one of the most efficient means has always been *material wealth*, in a Sensate society it is the *alpha* and *omega* of comfort, of the satisfaction of all desires, of power, prestige, fame, happiness. With it everything can be bought, everything can be sold, and everything can be gratified. Therefore, it is quite comprehensible that the striving for wealth is inevitably one of the main activities of such a culture, that wealth is the standard by which almost all other values are judged, that it is, in fact, the supreme value of values. *Pecuniary value thus becomes the measuring stick* of scientific, artistic, moral, and other values. Those who are excellent moneymakers are the *leaders* of such a society. Those who are wealthy are its *aristocracy*. They are simultaneously public leaders, high priests, moral examples, kings who ennoble others, the Four Hundred which is envied, if not deeply esteemed. Under these conditions, writers, artists, scientists, ministers, public officials, and men of the professional classes hope and act mainly to write a "best seller," to obtain the best-paying position, to have the highest scale of remuneration, and so on. If arms and force, not money, are the means to maximum happiness, then these instruments are the supreme arbiters of value, instead of money.

In this respect, the Ideational mentality differs from the Sensate once again. An Ideationalist is either quite indifferent to all these illusory and transient values, or is even inimical to them as the sources of the disturbances of the peace of mind and of the perdition of the human soul. In a thoroughgoing Ideational society, wealth or any other Sensate value cannot become dominant but at best will be tolerated only as turpitudinous. The most successful dealers in wealth do not have much chance to become the bearers of prestige, the leaders, the evaluators, the assessors of men, objects, and values, in such a society.

Enough of contrasts for the present. Table I will make plain at a glance by its arrangement in tabular form the results of this examination of the several types of culture mentalities.

The preceding pages outline the profound differences of various types of mentality, as they fall generally under the heading of Ideational or Sensate. Based on divergent major premises, they likewise differ throughout, if the implications of the premises are consistently carried through. A consistent adherence to these implications makes each type of mentality logical and integrated (according to the same canon of logic), in spite of their contrast.

The problems which next face us are these: first, to show that the above types of mentality have had actual historical existence; second, to demonstrate that in these historical culture complexes the combination of the elements and satellites of each type was indeed exactly as outlined

When these tasks are done, there still remains another major problem: that of the relationship between the mentality and the external behavior, manifestation, events, processes, and other externalities of a culture. The point is that the *mentality* of a given person or group may be quite

TABLE 1. SUMMARY OF THE MAIN TRAITS AND SATELLITES OF THE DISCUSSED TYPES OF ADAPTATION

MAIN ELEMENTS	TYPES OF CULTURE MENTALITY						
	Ascetic Ideational	*Active Sensate*	*Active Ideational*	*Idealistic*	*Passive Sensate*	*Cynical Sensate*	*Pseudo-Ideational*
1. *Reality*	ultimate reality, eternal, nonsensate, transcendental	sensate, empirical, material	both, with emphasis on the eternal and nonsensate	both approximately equally represented	sensate, narrow, and shallow	sensate, but with spiritual mask	painfully sensate; spiritual, but undifferentiated; felt and sensed but not thought through (unintegrated)
2. *Main needs and ends*	spiritual	manifold and richly sensate	both, with predominance of spiritual	both approximately equally represented	narrow sensate	sensate, with a spiritual mask	mainly sensate, with elements of spiritual not differentiated
3. *Extent of satisfaction*	maximum	maximum	great, but moderated	great, but balanced	maximum for narrow sensate needs	according to circumstances	very limited
4. *Method of satisfaction*	mainly self-modification	mainly modification of external milieu	both ways, with the prevalence of self-modification	both ways	utilization of external milieu	milieu's utilization through superficial and purely external change of the psychosocial traits of the person, without change of itself	mere enforced endurance of the milieu
LOGICAL SATELLITES							
5. *Weltanschauung*	Being (*Sein*): lasting value; indifference to transient values; imperturbability; statism	Becoming (*Werden*): transient values; full-blooded sense of life, joy, and grief; dynamism and endless readjustment (progress, evolution)	both, with emphasis on Being	both equally represented	narrow and extreme Becoming, ("*Carpe diem*")	narrow Becoming, with a mask of *Being*	undifferentiated and not thought through, vague and fragmentary ideas (lack of integration)
6. *Power and object of control*	self-control, repression of the sensual man and of "self"	control of the sensate reality	both, with emphasis on self-control	both equally represented	no real control of either self or milieu	control of assuming and putting off masks	no control: mere endurance of the effects of other forces acted on by external power

TABLE 1. SUMMARY OF THE MAIN TRAITS AND SATELLITES OF THE DISCUSSED TYPES OF ADAPTATION — *continued*

LOGICAL SATELLITES	TYPES OF CULTURE MENTALITY						
	Ascetic Ideational	*Active Sensate*	*Active Ideational*	*Idealistic*	*Passive Sensate*	*Cynical Sensate*	*Pseudo-Ideational*
7. *Activity*	introvert	extrovert	both, with emphasis on introvert	both equally represented	parasitism of introvert-extrovert type	specific introvert-extrovert	enforced extrovert-introvert; fatalistic
8. *Self*	highly integrated, spiritual, dissolved in the ultimate reality, aware of the sensual world as illusion or content of self; antimaterialistic	highly integrated, sensate, dissolved in immediate physical reality; materializes self and all the spiritual phenomena; materialistic, caring for integrity of body and its sensual interest. Sensual liberty, sensual egotism	both, with emphasis on spiritual, etc.	both equally represented	no real integration of self; mere flux of unintegrated physical sensations; self almost identical with stomach, sex organs, etc.	no real integration; similar to the passive sensate, but scheming and manipulating	no integrated self, except as a vague center of sensations; with some fanciful, animistic, or other, ideas and images; remains on a half-animal level (unintegrated)
9. *Knowledge*	develops insight into and cognition of the spiritual, psychical, immaterial phenomena and experiences; concentrates upon these exclusively; leads to arts of education and modification of man's inner life	develops science of natural phenomena and technical inventions; concentrates on these; leads to arts of technology, medicine, hygiene, sanitation, and modification of man's physical actions	both, but more moderately, with emphasis on the spiritual	both, equally represented	develops only the "culinary" and "bedroom" techniques of sensual enjoyment	same as in passive sensate plus the technique of deception and hypocrisy	does not give any real opportunity to develop any form of integrated knowledge and cognition except some fragments acquired through imposed "trial and error"
10. *Truth, its categories, criteria, and methods (of arriving at)*	based on inner experience, "mystic way," concentrated meditation; intuition and "revelation"; prophecy	based on observation of, measurement of, experimentation with, the exterior phenomena through exterior organs of senses, inductive logic	both, with the "inner way" emphasized	both, equally emphasized (Scholasticism)	nothing coherent, no truth except sensations	nothing coherent	nothing differentiated and thought through clearly

TABLE 1. SUMMARY OF THE MAIN TRAITS AND SATELLITES OF THE DISCUSSED TYPES OF ADAPTATION — *continued*

LOGICAL SATELLITES	TYPES OF CULTURE MENTALITY						
	Ascetic Ideational	*Active Sensate*	*Active Ideational*	*Idealistic*	*Passive Sensate*	*Cynical Sensate*	*Pseudo-Ideational*
11. *Moral values and systems*	absolute, transcendental, categoric, imperative, everlasting, and unchangeable	relativistic and sensate: hedonistic, eudaemonistic, utilitarian; seeking maximum sensate happiness for largest number of human beings; "morals of rightly understood egotism"	both, with emphasis on the absolute and the external	both, equally emphasized	no real moral values, except sensual, "Wine, women, and song"; amoralism; nihilism	no real moral values, except sensate masked by spiritual; cynicism, nihilism	no differentiated moral system, except apathetic and dull submission to fate, and sensual disapproval of hard blows and approval of easier times followed by vague ideas about the other world's justice
12. *Aesthetic values*	"ideational" subservient to the main inner values, religious, nonsensate	sensate, secular, created to increase joys and beauties of a rich sensate life	both, with emphasis on the nonsensate	both, equally emphasized	narrow sensual; refinedly pathologic	sensate, masked with spiritual	undifferentiated and vague
13. *Social and practical values*	those which are lasting and lead to the ultimate reality: only such persons are leaders, only such things and events are positive, all others are valueless, or of negative value, particularly wealth, earthly comfort, etc.; principle of sacrifice	everything that gives joy of life to self and partly to others: particularly wealth, comfort, etc.; prestige is based on the above; wealth, money, physical might become "rights" and basis of all values; principle of sound egotism	both, with emphasis on spiritual	both, equally emphasized; live and let live	narrow and extremely sensual; "*après moi le déluge*"	narrow and extremely sensual with a mask of spiritual values; Tartufeism	no choice given; undifferentiated; as God or boss decides

consistent and logical, but this does not entitle us, as yet, to conclude that it will be carried through in the activities, external patterns, and *behavior* of the person or group. A man may be a most brilliant commentator on Kant's *Critique of Practical Reason*, and yet in his behavior remain a scoundrel of the first degree.

In other words we must try to answer the question: What is the relationship between the mentality and the overt behavior or appearance of a given person, group, culture? Are they always also logically consistent with each other? or are they not?

3

CONCRETE ILLUSTRATIONS OF THE CHIEF TYPES OF CULTURE MENTALITY

It now becomes our main purpose to indicate by illustrations from the actual sociocultural world, both present and past, that the types of culture mentality distinguished in the last chapter are not artificially conceived abstractions without basis in empirical fact.

I. Individuals and Small Groups

We shall begin with a few generalized examples of the mentality and conduct of individuals and groups familiar to us in our daily experience.

With the characteristics of the chief culture types in our minds, even a superficial glance at our friends and acquaintances would show some of them to be conspicuously Active "Epicureans" to a larger or smaller degree; others to be Passive "Epicureans"; others Ideationalists with the traits of Active Ideationalism dominant (though in our culture this type is not common); and most of them to be of an intermediate type, providing examples of numerous varieties of the Mixed classification.

Innumerable Tartufes, so well typified in Molière's comedy; all the hypocrites, the insincere, the dissimulators in speech, writing, and action; all the cynics, flatterers, and "good mixers," who are acting so in order to attract the good will of the rich and mighty or for some material profit, and always with an eye in the direction whence in their opinion the profit is most certain to come — all these Cynical "Epicureans" have always been, and are still, among us.

Again, who does not know of those who "burn the candle at both ends" in an incessant search for sensate pleasures.

Moreover, all those in contact with the needy, the suppressed, the underprivileged, those bound hand and foot to follow what is ordered, who cannot do anything to change these conditions (slaves, serfs, prisoners, dependents, employees of inferior rank), would understand what is meant by Pseudo-Ideational adaptation. Large masses of individuals among the primitive tribes, as well as amidst a modern metropolis, have had a Pseudo-Ideational culture mentality.

Finally, most of our acquaintances, in all probability, belong to various of the Mixed culture types. Some even exemplify the balanced Idealistic class, though most will be dominated by Sensate elements. They like comfort, enjoy their meals and drinks, golf, bridge, and sex in a reasonable degree; they are respectable, follow the rules of propriety and etiquette ("slips" are merely incidental); they discharge their business conscientiously. pay their taxes, make some philanthropic contributions, do their other duties, go to church on Sundays.

What has been said of our living acquaintances is also true of historical personages. In order for us to test in a general way this assumption and more specifically to see to what cultural type a series of kings and popes belongs (these being groups for which we have perhaps the fullest extant records), and in order also to ascertain whether these two social categories exhibit any marked differences as groups in respect to culture mentality, the present author, in co-operation with Mr. J. W. Boldyreff, undertook a detailed study of the popes together with the kings of four countries.

The results are summarized in Table 2.

TABLE 2. DISTRIBUTION OF IDEATIONAL, MIXED, AND SENSATE TYPES AMONG POPES AND KINGS

GROUP AND PERIOD	*Total Number of Individuals Studied*	*Very Sensate*		*Sensate*		*Mixed*		*Ideational*		*Very Ideational*	
		No.	*Per cent of the total*	*No.*	*Per cent of the total*	*No.*	*Per cent of the total*	*No.*	*Per cent of the total*	*No.*	*Per cent of the total*
Roman Catholic popes 42–1932	256	3	1.2	34	13.4	116	45.3	101	39.3	2	0.8
Russian czars 1290–1918	32	5	15.6	14	43.7	8	25.1	5	15.6	0	0
Austrian kings 1218–1922	30	1	3.3	13	43.3	9	30.0	7	23.4	0	0
English kings 1027–1910	35	3	8.6	18	51.4	8	22.9	6	17.1	0	0
French kings 938–1793	32	4	12.5	16	50.0	4	12.5	8	25.0	0	0

These results suggest that not only individuals but social groups and classes differ from one another in regard to the frequency of each type of culture mentality and conduct within its limits. The group of Roman Catholic popes as a whole is more Ideational than is the group of monarchs. If we had taken the group of slaves or serfs or other submerged classes, we probably should have found the Pseudo-Ideational type quite prevalent, while among popes and kings it is practically absent. In other words, *the types and the traits of culture mentality and conduct are unevenly distributed among various social groups, and, as we shall see, in the systems of integrated culture created and maintained by these groups.*

Here is the distribution of types and traits which are perhaps typical, or at least most conspicuous in each group.

A. Within any society the Active and Passive Sensate mentalities probably occupy more prominent positions in the adaptation of the rich and privileged classes than in that of the poor.

(1) In the period of vigor and ascendancy the Active Sensate form prevails among the rich.

(2) In the period of decay of this class the Passive Sensate form dominates.

B. Of all the types of mentality existent among the poor and disenfranchised classes, the Pseudo-Ideational type is perhaps the most prevalent; it is less frequent among the rich and privileged.

C. In a given society the Active Ideational mentality, and to some extent the Ascetic Ideational, occupy a relatively greater place in the life of the clergy or priesthood, or their equivalents (Shamans, Brahmans, moral leaders, etc.), than in the life of other groups. On the eve of the decay of, or a crisis in, a given religion, or moral and social ideology equivalent to it, both of these types of mentality tend to diminish among the clergy as a whole, and to be replaced either by the Idealistic or Mixed type or by Active and Passive "Epicureanism." The data on the popes offer corroboration of this statement.

The reasons for the distribution indicated above are obvious. The rich and the privileged classes have more means (wealth) at their disposal for the satisfaction of their needs and therefore can indulge in more of such satisfaction than the poor. They have greater power to modify the external world and their social environment than the poor. Therefore, they do not practice giving up their fancies and needs, modifying themselves instead of their milieu to the extent to which the poor classes must. Hence the greater "Epicureanism" of the rich.

For similar reasons the poor and the subjugated groups are more exposed to the Pseudo-Ideational mentality than the rich. Their circumstances do not permit them to be Active or Passive "Epicureans." As a whole they are not capable of lifting themselves to the high level of Ideationalism. Neither have they an opportunity or possibility of elevating themselves to the level of Active Ideationalism. Hence they have to be content with whatever the circumstances give them, and this is not enough to permit their developing a full Sensate mentality and behavior.

As to the clergy and other religious and moral leaders, the nature of their profession requires of them a degree of Ideationalism, Ascetic or Active, greater than is required of other groups and classes. This, of course, does not mean that the clerical class always has it. Thus, during a period of the temporary or final decay of a religion, the clergy turn to

"Epicureanism," and sometimes perhaps even more than the other classes.

Taking everything into consideration, the behavior of the clergy is well above the average in morality. Even in our predominantly Sensate age, as we shall see, the clergy, though it probably does not have much purely Ideational mentality, has a Mixed mentality which contains perhaps more Ideational elements than the Mixed mentalities of the other classes, and this despite the notable "worldliness" of some members of the clerical profession.

It is also probable that the occupation of the clergy tends to bring into its behavior some of the Cynical Sensate type, and perhaps to an extent greater than for many other groups. Even those clergymen with the strongest leaning toward the Sensate must keep up appearances, otherwise they would lose their positions. Hence, hypocrisy, Elmer Gantryism, the putting on of the masks of decency, of Ideationalism, spiritualism, religiosity, and so on, which do not correspond to the inner *Gestalt* and to some of the outward actions of the persons involved.

II. Larger Cultural Systems

Let us turn now to a more thorough examination of the types of culture mentality, selecting these not from among individuals and small groups, but largely from the vast and long-enduring psychosocial systems established by the great historical religions: Hinduism, Buddhism, Taoism, Jainism, Judaism, Christianity, Confucianism, and others.

1. Systems Dominated by the Ascetic Ideational Mentality

A. *Hinduism (Brahmanism) and Buddhism.* Living in an age of a predominantly Sensate or Mixed type of culture mentality, we are prone to think that the Ascetic Ideational culture mentality is something rare, almost abnormal; and yet a brief survey of the mental patterns that have dominated and still dominate millions of human beings, that permeate the vastest systems of culture, shows that the Ascetic Ideational culture mentality comprises not an island but several of the largest continents in the world of culture. The systems of mentality of Hinduism, Buddhism, Jainism, Taoism, Sufism, early Christianity, and of many ascetic and mystical sects, groups, and movements (*i.e.*, the Cynics, Stoics, Gnostics, and the devotees of Orphism) have been predominantly Ideational, Ascetic Ideational at the highest level, Active Ideational on a lower, and Idealistic and Mixed on the lowest.

The slightest acquaintance with these systems of mentality shows that their major premises and secondary, implied characteristics are exactly like those ascribed in the preceding chapter to the Ascetic Ideational type.

In all these systems ultimate reality is considered to be immaterial, hidden beyond the reach of the senses. It is Being, eternal and everlasting, having none of the properties of the sensate and material world.

The world of external sense perception is considered, therefore, to be unreal, unstable, transient, illusory — māyā.

The highest mentality of these systems contains these four elements:

(1) Ultimate reality is spiritual, toward which one must strive by throwing off the illusion of personality and by being absorbed in the Ultimate.

(2) Needs are purely spiritual.

(3) The extent of their satisfaction is maximal.

(4) The method of satisfaction consists in a complete mastery of all sensate needs, even to the point of the annihilation of their very source — that is, a complete modification (dissolution) of self, social, psychological, and biological.

The philosophy of Hinduism and Buddhism is that of Being, not Becoming; it develops a high ability to control the self; its ideal of activity is entirely introvert, even to the point of advocating the relinquishing of sensations, contact with the external world, the disregard of the testimony of the "six entrances," and the assumption of a superhuman attitude of indifference to the whole external and material world. Of values it recognizes only the eternal, everlasting, and imperishable, rejecting all the transient and temporary as pseudo values. Likewise, its truth is not that of the senses, but is revealed in the mystic way, through intuition, meditation, revelation. Its truth is not relative; it is absolute. Absolute and eternal also are the moral and other values. They have nothing to do with relativistic and conditional utilitarianism, hedonism, positivism, eudaemonism, or any other empirical and transient values.

B. *Jainism.* What has been said of Hinduism and Buddhism also applies to Jainism. Founded by Parçva (about the sixth century B.C.), and remade by Vardhamaṇa Mahāvira (died *c.* 528 B.C.) about the time of the foundation of Buddhism, it was, like Buddhism, a reaction against Brahmanic Hinduism.

Jainism lays more stress than Hinduism and Buddhism on the torturing of the body and thus puts greater emphasis upon the physical aspect of the means to reach deliverance.

These principles, philosophies, and practices of Brahmanism, Buddhism, Jainism, extend throughout India, and not only in India of the ancient period, but in India of the Middle Ages and of the present; in India Brahmanic, Buddhistic, Jainistic, Mohammedan, Portuguese, and English.

C. *Taoism.* Another great system of culture mentality and conduct of the Ascetic Ideational type is represented by *Taoism* in its pure form. (It was supposedly founded by Lao-tse, born *c.* 604 B.C.) Like many other religious or moral systems, it has its highest forms which are within reach of only a few, and more "practical" forms accessible to the masses. In the latter forms the extremely pure are mixed with other, more earthly, and more sensate elements, and therefore the resulting mentality types on these levels are either Active Ideational or Mixed. But even such forms, just as in the case of "practical" Hinduism and Buddhism, bear the marks of the purer Ascetic Ideational nature of the system as a whole. In this sense the Taoist is not only an Ideational system of thought and conduct, but also to some extent a formula of the actual culture and conduct of millions of men who have been affected by it.

D. *Sufism.* In Mohammedanism the Sufist sect is a further example of the Ascetic Ideational mentality.

E. *Early and Ascetic Christianity and Other Ascetic Mystic Groups.* To the Ascetic Ideational type belong many branches of the Graeco-Roman currents of mentality: some Orphics, Cynics, Stoics, Gnostics, and Mystics; early and Monastic Christianity ("My Kingdom is not of this world"); and a great number of ascetic and mystical systems which in one way or another have existed, during all historical periods, among various peoples (many primitive tribes not excluded) in various countries and under the most different names.

This mentality is not a curious pathological or exceedingly rare case, but a form set forth and endorsed by, and incorporated in, the ideologies and practices of most of the world religions of the past and present and by innumerable smaller groups and sects, in comparison with which all the rationalistic, positivistic, scientific, intellectual, Sensate ideologies that have had historical existence are, in their diffusion and influence, as a flickering candlelight to the sun. In other words, contrary to the opinion of most of the contemporary scholars and scientists, who are inclined to underestimate the role played by this mentality, it has been one of the most widespread, one of the most persistent, one of the most influential; it has played a major part in the vastest cultural systems that have shaped and conditioned the minds of hundreds of millions of human beings. No scholar who studies the psychosocial reality, as it is, can ignore or pass by this form of mentality and culture.

II. THE ACTIVE IDEATIONAL CULTURE MENTALITY

Beyond the behavior of individuals and small groups, the Active Ideational mentality is found in the great systems which spring to life from the Ascetic Ideational point of view. In a way it is the tragic and immanent destiny of the Ascetic Ideational culture system to turn into the Active Ideational. As soon as the Ascetic initiators attract the attention of other men, they begin to acquire followers. As the number of followers increases, an organization appears; and with it the pure Ascetic attitude — the attitude of complete indifference toward, and non-interference in, the affairs of the empirical world — becomes impossible. An "organization" or an "institution" is a phenomenon of this world. It requires management, direction, guidance, and the administration of many needs and relationships which are purely empirical. Thus, any Ascetic current, as soon as it grows in influence, becomes an organization; as soon as it becomes an organization, it necessarily becomes more and more Active Ideational; and the more Active, the more rapidly it grows. Such is the inevitable chain of transformation.

One can see this in a great many cases. As soon as Brahmanism, or Buddhism, or Jainism, or Christianity, or Taoism, or, to take smaller groups, St. Francis of Assisi, or other hermits and ascetics, began to attract followers an organization appeared. Immediately the empirical world with its needs, affairs, relationships, pains and pleasures, sorrows and joys, poverty and property, sympathies and antipathies, became involved, and made pure Ascetic Ideationalism impossible for most members of the organization, and for the organization itself. The only form possible at this stage, when the moral powers of the current are still very strong and the demoralization of the stage of decay is as yet absent, is the Active Ideational. It stands for constitutions, rules, laws, and by-laws; often for empirical punishments and rewards, promotions and demotions, praise and blame; for the appearance of rulers and the ruled; in brief, for an organized network designed to enforce empirically the moral standard of life among the members of the organization as well as among outsiders. "The salvation of one's own soul turns into the salvation of the souls of others." The transcendental and the other worldly phenomena return to the empirical world and are more and more entangled by it.

Read from this standpoint the history of the growth of Brahmanism, Buddhism, Christianity, or Taoism, or of a religious order or center, or of a settlement which grew about some hermit or ascetic, or of many a minor current of mysticism. Everywhere you will find this transformation from Ascetic to Active Ideationalism. When we read about the activities of St. Paul, the great organizer of Christianity, we notice at once (from his Epistles) how he had to busy himself with worldly matters, and how the empirical world caught him more and more in its web. He had to give instructions to the brethren about this and that, censure them for some things, warn them of others, prohibit some activities, encourage others; and most of the matters in which his flock involved him, from riots and politics to property and wealth, were of this world. And the more that Christianity grew in that period, the more that this transformation progressed. It is true that the Ascetic aspect remained very strong during the earliest centuries of its history; but its Active aspect grew rapidly, especially from the time of its legalization (after A.D. 313 and 321). More and more Christianity had to enter into world affairs, and into affairs for the salvation of mankind as a whole.

What has been said of Christianity may be said of any other system which was Ascetic at its beginning. I have already pointed to a similar phenomenon with respect to Taoism. The history of Buddhism and Sufism offers further examples. This means that the Active Ideational type of mentality has always been widely spread in such systems when they entered the stage of attracting a large following and assumed an organized or institutionalized form. It is their destiny (until they become demoralized and lose their vigor and spirituality, and fall into the snares of the Sensate mentality).

The Active Ideational culture mentality can come to existence also directly, without passing through the Ascetic stage. Many groups have always been emerging in that direct way. As an example we may take the system of mentality of Mih-Teich in China — the system that was perhaps the most powerful in the fourth and third centuries B.C. It was rigidly organized as a sect. It attempted actively to transform the empirical world; it fought luxury, degeneration, egotism, anger, greed, by all means, including especially the compulsion, and autocratic enforcement, of its prescriptions. Logically moving along this line, the doctrine came to its culmination: to the *compulsory* introduction and maintenance of universal solidarity and love.

III. ACTIVE SENSATE CULTURE MENTALITY

This type of mentality is quite familiar to us. As we shall see, it pervades our contemporary culture. We find it in the behavior of most of the secular "executives" of history, be they great rulers, conquerors, organizers of political and business empires, efficient rebels against various "spiritual" limitations and bonds. It is very widely spread, especially now, among businessmen, energetic professionals, scientists, scholars, laborers, "practical" ministers of the liberal "Social Gospel" — especially revolutionaries, and all those human groups which seek a "full, rich, beautiful, and active life"; who want their cups filled to the brim with sensate experience; who enjoy overcoming obstacles of an empirical nature, of transforming the environment in all its aspects; who enjoy and seek power over inorganic, organic, and psychosocial Nature; who delight in taming rivers, cutting canals, turning wilderness into civilization, hunting, breeding, changing, or exterminating animal and plant organisms, creating artistic, scientific, or other sensate values, fighting for political position, for superiority, fame, glory, wealth, comfort, and other values of this world.

IV. PASSIVE SENSATE CULTURE MENTALITY

This type is also very familiar to us in contemporary examples of both groups and individuals practicing it. It is found, in greater or lesser frequency, in practically all societies and virtually at all times. When and why it tends to increase, or to decrease, will be discussed further. The formulas of such a mentality have long existed and have been frequently repeated with a monotonous lack of variation in detail. Here are a few typical examples.

> Look upon this [the coffin with the mummy of the deceased], then drink and enjoy yourself; for when dead you will be like this.
> Be glad now, that thou mayest cause thine heart to forget that men will one day pay thee also thy funeral honours.
> Follow thy desire, so long as thou livest.
> Do what thou wishest on earth, and vex not thine heart — until that day of lamentation cometh unto thee.

This is the old Egyptian expression of this type of mentality. It is difficult to find a more poignant example of the Passive "Epicureanism"!

Similarly, in ancient China and India, as practically in every other country, this type of culture adaptation not only was practiced but also found its rationalizing philosophy and ideology, as, for example, in such a hedonistic system as that of Yang-Choo who satirizes all values except those of hedonism, and preaches an absolute "*Carpe diem*" attitude and the complete disregard for any moral, social, religious, or other value which may hinder or diminish the sensual pleasure of a given moment, styling as fools all those who have sacrificed "wine, women, and song" to any such values. Yang-Choo offers perhaps the most radical formulation of the most complete Sensate mentality of any time.

In India the teaching and materialistic philosophy assigned to Chārvākā and to his followers gives a closely similar formula.

> There is no heaven, no final liberation, nor any soul in another world. . . .
> While life remains, let man live happily, let him feed on glee, even though he runs in debt.
> When once the body becomes ashes, how can it ever return again?

As for Greece and Rome, the philosophical systems of vulgar Epicureanism (not that of Epicurus which is much nearer to a combination of our Active Sensate mentality with partly Active and partly Ascetic Ideationalism) are at some periods, as we shall see, widespread. The works of many poets like Catullus, Horace, Ovid, epitaphs on tombstones, give a rich variety of examples of the formulation and practice of this mode of adaptation. The most famous brief formula is Juvenal's "*Carpe diem.*"

And so it goes with slight variations. Turning to later periods when such mentality and conduct were again in flower, we find that the Renaissance offers many similar formulas. Boccaccio's *Decameron* is one example of it.

This kind of formulation of the Passive Sensate mentality has never died and finds its expression in thousands of ideologies, moral systems, and so on, the mottoes of which are the same: "Enjoy life, for it is short!"; "Wine, women, and song"; or, as in the present-day advertising: "Unhappy? — Buy a Chevrolet!"; "Buy Swift's ham and be happy!"

V. THE IDEALISTIC AND OTHER MIXED CULTURE MENTALITIES

The Idealistic, the only perfectly integrated and logically consistent form of the Mixed mentality, is not very frequently met with. Probably at all periods and in all societies there have been individuals and groups who have been its bearers, but they are the minority among the mass of those who represent the other varieties of the Mixed mentality. Moreover, as we shall see, though there have been periods in the history of several cultures when the Idealistic mentality became dominant, such periods were comparatively few and short in their duration.

Despite the comparative infrequency of this type of Mixed mentality, its contribution to cultural value is qualitatively of a very high order. We shall meet it further in our consideration of the Greek and Western culture mentalities, where it will be properly analyzed.

As to the Mixed forms which represent a highly eclectic and low-grade integration of Ideational and Sensate elements, they have probably always been very widespread, except during periods of calamity and catastrophe. In fact, with all their variations in content, proportion, forms, mixtures of this sort probably represent the most common type of mentality to be found among individuals and groups. Since the major premises of such mentalities are eclectic, sometimes even irreconcilable, the mentalities as a whole are also eclectic and sometimes self-contradictory. Thus the logic of such a culture type is often nonlogical or illogical. In this sense the mentality is consistent with its mutually inconsistent major premises. This does not mean, however, that the whole mentality of those who represent this culture type is eclectic. Some compartments of their minds may be well integrated, to the extent that they are Idealistic in form.

All persons and groups who are "sensible," and "reasonable," who enjoy the life of this world but at the same time "give to God what belongs to God," perform their duties, do not go to extremes of sensualism or asceticism, are "good citizens," "honest men," who take good care of their bodies and at the same time do not entirely forget about their "souls" and the nonmaterial values, are the bearers of this form of mentality.

Among the great systems of human conduct Confucianism best embodies this culture type. To this I may add that, so far as the surviving fragments show, this mentality seems also to have been typical for the Ancient Egyptians in the "normal" (noncatastrophic) times of their long history. In the whole range of ancient Egyptian literature, one finds almost no real note of Ascetic Ideationalism but plenty of teachings of the Mixed form of life.

Confucianism. As a theory of conduct, system of mentality, and philosophical-religious-moral code, Confucianism also represents a Mixed type considerably integrated but in a form different from that of the Ancient Egyptians: "To search for what is mysterious, and practice marvelous arts this is what I do not do." "When you do not know about life how can you know about death." These quotations show the unwillingness of Confucius to go beyond the empirical world and its phenomena, and consequently the fact that the aspirations and interests of Confucianism have been mainly within the limits of the empirical world.

Free from ascetic elements, this system at the same time represents a remarkable combination of the Ideational and Sensate; its main purpose being to indicate the empirical mean, to keep the balance, or, in its own language, to preserve "the state of equilibrium and harmony," meaning by this the state "when those feelings [of pleasure, anger, sorrow, or joy] have been stirred, and all in their due measure and degree." "This harmony is the universal path in which all human actings should proceed." When it exists "all things [are] nourished and flourish."

Thus Confucianism defines itself, its main objective, and the conduct which it recommends, in such a way as to associate itself with our Mixed type. It recommends a proper gratification of all the important sensate needs but in due measure and degree, and with necessary limitations which are imposed by social duties, the general welfare of the people, and the commands of Heaven.

All the other characteristics of Confucianism are summed up in the system of means which facilitate the realization of this goal. Such means are the doctrine of filial piety; the system of five fundamental social relationships; the preaching of reverence and benevolence; the exhortation to all, beginning with the ruler, to follow the path of harmony; the highest social ideal — the Society of the Great Similarity; the moral code; the technical use of poetry, music, ceremonies, habits, etc., as helpers in this task; and so on.

VI. CYNICAL SENSATE AND PSEUDO-IDEATIONAL MENTALITY

As we shall see further, the Cynical Sensate form has not been endorsed *openly* by any great system or group. But, in fact, in a limited way, it enters the mentality and conduct of almost all human beings who do not always tell the whole truth, who follow the rules of courtesy and good education and often do not say what they think. In brief, those who are to some extent "liars," "hypocrites," "diplomats," "well-educated persons," "good mixers," "very pleasant and nice," "very courteous, polite, and polished men," and so on, all share, to some extent, in this type of mentality and conduct. Almost all adult human beings, in a slight or a great degree, are given to uttering falsehoods of the nature just indicated.

There are, of course, individuals and groups for whom this is the main form of culture mentality: "professional liars," so to speak, and those persons who are too ready to adapt themselves. "Flatterers" at courts, among the rich people, in business, in literature, in science, in the professions, exist everywhere. When a reviewer or critic praises a work which he thinks is bad but which he cannot afford not to praise in order to keep his job or to be praised in return; when the same is done by a scholar, a poet, an artist; when an employee is flattering to his employer; when these and other persons prefer not to say anything in spite of having a firm negative opinion, not desiring to "spoil the good relationship," and so on; all these are acting according to the Cynical Sensate mentality. And though such individuals have seldom composed a special class, they have nevertheless been present in every society.

Finally, the Pseudo-Ideational type has also existed at all times, in all societies, to a greater or lesser degree. All those who have been obliged to live in hard conditions, not because they chose them but because these conditions were imposed on them, either by other human agencies or by nature; all those who have had to bear their unfortunate lot, whether through their own fault like many imprisoned criminals or through the fault of the circumstances like slaves and serfs, the conquered, the subjugated; all those who have had, because of need and against their desire, to accept employment of a nature or under circumstances distasteful to them; all these are included under the Pseudo-Ideational type. Their number has always been legion.

The above discussion has made clear the nature of each type of mentality in its essentials. It demonstrates that each type has existed in the empirical cultural world and is composed of exactly the characteristics that are given to it in our abstract delineation. To this extent our first task is done. The classification of culture mentalities as proposed in the present work has thus shown itself a fruitful way of ordering the infinite chaos of cultural phenomena, at least in their inner aspect, into a few comprehensible systems. When the major premises of each of these systems are understood, all that is necessary is a logical unfolding of the rich content of each premise, uncovering all the detailed implications that are in it.

Thus the logico-meaningful reading of culture shows its "heuristic" value. It permits us to cast the logical net of relationship out over an enormous number of fragments of cultural phenomena often quite widely separated from one another; to establish a definite connection between them; and to find the proper place and the proper meaning for each fragment in the system.

We now have a grasp of one of the key principles for the study of the logical integration of cultural phenomena. The analysis of each type of mentality is far from having been exhaustive, but it has been sufficient to enable us to plunge into the main task of this work: a study of socio-cultural fluctuations. Let us, therefore, pass to a preliminary delineation of the principles involved in the study of fluctuation and change, or the dynamic aspects of cultural phenomena.

4

SOCIOCULTURAL FLUCTUATIONS: CONCEPT AND FORMS OF SOCIOCULTURAL PROCESS

Sociocultural fluctuations, *i.e.*, recurrent processes in social and cultural life and in human history — these are the main concern of the present study. The subject sounds fascinating but somewhat indefinite. The vagueness concerns not only the kind of processes the recurrence of which is to be studied, but also the very terms *process*, *recurrence*, and their derivatives. They have been used with such various senses and contain such a multitude of different connotations as to make necessary a special description of the meaning in which they are employed here. *By process is meant any kind of movement, or modification, or transformation, or alteration, or "evolution," in brief any change, of a given logical subject in the course of time, whether it be a change in its place in space or a modification of its quantitative or qualitative aspects.*

I. Fundamental Specifications of the Concept Process

Any process, in order to be meaningful, implies specification (1) of its *unit*, the logical subject — that which is changing or is in process, (2) of its *time relationships*, (3) of its *space relationships*, (4) of its *direction.*

Without the *unit* or the logical subject, no process, no dynamic state generally, is observable, thinkable, or describable. Even physical mechanics in its description of the simplest motion has always to give, implicitly or explicitly, the unit in the form of a material point or a material body. The same is to be said of any other more complex, process. The unit may be a thing; it may be a certain dynamic state, for instance, a process of integration, of disintegration, of growth, of degeneration, of expansion, etc. But some unit, as a logical subject, change, or modification of which we assert, must be given. Unitless or subjectless process is a word without meaning. More than that. This unit, though in a process or change, must be thought of as retaining its identity during the whole process in which it is involved. Any unit or subject exists as long as it retains its sameness or identity. When it loses this, it ceases to exist as a given unit, as the same logical subject. If it ceases to exist, it cannot be in any process or in any change, because the nonexistent cannot either change or remain unchangeable. At least, while concerned primarily with the change, we must think of this subject or unit as unchangeable, as a mode of *Being*. Whatever it is that changes,

This reconciliation of permanent sameness with change is not the illogical matter that it seems. It is based on the fact that if the unit of change A consists of the essential elements a, b, c, together with other elements which are not essential — now m, now n, now f, now k, now l, or some combination of these, A, as an integration of the elements a, b, c, can remain constant and at the same time be in a process of change with reference to m, n, f, k, l, or their combinations; and thus A may change without losing its identity.

Any Becoming, Change, Process, Motion, Movement, Dynamic State, in contrast to Being, implies *time*. Without entering here into a discussion of this intricate matter, it is sufficient to say that the time suitable for the description of the motions of material bodies is often unfit for the characterization of social and cultural processes. For these we often must use another kind of time — *social time*.

What has been said about time holds also, *mutatis mutandis*, for *space*. Any process takes *place* somewhere and in spatial relationship with other processes and phenomena chosen as points of reference. Otherwise, the process cannot be located and remains indefinite. A different problem is raised in dealing with the *kind of space* and the *system of space co-ordinates* (vector) to be used for the "location" of cultural processes. *Physical or geometric space and its system of co-ordinates (vector of mechanics), which are suitable for the description of the spatial relationships of physical bodies, are often quite inadequate for that of psychosocial processes and of cultural phenomena generally.* As a matter of fact, for their adequate description, *many sociocultural phenomena require a special category of social space with its own system of co-ordinates.*

Finally, the fourth essential specification with reference to process, namely, *direction*, is based on the fact that process proceeds *from* something *to* something, that change presupposes a passage *from* one status *to* another. Any dynamic state means some modification of the unit in the category of *From-To*. *This From-To movement is the direction of the process.*

The directions of a process may be various. *They can be reduced to four classes: time direction, space direction, quantitative direction, and qualitative direction. Time direction* is involved when we deal with such phrases as "from the past to the present," "from the Middle Ages to the Machine Age," "from 2500 B.C. to 1933," "from 6 P.M to 4 A.M."

The time specification of a process most frequently comes out in the form of *duration*. For many processes it becomes necessary to know whether they have lasted a second, an hour, a day, a year, an age.

Another variety of time direction is *time sequence*. Given the objects, qualities, events a, b, c, which comes first, which second, which last? In other words, what is their *order* in time?

In these and many other forms the time specification of the direction of a process is often one of the most important traits to know, whether for theoretical or for practical purposes. All such specifications are varieties of time direction.

The second form of the direction of a process is *spatial direction:* either a purely geometrico-spatial direction, as in physical motion, in any movement of a material body in geometric space (such as driving from Dakota to New England); or a direction in social space—"climbing the social ladder," social promotion and demotion, social rapprochement, social separation.

Thirdly, a process may have a *quantitative* direction. When we say of a process that it increases, decreases, or remains constant; that it grows, multiplies, declines, becomes scarce — for instance that the birth rate falls from 10.2 to 9.6 per 1000 and that the suicide rate increases from 0.2 to 0.5 per 10,000, the direction of the process here is neither purely temporal nor purely spatial, it is *sui generis* and stresses the quantitative modification of the unit as such, and for this reason it is to be styled by a special name.

Propositions specifying the quantitative direction are of two varieties, *verbal* and *numerical.*

The fourth form of direction is *qualitative* in the sense of a passage from one qualitative status to another, as from misery to happiness, childhood to senility, health to sickness, hatred to love, the state of an amoeba to that of *homo sapiens*, the Gothic to the baroque, capitalism to communism, and so on.

The four directions which we have just described are sufficient for the formation of a working concept of the nature of process and, together with the other specifications (unit, time), for the classification of an infinitely great variety of processes into a few kinds.

II. Forms and Degrees of Uniqueness and Recurrence

Phenomena (including the phenomena of process) are either unique or recurring. The uniqueness or recurrence of processes may, however, have different forms and degrees. Let us single out the main forms of unique and recurrent processes according to the process specifications which we have enumerated.

A. A process may be unique in *all its specifications.* This means that it happens only once in the eternity of time, only at one locus in the infinity of space, and also that the unit is unique in which the process occurs.

B. A process related to a unique unit may be repeated *within this unit.* Socrates is a unique individual; however, such of his activities as sleeping and being awake, wandering in the streets of Athens, listening to the scoldings of Xantippe, and many others, were repeated many times during his life. We can call such processes *recurrent in time only*. By definition, then, the *processes recurrent in time* only are those *which occur in a unique unit and are repeated in it.*

C. There are two or more units essentially similar to one another, but a given process occurs only *once in the lifetime of each unit.* Let us assume that all human individuals are essentially alike. Since there are many human individuals, then by definition there are many similar units in which processes take place. But in the life span of each many processes occur only once: each is born once, passes the stage of childhood once, and dies once. *All such processes are unique in the time existence of each unit but repeated in social space, i.e., in other similar units.* All such recurrences may be called *recurrences in space only.*

D. A process may not only occur in units which are not unique, but also be repeated several times in such units. Such a process is then *recurrent in time as well as in space.* Under the assumption that human individuals are essentially similar, the alternating processes of sleep and wakefulness, of fatigue and rest, of cheer and gloom, and others which occur many times in all human beings, are processes repeated in both time and space.

III. Are Sociocultural Processes Unique or Recurrent?

At this point it would be well to consider, at least briefly, the question: Are sociocultural processes recurrent? The problem arises from the fairly wide prevalence of the opinion that "history never repeats itself," that it is ever new, that there are no two sociocultural objects, values, groups, events, similar to each other either in time or in space. This is an abbreviated statement of the unicist conception of sociocultural and historical processes.

This conception has been stressed again and again, mainly by historians, though perhaps rarely in such a pointed form as in this work. Let us now ask to what extent it is valid. That it has some truth in it is beyond doubt: if one intentionally turns one's attention only to those characteristics of historical and sociocultural processes which are unique, one can find many traits unrepeated. However, because sociocultural processes have an aspect of uniqueness it does not follow that they do not also have an aspect of repetition. As a matter of fact not only historical and social phenomena but all inorganic and organic phenomena are likewise unique in a way. There probably do not exist two identical drops of water, two cells, two organisms, even two atoms or electrons. And yet this does not prevent the organic and inorganic phenomena from having an aspect of similarity and repetition which may be studied by physics and chemistry.

It is the same with the processes of social life and human history. If we set ourselves to ferret out only the unique traits in these processes we can do so. But if we wish to concentrate our attention on the repeated aspects of these phenomena we can find enough to suit us. Perhaps the uniformity of these repetitions is not so rigid here as in the inorganic world. Nevertheless it is still as important to recognize here as elsewhere the repetition of a given phenomenon, that is, the similarity of its essential traits in a given recurrence with those which occurred before or after, or here and there.

The great symphony of social life is "scored" for a countless number of separate processes, each proceeding in a wavelike manner and recurring in space, in time, in both space and time, periodically or nonperiodically, after short or long intervals. Briefly or for an extensive time, in the same or in several social systems, a process moves in a certain quantitative or qualitative or spatial direction, or in all these directions, reaches its "point of saturation," and then often reverses its movements. Economic processes fluctuate endlessly between prosperity and depression, enrichment and poverty; vital processes between births, deaths, marriages, divorces; all undergo their "ups and downs," which sometimes become monotonously uniform. Crime and licentiousness, religion and irreligion, social stability and revolt, recur endlessly. Social systems — associations, organizations, institutions — forever repeat the processes of recruiting, change, dismissal of their members, originate, grow, and dissolve. And so it goes with almost all social phenomena and process.

These reminders are sufficient, for the present, to enable the reader to detect the one-sidedness of the partisans of the unicist conception of the processes of social life and human history. They have taken only one side of the coin and forgotten the other.

A much stronger argument, which virtually demolishes the theory of the unicists, is that their position is untenable logically. No unique historical process can be narrated without the admission, explicit or implicit, that many essential traits are repeated. Suppose our historian wishes to describe Roman religion, or law, or the class composition of Roman society, or any other aspect of Roman history, as an absolutely unique event or process which has nothing in common with, or recurring in, other societies and other periods. Is such a task possible to accomplish? No, and for very obvious reasons. Let us take, for example, Roman religion. If any moment of any historical event or sociocultural process is unique, a difficulty arises at once: what moment of Roman religion is to be described? Is it to be the Roman religion of 8 P.M., July 1, 321 B.C., or of 7 A.M., May 10, 322 B.C.? If the historian wished to give such a description he could not because nobody knows what exactly were the religious beliefs, rites, and so on, at one of these moments, and how they changed from one moment to another. If he should say that so exact a concern with time is unnecessary, he would be denying his own claim that every process of history is unique. If he attempted to give a general picture of the religious situation in Rome during several decades or centuries, it would be not, as it were, a single photograph of a unique process but a composite photograph, a kind of average, a generalizing picture for a very long period. This would imply an admission that for decades or centuries a process had retained many traits unchanged or was recurring from generation to generation, was repeated in the actions and beliefs of numerous individuals and groups. In brief, it would mean a complete abandonment of the unicist contention.

The next obstacle, which is no less difficult to surmount, is that connected with uniqueness or recurrence in space. The thesis of uniqueness demands that any phenomenon which shows some differences from every other in space or time is to be described as unique. There is no doubt that the religious beliefs and convictions of thousands of Roman individuals, families, and groups were not absolutely identical. To some degree they were different with every individual as they are among people of today. Since this is so, the problem arises whether our unicist means to describe the religious beliefs and rites of Roman X, or Roman Y, or Roman Z, or any other Roman individual, or whether he intends to describe Roman religion generally as it existed within such and such a group in Roman society. His concept of uniqueness would have been carried through only when he had described the religious beliefs of specific individuals, each taken separately. It is evident that such a task could not be performed for all the individuals in Roman society. If the unicist confined himself to one, or five, or ten Romans, his work could not be styled a description of Roman religion generally, because it would be the religion of only a few different Roman individuals out of hundreds of thousands, each of whom, according to the thesis, would be unique. Moreover, even with respect to these ten Romans — or, for that matter, to one — adequate description would be impossible, because the religion of any individual is changing throughout life, from childhood to senility. Therefore, even in an individual every moment of religious belief is unique. Under such circumstances our unicist, to be consistent, may not talk or write about the religion of such and such an individual generally, but must deal with the religion, for example, of X at the age of 7 years, 4 months, 23 days, 7 hours, 53 minutes, and 24 seconds. But this is only the beginning. He must now proceed to record the religion of this individual at intervals of a year, a month, a day, perhaps even an hour — in any case at intervals of no more than several years. Without the performance of this insuperable task — impossible with regard to one Roman, and inconceivable for any large number of Romans — the unicist can make no generalizations about Roman religion. In effect, history becomes merely the meaningless setting down of microscopically minute facts. Any deviation from this becomes an admission of the fact of recurrence.

All these considerations show how the thesis of uniqueness, being consistently carried through, destroys itself.

But this is not all. The greatest difficulty, seemingly unconquerable, which the unicist meets with is that which springs from human language and human logic, from the elementary but important rule that he may style by the same term only phenomena which are identical, or at least essentially similar, and that he must style by different terms phenomena which are fundamentally different. From this standpoint when our unicist describes the *religion* of the Romans, the *art*, the *law*, the *class composition*, the *wars*, the *imperialism*, the *decay*, the *vices* and *virtues*, or the *sculpture* of the Romans — or when he talks of the Roman *rich* and the Roman *poor classes*, the Roman *bourgeoisie*, or of Roman *expansion*, and so on — he admits through his back door recurrences and repetitions of social processes which he tried to bar from his front door. In styling a certain complex of social phenomena in Roman society as religion or a rich class or decay or law or art, the historian indicates that it is in some essential respects the same as religion, art, law, decay, and so on, among other peoples and at different periods. Otherwise, none of these terms, which imply classification and therefore recurrence, could be used. The point is that, for example, the Roman, Greek, Persian, Egyptian, medieval Christian, Protestant, Hindu, and other *religions*, whatever their differences and however each may be unique, must all have certain essential elements in common in order to belong to *the same class* of social phenomena styled religion. And since they belong to the same class and have common elements, then this means that in certain characteristics religion is a recurring phenomenon, repeated in different societies — at different periods, that is, in space and time. This is true of all categories of sociocultural and historical processes.

The crushing power of this argument is clear now. It has shown that the unicist cannot make any of his scientific descriptions without using the terms of human language which imply inevitably and unescapably the existence of recurrent elements and traits in any of the phenomena which are viewed as unique.

If any phenomena have their unique aspects, they also have recurrent traits, characteristics which are common to other phenomena. In one sense sociocultural life and history never repeat themselves; and yet, in another, they always recur to some extent. Such seems to be the truth of the entire matter.

One may, therefore, as readily justify scientifically the study of the recurrent aspect of sociocultural processes as of their unique aspect. Hence, a discipline which specializes in the investigation of the first — be it called sociology, social philosophy, philosophy of history, or "abracadabra" — has as much right to exist as any unicist discipline that concentrates on the study of the second.

IV. Punctuation and Pulsation of Sociocultural Processes

If the unit and all the directions of a given process remain the same throughout its existence, it cannot have any "punctuation," "turn," "measure," "phase," "link," "beat," "rhythm." The unvarying nature of its directions in all their senses excludes, by definition, any pauses that separate one part of it from the others. This means that *a change in one or more directions, in any of their senses, of a process is necessary for its real punctuation.* More than this: *Any punctuation of a process is always the result of a change of one or more of its directions and their senses.* So far as a process is marked by caesuras, rhythm, "turns," change in tempo, or division into "phases," "links," "parts," and so on, all these marks are but a function of a change in any of the directions (in any of their senses) of a given process.

Thus, if the time direction in its various meanings remains the same, no time punctuation, no change of rhythm or tempo, no largo, prestissimo, accelerando, ritardando, is possible. On the other hand, as soon as the time direction changes (the tempo, let us say, passes from largo to presto), the process is divided at once into empirically existing links or phases, or, to speak in musical terms, measures and rhythms. Similarly, as soon as the quantitative direction shows any change (say the birth rate falls from 9.2 to 8.5 per 1000), this denotes a "turn" in the process, and breaks it into punctuated parts. When a process changes its qualitative direction (when something passes, for example, from health to sickness, red to blue, silence to noise, peace to war, prosperity to depression, childhood to puberty), the change of the qualitative direction divides the process into two or more different stages, phases, parts. In all such cases the punctuation is not imposed artificially, but exists within the process, and, when comprehended, provides an adequate indication of the real pulsation of the process.

From the principle thus explained there follows a series of conclusions which bear upon many important problems in the social sciences.

A. *The sharper the change in a given direction, the greater the modification of the process, so far as this direction is concerned.*

B. Other conditions being equal, *simultaneous change in two directions punctuates a process more markedly than an* equal change in either of these directions alone. In such cases the caesura that separates one phase from the other becomes double or cumulative.

C. From propositions A and B it follows that the greater the number of directions and their senses in which simultaneous change takes place, and the deeper or sharper the change in each of them, the greater will be the turn experienced by the process and the more easily this will be observed and understood.

The essential meaning of all three preceding propositions may be formulated thus: *the depth, magnitude, and sharpness of each punctuation of a given process is directly proportional to the number of the directions in which the process synchronously changes, and to the sharpness of change in each of these directions.*

A change in one direction usually marks some "phase" in the life history of a process; a change in two or more directions marks a much larger "period" or "epoch" or "era."

D. Finally, *when the unit in which the process takes place ceases to be identifiable, the process itself is to be regarded as ended.*

A few additional words in regard to the beginning and end of a process are not out of place here, since these extremes are the greatest, the ultimate, punctuations. *As long as the unit which is in process is identifiable, the process continues to exist in spite of all the changes in its directions. When the unit is changed to such an extent that it becomes unidentifiable, the process ends. The moment when the identification of the unit becomes impossible is the point at which the process ends. The moment when we observe the emergence of a new unit which, so far as our knowledge goes, did not exist before, a new process is started.*

V. Linear and Nonlinear: Cyclical and Varyingly Recurrent Patterns of Process from the Standpoint of Their Direction

As we have mentioned, processes have directions with their senses. If the sense of a given direction and the direction itself remain the same throughout the existence of a process, its pattern may be said to be *linear* so far as the given direction and sense are concerned.

With reference to *spatial direction* linearity means a steady movement of the unit of process along the same line from one spatial center to another.

As applied to *quantitative direction* linearity means that the process either increases, or decreases, or remains constant during the time of its existence.

In application to the *time direction* linearity, *in combination with spatial and other directions it can have a very distinct significance.* For instance, in such concepts as the acceleration or slowing of a process, time is a necessary element: acceleration means an ever-increasing tempo.

Finally, with regard to the *qualitative direction also, linearity is not quite applicable.* Linearity means in all such cases a certain *uniform order of sequence of the qualitative states.* This is, in fact, the only meaning which qualitative linearity may have.

In recurrent processes, and in those aspects of each process which are repeated, linearity may be of the *oscillating*, *spiral*, or *branching* type, but not of the *unilinear.*

Let us now turn to one special type of recurrence: the *cyclical.* This type may be subdivided into the *completely cyclical* and the *relatively cyclical.* In the *completely cyclical* process the last phase of a given recurrence returns to its first phase, and the cycle begins again, traversing the same route through which it has passed before. In the *relatively cyclical* process, on the other hand, the direction of the recurring process does not coincide completely with that of the series of previous recurrences. There is some deviation from cycle to cycle. But in contradistinction to the linear pattern and especially to its oscillating and branching varieties, the relatively cyclical process does not have any main route *ex definitione* and returns partly to its previous direction, while the oscillating and branching linear processes do have such a route and in their recurrence never run twice over the same tracks.

As is true of linearity, the cyclic nature of a process may concern the *spatial* direction.

A process may be cyclic with respect to its *quantitative* direction. In the completely cyclical process the "curve" of the quantitative senses of each cycle (increase, decrease, constancy — in whatever combination) is the same not only in the sequence of these senses but also in the amplitude of each.

A process may be cyclic in its *qualitative* direction. The completely cyclical process would effect the passage of the unit of the process, in a uniform sequence through the same qualitative phases in each recurrence.

Finally, cyclical recurrence may relate to *time direction*, but only, however, when the temporal is combined with other directions of the process. Such recurrence means a *periodical time rhythm*, of whatever kind of periodicity, in regard to the phases of the cycles or the entire cycles themselves (rhythms: 1–2; 1–2–3; 1–2–3–4; etc.).

When a process is completely cyclical in all directions it becomes *absolutely cyclical.*

The third fundamental pattern of recurrent processes may be styled *variably or creatively recurrent.* This applies to recurrences which are not absolutely identical, and the successive stages of which are not always linear or cyclical, or unchangeable or regular, but vary. In one link the movement may be unilinear, in another oscillating, in a third cyclical, in others curvilinear, and so on.

Thus the *variably recurrent pattern is the broadest and richest of these conceptions*. It does not ascribe to an entire historical process or to all sociocultural processes any perpetual tendency or direction which must be followed without change. It does not assume that social and historical processes must always proceed either along a straight line, or spirally, or in cycles, or in any other single manner or direction. Some social processes entire, and others in part, do indeed run along a straight line, but within definite limits, after which they continue, here in loops, there in irregular oscillations, elsewhere in waves and in other different forms. Since sociocultural processes are as manifold in pattern as life itself, as rich and creative as the activity of the highest human genius, it would be strange if they should in fact be so poor in creative variations as to follow eternally one route, one direction, one pattern of trajectory which the limited sense or the nonsense of a theorizer would like them to follow.

Differing thus from the other two, the variably or creatively recurrent pattern stresses particularly the following three points. First, since there is no one permanent linear trend, and since the directions change, historical and social processes incessantly undergo ever new variations of the old themes. In this sense they are filled with surprise and are seldom predictable in their totality. In this sense history as a whole never repeats itself, and the entire historical process has a unique aspect at any point of its existence, an aspect which is perhaps predictable only in its unpredictability.

So far this conception agrees with the unicist conception. However, as has been mentioned, processes with a unique aspect are not woven of entirely unique materials. They have recurrent and repeated elements. To the extent that they repeat themselves, either in units, or in space, or in time, or in two or more of these factors, this conception is congenial with the cyclical theory, which views all the processes as recurrent, absolutely or relatively. It fits with the linearists' point of view in admitting a linear trend for a portion of a process, and during a limited period, but sharply disagrees with them in their main contentions. This leads to the second point.

The variably recurrent conception stresses the *existence of limits* in the linear direction of most social processes. This is the point at which the conception differs radically from those of the linearists and cyclicists. The latter either do not recognize the existence of limit in a given direction, or are obliged to claim that the direction changes all the time (since the process goes in a circle) but that the whole process runs in the same, or a similar, circle again and again. The variably recurrent conception, on the contrary, claims that many processes go on for some time without any appreciable change in their direction, but that sooner or later the trend reaches its limit, and then the process turns aside into a new path. This means the denial of the existence of a perpetual main linear trend in history and most of the social processes. As to history as a whole, since it is not finished as yet and since the future is unpredictable, we do not and cannot know whether there is any continuous and main trend and any terminal point to which mankind is being led.

The third point involves the so-called principle of *immanent causation*, or self-regulation of sociocultural processes. According to this principle, when the unit is integrated the change in the direction of the process is caused not only and not so much by the interference of external forces but by the inner forces of the process itself and by the nature of its unit. Just as the living activity of an organism breeds its death, regardless of any external accident or external forces, so any sociocultural process occurring in an integrated unit and moving in a certain direction generates, by virtue of this activity, "forces" or "causes" which change the unit of the process and its direction.

The subsequent scheme recapitulates the discussed classification of processes.

- **Becoming (process) *versus* Being**
  - Unique
    - (1) absolutely
    - (2) in the unit only
    - (3) in the unit and in space only
    - (4) in the unit and in its time span only
      - No identity or similarity of the processes in the aspects in which they are unique
  - Recurrent
    - (1) in space only
    - (2) in the life span of the unit only
    - (3) in the lifetime of the unit as well as of that of other units
    - (4) in the unit, in time, and in space (absolute)
      - Gradation of the recurrences from complete identity to a partial similarity
        - *Linear*: oscillating, spiral, branching
          - spatially linear, quantitatively, qualitatively, cumulatively
            - periodical
            - nonperiodical
        - *Cyclical*: absolutely, completely, incompletely
          - spatially cyclical, quantitatively, qualitatively, cumulatively
            - periodical
            - nonperiodical
        - *Variably recurrent*
          - spatially, quantitatively, qualitatively, cumulatively
            - periodical
            - nonperiodical

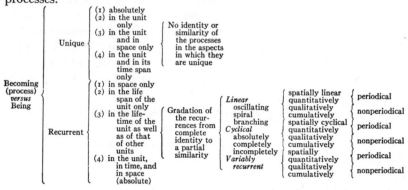

We are now about to turn to a study of sociocultural fluctuations mainly in the Graeco-Roman and the Western cultures, concentrating on the period from about 600 B.C. to the present time. These cultures are taken because they are better known to us than the others: they have left fuller and more accurate records than possibly any other culture. A period of, roughly, 2500 years is taken because long-time fluctuations cannot be studied properly in a shorter space of time, especially the profounder "waves" of history. Even this period is too short for the purposes of this study. But a lack of any even remotely satisfactory data for the time previous to 600 B.C. prevents our going beyond it into the past. But, though concentrating on these cultures and periods, we shall at the same time, in a study of the fluctuations of each class of phenomena, make additional, but much shorter, excursions into the sociocultural fluctuations of several other cultures.

Now comes a more important question: What is studied in these cultures? What kind of fluctuations? What kind of problems? How are they investigated? For what purposes? A full and adequate answer to these questions is offered in the subsequent parts of the work. At the present we need only to indicate briefly a few of the main problems investigated. The questions dealt with are these: (1) Have the Graeco-Roman and the Western been logically integrated cultures? (2) If they have been, around what major premises have they been integrated? (3) Do the principles of the Ideational, the Sensate, and the Mixed types of culture offer a key for the solution of the problem of their integration? (4) If these principles do furnish a key, do they make it possible for the observer to comprehend the main forms of the science and philosophy, art and ethics, law and politics, economic and social organization, psychology and ideology, of the bearers of these cultures? (5) Has the logico-meaningful integration in these cultures been accompanied by the causal-functional? (6) Have these cultures and their main compartments remained unchanged in the course of time with respect to their predominant culture type, or have they undergone a substantial change in this respect? If they have experienced such alterations, then at what period were they predominantly Ideational, or Sensate, or Idealistic, or Mixed? (7) If there were these variations, what have been the main waves and alternations in these cultures? How long did each type last? Is any regular periodicity observable in the alternation of these types? (8) What have been the relationships in this process of various compartments of the cultures? Have they all been changing synchronously? Have some compartments been changing earlier than the others? Has the change in the direction of the cultural changes been always parallel or opposite or independent? (9) What have been the "causes" and factors of the change? And so many more questions might be specified without, however, exhausting the problems touched upon and discussed in the present work.

The work represents a kind of grand fugue, the scoring of which involves the weaving into it of countless smaller fugues played by various sections of the orchestra. If the grand fugue is scored poorly, there is consolation for the composer: each little fugue may stand on its own feet and may have its own value, regardless of the value of the larger work which is intended to absorb all the smaller parts and to be the crowning climax of all of them.

If not for logical, then at least for pedagogical reasons, the study opens with a treatment of the fluctuation of the arts in the cultures studied. The pictorial and "concrete" nature of some of the art forms, particularly of painting and sculpture, and partly of music, architecture, and literature, seems to provide the best conditions for introducing the reader into the heart of the problem. Hence, we turn directly to a study of the arts.

PART TWO

FLUCTUATION OF IDEATIONAL, IDEALISTIC, AND SENSATE FORMS OF ART

5

IS THERE ANY UNIFORM SEQUENCE IN THE FLOURISHING OF VARIOUS ARTS IN THE HISTORY OF A GIVEN CULTURE? PRELIMINARY CRITICAL SURVEY OF THEORIES ON THE SUBJECT

I. Introductory Remarks

The purpose of this section is to inquire into the meaning of the Ideational, Sensate, Idealistic, and the Mixed categories in the field of art phenomena.

Before passing to the realization of this plan and to the present writer's theories, it will be illuminating for us to glance, at least briefly, through the main body of theories in the field of these problems. Such a glance will disclose generally the status of contemporary knowledge of the subject. Thus, it will serve also as an introduction to the development of the special position taken in the present work.

II. Theories of the Recurrence of Art Phenomena in Space, in Time, and in Both Together

Like most of the cyclical theories of social process, the theories of recurrence in the field of art phenomena belong mostly to the class of those which hold for a repetition of certain uniformities in space.

As the first problem of the recurrence of art phenomena in social space we ask ourselves: Is there any uniform sequence in the development and blossoming of various forms of art in cultures? For instance, in all cultures is it architecture (A) that develops and blossoms first, then sculpture (S), then painting (P), then music (M), and finally literature (L)? Does architecture lead, always and in all cultures, in the change of style, while all the other forms of art lag behind in the above sequential order? Does, therefore, this uniform sequence A, S, P, M, L recur universally in social space (in all cultures)? If not, then is there any other uniform sequence?

Of several recent works which deal with this problem two of the most interesting, if not most important, are Sir Flinders Petrie's *The Revolutions of Civilization*, whose contentions were recently reiterated in his article "History in Art," and Paul Ligeti's *Der Weg aus dem Chaos*. According to Petrie not all forms of art in a given culture, or in its great period, blossom simultaneously. Some branches of art always reach the stage of liberation from archaic, and advance into free and finer, forms earlier than others. Generally, there is a uniform and regular sequence: such a turning point appears first in architecture and sculpture,

> next comes Painting, then Literature, Music, Mechanics, Theoretic Science, and lastly Wealth. When there is no survival of useful abilities, then the race is doomed, and only lives on its prestige and savings, until its wealth attracts a more vigorous people.

The theory of the eminent Egyptologist is undoubtedly very stimulating and suggestive. Is it, however, valid? I am afraid that he, like many others, ascribes to social and historical processes a uniformity which they do not have.

His sequence is based upon the "turning point from archaism to freedom" of each cultural class. Is the meaning of "turning point" clear enough and sufficiently definite so that such a point may be located and fixed? I am afraid not. And since the meaning is neither clear nor definite, it is not possible to locate the "turning point" objectively, whether in art, literature, music, or science; hence, any attempt to make such a location for each class of cultural phenomena is doomed to be questionable, and the entire sequence remains subjective.

Let us now turn to a recent theory of Paul Ligeti, set forth in his interesting and impressive work *Der Weg aus dem Chaos*. In contradistinction to Petrie he does not think that "Sculpture and Architecture go closely together in all ages." Ligeti thinks that the blossoming of architecture in all cultures always precedes that of sculpture. The essence of Ligeti's theory of the art sequence is as follows: in any great culture, at the beginning of its development architecture is the first and earliest form of art to blossom; then comes the blossoming of sculpture, which happens at the period of maturity; and finally, the blossoming of painting takes place at the declining stage of the culture. This order is invariable and uniform in the development of all great cultures. In European culture the Middle Ages are marked by the greatest development of architecture, while sculpture and painting remain primitive and undeveloped. The Renaissance is the period of the triumph of sculpture, as the synthesis of architecture and painting.

> Behind the rhythm of these arts there is a law, or the uniformity which operates everywhere that human culture is given. . . . Each culture begins with the architectonic period and ends with the period of painting.

Side by side with these long waves, on which are based Ligeti's "law of the three states" in the development of art and culture, there are waves of a still longer duration, as well as other waves which are shorter. Thus, with regard to the longer waves, not only does every culture pass through these three states enumerated by Ligeti, but when all the cultures are taken together in their time succession, the same uniformity operates:

the great ancient cultures, like the Egyptian, are predominantly architectural; later cultures, like those of Greece and Rome, are predominantly plastic; while modern cultures, like the European, are predominantly *malerisch.* Such is the long rhythm of the development of human art generally and human culture as a whole.

As to the shorter waves, there are periods about one hundred and thirty years long, in which the same rhythm, architecture-sculpture-painting, takes place.

It goes without saying that such a construction involves an estimation of what is the highest achievement in each of these arts, and as with all such evaluation, it contains an element of subjectivity. For one investigator the highest achievement in a given art may be of one kind, for another of a different kind. Correspondingly, the periods of the highest accomplishment would be different for such investigators. If, however, an investigator claims to have discovered a uniform law, the least that his theory must do is to run in general agreement with the estimates of the highest points as established by many competent investigators. When we take the statements of Ligeti and confront them with the estimates of other authorities, the result is that Ligeti's "uniform law" does not appear to be uniform at all, ceases to be a general law.

Let us consider the cultures of Egypt, India, China, Japan, France, Italy, Germany, England, Greece, and Rome, the time sequence in which the specified arts reached the zenith of their blossoming, and the periods in which this blossoming took place, according to several historians of the respective literature, art, and music of each country. It becomes clear at once that Ligeti has elevated into a uniform law something which exists only in a limited number of cases: in only three cultures out of the ten considered — that is, in Greece, Germany, and France — does his sequence occur. In the other seven cultures the sequence is either the reverse of or quite different from his "law of lag" and his sequence. Thus we again have a case in which "an ugly fact kills a beautiful theory."

Postponing for a moment a characterization of the subsequent part of Ligeti's theory, let us review briefly some other theories of the uniform sequence of the development of various arts in various cultures or, what is the same, theories which claim that in all cultures certain arts always lead in the change of style while other arts always lag. Such a theory of a uniform lag is but the theory of uniform sequence of change in various arts. In either a systematic or an unsystematic way such contentions have been set forth many times before Ligeti and Petrie. For instance V. de Laprade developed a theory that the art of the Orient (India, Egypt, Persia, China) was predominantly architectural; the art of Greece and Rome, predominantly sculptural; of Christian medieval Europe, mainly *malerisch;* and of the modern time, essentially musical. "Architecture responds to God; sculpture and painting, to an ideal or real man; music, to the external sensate world."

The theories of Ligeti and Laprade, as well as several others of this type, are possibly influenced by the theory of G. W. F. Hegel's *Aesthetik*. In any case, there are several resemblances between Hegelian theories and the theories of these men. The essentials of that aspect of Hegel's theory which is relevant to this problem are as follows. In conformity with the chief principle of his philosophy, Hegel views the evolution of art as the process of self-realization, or of an unfolding of the Idea or Spirit, in the course of time. In this process of unfolding there are three stages (*Hauptstufen*), each with its characteristic type of art: the *symbolic*, the *classical*, and the *romantic*. In the symbolic stage and type of art

> The Idea is still seeking for its true artistic expression, because it is here still essentially abstract and undetermined, and consequently has not mastered for itself the external appearance adequate to its own substance.

Therefore, only by symbolism can it express itself, in crude forms in which there is little real resemblance between the idea and the exterior forms in which it is clothed. Here matter dominates the Idea, and the Idea does not find an adequate expression in Sensate forms.

> The second type of art, the classical, is based upon an absolutely homogeneous unity of content and form.

Here is an adequate bridge between the Idea and its expression. Finally

> The romantic type of art annuls the completed union of the Idea and its reality.

But as "Mind is the infinite subjectivity of Idea," it does not find a quite perfect expression in the finite nature of the sensate means of its objectization, even in the classical art.

> To escape from such a condition the romantic type of art once more cancels that inseparable unity of the classical type, by securing a content which passes beyond the classical stage and its mode of expression.

Hegel develops these principles further, showing that the most adequate objectization of the symbolic stage and type is architecture; of the classical type and stage, sculpture; of the romantic, painting and then, especially, music and poetry. This is not all. Each of the arts, in the process of its evolution, passes through these three stages; for instance, architecture evolves through symbolic, classical, and romantic periods. The same is true of other arts: sculpture, painting, music, poetry (though Hegel prefers to use somewhat different terms to designate the stages of poetic evolution).

We have, then, a complex scale of progression from the smallest to the fullest unfolding of Spirit in the movement from architecture to poetry, and in the movement of each of the arts from the symbolic to the romantic stage. Viewed from the standpoint of the Hegelian classifications the art of the Orient has remained almost exclusively at the symbolic, the art of Greece and Rome at the classical, stage. The only art to reach the romantic stage has been the European, especially that of modern Europe.

Since this whole work is a refutation of linear conceptions of socio-cultural processes there is no need to make a special criticism of the Hegelian theory at this point. As far as its factual side is concerned the above data and the data of the subsequent chapters will be sufficient to show its inadequacies and blunders.

A further type which it is necessary to discuss is represented by the theory of J. Combarieu, according to which music, in the change of its style, uniformly lags behind the other arts.

> Music almost always lags in social evolution. Schütz, Bach, Händel should be pushed back a century if one is to find a social mentality corresponding to their artistic mentality. In their sonatas Mozart and Beethoven express the charming conception of life which existed much earlier. The Germans had their musical romanticism about two generations later than their literary romanticism. Even Weber, in the songs of his *Freischütz* (1821), was lagging behind Herder and Bürger.

The invalidity of this generalization follows from my previous remarks and from the data.

In brief, there are so many exceptions to the rule of Combarieu, D'Indy, and others, that there remains no rule at all. Only by disregarding the extensive array of contradictory facts can one insist upon it.

Mutatis mutandis, the same may be said of many other theories of the existence of a universal and uniform lag of certain arts when compared with others.

Of the several theories under discussion in this chapter which try to establish a definite and universal sequence in the development of various arts in all cultures and civilizations, we are obliged by the facts to adjudge their claim as, at best, only partially valid. No such uniform and universal sequence exists, and however valuable and interesting in other respects are the theories which have been tested, in this respect they must be regarded as a distortion of the truth.

6

IS THE CURVE OF ART DEVELOPMENT UNIFORMLY SIMILAR IN VARIOUS SOCIETIES AND CULTURES? PRELIMINARY CRITICAL SURVEY OF THEORIES ON THE SUBJECT *(Continued)*

The preceding chapter shows that the sequence of the blossoming of the various fine arts — painting, sculpture, architecture, music, and literature — is different in various cultures. In this chapter I am going to discuss a problem somewhat similar, namely: *Are the curves of art development in general, and of the specific arts in particular, essentially the same in various cultures? Do they pass through the same stages?*

Since, as we shall see, the nineteenth and the beginning of the twentieth centuries have been periods of belief in the existence of rigid uniformities and, to a considerable extent, of a linear evolution in cosmology and biology, as well as in sociology, it has been believed also that various cultures and their art pass through the same stages of evolution. A very great number of social scientists and journalists, from Auguste Comte, Herbert Spencer, and E. B. Tylor, to Letourneau and other *dii minores*, have been busy with the formulation of "the laws of evolution," of "progress," of "stages of development," of the historical trends and tendencies in all fields of culture, including art.

During these years even many partisans of what may roughly be called the creatively recurrent or cyclical interpretation of the direction of sociohistorical processes have also believed, despite the difference of their conception from the linear, in the uniformity of the "curve" of cultural development in general, and art development in particular, in various cultures and in various societies. Oswald Spengler may serve as an example of a "cyclicist" who has succumbed to this obsession by "uniformity" in space. In spite of his contempt of the social science of the nineteenth century, like most of the "cyclicists" he did not succeed in freeing himself from the tenets of the nineteenth-century dogmas of the "universal uniformity" and "invariable rigidity" of the "laws of social development" for all cultures and societies. "Cultures are organisms, and world-history is their collective biography." "Every culture passes through the age-phases of the individual man. . . . Each has its childhood, youth, manhood and old age." This is not much different from Auguste Comte's "law of the three states" through which, supposedly, all cultures must pass, nor is it much different from most linearist conceptions.

Since the linearists as well as the cyclicists have believed in these dogmas in regard to the evolution of whole cultures, it is natural that the majority of theories of art evolution in various cultures have been formulated with the same assumptions as to the uniformity of the curves of evolution in various cultures.

They claim that any art system is finite in its existence: it appears, blossoms, and declines. I agree with this, because not only art but, as Plato says, "everything [on this earth] which has a beginning has also an end"; and therefore any empirical system, not only art, "will in time perish and come to dissolution." There is no reason to insist further upon this platitude in special reference to art, nor painfully to try to prove its truth.

The second claim advanced by those holding such theories seems to be worthy of more serious consideration, namely, that the art systems of various cultures have the same or similar curves of development: origin, growth, zenith, and decline; or childhood, maturity, and senility. If they can show, with evidence, what the essential characteristics of art at each of these phases are, and that these phases, each with its special characteristics, are similar in the art systems of various cultures, then their contention becomes quite important, and is no longer platitudinous.

Do most of the theories discussed meet with these requirements? Unfortunately they do not. Most of them give only figurative expressions without any serious attempt to substantiate them in the ways indicated above. Without such a substantiation they hardly can be taken seriously and are of no scientific value.

The situation is different with all theories of uniform development in art which are supported by a solid factual substantiation and corroboration of their general contentions. Let us take the theory of a distinguished historian of art, W. Deonna, which is brilliantly developed in his several works, and especially in the three large volumes of his *L'archéologie, sa valeur, ses méthodes*.

Deonna takes four great art systems in sculpture and, in part, painting — the paleolithic, the neolithic, the Graeco-Roman, and the Christian — and tries to show that each of these systems has passed through similar fundamental periods of archaism, classicism, and finally decadence. In each of these phases the traits and style of all four systems of art are strikingly homogeneous and similar. The similarity is so great that the statues of early medieval Europe (before the twelfth century) can easily be mistaken for those of archaic Greece (before the sixth century B.C.). On the basis of an enormous amount of material, he proceeds to demonstrate the similarity of the phases in all four systems and the likeness of the art of the four in corresponding phases.

The *archaic phase* of art of the paleolithic, neolithic, Graeco-Roman (up to the sixth century B.C.), and the early medieval (up to the twelfth century A.D.) periods exhibits the same primitive technique, frontality, "horror of emptiness," lack of perspective or perspective by superposition of planes, lack of unity in the composition, triangular heads, "archaic smile," low foreheads, and a similar composition of ears, nose, hair, beard, and other parts of the human body. Likewise, when the *classical phase* in these four art systems is considered, particularly the Greek art of the fifth century B.C. and the Christian art of the thirteenth century, one finds a complete similarity between them. The technique becomes perfect, the statues begin to live, frontality disappears, and simplicity of perfection takes place. Idealism becomes supreme, and art now reproduces either the positively valuable and ideal object only, or idealizes natural objects: mortals are produced like young gods; human beings, even though old, are shown as young and perfect; nothing prosaic, ugly, defective, low, finds place in it. Both these arts are profoundly religious. Both are essentially anonymous, and the artists retreat before the community; both are local in detail but universal in topic; both incorporate the unity of mind of their entire society and are the work of the entire society; both are rationalistic, meditatively speculative, and free from any sensuality.

If we then take the period of "overripeness" — the end of the classical period and the beginning of the period of decline, in the Mycenaean, the Hellenistic, and the modern European arts — we again find, in all of them, a series of striking resemblances. In spite of being separated by great intervals of time, they show the same style, the same spirit, and similar forms and content. We find skilled technique which can reproduce anything, but, having no strong "soul" of its own, it mixes all kinds of styles incongruously, and conscientiously imitates the "primitive" style. Not idealism but sensory (visual) naturalism is now supreme. Art is down to earth. While the idealistic art deified mortals, this naturalistic art mortalizes the immortals. It imitates sensate nature and empirical reality. It has a particular inclination to the reproduction of the negative, the macabre, the pathetic, the passionate, the prosaic, the picturesque, and the ugly phenomena of life.

The outline shows that Deonna was not content merely with vague generalizations, but presented a vast amount of factual material for its substantiation and verification. Whether or not the main claims of his theory are valid we shall see on further investigation. For the present let us take some other theories of the same type. A theory set forth by Frank Chambers will serve as a good example.

Frank Chambers also tries to prove that the curve of art evolution, and its essential stages, are very similar in Ancient Greece and in Europe.

Making use of literature and literary criticism as the main body of his material, he comes to the following conclusions. Both arts have passed through two similar stages. The first stage is characterized by a nonaesthetic estimation of beauty and the fine arts. In this stage all the great art creations are produced, not for art's or beauty's sake but for the sake of religion, morals, patriotism, civic virtue, and other nonaesthetic ends. The fine arts as such, and beauty as beauty, are viewed negatively and resisted. However, this does not hinder the creation of the greatest art values. Such was the stage in Greece up to the fourth century B.C., and in Europe up to the Renaissance and the fall of classicism, *i.e.*, the Academies. In the second stage there appears an appreciation of the fine arts as such, and beauty for beauty's sake. At this stage the arts become free from their duties as the handmaid of religion or of other nonaesthetic values. "Aestheticism," art collecting, the connoisseur, art education, art criticism, and so on, now make their appearance. In spite of this, the art of the second stage hardly achieves the summits that were reached during the first stage, and it is soon destined to disintegration and decline.

While the theories of Deonna and Chambers deal mainly with the fields of *sculpture* and *painting*, other theories, making similar contentions concerning the uniformity of the main phases of art in various cultures, try to establish their claim with regard to *literature* and *music*. The theory of E. Bovet may be taken as an example for literature, and that of Charles Lalo for music. Both of these theories, however, go further than those of Deonna and Chambers and insist not only on the uniformity of the stages of the evolution of these arts in various cultures, but also on the recurrence of these stages (or cycles) in time in the same cultures: when one cycle ends, another, in a different concrete form but with similar stages, begins and, having run its course, is again succeeded by a new cycle with the same stages, and so on.

These theories do not, of course, exhaust the list. There are numerous other theories of the uniform development of art among various peoples and cultures. Such are, for instance, the theories which claim that among all peoples art passes from the "physioplastic" to the "ideoplastic" style (Max Verworn); from the expressionistic to the impressionistic (H. Schäfer and, in part, A. Rigle and A. Schmarsow); from the architectural, through the sculptural, to the *malerisch* style (Victor de Laprade, P. Ligeti, and others). Other theories claim that the art of all cultures passes, in the course of its development, through the stages decorative, plastic, architectural, and *malerisch* in conformity with a corresponding *Weltbegriff* (L. Coellen), and so on. As many of these theories will have to be dealt with further on, and as their defects are somewhat similar to those of the theories of Deonna, Chambers, Bovet, and Lalo.

It can hardly be questioned that between the art systems of various cultures there exist many similarities in both small and great matters. Whether they are due to diffusion or to independent and spontaneous creation, or to both factors, such recurrences of similarities in space and time are readily observable.

Quite different, however, is the claim that the essential stages of the life history of all art systems are the same, that there exists a uniform sequence of these stages, and that therefore the life curve of all art systems has practically the same configuration, with its height in the classic period and a decline in the direction of the initial (archaic) and the final (postclassic) periods. These claims appear to me to be questionable.

Not only in regard to the general form of the curve of art development and its phases, but also in regard to many, if not all, of the most important changes in the style of an art, the character and sequence are different in the art systems of various cultures. Here are a few instances:

(1) In some cultures the earliest art style is predominantly ideational or symbolic or ideoplastic (Max Verworn), or expressionistic (H. Schäfer); in other cultures it is predominantly visual, impressionistic, perspectivistic, illusionistic, or naturalistic; in still others both styles are found simultaneously.

(2) The alternation of these styles from the standpoint of the length of domination, of the frequency of alternations, of the intensity of the shifts from one to another, and so on, are again considerably different in various cultures.

(3) The art of some cultures (*e.g.*, the Hindu) remains predominantly ideational throughout its history, while the art of other cultures (*e.g.*, the paleolithic, the Creto-Mycenaean, and, in part, the Greek) remains predominantly visual or naturalistic.

(4) The same propositions can be made with regard to the idealistic (not to be confused with ideational) and impressionistic (as the extreme form of the visual styles), their presence or absence, their alternations, and so on.

In all of these and in many other respects the art systems of various, and especially of very different, cultures offer a considerable diversity, and exhibit a clear lack of any uniformity. If we grant that this is really the situation, which it will be our attempt to prove in subsequent studies in the present work, then the laws of the uniform development of art in various cultures, of the uniform lagging of certain arts behind the others, of uniform curves of the quantitative and qualitative rhythms of the arts — all these and similar claims so dear to the linearists, cyclicists, evolutionists, and uniformists, in social sciences of the nineteenth and twentieth centuries — are not laws at all.

7

IDEATIONAL, SENSATE (Visual), AND MIXED (Idealistic, Cubistic, and Other) STYLES IN ART: PAINTING AND SCULPTURE

I. Ideational and Sensate (Visual) Styles

Both per se and for the aims of this work, one of the most important forms of recurrence is the repetition (in space and time) and fluctuation of the Ideational, the Sensate (Visual), the Idealistic, and other Mixed styles in all their varieties and with all their secondary characteristics. It is important because, when it is understood, it makes comprehensible many essential traits of a given art in a given period, which otherwise would appear as meaningless *membra disjecta*. It is important also from the standpoint of the mentality incorporated in a given art. Enough for the preliminary remarks. Now for the definitions.

The pictures of Plate I reproduce a few of the familiar geometric designs of the Indians. Their meaning is quite different from and infinitely more complex than their visual form shows. The real meanings of the pictures are as follows:

In No. 1, the upper zigzag line (*a*) represents a snake; the rectangular fields under it (*b*), the sea moved by the wind. The dark corners of the rectangle (*c*) indicate calm on deep water, etc.

The design of No. 2 is called "cloud all alone." Its meaning is still more complex. It is as follows, according to the Zuñi Indians.

When a person does not go to the dances when they dance for rain, after her death she goes to the Sacred Lake and when all the spirits of the other dead people come back to Zuni to make rain, she cannot go, but must wait there all alone, like a single little cloud left in the sky after the storm clouds have blown over. She just sits and waits all alone, always looking and looking in all directions, waiting for somebody to come. That is why we put eyes looking out in all directions.

In No. 3 the main meanings of its various parts are as follows: (*a*) centipede; (*b*) savannah grass; (*c-f*) periwinkles; (*g*) butterflies; (*h-j*) snakes.

The meaning of No. 4 is:

The cross in the center represents four clouds on the horizon, the colored segments completing the inner circle represent red and blue birds soaring above the clouds. In the second circle are shown crosses representing red, yellow and blue corn. In the outer zone is a zig-zag line representing Mother East-

PLATE I

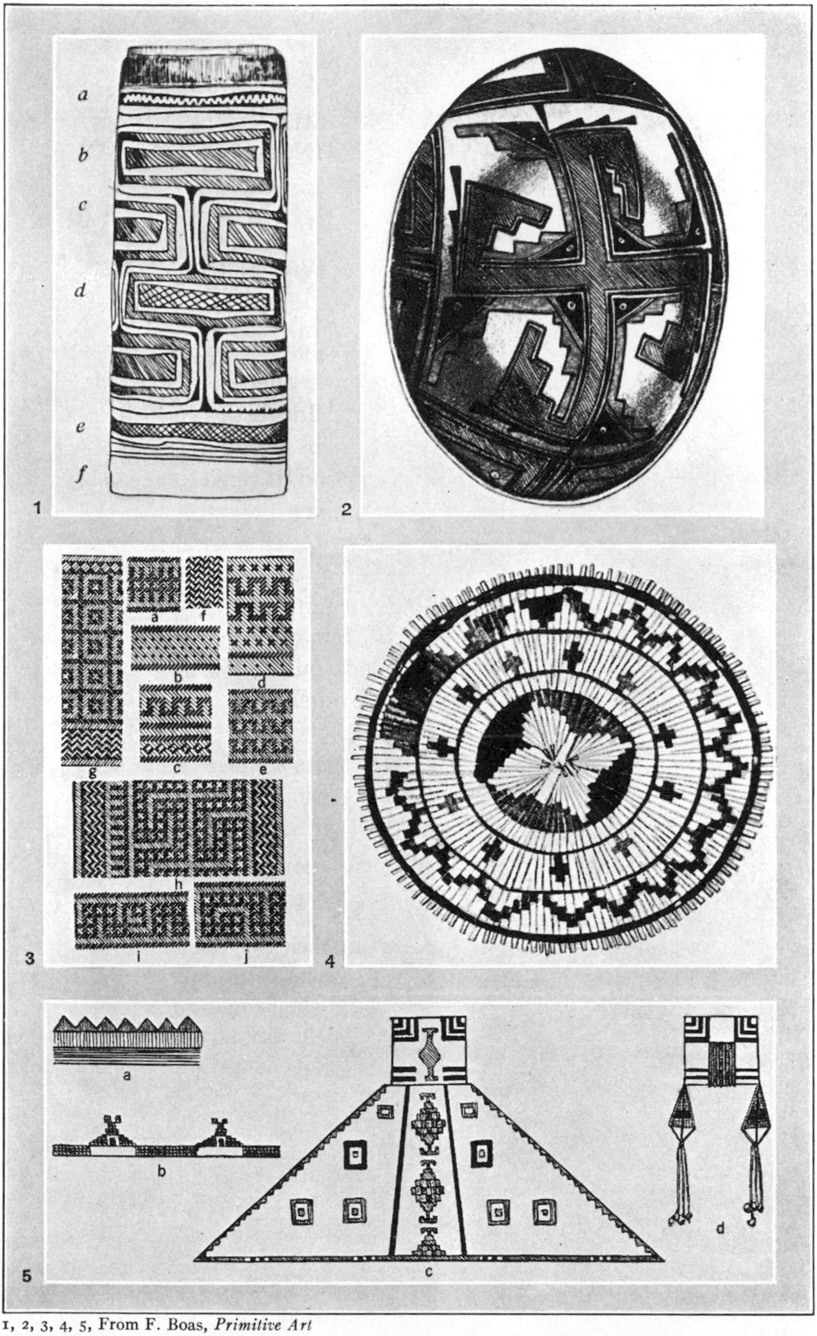

1, 2, 3, 4, 5, From F. Boas, *Primitive Art*

1, Bamboo case, from Melanesia. 2, Fragment of bowl, by the Zuñi Indians, New Mexico. 3, Patterns from baskets, from British Guiana. 4, Sacred shield, from the Huichol Indians, Mexico. 5, Designs, from the Cheyenne Indians, northwestern United States.

PLATE II

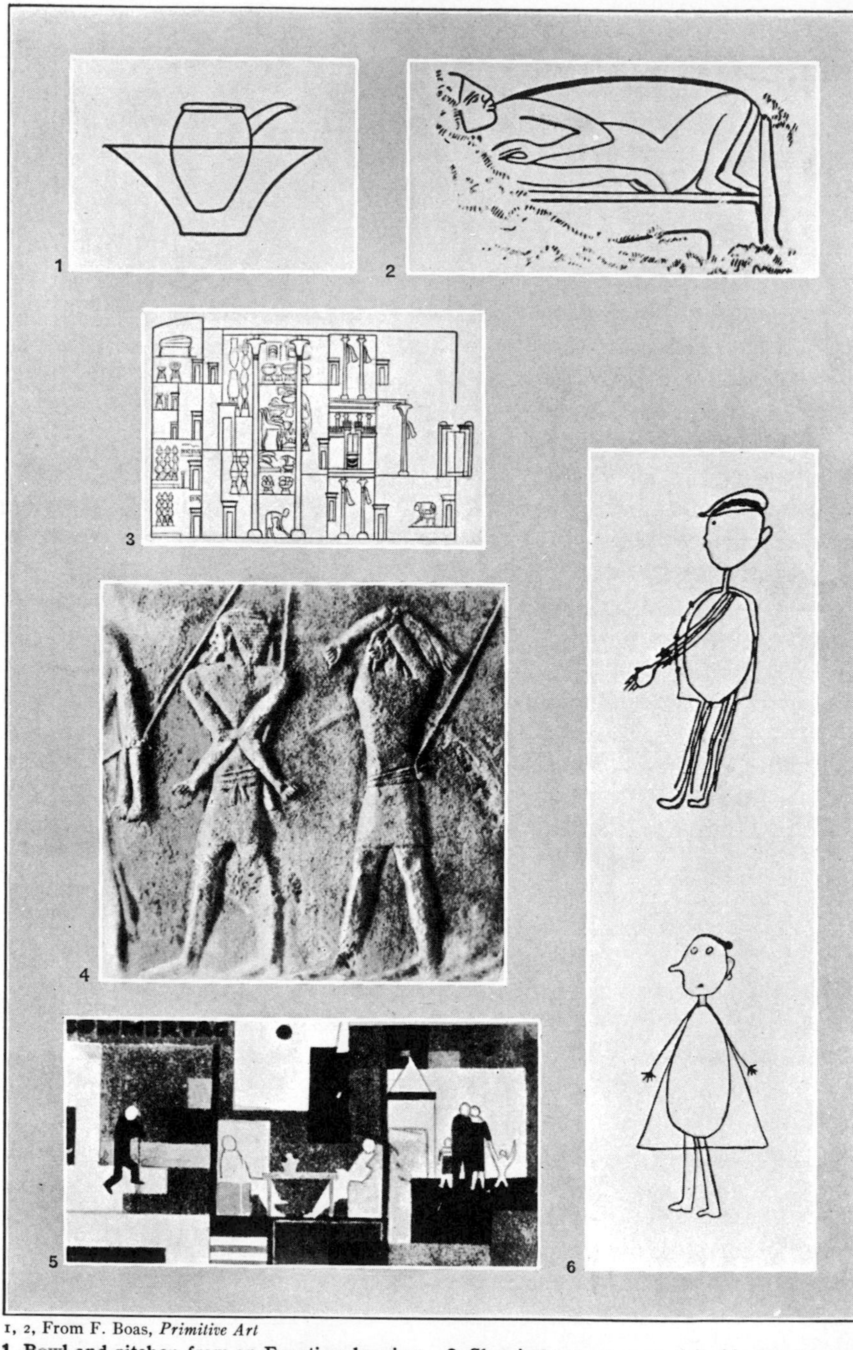

1, 2, From F. Boas, *Primitive Art*

1, Bowl and pitcher, from an Egyptian drawing. 2, Sleeping person covered by blanket, from an Egyptian drawing. 3, Palace in Amarna, from an Egyptian drawing. 4, Egyptian sculpture of prisoners, from the Temple of King Sahure. 5, Summer's Day, by O. Nerlinger. 6, Drawings, by contemporary children.

water, a Deity. Nine triangles between head and tail of the serpent represent mescal which is . . . held as a prayer for rain and for health.

In No. 5 figure (*a*) means mountains, a river, and a trail; figure (*b*), tents with fires in front. The meanings of the figures (*d*) and (*c*) are still more complex and abstract. There "the middle field represents the path of life of the child." The green dots in it symbolize "the child's good luck or the success that he will have in life. In this case green symbolizes growth and development; yellow, maturity and perfection; red means blood, life and good fortune." Other parts of the figures represent the age of the child, the heart, the unexpected events of life, and so on.

These examples show the existence of a style in painting or drawing where the designs have no or an exceedingly remote visual (sensate) resemblance to the meanings symbolized by them.

Figures 1 to 4 of Plate II reproduce respectively Egyptian illustrations of a jug in a basin, a woman sleeping under a blanket, an Egyptian palace (in Amarna), and several prisoners. With these there are a picture (No. 5), entitled *Summer's Day,* by a distinguished modern artist (O. Nerlinger), and drawings by contemporary children (No. 6). A mere glance at the pictures is sufficient to see their visual (sensate) "unnaturalness." Here again we have a set of pictures which seems to depict various objects not as they look to our eyes but as they exist in the mind of the artists, regardless of whether the picture has any visual resemblance to the objects when we look at them.

In Plate III, No. 1 is a reproduction of a famous work by Picasso. It depicts a cello or a violin, but again in a form quite different from that which it naturally impresses on the eye. The same is to be said of his *Lady with a Lute* (Plate IX), or of any "cubistic," "futuristic," or "modernistic" picture. They do not depict objects as they look to our eyes, but as they are in the mind of the artist, in their ideational essence, as it is thought of by the artist.

A few more examples. The next pictures we observe are a scene from a sarcophagus of approximately the fourth century A.D. (No. 2), and two scenes of the Crucifixion (Nos. 3 and 4) taken from the covers of a copy of the New Testament of about the ninth century. However the illustrations on Plates II and III differ from one another and from those on Plate I, these illustrations all have in common the trait that they do not reproduce the scenes and objects as they appear to our sight: such a conglomeration of figures and objects piled one upon another is impossible from the point of view of natural perspective. These pictures are ideational rather than visual or "natural."

If now we compare with these either the pictures created by paleolithic man, a sample of which (bison, No. 1) is given in Plate IV, or those of several contemporary primitive groups, a sample of which is also given (bushman rock paintings, No. 2), or the dying lion (No. 3) and the gazelle in the steppe (No. 4), from Assurbanipal's Palace in Nineveh, or virtually any other picture known to us as "natural," and the product of "skill," the contrast is clear: while the preceding group does not strive to depict the objects as they appear to our eyes, these last all attempt to depict them in their exact visual impression — as we see them and only so.

After these remarks and examples the profound difference between what I here style the Ideational and the Visual (Sensate) styles must be clear in its essentials to the reader before we can proceed to a more detailed and more precise and more meaningful analysis of these styles and their intermediary or Mixed forms.

In their pristine nature, the Ideational and the Visual (Sensate) styles, from the standpoint of the mentality which they represent and the purposes and forms of depicting objects, are directly opposite and as different as can be. One is "transcendental," the other "empirical" or "naïve realistic." One lives in the supersensory world of Being, the other in the sensate world of Becoming. One is symbolic in its striving to depict by "visible signs the invisible world," the other is "impressionistic" and "illusionary." One is static, because the world of Being is unchangeable and remains always equal to itself, like Plato's Idea or the believer's God, or the philosopher's Ultimate Reality. The other is dynamic by its very nature, because its sensate world changes incessantly.

Which of these styles and mentalities is real or realistic? It is useless to ask. The answer depends upon what is meant by real, reality, realistic. If by these is meant the "unchangeable essence of an object," then the Ideational style is realistic. If the elusive appearance of the sensory-perceptual world is meant, then the Visual style is realistic.

II. Main Subclasses of Ideational, Visual, and Mixed Styles in Painting and Sculpture

Each of the two chief styles has different degrees of purity, beginning with the purest and ending with such a mixture of the elements of both styles that one cannot recognize in it either the Ideational or Visual and is obliged to put it into an intermediary Mixed, or Ideational Visual, style.

I. IDEATIONAL STYLE

A. *Purest.* The subject matter is superempirical (supersensory) and immaterial (like God, the Virgin, the soul, the spirit, the Holy Ghost, and other religious and mystical topics) and its form (*i.e.*, the design, the picture, the sculpture) is purely symbolic, having no resemblance to the

PLATE III

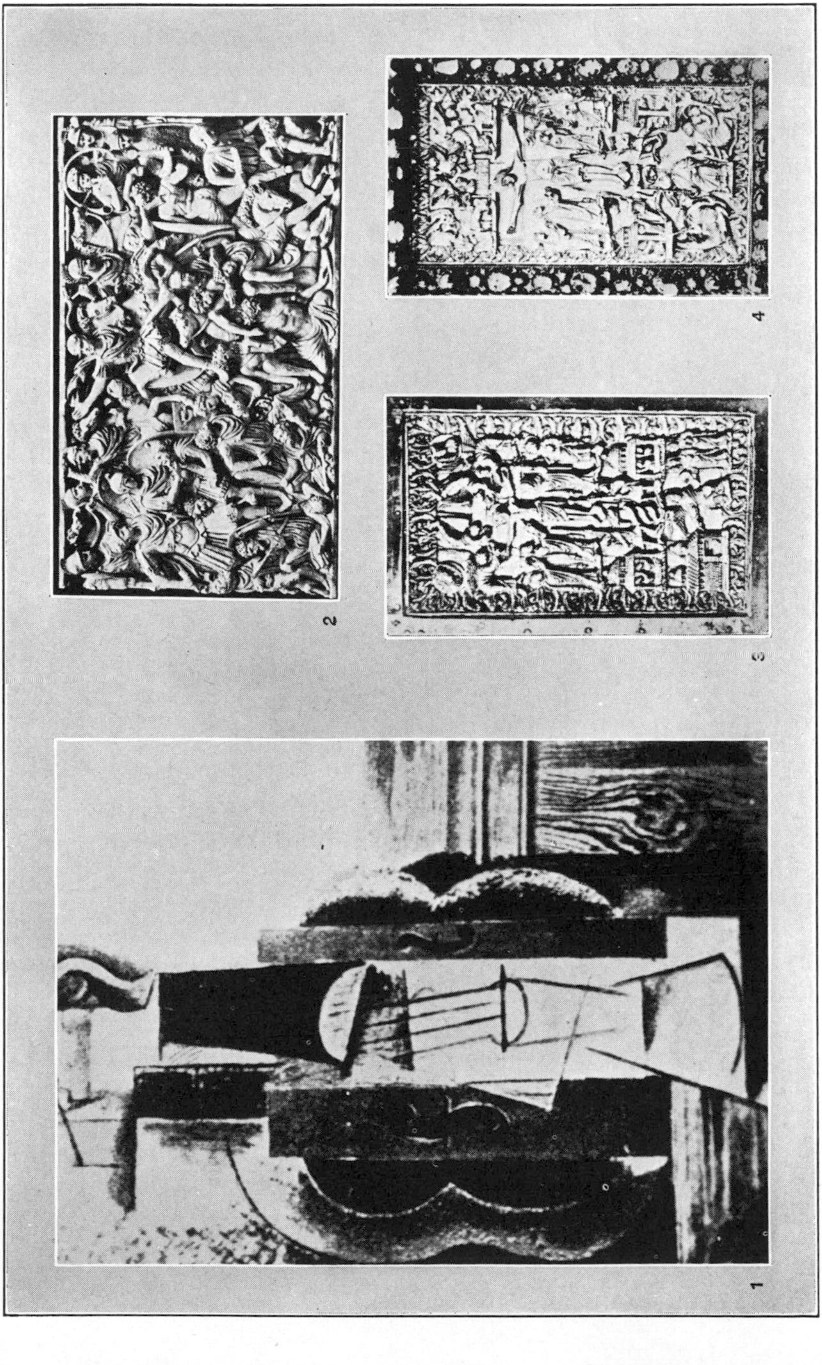

1, Cello, by Picasso. 2, Relief, from a Ludovisi sarcophagus of the fourth century. 3 and 4, Scenes of the Crucifixion, as represented on the covers of a New Testament of about the ninth century.

PLATE IV

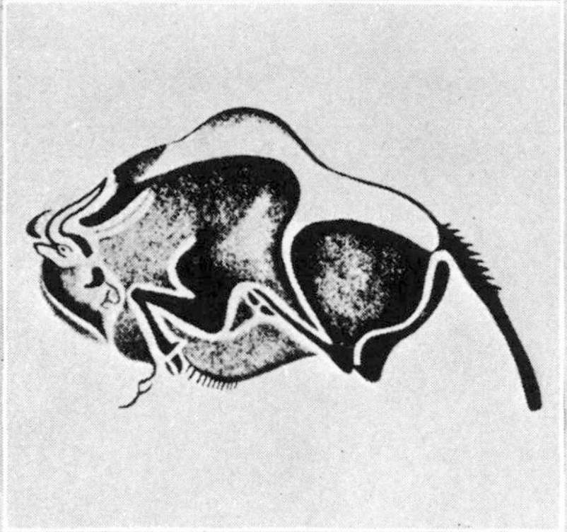

1

2

3

4

1, Cave painting of a bison dating from Paleolithic times, from southern France. **2**, Bushman rock paintings, from South Africa. **3**, Dying lion, and **4**, Gazelle in the steppe, from Assurbanipal's Palace in Nineveh.

visual or sensory appearance of the object depicted. Since the topic is "invisible," its visible symbol naturally cannot have any visual resemblance to it. Examples of such an art are to be found in the Christian pictures in the Catacombs — an anchor, a dove, an olive branch, etc. — which signify ideational phenomena quite different from these objects.

B. *Impure Ideational Style.* (1) Though the subject is superempirical, the form in which it is rendered attempts to embody some visual resemblance to what is considered to be its empirical aspect, *e.g.*, pictures of Paradise, Inferno, the Last Judgment, *Pietà*, allegorical figures of Virtue, Vice, Patience, Temperance, the Muses, and similar topics, rendered in the conventional visual form in which they supposedly exist or will exist.

(2) The subject is empirical but the form is symbolic, having little or no visual resemblance to the physical appearance of the subject. The geometric designs of many primitive peoples, symbolizing buffalo, snake, hunting, fishing, etc., like the Indian pictures discussed above, belong to this type.

II. VISUAL (SENSATE) STYLE

A. *Purest.* The topic is purely empirical and material and the rendering is purely impressionistic, that is, illusionistic, in its visual similarity to a momentary appearance of the empirical and sensory reality depicted. A good camera snapshot and the most completely impressionistic pictures are the best samples of the purest Visual style. Such a style is dynamic, because the visual empirical reality, through incessant play of light and shade, incessantly changes. It must be impressionistic in the sense of catching visual appearance at a given moment. In this sense it is necessarily illusionistic, showy, presenting material objects in as illusionistic a form as they offer to our sense perceptions. The pictures of the leading French impressionists of the end of the nineteenth century are conspicuous samples of such a purely Visual style. Their rendering, as well as their theory, stresses the essentials of this purest Visual style.

For them in painting the only reality was the visual appearance of the objects. Behind and beyond it there was nothing. This visual reality was ever fugitive and changing. Therefore the task of artists like Manet, Degas, Renoir, and especially Claude Monet, was to catch the momentary glimpse of the empirical phenomena as illusionistically as possible. What phenomena? It does not matter at all what is depicted.

The more completely Visual is the style, the more *dynamic* the picture. Since it strives to catch just a passing moment in the ever-fugitive appearance of the visual surface of the empirical world, the impression of change, of becoming, of dynamism, is unavoidable in such an art. Hence in conspicuously Visual pictures or sculptures or architectural creations (even in pictures of *nature morte*), the impression of dynamism, of restlessness, of fugitiveness, is, as we shall see, a usual satellite.

Moreover, the conspicuously Visual art in painting, sculpture, and, in part, even architecture, must be *malerisch*, and the more *malerisch* the more Visual it is. I use the term *malerisch* in H. Wölfflin's sense. Visually almost no material objects are separated from the rest of the world by a clear and unbroken line. Similarly the parts of the object are not separated from one another clearly. The visual world is the world of patches of different colors, of light and shade, imperceptibly merging into one another. It is not a world where the boundaries of each object are clearly outlined by an unbroken line definitely separating one object and one color from the others. It is a world of somewhat indefinite forms and colors merging into one another.

As we shall see (and this has been excellently shown by H. Wölfflin), the painting of the second half of the sixteenth, and especially of the seventeenth and subsequent centuries, tended to be more and more *malerisch* in comparison with the linear character of the painting, sculpture, and architecture of the preceding centuries. In order to see the point a glance at Plate V is sufficient.

The first pair of pictures (Nos. 1 and 2) represent similar subjects — a woman, as treated by the linear Dürer and by the *malerisch* Rembrandt. Dürer's etching gives a clear linear representation of the body with all its details. It is sculptural, corporeal, tactile, architectonic. The artist separates the figure clearly from its surroundings not because it so clearly stands out from the rest of the world to our eyes but because he knows by his other organs of perception that it is a separate object with each part having clearly defined individuality. He supplements and "corrects" ideationally its visual appearance as this is given by our eyes only. Quite different is the sketch by Rembrandt. The figure imperceptibly merges into the rest of the world. No part is linearly defined; instead, the patches of light and shade (and in other pictures the patches of various colors) serve to give the visual and illusionistic impression of the subject. Nothing tactile or sculptural is in the picture. It is an illusionistic representation of a fugitive appearance.

The same difference is clear in the second pair of pictures, No. 3 by Dürer, No. 4 by Ostade, which treat a somewhat similar set of conditions. Ostade is *malerisch*, Dürer linear. One is purely visual, the other is only partly so. Finally, Rubens's picture (No. 5) stresses the dynamism of the *malerisch* style.

B. *Impure Visual Style.* Like the Ideational style the Visual has different degrees of purity, running from the ideally pure — as outlined above — to less and less pure forms until the result becomes so mixed

PLATE V

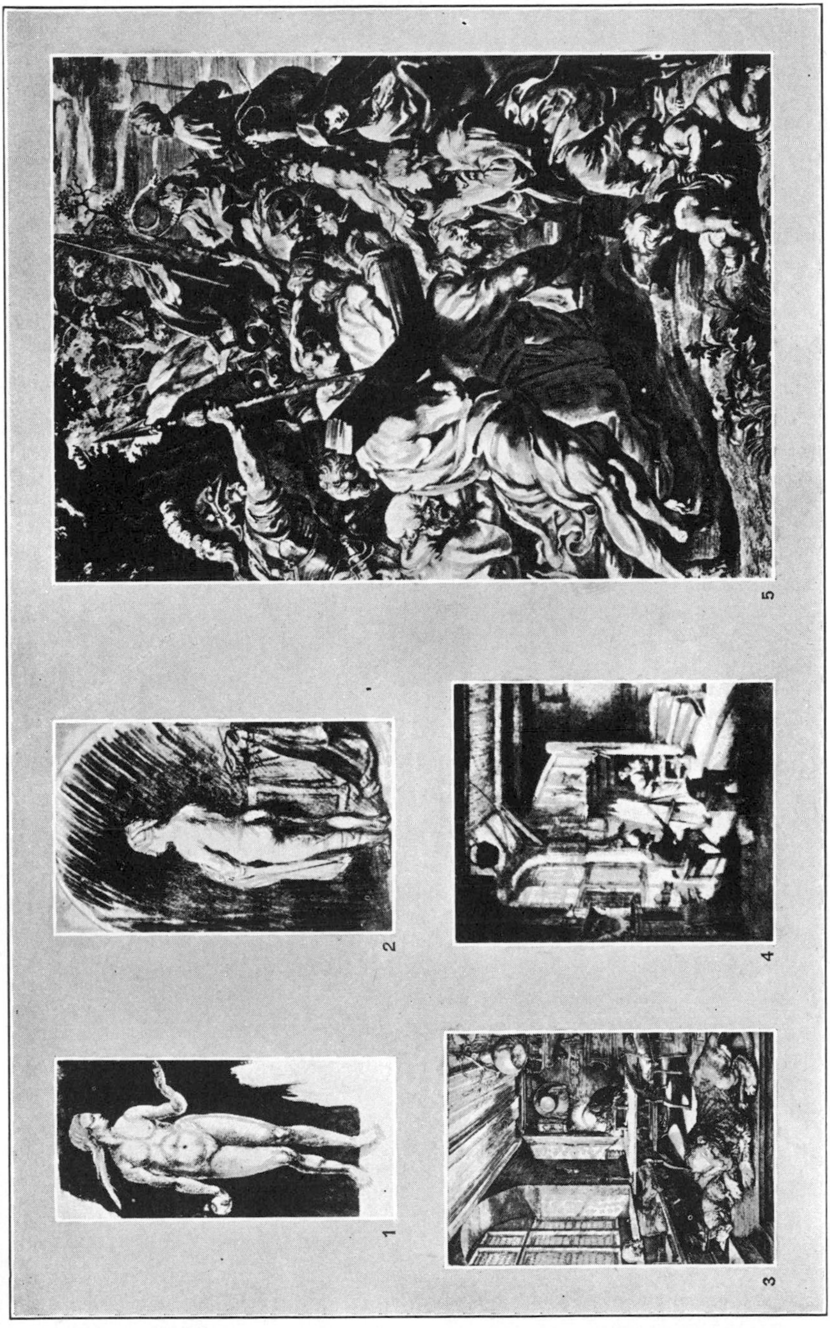

1, Study for Eve, by Dürer. 2, Woman dressing, by Rembrandt. 3, St. Jerome in His Cell, by Dürer. 4, The Artist in His Studio, by Ostade. 5, Christ Carrying the Cross, by Rubens.

PLATE VI

1

2

3

1, Old Woman with a Rosary, by Cézanne. **2**, Etching, by Heckel. **3**, Egyptian bust of Akhenaton.

that the Visual strain in it ceases to be dominant. The main Impure varieties of the Visual style are as follows.

(1) The *topic* is empirical or visual, but the *rendering* is not based exclusively upon the visual impression. It gives something not presented by the momentary appearance of the object to the senses, or suppresses some "incidental" and "secondary" visual elements, or introduces some generally ideal and nonvisual elements either in the content or in the style of the picture, sculpture, or architecture. Such are, for instance, "character paintings" and "character portraits." In these the artist tends to render not merely the momentary appearance of the subject, but his essential, lasting, dominant nature. Moreover, many so-called expressionistic paintings conveying some central idea are of this sort; and this is true also of most of the "classical" paintings and sculptures with their careful selection of subject, of setting, of every detail of the picture or sculpture, and their elimination of everything incidental, unimportant, unclassical, debasing, and so on.

The works of most of these periods, schools, and individuals belonging to the present subclass do not require to be represented by illustrations. The case of the modern Expressionists like Cézanne is less clear. Therefore, illustrations of this school are not out of place here. It is enough to glance, on Plate VI, at the picture by Cézanne (No. 1), or E. Heckel's portrait of a woman (No. 2), or the Egyptian bust of the reformer-pharaoh Akhenaton (No. 3), to see clearly the point we have been discussing. Their technique is either impressionistic and *malerisch*, or linear (portraits). In content they represent "character painting" with much that is nonvisual worked into the rendering.

(2) Another main form of an Impure Visual style results when the topic is only partly empirical but the rendering is conspicuously visual. Such is, for instance, a purely "naturalistic" rendering of the Last Judgment, of the Christ Child sucking his finger, of the Madonna in the form of a lady of the world about us, of Virtues and Vices, of the migration of the Soul, of Justice, of Sin, and so on.

III. MIXED STYLE

Though the Impure forms of the Ideational and of the Visual are in fact Mixed styles, the preponderance of the elements of one permits us to classify such renderings with the dominant style. By the *Mixed*, on the other hand, is meant a style containing such a mixture of the elements of both main styles that one cannot without difficulty decide which elements are preponderant.

The varieties of the Mixed style, as this occurs empirically, are many. Of these I shall mention here especially three.

A. *Idealistic Style.* Exemplified most strikingly by the Greek art of the fifth century B.C. and the religious art of Europe in the thirteenth century, the Idealistic style is simultaneously Ideational and Visual. It is visual in the form in which it renders its subjects, but not entirely: as we shall see, it ignores on principle the profane, the incidental, the negative aspects of visual reality and adds the noblest, the sublimest, the most beautiful and typical values, which are not apparent in the objects perceived visually. It idealizes, modifies, typifies, and transforms visual reality in conformity with its ideals and ideas. To this extent it is not Visual, but Ideational. The same is true of the subjects represented. They are carefully selected and in most cases are either of the nonempirical kind, or of the half-empirical — typical, generalized in their nature. Nothing vulgar, debasing, ugly, unmoral, eccentric, can be the subject of such an art. If negative values are chosen for depiction, even these are beautified, are used mainly for stressing, by means of contrast, the positive values. If an individual is represented in portraiture, he is typified according to the idealized type. In all these respects the Idealistic art presents a marvelous balance and "organic" union of the elements of the Ideational and of the Visual style with some slight domination of the Ideational. Thus it is a specific form of the Mixed style. It has, of course, its own gradations and degrees with respect to the amount of dominance of, or the closeness of approach to, one or the other of the two opposed styles. But in its sublimest form the Idealistic maintains a steady balance between the two.

A glance at Plate VII, in which the Idealistic is confronted with a purely Visual or "naturalistic" rendering, will make clear the nature of the Idealistic art. Two sculptures of Pericles (Nos. 1 and 2), one of Christ (No. 4), two of the *Pietà* (thirteenth century — No. 3, and sixteenth century — No. 7), and two representing Church (No. 5) and Synagogue (No. 6, thirteenth century) offer examples of the Idealistic treatment of subjects. The five illustrations of Plate VIII give examples of an impure Visual or "naturalistic" rendering of, respectively, Caracalla (No. 1) and Christ (Nos. 2–5). The contrast is strikingly conspicuous. The Idealistic treatment does not show anything of decay, senility, death, imperfection, even of a purely human excess of emotion and passion. Even mortals are depicted as immortal, or noble, or sublime, or as an idealized type. The "naturalistic" or impure Visual treatment depicts even the immortals (Christ) as mortal, the noble as vulgar, the great as debased. It is in a sense a "debunking" rendering which takes from its subjects most of their greatness, virtue, romance, charm, heroism, divinity, sublimity, and depicts them, naked, in their vulgar aspects. This is clearly shown by the pictures of Plate VIII. Christ in these pictures does not have anything divine or great. He is just a corpse, an imperfect

PLATE VII

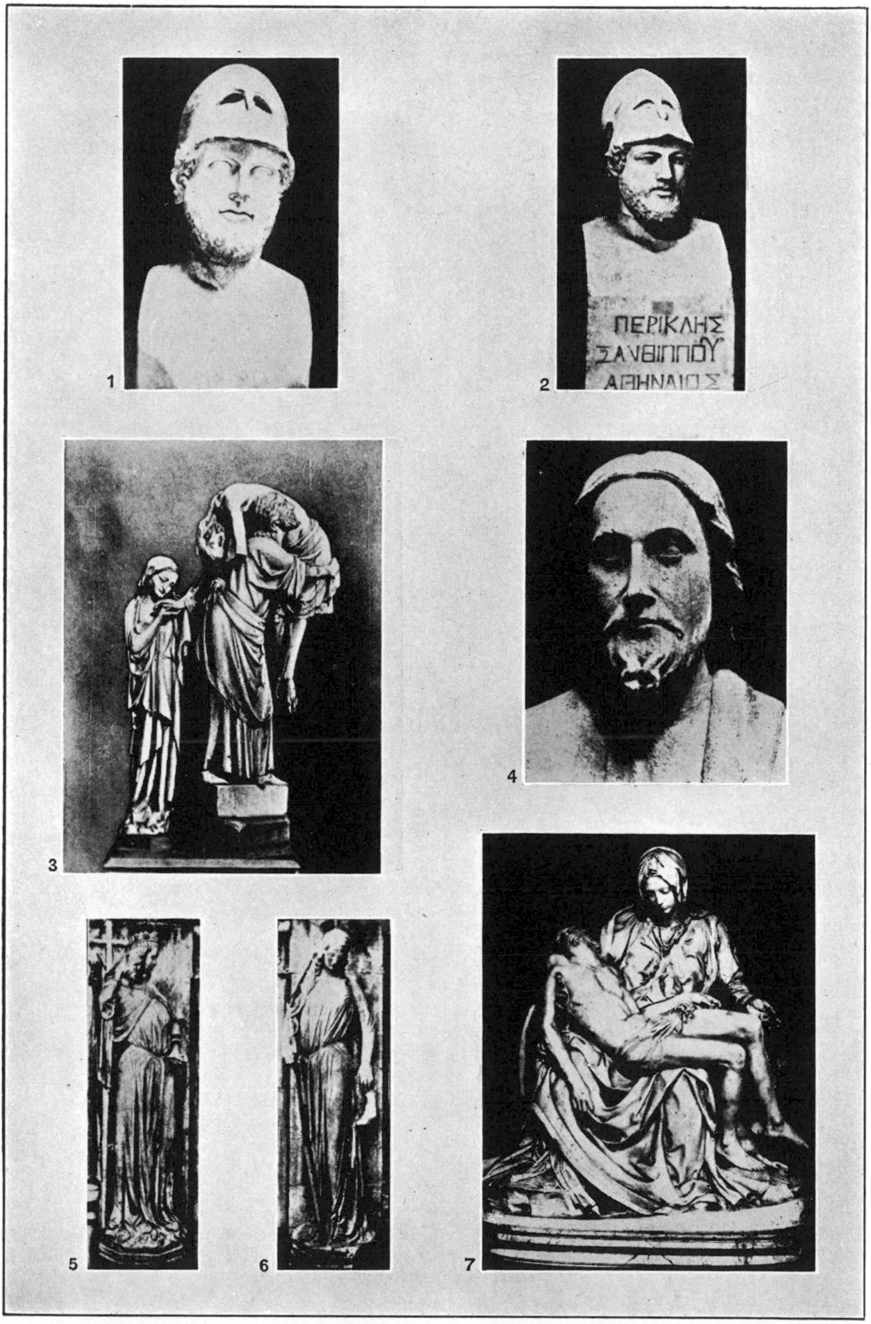

1 and 2, Greek busts of Pericles. **3,** Pietà, eleventh or thirteenth century. **4,** Head of Christ, thirteenth century. **5,** Statue representing the Church, thirteenth century. **6,** Statue representing the Synagogue, thirteenth century. **7,** Pietà, by Michelangelo, sixteenth century.

PLATE VIII

1

2

3

4

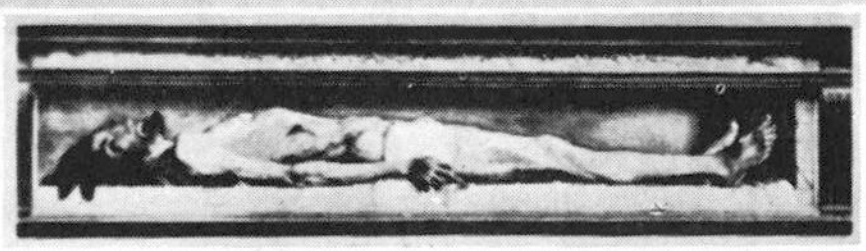

5

1, Head of Caracalla. 2, Head of Christ, Museum of Beauvais, fourteenth or fifteenth century. 3, Christ on the Cross, by G. Duvall. 4, The Crucifixion, by N. Gay. 5, The Dead Christ, by Holbein the Younger.

corpse, an imperfect ordinary human being. The same contrast is easily seen in the busts of Pericles and of Caracalla. In the first we are given an ennobled and idealized type rather than an individual portrait with real — *i.e.*, visual — traits. In the second, we see an individual as he "really" looks without idealized typification.

From these lines one can see that the Idealistic style of art is based on a specific *Weltanschauung* and philosophy of life, intermediary in nature between that of pure Ideationalism and pure Visualism (Sensatism).

From the very nature of the Idealistic and the Visual styles and the mentalities on which they are grounded, a series of associated traits follows. The most important of them may be mentioned here.

(1) To the extent that it does not try to reflect indiscriminately empirical reality as it is, but selects primarily those phenomena which conform to the supreme ideal, *the Idealistic art is almost always both a self-sufficient value created for its own sake, and a means to express, to manifest, to convey, to teach, to propagate the ideal and its values, which lie outside art.* Such an art is rarely art for art's sake, but almost always a partner or a companion, sometimes a handmaid, of religion, moral and civic virtue, or of other values of a nonaesthetic character. This does not, however, prevent such an art from reaching a position of supreme achievement in the realm of art alone.

The Visual (Sensate) art tends to be an art for art's sake so far as it does not tend to be a means to express anything except itself. It sees its main purpose and objectives in its reflection of the empirical reality as accurately as may be. It therefore is often associated with "aestheticism" in a particular sense, with that period in art history when art for art's sake appears, with its crowds of aesthetes, connoisseurs, collectors, professional critics, theorizers of beauty, professional artists who want to be artistic and nothing more. This is the period where art "liberates" itself, or rather believes that it liberates itself from any companionship with or subordination to anything outside of art itself: from religion, morality, civic duty, etc.

This means, in a straight formulation, that such a "realistic" and supposedly absolutely "free" art is, in fact, the victim of its illusion. In fact it becomes also a servant, but a servant to different bosses from those of the Idealistic or Ideational art — to the Golden Calf; to the empirical visual reality; to the sensate — *i.e.*, eudaemonistic, hedonistic, and utilitarian — needs; to the sensual fancies of the Epicureans, the rich, the powerful.

(2) Since the Idealistic art has behind it, as its inspiration and soul, some great ideal, such an ideal or value is always the value of a genuine collectivity. It is not, and cannot be, mere individual fancy. It is

logical, therefore, to expect that this value embraces within itself the collectivity as well as the individual artist creators. The creation then tends actively to involve the collectivity in which the individual artists are only the leaders. Everybody strives to contribute what he can to such a creation because the value is the common value of all. Hence the art of such periods tends to be stamped by the collective character of its creation, by the participation of masses in it, and by the anonymity of its individual artists. In this sense it is *nonindividualistic*, *collectivistic*, or "*familistic*." Often, as in the creation of many medieval Gothic and Romanesque or of early Byzantine cathedrals, or of some of the great Greek edifices, even the names of their builders and creators are either not preserved or were regarded as the names of the leaders only. Even when the real creator is an individual artist, his creation, if it is idealistic, reflects always a collective value and therefore remains collectivistic.

The Sensate (Visual) art, for the same reasons, tends to be, on the contrary, highly *individualistic*. It expresses the value of the artist, a value which may or may not be shared by the masses; here the artist is the creator; his name is attached to the creation and is inseparable from it. Since his creation is for him self-value, not a means to something else behind it, he is anxious to get a "copyright," to "immortalize" himself in it, to attach his name to it. Individualism in this sense and the Sensate (Visual) art are correlated to a high degree.

(3) Since the Idealistic art embodies some great values, any individual person of the common sort, any common landscape per se, any common event — unless they are symbols of the great value — can have no interest, or at best only a secondary interest. Only that object, person, or event which incarnates the value — has a direct relation to it — may properly be the subject of the Idealistic art. As to all other subjects, it either passes them by or strips them of any real individuality, turning them into rationalized and idealized types, a kind of algebraic formula without any concrete arithmetical value. Hence, the rationalistic, abstract, "typifying" nature of the Idealistic art. Under such circumstances, *the individual portrait, the empirical genre, the landscape, the historical scene, and anything concrete, not related to the ideal, are rare in such an art.* Its main content centers about its chief idealistic values. If these be religious, then it would represent deities, great religious events, religious history, doctrines, beliefs, and everything else of great significance as judged from the standpoint of these values.

In the Visual art the situation is the reverse. Only the empirical world, which always consists of individual objects, persons, events, is and can be the concern of such an art. It is the art of the portraiture of individuals; the art of the depiction of the daily *genre;* the art of empirical events, historical scenes, landscapes.

(4) The choice of the Idealistic art with regard to subject matter and treatment is determined by the nature of the *ideal value*, not entirely separated, however, from the empirical world, as it is in the Ideational art. All that is foreign to this value is unimportant for such an art and is passed over by it. The nonidealistic phenomena, especially, or the phenomena which are contrary to the ideal (unless they can be made to serve, by contrast, for the augmentation of the glory of the ideal value) are out of place in such an art. *It passes by the prosaic, the debased, the defective, the common, the earthly.* It does not see the baby as a baby, the old man as senile, the woman as womanish; what it sees is some general and perfected type of man. Therefore its babies are grown up; its old men are youthful; its women are manly — there is no sex in them.

The Visual art is *earthly* in its principle of selection. It depicts what may be interesting from the earthly standpoint, what may be "picturesque" ("Ah, how interesting!"), "stunning," "pretty," "effective," "romantic," "truthful," "sensational," "marketable." By the law of contrast, it tends to concentrate on common aspects of life and the world, on the low, debased, perverse, evil, disgusting, sensual. Hence its tendency to depict scenes of common or low life, historical events, the drunkard, the prostitute, the street urchin, the criminal, the pretty face, the seductive body, the nude erotic figure, the portrait, and so on; or to render something that gives gratification to the eyes by its configuration of forms and its play of colors.

(5) The world of the ideal is *thought to be eternal.* It is the world of Being. *Eternal means static. Static means quiet, calm, serene, immovable, and unagitated,* unshakably grounded and immersed in the ideal. The world of the empirical, and especially of the visual empirical reality, means *incessant change:* its forms, lights and shadows, colors and configurations, sounds, objects, and events, are in a ceaseless flux, moving along the scale of time. It is dynamic par excellence. Its human subjects are eternally agitated, full of passions, emotions, activity, effort. Their life is an endless succession of joys and sufferings, defeats and victories, comedies and tragedies, drama and boredom. Shall we wonder, then, that the Idealistic art tends to be relatively static? Its abstract figures are not agitated; they are calm and serene. Their whole world is also a kingdom of undisturbable, eternal, motionless unchangeableness. The Visual art, on the contrary, is charged with emotions, passions, agitation, and dynamics. It is dramatic, even comic and humorous, par excellence.

(6) Since sensate gratification is not the object of the Idealistic art, one cannot expect from it gratification of sensate needs or desires. It is not and cannot be frivolous. Therefore the figures of women are relatively rare in it; figures, faces, and scenes which are frivolous, seduc-

tive, sexual, tempting, gratifying as "pretty," are out of place in it. In the Visual art the situation is the reverse.

(7) Since the Visual art depicts, not the lasting, but the passing visual aspect of things, an incessant novelty, change, and variety in its pictures and sculptures are its traits also; otherwise, the same thing becomes sensuously boring, too familiar, devoid of a sense of novelty. The Visual art must change incessantly; therefore it is and must be an *art* of *mode* and *fashion* and *fad:* the newer the better; the more variety the more enjoyment. Its fascination is in its looks; beyond and behind it there is no infinity of ideational content as in an Ideational art work. The Ideational art, on the contrary, is of necessity associated with slow change; it is an art of *lasting, ever-meaningful tradition:* ever old in its form and ever new in the content which it does and can absorb because it deals with infinity. Its values are the eternal values, well selected and well chosen: they do not require incessant change. Absolute value is the supreme value; and the supreme value need not be replaced by other, inferior values, even if these are quite new, ever-changing, perfectly "modern." Therefore the period of the domination of the Ideational art is the age of tradition and convention. The period of the domination of the Visual art is the age of mode, fashion, seeking for the newest and the most modern. In such an age "*tout nouveau, tout beau.*"

Therefore there are no traditional and conventional forms in style; every artist tries to create his own style, different from the others. Hence, an incessant change of the forms and styles of art in such periods.

Such are some of the typical traits of the Idealistic as contrasted with the Visual (Sensate) art. As to its difference from the Ideational art, it must be clear from the above characterization of the Ideational style. The main difference between them is that while the pure Ideational art is not attached in any way to the empirical (visual, sensate) reality either by its subject matter or by its form, the Idealistic does have such connections. Many of its ideals are not transcendental but empirical; its forms are visual; with one foot it stands in the ideational, with the other in the empirical, world.

As we shall see, the *Idealistic* style usually occurs when the Ideational begins to decline, but without breaking entirely free from its "super-empirical" moorings; and when the Visual style begins to grow, without becoming, as yet, completely materialistic, mechanistic, hedonistic, and antireligious.

B. *Cubistic Mixed Style.* Another fundamental form of the Mixed style is represented by such styles as cubism, futurism, "imaginism," expressionism (as it is called often), and similar "modernistic" radical currents in art. These styles are neither predominantly Visual, nor Ideational. They are not Visual because they do not try to render the

PLATE IX

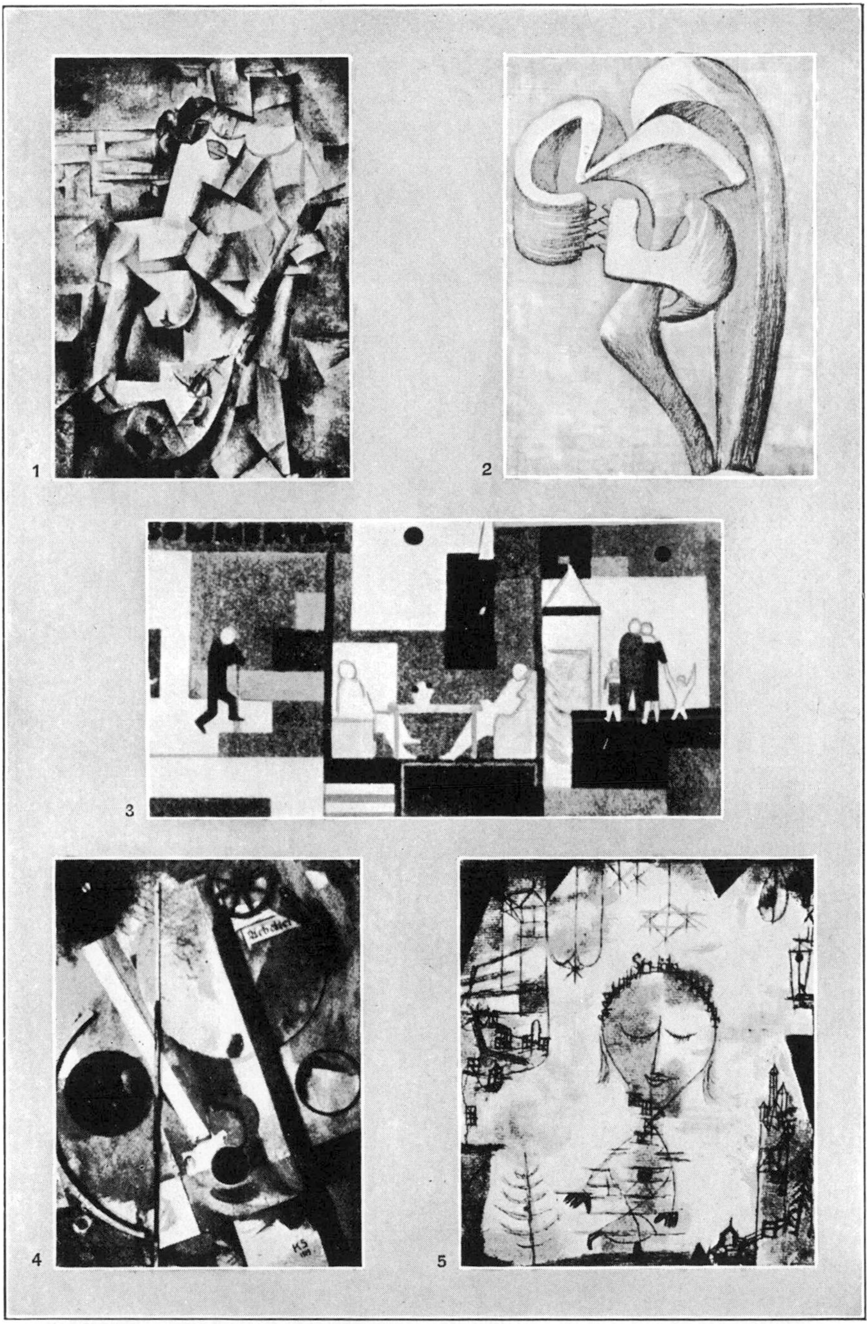

1, Lady with a Lute, by Picasso. 2, Abstract painting, by Picasso. 3, Summer's Day, by Nerlinger. 4, Das Arbeiterbild, by Kurt Schwitters. 5, Entfernung, by Paul Klee.

PLATE X

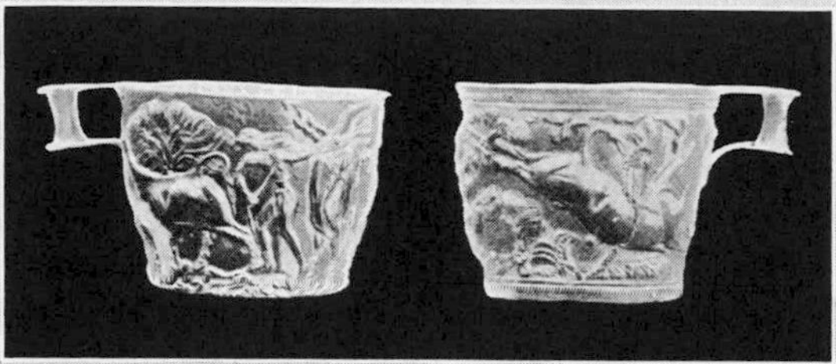
1

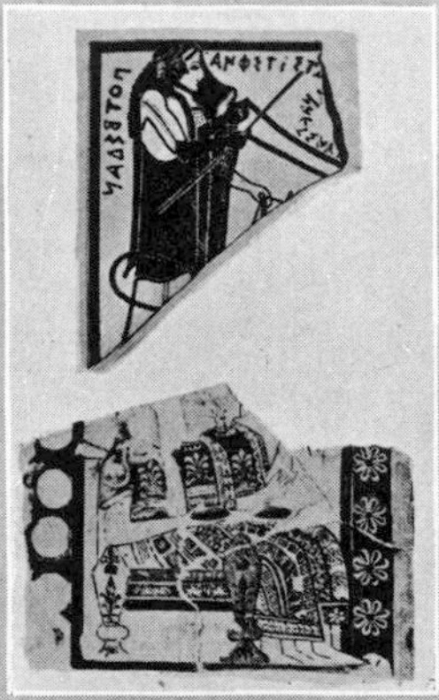
2

3

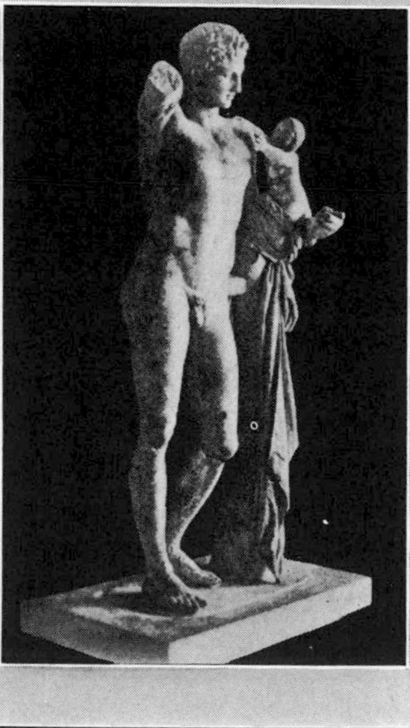
4

5

1, Vaphio gold cup. 2, Votive tablet and painted metope, from early Corinthian paintings. 3, Head of a strategos. 4, Hermes with the Child Dionysos, by Praxiteles. 5, Head of Anakreon.

object as it looks to our eyes. No cubistic, futuristic, or other picture of a similar nature gives a purely visual impression of the object (see Plate IX). When painters of these schools try to depict the three-dimensional corporeality of a material object in the forms of cubes, they aim to represent not its visual form — because these three dimensions we cannot see — but its ideational form : its three-dimensional solidity known by other organs of sense and "stored" in our mind. It is rightly said of Picasso and can be said of most of the "modernists" that they try "to substitute a conceptual reality for the visual one."

On the other hand, by these symbolic cubes or other nonvisual signs the artists of these schools do not try to represent something superempirical, nonmaterialistic. On the contrary, these "modern" styles are in the realm of empirical reality from top to bottom, and are perhaps more empirical, sensate, materialistic, than even pure Visualism. They aim to depict all the solidity, spaciousness, weight, and other properties of the *material* world.

C. *Other Mixed Styles.* Besides the Idealistic and the Cubistic forms there are many other varieties of the Mixed style. When one studies, for instance, Egyptian sculpture, one notices, even in the sculpture portraits from the Old Kingdom, the clearly and beautifully rendered Visual style of the face or of the head of the person, and the quite "unnatural" (from the Visual standpoint) rendering of the rest of the body: its posture, anatomy, configuration. The Visual style is thus closely combined with the nonvisual, sometimes conspicuously Ideational, form in the same sculpture or bas-relief or design. In this way we have an example of, so to speak, *the mechanical unification or the spatial adjacency of the elements of both styles in the same sculpture or design.*

Another variety of the Mixed style is exemplified in the predominant character of the early Chinese painting or pictorial art. It also often combines, in a peculiar way, elements of both styles. It is neither Ideational nor Visual; it is neither Idealistic nor Cubistic; nor is it even a mechanical mixture like that of the Egyptian. In one sense it is even extremely Visual, almost Impressionistic (especially in many a *paysage*); on the other hand, it is Ideational in several respects.

Such, in outline, are the main styles into which fall all painting, sculpture, and (in a slightly modified form) architecture, music, literature, and drama. Each of these styles has many gradations; the main forms that we have discussed are only a few of the chief marks on the scale of these numerous gradations. But these signs are very useful for orientation in the tremendously vast and complex ocean of the art world, and especially in the study of the life of art: its courses, fluctuations, "cycles," turns, and changes, in the course of time.

The analysis which we have just made constitutes the first test through which our categories of culture mentality must pass. The fact that they happen to fit perfectly for the classification of the main styles in art — that painting and sculpture fell quite naturally, so to speak, into these categories — indicates that they are not mere bloodless phantoms, a mere exercise in abstract logical classification. On the contrary, these preliminary concepts of Ideational, Sensate, and Mixed styles embrace principles which are conformable to and expressive of the actual, empirical reality, which bring clear meaning to the complexity and confusion in the field of art. We shall see further that this classification of the styles in art is one of the most "natural": it goes to the core of the predominant mentality shown in each style; it uncovers the essentials of the *Weltanschauung* of the artist and of his society; it stands in the closest relationship with the characteristics of other aspects of a given culture: its science and philosophy, religion and morals, forms of social and political organization, the nature of the social relationships — in brief, with all the essential traits of the given culture and its mentality. In this sense, an understanding of the *Gestalt* of a given culture at a given period helps us to understand the meaning, the origins, and methods of the predominant style of art; and an adequate knowledge of the art style and its proper interpretation in terms of these categories throws a peculiar light upon the culture in which it is born and prospers.

8

RECURRENCE IN SOCIAL SPACE AND FLUCTUATION IN TIME OF THE IDEATIONAL, VISUAL, AND MIXED STYLES IN PAINTING AND SCULPTURE (Qualitative Outline)

We shall begin our investigation with the problem of the existence or nonexistence of any perpetual trend from one of the two opposed styles to the other in the course of time generally and particularly in passing from the earlier to the later stages of the history of the Graeco-Roman and Western cultures. These cultures will be at the center of our study of the problem.

I. Is the Style of Primitive Art Visual or Ideational?

In the nineteenth century, with its evolutionary and linearly progressive theories, it was pretty commonly accepted that in the development of art style there was a perpetual linear tendency — unilinear, or spiral, or oscillating — from primitive art, devoid of skill and technique, to the present art, which supposedly is perfect and highly skillful. Most writers viewed almost all the forms of what is termed here the Ideational style as the "primitive" style, which results from the inability of the artists to draw or to paint or otherwise to reproduce the object properly. Ideational and primitive were often taken to be identical, while any competent rendering in the Visual style was regarded as a manifestation of artistic skill, maturity of technique, progress in art and in aesthetic genius. Even now many people, looking at the paintings of Indians or Eskimos or Egyptians or other ancient peoples, consider them certainly to be the result of a lack of artistic skill and as a manifestation of the primitiveness of the art of the ancients. However natural such opinions seem to be, in most cases they are wrong. The fault of such theories consists in their identification of Ideational with immature, of Visual with mature. As a matter of fact, the real situation in many cases is quite different. Often the Ideational and Visual styles are not so much a manifestation of the presence or absence of skill and highly developed technique, as the expression of quite different mentalities and different outlooks. One, as we have already observed in its definition, is the mentality of the Being; the other of the Becoming.

The sensory mentality strives to depict physical objects visually. Therefore, it practices and learns how to do this. The Ideational mentality does not care to do this. Therefore it lacks practice. Instead, it trains itself to render things ideationally.

If this be true, then we must expect that the *primitive art of all cultures may have either of the two opposing styles at the same "stage" of development. This expectation is justified in fact. Some of the primitive peoples have predominantly Ideational, some predominantly Visual, and some both styles.* Such a situation evidently gives a decisive blow to most of the linear theories mentioned above. Here are the corroborative data and the references.

The paintings, drawings, and sculptures of paleolithic man, as far as they are known to us, are predominantly Visual. Some of them may be styled even Visual-Impressionistic, being excellent "snapshots" of an animal in motion — a reindeer, a buffalo, a mammoth. When we pass to the drawings, paintings, and sculptures of neolithic man, we observe that they are less Visual and much more Ideational.

If we turn to the styles of the *living primitive peoples*, we find both styles present among them. Among some the Visual predominates, among the others the Ideational; among many both are found. But all in all there is no possibility of saying that one is dominant among the "more advanced," the other among the "less advanced," peoples. The distribution of the styles does not show any such uniformity.

Side by side with this it may be noted that the *Ideational style tends to occur particularly in the fields of religion, magic, and other "sacred" and "hieratic" compartments of social life — no matter what they are concretely, while the Visual style more frequently occurs, even within the same culture, in the "profane," daily, routine, earthly fields of social life.* Even when the Visual art dominates the given society, the Ideational style often still continues to exist in such "hieratic" compartments, whether they be the fields of religion, of magic ceremonies and symbols, of the important state functions and festivities, or of what not.

The reason for such a gravitation of each of these forms is evident: since the sacred and hieratic compartments of social life deal with "super-empirical," "transcendental," ideational abstract, noncorporeal and somewhat nonmaterial, complex values (whether religion, magic, or the dignity and honor of the nation, or family pride, or the glory of a group, or patriotism, justice, sacrifice, virtue), they cannot be expressed in any adequate Visual form because they do not have any. Hence the necessity of the Ideational signs or symbols — pure or impure — for denoting such phenomena and for making them "visible." On the other hand, purely empirical, daily, material phenomena have in the majority of the cases a visible form. Such a form can be rendered visually. Hence the existence of Visualism in such fields.

II. Fluctuation of the Ideational, Visual, and Mixel Styles in the Course of the Greek Culture

If we pay attention only to the greatest waves in the alternation of styles during the course of the Creto-Mycenaean and Graeco-Roman cultures up to the beginning of the Middle Ages, then the main periods of domination of each of the main styles may be delineated roughly as follows.

A. The known phase of the Creto-Mycenaean culture, extending from the twelfth to the ninth century B.C., exhibits the domination of a Visual style of very refined form, amounting sometimes to an extreme Impressionistic Visualism.

B. Whether the Greek culture properly was or was not a continuation of the Creto-Mycenaean culture, the period from about the ninth to the sixth century B.C. is marked by the domination of the Ideational art. If the Greek was a continuation of the Creto-Mycenaean culture, then such a fact means that a decay had taken place in the Visual style together with its passage into the Ideational. If the Greek culture was not a continuation of the Creto-Mycenaean, then all we can say is that the earliest known phase of the Greek art must be regarded as predominantly Ideational.

C. From the second part of the sixth century B.C. on, the Ideational pattern of Greek art seems to have been relatively weakening while the Visual was rising. The descending course of the one and the ascending course of the other crossed in the fifth and fourth centuries B.C. and as a result gave the marvelous blend of both styles in the form of the great Idealistic art of Greece.

D. Toward the end of the fourth century B.C. the Ideational stream thinned so much and the Visual stream swelled to such an extent that the Visual style became already slightly dominant. Its swelling continued, at the cost of the Ideational, during the subsequent centuries of the Hellenistic culture. Therefore the period beginning with the end of the fourth century, and Hellenistic culture generally, were marked by a decisive domination of the Visual art with its centers at the Island of Rhodes, Alexandria, Pergamum, and other foci of the Hellenistic culture. In other words the purely Greek and Hellenistic phases of Greek culture ended with the domination of the Visual (Sensate) art and mentality.

E. The Etruscan art, the early "native" art of the Romans, was, before the influence of Hellenistic culture, a mixture of an Ideational with a Visual stream. Such a blend, not being perfect, yielded some Idealistic forms, but these were neither dominant nor perfectly balanced as in the case of Greece of the fifth century.

F. The free and autonomous development of the Roman art was sharply interfered with by the powerful influence of the Hellenistic and, in part, the Greek culture, especially from the end of the second century B.C. This interference led to a peculiar mixture of the native Etruscan and late — Hellenistic — Greek forms of art, which resulted in a kind of rugged Idealistic mixed with overripe Visualism. The main effect of this was a series of imitative waves of Roman art: imitation of the Hellenistic Visualism in the first century B.C.; then imitation of the Idealistic art of Greece in the time of Augustus; then again several waves — all of a short duration — with quantitative-qualitative ups and downs of more or less extreme Visualism, followed in some periods by a tiny stream of imitative — primitive — Ideationalism. Such is the essence of the Roman art (omitting here the Christian) during the first century B.C. and the first three centuries A.D. In no period during these centuries was it conspicuously Ideational. On the contrary it was predominantly Visual, but more at one time and less at another.

G. However, into this world of Visualism, with the beginning of Christianity, there entered a stream of pure Ideationalism in the form of the early Christian art, the art of the catacombs. At the beginning it was just a tiny rivulet, almost unnoticeable and running far away from the highway of Roman art. Very rapidly, to the surprise of the intellectuals of the Graeco-Roman world, Christianity grew into major power, and with it the tiny rivulet of its Ideational art swelled into a broad river. Partly because of this fact, partly because the Roman (non-Christian) art itself, especially after the third century, began to show more and more a swing toward a bizarre Ideationalism which was somewhat like one of the Mixed styles — because of these circumstances the non-Christian Roman art underwent a comparatively rapid transformation from the dominant Visual into an incongruous mixture of the extreme Visual with the Ideational elements (Roman "cubism" and "impressionism" of a cinematographic type) and finally, after being engulfed by the Christian art, became, beginning with the end of the fifth century, predominantly Ideational. In this way it ushered art into the Ideational stream of the Middle Ages.

Such schematically are the main waves of the alternation of the styles and the main periods of the domination of each of them in the history of the Creto-Mycenaean and Graeco-Roman cultures.

In order not to be accused of the usual sin of a sociologist, that of fitting the facts to preconceived generalizations and of a superficial playing with the facts of history, and for the sake of unfolding the sufficiently rich content of the dry scheme presented above, I add a few typical details, colors, and factual "shadings."

Whether the early stage of the Creto-Mycenaean art (*c.* 2500-900 B.C.) failed to survive, as some investigators think, or whether it was from its beginning predominantly Visual, the fact is that most of what we have left from the Creto-Mycenaean art is of a highly Visual nature, and many of its objects, like the famous Vaphio cup (No. 1 on Plate X), are as perfect in their Visual artistry as anything produced later. It is true that there are some Ideational designs — geometric and others — on vases and painted pottery of Mycenae and on the ivory casket from Enkomi, Cyprus; but these are few in number. The bulk of what we know of this art is clearly Visual, even impressionistic. Of this nature are the excellent renderings of animals and human figures, with the mature knowledge of their anatomy which the art works show; such are the slender, pretty, voluptuous feminine figures, the Visual landscapes, the *genre* of daily life, the depiction of the common run of people; such are the picturesqueness, drama, dynamism, and sensuality. These are the essential traits of this art. If a skillful Visual art is to be styled ripe or overripe, this art appears to us to be so.

This culture which existed between 2500 B.C. and 900 B.C. supposedly "disappears" as suddenly as it appears. We can leave it to historians to unravel the mystery of this supposedly sudden change. What is important for us is that the Greek art which comes after the Creto-Mycenaean, the art of the so-called Archaic period (*c.* 1000 or 900 to 500 or 460 B.C.), is fundamentally different. The art of the ninth and possibly of the eighth century shows a growth of the geometric type (No. 2 on Plate X) — which in most cases is but a symbolic or Ideational art — together with another stream, exemplified by the shield of Achilles described in Homer which, with its visual delineation of daily life, bears the clear stamp of the Visual type. These and other remains of the art of this period suggest its transitory nature, as it moves from the dominant Visual of the previous age to the Ideational type. Hence, the mixture of these two streams. From this standpoint the art of this period seems to have been similar to the art of the fourth and fifth centuries A.D. in Rome when, as we shall see, art and culture were also in a transition from the Visual to the Ideational.

During the seventh and as late as the first half of the sixth century, the Ideational wave seems to have been rising higher. The geometrical and other forms of the Ideational style predominate; the subjects, as they are exemplified by the Chest of Kypselos and the throne of Apollo at Amiklae, become almost exclusively religious and mythological. Of the previous refined Visualism there remains little, if anything, either in technique or in the content of art. Art becomes quite "conventional" and "formal" — terms which mean in most of the cases what I style Ideational.

Beginning with the sixth century, especially the latter half, the first signs of a shift from the Ideational toward the Visual style appear in sculpture as well as in painting. An effort to render subjects somewhat more visually seems to have taken place in the Athenian school of sculpture and to a less degree in the school of Samos (Theodorus, Rhoikos, Smilis, Telekles) and of Chios (Melas, Mikkiades, Archermos, Bupalos, Athenis). The same seems to be true of the vase painting of the schools of Corinth, of Sikyon, and especially of Athens (Eumaros, *c.* 600–590 B.C.; Kimon of Kleonae, *c.* 520–500 B.C.). However, the art still remains predominantly Ideational, though the Ideationalism is progressively declining before a growing Visualism. But soon the descending curve of Ideationalism and ascending curve of Visualism cross each other and produce a marvelous blending in the form of the *sublime Idealistic art* of the fifth century B.C. It has all the perfections of the mature Visual technique. At the same time its "soul" is still in the Ideational — religious, ethical, and nonsensate — world. We are in the age of the "predecessors" of Phidias: of Aegeladas of Argos (*c.* 520–516), of Myron, of Onatas (*c.* 480), of Kalamis, of Pythagoras of Rhegion, and others. The culmination point of the period — and of all time — in sculpture was Phidias (500–432 B.C.),

> the first sculptor to produce ideal embodiments of the highest moral qualities of which a Greek could conceive, such as majesty, wisdom or beauty. He was the first sculptor who combined the idealism with the perfect mastery of his material, thus producing a completer harmony than was attained by any before or since.

Then comes Polycletus (*c.* 440–410 B.C.), not to mention others like Agorakritos, Alkamenes, Kolotes, Kallimachos.

The subjects of the sculpture of the fifth century are gods, heroes, or ideational entities like Victory, Nemesis, and so on. In this sense the art is Ideational. But the perfect technique is Visual. Hence it unites in itself both styles in an unrivaled form, and gives what I call the Idealistic art.

Greek painting of the fifth century is Idealistic. The culmination of the fifth century painting was Polygnotus (*c.* 475–430 B.C.). He is rightly styled the Phidias of painting.

In view of the exceptional perfection of this Idealistic art of the fifth century, it is advisable to outline its characteristics a little more substantially. Such an analysis should help us to understand several typical traits of the Idealistic style. A few quotations from specialists will help us in this purpose.

This Idealism of the Greek painting and sculpture of the fifth century shows itself first in an excellent knowledge on the part of the artists of human anatomy and the means of rendering it in its ideal or perfect form, in the type of the persons represented, in their postures, in the abstractness of the human type; there are no concrete portraits, no ugliness, no defective traits or types; before us are immortals or idealized mortals; old age is rejuvenated; the baby is depicted as grown up; the women have little that is specifically womanish and appear like perfect athletes; there are no concrete landscapes. The postures and the expressions are free from any violent or debased or too human emotion and distorting passion. They are calm, serene, imperturbable like the gods. Even the dead shine with the same calmness and serene beauty. All the statues have a "Greek" profile; not because the Greeks were such, as Winkelmann thought, but because it was the profile thought to be perfect. The *chevelure* is simple but perfectly ordered; the drapery is perfectly adapted to the body, simple and marvelous in its orderly beauty. Eyes are natural and perfect, and shine with calmness and serenity; the lips and mouth are ideally cut; the postures are dignified and idealized.

This Greek art was deeply religious, patriotic, instructive, moralizing, educating. It was created not only for its own sake, but also as a means for such instruction and education. It was not separated from, but was the partner of, religion, of civic and social morality.

From the same spirit comes its collective and in a way anonymous character. "Temples and their art were the expression of the popular beliefs and were the collective work of all the citizens." After the Persian wars, it was necessary to thank the gods for the victory, for peace, for prosperity; and "the whole Athenian people wanted to devote themselves to that national work which was to honour the gods and their own country." There was a universal *élan*, ardent and enthusiastic desire to exalt the religion and the country. Hence all tried to participate in the creation of the great national monument — the art of the fifth century. There was this idealism, there was unanimity, there was exaltation; hence the unity, harmony, and marvel of the art of that period.

The period of pure Idealism in Greek art was short. Though it remained Idealistic throughout the fifth and a part of the fourth century, nevertheless, after Phidias and Polygnotus the Ideational stream continued to become thinner, the Sensate ampler. The marvelous balance of the Idealistic art was then more and more lost and this led to a gradual decline of the purity of the Idealistic style.

In sculpture, the first signs of a contamination of the pure Idealism of Phidias appear already in the works of Polycletus (active *c.* 440–410) with his idealization of the body (mainly athletes) rather than of the soul. However, his works and that of the contemporary artists remain predominantly Idealistic still. Idealism, though more and more contaminated, continues in the works of the first part of the fourth century, in those of Kephisodotus (active *c.* 395–370 B.C.), Praxiteles (*c.* 370–350 B.C.) (No. 4 on Plate X), Scopas (390–350 B.C.), and even partly of Lysippus (*c.* 330–315 B.C.), not to mention lesser sculptors.

Toward the end of the fourth century Idealism is over and the rising tide of Visualism definitely triumphs. Beginning with that period we have the Hellenistic sculpture, which is clearly and conspicuously Sensate or Visual, with all the traits of such an art. A similar change took place in painting during the fourth century.

Here are most important characteristics: (1) The figures of women which before were rare now become quite common subjects of sculpture and painting. (2) They are represented, not as robust and athletic — almost sexless — youths, but as slender, voluptuous, sexual, seductive figures, side by side with realistic figures of old women. (3) A similar change takes place in regard to the figures of men. (4) Portraits of individual persons, especially rulers and others on whom the artists depended, become more and more common. (5) There appears more and more the representation of real landscapes and dramatic historical scenes. (6) The everyday life, in form of the realistic *genre*, becomes a very common topic. (7) Crowds, mobs, the common run of people, and especially pathological types: prostitutes, criminals, street urchins, etc., more and more replace the heroes and ideal men. (8) The postures and expressions of the persons lose their idealized patterns and become realistic: serenity and calm are replaced by the pathetic, by passion and emotionality, including suffering, sorrow, pain, fear, agony, and distortion; static immobility is driven out by dynamism and violent movement. (9) Picturesqueness takes the upper hand over idealism: a street urchin in his rags is preferred to the idealized demigod. An inclination to the macabre, nudity of a sexual nature, etc., is another aspect of it. (10) If before mortals were depicted like the immortals, now the gods tend to be depicted like mortals. (11) It is natural that now the baby is depicted as a baby, and the old man as a senile person, the woman as very different from the man; and if before the women were masculinized now the men are frequently effeminized. (12) Behind the art object there is hardly noticeable any other ideal or value. "Art for art's sake" (just for a sensuous gratification!) becomes a norm; and the art's sake is considered purely sensuously, destined to give a sensate pleasure to the sensate man. (13) A tendency to gigantic quantitative proportions shows itself. What is lacking in quality is compensated for by hugeness, by large quantity (in size, in mass, in caliber). "The biggest" becomes one of the main means to be impressive. "The biggest," the "largest," tends to become the criterion of the best. Quantity tends to replace quality. In brief, we are on the earth, in a fleshy world, sensate, utilitarian, material, Epicurean.

PLATE XI

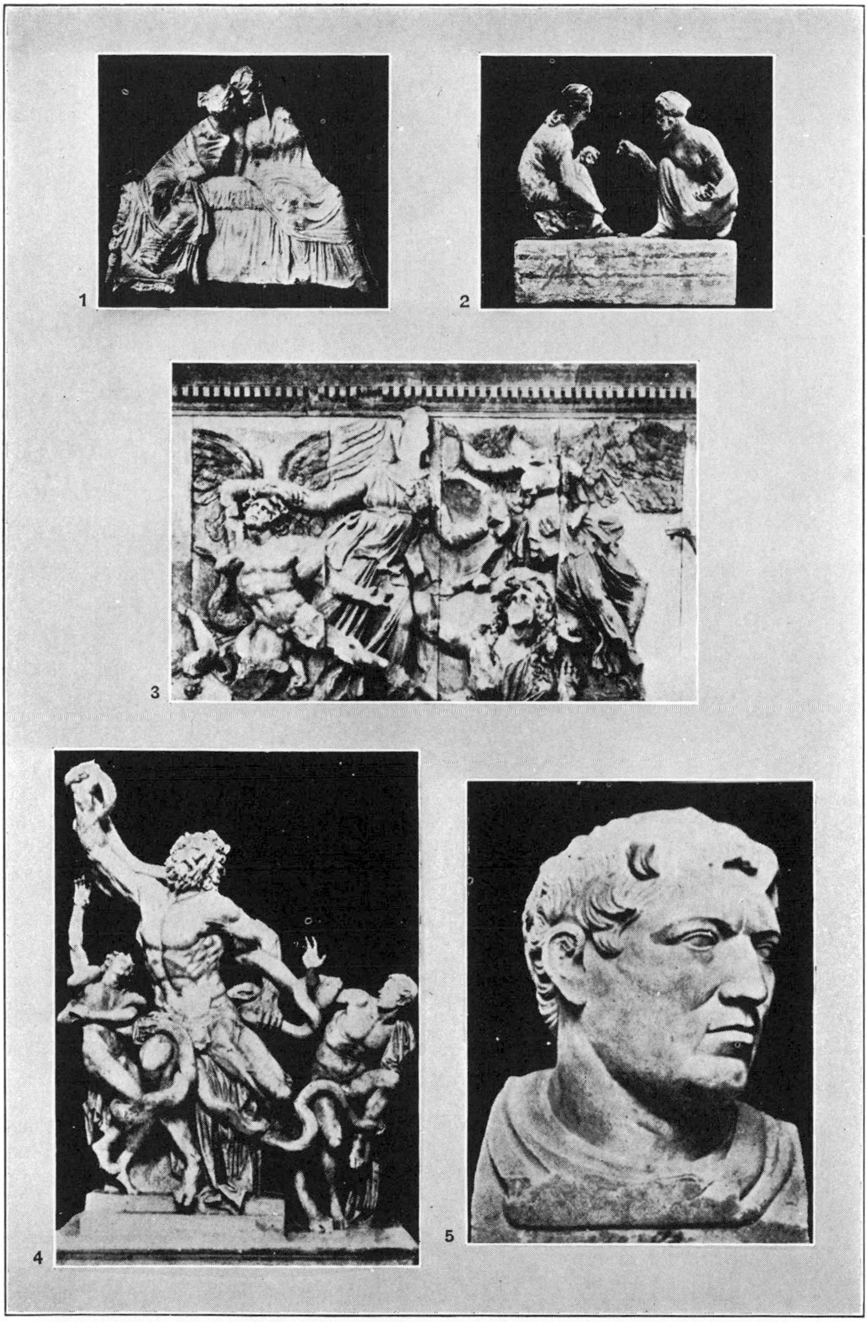

1, Women conversing, from Myrina. **2,** Women playing, from Capua. **3,** Relief, from the altar of Pergamum. **4,** Laocoön. **5,** Philetaerus of Pergamum.

PLATE XII

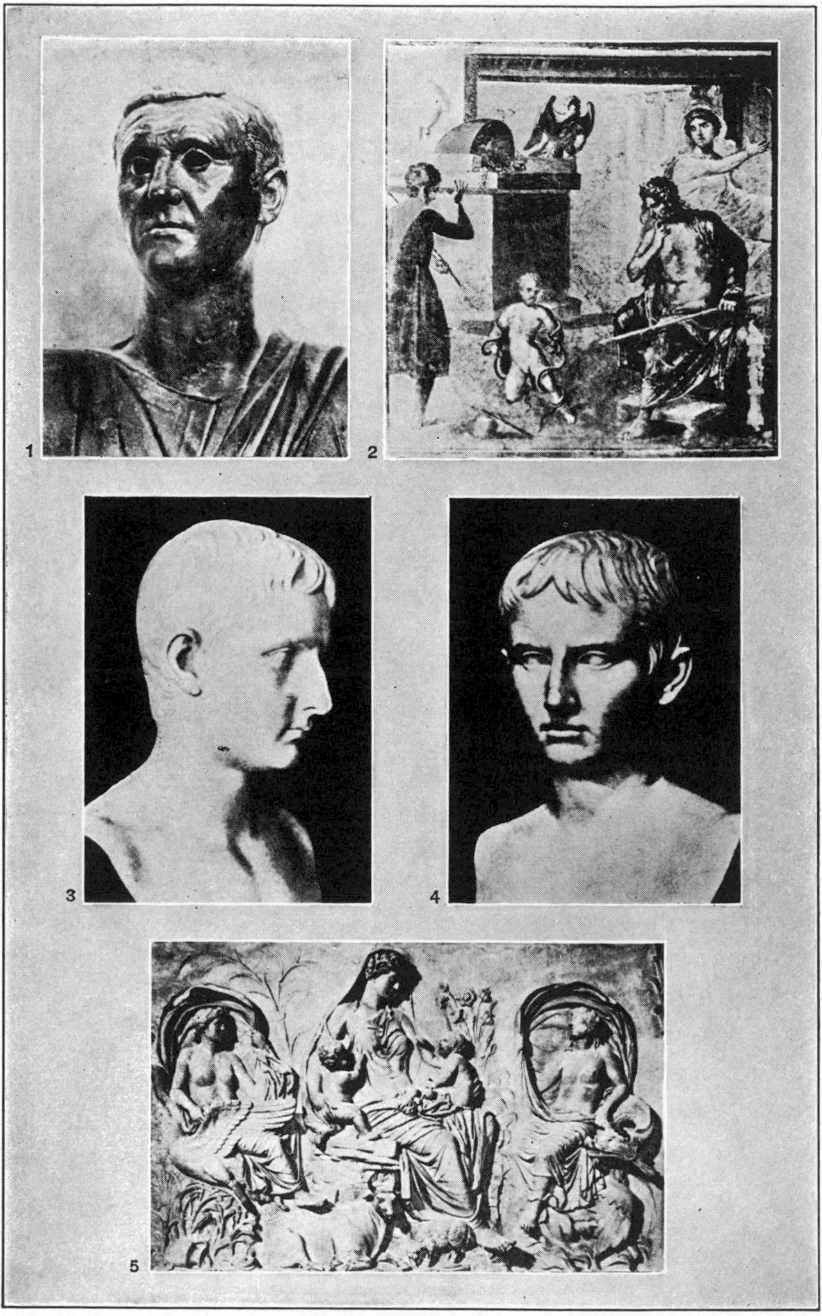

1, Portrait of Arringatore. 2, Pompeian wall painting. 3 and 4, Portrait of Augustus. 5, Ara Pacis, from the Augustan Parthenon.

On Plate XI, Nos. 1 and 2 show examples of everyday-life topics, with common type of people — females, "playing bridge" — which became the common topic of Hellenic art; Nos. 3 and 4 show the pathetic, dramatic, theatrical tendency, together with Visual dynamism. Nothing in the sculptures is at rest. Everything is in a violent motion. No. 5 is a sample of a Visual, matter-of-fact portrait, with all the peculiar traits of a given individual, without any idealization.

Finally, the position and the mentality of artists also changed greatly. The artist became "emancipated" from the "fetters" of religion, community, *mores*, and what not. From now on he became a servant of art for art's sake. Thus he began to depend upon various patrons, the rulers and the rich.

In this way there appeared a new type of artist in Greece, that of the court; later on, that of the rich and influential men. Thus, instead of being free servants of the community and of the transcendental values, they became "friends and valets" of the rich and of the powerful.

Take further, for instance, the treatment of gods, like Apollo, Dionysos, or Eros:

What has the Eros of the fifth century, the serious young euphebus, in common with the boy-loves of the Alexandrian period? Or the Aphrodite of the fifth century, a vigorous woman chastely clad, with the soft voluptuousness of the naked goddess of Hellenistic times! What is there in common between the bearded and garbed Dionysus of archäism and the youthful god, nude and effeminate, of the Graeco-Roman?

Or take:

The Aegean Cretan avoided stripping completely, and the Egyptians, Chaldeans, Assyrians and Etruscans were averse to it except in the cases of the lower orders. . . . Woman . . . was draped from head to foot in the sixth century and the first half of the fifth. [The second half of the fifth introduced some beginning of nudity.] The fourth century went far along this road. . . . The draperies now slip off the shoulders altogether and only stop at the hips [Aphrodite of Milo, the Praxitelean Aphrodite of Arles, for instance]. Praxiteles is the first completely to undrape the goddess [*e.g.*, Chidian Aphrodite]. No garment enwraps her. She is nude and completely displays all her beauties.

Later on "Woman invaded art." Eroticism and Sensate Epicureanism generally reign supreme in these Visual art creations.

And so it was with other human figures.

These tendencies became still more pronounced in the Hellenistic period. Here women became one of the main subjects of art. And, if the Aphrodites of the fourth century still retained something of the vigor and chastity of the fifth century, the Hellenistic Aphrodites, the Nymphs, the Menades became charming and sensual women, of an easy virtue, somewhat similar to the influential courtesans, and from their bodies emanated the restless charm of voluptuousness.

Male visages are now rendered mainly as smooth shaven, in contrast with the preceding period.

The love of nature, of landscapes, grows, parallel to the preoccupation with the picturesque, assuming often the half-romantic tendency of the tired urbanist to find rest in the country among "pastoral" scenery. Likewise, an accurate rendering of animals and the frequent use of them as subjects became common in art.

All this is followed by the disease of "colossalism" — by a tendency to substitute quantity for quality, the biggest and largest for the best. One can see this in virtually all forms of the Hellenistic art: in music and architecture, in literature ("the best sellers!"), in sculpture and painting. It is enough to remind the reader of the Colossus of Rhodes, about 105 feet high; of the Halicarnassus Mausoleum (or tomb of Mausolos), 140 feet high; of the large scale of the Pergamene Frieze (No. 3, Plate XI), and other sculptures; of the large buildings, and large paintings; in order to make clear this trait of the Visual art.

Such are main traits of this Visual art as they are manifest in the Hellenistic period. No doubt, during that period Idealism and even Ideationalism in art did not disappear entirely. But they became quite a thin stream just as Visualism had been a minor rivulet in the Greek art of the fifth and of the preceding centuries.

III. Fluctuation of the Styles in Roman Painting and Sculpture

The course of Roman painting and sculpture, considered from our present standpoint, can be briefly told. Its first source, the Italic art, was rather geometric cubistic (Ideational); its second source, the Etruscan art, so far as we know it, belonged to a mixed or moderate Visual ("naturalistic") style. The portrait busts, of which a sample is given (the so-called bust of a prominent orator, Arringatore, shown in No. 1 on Plate XII), show a clear inclination to the Visual style without any notable Ideational or Idealistic tendencies.

When the Greek art, unfortunately in its Hellenistic Visual style, began to influence Roman painting and sculpture, the result was, from about the end of the second century B.C., an interruption in the spontaneous development of the Roman arts, the development of eclecticism, and imitation, decay of Italic Ideational, and a softening and an extreme development of the Etruscan naturalism along the lines of the Hellenistic art. The somewhat "rugged" Etruscan Visual art was turned into a Visualism that was overripe, effeminate, exotic, idyllic, and impressionistic. This is partly exemplified by the paintings of Pompeii, and by other surviving pictures (see No. 2, Plate XII, an illustration of Hercules, from the paintings of a Pompeian house), partly by the rococo style of Arcesilaus and other painters of "boudoir mythology." Since that time the Roman arts became imitative, in a considerable degree, and remained so up to the end of the Visual (Sensate) culture of the Roman Empire, the change being mainly in the replacement of the models of the Greek art which were imitated. Of course, it was not a mere imitation: the Etruscan source remained and modified imitation. Nevertheless the main patterns were taken from Greece.

Throughout its history, from the first century B.C. to the fourth century A.D., Roman sculpture and painting were predominantly Visual. Their sculpture and painting remained "photographic" and large in size. But their Visualism had various shades and degrees. In the second part of the first century B.C. it imitated the sixth-century archaistic patterns (Pasiteles, Stephanus), and the Alexandrian effeminate rococo (Arcesilaus and his school). In the Augustan period it was pseudo-Idealistic Visualism, imitating the Idealistic art of Greece of the fifth century, but with a specific flavor of Visualism. It was not a real Idealism spontaneously springing from deep sources, it was rather a change of a fashion, of the pattern for imitation, as a reaction against the imitation of the Archaic Attic and of the overripe Hellenistic patterns of the preceding century. Hence, the Augustan imitative Idealistic art exemplified in the portrait statues, in the Augustan Parthenon, and in other sculptural and pictorial monuments of the time. Here are two examples of this art: an Idealized sculpture of Augustus (Nos. 3 and 4, Plate XII) and a part of the Augustan Parthenon — the *Ara pacis Augustae* (No. 5) — with its overabundance of decorations, and a lack of cohesion in the scheme.

This pseudo Idealism was short-lived, and soon after Augustus was replaced by a more extreme Visualism — impressionistic, photographic, singularistic, and illusionistic. In the Arch of Titus "each portrait is like a modern photograph, the reproduction of a passing impression."

The chief post-Augustan fluctuations in the history of art may be summed up as follows.

Under the Flavian dynasty the chief aim of the artist was an imitative naturalism illusionism. Under Trajan (A.D. 98) a different tendency is at work. It is historicism, concentration on the rendering of the real historical scenes and personalities as they are. Lastly, under Hadrian (A.D. 117) we have an archaistic reaction in the form of a cold academic imitation of the archaistic and idealistic art of Greece, but without its soul and mentality and with a sensuousness quite foreign to the Greek models. Under Marcus Aurelius (A.D. 161) we are in a "rococo" age of an insipid refinement and effeminate elegance. Under Caracalla (A.D. 212) came exaggerated passion, particularly rage, dynamism, and colossalism. Then soon comes a "decay" of Roman art; more exactly, a decline of the Visual style and the reappearance of the Distorted Ideational style. Their mixture, in the fourth and fifth centuries, gives a peculiar Mixed style — transitory, neither Ideational, nor Visual. With the continued decline of Visualism and the continued rise of the Christian Ideational style, we come to the Ideational art of the Middle Ages, as a new wave which replaced the preceding Visual wave of the Hellenistic and Roman Visual art. (See the illustrations of these waves in the sculpture portraits Nos. 1, 2, 3, 5, 6 on Plate XIII.)

Whatever the models imitated, the Sensate and Visual character of the Roman art during these centuries remains unquestionable. It manifests itself in the photographic rendering of persons, even in the periods of Idealization; in everyday or historical topics; in an inclination toward huge size (*e.g.*, Farnese Heracles, the Arch of Titus, the Column of Trajan, the Column of Marcus Aurelius, the Column of Constantine, huge palaces, etc.); in profuse overdecoration; in the spirit of sensuality, voluptuousness, eroticism, pervading even the idealized portraits (see the reproduction of portrait of Hadrian's favorite, Antinoüs, No. 4 on Plate XIII); in the cinematographic method of rendering figures; in the restless dynamism of their posture and setting; in the pathetic, emotional, and passionate rendering of feelings, in endless *amoretti* and sexuality; and in many other features which are the traits of the Visual style.

Similar, in essence, were the character and the changes in the styles of the Roman painting from the second century B.C. when the Hellenistic influence affected it. As we pass from the "Incrustation Style" (second and first centuries to about 80 B.C.) to the "Architectural Style" (80 to 10 B.C.), then to the "Ornate Style" (10 B.C. to A.D. 50), and then to the "Intricate Style" (from A.D. 50 on), we observe an increase in the occurrence of the various signs of Visualism and Illusionism.

During the subsequent times, from the end of the first to the fourth century A.D., there were various imitative waves, somewhat similar to those in sculpture, but whatever was the pattern imitated — whether the Hellenistic refined and oversweet style, pastoralism and superannuated idyllic themes, "classical examples," archaic, chilly academism, or what not — the dominant tone of all these varieties continued to be predominantly Visual, with all the traits of the Visual art, including complexity, colossalism, Epicureanism, and sensuality. Vitruvius, Tacitus, Petronius Arbiter, Pliny, Dionysius of Halicarnassus, all stress the Visual character of the painting and unanimously complain of its

PLATE XIII

1, Colossal bust of Titus. 2, Colossal bust of Domitian. 3, Head of the raging Caracalla. 4, Hadrian's favorite, Antinoüs. 5, Colossal bust of Constantine. 6, Colossal bust of Valentinian I. 7, Sarcophagus of the fourth century A.D.

PLATE XIV

1

2

3

4

1, 2, and 4, from the Dance of Death, by Hans Holbein the Younger. 3, Melancholia, by Dürer.

complexity, overdeveloped technique, colossalism, voluptuousness, and contrast it unfavorably with the earlier painting, simpler but more original, more talented, more sound, and more beautiful.

Thus in sculpture as well as in painting — and further on we shall see also in music, literature, architecture, and drama — the Roman art (pagan) up to the second part of the fourth century remained predominantly Visual, with all the characteristics of such an art.

These, as schematized, were the main "pulsations" of the Ideational, Visual, Idealistic, and Mixed styles in the Graeco-Roman painting and sculpture. The periods of rise, domination, and decline of each of these styles are only approximate, but that they did exist we can be sure.

9

FLUCTUATION OF THE MAIN STYLES IN THE PAINTING AND SCULPTURE OF WESTERN EUROPE

(Qualitative Outline, *Continued*)

I. Rise and Domination of Ideational Christian Art from the Sixth to the Twelfth Centuries

Even a layman, when he glances at the sculpture and painting of the time from the fifth century B.C. to the third A.D. and then at the colossal "cubistic" heads of Constantine and Valentinian, cannot help feeling that something "catastrophic" happened to the art in the fourth or the fifth century of our era. Indeed, all the artistic skill of the preceding centuries seems to have vanished; instead, we have very rough "blocks" cut apparently without any skill, very primitively, without showing any ability to render the individual traits of the persons rendered or even the anatomy of the head and other parts of the human body. It is as though we were suddenly plunged from the world of "skillful" and "mature" art with perfect technique into the world of the "primitive" art devoid of any artistry.

The change was neither "decay" nor the "end" of the Graeco-Roman art, but merely one of its great transformations, that is, a decline of the Visual and a rise of the Ideational form of art — a process which seems also to have occurred in the passage from the overripe Mycenaean to the Archaic Greek art in the period from the ninth to the sixth centuries B.C.

The emergence of Christianity at the beginning of the first century meant, as we shall see, the beginning of a great transformation of the Sensate Graeco-Roman culture into the subsequent Ideational culture of the Middle Ages. Christianity was an Ideational cultural stream from its very emergence. Hence it necessarily gave rise to an extreme form of the Ideational art, as any such culture must if it is truly integrated. And, indeed, the earliest Christian art, that of the Catacombs, was practically pure Ideational art: symbolic and transcendental in form as well as in content. Symbols of a dove, an olive branch, an anchor, a fish, the cross, a Good Shepherd, and a few others comprised its subjects. They meant not a fish nor an anchor, but a transcendental value quite different from these Visual signs. They were just the visible signs of the invisible world. Even the scenes from the Bible or from the lives of the saints were Ideational also — "imperfect" in their Visual technique and carrying much of symbolic meaning. In brief, it was "otherworldly" art as Christianity itself was based on an "otherworldly" mentality.

In spite of that it was still Graeco-Roman (plus Oriental) art, being "a marriage of the antique Greek beauty with the Christian genius," "pure, innocent, and tender," "radiating peace and serenity." Appearing as a small stream in the total Graeco-Roman — Visual — art, with the growth of Christianity grew also more and more, until in the fourth and the fifth centuries it became practically a major stream.

This Ideationalism continues throughout the subsequent centuries of the Middle Ages, almost up to the thirteenth century. Beginning with about the sixth century the pagan art practically disappears, being engulfed by Christian art, which from that time became the only art of high achievement during the rest of the Middle Ages.

Its topics are mainly superempirical and "transcendental." Its technique is Ideational, only in a minor part Visual, and even then Idealistic rather than purely Visual.

The Ideational otherworldliness of this art manifested itself in a kind of extreme asceticism and radical "puritanism," partly consciously, partly unconsciously, opposed to any sensuous objective as well as to sensuous enjoyment of art. The history of Christianity is marked by numerous explosions against any art and any representation of religious topics in painting or sculpture. This was one form of asceticism, the form of the rejection, prohibition, and persecution of any icons and iconography and painting. Its other form was manifested in innumerable demands and measures directed against any seductive, sensuously enjoyable forms of art.

St. Jerome, St. Ambrose, St. Bernard, St. Anthony, St. Thomas Aquinas, the Cistercians, the Cluniacs, and many other leaders of Christianity as well as the Christian orders and institutions, did not weary of protesting, warning, prohibiting any art or any element in it that was for sensuous enjoyment. They indefatigably cleansed it of such elements.

Such an asceticism is a clear evidence of the Ideational character of that art.

Its Ideationalism is shown no less clearly by its *symbolic* character. Even more, it is shown by symbolism of a superempirical and transcendental nature. By very definition the Ideational art is that in which the visible signs are mere symbols of the invisible world. And this is exactly what we have in the Christian or in the central medieval art.

Medieval painting and sculpture are virtually iconography. An icon is not the same as a picture. After the thirteenth century the difference tended to decrease and the icon was in a sense swallowed by the picture. But before that time the picture was in a sense absorbed by the icon.

This means that the icon is a *symbol* of the transsensory world and values. Hence any real iconographic painting and sculpture are necessarily symbolic, that is, Ideational. Since this deduction is self-evident, the transcendentally symbolic character — so many times stressed — of the medieval art (and mentality) becomes comprehensible at once, and is seen to be inevitable if the contention that it was predominantly Ideational is true.

It is unnecessary for me to endeavor to prove that the medieval painting, sculpture, and other arts, as well as their whole mentality (as we shall see) were symbolic and therefore Ideational. Almost any competent investigator of the medieval art knows its symbolic character. As we have mentioned, the early Christian art was symbolic. Medieval architecture — Gothic and pre-Gothic — is symbolic, in the whole as well as in the details. In the thirteenth century Guillaume Durand, bishop of Mende in France, explained the symbolic meaning of every important detail of that architecture. And the same is still more true of the medieval sculpture and painting. As shown elsewhere, the other forms of art and the whole mentality of the Middle Ages were transcendentally symbolic or Ideational. Finally, the art theories and the entire aesthetic mentality of the Middle Ages were again transcendentally symbolic. Thus, according to St. Thomas and the great Scholastics:

> Beauty is essentially an object of *intelligence*, for what *knows* in the full meaning of the world is the mind, which alone is open to the infinity of being. The natural site of beauty is the intelligible world: thence it descends. . . . [It is] *splendor formae* . . . for *form*, that is to say the principle determining the peculiar perfection of everything which is, constituting and completing the things in their essence and their qualities, the *ontological secret, so to speak, of their innermost being, their spiritual essence*, their operative mystery, is above all the peculiar *principle of intelligibility*, the peculiar clarity of every thing.

The characteristics of the Ideational art which we expect logically do in fact occur in it. No prosaic or profane topics are rendered in it. It is an art which instructs in, propagates, testifies to the victorious religion — a visible symbol for the invisible values. No sensatism is in it; nothing appears for a merely sensate enjoyment. It is limited to the religious symbols and the images of Christ, the Madonna, and the saints, and to Biblical scenes.

A. *Byzantine Art.* This concerns not only Western art but that of Byzantium, which was a peculiar synthesis of the Graeco-Roman and Syrian-Egyptian styles. Here the Ideationalization of the abstract types of the triumphant Christ, the Madonna, the saints, became in a way still more pronounced and led to the marvelous creation of the image of God as a celestial emperor, the *Pantocrator;* to a similar standardized image of the Madonna — Odigitria — somewhat ascetic, free from any mortal traits, a symbolic image of the all-powerful and all-sublime Madonna, reminiscent now of the blonde Athena (*flava*), now of Pallas (*casta Pallas*), courageous and vigorous, the most wise (*doctissima domina*), stern and austere (*cruda virago*), pure and stainless (*innupta, intacta*), the protectress of mortals (*patrona*). All real mortal traits vanished from such a conceptual image.

In the thirteenth century, however, the Ideationalism commences to decline and Visualism to ascend, giving as a result the balanced Idealistic art of the thirteenth and partly of the fourteenth centuries. In the fourteenth century Visualism continues to grow and becomes even slightly dominant at its end and especially in the fifteenth and sixteenth centuries. As we shall see, these great fluctuations in the course of the Byzantine art were almost parallel with those of the Western art.

B. *Western Art.* For the period from about the sixth to the thirteenth century the Christian art was the only major, logically integrated art. The division of high art into the religious and the secular was practically nonexistent at that period. The course of this Western Christian art was in essentials similar to that of the Byzantine art. Throughout this period it remained essentially Ideational with an Idealistic treatment of the empirical-visual phenomena. It is true that from about the ninth century (the Carlovingian Renaissance) the elements of Visualism began to filter into that art. Nevertheless, up to the end of the twelfth century Ideationalism was the dominant characteristic of that art. It was somewhat different from the Ideationalism of the Byzantine art for that period: it was, so to speak, a more Greek than Oriental (Egyptian-Syrian) Ideationalism; less ascetic and less stern than the Ideationalism of the Byzantine art. Here Christ is more often depicted as a beautiful young Orpheus, or good youthful shepherd, than as a bearded Jewish prophet. Likewise, the figures and postures and expressions of the Madonna, of the saints, of the prophets and sages, were less stern and hieratic than in the Byzantine art.

Being almost entirely religious, it is concerned mainly with religious, transcendental, and conceptual symbols, and when it deals with "worldly" scenes, animals, and persons, it represents them in an Ideational Idealistic form.

II. The Thirteenth-century Idealistic Art

The rising tide of Visualism and ebb of Ideationalism that appeared in the twelfth century resulted in the next two centuries in one of those rare but recurrent sublime blends of both styles in the form of the supreme Idealistic art of these centuries, an art in all its essential traits similar to the great Idealistic art of Greece of the fifth and, in part, of the fourth centuries B.C. It should be noted here that such an Idealistic art appeared again when the dominant Ideational style was declining and the moderate Visualism was rising. But not when Visualism was falling and Ideationalism rising. *The periods of a declining Visualism and of an ascending Idealionalism, like the transition from the Mycenaean art to the Archaic Greek art, or from the overripe Hellenistic Roman art to the Christian art of the fourth and the fifth centuries* A.D., *or perhaps like the change in the present period in which we live (as we shall see), seem to give not this marvelous Idealistic art but the incongruous results of a search for something different from overripe Visualism: cubism, futurism, and other Mixed "isms" which are neither the fish of Ideationalism nor the flesh of Visualism; nor are they a harmonious blend of both styles. They are just a revolt against, and a striving for, something different from the infatuated Visualism; but this search yields hardly any organic synthesis at all. Such periods seem to produce "modernistic incongruities," important as symptoms but far from representing the realization of the hopes of the Visual-Sensuous man who seeks to find the "bluebird" or a new and grand Art.*

Only the Ideational man and the Ideational culture which begin to pay more and more attention to the empirico-sensory world but which by one half, at least, are still in the supersensate world of Ideationalism, seem to be able to produce the great Idealistic art, as a blend of both styles. Such exactly was the situation in the thirteenth century in Western culture generally, and especially in its art. As in Greece of the fifth century B.C., here again we are in an age of faith, all-embracing, understanding, and justifying all, including this world. It still does not see the central value in this world and in the earthly life. It sees this in the supersensory world; but the divine plan of this supersensory world somehow now includes also this earthly world and gives to it its meaning, blessing, and justification. Hence the art of the thirteenth century included (like the *Speculum majus* of Vincent of Beauvais): (1) the mirror of nature (humblest animals and plants), (2) the mirror of science (seven Muses of the *trivium* and the *quadrivium*, plus the eighth of philosophy), (3) the mirror of the virtues and of religion. This was the chief division. For the main place in art was given naturally (naturally in an Idealistic culture) to the representation of the providentially controlled march of humanity, in which "it sees only Christ and looks only for Christ in it."

All the other earmarks of the Idealistic art are clearly shown by the art of the thirteenth century, this apex of the Christian European art. Here are a few of its characteristics — already familiar to us.

(1) It was not an art for art's sake, but the "Bible in the stone." Art was a means for the expression of the sublime religious conscience of the people.

(2) We have already seen that its figures were idealized, even the dead. Most of its statues are remarkable from this standpoint. Their postures, gestures, expressions, appearance, all are lighted by the sublime serenity of the religious and moral ideal.

(3) The art of the thirteenth and of the preceding centuries, like that of the fifth B.C. and before, was an expression of a collective ideal, and thus it was a collective work. All in some way participated in it, especially in the building of the cathedrals.

(4) Again like the art of the fifth century B.C., the art of the thirteenth century "tends to convince but not to disturb emotionally."

(5) Since it was a collective work and a realization of the ideal of the collectivity, the leading artists played only the role of the *primus inter pares*. They themselves neither regarded it as their own achievement only, nor were anxious to stamp their names and to take copyrights for it. Nor did they do it for the art's sake only. They did it as their service to God, *ad gloriam Dei*, for the realization of the ideal and not at all for the sake of a sensuous beauty or for a sensate enjoyment. Though the names of some of the leaders, like Villard de Honnecourt, are known, most of the artists remained anonymous, and their mood was very different from the Visual-individualistic artist who, at least, wants to immortalize himself through his creation. The spirit and mood of these artists are the same as those which were expressed somewhat earlier by the famous Theophilus, who as the only recompense for his work and instruction asks: "Pray for me for the pity of all powerful God."

(6) The technique of art of the period was already so greatly developed that not without reason most of the investigators compare it and its creations with the technique of Phidias and of other great Greek masters of the fifth century.

(7) As in the Greek classical art, there is calm and quiet and a lack of dynamism (the Platonic ideas do not change); there is no "show" and nothing *malerisch;* there is no patheticism, no sentimentality, no emotionalism; and there is no disorder.

Such was this golden age of the idealistic art of Christian Europe.

III. Rise of Visualism from the Fourteenth to the Sixteenth Centuries

The tide of Visualism continued, however, to rise and the "optimum" point of the marvelous blending of the two opposite styles was soon passed. Its duration was short (as was the case with the Greek Idealistic art). Already at the end of the thirteenth century the "optimum" point was left behind, and the art of the fourteenth and fifteenth centuries already represents the period of transition from a waning Idealism toward a full-blooded Visualism. "The 'fact' is that after the climax of what is styled 'idealism' there followed a birth of 'realism.'"

The visual tendency grew in the fourteenth and the fifteenth centuries, but "this attractive art lacked vigour."

Its topics began to become more and more secular and, of the secular, more and more everyday and common. They become increasingly "fleshly." The drapery of the thirteenth century was architectural; now it becomes complicated, plaited, picturesque, even burlesque, imitating real drapery in its numerous details and losing more and more in unity and sobriety of texture. Agitation, dynamism, passionateness, emotionalism, particularly pathetic and macabre moods, combined with voluptuousness, all this begins to permeate the figures, the scenes, the expressions, the postures, the clothing as reproduced in painting and sculpture.

If previously mortals were idealized like gods, now the gods are depicted as mortals, with the exception of the few powerful mortals who are rendered godlike out of flattery. Individualism of artists, Epicureanism, voluptuousness, sensuality, all are rising. Virtually all the traits of the transitional period from Idealism to Visualism, which we saw in the Greek art of the fourth century B.C., are repeated, in a new setting and under different conditions.

Unflinching faith having been lost and man being thrown upon himself, emotionality, passionateness, dolor, pessimism, suffering, side by side with the attempt to see salvation in pleasure, seized the Christian world. With the previous world (which once seemed unshakable) falling to pieces, and a new world not yet assured, such dolor and despair are rather comprehensible. Shall we wonder that exactly at that time such themes as Death, in its ugliness, the dance macabre, corpses (including Christ) in all their reality, became, as it were, epidemic?

Beginning with the opening of the fifteenth century and continuing in the sixteenth, the images of corpses, and death's heads, and skulls, multiplied in the churches, on the church glass, in pictures.

Finally, art itself was greatly influenced by the religious theater, by its mysteries, and as a result became more and more *theatrical*, that is Visual, with representation of all the passions, emotionality, and sensibility described above.

Religious art thus ceased to be not only all of art exclusively, but even the main form of art; it tended more and more to become a small stream, and even this small stream ceased to be a united stream but was broken into a series of small individual rivulets. Since that time "there have been Christian artists; but there is no more a Christian art."

Now the verdict "like life itself" becomes the highest praise of a work of art. And *visual illusionism* becomes more and more the fundamental criterion of the perfection of the artistic technique. An exactly similar thing occurred in the Greek art of the fourth and following centuries and in Roman art, where to find in a work such an illusionism was also the greatest compliment to the artist. Just as stories once began to circulate about a painted picture of grapes or of something else so similar to the reality that animals were deceived and took the painting for the real thing (*e.g.*, the grape painted by Zeuxis), so it was now; and Vasari tells us with pride that he painted a strawberry bush with such success that the peacock was deceived and tried to pick the berries from the picture!

In conformity with this the *technical style of sculpture and painting* begins to move also toward an ever-increasing *malerisch* quality, illusionism, and their satellites: dynamism, emotionality, sensuality, and so forth.

It now becomes easy to understand how the European painting and sculpture in the period from the fifteenth to the seventeenth century passed from the clear-cut linearism of the Primitives of the fifteenth century, through the Classics of the sixteenth century, to the baroque of the seventeenth, which is a clear-cut *malerisch* art (*i.e.*, from the linear classics, like Leonardo da Vinci, Botticelli, Dürer, Raphael, Massys, Wolf Huber, Holbein, Sansovino, H. Aldegrever, Benedetto da Mariano, Michelangelo (partly), Altdorfer, Ter Borch, etc.; to the *malerisch* Frans Hals, Van Dyck, Rembrandt, Velasquez, Grünewald, Ostade, Jan Lievens, Metsu, A. van de Velde, Bernini, Puget, Rubens, Van Goyen, Vermeer, Ruysdael, and so on).

This trend toward an ever-increasing *malerisch* quality continues with slight fluctuations, up to about the end of the eighteenth century. Then comes a temporary lull in the form of neo-classicism, an imitation of the imitation of the antique by the Renaissance. Though in technique it is somewhat less *malerisch* than the baroque (and the rococo), it still remains conspicuously Visual in form and especially in content; in fact the neo-classicism of the end of the eighteenth and of the beginning of the nineteenth century is rather more sensate and "worldly" than the baroque.

As to *the other traits* of the art of the fifteenth and in part of the sixteenth century, the sculpture as well as the painting shows the same trend toward Visualism, being in this respect an art of a transition.

The Middle Ages and Ideationalism are still alive, still noticeable, but they are waning. Individualism grows. Portraiture also. *Genre* also. Dynamism and emotionalism also. A secular spirit rises both in subjects and in manner. Similarly to the Greek art of the fourth century sensualism, voluptuousness, eroticism make further headway.

In the sixteenth century — the century of the Renaissance — all these tendencies became quite clear and pronounced. Ideationalism in its pure form is practically dead; Visualism triumphs. Only a somewhat diluted Idealism still lingers and temporarily flares up; but even it is moored to the earth rather than to heaven. It is in most cases an Idealism of the empirical and of the sensory human body, of landscape, of visual form generally; but not the idealization of the transcendental and supersensory. The Flemish school develops as entirely Visual, undilutedly "naturalistic." The Italian classics idealize and select and beautify the objects rendered, but do this in a purely empirical sense, from an empirical standpoint, and with empirical objects mainly. However, their nature is almost exclusively Sensate and they perfect it in a purely empirical sense. Even when they paint the religious subject it is "visualized," "materialized," dragged from its transcendental heaven to an earthly Sensate form, and treated from the standpoint of a purely Sensate psychology. (See No. 1, Plate XV, and No. 5, Plate VIII.)

The reason is that their idealism was purely humanistic, earthly, scientific, wingless, to soar to the heights of transcendental idealism, an idealism which does not fear anything, does not question itself, in a way is blind and unreservedly believing. Here in the earthly idealism, vested entirely in mortal man, such a power was impossible. In the second place, being an earthly idealism it was bound hand and foot to the empirical appearance of man and his milieu. It could not divorce itself decisively from this empirical reality, as does the Ideational and purely Idealistic art. Since it rejected the transcendental world, it had only the empirical world; it had to study it and to render it as it appeared to the eyes, at the best beautifying it but again on the basis merely of this Visual reality. "The main thing in the art of design," says Cellini, "is to cleverly fashion a naked man or woman."

Such is its motto. These masters studied, studied most patiently; and, as Leonardo da Vinci said, this seems sometimes to have led to a mere pedantic and scientific exercise instead of an art creation.[78] Being so closely bound to that reality — the only reality they really believed in — they could not get free from it entirely.

But the main thing was the whole mentality of the age, reflected by and in the art.

> This art is neither mystic, nor dramatic, nor spiritual. . . . Its aim is not to present to the eye the incorporeal and sublime world, the innocent and ecstatic spirits, the theological or ecclesiastical dogmas . . . it abandons the Christian and monastic period to enter on the laic and pagan period.

The whole process of transition from the fourteenth to the sixteenth century in Italy is depicted as follows.

PLATE XV

1, St. Anne and the Child Jesus, by Leonardo da Vinci. 2, Sleeping Venus, by Giorgione.

PLATE XVI

1

2

1, Saint Teresa, by Bernini. 2, Christ Carrying the Cross, by Rubens.

The order of painting remained symbolic and mystic up to the end of the fourteenth century, under the control of Christian theological ideas. It perpetuated the symbolic and mystic school down to the middle of the fifteenth century (Paro Spinello and the Bicci), during the long contest between the Christian spirit and the pagan spirit. In the middle of the fifteenth century its most angelic interpreter (Fra Angelico) is found in a holy spirit preserved from paganism by the seclusion of the cloister. It began to be interested in the real and substantial body during the early years of the fifteenth century . . . and substituted for the hope of celestial felicity the search for terrestrial happiness. It passed over from exact imitation to creative beauty (at the time of Leonardo da Vinci, Michael Angelo). . . . It maintained itself at Venice half a century later than elsewhere. . . . It became enfeebled in the time of Correggio, and chilled under the successors of Michael Angelo . . . when habits assumed a decorous air and minds took a sentimental turn; when the painter . . . became a polished cavalier; when the shop with its apprentices gave way to an "Academy"; when the bold and free artist . . . became a diplomatic courtier convinced of his own importance, a respecter of etiquette, a defender of rules, and the vain flatterer of prelates and the great.

In other countries which occupied a leading place in the art of the fifteenth and sixteenth centuries, even this reaction of a feeble Idealism scarcely took place. I mean first of all the Netherlands. Its art, beginning with Hubert van Eyck, grew in Visualism and became Visual par excellence during the first half of the sixteenth century.

Here is an excellent summary of the Flemish school. After the art of the thirteenth century almost entirely devoted to God, to Moral Order, and to Physical Order as a Work of God, the Flemish art now devotes itself to rendering such empirical objects as:

the armour, the polished glass of a window, the scrolls of a carpet, the hairs of fur, the undraped body, a canon's massive, wrinkled and obese features, a bourgomaster's or soldier's massive shoulders, projecting chin and prominent nose, the spindling shanks of a hangman, the overlarge head and diminutive limbs of a child, the costumes and furniture of the age; their entire work being a glorification of this present life. . . . Art falls from heaven to earth, and is no longer to treat divine but human incidents.

If to this list we add the tavern, the kitchen, the bedroom, the mill; the prosaic figures of merchants, of beggars, of housewives, some comely, some ugly; of fish, game, ham; club and council meetings; scenes of brawling, love making; street boys; farms, landscapes.

Other countries of Europe, France, Spain, Germany, England, occupy an intermediary position between the earthly Idealism of Italy and the purely Visual naturalism of Holland.

To sum up the general trend in all the European countries at the end of the fifteenth and in the first half of the sixteenth century we can say: During that period the art of "humility, of suffering, of sorrow," or resignation, of acceptance of divine guidance, was replaced by another art which Pascal defined as "concupiscence of eyes, concupiscence of flesh and lust (*orgueil*) of life."

At that time there began a clear separation and even an opposition of the secular and of the religious art, which up to the end of the fifteenth century had been one, that is, religious. The fact of the separation and the fact that the religious art from now on becomes a minor stream are in themselves most important symptoms of the great shift from Ideationalism toward a secular and sensuous Visualism.

IV. The End of the Sixteenth and the Seventeenth Century. The Baroque as a Further Growth of Sensate Visualism

A superficial glance at the art of the end of the sixteenth and of the seventeenth century may suggest that during that period painting and sculpture make a shift from Visualism toward Ideationalism. The main reason for such a contention would be the fact of a tightening moral and religious control over paintings and sculpture, and their "cleansing" and "purification," carried on by the Church after the twenty-fifth session of the Council of Trent in 1563, as well as by other, secular agencies of the Western society of that time, including Protestantism and its "iconoclastic" and "puritanic" tendencies.

Side by side with this, in the field of the purely secular art the establishment of the Academies of Art, especially in France around the middle of the seventeenth century, with their Academic classicism, modeled supposedly on the Greek "classic" art and the art of the classics of the Italian Renaissance; with Academic rules — at the beginning stressing line at the cost of color, proscribing the incidental, the ugly, the individual, and, in part, landscape and *genre* and portraiture; demanding an idealization of the typical and beautiful: all this seems to suggest also a shift from a comparatively strong to less strong Visualism, from a comparatively weak to a stronger Idealism.

However, such a conclusion would be wrong. It would have been based upon a few artificially selected data favorable to it, and would have overlooked an infinitely greater body of quite contradictory facts. In brief, the period in reality undergoes not a shift from Visualism but a further promotion of its success at the cost not only of the weak remnants of Ideationalism but even of Idealism. A very concise survey of the main features of both the religious and the secular painting and sculpture of the period is sufficient to make this clear.

A. *Religious Art.* Protestantism assumed an iconoclastic attitude; therefore it would not and did not have a religious art, though several Protestant painters treated religious topics. As to the Catholic religious art, the austere censorship applied, after the Council of Trent of 1563, to religious pictures and sculpture succeeded somewhat in achieving a mechanical suppression of "indecency," "nudity," and "light-mindedness." However, even in this the success was not complete.

Aside from this all the other traits of the religious art of the period, in the content as well as in the technique, were more Visual than the art of even the preceding period.

(1) It became controversially propagandist and political in the fight with Protestantism and other sects. Therefore the spirit of calmness, untroubled faith, serenity was gone from it: it was now on the earth and heavily engaged in a political conflict.

(2) Idealistic art is serene and calm. The religious art of the seventeenth century was supercharged with an almost pathological, in a sense sadistic, terrible and terrifying emotionalism and patheticism, particularly in the pictures of the martyrs, in tortures and sufferings, which are depicted in all their Visual horror. The scenes of the cutting of tongues, of the putting of people into a grave alive, of cutting the stomach and pulling out the intestines and kidneys, and so on — these scenes, depicted in all their last horrible details, evidently are even farther from Ideationalism or Idealism than the Laocoön group or emotionally Visual creations of the Hellenistic and Roman Sensate art.

(3) The same absolutely un-Ideational and un-Idealistic — almost pathological — emotionalism is shown by the appearance of a great multitude of pictures of ecstasy, visions, ecstatic and convulsed expressions on the faces, in the postures and attitudes of saints and other persons depicted. In the religious as well as in the secular art these scenes and expressions are everywhere. Nothing remains of the inner calmness, serenity, imperturbability of the Ideational and Idealistic art.

(4) The period is marked by a great multiplication of the scenes of death and of death itself, rendered in all their Visual reality and morbid appearance (Plate XVI and No. 5, Plate VIII). Skulls, corpses, disintegration, skeletons, rotten bones, graves, coffins, and similar topics are to be found everywhere.

(5) As to the form, it became, so we have already observed, much more Visual — more *malerisch* — and less linear; more dynamic and less static; more showy than before; more allegorical and less symbolic. Artificial perspectives to give illusion, *malerisch* technique, dynamism of postures and expressions, invention and application of several new devices to give "realistic" effects and to increase the Visual deceit — the growth of all this is unquestionable, has been stressed by many historians and critics, and need not be discussed here at length. (See Plate XVI.)

If, then, the seventeenth-century art shows an increase of Visualism, we must expect logically a further decline in the transcendental symbolism of the Ideational Art of the Middle Ages and its replacement by Visual allegories. This deduction is corroborated by the facts.

> The Middle Ages were the age of symbols. . . . Art was profoundly symbolic. . . . Already weakened in the fifteenth century the symbolic genius declined entirely in the seventeenth century.

Instead there came the abstract and "worldly" allegories, a flood of allegories in the art of the period: innumerable pictures and statues of *Simplex, Humilis, Fidelis, Verecunda, Secreta, Lacrimabilis; Verity, Justice, Benignity, Poverty, Vigilance, Force, Possession, Prudence, Memory, Volition, Intellect, Liberty, Friendship, Sleep*, and all the other abstractions of Cesar Ripa's *Iconologia* compiled soon into a whole encyclopedia of abstractions.

Yes, we are in an age of a premeditated theatricality, the planned and "scientific" Visualism of Despair; in an age of "illusion," of exalted "show."

B. *Secular Art.* The religious art is now already a minor stream, as compared with the secular, which became from now on the major current; second, that in the total of both the streams the proportion of religious topics continues rapidly to decline. These two facts are eloquent enough testimony that art was moving farther and farther away from its Ideational form toward the Visual.

In other respects the essential characteristics of the secular sculpture and painting of the period are similar to those of the religious art. This happens because both are manifestations of the predominant mentality and of the cultural configurations of the period.

If we wish to characterize the specific traits of the art of the end of the sixteenth, of the seventeenth, and, with modifications, of the first part of the eighteenth century, we must use several terms which, as a matter of fact, are employed by nearly all the historians of the art of that period and which by themselves point to its particularly conspicuous Visualism. These words are: theatricality, illusionism, illusionistic artificiality, showiness manifest in the ostentation of art, sumptuousness, pomp, luxury, overabundance of decoration, impurity, latent or open sensuality and sexuality, paganism, dynamism, patheticism, twisted and convulsive exaltation of ecstasy and other strong emotions, imitative, purely cerebral and chilly Academism with its pseudo idealism paralleled by the pure Visual naturalism of the Flemish school. Such are the characteristics of the baroque.

Baroque first of all is a theatrical pomp, an exaggerated "show," and therefore Visualism. It is enough to glance at a typical baroque architectural creation in order to see this.

When its other traits are observed, its restlessness, dynamism, fluidity, this theatrical Visualism comes out still stronger. When, besides the exterior, the interior decoration of the baroque is considered, with its gluttony for mirrors, damask flowers, gilt, stucco, garlands (even petty angels, which are hybrids between the angels of religion and vulgar cupids), the baroque is at once recognized as the world of theatrical and ostentatious Visualism.

When this ostentatious and sumptuous display became tiresome after some fifty or sixty years, the same visual and theatrical mentality changed the decorations of the baroque into its direct descendant, the rococo. The rococo of the eighteenth century is the direct outcome of the baroque and belongs to the same family of theatricality and show, but the decorations are changed for the sake of variety. The rococo world is the same illusionistic artificial world, the world of seen surfaces and appearances, but they now are made in an effeminate, enfeebled, idyllic, pastoral, coquettish fashion. It is the "boudoir" world with its "bosoms," with artificial and illusionistic rocks, waterfalls, gorges, fountains, idyllic shepherds and pastorals, cupids and nymphs, with artificial disorderliness of shrubbery and trees (trimmed and clipped to give this effect), with theatrical "simplicity," in most cases fashioned supposedly *à la* Chinese, with other exotic freaks and illusionistic devices of an enfeebled, weary, bored, overripe, and half-senile society. This play with "freaks" was styled and believed to be a "return to nature," to "simplicity," to "innocence."

However different is the sculpture and painting of the period in various countries, especially in the Netherlands on the one hand and in Italy, France, and Spain, on the other; however profound are the contrasts between the artists of the same country (*e.g.*, Rubens and Rembrandt; Caravaggio and Carracci and Bernini in Italy; Poussin, Le Brun, and Claude Lorrain in France; El Greco, Velásquez, Murillo, Zurbarán, and Montañés in Spain); almost all of them are similar in having in common the properties of the Visual art of the baroque described above.

The Visualism took two main forms in that period: the Flemish naturalistic, and the Italo-French theatrical. In conformity with this main trend, its satellites, like the growth of individualism; the transformation of the artist into the professional who is paid for his art by fame, by popularity, by wealth, by nearness to the powerful of the period; the growth of so-called aestheticism in society; the development of a literature devoted to the problem of art; the reasoning and chattering about it; the rise of connoisseurism in art; the appearance of professional critics; the increase of art education; and so on — all the satellites already familiar from the Visual phase of the Graeco-Roman art did not fail to appear. In many respects the period was indeed similar to the phase of the Hellenistic and of the Roman art after the second century B.C. Generally its "increasing sensualism ushered into painting [and also sculpture] what Pascal styled 'vanity' and what Mother Angelica accused as satisfying 'two senses at once'!" The age and culture of Ideationalism was over; over was the age of Idealism of the thirteenth century. The European world passed definitely into the Sensate Visual stage of its culture.

V. Eighteenth Century

I have remarked, in regard to the Hellenistic and the Roman post-Augustan art, that their subsequent course was a series of waves of imitation of previous forms of art, changing more and more quickly as we pass to the later centuries of these cultures — imitation of the early "archaic," the "classic," then the previous Idealistic and purely Visual forms, and so on. *In this sequence of the various fashions and imitations the previous Ideational form as well as a real Idealistic form was never successfully achieved, all the imitative waves remaining generally in the Visual stream and the change consisting in a variation of different Visual forms in spite of the efforts to give a real Idealistic or even Ideational art.*

This fact comes spontaneously to one's mind when one is following the destinies of the European art after the Idealistic art of the thirteenth and in part of the fourteenth century. There have been many waves of changed styles, several attempts to revive the "idealistic classicism," and to achieve an Idealistic art; quite recently there has been attempted even something near to the Ideational style. But in spite of all this, all these changes have moved in a Visual stream, never giving real Idealistic or Ideational art. And Visualism, since the fifteenth century, has steadily progressed up to the end of the nineteenth century.

About the beginning of the second part of the eighteenth century the rococo was practically worn out and the first signs of a return, for the third time, to "classicism" appeared. This return was an accomplished fact at the end of the eighteenth century. Thus within one century art made a whole circle: beginning with classical Academism, it went to the romantic rococo, and at the end of the century returned to classicism. The domination of the third imitation of classicism was short, however: around 1825 it was almost over and soon was replaced by the romanticism of the second quarter of the nineteenth century. Romanticism did not last longer, and within one quarter of a century was outmoded. It was replaced by something like "naturalism," and several other currents, one of which developed into the impressionistic school of the last quarter of the nineteenth century. In it Visualism reached its extremest and purest form: there was and there is no possibility of going further along the line of Visualism. Its triumph was again short, and toward the end of the nineteenth century its fashionableness was already on the decline: "expressionists," and especially "cubists," "futurists," "symbolists," appeared as the opponents of not only the impressionistic school but almost the Visual style itself.

At the present moment we have a most diversified conglomeration of many schools and currents, among them even the challengers of the Visual style generally and the first symptoms of the search for something akin to the Ideational style. But these symptoms as yet are weak; the searchers look but have not yet found what they desire.

Thus within the nineteenth century we have several waves, each of a duration hardly longer than a quarter of a century. In the eighteenth century the duration of the rococo and of classicism was about half of a century; in the seventeenth century the baroque and Academism lasted almost a century; the Flemish naturalism lasted even longer; and the Renaissance "classicism" also continued for more than a century.

Such, roughly speaking, was the main course of European art, with its trend to an acceleration of the change of the fashionable varieties of the Visual style. This acceleration seems to mean that Visualism is perhaps beginning to wear itself out, since one variety of it after another is tried and quickly discarded, and this trial and discarding, becoming quicker and more short lived, is perhaps an indication of the decline of the Visual style.

VI. The End of the Eighteenth Century and the Nineteenth Century

As we have mentioned, beginning with about the second part of the eighteenth century a reaction against the rococo and romanticism began to appear. Around 1780 it triumphed and ushered in again a "neo-classic" style in the work of David and his school in France, and similar painting and sculpture in other countries.

In reality it was a simulacrum of all this, an even poorer simulacrum perhaps than the Academism of the second half of the seventeenth century had provided. Even more artificial, cold, and boring than the earlier imitation, it followed the purely external traits of the classic art, without its inner spirit. The results were about the same as in several of the ancient Roman waves of pseudo classicism: cold theatricality, *ennui*, incongruity (especially when some contemporary persons were represented either naked or in Roman togas), and other traits of a purely imitative movement.

In the anarchical and many-colored conglomeration of numerous and various schools of art of the nineteenth century — all of which, to the end, remained in the Visual stream — there were some alternations in the slight domination of the neo-neo-neo-classic and of the neo-neo-neo-anticlassic, the neo-romantic, the neo-Primitivist, the pre-Raphaelite, the rationalist, and other currents. The neo-classicism of the David-Winckelmann school continued to about 1820–1830. Its place was taken by the anticlassical Romantic school, which dominated up to about 1848- 1850. Then its place was taken in turn by the realism (practically the Visual naturalism so excellently developed before by the Flemish artists of the seventeenth century) of Gericault, of the *paysagists* of the Barbizon school (Courbet, Daumier, Millet, and others). It flourished from about 1848 to 1870. Its further development, and purest form of the Visual art, was *impressionism*, which succeeded realism and dominated from about 1870 to the end of the nineteenth century. All these currents were Visual. Impressionism is Visual par excellence.

Then only, as a reaction to it and to Visualism generally, appeared symbolism, constructivism, expressionism, neo-Primitivism, cubism, futurism, and similar movements which at least in their negative program and aspirations broke sharply and decisively with Visualism for the first time since the entrance of Visualism into the Western art. As I have pointed out, they did not succeed in becoming real Ideationalism or even Idealism; they are just transitory, incoherent movements, whose aversion to Visualism is clear and determined. In this sense they are a real landmark in the course of the Western art. But in their positive search for a new form of art they remain, so far, unsuccessful. The result is incoherence, inner contradiction, "queerness," and, in a sense, sterility. They are the children of divorce from Visuality; they have lost the old family shelter, but they have not found, as yet, a new family. Therefore they are "in the street," a kind of homeless, formless wild urchins running here and there and failing in their attempt to find a safe and pleasant place to live and really creative work to do. This is a tendency common, as we shall see, to practically all the main forms of contemporary art: painting and sculpture, architecture, music, drama, and literature.

That romanticism, realism (or rather Visual naturalism), and impressionism are quite Visual currents is evident. They do not even pretend to be Idealistic or Ideational. For this reason it is needless to discuss them. What is worth doing here is to point out some of the traits of impressionism which make it the last and the extremest development of Visualism to the limit beyond which there is *non plus ultra*. It replaced composition (choice, selection, arrangement — omitting the incidental, stressing the essential) by the impression of a moment. It painted things as they looked at a given point in an incessant fugitive change of Visual appearance due to the vibration of light and shade. It did not aim to stress anything essential, lasting, eternal in the objects. It was *malerisch* par excellence. There were no fixed linear forms, no constant color, because "forms and colours incessantly change from moment to moment," and because "all shades are transparent and coloured, animated by thousands of reflexions." Accordingly they painted out of doors, in full sunlight, *sub Jove crudo*, with a specially elaborated technique of extreme *malerisch* characters (patches of various colors put side by side) made possible through the photographic and optical discoveries of Chevreul.

The theorizers of impressionism and the artists claimed quite consistently that such an art did not need either mind or thought or any idea; all that it needed was a sharp eye and a trained hand to render the impression of the eye either in painting or in sculpture. Also, they contended quite consistently that it was a matter of indifference what was painted; the subject was a secondary matter and anything would do. "*Sujet* is quite unimportant: a pile of earth or the most vulgar and common object may become, in certain moments, quite fascinating." The same object could be rendered many times, each time giving a new picture or new sculpture because at different moments this object would look different. And many of the artists indeed painted the same landscape or other object several times. *Paysage* and portrait — these two forms of art profited essentially from impressionism. No particular selection in the topics, no idealization, no ideationalization, have a place in impressionism. It aimed to be "empty minded," like a photographic camera that would "shoot" anything. Like the camera, impressionism desired to take "snapshots" of the passing Visual surface of objects. It was not an accident that impressionism developed simultaneously and in connection with the development of photography: both were the offshoots of the same deep forces which concentrated the attention mainly on the Visual appearance of the world, on its "surface," on its "visible illusion" — moreover, on the surface of a given passing moment, proscribing and refusing to go "deeper" into what is behind the visual aspect, behind the world of the senses. In all these respects the principle of Becoming and of the Visualist outlook on the world (*Weltanschauung*) reached its climax in impressionism. There is no possibility of going further along that path. Even photography; even "movies," which also began to develop almost simultaneously with all this and the appearance of which at the end of the nineteenth century is again not purely accidental; even these can hardly go further along the line of Visualism than impressionism has already gone.

Plates XVII, XVIII, and XIX give an idea of the moderately impressionistic, impressionistic, and imitative sculptural and expressionistic pictures, with the sex motive, of the second part of the nineteenth century and the beginning of the twentieth. In Plate XVII, No. 1, *Naked Woman* by Gustave Courbet (1819–1877), is sculptural; No. 2, *Street in Bern* by Edouard Manet (1832–1883), is mildly impressionistic. Nos. 1 and 2 on Plate XVIII, *Boulevard* and *The Breakfast of the Boaters* by Auguste

Renoir (1841–1920), and No. 3, *Ugolino and His Sons* by J. B. Carpeaux (1827–1875), and No. 4, a bust of H. von —— by Auguste Rodin (1840–1917), represent the impressionistic in painting and sculpture. Plate XIX shows *Scene from Tahiti* by Paul Gaugin (1848–1903) with "primitivistic" tendency, and *Field in Spring* by Claude Monet (1840–1928) impressionistic especially. For an example of the *pathétique* similar to the Laocoön group (Plate XI), Carpeaux's group may be taken. Cubistic and other expressionistic works may be found on Plate IX.

Impressionism, photography, movies — all three are excellent testimony that at the end of the nineteenth and at the beginning of the twentieth century the mentality of the Western society, so far as it was expressed in art (and, as we shall see, in philosophy, science, and all the compartments of culture), became extremely Visual and illusionistic. Reality was reduced in that mentality to the mere surface of the sensory phenomena; even in that surface the reality was thought of as a purely momentary, fugitive, and passing glimpse. "The real is only what your eye sees at a given moment." Such is this "visually solipsistic" philosophy of illusionism and radical illusionistic Visual "shallowness." "All the world is but a momentary Visual appearance," a "momentary Visual impression," such is another formula. And all this results from the development of Visualism to its logical limits. When this limit, in the form of impressionism (and other illusion philosophies), has been reached, Visualism, and its foundation Sensatism (*Nihil esse in intellectu quod non fuerit prius in sensu*), suddenly find themselves at "the end of their rope," in a blind alley, in imminent danger of self-annihilation. Since the whole of reality has been reduced by Visualism to the mere passing impression, to the momentary appearance, the reality amounts to mere illusion and mirage, to self-deceit and dreaming; even these being purely fugitive and momentary.

Such a "reality" became so "thin" (thinner even than the outermost surface of the things), and so "immaterial," that it reduced itself to something less substantial than even the proverbial ashes. Ashes have at least some material being; in the Impressionistic Visualism there is left nothing but the passing mirage. Paradoxically Visualism and Sensatism, pushed to their limits, came to self-destruction. Both rejected any "Ideational" reality, any mind, any thought, any planned construction in their purposes and creations. Their ultimate foundation, at the beginning, was the materiality of the external world. Now this materiality has evaporated in "illusionism." Therefore this basis has disappeared. The Ideational foundation had been rejected from the very beginning. Therefore it could not become the new foundation. In this way reality was reduced to almost nothingness, and the mentality of Visualism found itself in emptiness.

For a time it could live in the illusionistic world of fugitive phantasmagorias, amidst the restless mirages of incessant Becoming; but nobody and no movement can live for a long time in such a world of illusionistic appearances. Impressionism could not do it; and at the beginning of the twentieth century its triumph was over; it destroyed itself; it called forth a vigorous reaction and criticism. And since it was the most extreme form of Visualism; and since other, more moderate, forms had been tried before, there seems to have been no possibility of advancing along this path. The only "new" way or way further was the *non-Visual* way. Hence, "the blind alley" of Visualism suddenly began to be abandoned and there appeared an ever-increasing number of artists who decisively refused to enter into any part of the Visual highway. They believed that all Visual routes had been tried and that all led, after a time, to a blind alley. The only possibility was to try to find a new, non-Visual road. Expressionism, constructivism, cubism, futurism, "pointilism," "dadaism," "surrealism," "tactilism," and many other modern "isms" were exactly this "getting-off" the Visual highway and searching for a new non-Visual pass leading to new horizons and to new summits of artistic creation. "The dominant trait of the contemporary painting is a vigorous reaction against Impressionism. Almost all the post-Impressionists are anti-Impressionists."

The main criticisms raised against impressionism are:

(1) Absence of thought, style, and construction.

(2) Its purely Sensate nature — "an acephalic art." It notes only sensations, without any judgment of thought; "eye eats the brain in it."

(3) Its nihilism. For impressionism there is nothing noble or ignoble.

Since the most anti-Visual currents are neither Ideational nor Idealistic, and besides are still the minor currents in the river of contemporary art, this means that the art of the end of the nineteenth and of the twentieth centuries is still conspicuously and extremely Visual. Therefore we should expect the usual satellites of the Visual art also to be displayed in it conspicuously. The expectation is sustained by the facts. Is this contemporary art *individualistic?* Of course. From this follows the contemporary "anarchy" of art. "The word school has no longer its old significance. Individualism which has shattered this uniformity, has destroyed both state and school in the early sense. There is no longer either victor or vanquished [but as many schools as there are artists]." To call any artist unoriginal and without individuality is an insult. Right or wrong, the artists want to be individualists, original, peculiar, especially free from any restraint, even extravagant and queer. Likewise the contemporary artist is a highly professional artist. He wants to be free from any tutelage of religion, moral decency, of anything except his fancy. He wants to mark his creation with his name and is willing in no way to be just an anonymous creator, the *primus inter pares* of a collectivity, as the Ideational artists were. On the other hand, he is a member of the professional union of artists, a kind of caste separate from the rest of the collectivity and ready to protect its interests at the cost of this collectivity.

What is the basis of the selection of the topics by artists of our time? There are several, among them in a few cases some which are purely Ideational. But in the bulk the basis is neither the glory of God nor the glory of the country nor a service to some ideal as such, but the *market demand, profit,* either through commercial sale of pictures and sculptures or through getting an order from a rich magnate, from politicians, or from the state. In all such cases, with publicity as an instrument toward such a commercial goal, Mammon is what dictates the patterns as well as the topics of the art of today. The professional artist has to make his living. To make it he must be able to sell his services or creations. To sell them he must adapt them to the existing demand of the market. Hence the highly commercialized character of his work and the vulgarism which controls it. The artist, instead of lifting the vulgar tastes to sublime heights, must debase himself to the low level of vulgarism.

Further, we have seen that colossalism is one of the satellites of the Visual art. Do we have it with us? More than enough. Sheer quantity springs to the eye everywhere and tends more and more to replace quality. We build one art museum bigger than the others. A strenuous competition exists in that respect. And if a building is the "biggest in the world," this is advertised *urbi et orbi;* and the building is proudly thought of as the best in the world. The same is true of the pictures, of the mural frescoes, of the statues and sculptural decorations. "Biggest in the world," or "the greatest number of art galleries, art schools, art courses, art trades" — as with the best sellers, this is thought of as equivalent to being the leader in art, the highest and the best! We are in the grip of this mania of colossalism, and it manifests itself everywhere and in all fields of art, as will be shown further.

Moreover, as has happened before, the main topics of our art are the persons, the events, the sights of common, daily life, with an inclination for the picaresque, picturesque, for the doubtful aspects and types of life: to crime, to criminals, to prostitutes, to ragamuffins, to urchins, to the "poorer classes," to abnormal types, and so on. The "proletariat," labor, the "misadapted," Cinderellas, tramps, criminals, and so on, play a very large part in the paintings and sculpture of our time. Here again we are simply repeating what has happened several times before.

Sex, eroticism, voluptuous nudity, the invasion of the pretty — and not too chaste — woman, have been the usual satellites of such a Visual art. It is enough to pick up almost any copy of one of our

PLATE XVII

1

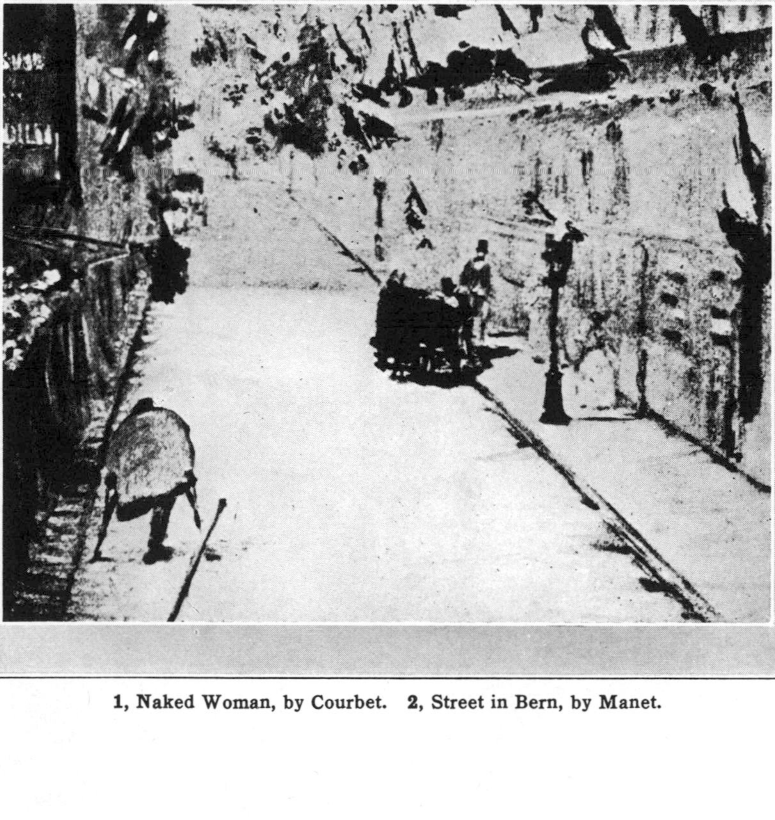

2

1, Naked Woman, by Courbet. 2, Street in Bern, by Manet.

PLATE XVIII

1

2

3

4

1, Boulevard, by Renoir. 2, The Breakfast of the Boaters, by Renoir. 3, Ugolino and His Sons, by Carpeaux. 4, Bust of H. von ——, by Rodin.

contemporary magazines, in order to find such a pretty face, be it a movie star, a prostitute, a pretty stenographer, society lady, or just the anonymous mistress of the artist or of the editor. It is enough to go to any annual salon of the new pictures in order to see everywhere old and young female bodies, sitting, lying, standing, quite nude, almost completely nude, three-quarters naked, half-naked but coquettishly dressed so that the figure looks more sexual, having a stronger voluptuous appeal than many naked contemporary Venuses. The same is true of the males: they also are depicted either as "brutes" and "cave men-like" or "fine and dandy," effeminate, and with "sex appeal." One can go at random a dozen times to the movies and see all this in this modern and most Visual form of art.

Other satellites are not lacking. Patheticism, emotionality, dynamism — we have all that in an even supermelodramatic portion. *Satirical, cynical, skeptical* topics abound. In the Ideational and Idealistic there is no place for such an art, because there is no such mentality. The Sensate Visualist cannot help having them. Hence widespread development of caricature, satirical cartoons, pictures, sculptures, portraits, and the satirization of all kinds of events, persons, values. Each newspaper copy has a section containing such satire and caricature; and there are dozens and dozens of special magazines (*The New Yorker, Ballyhoo*) devoted exclusively to satirizing and caricaturing and ridiculing everything and everybody. This is our "stimulant" and refreshment.

We have also seen that the development of *paysage* is connected with Visualism. We, too, have a great development of landscape painting, landscape architecture, and decorative art.

Finally, as the crowning jewel of the four-hundred-year development of Sensate Visualism we have — not by chance — photography, television and movies. That they were invented when Visualism in form of Visual realism and impressionism was reaching its extreme development is not to be overlooked. It is in an excellent harmony with the style of time.

In the original four-volume edition, the verbal and qualitative outline of this chapter is substantiated in the next by a quantitative description of the fluctuation of the main styles and their satellites in the painting and sculpture of Western Europe.

However, given below is a summary of the main results of that quantitative study:

A. The data show that art before the thirteenth century, and especially from the tenth to the thirteenth, was almost exclusively Ideational. The art of the thirteenth century was predominantly Idealistic. After the thirteenth century the Visual tide began to rise, the Ideational to ebb rapidly, and the nineteenth century was the climax, so far, of this Visualism.

B. Side by side with these big waves, there have been minor ripples, but they are not caught in our net of big periods of half a century, a century, and even of two centuries.

C. This main course has manifested itself in several changes in the content as well as in the form or style of painting and sculpture, during the period studied, which content and style are the essential traits of the Ideational and the Visual styles.

(1) Art subjects have been, after the thirteenth century, more and more secular and less and less religious, transcendental, superempirical. At the present time more than 96 per cent of all art is secular, while in the period before the fourteenth century the situation was reversed. A slight reaction, however, is noticeable in the twentieth century.

(2) The style of depicting the objects of painting and sculpture was predominantly Ideational before the thirteenth century; Idealistic in the thirteenth and part of the fourteenth; then it became more and more Visual, until at the end of the nineteenth century it reached the limit of Visualism, becoming impressionistic. The twentieth century is marked by a strong anti-Visual reaction, showing itself in a notable increase of such anti-Visual forms as cubistic, expressionistic, constructistic, and other Mixed styles. They are not as yet, however, Ideational.

(3) Parallel is the course of the spiritual and sensual character of art in these centuries; likewise, Visual centuries are marked by a quantitative increase of nudity, and by a growth of the sensuous, voluptuous, erotic, fleshy nudity at the cost of ascetic, martyrlike, or nonhuman nudity of the Middle Ages.

(4) Parallel is the course of the Visual portraiture, *paysage*, *genre*, and partly of the *nature morte*. They all increase in the centuries after the thirteenth, while in the Ideational period before that they occupy little space in art, and even so not in the visual sense but as mere symbols of the superempirical realities.

(5) Many subclasses of each of these main classes of painting and sculpture move in agreement with the expectations given by the very concepts of Ideational, Idealistic, and Visual art, and in this way support the whole hypothesis as well as many of its details.

D. As an additional conclusion given by the data and directly sustaining the theory of the whole pattern of the Ideational and Sensate cultures and mentality, we can say that the following "variables" are

PLATE XIX

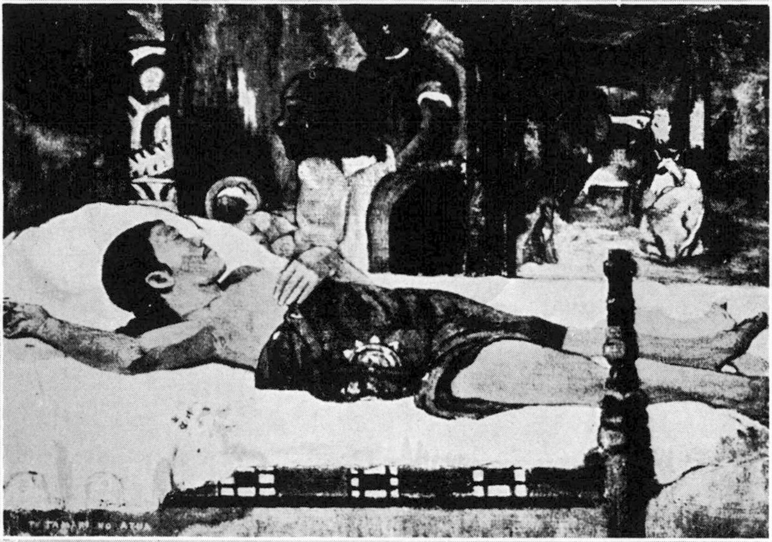

1

2

1, Scene from Tahiti, by Gaugin. **2,** Field in Spring, by Monet.

PLATE XX

1, Doric column and capital, from the Parthenon. 2, Ionic column and capital, from Erechtheion. 3, Corinthian column and capital, from the monument of Lysistrates. 4, Roman Composite column and capital, from the Arch of Titus. 5, Pyramid of Ne-woser-re, reconstructed by Borchardt. 6, Grave temple of Mentuhotep III, restored.

usually associated with one another, and in their quantitative ups and downs move parallel, or almost so, in their essential fluctuations.

Ideational Art	*Visual Art*
Prevalence of religious topics	Prevalence of secular topics
Spiritual character of the objects rendered	Sensual character of the objects rendered
Ideational style	Visual, especially impressionistic style
Lack of or little nudity	A considerable nudity (quantitatively)
Ascetic and nonsensual and nonerotic nudity qualitatively	Sensual and erotic and fleshy character of it, qualitatively
Lack of, or little place occupied by, portraiture, *genre*, *paysage*, and fantastic subjects (in a merely imaginative sense)	Ever-increasing proportion of *paysage*, portraiture, *genre*. Portraiture tends to become more and more "democratic," replacing the hero, the aristocracy, by the man of the lower classes, *bourgeoisie*, and in part intellectuals.
Lack of the daily events, exotic, picturesque, and negative types, values, and events	*Genre* becomes also more and more erotic; more and more of "everyday life," more and more devoted to the exotic, negative, and pathological types and events

E. All the European countries studied show, in these changes, that they belong to the same "cultural continent," and the main changes are essentially similar in all of them, though not in all simultaneous and synchronous.

F. The data and the curves support the theory of limit, the variationally recurring character of social processes, the theory of autonomous self-regulation of sociocultural processes, and a lack of any permanent and perpetual tendency.

G. When the whole period studied is taken, beginning with the Creto-Mycenaean and Graeco-Roman cultures and ending with the present time, the curves of Ideational and Visual art give several alternating big waves of domination of either one of these main styles.

H. When art enters a transition from the dominant Ideational form to the coming-to-dominate Visual form, the descending line of Ideationalism and the ascending line of Visualism usually give an "optimum point" of perfect balance of both styles, which results in the marvelous Idealistic art similar to that of the fifth century B.C. and the thirteenth century A.D. When art passes from the domination of the Visual art to the domination of the Ideational, the art of that transitory period is marked by an incoherent, impure, queer form of anti-Visualism.

I. The art of various countries, and especially of quite different cultures, shows different proportions of general domination of Visualism and Ideationalism.

10

FLUCTUATION OF IDEATIONAL AND VISUAL FORMS OF ARCHITECTURE

Having treated in considerable detail the fluctuation and recurrence of the Ideational and Visual and main intermediary styles in painting and sculpture, in this and the subsequent chapters I want to show briefly, first, that the same categories can be applied to other classes of art phenomena — namely, architecture, music, literature, and criticism; second, that somewhat similar recurrences and fluctuations of these styles go on also in these fields of art; third, what the relationship is to one another of the waves of Ideationalism and Visualism in each of them.

The first question which confronts us is whether the concepts of the Ideational and Visual (Sensate) styles, with their intermediaries, are applicable to architecture as a whole.

Regardless of the variety of the architectural types from other standpoints, it is possible to distinguish the elements of both the Ideational and Visual styles (with the linear and pictorial, static and dynamic, open and closed forms, unity and multiplicity, and other satellites of these fundamental categories) in architectural creations. As to the "content" or *inner characteristic* of Ideational architecture, it is the same as in other Ideational forms: dedication of the building to the transcendental values. In its form it is marked by symbolism: the symbolism (and allegory of impure Ideational style) permeates the building in its entirety as well as in its details.

The meaning and value of Ideational architecture lies not in its visual aspect but in what is beyond and behind it, and of which it is only a visible symbol. If, for instance, the foundations of many churches are in the pattern of a cross, the pattern is chosen and valued not so much because it visually is a cross but because the cross is a symbol of Christianity, of Christ, of His Cross, and so on. The same is to be said of many details. If, for instance, the buildings of many churches in the Oriental Christianity have one central cupola with four smaller cupolas around it, its "beauty" or "value" lies not merely in the visible pleasant effect but in the fact that the central cupola represents Christ, and the other four, the four evangelists. In the Visual style of architecture such a symbolism is absent: its value lies in its visual effects and in its success in meeting the utilitarian needs which it has to serve, and that is all. Behind or beyond that, no symbolic meaning is to be looked for. The quality of the building depends entirely upon its visual form and utility as such. Therefore, most of the Ideational architecture is to be sought for mainly in the religious, magical, or other fields, where buildings are constructed to serve these — at least in part — superempirical and transcendental purposes. In a word, the characteristics of Ideationality, from the standpoint of the "inner content," are the same in architecture as in painting and sculpture. This is also true of the "*external*" forms of architecture: here the *criteria* also remain the same as in painting and sculpture. The Ideational architecture (in any concrete pattern) is marked by a relative simplicity and external unpretentiousness of form; by freedom from anything merely "illusionary" and "showy"; by the static nature of the building; by the perfect fulfillment of the structural functions of all its important parts; by a strong atmosphere of independence of its empirical surroundings; by its inner richness and harmony and beauty, compared and contrasted with its exterior simplicity; it is "solid, definite, enduring," built for eternity, tactile, clear, complete in itself, and "architectural."

In the Visual architecture, the principles of dynamism (catching in stone or steel or wood the passing glimpses of phenomena), movement, "show," change, mere exterior appearance, illusion, and artificiality (for instance, various devices of the baroque to prolong the perspective and size and other "light and shade" effects in their purely visual illusion), intricacy of forms, superabundance of embellishments and decorations to catch the eye but having no structural functions; unclearness; inner plainness in comparison with the external ornateness, etc. — such are its traits. What is meant will be much clearer after a glance at the plates.

Numbers 1, 2, and 3 of Plate XX show three main orders of Greek columns, the Doric, the Ionic, and the Corinthian, and No. 4 is a Roman Composite order, made, in a way, out of all the other three. As we pass from the Doric order to the Ionic, then to the Corinthian, and finally to the Roman Composite order, we see a progressive growth of complication, ornamentation, and "showiness." The Ionic column begins to portray this element of show and illusion and deceit: its façade is all right but its side view is already less satisfactory than the Doric and impresses us as though, after taking great care to wash its face (façade), the builders neglected to wash (to take care of) its sides. The showy nature of the Corinthian order, with its abundance of purely decorative and purely Visual elements, is obvious. Finally, the Roman Composite order is the most overdecorated, most complicated, and most Visual, in the sense that these decorations have almost no architectural function; they are placed entirely for visual effects.

Numbers 5 and 6 on Plate XX depict two Egyptian architectural monuments very similar in their form, but one much simpler and Ideational in character, while the other is decorated externally with rows of columns which have hardly any real architectural function and are placed mainly for visual effect. (No. 5 is the pyramid of Ne-woser-re, reconstructed by Borchardt; No. 6 is the grave and the temple of Mentuhotep III.)

Pictures 1 and 2 of Plate XXI show the exterior and the interior appearance of the Hagia Sophia, sixth century A.D. (the exterior appearance was complicated by the minarets, added by the Turks) and 3 and 4 of the San Giovanni in Fonte, Ravenna, ninth century A.D. Externally both buildings are extremely simple, having almost no purely decorative elements and nothing for effect. They are just cutting a part of real space from the rest of the world in a real way by real walls. Internally, they represent a creation of their own world, perfect and harmonious. They remind one of a man dressed very plainly and modestly but with a beautiful, pure, and harmonious soul.

Finally, if one looks at the two baroque churches on Plate XXII, their dynamic, showy, overdecorated character hits the eye. Their Visualism is shown also by the fact that being overdecorated on the façade, their sides impress us as forgotten. The face is "powdered and rouged," the ears and other features are neglected.

These illustrations possibly make clearer the idea of the Ideational and Visual externality in architecture, at least for the nonspecialists in the field.

Viewed from this standpoint, the life history of the architecture of various cultures, as well as that of a certain and definite architectural style, like the Gothic or the classic, shows long-time and short-time oscillations between Ideationalism and Visualism with their intermediaries.

The "swings" between Ideational and Visual styles are more noticeable in the life history of the Graeco-Roman architecture.

Let us take the main forms of the columns — the Doric, the Ionic, and the Corinthian — and the respective place which each of them occupies in the Graeco-Roman architecture at different periods, and consider the swings. The Doric column is the most Ideational. It is structural and organic in its pure simplicity; in its pure form it has nothing for decorative purposes. The Corinthian, the most Visual in its relatively rich ornamentation, existed in great part for the sake of ornamentation, from the visual standpoint. The Ionic occupies an intermediate place between these two forms.

At the earlier stages of the continental Greek architecture, the Doric order was used almost exclusively. Then the Ionic order, somewhat Doricized, began to spread more and more. Finally, about the beginning of the fourth century B.C., while "the Doric style was almost abandoned by the middle of the fourth" the Corinthian style appeared. The Ionic and the Corinthian both grew at the cost of the Doric. The Hellenistic and the Roman architects used more and more the Corinthian,

PLATE XXI

1

2

3

4

1, The Hagia Sophia, Constantinople. 2, Interior of the Hagia Sophia. 3, Exterior of San Giovanni, in Ravenna. 4, Interior of San Giovanni.

PLATE XXII

1

2

1, Baroque façade of the San Andrea della Valle in Rome.
2, Baroque façade of the Santa Crocé in Lecce.

and ever more complicated forms of it, until they produced a still more complicated "Composite order" where all the styles were mixed and decoration and Visualism reached a kind of climax.

If now we turn to architecture as a whole, its early stage *before the fifth century* B.C. was simple Doric, externally; and internally the grand buildings were temples, devoted to the worship of deities and other super-empirical purposes. In other words, it was predominantly *Ideational*, according to the *internal as well as external criteria of Ideationality*. Internally it was a temple, "*not a civil but a religious building*." "*It served the gods and the dead*." "Luxury and beauty were entirely reserved for the gods."

Externally this Doric architecture was simple even in details. It was free from any colossalism. The Greek artist of that period "saw beauty not in material grandeur or riches but in proportion and simplicity"; likewise he "did not care for rare and glittering materials, such as gold, silver, and precious stones."

In brief, just as painting and sculpture before the fifth century were pre-eminently Ideational, the Greek architecture was also Ideational in that period.

The fifth century was the Idealistic period in Greek painting and sculpture. And it seems to have been *Idealistic also in architecture*. The Parthenon is its evidence and incarnation. Internally it was still devoted to God but also to the civic virtues, and, to a degree, to the noble empirical values. Externally, this manifests itself in a marvelous harmony and proportion between the Ideational otherworldliness and visual beauty. Hence, its greater decorativeness and visual appeal as compared with the preceding period. It is larger in size. It is more ornamented. Instead of an almost complete lack of decorative elements "now, in the design of the Parthenon, all the metopes of the external Doric order were filled with sculpture, and a continuous Ionic frieze was added around the cella."

Since about the middle of the fourth century, the balance line in the rising tide of Visualism and falling tide of Ideationalism seems to have been passed. From that time on, the architecture becomes, with minor fluctuations and reactions, more and more Visual, like the Greek, the Hellenistic, and then the Roman painting and sculpture. Again a change takes place in the inner character of the buildings as well as in their externality: both become more and more Visual. From the inner standpoint, side by side with temples, the princes' palaces, the theaters, public civic buildings, triumphal arches, aqueducts, mansions of the potentates and other secular buildings, "for every variety of purpose which public and private life on a scale of magnificence demanded," became more and more the incarnation of the grand architecture. It begins to serve less and less the gods and the dead and more and more the empirical needs of the powerful, the rich, and the privileged. It ceases to be symbolic and becomes Visual in its beauty or ugliness.

"Luxury, love of the colossal and grandiose, pompousness and theatrical display, the very things Greek art had once avoided, now appeared."

All this is manifest throughout the whole of the buildings as well as in their details: in the Roman architecture which "is entirely founded on Greek and forms indeed a kind of continuation of the latter in the spirit of lavishness and display and inferior refinement" — all this reached a kind of climax of Visualism.

To sum up, then, *the Graeco-Roman architecture in its Ideational Visual aspects seems to have had main waves fairly synchronous with those in the Graeco-Roman painting and sculpture: it was predominantly Ideational up to the fifth century* B.C.; *in the fifth century it became Idealistic; beginning with the end of the fourth century* B.C. *it began to be dominated more and more by Visualism. Temporary and shallow short-lived reactions and minor fluctuations occurred, but they were only ripples upon the above main tides. Beginning with about the end of the fourth century* A.D., *the Visual phase of that architecture began to decline more and more and a new rising tide of Ideational-Christian architecture began to replace it until that became triumphant during the next century. In this way, the wave of Visualism which dominated for some seven or even eight centuries was ended and succeeded by a new wave of Ideational Christian architecture.*

This Christian architecture — the basilica type, the Byzantine dome style, and then the Romanesque and the Gothic — was but a continuation of the Graeco-Roman architecture, not its absolute end and an absolutely new beginning and therefore new form. It is a continuation of it, but in a form of a new Ideational wave which replaced the Visual wave, just as the Visual wave succeeded the Ideational and Idealistic, after the fifth century B.C.

As to the early Christian (the basilica type) and the early Byzantine architecture (dome style) their Ideational character is shown by both their internal and external traits. Internally again the *grand buildings of architecture are churches and cathedrals, serving religious purposes and devoted to God and to the superempirical values.* Even the external trait of the comparative size of the religious and secular buildings shows that "however tall and threatening the houses of noblemen and merchants might be in the aspect of the town, the lofty mass of the churches always remained dominant."

When we are approaching a contemporary city or village, especially in the countries which have been built recently, and do not have buildings left from the Middle Ages, like the United States of America, we do not see on the horizon church domes or Gothic church towers looming above and dominating all the other buildings. They are lost among the contemporary skyscrapers built for business and other secular purposes. Among these the cathedrals and churches are overshadowed as insignificant midgets. The landscape and the skyline of the Middle Ages were quite different.

The city announced itself from a distance by the high uprising roofs and towers of its numerous churches and monasteries, and in a flat country the extremely stately buildings of the rich old abbeys and convents struck the eye far more than the fortresses and castles.

Cologne's landscape in 1562 was determined by 19 parish churches; 22 great monasteries; 11 religious foundations; more than 100 chapels; 76 religious convents; 106 houses of Beguines; 12 religious hospitals.

Mainz (in 1450) with 7050 inhabitants had 19 religious foundations; 8 monasteries; 7 nunneries; 3 establishments of the Spiritual Orders of Knights.

Such was the landscape and the situation up to the fifteenth century. Beginning with that century the grand architecture becomes more and more secular: the palace, the *Rathaus*, the mansion, the commercial edifice, the parliament buildings, and so on become more and more dominant.

Being religious, the buildings and their important details are *symbolic:* in the basilica, or in the Romanesque, or in the Gothic cathedral, almost every part has its definite symbol: a visible sign of the invisible values. And the "beauty" of the whole or of the part of the building is, so to speak, not in its visible form, but in the value of the invisible which it symbolizes.

Judged as a whole the Early Christian architecture "is a self-sufficient style, amply providing the early Church with buildings beautiful in themselves and even finer in their complete fulfillment of the needs for which they were designed."

The same is to be said of the Byzantine early architecture up to its climax, represented by the Hagia Sophia (A.D. 537–563). Even this marvel "externally seems a mass of huge and not very shapely buttressing, and it must be admitted that its architectural glory is rather internal than external." Its "decoration is drab on the exterior but brilliant in the interior."

This Ideational character — innerly as well as externally — architecture retained throughout the few subsequent centuries, in Byzantium as well as in Western Europe, having smaller and shorter swings between the main types discussed.

When, after the experimentation and transitional period from the basilica to the Romanesque — a style not quite definite, up to the emergence of the Gothic in the twelfth century — the style crystallized, it revealed itself as conspicuously Ideational.

In the course of existence from about the sixth to the twelfth century, there seem to have occurred minor swings to more or less Ideationalism versus Visualism. Nevertheless, the Ideational style was dominant up to the eleventh century. Beginning with that time, the Visual tide began to rise and manifested itself in the late Romanesque of the eleventh and the twelfth centuries, typified by the Cathedral of Pisa and by several French, German, and Italian buildings, with their much greater complication, picturesqueness, and theatrical decorativeness, and with the reduced massiveness, simplicity, and other traits of Ideationalism.

This increasing tide of Visualism finally manifested itself in the emergence of the Gothic of the twelfth and of the thirteenth centuries — the style which is a marvelous balance of the Ideational and the Visual elements and is neither one nor the other but a straight Idealistic style, like the Idealistic sculpture and painting of the same centuries. Its course of development from the early to the late "flamboyant" Gothic of the fifteenth and sixteenth centuries, which evolved into the baroque and the late baroque, or the rococo, is a steady rise of Visualism, which with the late "flamboyant" Gothic became dominant and in the baroque reached its great heights.

Like many another great style, "Gothic architecture, continually on the strain for improvement, arrived in the sixteenth century at the point where it seemed nothing further could be done." It had "exhausted its resources." "From the end of the fourteenth century up to the Renaissance, the flamboyant Gothic did not produce any new principle . . . but brought only a taste for complexity."

Its course was run; in the rising tide of Visualism it could not continue; either a new architectural style had to be created, or there had to be a return to one previously abandoned. This latter happened to be the Renaissance form of architecture.

Beginning with the Renaissance, "architecture, for the first time in her great history, took to looking not forward but backward, to the precedents of what was considered to be, and was in some senses, a greater age."

In spite of its seeming simplicity in its initial stages, represented by Brunelleschi (1377–1446), Michelozzo (1391–1472), L. B. Alberti (1404–1472), the Renaissance architecture represented a further step toward Visualism. *Innerly*, since that time, the grand architecture has ceased to be exclusively religious, but has tended to be more and more secular: the palace of a prince, king, monarch, magnate, the rich, the powerful; the public building, and so on, began to be the form more and more often used to incarnate the grand architecture. So far, it ceases to be symbolic and loses any "invisible meaning" of its visible sign. The visible, visual form becomes more and more self-sufficient. This means a waning of the inner criterion of Ideationalism.

Externally, all the earmarks of Visual architecture emerged and grew with the beginning of the Renaissance and continued with the subsequent forms of the baroque and the rococo.

Whether through an intermezzo of the Renaissance classicism, or continuing directly from the flamboyant Gothic, at the end of the sixteenth and in the seventeenth century, Western architecture assumed the so-called baroque style. The mere word "baroque" is quite sufficient to suggest its excessive visualism. "The Baroque style . . . is characterized by a taste for contrast and movement, by an appetite for the colossal, by search for theatrical effects, and by arbitrariness in the treatment of the combination of forms."

Richness of decoration was pushed to the limit: sculpture, painting, color, gold, polychrome marble, all were used in this age of the *goût de luxe*. All the other satellites of an extreme Visualism in architecture were not lacking. Ligeti rightly stresses the visual mania of the period as well as the growing victory of the *Schein* over the *Sein*, beginning with the Renaissance and ending with the nineteenth century.

After the baroque came the rococo, still more Visual, erotic, futile, reduced almost entirely to puerile decorations: it was a confectioner's sweet and toyland architecture.

Then came the neo-classic reaction, but it was, exactly as in painting and sculpture, a change of one form of Visualism for another, but not an abandonment of Visualism, or even hardly its moderation.

After that, during the nineteenth century we had several waves of romanticism and classicism, a revival of the Gothic, of the Renaissance, and several other hopeless revivals, but none succeeded in creating an Ideational style, or any original style at all. And all were visual with a passion for size, external appearance, decorativeness; purely sensual; devoid of any symbolism; aimed entirely at a pleasant impression upon the eye and utilitarian convenience for the satisfaction of economic and physiological needs.

And these "revivals" and "eclectic mixtures" have been going on up to this day, up to the "new architecture" of the skyscrapers and other modern designs. Whether the skyscraper architecture represents a departure of a new — and a real — style in architecture, as some are claiming, remains to be seen. But compared with most of the imitative styles of the second half of the nineteenth and of the beginning of the twentieth centuries, this modern architecture shows undoubtedly a trend toward structural simplicity, but hardly Ideationality.

Its simplicity and structural form suggest that it is perhaps the *anti-Visual* (cubistic) *reaction* in architecture, similar to that in painting and sculpture at the end of the nineteenth and of the twentieth century. Its many traits support such an interpretation. On the other hand, it is, so far, not an Ideational architecture. Practically all these buildings are secular. They do not pretend to symbolize any transcendental reality. On the contrary, they are mainly railroad stations, commercial buildings, theaters (especially the movie theaters), Radio City, the Woolworth, the Empire State, the Chrysler buildings, and others, serving the most material, the most commercial, the most empirical, and the most visual needs. There is nothing of the characteristic of the Ideational style. Outwardly, in spite of their greater simplicity, they have all the earmarks of Visualism: first of all, their main passion for quantitative size: The biggest building in the world! — this is regarded as the highest praise, its glory and pride. In this respect we witness a real race for the biggest and largest. A real mania of quantitative colossalism, typical of an overripe era of Visualism. Next to it comes the "scientism," and "the rationalistic cerebrality" of this simplicity. It is not an outflow of a spontaneous creation, but mathematically calculated, from the real-estate standpoint of profit. It is perfectly, geometrically accurate, measured, thought through, especially from the standpoint of dividends and profit. But "the Parthenon was not geometrically regular. It obeys a very much higher logic and regularity." And irregular also were the great cathedrals of the thirteenth century.

This too cerebral, mathematical, commercial, "scientific" planning — quite regular, almost deadly correct — so far has not resulted in the creation of any new style, except hugeness and a new type of decoration of the buildings. They are the fruit of the "interior decorators": eclectic, luxurious, representing a mixture of everything, from Greek frescoes to the baroque and the rococo, from the Gothic to the "Primitives," and almost all imitative even when the subjects of the decorative ornaments are supposed to be perfectly modern, like the industrial world, the machine, and, of course, a proletarian blessed by Lenin. So far, there is nothing from Ideationalism. It is, from a purely empirical standpoint, quite a justifiable "cubism" and "constructivism" in architecture, similar in its nature to the anti-Visual reaction in painting and sculpture. Whether, as such, it is the forerunner of a coming Ideationalism, or just a temporary reaction of the twentieth century, remains to be seen.

Summing up this sketch, we can make these conclusions.

(1) Our main categories fit, without any difficulty, the field of architecture also. They help to order into graspable systems the perceptional chaos of architectural phenomena and show that in its main traits architecture is not something incidental, but a logical manifestation of the respective Ideational, Idealistic, Sensate, and Mixed mentality

of a given culture. Thus the second installment is paid on the "promissory note."

(2) In architecture, as in painting and sculpture, there are long-time and short-time waves of ascendance and domination of the Ideational and Visual styles, with their intermediary ones.

(3) So far as the short and long waves of this alternation are concerned in the course of the Graeco-Roman and the Western Christian cultures, these waves in essentials have been running parallel to those in painting and sculpture. The architecture of Greece, up to the fifth century B.C., was predominantly Ideational, as were Greek painting and sculpture. The architecture of the fifth century was mainly Idealistic, as were painting and sculpture. The architecture after the first part of the fourth century became more and more Visual and remained such up to the fifth century A.D. So with painting and sculpture. After the fifth century, the architecture began to grow more and more Ideational and remained so, small fluctuations disregarded, up to the twelfth century. So it was with painting and sculpture. The architecture of the thirteenth century was pre-eminently Idealistic. So were painting and sculpture. Since the fourteenth century, the Visual tide has been rising and dominant up to the present time. So it is in painting and sculpture. At the present time, we have an anti-Visual reaction in architecture, painting, and sculpture. But this reaction is not as yet Ideationalism. It is the symptom of a possible end of the Visual wave and of the coming domination of the Ideational wave; but that is a guess.

(4) Thus the main waves in all these fields are more or less synchronous, when only the main waves are considered and in such relatively long units of time as century periods. In their minor fluctuations there seem to be present some "lags" and "leads" in time, when the time units are shorter. But as shown before, these "non-synchronisms" concerned only the smaller waves; and in these lags and leads there hardly is present any universal uniformity as to which of these three fields uniformly lags and which uniformly leads.

(5) If to the foregoing data one adds that similar swings from Ideationality to Visuality and vice versa took place in the history of the Persian and the Saracenic architecture, where the later stages of a given style exhibit a similar trend toward visuality, decorativeness, complication, etc., then the above sketch is sufficient to claim that the contended swings and the rhythm of Ideationality and Visuality indeed exist and indeed are shown by the dynamics of the architectural styles of almost any culture.

(6) This sketch shows also that the swings are not periodical; that the duration of the domination of each of the fundamental forms studied varies from country to country, from period to period.

II

FLUCTUATION OF IDEATIONAL, SENSATE, AND MIXED FORMS OF MUSIC

I. Ideational, Sensate, and Mixed Forms of Music

The generic categories — Ideational and Sensate — are as fundamental in and applicable to music as they are to painting, sculpture, and architecture.

Just as in Ideational painting visual impression (through the eye) plays a secondary role, and the aim of the picture is to give the idea of the object as it exists in the mind, likewise in Ideational music the main thing is not how it sounds — pleasant or unpleasant — but what is hidden behind the sounds for which they are mere signs or symbols. The music is not in the sounds as they are heard by the ear but in this "behind the sounds," which can be grasped only by the mind and not by an organ of perception like the ear.

In the Sensate music, on the contrary, the aim is to please the ear. The criterion is its "audible beauty," at its face value, regardless of any hidden meaning. If there is such a meaning, as in so-called program music, it is the meaning of this perceptional, empirical world (descriptive music, program music, etc.). The ear is here the supreme judge and it decides whether the sounds are pleasant, enjoyable, charming, ravishing; whether they describe well "clouds," "love," "summer night," "dreams," "terror," etc. The music stands or falls by its "audible beauty" just as in the Visual painting the picture stands or falls by the purely visual impression made on the eye by the object perceived.

These two forms of music represent two different mentalities, two different mental attitudes toward the world of sound and the world of reality.

Let us take the predominant form of medieval music, the plain chant, and more specifically the Gregorian chant, in order to clarify the differences in these two types of music. Many readers probably know that the plain chant was not only the main music in the Middle Ages, but almost the only great music that existed. All the other forms were absorbed or eliminated by it. "During centuries it was the only music known, practiced, and taught."

From the standpoint of a sensually audible criterion, the medieval chant is no music at all; it is something queer; unenjoyable, primitive, dry; in brief, it has none of the earmarks of what we are accustomed to style music — neither measure, nor harmony, nor polyphony.

From the standpoint of melody, the plain chant seems to contradict every common sense. . . . It has a very mediocre respect for words and their rhythmic disposition. . . . (It divides the words and phrases without any regard for their sense and unity.) Another queerness — there are vocalisms in it (which again go contrary to every rule of music).

These defects are already sufficiently enormous. But they are not all and not the most apparent. . . . This music is disconcerting. It is devoid of everything that constitutes our musical art. It ignores measure. It does not care at all, or very rarely, for what is styled "expression." . . . It does not have any indicated tempo. It does not have the advantages of the nuances of intensity (*forte*, *piano*); the tones it employs are practically unrealizable; also it does not make any transposition; it permits the basso to sing all that is written in the seventh tone! Finally, does this music give at least enjoyment to the ear? That is very doubtful. . . . We can add that it is unfit for any audience (concert hall). It was not made to be listened to. In the church there were not meant to be present any listeners, but only the performers. All this means that the plain chant is . . . in opposition to all our ideas and all our habits. In brief: it is anti-musical."

Such is this music. It has nothing musical in the sense of Sensate music. But is it indeed of purely negative value? If one tried to say that, he would have an unconquerable difficulty in explaining why and how it was able to be not only the supreme, but the only grand music in the whole Western Christian world for almost a thousand years. It is absolutely incomprehensible that a purely negative value could exist, dominate, and be performed unquestioned for such a length of time and on such a vast "cultural continent." And many other — no less important — difficulties will beset the partisans of such an answer. All these unconquerable contradictions indicate that the answer is wrong. And it is wrong, indeed. Its main mistake is that it applies to Ideational music the criterion of perfection of Sensate music, a perfectly wrong procedure which leads to an absurd solution. The point is that the plain chant is one of the most conspicuous, perhaps even the *most* conspicuous, pure, and the most characteristic example of Ideational music. When this is understood, then, it will appear as a marvel.

Does all this mean that its "originality" is purely negative? On the contrary, it is admirable. Enumerating all the embellishments of which the plain chant is voluntarily and conscientiously devoid, we . . . were doing that in order to stress the following proposition: the plain chant is above all forms of expression of profane art because it is connected with such a disposition of soul which itself is above all the [empirical] sentiments in which the musical expression takes habitually its place. Perhaps it would be too much to say that the plain chant is mystic and that it has a kind of spiritual richness, where the followers of the profane, viewing the matter from a purely exterior standpoint, see in it but an apparent poverty. To say this would be to ignore its fineness and variety (because in fact it is not dry, not abstract, and not incapable of touching and of impressing). . . . It is an admirable expression of Christian idealism. . . . It is serene. It is a triumph of pure form. . . . It is an epoch.

These statements are sufficient to show the Ideational nature of the dominant medieval music and to clarify still more the concept of the Ideational and Sensate forms of music.

Sensate music is hedonistic in its nature. It has its *raison d'être* only as much and as long as it has its sensual beauty (like a woman physically beautiful, but mentally flat, who is appreciated so long as she keeps her beauty — physical loveliness gone, she becomes uninteresting, lifeless, boring). If the sounds are pleasing, it is good music. If they are not, it is poor music.

As in the field of painting, sculpture, and architecture, there are *Mixed forms of music:* one of the most important variety is the *Idealistic* and the *cubistic* music, corresponding to the nonvisual style of painting.

In the *Idealistic* music the Ideational values are perfectly blended with sensual beauty. Such, for instance, are many compositions of Palestrina, of Bach, of Beethoven. They are neither quite Sensate, like many sensually beautiful musical pieces, nor quite Ideational, like the Gregorian chants.

Similar gradations are given in the Sensate music, from the purest to the impure, passing into Mixed.

A. Ideational music tends to be "inner," while the Sensate is inclined to be theatrical and external. Being "inner," the Ideational music does not need either impressive technical means or any external impressiveness aimed to "hit," to "stun," to impress sensationally. No "smartness" is necessary to it. It is like the silent communion of a soul with God. It can achieve its purpose with the simplest means. Therefore it is not intended for popularity, for success, for public approval; nor to be considered the biggest, the loudest, the best selling. Neither does it demand enormous choruses, concert halls, advertising, applause, etc. Take the Gregorian or the Ambrosian chants as the purest form of Ideational music. How small and simple, then, was its technical apparatus. The Roman *Schola* had, in the time of St. Gregory, only seven singers. Later on, with all the luxury of the Papal Sistine Chapel, there were hardly more than thirty-seven singers, which number was reduced to twenty-four in 1565 (the year of Palestrina's *Mass of the Pope Marcel*). No orchestra; no instrumental means.

Sensate music cannot, however, be blamed for its theatricalness, its bent to stun, to be "smart," to be a sensation, and for these purposes to utilize anything that may be useful — the deadening quantity and the tricks. It cannot be blamed for all that because it is its very nature. It has to be interesting, enjoyable, entertaining, successful, popular. Otherwise it will not exist at all.

This difference shows itself not only in the quantity of the technical means employed by each type of music, but in many other traits. The Gregorian chants use no instrumental accompaniment; only human voices. And these voices sing in unison: there is no polyphony. And the melody is almost all within one octave. What a poverty of means, indeed!

Sensate music uses and abuses any means which can increase the sensual effects, be it massing of voices; their enormous range; their modulations; all kinds of consonances, and especially dissonances; chromatics; contrasts of rhythms, intensity, etc.

B. Ideational music tends to be and is comparatively *pure* in its style, meaning by purity its inner self-consistency and the elimination of everything that does not belong to it. The Sensate music has to be the opposite; it is not and cannot afford to be pure. Like a movie "star," as long as it captivates it lives; as soon as the charms are lacking, nobody employs it. It is in its nature to seek popularity; to adapt itself to all the fancies and tastes of the large masses — or those who pay — and to make the front page and "fame" and "glory"! Therefore it has to contaminate itself with all the tricks which are necessary for a "success." The intermediary forms occupy intermediary positions. Palestrina, Vittoria, and Orlando di Lasso, Bach, Handel, Mozart, and Beethoven, all have a considerable purity of style (because their music is Idealistic in greater part); but it is not so "pure" as that of the Gregorian chants. It has already an admixture of the noblest music with elements heterogeneous to the main theme.

C. Ideational music, being "inner," does not force its author or creator to protect his rights, insure his name and authorship. Since it is not music for the listeners but a communion of a soul with itself or its god, there is no motive for all that. In the Sensate music all this is inevitable. It has to be "individualistic."

D. Since Ideational music is an audible sign for inaudible great values, these values are and have to be, ordinarily, the values of a collectivity. Purely individual values are too weak, too fragile and uncertain to be great.

Grand Ideational music must have a fairly homogeneous society mentally; otherwise its "audible signs" would be incomprehensible and as such unrecognized. For Sensate music all this is unnecessary. It is music for a heterogeneous market, just for a buyer.

E. Purely Ideational music does not need any special aesthetic theorizing and aesthetic critics and professional art appraisers. Instead it needs and usually has religious and moral *censors*, whose business is to find whether it conveys properly the superempirical and other values which lie behind the sound symbols. As the symbols chosen to convey these values are usually pre-existing in the social *milieu* and precede the individual creators of such music, these creators usually accept them and only purify and modify them, without a radical alteration.

Different is the situation in the periods of the domination of the Sensate music. Its very nature calls for a criterion of its beauty and perfection, therefore for a development of theorizing and professional criticism. As the field of sensual tastes is exceedingly variable and changes from man to man, from group to group, from period to period, this diversity calls forth an ever-increasing number of theories of beauty, aesthetic perfection, and of aesthetic theorizing by professional critics, "reviewers," "estimators," etc. Such is the inner connection between these.

When we have the stage of marvelous mixture of the Ideational and Sensate music — the great idealistic period in the history of any art — the theorizing and criticism, though already present, are not fully developed as yet. The art itself is so beautiful and perfect that it needs no theoretical justification and reasoned proofs that it is great and beautiful. Art itself is the best and the most convincing incarnation of its perfection and beauty — far more convincing than any literary or critical essay on what is beautiful and what is not.

And the grandeur of their creations is so convincing to all that the critics themselves have to bow and accept the criteria given in the creations. For such a period Tolstoi's caustic statements about professional art critics is quite applicable. In comparison with the real great master,

> the professional art critics are the fools who dispute the sages. They say that their function is to explain the art objects. Explain and interpret! What is it in art that they have to explain? An artist, if he is a real artist, through his work transmits most successfully to other men the sentiments which he experienced. In such conditions what remains or needs to be explained?

These considerations explain why in such periods art criticism and art theorizing, with all its crowd of professional art critics, art guides, art managers, are little developed, though not absent.

It is only when the Idealistic stage is passed and even when the Sensate art has passed its peak and begins to decline that a great development of all these phenomena becomes necessary. Why? Because there is no grand work equally convincing to all; and there are a great many works, very different from one another, each of which is admired by some and detested by others. In these circumstances, as in a court case with incomplete and contradictory evidences, each party needs many "lawyers" and a crowd of witnesses and helpers, to show that their party is right and the other parties are wrong. Hence an enormous development of "the professional art lawyers," that is, critics and theorizers. Hence a blossoming of heated disputes in the incessant controversies; hence, in brief, a development of art criticism, in the period when the grand works of art are absent.

II. Fluctuation of the Main Styles in Time and Space

Like painting, sculpture, architecture, and literature, music, so far as these forms are concerned, has different dominant styles in various cultures at the same moment, and at various stages of the same culture in the course of time. As mentioned, both forms are found in practically all cultures at all stages. But the proportion of each form as well as its purity is not constant. In one culture or in one period the Ideational form may be dominant; in another culture or period the Sensate music may be the main form. Side by side with these conspicuous differences, the purity or intensity of each style may also fluctuate. In this way we have short-time and long-time, strong and weak, waves of domination, now of one, now of the other form. Besides the periods of domination of one of these forms, there are their periods of either mechanical or organic mixture, where neither form is dominant. When the periods of organic, harmonious, and well-balanced mixture occur, these periods, as we shall see, give possibly the highest peaks of musical creativeness and the greatest music.

A. *Preliterate Cultures.* So far as the primitive peoples are concerned, they all seem to have had in some form and in some proportion both forms of music: Sensate and non-Sensate, or rude Ideational. Any primitive people, so far as known, has some form of magical and religious music chants and incantations, and some instrumental music used in these performances and ceremonies; in so far, any people has a non-Sensate form approaching Ideational music. And any people has, side by side with such a music, a form of music performed just for the sensual joy of it, without any magical, religious, or ideational implication.

B. *Oriental Cultures.* For lack of data, and especially data as to the nature of the music predominant at various periods of the history of the Oriental cultures, there is no possibility of indicating directly the cycles of the domination of each of the types studied. What can be said with a reasonable certainty is that both types existed in the music of Ancient Egypt, Assyria, China, India, and of the Hebrew culture. That the Ideational music existed is witnessed by the beliefs in the divine and mysterious origin of music; by its use in magico-religious activities; by a belief in its magic power; in its connection with the laws of nature; by the social control of music by the State and by religious authorities;

and by direct testimony of the writers and thinkers of these cultures, who clearly distinguish between music for pleasure and the other kind of music which has mysterious social, moral, educational, magical meaning and value. On the other hand, music for pleasure, purely Sensate, in a class with "wine, women, and song," is also certain from the evidences which have survived.

Likewise in all these cultures the music was credited with a magical and mysterious power which has led to careful formal discrimination of various forms of hieratic music suitable for various occasions.

Similarly the oldest forms are met in religious and magical ceremonies.

In all of these cultures, music was carefully controlled either by the religious or State authorities, and the earliest musicians were the religious priests, the prophets, the seers, or other persons and groups in whose hands were the social, mental, and moral control of the people. Among the Chinese, the Egyptians, the Hebrews, the Assyrians, the Hindus, we find evidences of an existence of a special corporation (the Chinese Board of Control of Music; the School of Samuel and the Levitic corporation among the Hebrews; a similar board of music among the Egyptians; and so on) which created, chose, and controlled music as the magical and sacred power for religious, social, and moral purposes, which had little, if any, relationship to sensual enjoyment. Therefore, as such a sacred power, it was formal, in the sense of being Ideational and serving as a symbol of the superempirical values. As such it was forbidden to be changed and tampered with.

Like a doctor's prescription for various diseases, for each ceremony, for each occasion, there was its own appropriate music, and sometimes the deviation from the rule was regarded as a great sin or blunder.

In accordance with that, each musical phrase, often each tone, was a special symbol of some value.

Usually the main topic of the Sensate music — love — played little, if any, part in such a music.

Side by side with it there existed also Sensate music. The contemporary thinkers and the sources make the distinction between these two forms rather clear and fundamental. It is the music used in secular feasts, orgies, during repasts, in places of sensual pleasure — the court, the harem, the palace of the noble, the house of the rich man, the house of love sold and bought; in brief, the place and activity of sensual enjoyment. And curiously enough, for such music the musicians were often women with a not particularly enviable reputation.

Finally, between these two types there were several intermediate forms of music, partly Ideational, partly Sensate. Such, for instance, was the music used in military activities, festivities, and so on.

C. *Graeco-Roman Culture.* (1) So far as the existing evidences show, the earliest stages of the Greek music (not of the Creto-Mycenaean, of which little is known, nor even of the later stage of the Ionic music) seem to have been predominantly Ideational. And this domination of Ideational music seems to have continued up to the middle of the fifth century B.C. and, with an admixture of the growing Sensate as a subordinate factor, throughout the fifth century B.C.

(2) The fifth century gives a marvelous balance of both kinds, with a still notable domination of the Ideational music. It is the period of Idealistic music.

(3) After the fifth century, or even at its end, the Sensate music continues to rise, and becomes particularly dominant in the Hellenistic culture, especially in Alexandria, Pergamum, and other centers.

(4) As to Roman music, its earliest stages, not yet touched by the pronounced Greek influence, were also mainly non-Sensate, crudely Ideational, though the Ideationality seems to have been of a lower grade and more primitive than that of the Greeks, particularly in the classic period of the times of Terpander, when were produced the great classics of Greek choral religious music. The Roman music seems not to have had either the marvelous balance of the Ideational and Sensate music, reached by the Greek music in the sixth and fifth centuries, the period of Aeschylus (525–456 B.C.), Pindar (522–448 B.C.), Sophocles (496–406 B.C.), Euripides (480–406 B.C.), and others. The Roman music, from its primitive predominant Ideationality, passed, under the influence of the decadent Sensate music of the Greeks, directly to the stage of predominating Sensate music of possibly a coarser and more decadent type than the Greek Sensate music at its best period.

(5) This predomination of Sensate music in the Hellenic as well as in the Roman world continued during the first three or four centuries of the Christian era, when it was gradually replaced by the conspicuous forms of the Christian music, which, after the fourth century, became Ideational par excellence, since the Ambrosian and then Gregorian chants had swept away the Sensate music from the "highway" of grand music.

Such, in a schematic way, were the grand waves of Ideational and Sensate music in the history of the Graeco-Roman culture.

Now a few data to explain and corroborate this "curve of the waves."

(*a*) The predominant Ideational character of the early Greek music follows from the fact that it was principally for magic and religious use, and as such was Ideational in its essence, though perhaps of not a very high quality.

(*b*) The high degree of Ideationality of the "classic" period of Greek music — the period of Terpander, his contemporaries, and immediate successors, like Archilochos (b. *c.* 720 B.C.), Clonas of Argos, Aristonicos of Argos, Simonides of Samos, Thaletas, Olympus, Polymnastes of Colophon, Tyrtaeus, Stesichoros, Alkman, Sakadas, and many others who lived at the end of the eighth, in the seventh, and during the first part of the sixth century — can hardly be questioned.

The essential traits of their music can be summed up as follows. It was religious and religiously civic, as indicated by the very terms of the musical forms: *nome* meant a religious chant in honor of this or that god of a given province; *dithyramb*, a lyric hymn to Dionysos; *paean*, a chant to Apollo; other terms — like the *prosody* — the chants of the march of the religious cortege to the temple; the *threnody* and other terms are equally of religious (or magic) nature. At that stage, these forms of the grand music were all religious.

Altar, temple, or religious theatre was the place of their performance. They were one of the most important functions of the state and religious authorities. All performances were in charge of the first *archon* and of special authorities. How seriously the task was regarded can be judged from Demosthenes' speech (*Contra Midias*), where for a supposedly unlawful interference in the functions of the person given charge of the chorus in these festivals, capital punishment was demanded. And this in the fourth century when the previous severity and religious character of music were already considerably weakened. The State and religious authorities controlled and censored the music produced quite as severely as the early Christian Church did. Any transgression of the rules was a sacrilege.

At that period, and not even in the fifth century B.C., the main and almost the only theme of our music, operas, dramas, oratorios, and so on — love, romantic, and sexual — did not enter at all into the music and ceremonies. Still less were the common man and his daily life the theme. The music was highly symbolic. It was merely a sign for the invisible and superempirical realities.

As religiously Ideational, it was a collective task and performance. Creators were regarded as one of the many agencies, and as such did not have the spirit of professional individuals nor other qualities of modern composers in regard to personal ambitions, professional vanity, and high commercial returns. They created *ad gloriam Dei* and regarded their work as a performance of their religious and patriotic duties. All they aspired to was to be the victor at the national contest, usual during these religious festivities. Hence the central role was that of the chorus, and not of the individual performer. For the same reasons, only the fully pledged citizens were admitted to the audience. Noninitiates and strangers were not permitted to participate in this sacred activity, either as listeners or performers.

The topics were the gods and their actions and their relations to man.

Later on, came man's struggle against the Invisible, the gigantic duel against the superhuman and superempirical forces, as in the tragedies of the fifth century B.C. Nothing vulgar, of everyday occurrence, of the "Main Street" life, was to be found in this nonnaturalistic Ideational art.

(*c*) This magico-religious ideationality of music of the eighth to the sixth century did not continue in the subsequent period. Parallel to the change in other arts — from Ideationality to Sensateness — music underwent a similar change. In the sixth century the Sensate form began to gain. Toward its end and in the fifth century B.C. — roughly speaking — the descending line of Ideational music and the ascending line of Sensate music crossed each other, and this crossing resulted in the marvel of the Idealistic music of the fifth century. It reached its point of maturity or a perfect equilibrium between religion and pure art in the music and, associated with it, poetry and drama (tragedy and comedy) of Pindar, Aeschylus, Sophocles; partly Euripides, Aristophanes, Simonides of Klos (likened often to P. E. Bach), Agathocles, Melanippides the Older (master of counterpoint), Bacchylides (likened often to Mozart), Lamprocles, Diagoras, Likymnos, Damon, and others.

The main changes in comparison with the preceding stage were schematically as follows:

(i) Progressive abandonment of the purely sacerdotal art in favor of music to please.

(ii) Increasing substitution of Destiny for the gods and other "metaphysical abstractions" (as August Comte would say).

(iii) Complication of the technicality of music, intended to make a greater impression and to please more.

(iv) Increase of the purely "human" theme of music and drama associated with it.

(v) Increase of the comical, satirical, and sarcastic veins, in ridiculing and satirizing, in a roughly human way, human affairs and events and relationships. (Aristophanes and the increasing number of comedies.)

(vi) Decreasing role of the chorus and increasing role of individual performers. Likewise the increasing individualism at the cost of collectivity is seen in the authors also. They begin to be more and more individualistic and less and less to erase themselves before anonymous collectivity.

(vii) Progressive permeation of the profane spirit in art.

(viii) Progressive loss of calm serenity in music in favor of its increasing passionate, pathetic, individual emotionality.

(ix) Even such details as the introduction of the feminine element upon the stage are not lacking. "Such an introduction (by Euripides) opened to the melodic imagination unexplored domains. The heroines of Euripides chant beautifully. Wherever a violent emotion is to be expressed, or a cry of the heart to be issued, three-metrical iamb gives place to the melic rhythms. Hence these monodies and duets — the predecessors of our operas — as characteristics of the new tragedy," rightly says Gevaërt. "The music of Venus could be but ardent, nervous, and dissolving. Euripides was already on the border of decay."

(*d*) After the fourth century B.C. the Sensate music, already strong, continues to grow and to dominate over the Ideational music of the preceding period. The marvelous balance of the fifth century is disrupted in favor of Sensate music. The contemporary and subsequent thinkers used to mention the names of Euripides, Melanippides the Younger, Phrynis, and his disciple Timothy (446–357) as the "corrupters of taste." From now on, to please sensually becomes the ever-increasing aim of music (and of other arts also). Subsequent masters, like Philoxenes of Cytherea (b. 436), Telestes (b. 420), Agathon (b. 415), Cleomenes of Rhegium, and a crowd of parodists continued this tendency, and introduced important innovations most favorably accepted by the public but denounced by Plato, Aristophanes, Aristoxenes, who accused these composers of "corruption" of "real music."

The essential traits of this Sensate music were as follows. It became

(i) More and more profane.

(ii) More and more sensual.

(iii) More and more "human," free, individualistic.

(iv) More and more intended to produce "effects," sensation.

(v) More and more impure, complicated, with ever-increasing tendency to be "bigger" in mass and quantity.

(vi) More and more "professional."

(vii) Not the gods, nor even the metaphysical abstractions and entities, nor even the half-mythical heroes, but just the "common man" and his affairs tended to be the theme of that music. Respectively the spirit of profanity, love, sex, "wine, women and song," the hunt for popularity and applause, with commercial returns, and all the earmarks of modernism permeated it.

The purity of the Ideational style was lost. The new music was a mixture of all types and *genres*, of tragic and comic elements, and all sorts of tricks which might be successful. It was transformed into theatricalness, with all the impurity of styles typical of the ripe Sensate music. In a way it became on the one hand the Wagnerian theater, on the other the hodgepodge of Radio City theaters.

If the forms of Melanippides' music are not yet quite gone, Kinesias of Athens is already lost in these bizarre researches. Timothy plunges into the depths of impressionism and embarrasses his contemporaries with the audacity of his realistic innovations. . . . Philemon of Cythera — a remote predecessor of R. Strauss — pushed naturalism to an imitation of a goat's bleating in his tragedy *Cyclopes*. Agathon imagined grand operas, where the accompaniment supported easy and sweet melodies, which prolonged themselves into the interminable solos and duets — vain efforts to achieve the sublime by virtuosity and "effects." Naturally the parodists took their part. . . . Already Aristophanes in his comedies caricatured, with an infinite *esprit*, the musical and literary style of the grand masters. His successors are but just insipid clowns. Before us is a plain dilettantism, and this dilettantism had a long existence because it amused the masses during the whole Alexandrian period and up to the Renaissance of music in the medieval plain chant.

Side by side with this transformation, music and its instruments tended to become more complicated and more numerous. What could not be achieved by creative quality was attempted by mere quantity, by huge masses and ever-increasing scales. Huge private buildings were erected for musical and other performances. Monster concerts, with hundreds and even thousands of artists were given. At the funeral games organized by Alexander the Great in honor of Ephestion, more than three thousand artists gathered from all parts of Greece. Other similar monster performances were not lacking in Greece, as well as later on in Rome.

Add to this a fundamental transformation of the status and the functions of the music maker. At the early stages he was a priest, a prophet, a magician. Then he was a moral and social leader. Now he became a professional and an individualist. His creation was his own monopoly. Through it he sought to make his living — and a most luxurious one — to be famous, to be popular, to be the idol of a crowd of emotional and half-hysterical followers. All of this would arouse in the creator an insatiable vanity and appetite. In order to protect better their individual interests, a crowd of such professionals would unite themselves into unions, those numerous *Dionysiae Synodes* (*c.* 300 B.C. and later), *Dionysiac Associations of Artists of Ionia and Hellespont* (*c.* 279 B.C.), *Union of the Itinerant Musicians*, etc. The popular musician was sums were paid for their concerts. In brief, the popular musician was a manufacturer of an important sensual pleasure, and as such he was paid well by sensual values, from applause and fame to wealth and sensual and sexual love. In this way the situation continued (with slighter ups and downs) until the victorious Ideational music of Christianity put an end to this sensual music, great in a way in its initial stages, but completely degenerated during the Alexandrian, Pergamene, and the Roman period.

(*e*) As for Roman music, its story can be told briefly. The Etruscan and early Roman music seems to have been predominantly Ideational, at least in its religious, social, and public forms. As mentioned, the Ideationality must have been of a low grade. Before it was fully developed and before the "homemade" Sensate form had time to grow, the Greek music infiltrated and was superimposed upon the Roman music, still native and primitive. The result was that the intermediate stage, the "classic miracle" of the Idealistic music, was hardly known to Rome, as it was unknown in painting, sculpture, and architecture, except by imitation. It skipped this greatest stage and from the predominance of the primitive Ideational jumped directly to the superannuated and overripe Sensate music which was imported from Greece. "Generally the Romans imitated and continued merrily and in a poorer form the music of Greece. They developed it in an inartistic way, bringing it to the terminal point of decadence."

Therefore in that stage of imitative music, the Roman musical art had all the above traits of the Greek Sensate music still more conspicuous and overemphasized. Here the principle of quantitative hugeness reached an enormous development. The theaters they built, like that erected by Pompey in 55 B.C., were enormous, being intended for forty thousand persons, as Pliny the Elder tells. "Not being able to make it beautiful, they made it rich." Such is the moral of this "quantitative bigness," formulated by Pliny.

This colossalism comes out everywhere. Their musical festivals often were on a gigantic scale. Concerts where simultaneously a hundred trumpets blared, a hundred players accompanied thousands of actors and acrobats, were not rare. Purity of style disappeared. "The contemporaries of Terentius and Plautus, Livius Andronicus and Attius, were incapable of enjoying a melody as such without words, gesticulation, and pantomime."

Cicero's letter to Marius in 55 B.C. gives a fairly accurate idea of this Roman art. Describing the theatrical performances he attended, Cicero complains:

I must tell you that though our entertainments were extremely magnificent, yet they were by no means such as you would have relished. . . . The enormous parade with which they were attended . . . destroyed all the grace of the performance. What pleasure could it afford to a judicious spectator to see a thousand mules prancing about the stage, in the tragedy of *Clytemnestra;* or whole regiments accoutered in foreign armor in that of the *Trojan Horse?* In a word, what man of sense could be entertained with viewing a mock army drawn up on the stage in battle array? These, I confess, are spectacles extremely well adapted to captivate vulgar eyes; but undoubtedly would have had no charm in yours.

Then comes an increase in the size of the instruments; complication of their character; and an enormous increase of their number.

It is needless to describe in detail the popularity of music, from the emperors to the *bourgeoisie;* the musical training of children; musical aestheticism and aestheticians; the lucrativeness of the musical profession; the vanity of the artists; the crowd of admirers (especially female) of the popular musicians; the sex scandals about them.

In brief, all the traits of the Greek Sensate music were present in the Roman Sensate music in an exaggerated and cruder form.

Such a music continued during the first few centuries of our era, degenerating more and more, parallel with the decay of the Sensate Graeco-Roman civilization. Christianity early enough rejected it and soon intentionally began to purify music of all its sensual embellishments, at the same time elaborating from the Graeco-Hebrew sources of its own music. In the form of the plain chant, Christianity put an end to the eight-hundred-year (from about 400 B.C. to A.D. 400) domination of Sensate music and ushered in the domination of Ideational music on the level of the grand art. And this domination also continued during some eight hundred to nine hundred years (from about A.D. 400 to 1300–1400). Then we come to the medieval period, with its unquestionable and almost monopolistic domination of the plain chant — one of the sublimest and purest forms of Ideational music.

(*f*) In the above, I have indicated the abundance of art critics and professional aestheticians during the period of the domination of Sensate music and their absence — with the presence of socioreligious and moral censorships — in the period of Ideational music, especially in the initial stages of its decline. The association claimed is well corroborated in the history of the Graeco-Roman music and musical theorizing and criticism.

D. *Medieval Music.* The movement of medieval and modern music can be characterized from the standpoint of the forms discussed, as follows.

(1) On the highway of the great music, the medieval music, during almost nine hundred years (from about the fifth century A.D. to the fourteenth century) was either exclusively Ideational, or (from the twelfth to the fourteenth centuries) predominantly so.

(2) The Ideationality of this music was of the purest and most sublime.

(3) Up to the end of the eleventh century, Ideational music was almost the only grand music existing; after the end of that century, there appeared the first signs of its mixture with the Sensate, in the music of troubadours, trouvères, minnesingers, and other forms of secular music, which had acquired many traits of the Sensate. After that time, this stream of Sensate music — not without fluctuations — tended to increase, in the form of secular motets, madrigals, and later on, in the form of the *ars nova*, and then in that of symphonies, operas, musical comedies, and so on. The growing sensatization of music manifested itself in the

Sensate musical mentality, in the rapid increase of Sensate music, in its technical forms, in its themes, in the occasions for which it was written, in the social events which it immortalized. In brief, in the inner nature as well as in the external traits.

(4) In contradistinction to some other forms of art, especially of painting and sculpture, which attained, as we saw, the marvelous Idealistic phase in the thirteenth and fourteenth centuries, *music seems to have reached the Idealistic point somewhat later:* around the sixteenth and seventeenth and partly the eighteenth century (Palestrina, Vittoria, Bach, Handel, Mozart, and Beethoven) when these forms were wonderfully blended and resulted in the miracle of the Idealistic music of the sixteenth to the eighteenth centuries, inclusive.

This marvelous balance, though with a slightly and slowly increasing predominance of the Sensate music, was not broken during the eighteenth century. Great masters of the period, like the Bachs, Gluck, Handel, Rameau, Mozart, Haydn, Beethoven are still mainly within the borderline of this balance; therefore the Idealistic period may be extended up to the very beginning of the nineteenth century, including such great masterpieces as Beethoven's last five quartets and the *Ninth Symphony*, with the transcendental heights of some parts of these works. Though in some of the works of these great masters there is little Ideationality, nevertheless all the while in the bulk of these creations, the balance — more and more sensualized — still persisted.

(5) After the beginning of the nineteenth century, the Sensate form begins to predominate definitely and more and more radically. In the music of Wagner and other Romantics, it possibly reached its highest peak. After that, and especially after the end of the nineteenth century, it began to show all the symptoms of disorganization, demoralization, and degeneration, which — again not without exceptions and oscillations — has been continuing up to the present time. It witnesses on the one hand an utter degradation, vulgarization, "jazzing," and modernistic-impressionistic musical anarchy and impotency (in spite of the gigantic technical skill and complexities of many a modern composition); on the other hand, it exhibits the first signs of the efforts to seek new, anti-Sensate forms of music.

That the grand music of the fifth to the twelfth centuries was almost monopolistically Ideational is testified to by the fact that the main and almost its only form was the plain chant, first the Ambrosian version, then the Gregorian classical improvement, and then the religious hymns and psalmodies. (The same is still more true of the religious grand music of the Eastern Church.)

During the centuries of the domination of this music, in the circles of the common people there was undoubtedly circulating another —

more Sensate — type of music, of folk songs; but these do not belong to the grand music; they do not stamp the integrated culture of the period; and besides, even these were considerably influenced by the plain chant and its forms and spirit. For this reason they are out of the field of our study.

Plain chant dominated monopolistically up to the end of the eleventh century.

Then on the highway of grand music for the first time appears secular music, more worldly, more embellished and less Ideational than the chants. I mean the debut of the music of the troubadours, trouvères and their German replicas, the minnesingers. The curve of their rise and decay stretches from 1090 to 1290. Their *chansons* were numerous (more than 260 *chansons* of trouvères and about 2000 *chansons* of troubadours are preserved). In its spirit and character this music and its themes are very different from the chants. Its subjects — mainly love and sentiment — are of this world; its nature is much more Sensate. These songs and their words signify the first break in the domination of the purely Ideational music. This is shown also by the technical traits of this music. It introduces some of the embellishments expelled from the chants. Their monodies were sentimental and gallant. Instrumental accompaniment was used. Some other novelties of a nobly Sensate nature were introduced. Nevertheless in spite of profane love being the main subject of these *chansons*, they do not differ in their music and technique radically from the Ideational music.

The reason for this situation, just as the reason for the almost contemporary "Courts of Love," is that profane love and otherworldly subjects are still shot through by the modified, idealistic, Platonic spirit. They are but a transposition of the Divine love. Their subtleties of "fine amour" maintain the cult of an ideal lady, like the Madonna, the mother of the Savior, the object of devotion, adoration, pure and ideal. It is the idealization of love and the elevation of this tender emotion of mortals to the heights of immortal forms — a phenomenon typical of any period when the Ideational forms begin to be mixed with a moderate injection of the nobler Sensate elements.

After the thirteenth century, then, with some ups and downs, the Sensate music rises, in the secular as well as in the religious fields, and its rise leads to the wonderful balance of both forms, which gives, as it often does, the peak of musical art.

As for the technical side, it acquires one audible embellishment after another, and becomes steadily richer and more beautiful. After the thirteenth century it becomes "measured" (quite a symbolic phenomenon in its significance); it develops polyphony; it produces and develops counterpoint (the fifteenth century being its "golden age"); introduces and cultivates the richest variety of rhythms; then develops harmony and "vertical" writing, as well as the "horizontal"; begins artistically to use intensity — *piano*, *forte*, etc.; achieves wonderful perfection in its use of chromatics, consonances, and dissonances; tends to become more and more expressive; introduces and expands and perfects the use of instrumental music and blends it with vocal; enlarges the scale of the choruses as well as that of the orchestras; combines the sound impression with the visual in form, color, motion, and so on.

These tendencies in both music and technique are equally clear in the *ars nova* in its Italian and French branches (Philippe de Vitry, 1290–1361; Francesco Landino, 1225–1377; Francesco da Cesaro; Guillaume Machant, d. 1367; and others); in the Flemish Polyphonic school (John Dunstable, d. 1453; Guillaume Dufay, 1400–1474; Pierre de la Rue, d. 1518; Okeghem, 1430–1495; and Josquin Deprès, 1450–1521, to mention only the main names); in the French school (Clément Jannequin; Goudimel, 1510–1564; Claudin Le Jeune, 1530–1564); in the Italian schools (Costanzo Festa, b. 1505; Wallaërt, 1510–1562; Cyprian van Rore, 1516–1565; A. Gabrieli, 1510–1586; G. Gabrieli, 1557–1612; Gesualdo, d. 1614; Palestrina, 1524–1594; Orlando di Lasso, 1530–1594); and even in the Spanish school (Christobal Morales, b. 1512; Vittoria, 1540–1608, and others); in the English school (R. Fairfax, John Taverner, William Bird, and others); among the German Meistersingers and other currents there (Hans Sach, 1496–1576). The trend was general for Western European culture.

So far as the inner character of the change is concerned, the trend of Sensualization shows itself unquestionably in many forms.

First of all the proportion of religious music tends to decrease while that of the secular music tends to increase.

In co-operation with I. Lapshin, I computed the changes in the proportion of religious and secular music, according to the number of composers of each type as well as to the compositions belonging to the grand music (see Tables 32 and 33).

The results of Tables 32 and 33 are rather close. The trends are the same — toward ever-increasing secularization which in the nineteenth and (especially) in the twentieth centuries has become not only dominant but crushingly so.

This secularization has been proceeding not only quantitatively but qualitatively. As mentioned, even the religious music after the fourteenth and fifteenth centuries has been showing an increasingly profane and worldly character.

Since religious music has been dwindling, becoming less and less Ideational and more Sensate, it follows that the Sensate music for the last eight centuries has been correspondingly increasing.

TABLE 32. PROPORTION OF RELIGIOUS AND SECULAR COMPOSERS BY CENTURIES

Century	*Period*	*Number of Religious Composers*	*Number of Secular Composers*	*Per Cent Religious*	*Per Cent Secular*
XVI	1500–1520	26	19	—	—
	1520–1540	19	30	—	—
	1540–1560	22	16	53	47
	1560–1580	18	16	—	—
	1580–1600	31	21	—	—
XVII	1600–1620	28	47	—	—
	1620–1640	22	25	—	—
	1640–1660	31	37	46	54
	1660–1680	47	48	—	—
	1680–1700	64	64	—	—
XVIII	1700–1720	68	57	—	—
	1720–1740	69	72	44	56
	1740–1760	41	55	—	—
	1760–1780	27	55	—	—
	1780–1800	28	52	—	—
XIX	1800–1820	27	73	—	—
	1820–1840	31	67	—	—
	1840–1860	47	87	24	76
	1860–1880	22	126	—	—
	1880–1900	35	163	—	—

TABLE 33. PROPORTION OF RELIGIOUS AND SECULAR COMPOSITIONS BY CENTURIES

Century	*Period*	*Number of Great Religious Works*	*Number of Great Secular Works*	*Per Cent Religious*	*Per Cent Secular*
	1600–1620	19	47	—	—
	1620–1640	19	25	—	—
XVII	1640–1660	25	37	42	58
	1660–1680	42	48	—	—
	1680–1700	54	64	—	—
	1700–1720	60	57	—	—
	1720–1740	60	72	—	—
XVIII	1740–1760	40	55	42	58
	1760–1680	27	55	—	—
	1780–1800	27	52	—	—
	1800–1820	25	73	—	—
	1820–1840	29	67	—	—
XIX	1840–1860	42	87	21	79
	1860–1880	19	126	—	—
	1880–1900	25	163	—	—
	1900–1920	7	138	5	95

It is to be said, on the other hand, that in the period from the end of the fifteenth century to the beginning of the nineteenth, all in all 'the grand music represented (special currents exempted) a mixture of both forms, without an extreme or monopolistic preponderance of either.

The Idealistic music of these centuries incorporated in itself all the purest, noblest, and richest there is in Sensate beauty. The supreme inspiration still comes from the sublime ideals and idealistic values, which were a substitution for the entirely otherworldly values of the pure Ideational music.

It is not incidental that the religious and the secular music of this period differ from each other very little. Bach, Mozart, Handel, Beethoven often use similar airs and music in their secular and religious compositions. This means that both kinds are Idealistic, neither otherworldly religious, nor sensually hedonistic.

The trend toward ever-increasing sensatism in music is shown by various data. One of these concerns the *theatricalism of music*. This is manifest in the fact that opera, especially comic opera, not to mention vaudeville and entertainments of a similar low order, emerged only at the end of the sixteenth and in the seventeenth centuries.

In the field of religious music, oratorio, as a theatrical form of music, emerged in the seventeenth century.

These theatrical forms of music have been rapidly growing during the last three centuries. We divided the important musical works mentioned in the above histories into the "theatrical" (oratorio, opera, and comic opera) and the nontheatrical (cantata, organ and chamber music, symphony, concerto, suite, etc.) and roughly computed their number in these centuries. The results are shown in Table 34.

TABLE 34. FLUCTUATION OF THEATRICAL AND NONTHEATRICAL COMPOSITIONS BY CENTURIES

Century	*Number of Important Theatrical Combinations (opera, musical drama, musical comedy, oratorio)*	*Number of Important Nontheatrical Compositions*
XVII	.96	317
XVIII	163	353
XIX	207	395

Thus while the number of nontheatrical works increased but slightly, that of important theatrical works increased more than twice, an additional evidence of the "theatrical" nature of modern culture, shown by other compartments of art.

C. Lalo indicates, in his own way, the sensate and superficial nature of theatrical music, as opposed to "classic" music.

The great classics are not dramaturgies and the great dramaturgies are not and cannot be classics. The reason for that is that by its nature the technique of drama is a hash, an inevitable impurity.

The next satellite of the sensual art generally, and of sensual music particularly, is *quantitative colossalism*. We saw how successfully it invaded the Graeco-Roman music in its Sensate stage. The same is evident in the music of the last three centuries, and especially of the nineteenth and twentieth.

Take, for instance, the *size of the orchestra* for which musical compositions are scored. Here are typical data. Monteverde's *Orpheus* (1607) is scored, all in all, for about thirty instruments. The orchestras of Lulli, Bach and Stamitz were ordinarily not larger. Even the orchestra for which Beethoven scored his first to the fifth symphonies was still moderate and well balanced.

When we come to the nineteenth and twentieth centuries the size notably increases. Berlioz's *Fantastic Symphony* (1830) is scored for more than a hundred instruments. His *Tuba mirum* (1838) for a still larger orchestra (not to mention the chorus). About the size of the *Fantastic Symphony* orchestra was that for the *Rienzi* of Wagner (1840). As we come to Wagner's *Gotterdämmerung* (1877), Bruckner's *Eighth Symphony* (1884), Mahler's *First Symphony* (1888), Richard Strauss's *Heldenleben* (1899), the size and complexity of the orchestra still further increase. In Strauss's *Electra* (1908), Mahler's *Fifth Symphony* (1904) and then his *Eighth* (1910), Schönberg's *Gurrelieder* (1901), and Stravinsky's *Sacrê du printemps* (1913), the necessary instruments number one hundred and twenty and more.

From seven singers in the Gregorian *Schola*, from four to twenty for Palestrina's music, from some thirty to sixty instruments in the regular orchestras of Bach and Mozart, the orchestra of the nineteenth and twentieth centuries has certainly grown to be colossal.

The same is true of the choruses and other instrumentalities of music, beginning with the buildings and ending with the stage.

One sees the same trait in many more intimate forms of music: the scale of tonality has grown wider in range; the polytonality greater; the contrasts sharper, more used and more abused, especially in the *fortissimo;* the scale of dissonances has been growing; the proportion and character of noises, which tend more and more to replace melody; also the variety of chromatics, of timbres, of rhythms, of tempos, as well.

The evidences of the trend discussed and of the powerful domination of Sensate music in the nineteenth and twentieth centuries are not limited by the above. There are many others. Such is the *ever-increasing complication of the texture of music and the deliberate creation of technical difficulties*. While ordinary orchestras can play the works of the classics, many a modern work, like some by Stravinsky, Smidt, Schönberg, Honegger, Mahler, taxes to the limit the resources of even the very best and most virtuosic orchestras. Another aspect is the *ever-increasing role of technique*, not of genius or talent, but technique which is the result of long training in order to be capable of the most difficult "tricks," whatever they may be. The great masterpieces in art and literature and science have mostly been spontaneous in the sense that they were the result of a free flow of the creative forces of a genius not dominated by technique, to whom technique is a minor matter and who creates his own.

The decadent periods, whether in art or science or religion, have often been marked by this substitution of technique for genius; of specific training in technical skill rather than real creativeness or inspiration. *In such periods as these, technique usually dominates the field.* All these things are various aspects of the same phenomenon: the Sensate character of art. And of all that we have more than enough, in the music of the last part of the nineteenth and the twentieth century.

I shall mention just a few additional satellites of Sensate music which have appeared during the nineteenth and twentieth centuries. Such are the *professionalism and individualism* of the music composers. Anonymity and collectivity of creative activities do not exist. Everybody wants to attach his name to his work. Everybody wants to be "original," "singular," "individual." Collective creation, whether it be folk song or just a tune, has practically disappeared. Instead, the last "hit" of the crooner or of a successful song writer is broadcast over the country.

On the other hand there are professional unions of composers, singers, musicians, quite similar to the Dionysiac unions of musicians in Greece and similar unions in Rome. But the collective creation in music by the body of the people, as it was practiced in the Ideational and Idealistic periods, has practically disappeared.

Another satellite and symptom of the trend discussed is the *enormous development of musical education, musical criticism, musical discussion, and musical aestheticism.* Nowadays almost every boy and girl of good family is obliged to be "musically educated." Innumerable public and private agencies strive to give a musical education to every child through singing clubs, governmental organizations, public schools, etc. Musical criticism blossoms in every copy of practically every newspaper. Musical journals, musical schools, musical discussions, departments of music in every college and high school — all these are present in abundance. If the production of masterpieces depended upon the number of people involved in musical activities, then certainly we should expect a generous crop. The reality, however, does not agree with that expectation.

Sensate art is created for a market. Nowadays, when the artist is a professional and makes his living by his activity, he has to create a marketable commodity. Therefore he has to create, not perhaps what he would like to, but what can make money. In order to do this, he has to adapt his work to the prevailing taste of the largest class of consumers. Such an adaptation means *vulgarization and commercialization.*

Its other aspect is a *cheap sensationalism.* If an artist is to make money, he has to make a "hit." All this we have to a degree hardly equalled before.

Sensate music and culture are of the world of Becoming, of incessant and rapid change. Since the value of Sensate music is in its *sounds* as such; and since many repetitions of the same combination of sounds soon become familiar and boring, *musical art, under such conditions, demands an incessant change, unceasing variety, contrasting fashions.* Of all this we have also more than enough. The best sellers in music, like those in literature, are acclaimed, and then forgotten the next season; something new has to come incessantly, and not merely new, but contrastingly new. Hence the rapid change in fads and fashions in the music of these centuries. Within the nineteenth century alone, there were at least three waves of classicism-romanticism. As for smaller changes, they are almost seasonal. Even the leading musical critics, in their reviews of the performances of the great orchestras or conductors, make it almost a rule to complain that "only last season such and such a composition was played, and now it is again on the program."

We are so accustomed to this psychology that we do not notice the extraordinary character of such everyday statements. Imagine a medieval "highbrow" saying that only last season the Chants, or the Kyrie, or the Gloria was performed, and now it is again on the program!

The result of this unceasing change is an ever-increasing trend of Sensate music toward something not just beautiful, but *striking, extreme, exotic, picturesque, and monstrous.* Sensual beauty of normal form soon becomes familiar and tiresome.

The sensual music is bound to take something that is either perverse, exotic or negative, or empirically dramatic or just mediocre — types such as *The Emperor Jones*, *Heldenleben*, *Sinfonia Domestica*, or the urbanized cavemen (in the *Sacré*), with human sacrifice, of course, interwoven around sex (also of course), or comedians (*Petrushka*) or clowns (*Pagliacci*), or a pregnant woman with her lover (Schönberg), or gypsies and smugglers (*Carmen*), or railroad business (*Pacific*), or romantic brigands (*Robert le Diable*), or the Voceks, and so on. As we shall see, in literature and dramatic art, this trend is still more conspicuous (remember the success of the series of perverse types given in O'Neill's plays), but it is quite tangible in music also.

One of the most important evidences of that is the *growth of musical comedy.* In the form of the *opera buffa*, it appeared in the sixteenth century and has been growing ever since. In our sample we got twenty-four for the seventeenth century, ninety-seven for the eighteenth, and one hundred and six for the nineteenth. Quite a growth! Like caricature and satire in painting, comedy in literature and drama, the musical comedy, by its very nature, deals with the ridiculous, stupid, perverse, criminal aspects of life.

Besides the directly negative and perverse subjects, another refuge and source of supply for new and unusual subjects is the *types, phenomena, and values on the level of commonness and mediocrity, devoid of any heroism or halo.* Since these fields were also intentionally avoided by the Ideational-Idealistic art, the sensational art naturally appropriates them, depicts them with all the empirical circumstances of real life, and proudly parades them as "naturalism," "realism," and truth. This naturalism, in all its flatness, is another variety of the phenomenon typical of a sensual mentality and sensual music and is present abundantly in contemporary music. The railroad-airplane (Honegger), factory (Molotov), toccata (Prokoffieff), *May First Symphony* (Shostakovitch), *Noises of London* (Elgar), football (Martinou), are just a few recent examples of that.

Another source for the novelty to which the musician of sensualism turns is something exotic, sensually exotic particularly, which, like a cocktail or mystery or detective story, can provide a diversion from the boring routine of life (office hours, day-in and day-out drudgery). Hence the *exotic, the picturesque, the sexually charged "romanticism"* of the Hollywood type — "Isn't It Romantic?" Egyptians, Chinese, Persians, Africans, Turks, Mongols, ancient peoples, cavemen, Romans, Jews, are presented in the most naïvely fantastic but picturesque manner, quite different from our own society. These and many other exoticisms (woven around sex chiefly, of course) have been one of the most popular sources of supply of the ever new and different to which sensual music is doomed. *Samson and Delilah, Islamey, Salammbo, Île de Calypso, Oberon, Salomé, Aïda, Thaïs, Astarté, Thamara, L'Africaine, Coppelia, Sappho, Faire, Othello, Le Prise de Trois, Ariadne, Bacchus,* the whole Wagnerian series of the Ring, *Tristan and Isolde,* each more exotic than its predecessor! The majority of the operas and a considerable part of other musical compositions of the end of the eighteenth and of the nineteenth and twentieth centuries have subjects of this kind.

Finally, *pathos, dramatism, emotion* — especially woven around love: love tragic and comic, light and heavy, of the caveman type and of the chorus-girl type, Don Juanish, Othelloish, of the Romeo type; love ancient, medieval, of modern Broadway; love of gods, of devils; love angelic; love in every imaginable form, with veiled and unveiled sex — all this naturally pervades our music and our art generally, as it always does in the period of dominant sensual art and mentality.

One of the manifestations of this emotionality and pathos is an increasing sentimental sadness of grand as well as of the vulgar contemporary music. This has been noticed by several historians of music. Speaking of that Combarieu says that this *triste sentimentality* has been growing, even in comic opera. "Music of the comic theater, which by definition has to be gay, has become sad and dolorous. Already in the melodies of Massenet, in *Werther* and *Manon*, the intensity of the expression of love is a voice of suffering. In the *Louise* of Charpentier, it is a poignant sadness."

In agreement with this is the moronic and sentimentally sad crooning in the field of contemporary vulgar music. Our study of the major and minor keys in which great compositions are written indicates that the proportion of those written in the minor key has been increasing.

Though the sad or the gay impression of music depends upon the total means used, and among them the minor may sound gay and the major dolorous, nevertheless, normally the statements expressed many times from Aristotle up to Pierre Maillard, - that the minor usually sounds sad, dolorous, lamentable, are hardly wrong. Under such an assumption — and I subscribe to it — an increase of the minor is also a symptom of growing sentimental sadness, emotionality, and lamentability of music. We have seen that these qualities and the pathetic are the usual satellites of Sensate art in all its compartments, and this is an additional corroboration of the growth of Sensate music in the last two centuries.

The growth of all these tendencies to ultrasensatism, sexualism, exoticism, and naturalism in the effort, on the one hand, to reflect in music the empirical Sensate reality — and especially its common, everyday, or pathological aspects — and, on the other — as a counterpoison — some exotic and fantastic aspects of it as a remedy for the boredom of prosaism is shown also in the approximate statistics of the main subjects or themes of the prominent operas for the last three centuries. Table 35 gives the figures from our sample taken from the same sources.

In the classification, by mythological and pseudo-historical operas are meant the operas and music where the subject is taken from ancient mythology and pseudo history, like most of the operas of Lulli, the aristocratic operas of the Venetian school, and the *galant* operas of Rameau. Similar subjects have been used in symphonic poems, like the *Prometheus* of Beethoven, the *Orpheus* of Monteverde, Glück, and Liszt, the *Ariadne* of Richard Strauss, the *Oedipus* of Stravinsky, *Psychée* of César Franck, etc.

By comic and *genre* music are meant most of the classical comic operas and similar works, like Rossini's *Barber of Seville*, Pergolesi's *Serva-Padrona* (1733), Moussorgsky's *Fair of Sorochnitzy*, Smetana's *Bartered Bride*, and the works of Weber, Cherubini, Cambini, and others.

By revolutionary and war types are meant works like Tschaikovsky's *1812*, Gossek's, Catel's, Lesueur's, Cherubini's, Cambini's revolutionary music; Cretri's *Dionys le tyran*, Beethoven's *Leonora* and *Fidelio*, Rossini's *William Tell*, Meyerbeer's *Huguenots* and *Prophet*, Moussorgsky's *Khovantzchina*, etc.

By animalism and *paysage*, clouds, sea, morning, night, seasons, forest, thunderstorm; songs about a flea or a rat or a lion; the waterfall, desert; birds and other creatures and the *paysage* subjects expressed in musical terms, like Debussy's *Clouds* and *Sea;* Rimsky-Korsakoff's *Scheherazade*, Wagner's *Siegfried's Idyll*, Berlioz's *Damnation of Faust*, Haydn's and Glazunoff's *Seasons*, and so on.

By historical works, those like Moussorgsky's *Boris Godunoff*, Wagner's *Meistersinger*, the *Kitege* of Rimsky-Korsakoff, etc.

By exoticism, works like Lesueur's *Île de Calypso*, Beethoven's *Ruins of Athens*, Weber's *Oberon* (Turkish theme), *Tourandott* (Chinese), Glinka's *Ruslan*, Balakireff's *Islamey*, Strauss's *Salomé*, etc.

By urbanism and *nature morte*, the naturalistic reflection of the industrial, urban, and mechanized or still-life phenomena, like the factory, railway, airplane, subway, machine, engine, skyscraper, noises of the city, football, city crowds, etc.

TABLE 35. FLUCTUATION OF COMPOSITIONS BY CONTENT

Period	Mythology Pseudo history	Genre Comedy	Revolution War	Folk Legend Paysage Animalism	Historism	Exoticism	Urbanism Nature morte
1600–1620 }	30	5	—	—	—	—	—
1620–1640 }	—	—	—	—	—	—	—
1640–1660	18	2	—	—	—	—	—
1660–1680	25	7	—	—	—	—	—
1680–1700	50	10	—	—	—	—	—
1600–1700	*123*	*24*	—	—	—	—	—
1700–1720	23	10	—	—	—	—	—
1720–1740	34	6	—	—	—	—	—
1740–1760	17	13	—	—	—	—	—
1760–1780	26	47	—	—	—	—	—
1780–1800	12	21	11	—	—	—	—
1700–1800	*112*	*97*	*11*	—	—	—	—
1800–1820	14	26	3	—	—	—	—
1820–1840	14	14	5	2	4	—	—
1840–1860	14	12	4	16	5	8	
1860–1880	9	40	15	20	10	13	12
1880–1900	12	14	3	25	8	20	8
1800–1900	*63*	*106*	*30*	*63*	*27*	*41*	*20*
1900–1920	15	15	6	19	6	11	20

The sample is of course incomplete and only approximate, but roughly it reflects the reality. It shows that animalism and *paysage*, *nature morte*, exoticism, and urbanism emerged only in the nineteenth century; here the trend is identical with what we have seen in the fields of painting and sculpture. Urbanism reflects in the most naturalistic way the routine of daily life of the common average type of man. The same is shown by the increase of the *genre* and comedy music. Historism, which grows usually only in the period of the domination of sensatism in art, appears also here only in the nineteenth century. Revolution and war is an incarnation of the pathetic, dramatic, and emotional. It emerged in the eighteenth century.

As a contrast to these growing classes, "mythology" and "pseudo history," which deal mainly with the hero, with the deeply tragic and heroic aspects of life, the class which is the favorite subject of Idealistic art, shows a rapid decrease; the little halo of the heroic, not to mention the divine, fades in the realm of the growing Sensate. From the heavens and heroic heights it always descends to social gutters and cellars. That is its destiny!

It is really an interpretation of man and of all the sociocultural values on a decidedly low level, and is a general characteristic of the overripe phase of any Sensate culture and mentality. From the heavens and heroic heights it always descends to social gutters and cellars. That is its destiny!

Inner emptiness and the most complicated and brilliant techniques are the destiny to which it is doomed until it is replaced by the Ideational music, which has still to appear, but will probably grow eventually. The first clumsy signs of it, in some of the modern "isms," seem already to have come to the surface. The works of many of the most modern composers, like Stravinsky and Honegger, show already a rupture with the purely Sensate music, quite similar to the reaction of the anti-Visualists in painting. These modernists, or "Cubists in Music," are in real revolt against the prevalent forms of Sensate music. Some of them quite openly brush aside the sensually pleasing functions of music and profess something quite different from them, as the objectives of their compositions. So far, like the anti-Visualists, they are reactionists. Like the cubists, they have cut their moorings from the shore of sensualism, but they have not arrived at any new and real port where they and their music can settle permanently. They are still searching, but they do not know what they are looking for, or, if they think they know, they still remain children of the Sensate age, with all its Sensate mentality.

Whether they constitute one of the "twists" of the sensual stream, or are the forerunners of a coming Ideational wave remains to be seen. What is significant is that here in music we find exactly the same situation as in other fields of art studied.

The above sums up the main waves of the Ideational and Sensate music, during some twenty-five hundred to twenty-seven hundred years studied. Besides these tidal fluctuations, there have been many minor ones, but they are outside the scope of this work, though the most important are reflected in the data given. So far as the tidal waves are concerned, they have proceeded in their essentials parallel with similar waves in other fields of art. The main discrepancies in time are as follows.

First, music became classically Ideational in the fifth and sixth centuries A.D., while other arts — painting, sculpture, architecture — achieved their classic Ideationality somewhat later, by two or three centuries.

Second, the Idealistic phase of music lagged, compared with that phase in the other arts; while these reached the Idealistic stage in the thirteenth century, music entered it in the fifteenth and stayed in that phase longer, up to the beginning of the nineteenth century.

Such are the main differences. They answer the problem to what extent various generalizations of the theories considered in Chapters Five and Six are valid. The answer is rather negative in regard to the existence of a universally uniform sequence of leading and lagging claimed by such theories. In one period music was leading painting, sculpture, and architecture; in another, it was lagging. We shall meet these phenomena many times.

Finally, the results show that, all in all, the four forms of art studied moved together in their changes, but the simultaneousness of the change was neither very close nor perfectly integrated.

12

FLUCTUATION OF IDEATIONAL AND SENSATE FORMS OF LITERATURE AND CRITICISM

I. Preliterary Groups

Literature, like the other forms of art, may be of two fundamental types: Ideational and Sensate. And between these extremes lie the many Mixed varieties. The literary work which deals with the "invisible" world, superempirical and transcendental, and in which words and images are but symbols of this world, is, according to definition, Ideational literature. The work which depicts and describes empirical phenomena in their sensory aspect, where words and images have nothing but their empirical meaning, is Sensate literature. A considerable number of purely religious and magical literary works (hymns, dithyrambs, prayers, odes, narratives, proverbs, riddles, incantations, etc.), on the one hand, and such works as Dante's *Divine Comedy*, on the other, are examples of the first type; purely "realistic" and "naturalistic" novels, dramas, plays, lyrics (for example, the works of Zola and Sinclair Lewis) are examples of the second.

In a rough or highly developed form both of these types of literature seem to have coexisted in virtually all cultures, at all periods.

Though present in almost every sociocultural constellation, both styles naturally occur, however, in different states of purity and in different proportions. Among primitive tribes both forms, and especially the Ideational, are to a large extent impure. Most of the literature of such peoples is of a Mixed form, where the Ideational and Sensate elements are interwoven — in some cases exceedingly well, in others rather poorly. For instance, most of the early epics, anonymous or connected with some individual name, whether the *Mahabharata* and *Ramayana*, the *Gilgamesh* epic, or parts of the Bible, the *Iliad*, the *Odyssey*, the *Edda*, the *Scop's Song*, the *Song of Beowulf*, or the Russian folk epics about the great heroes Iliya Murometz, Dobrynia Nikititch, Sviatopolk, Mikula Selianinovitch, and others — these and many other early epics represent in principle the Mixed — that is, the Ideational-Sensate — literature in their character. Some of them were to all purposes Idealistic in the sense given to that term in this work.

When one studies in detail and makes an analysis of the main waves of the transformation of literature from the Ideational to the Sensate types with their Mixed forms, or vice versa, one is led to the conclusion that in their main movements *these fluctuations follow in a close parallel those in the fields of painting and sculpture, and also, to a less degree, in other fields of art.* At least such is the conclusion obtained after a study of the literature of the Western Christian and, to some extent, of the Graeco-Roman cultures. Whether such a parallelism is universal for all cultures and times, I am not prepared to say.

II. Graeco-Roman Literature and Criticism

As to the Graeco-Roman literature (omitting the Creto-Mycenaean), it seems that in the centuries from about the eighth to the fifth B.C. this was predominantly Ideational. The precise century to which Homer and Hesiod belong is unknown, but it is possibly the eighth. The same is true of the legendary Orpheus and the Orphic literature. If the great works of these writers and groups cannot be styled purely Ideational, they are mainly so, for the rest being at least Idealistic. The poets of the Homeric, the Orphic, and the Hesiodic schools are all mainly the "spokesmen of deity" and "prophets." To their contemporaries and to the Greeks up to about the time of Plato and Aristotle they were, in all probability, much more Ideational than they now appear to us. To the Greeks before the fourth century the *Iliad* and *Odyssey* were religious, moral, and educational, rather than art creations.

Still more indicative is the bulk of the literature, which was represented by the Doric choral lyric of religious *nomes, dithyrambs, paeans, prosodies, threnodies,* and other magico-religious songs, hymns, and literary-musical creations (Terpander, Alkman, Lasos, Simonides of Samos, Arion, Stesichoros, Simonides of Keos, and others). In so far as these were predominantly Ideational the literature of the period may be said to be predominantly Ideational. There is no doubt that the Sensate literature, especially the Ionic stream of literature somewhat later (Theognis, Sappho, Anakreon, the Sicilian comic but moralizing and philosophizing poets such as Epicharmos, Sophron, and others of the sixth century), existed side by side with the Ideational stream; but it was, to all appearances, a subordinate and minor current, and even this current was greatly permeated by Ideationalism and Idealism.

The end of the sixth and the fifth century B.C. — the period of the great Ideational-Idealistic lyricist Pindar and of the great tragedies and comedies (Aeschylus, Sophocles, and to some extent Euripides and Aristophanes) — was, as was indicated in Chapter Twelve, the *Idealistic period of Greek literature* (and of other arts).

After the first half of the fifth century, and especially beginning with the end of the fourth century B.C., Greek literature as well as Greek literary criticism, like the other forms of art already studied, definitely move toward ever-increasing Sensatism. *The manifestations of this rising tide of Sensate literature are exactly the same as those which we have pointed out in Greek painting, sculpture, music, and to some extent, architecture.*

A. The subject matter becomes more secular and less religious.

B. Gradually not only gods but even heroes are depicted as mortal. The common, vulgar type of personages, the negative, the picturesque, the subsocial types begin to become more and more popular as themes for works.

C. Description itself, especially in the Alexandrian school, becomes more "realistic" and empirically "scientific." Symbolism, especially transcendental symbolism, practically disappears. Its place is taken by a "naturalistic realism," by a correct, detailed, scientific characterization of personages, events, places.

D. The portrayal of *genre* of a banal character ("here, certainly we are in the very heart of a banal and everyday reality"), on the one hand, and the paysage, the pastoral, the idyll (whether in the style of Theocritus or others still more sentimental), on the other hand, develop increasingly — a fact analogous to what we have observed in painting and sculpture.

E. Tragedy slowly begins to give way to comedy, to satire, to burlesque, to picaresque — again a trait indicated in the preceding chapters as one of the usual satellites of the Sensate art.

F. Just as the Western literature of the Renaissance and the period of the Academies, in attempting to revive antiquity, of necessity hid under the forms of antiquity the sensational subject matter and interests of the sixteenth and seventeenth centuries, so did the Greek, especially from the third century B.C. in its "renaissances" of the archaic forms, including many of ancient legendary and mythological content. For "these false archaisms were but mere mannerisms."

G. Sensualism and eroticism, sometimes crude, sometimes refined, occasionally in the form of "innocence" of the type of Greuze's "innocent doves," permeates the literary work.

H. Sensual pleasure becomes, more and more, the main and often the only objective.

I. In conformity with this we find "art for art's sake," aestheticism, art criticism, art education, art fashion, "art appreciation," and so on, developing rapidly.

J. We find the growth of individualism, among the literati, and of their "professionalization," mannerisms, vanity, influence, and the improvement of their position in social and material respects. In brief we have all the familiar satellites of the art dominated by the Sensate form.

Instead of my offering a detailed historical corroboration of these statements — which is beyond the scope of this work — it will be enough to remind the reader of a few of the "milestones," a few of the chief names which mark the long course of Greek literature. After Euripides and a few epigoni, Greek tragedy died and was replaced by the *Old Greek Comedy*, with Aristophanes as its chief creator. The replacement of the Old Comedy by the so-called *Middle Comedy*, and this by the *New Comedy*, were further milestones in the movement of Greek literature toward an ever-increasing Sensatism. The movement from Aristophanes to Menander and Philemon and other representatives of the New Comedy was a great shift from the world of gods and heroes to that of ordinary men, and even to that of negative subsocial personalities and affairs. In the New Comedy there is nothing mythological, religious, heroic. Practically all the comedies deal with very ordinary people, often with the sexual, with low morality and with all the ordinary and pathological paraphernalia of such a social world. We are virtually in the same world as that of today's Broadway "shows" and musical and other comedy.

When we pass onward to the Hellenistic literature, we are practically at the extreme point of the Sensate. What this literature consists of is imitative epics with old gods and heroes in whom nobody now believes and in whose trappings are dressed the potentates of the time, those patrons on whom depend the well-being and position and income of the writer (Ptolemy in the guise of Zeus or some other deity or mythological hero); or the pedantically learned and superscholarly poetry of the rococo type, thoroughly "technical" and "scientific" and therefore perfectly mediocre even in the works of its greatest representatives, like Kallimachos, Apollonius of Rhodes, Aratos (with his versification of a textbook in astronomy), Nikandros (who does the same with medicine); or the bucolic and pastoral poetry of Theokritus with his sugary shepherds and shepherdesses; or the still more typical riddle and the figure poetry of Lykophoron and others, where the supreme end was to write a poem with the length of the lines so shaped as to give the figure of an ax or an altar or wings or some other shape — and all this permeated with the notorious Alexandrian eroticism and indecency, as represented not only by such specialists in this line as Sotades and others, but also in almost all the other works, the pedantically learned not excluded. Add to this the development of epigrammatic, satirical literature, the "detective and mystery stories" — and the general character of the Hellenistic literature (about its criticism much more will be said further) will be comprehensible. We are in a world of overripe Sensatism, pushed to the extremes of sensuality and matter-of-fact empiricism and "positivism" even in poetry and literature.

This picture will appear still clearer if we glance briefly at the evolution of literary criticism before and after the end of the fourth century B.C. As has previously been mentioned, before Plato and Aristotle literary criticism as such virtually did not exist. Saintsbury finds the first weak glimmerings of it in only one of the six writers named Democritus. Its place was taken by estimation and censorship of the literary works from the standpoint of religion, moral and philosophical values.

The period from Plato to Aristotle was transitory in art, literature, and criticism, from the Idealistic to the Sensate. Hence the intermediary character of their positions in the field of art criticism. Plato, with the exception of some "aesthetic" liberalism of a very modest type in *Phedrus*, remains "nonaesthetic" like his predecessors. We all know how in his *Republic* and *Laws* he admonishes poets and artists, calling them "drones," when they were not endeavoring to inculcate appropriate moral, religious, political, and social values; considering them dangerous; prohibiting unexpurgated in his Commonwealth Homer, Hesiod, and Euripides; prescribing the kind and the style of art creations, and banishing all the artists who would not comply with these prescriptions, and so on. "We shall request Homer and the other poets not to be indignant if we erase these things; . . . the more poetical they are the less ought they to be heard by children, and by men who ought to be free, and more afraid of slavery than of death."

Aristotle stands essentially in a somewhat similar position. Saintsbury is right in saying that "Aristotle . . . is doubly and triply ethical" in his attitude and appraisal of art phenomena.

After Aristotle the literature as well as art criticism rapidly changes and shows all the characteristics of the Sensate literature, and these changes become increasingly conspicuous. A considerable and ever-increasing literature of art criticism from a purely aesthetic standpoint develops. Professional art criticism and art critics make their entrance and multiply, especially in the Pergamene and Alexandrian schools, during the third and second centuries B.C. Zenodotus, Crates of Mallos, Aristarchus, and the grammarians Aristophanes and Zoilus, are typical. Criticism also becomes erudite and scholastic. Scholia are piled upon scholia, commentaries, notes, references, grow. For instance in scholia on Homer

> . . . . We find [there] laborious comment on etymology, on grammar, on mythology, etc., etc. We get the most painstaking discussions on the poet's meaning, handled simply, handled allegorically, handled "this way, that way, which way you please." Two volumes of comment on the Odyssey contain endless discussion of the aesthetic technique of it concerning accentuation and punctuation, athetesis, anakephalaiosis; endless classifications of narratives into classes: homiletic, apangeltic, hypostatic, mixed, etc., etc.

In this way the Sensate "art for art's sake" and the no less Sensate criticism began to defeat their purpose. They became more and more futile, sterile, and uncreative.

This second stage of Greek art merges into the Hellenistic, and then into the Roman literature and criticism. Being archaic but sincere, the art and literature of the Romans before the Greek influence, though it never reached the height of the Greek at its peak of glory, were also predominantly Ideational or Idealistic, and mainly religious, magical, and moral. Even here, however, we sense a strong undercurrent of "rugged" naturalism and rough but subdued Sensatism. Greek influence, mainly in the Sensate Hellenistic form, shortened the life of this primitive Ideational and Idealistic literature and quickened the growth of its Sensate form. At the intersection of this decline of the Ideational stream and the forced rise of the Sensate stream we have the period of the Mixed type, the Roman Idealistic literature of about the first century B.C. and the beginning of the first century A.D. Similar to Roman painting, sculpture, music, and architecture of the same period, it never reached the sublimity of the Idealistic originals of the Greeks; nevertheless it gave a "golden age" to Roman literature, and its main stream was essentially Idealistic. I refer to the creations of Virgil and, to some extent, of Horace, Lucretius (whose materialistic poem was permeated by a specific kind of "materialistic idealism" or "idealistic materialism" presented as gospel), Livy, Sallust, Cicero, Seneca, Varro, Cato, and others. Although simultaneously with this stream there existed an almost purely Sensate stream — represented by Horace, and especially Catullus, Ovid, and a few others — it was secondary to the other. In brief, the literature of the period is a counterpart of the "neo-classic" forms of painting, sculpture, music, and architecture of that time. All, for a short time, undergo a transition, and we find the traits of a waning Ideationalism mixing with a ripe Sensatism, a reflection of the Graeco-Hellenistic Sensate influence. The period was short, however, corresponding to the pseudo-Idealistic, neo-classic period in other forms of art, which we have already dealt with. The rising tide of Sensatism in art and literature generally was progressing rapidly.

Roman society became aesthetically minded, as the works of Persius, Petronius, Seneca the Younger, Juvenal, and Martial show. "The literary discussion was as indispensable at a Roman supper of the better class as broiled bones at an English one . . . while supper lasted. . . ." Persius tells us: "Ecce inter pocula quaerunt Romulidae satieri, quid dia poemata narrent. . . . Ventosa et enormis loquacitas" was going on. There appeared literary salons; women took most intense interest in art and literature. There appeared groups of hysterical and enthusiastic admirers of this or that artist. Literary and artistic novelties stirred and excited cities — as the bigger football games in our day. Tacitus, in a work ascribed to him, *Dialogus de claris Oratoribus*, tells us, for instance, that C. Maternus's tragedy on Cato was such a sensation. Everybody seems to have aspired to become a professional artist, writer, orator, etc., and for this purpose subjected himself, or herself, to a long training under professionals. There was an enormous production of texts in every field, which multiplied as time went on. These characteristics of the times are pictured in a few lines of the *Arbiter elegantiarum* of Petronius. At the opening of the work he denounces the dominance of the bombastic and polished language of the writers and critics of his day.

If you will excuse my saying so, you rhetoricians were the first to ruin literature [with your polished, bombastic, and empty phraseology]. . . . Youth had not been enslaved yet to declamations when Sophocles and Euripides devised the words in which they were to speak. [Likewise Plato and Pindar were not subject to the rules of these] schoolmasters. . . . Of late this windy and extravagant loquacity has shifted from Asia to Athens. And forthwith true eloquence, its rule corrupted, has been . . . put to silence. Tell me, who has since equaled the fame of Thucydides, of Hyperides? Not so much as a lyric of wholesome complexion has appeared, and everything, as if poisoned with the same food, has been unable to last to a natural grey old age. Even painting has made no better end. . . .

Similarly, Seneca decries all this literary and artistic bustle; Persius satirizes the common figure of "a literary dandy" in hyacinthine garment, mincing and twanging through his nose some rancid stuff (*rancidulum quiddam*), "these effeminate drivels" who are scribbling in their study, arraying themselves in their best clothes before sitting down to read — and he adds in a hopeless *desiderium*, "Whatever you write, write it in a manly fashion, with no aesthetic trifling!" Still more sharply Juvenal (in his tenth *Satire*) denounces all this Sensate aestheticism, beginning with "the learned lady who talks for hours on the comparative merits of Homer and Virgil."

To be a bookish aesthete became popular. Pliny the Younger tells us that he himself, even during boar-hunting "sat at the nets with a pencil and notebook." And quite naturally he coins the formula so familiar to us: "The bigger the better." ("Ut aliae bonae res, ita bonus liber melior est quisque, quo major.") A picture essentially no different is given by Tacitus. Just as in Hellenistic Greece, erudition goes hand in hand with aestheticism. The age was polyhistoric, and a disproportionate place was given to rhetoric, oratory, criticism, literary occupations; and withal there was little if any originality or creativeness. Pure aestheticism found its best expression and theoretical formulation in the works of Quintilian and other leading critics. Quintilian, the best of these, laid down the canons of style for various types of writing: how to write jokes;

what is the difference between *venustum*, *salsum*, *facetum;* what makes for perspicuity, elegance, beauty of style; what are the forms of tapeinoisis, meiosis, homology, macrology, pleonasm, cacozelon, tropes, figures, and so on. Other critics and writers, as Aulus Gellius, Macrobius, Servius Honoratus, Curius Fortunatianus, and so on, are still more "learned" and more sterile.

At the beginning of this rising tide of Sensatism, the demands for the absolute freedom of a poet, a writer, an artist, were naturally not lacking. Already Cicero pleads for it. In the second century A.D. Lucian gives its formula: "Poetry enjoys unrestricted freedom; the poet's fancy is her only law." Thus a literary man declares that he "*legibus solutus est.*" Sensate art carried to an extreme, as if it had dried up the springs of creativeness, could offer only imitation and second-rate productions. And the contemporaries themselves well understood this. Longinus speaks of "the world-wide bareness that pervades our lives." The creative spirit was gone. Not the imitative idylls or sentimental pastorals, nor sham-heroic poems, nor mystery-adventure-detective stories, nor realistic and naturalistic novels, nor mannered and sensual poetry, nor still cruder erotic literature, nor different kinds of propaganda literature (from the antireligious and materialistic and erotic works of Lucian to the moral propaganda pieces), nor divers imitations of the archaic, classic, Oriental patterns of literature — none of these varieties, quite common in the literature of the period, produced anything great or durable. Thus, during the last decades of the fourth, and beginning of the fifth centuries the Sensate wave of Graeco-Hellenic-Roman literature had worn itself out. It had run its span of life and now was dead. In its place there came the rising tide of Christian Ideational literature, a tiny stream at the beginning of our era but the dominant stream in the fifth century and after. Thus, in all essentials, the main fluctuations in the alternation of Ideational and Sensate forms of literature in the course of a Graeco-Roman culture went parallel with similar waves in painting, sculpture, music, and architecture.

III. Medieval Ideational Literature and Criticism

Originating as an insignificant current at the beginning of our era, the Ideational literature of the Christians grew and, as we have already observed, about the end of the fifth century became the main current, pushing underground the dried-up Sensate stream which had dominated from the end of the fourth century B.C. In turn the Ideational stream remained dominant for about seven or eight hundred years. And in the thirteenth and, in part, the fourteenth centuries, when its decline began to be paralleled by the growth of the Sensate stream, it gave rise to an Idealistic literature, which was a balanced mixture of the two currents.

Subsequently, from the fifteenth to the twentieth centuries, the Sensate literature was once again dominant. Such in brief is the great pulsation of the Ideational and the Sensate in the course of the Western Christian literature. Let us now glance a little more closely at this pulsation.

That the chief literature of the centuries from the fifth to the end of the twelfth was mainly Ideational is beyond question. Its characteristics and the quantitative-qualitative changes in its nature were exactly the same as those which we have studied in some detail in the field of painting, sculpture, and other forms of art.

A. *Inner Traits.* From the point of view of its inner character *the literature of the centuries from the fifth to the tenth was almost entirely religious. In that period there is almost nothing which can be styled secular.* From the beginning Christianity assumed a purely negative attitude toward secular and Sensate literature, well exemplified by the famous case of St. Jerome's vision, in which he was warned of celestial condemnation for his "Ciceronianus," that is, for his being fond of great secular literature. Tertullian called the whole *doctrina secularis literaturae* stupid in the eyes of God. Hence the religious character of the literature of the period indicated. We must wait then until the second half of the twelfth century before secular literature really emerges.

B. *External Traits.* Being Ideational inwardly, in its external form the literature is also Ideational, that is, mainly *symbolical.* The symbolic, or as it is sometimes called, "allegorical," language appeared in the Western writings almost as early as the Christian literature itself. The Church Fathers used it widely, whether in the interpretation of the Bible or any other religious source, or in the interpretation of the pagan writers: of Cicero, or Ovid, or Virgil, or others. Origen, Gregory the Great (especially in his commentary on the Book of Job), Dionysius the Areopagite, Cassiodorus, Martianus, Boethius, Scotus Erigena, and practically every other Christian writer (and simultaneously many of the neo-Platonists and mystics among the pagan writers of the first centuries of our era, like Porphyry, Plotinus, Ammonius, and others who were in the Ideational stream of the period also) made *symbolism and allegory a fundamental category of thought, which from that time on dominates all the thinking and writing of the Middle Ages.* In everything and everywhere the hidden meaning was looked for, found, and interpreted. "The symbol has become a reality." "Allegory became an obsession."

This concerns equally the theological, the philosophical, and the poetical compositions. Just as the empirical world is mere appearance, a mere congeries of "accidents" which come into being and pass away whereas the real essence of things is superempirical and eternal, so language itself is but an imperfect sign using empirical terms and images for pointing out the superempirical realities in the world of God. In conformity with this even the most difficult and the most obscene passages from the Bible or from Ovid or Virgil or any other source, were symbolized, reinterpreted, and Ideationalized.

This symbolic language of writing and thinking was dominant up to the thirteenth century. Thus, here again, not accidentally but quite logically, we find the Ideational content of literature associated with symbolic external form; and both taken together testify definitely to the fact of the Ideational character of the literature of the period.

There is no need to point out that this Ideational literature was free from all the characteristics of the Sensate art and literature.

C. *Literary Criticism.* Finally, in conformity with all this, stands also the character of the *literary and art criticism* of the period from the fifth to the thirteenth century. This character, in contrast to that of the preceding Sensate criticism, is purely Ideational.

The criterion of beauty and art became again religious and moral. Whatever contradicted this criterion became nonart, nonbeauty. Such a situation continued almost unbroken up to the twelfth century. In the works of the Church Fathers — Augustine, Cassiodorus, Boethius, Martianus, Venantus Fortunatus, Fulgentius, Isidore of Seville, Bede, Scotus Erigena, St. Bernard, St. Benedictine, St. Francis — one does not find anything of this aestheticism and pure aesthetic criticism. Even the great theorizers of the twelfth and thirteenth centuries, like St. Thomas Aquinas, do not exhibit much of it. Whatever criticism there was — and there was certainly a great deal — it was not Sensately aesthetic, but religious and moral.

IV. Idealistic Literature and Criticism of the Thirteenth and Fourteenth Centuries

Just as in the various fields of art the first observable emergence of a mildly Sensate form took place in the twelfth and the thirteenth centuries, and led to the Idealistic style in painting, sculpture, architecture, and — somewhat later — music, so also is it with literary work during this same period. *In literature also these are transitional centuries of an Idealistic mixture of the declining Ideationalism and the reawakening Sensatism. The Idealistic character is manifest in all the main aspects of what is styled here Idealistic art, namely, in the inner content of the literature, in its external forms, and finally in the character of the art and literary criticism of the period.*

A. *Inner Traits.* As to the *inner content* of the literature of these centuries, it now represents, first of all, a *mixture of religious with secular topics*, though the secular is still predominantly *heroic*, and still does not deal with the banal, everyday events and personages and still less with the vulgar, negative, low, debased, pathological aspects of empirical life.

This mixture is one of the inner characteristics of the Idealistic art.

On the level of the major literature, according to our rough computation, the proportion of the religious writings, which was about 95 per cent previously, now falls for these centuries to about 30 to 55, in the French, the German, and the English literatures; the remaining 70 to 45 per cent being secular or semisecular. Somewhat similar is the situation in the literature of the other Western countries of Europe (with the exception of Russia, which lags here also). This decrease is due not to an absolute decrease in the quantity of religious literature, but to an enormous increase of secular and semisecular writing. In Germany this is the period of the *Ruodlieb* (a chivalric romance written by a monk, begun in the eleventh century), of the *Kaiserchronik*, *Rolandslied* (a secular heroic poem, but still permeated by the religious point of view), *Alexanderlied*, *Tristrant*, *Lanzelet*, *Nibelungenlied*, *Salman und Morolf*, *Gregorius*, *Barlaam*, *Parzival*, *Iwein*, *Lied von Troye*, the works of Hartmann von Aue, of Wolfram von Eschenbach, of Ulrich von Lichtenstein, of Gottfried von Strassburg, of Walter von der Vogelweide, and of a number of other "historico-legendary romances" and epics, with a little sprinkling of somewhat less heroic and more Sensate works. The character of these writings shows that even in the secular world they deal mainly with heroes, with outstanding persons, and with the positive values of empirical reality as they were understood then. Even these secular works are permeated considerably by the Ideational — religious and moral — atmosphere. The remaining portion of the literature, some 40 per cent, was still religious.

Not much different is the situation in the French or English or general Western European literature of the period.

In France the secular literature is represented by similar epics and heroic romances: *La Chanson de Roland*, *Le Couronnement de Louis*, *Raoul de Cambrai*, *Tristan et Iseult*, and so on; by a number of shorter narratives like Marie de France's *Seven Lais*, *La mule sans frein*, *Richeut*, by the *De amore* of André Chapelain; by a few secular dramas, like Adam de la Halle's *Jeu de Robin et Marion;* by fables, like the *Roman de Renard;* by lyrics and by fabliaux (thought they were on the lower level of literature); and at the end of the fourteenth century by historical works (Joinville and Froissart); and finally, by probably the greatest of all these writings, the *Roman de la Rose*.

As we shall see, the character of these is very like that of the German works of the same period. It is mainly heroic, positive, ennobling, moralizing, permeated still by the religious spirit. A few more "earthly" and, among the *fabliaux*, even indecent works emerged; but they again were a much smaller stream and even part of that stream circulated not as literature but as a kind of stories told ("not for the children and the ladies") while drinking and under similar circumstances.

In England, side by side with still predominant religious literature, the secular literature is represented by similar Arthurian romances and epics, by fables, by modified *chansons de geste*, by political songs, and at the close of the fourteenth century by Langland's *The Vision Concerning Piers Plowman*; and it culminates in the appearance of Chaucer, who by all rights not so much closes the period as opens the next one.

Similar was the situation in other Western European literatures, the peak and the summit of which, as well as for all Europe, was Dante's *Divine Comedy*.

Thus the quantitative proportions of the religious and secular literatures and their general qualitative character, so far as their inner content is concerned, testify to the Idealistic nature of the literature of those centuries.

If one should go into a deeper study of the inner character of this literature — the religious and especially the secular — one would find this Idealistic nature more fully confirmed. Here are some of the symptomatic items and the manner in which they are treated in the literature of the preceding period, and that of the period under discussion.

If we glance at the literature of the preceding period (before the twelfth century) and of the period under discussion from the standpoint of *asceticism versus sensuality*, the result is that the literature of the preceding period is seen to be ascetic and even extremely ascetic in a considerable part. If a few references to sex immorality are found, as for instance in the eighth-century *Altdeutsche Gespräche*, or in *Modus Liebung*, they are condemnatory mostly and serve as a contrast to what is held to be good and proper.

When we pass to the period of the twelfth to the fourteenth century, inclusive, the atmosphere notably changes. The ascetic strain decreases, quantitatively and in part qualitatively, and the Sensate strain increases. First of all, love now begins to occupy a much larger place. It becomes one of the main topics of the epics and of the romances, not to mention the *fabliaux* and the lyric poetry.

From this standpoint the famous *Roman de la Rose*, perhaps the greatest and the most popular work of its kind in the period, composed by two different authors in the thirteenth century, is in many respects typical. Its topic is love. In the first part composed by Guillaume de Lorris, we have an allegorical treatment of sensate love in its sublimest (but not ascetic), noblest, most decent, most delicate, and most romantic form.

On the other hand, in the second part of the same *Roman de la Rose*, composed somewhat later by another author, Jean de Meung, we face a different symphony of love — more fleshy, more sensate, partly cynical, erotic, and scoffing. Its motto, *Fais ce que tu voudras*, repeated later on by Rabelais, gives an idea of the change. After the first part where there is nothing of the "physiology of sex," we are thrown into a love romance where procreation and physiology and "sex appeal," in the modern sense, play a considerable part. In addition to this Jean de Meung attacks satirically chastity, the clergy, kings, the nobility, the monastic orders, and other qualities and institutions. His advice with regard to success in love is: Have "a great heavy purse."

Thus the *Roman de la Rose* in both its parts is typical for the period in regard to asceticism versus Sensatism, and represents the situation accurately. When along with these two streams of Sensate love — Platonic and physiological — the ascetic stream is also considered — then one can hardly question the validity of my statement that the literature was Mixed in its character, and that as a result of this mixture it was indeed Idealistic.

The ascetic and, more generally, Ideational stream, strongly present in that literature, found its greatest expression in Dante's *Divine Comedy*. When all the works of the Italian poet are considered, including his sonnets and lyric poetry in which the Sensate motives are conspicuous, he alone is found to incorporate in his works the perfect balance of the Ideational and Sensate currents and to be in this sense a manifestation of the Idealistic art of the period. In his *Divine Comedy*, however, he is much nearer to Ideationalism than to Idealism.

Thus when what are probably the two main works of the period are taken into consideration — the two differing parts of the *Roman de la Rose* and the *Divine Comedy* — these two works are found to incorporate in themselves all the three main streams of the literature of the period: predominantly Ideational, nobly and idealistically Sensate, and openly erotic. The presence and the mixture of these three streams in the literature are themselves excellent evidence of its Idealistic character. The fact that the period created these great masterpieces, not to mention many smaller ones, is additional evidence of such a character because, as has been indicated several times in this work, the greatest blossoming of art usually occurs in the Idealistic periods when the Ideational stream begins to decline and the Sensate to rise, and these streams cross each other and blend together and produce, as the result of such a blending, the great Idealistic art, not yet loosened from its Ideational moorings and at the same time dressed in the dazzling and noblest and purest forms of Sensate beauty.

From this standpoint the very fact of the creation of these two works — so different and at the same time so congenial — is not an accident but the manifestation of the deep and subtle logic of an integrated culture and art.

If now we take another item relevant to the problem under discussion it gives similar indications: for instance, *divorce* as the outlet for a sensately unhappy marriage. In the literature before the twelfth century it is practically absent. In the period considered, a few mentions of divorce already occur (Marie de France's *Eliduc*, and *Le Friesne*, and the *Oesterreichische Reichschronik*, and a few others). Another item which appears concerns *economic problems* in whatever form. Nowadays, in our Sensate culture there is hardly any problem and any work, whether in literature, art, philosophy, social science, which does not start with, or at least consider as one of the important factors, the economic problems. In the Ideational culture this "economic mentality" is practically absent. Idealistic literature is expected to consider it as one among many other — and no less important — problems and to consider it from the Idealistic — religious, moral, social, or other — standpoint. The literature of the period considers it exactly in that fashion, and therefore this symptom shows once more that my qualification and diagnosis of the literature as Idealistic are supported by the facts.

As a further test of the Ideationality, Idealism, or Sensatism of the literature before the twelfth century and from the twelfth to the fourteenth, I considered the attitudes which may be expressed in the terms *duty versus revolt*, that is, willingness or unwillingness to carry on acts or ways of life recognized as obligatory in painful and uncomfortable empirical conditions. Again the results corroborate what we should expect. In the Ideational literature and mentality, duty, especially the religious and moral duty, is absolute and the only category which counts. The cases in which this attitude is violated are exceedingly few in the literature before the twelfth century and are followed almost always by a statement of disapproval and by retribution.

In the literature of the Idealistic period, it is to be expected that such a rigidity will be somewhat mitigated; some violations of duty and in a moderate degree will be somewhat excused. And this is exactly what we find in fact. The fulfillment of duty under all circumstances is still the main ideal. But in several cases, as in the instance of the fatalistic passion in the *Tristan*, or in the instances of *Parzival*, *Meier Helmbrecht*, *Pfaffe Ameis*, and Ganelon of the *Chanson de Roland*, where in certain circumstances the Sensate point of view finds an excuse, or much more often in the case of the literature of the bourgeoisie — the *fabliaux* — duty begins to yield fairly often to material convenience and personal advantage. In the fourteenth century even in some epics, for instance in the *Hue Capet*, self-interest becomes more and more dominant at the cost of duty. This concerns equally the religious, the feudal, the chivalrous, the moral, or the patriotic duty.

Of the other inner "symptoms" studied I shall mention only five more: (1) *What proportion in the literatures of both periods is occupied by description of nature* (*paysage*, landscape)? (2) *What proportion is occupied by the genre of everyday life?* (3) *How often are real historical personages in their real empirical settings of time, place, and social conditions found in that literature?* (4) *How often do persons of low grade, of the lower classes, of mediocre nature, especially of picturesque, picaresque, negative, debased, and similar character, figure in the literature of both periods, and what place do they occupy?* (5) *What is the "emotional tone" of these literatures: Is it calm and serene, or is it dramatic, emotional, pathetic, and if the second, in what specific form: joy, pessimism, sadness?*

The brief answer to all these questions is that in the literatures of the two periods compared, we find the situation similar to what we found in the study of painting and sculpture for the same times. Landscape as landscape and appreciation of nature; the realistic *genre* of everyday life; historical romances, novels, or biographies, as well as descriptions of characters in their realistic types; persons and events of the debased and low order, or of picaresque and picturesque character, occupy little, if any, place in the literature before the twelfth century. And this shows again its Ideational character. Likewise, in emotional tone the literature is simple, serene, calm, unperturbed by anything empirical in its unfaltering faith in God and His providence. The literature of the second period shows already an increasing tendency to give place to *paysage*, to the daily *genre*, to mediocre types of men (especially in the *fabliaux* and in the "bourgeois" literature). In that period emerges *historical narrative* (*e.g.*, the work of Froissart, Joinville, and several other chroniclers); there appears a kind of biography as person portraiture. The emotional tone of the literature becomes less serene and calm, more alive; and in the fourteenth century, especially, it becomes *very* melancholy, sad, pessimistic, particularly in the lyric poetry — for instance, of E. Deschamps, Jean Meschinot, Georges Chastellain, Jean Gerson, and many others. So it happens almost always, when one fundamental form of culture comes to an end and the next form has not yet arrived.

If, further, we consider that most of the literature of the first period is *anonymous* and in a sense *collective*, while in the second period a considerable part of it becomes *individualistic*, in the sense that its single maker begins more and more to stamp his name upon the creation and to regard it as his and his only; in this trait again we see a complete parallelism with what we have observed of painting and sculpture. This trait shows once more the Ideational nature of the literature of the first period and the Idealistic character of that of the second.

Thus the totality of the inner symptomatic traits leaves no doubt about the predominantly Ideational character of the literature from the sixth to the twelfth century, and its Idealistic character from the twelfth century. The main fluctuations in literature accompany those in painting and sculpture.

B. *External Traits.* The Idealistic character of the literature of the period comes out no less clearly from a consideration of its *external* form or style. The external form of the Ideational art is transcendental symbolism, in which the sensory signs and images are but "visible symbols of the invisible world." The external form of the Sensate art is sensory realism or naturalism, or visualism. The characteristic external form of the mixed Idealistic art is a union of these different styles, resulting either in their simple intermingling, or in *allegory*, which is the organic or "chemical" synthesis of the two and not mere mechanical and spatial existence. In the preceding chapter I pointed out *the deep difference between transcendental symbolism and allegory.* The second is a metaphorical personification and hypostatization of abstractions taken mostly from this sensory world. The first is the representation by signs from the empirical world of the superempirical realities, which are beyond the empirical world and which can be but imperfectly indicated by the code of sensory signs. From this standpoint the literature of the preceding period, that is to the twelfth century, is mainly symbolic but not allegorical. The literature of the period under consideration displays the coexistence of all three styles: symbolism, for instance, in the *Divine Comedy;* "visual naturalism" in the *fabliaux,* in many short novels, and to some extent in the epics, romances, and lyrical poetry; and "allegory" in the *Roman de la Rose.* Such coexistence, with each style represented in a strong proportion, is by itself evidence of the Mixed Idealistic character of the literature. What, however, is more important, is that allegory is a new trait. It is in the period following the twelfth century, whether in the *Roman de la Rose* or in other literary works, that all the innumerable allegorical personifications emerge: Love, Beauty, Wealth, Youth, Gaiety, Leisure, Frankness, Liberty, Hope, Fear, Sweet Thought, Sweet Speech, Sweet Looks, Courtesy, Danger, Shame, Reason, Virginity, Seduction, Purity, Innocence, and so on. I have taken these allegorical figures from the *Roman de la Rose* only, and they are but a small part of those which occur in that work.

Thus, the external forms of the literature show its Idealistic nature no less clearly than its inner character. We have the coexistence of the symbolic, the allegorical, and the naturalistic forms; and we witness the emergence and rapid rise of Allegory as a particular style.

C. *Art Criticism.* If, finally, we turn to the *art and literary criticism* of the period, we find it consistent in character with the inner and external nature of the literature proper. In the preceding period, as has been indicated, there was but an Ideational appreciation or judgment of art and literature. Sensate beauty, Sensate art appreciation, and Sensate criticism did not exist at all. Now the situation begins to change. The Ideational standpoint is still strong and dominant, but its monopoly is broken: art and literary criticism, as we understand it now, begins to emerge. The first signs of this are seen in St. Thomas Aquinas's conceptions and in Dante's *De vulgari eloquentia* and even in such a mystic as Meister Eckhart (b. *c.* 1260). Others soon follow in their footsteps, and in the fifteenth century the literary (Sensate) criticism is already quite widespread, especially in Italy.

Thus, the inner nature of the writings, their external forms — especially the allegorical style—and, finally, the character of the art appreciation and what we call art and literary criticism all demonstrate unequivocally the Mixed, and Idealistically Mixed, quality of the literature of the twelfth to the fourteenth century, inclusive.

V. The Period of the Domination of Sensate Literature and Criticism

After the fourteenth century the decline of the Ideational stream and the rising tide of Sensatism progressed and led to the domination of the Sensate form of literature from about the fifteenth century to the present.

A. *Inner Traits. First of all, the literature becomes more and more secular and less and less religious in its topics.* In our rough quantitative estimation of the masterpieces in France, the percentage of the literature dealing with religious subjects, which had been about 100 up to the twelfth century and had fallen to some 55 to 30 during the period from the twelfth to the fourteenth centuries, decreases to some 25 to 20 per cent in the fifteenth century, rises to 25 to 35 in the sixteenth, seventeenth, and eighteenth centuries, and then falls again to some 10 per cent in the nineteenth and twentieth centuries. The figures are very approximate, but indicative of the trend. It is similar to what we have seen in painting and sculpture and music and architecture.

What is much more important, however, is not so much the quantitative proportions as the qualitative aspects of this literature of religious interest. If its proportions increased somewhat from the sixteenth to the eighteenth century, as compared with the fifteenth, the increase is due mainly to the purely controversial and, especially in the eighteenth century, antireligious character of this body of writing. It deals with the religious topics, but deals with them either by way of dispute (the quarrel of Protestantism with Catholicism, of various sects with one another, in which the authors are busy mainly with denouncing and slandering their opponents), or in a purely aesthetic or negative way, like the work of Rabelais, Jodelle's *Eugène* (1552), Régnier's (seventeenth century) work, Diderot's *La religieuse*, most of the writings of the Encyclopedists, of the men of the Enlightenment, of the materialists, of the Communists Mably, Morelli, and the like. Even in the writings of somewhat more positively religious type, for instance that of the Deists, the religious question is reduced to the almost purely empirical problem of finding what line of conduct and mentality is most conducive to the happiness of the empirical nature.

Somewhat similar is the situation in German, English, Italian, Dutch, and other European literatures, except for Russia and the Slavic countries generally, which lagged here also and where the same trend appeared later but, once it had appeared, proceeded much faster in its tempo. The fact of this quantitative and qualitative decline of the religious content of the literature is so evident and so indisputable, and is in such an agreement with the same trend in other fields of art, that there is no need to argue it extensively.

Other *inner* characteristics of the literature of the period clearly show the same symptoms of the rise of the Sensate and a progressive drying up of the Ideational. Take *asceticism and Ideational otherworldliness versus Sensualism* (erotic, nutritional, *i.e.*, gluttony and drinking, immoderacy in various kinds of refined and coarse sensual pleasures). Our study particularly of the German and the French literature shows, first, that *the ascetico-religious ideals and aspirations sound less and less often, and less and less strongly, as we pass from the fourteenth to the twentieth century.* From the fourteenth century to the twentieth century, the satirical, the condemnatory, the ironical, and generally the adverse attitude toward asceticism, religious piety, monasteries, monks, the clergy, the Church, Scripture, chastity, celibacy — in brief, almost all the religious-Ideational values of Christianity — systematically increases. These topics become more and more the favorites for every kind of denunciation, for ridicule, for satire. To them are ascribed all imaginable evils, especially erotic and sexual depravity and immorality. Various types of this adverse criticism are exemplified in Boccaccio's *Decameron*, with its sex-conscious nuns, monks, and priests; in Jodelle's comedy *Eugène* (1552), in which an abbé hires a chaplain to serve as a pimp and to find a husband for his mistress; in Antoine de la Salle's *Cent nouvelles nouvelles;* in Cyrano de Bergerac; in Rabelais's *Gargantua;* in Molière's comedies; in Diderot's *La religieuse;* in the satires of Régnier (especially the eighth); in Swift's *Tale of a Tub;* in Le Sage's *Gil Blas;* in several works of the Enlightenment, like Voltaire's *Pucelle;* and in hundreds of others, like the writings of Anatole France, Flaubert, Zola, like Sinclair Lewis's *Elmer Gantry*, and other iconoclastic and muckraking works of recent years in all the Western countries, including America.

This decline of religious and ascetic Ideationalism was followed by the *progress of straightforward Sensatism from the fourteenth to the twentieth century.*

First, let us take the main changes in the description of *love.* In Italy, in place of the Idealistic love of Dante for Beatrice, a love almost free from any signs of Sensatism, comes Petrarch's love for Laura, still delicate and not devoid of Idealization, but certainly more permeated by the Sensate motives than Dante's. Then comes Boccaccio's *Decameron*, where love is already sensual, though served lightly and with gallantry. It is already a love almost purely of the bedroom. And this strain continues and more openly develops into a mere sex physiology, an even perverted sex physiology. It is enough to mention Aretino's obscenities in his *Ragionamenti* and other works, Beccadelli's *Hermaphroditus*, Giraldi's *Hecatommithi*, Lorenzo Valla's *Voluptas*, Lorenzo the Magnificent's *Carpe diem* and the *Facetiae*, Berni's burlesque lyric, Politian's buffoonisms, and other works of high literary attainment, to see the enormous change in the modes of the treatment of love. From the heavenly love of the first medieval period, and the sublime and delicate knightly love of the second period, we are now reduced to mere sex affairs and bedroom entertainment.

Even somewhat less sensual works, perfectly decent and good, according to the time, in their advice and standards (like the popular and widely

The second part of the *Roman de la Rose* had already exhibited the trend. In the fifteenth and the subsequent centuries it was sharpened. Instead of the Idealistic love found in the works of Marie de France, in the first part of the *Roman* and in the *Livre des cent ballades*, and instead of the gallant and still Idealistic (though less than before) pattern of love of the romances and epics, there come now in the fifteenth and sixteenth centuries the open sensuality of Antoine de la Salle's *Cent nouvelles nouvelles*, *Les quinze joies de mariage*, and *Petit Jehan de Saintré*, the riotousness and sensuality of François Villon, the sophistication and eroticism (with a religious flavor) of Charles d'Orleans, the sensuality and realism of Jodelle, the unruliness and satiric sensuality of Rabelais, the more delicate sensuality of Marguerite of Navarre (imitator of Boccaccio's *Decameron*), the romanticism even of the Pléiade (Du Bellay, Ronsard, and others in whose works the *Carpe diem* motive is observable), and the salty coarseness of large numbers of the comedies and *sottises* and *farces*. In the seventeenth century there are Cyrano de Bergerac, Régnier, Scarron, C. Sorel, Furetière, and others with their satirical, picaresque, "naturalistic," and cynical novels and lyrics.

After a slight reaction in the second part of the seventeenth century, with its "classical revival," the trend is resumed in the eighteenth century and proceeds *crescendo* in the disreputable works of Voltaire, like *La Pucelle* and the less obscene *Jeannot et Colin*, and others; in Le Sage's novels of the interminable sexual adventures of a traveler, *Gil Blas*, from one bedroom to another; in the works of Marivaux; in the half-obscene *La religieuse* and *Les bijoux indiscrète* of Diderot; in Rousseaux's *Con-*

fessions; and in other works. In the nineteenth and twentieth centuries the main topic of French literature is sensual and sexual love, both normal and pathological: the love of the old and of the young; of the poor and of the rich; love bought, love granted; love in this way, love in that — but love always hovering near the bedroom and rarely if ever idealized and never ideationalized. This concerns equally Chateaubriand, Mme. de Staël, George Sand, Musset, Stendhal, Balzac, Hugo, Mérimée, Baudelaire, Zola, Maupassant, Verlaine, Daudet, France, Flaubert, Goncourt, and others. The main difference between them is that some, like Maupassant, made the sex affair their main and almost only topic; some enjoyed particularly poetizing and depicting either sadistic forms of sex (Mirbeau and others), or pathological forms (for instance, with a corpse, Baudelaire, Verlaine); while others described mainly the predominant sexual-sensual life of married or unmarried heroes who did not show any sadism or abnormality.

It is true that the Idealistic representation of love did not disappear at once from literature after the fourteenth century. A few writers, like Christine de Pisan and others, continued the earlier tradition. But their voices were drowned out by the large Sensate chorus of the majority of the writers and literati. Even such Idealistic voices as these grow fewer and weaker in the high literature as we move from the fifteenth toward the twentieth century.

The trend unfolded itself more slowly in Germany and the Scandinavian countries. But in essentials it proceeded there in the same direction.

In other countries, such as Spain and England, the trend was the same, though in each of them there have been local variations in accordance with local conditions.

So much for the trend toward Sensatism as it is reflected in the treatment of love. All in all, it is the same as that which we found in the field of painting and sculpture and music.

But there are also other inner traits which make the trend still clearer. Take such a matter as the reflection of *economic problems* in literature. We saw that in the first medieval period such problems were virtually absent from the literary work. In the Idealistic period they emerge but still occupy a small place and in very few writings. As we pass from the fifteenth to the twentieth century, they begin to occupy more and more space and become increasingly important, until, finally, in the nineteenth and twentieth centuries, they rank among the most important topics of literature, almost as important as love. The economic aspects of life, of love itself, began to be depicted, dissected, chewed over by almost all the literary men, who now depicted poverty, exploitation, the wickedness or generosity of the rich, the perpetration of crimes through poverty; who now made apologies for scoundrels, "unfortunate" criminals, prostitutes, idiots, paranoiacs, and all those whose failure is conceived as the result of poverty. Side by side with these the laboring and poorer classes enter literature; and this has given many an opportunity to depict the avarice, greed, unfaithfulness, hypocrisy, and so on, of many types of personality and social groups. In brief, in the nineteenth- and the twentieth-century economic problems, economic motives, economic behavior, economic ideology, the economic interpretation of almost all the actions of the heroes of literary works, became a mania, an obsession, a fashion, the sign of a supposedly deep insight into human nature, and the prophetic and scientific sense, mind, and intuition of the author. In this respect literature reflects the same physiological-sensual interpretation of man — so inescapable in a ripe Sensate culture — which by so-called science is reflected in the economic interpretation of history and of all social life and of almost all human behavior.

Another symptom of the nature of a culture mentality is found in the *kind of heroes* depicted by its literary works. In the first period — the Ideational — of painting, sculpture, music, and literature, the heroes were God Himself, other superhuman beings (the Madonna, the Holy Ghost, the apostles and saints), and a number of absolute values. In the Idealistic period, the personages were semideified heroes: great knights and other incarnations of the positive values of empirical and semiempirical reality. After the fourteenth century their place is taken by the common run of people, by merchants, servants, peasants, polished courtiers, artisans, etc.; then by rogues, criminals, prostitutes, failures, derelicts, and the wretched; by pathological types; by murderers, swindlers, exploiters, hypocrites, scoundrels, profligates, idiots, morons; by various picturesque and picaresque personalities.

From the seventeenth to the twentieth century this gallery has been enriched *crescendo* by a more common, negative, and disgusting collection of still lower, still less noble types of human derelicts, and of the sweepings of social sewers; until finally we are faced with the overwhelming crowd of pathological and negative personages which monopolize contemporary literature.

Any careful reader of present-day writing can but agree with the following statements: from the seventeenth century on, most of the heroes of literature

are either pathological or are on their way to becoming such. Shakespeare attentively follows their insanity and makes them exhibit scientifically all the stages which lead from soundness to insanity. The folly of Lear is complete; also that of Ophelia; Hamlet is rather sane than insane at the beginning, but the events give him such a great shock that his mind is disturbed. The pretended folly becomes real without the possibility of our marking the moment of this transformation. . . .

This is said of Shakespeare and early "naturalism." Of our contemporary realistic-naturalistic literature, the same author says:

The persons of the realistic novel and the theater of our times do not fare better than the Shakespearean heroes. These are also maladies, vice, passion, virtue itself being, according to the materialist doctrine, a mere consequence of a certain nervous situation. . . . Psychology is reduced to pathology, and physiological anatomy replaces the ancient moral anatomy. Try to pay attention to the moral aspect of every book, every play, every picture that appears: you will not find in any either beautiful sanity or genuine virtue. Everything that is not quite negative is of an honest mediocrity and quite hopeless. Virtue is more and more despised and outfashioned; it ends by being put into the group of manners and usages which our scepticism ridicules pitilessly. . . . On the other hand, the bad subjects of every kind, the immoral, the debauched, the criminal, abound. Each personage has his own "neurosis," his own ulcer; and each limps somewhat. These persons wear, now the blouse of a laborer, now the full evening dress of society; but they rarely differ from one another under these disguises. One can see at once where they came from: they escaped one fine night from the insane asylum (la cour des Miracles).

Thus knights and aristocracy, kings and saints, were replaced (as in portraiture in the field of painting) more and more by merchants, the rich, the bourgeois, and the powerful upstarts; then these began to be replaced more and more by serfs, servants, valets, artisans, peasants, farmers, laborers, proletarians; then side by side with these classes there began a big parade of the poor, of the oppressed, of the unfortunate of all kinds in company with rogues, gamins, ragamuffins, hypocrites, mistresses, profligates of both sexes, married and unmarried, prostitutes; the victims of gigantic passions, unbalanced and abnormal. Then came the romantic criminal and adventurer, the pirate and buccaneer; the savage, either of the Rousseau type, or the "caveman," or enchanting sheik, the exotic Oriental; then just criminals — terrible and plain, with the detective, of course, either clever or stupid. Then, to put the final touches on the trend, the most varied collection of pathological types is let out upon the front page of literature: idiots and morons, often romantically introduced; paranoiacs of different kinds; the pathological in sex, in crime, in virtue (rarely), in body, in mind, in general behavior, in everything imaginable. Side by side with them there parade the common — quite common — and almost always dishonest and hypocritical, and often sexual, Babbitts, or Elmer Gantrys, or Arrowsmiths, or Forsytes, or the Wang-Lungs, or the Trader Horns, or this or that farmer, merchant, duke, proletarian, secretary, stenographer, doctor, newspaperman, teacher, housewife, miner, carpenter, minister, or other ordinary, mediocre, insignificant, unheroic, flat kind of human beings.

Such has been the trend — a trend identical with what we have seen in painting and other fields of art.

I have somewhat overstressed the case, for the sake of brevity and clarity, but even if we introduce all the necessary shadings and all the more complex variations of the general tendency, the essence of the characterization which we have just discussed remains perfectly valid. This can be demonstrated in detail, step by step, century by century, in the major literature of practically all the European countries. If we take *epics* and *novels*, for example, and examine the nature of their heroes, we get the following sequence as we move from the fifteenth to the twentieth century. *In the fourteenth, fifteenth, sixteenth, and the first part of the seventeenth centuries the heroes of epics are still drawn on a grand scale, and the epics deal with persons and events far above the level of the mediocre, the vulgar, the everyday, the banal.* This is true of almost all the writings of this class, whether the heroic, mythological, or Christian. Take, for example, in Italy, Boccaccio's *Teseide* and the *Nymphs of Fiesole*, Pulci's *Morgante*, Boiardo's *Orlando Amoroso*, Ariosto's *Orlando Furioso*, Tasso's *Jerusalem Delivered;* in Spain and Portugal, Marini's *Adonis*, Camoëns's *Lusiada*, Ercilla's *Arancana;* and generally in Europe, Ronsard's *La Franciade*, Zrinyi's *The Zriniade*, Spenser's *Faerie Queene*, D'Aubigné's *Tragiques*, Guillaume du Bartas's *Judith*, Arrebo's *Hexaemeron*, Sternhjelm's *Hercules* and, stretching into the middle of the seventeenth century, Milton's great epic, *Paradise Lost.* These are but the outstanding representatives of a much larger group of such epics, which were produced in these centuries.

"Beginning with the end of the seventeenth century, the classical, the romanesque, or the religious epics lose their ground." And with their disappearance the heroic and grand personages and events disappear also from the literature of that kind, to give place to the less and less heroic persons and happenings.

Similarly heroic are the leading characters of the *roman*, the *novel*, and the *story* of the same centuries. This is true, for example, of the heroes of the chivalric romances so widely produced and read at this time: the cycle of the Arthurian romances (Malory) and especially the innumerable Amadis epics beginning with the *Amadis de Gaule* by Montalvo (1492) — still idealistic, clean, and romantic — and ending with countless imitations of it: *Esplandian*, *Florisand*, *Primaleon*, *Palmerin of Olive*, *Palmerin of England*, *Lisuart*, *Florisel*, *Clarisel*, *Belianis*, *Amadis of Greece*, and so on, by F. de Silva, F. de Moraes, and many others, who flourished mainly between 1510 and 1580. Their heroes are still wonderful knights, marvelous in their achievements, brave, unconquerable, audacious, just, noble, loyal, enchanted by love and, for its own and chivalry's sake, performing great and heroic deeds. With the end of the sixteenth century the chivalric romances, like the heroic epics, disappear, and the place of their heroes begins to be taken by much less heroic persons and types. The note of mockery at these heroes and heroic epics and romances had of course already appeared in the sixteenth century (Rabelais's *Pantagruel and Gargantua*, 1535–1552; Cervantes's *Don Quixote*, 1605–1615), but in the fourteenth, the fifteenth, and even in the sixteenth century they still blossomed, and their decline began only in the seventeenth, in which only a few of such works still continued, by way of imitation, to appear (for instance, Georges's and Madelaine's romances imitating the Amadis type).

Then as we move on toward the twentieth century, in the novels and romances and tales and in the more prosaic literature, the heroic element tends to be replaced by nonheroic heroes, by "average" mortals, as well as by the picturesque and picaresque characters and then later by the negative and pathological types.

In the sixteenth century already side by side with the declining heroic epics and romances there appeared the *pastoral romances*. They are represented in the sixteenth and seventeenth centuries by innumerable Arcadias (of Sannazaro, Lope de Vega, Philip Sidney, and others), by numerous Diana Amorosas (of J. de Montemayor, Gil Polo, and others), by the *Galatea* of Cervantes, by the *Young Girl and the Woman* of Ribeiro, by *L'Astrée* of Honoré d'Urfé, by the *Euphues* of John Lyly, and so on. Even in this brand of romances the heroic element tends to decrease as we pass from the pastorals of the end of the fifteenth to those of the end of the seventeenth centuries.

The next step in this trend among the novels and romances leads to the *picaresque*, *satirical*, and *realistic* tales, novels, and romances.

The *picaresque* novel as a notable current emerges a little later than the pastoral, somewhere in the second part of the sixteenth century (before the fifteenth we have hardly any of it in artistic literature, and of course it is entirely absent in the Ideational period), and reaches its climax only in the seventeenth and eighteenth centuries, when the pastoral romances had somewhat declined.

It is evident that this type is a further downward step from the idealistic and noble personages of the heroic and pastoral epics and romances. Examples of this kind of picaresque novels are the anonymous *Life of Lazarillo of Tormes* (1544), Mateo Aleman's *Life of the Picaro Guzman*, the *Picara Justina* (with its woman hero), Quevedo's *El Buscon* (1626), Espinel's *Marcos of Obregon*, *Till Eulenspiegel*, Grimmelshausen's *Simplicissimus* (1669), Cervantes's *Don Quixote*, the imitative works of Thomas Nashe, and others.

Here again as we move from the earlier to the later types of the *picaro*, especially to some of the eighteenth century, like *Gil Blas*, he becomes, as it were, more and more picaresque, more sexual, of a lower order, less heroic, and even less romantic.

Then, simultaneously with the picaresque novel or a little later (mainly in the seventeenth century), there emerges and grows the *realistic novel* (in its diverse varieties: classic, romantic, sentimental, etc.) and *satirical works*. The very name *realistic* or *naturalistic* implies that such a literature reflects mainly what is seen and met with most frequently and most commonly in the empirical reality. This means the average, mediocre, most common type of human. In the earlier stages of the realistic novel people and events were rather normal and sound, though neither heroic nor sublime; in the later stages the pathological, the diseased, the unsound aspects of empirical reality, the social dregs and sweepings, began to be depicted more and more, thus dragging even the realistic literature down from its common and normal level to the very gutters of social life and to the debased and perverse types of human personality.

Simultaneously with the realistic novel there arose to the level of conscious literature, the *satirical*, *ironical*, and *comical* tale and novel.

Now even within the satirical literature itself, as it developed, there was manifest the same downward movement in its debasing, tearing to pieces, ridiculing, smashing, slandering progressively greater and more fundamental values. If the satirical works of the earlier phase ridiculed the stupid or comic or silly aspects of an old husband married to a young wife or vice versa, the gluttony of an abbot, the difficulty of an adventurous lover, the shortsightedness of an elderly chaperon, they rarely if ever attacked the fundamental sociocultural values and institutions — religious, scientific, moral, artistic: God and the saints and the credo of religion, the family, the government, the Church, chastity, heroism, genius, duty, sacrifice, and so on. As time went on and as we move into the eighteenth, the nineteenth, and the twentieth centuries, the black and poisonous brush of satire reaches higher, and more boldly stains and vilifies the fundamental values, until at the present moment there is nothing left which has not been slandered, ridiculed, and debased by it. Religion, God, the saints, the Virgin, angels, devils, sacraments, Paradise, Inferno, the Credo, the State, the Government, aristocracy, nobility, talent, genius, sacrifice, altruism, marriage, the family, asceticism, idealism, chastity, faithfulness, loyalty, science, philosophy, moral duty, property, order, truth, beauty, righteousness, man himself — everything and everybody is slandered and satirized and defiled. I cannot find any single value whatever which has escaped.

To sum up: *from God and His Kingdom and His saints, the heroes of literature became the semideified knights of the Idealistic period; from these they turned into more and more human beings, until everything heroic disappeared almost entirely in the realistic literature and the scene was entirely occupied by ordinary mortals with their ordinary life events, which in their turn began to be replaced more and more by the subnormal and negative types and events of human society. The sequence — purely religious literature, heroic epic, chivalric romance, pastoral romance, picaresque story, realistic and satirical fiction — is the track along which these landmarks denote the main stages of the long-distance descent of literature from the Ideational heaven to the Sensual sewer.*

Thus far we have been concerned mainly with narrative prose (epics, stories, romances, novels, etc.). The *drama* and *poetry* have been intentionally excluded. But now let us briefly consider the "evolution" of these forms as well. All in all, the trend toward the progressive lowering of the type of heroes occurs in the drama no less than in narrative literature. The chief figures of the *medieval mysteries* were God, the saints, the angels, and other divine beings. The heroes of the subsequent semireligious plays and *moralities* were already of a lower order, but side by side with the mortals or with even the sinful types there always were present the religious or allegorical figures of the positive virtues and the semidivine and divine beings.

For the fifteenth and sixteenth centuries (except the comedies and the farces) this concerns the plays in Spain and Portugal of Juan del Engina (1465–1539; *Resurrection*, *Christmas*, etc.), of Gil Vicente (b. 1460), in part of Ines Pereira (*c.* 1523), of Juan de la Cueva (1550–1610), all with their religious or moralizing or national dramas; or even many of the dramatic pastorals of the sixteenth and of the first part of the seventeenth century.

The heroic characters still remain the main figures of the drama and tragedy of the seventeenth and of the beginning of the eighteenth century. This is true of the greatest plays of the period in England, from Shakespeare to Dryden, in France from Corneille and Racine to most of the tragedies of Voltaire, in Italy from the atrocious tragedies of Cinthio or Speroni to the less violent pastorals and operas. Similar was the situation in Spain, and also in Germany, though in a somewhat different way (Schiller, Goethe, the earlier Gottsched, Lessing, C. F. Weisse, and others).

In all these dramas and tragedies of Europe the heroes are often abnormal, often pathological, sometimes insane, but they are "heroic" in their passions, deeds, vices, and virtues.

From about the second half of the eighteenth century (with the short interlude of the Revolutionary theater at the end of the eighteenth and the beginning of the nineteenth) the classical tragedy declines, and with its decline the heroes of the drama become decidedly more "human," less heroic, and more the common type of persons.

Even in this respect there has also been a steadily increasing fashion to choose the hero or the heroine from somewhat abnormal, pathological, and defective types or criminal groups. Here, as in other fields of literature and art, the same gravitation toward the "social sewer" is also quite noticeable.

This trend in the theater is still more conspicuous *in comedy*, considered separately. Comedy did not exist — on the level of the great literature — in the Ideational period. It appeared but was still rare and mild in the period of Idealism. Its real emergence as a strong current in the main stream of literature was about the fifteenth and the sixteenth centuries. And it reached great heights in Spain in the sixteenth and seventeenth centuries with the plays of Lope de Rueda, Torres Naharro, Juan de la Cueva, Lope de Vega, de Castro, Tirso de Molina, Alarcón, and Calderon. In other countries comedy emerged somewhat later still. Thus from its beginning it is a specific brand of the Sensate literature. It has been developing progressively in Sensate quality during the subsequent centuries, not only quantitatively but also qualitatively, ridiculing, satirizing, and stressing the comical and the negative aspects of greater and greater values. The early comedy was rather mild, poking fun mainly at the delicate situations of a passionate love, with its bouffon its dame, its old husband and young wife. But soon it began to touch more sharply ever higher institutions and values, until in the nineteenth and twentieth centuries practically nothing has remained sacred, nothing has escaped being ridiculed, satirized, sometimes defiled by comedy and theatrical satire.

Of other *inner* evidences of the predominantly Sensate nature of the Western literature after the fourteenth century I shall mention briefly only a few. If we take such symptoms as *duty versus sensate comfort* (and this symptom is certainly a good indicator of the Ideational or Sensate mentality), the study of the conduct of persons in literature shows that, as we pass from the fourteenth century to the present time, duty begins to be sacrificed more and more in favor of comfort, and the consequent growing neglect of obligations — whether religious, moral, civic, familistic, political, or what not — is more and more approved by writers.

Statistical study of the problem is impossible for obvious reasons. But roughly, the change in this respect may, on the basis of our study of the French and partly of the German literature from this standpoint, be represented by the following figures.

The percentage of cases in which duty is placed above comfort and material convenience is, in the literature before the twelfth century, about 100; in the twelfth about 75; in the thirteenth and fourteenth, about 60; in the fifteenth, about 50; in the sixteenth and the first part of the seventeenth, about 60; in the later seventeenth, about 50; in the eighteenth, 35; in the nineteenth and twentieth, about 30 to 25. The figures for other countries would probably be somewhat different; but there is hardly any doubt that their main trend would be roughly the same. This quantitative increase of the frequency of the violation of duty in favor of Sensate comfort, convenience, and expediency is in perfect agreement with a similar trend in the ethical mentality for these centuries as will be shown in subsequent parts of this work.

Now we may add to this increasing frequency of the violation of duty, the evidence of the changing tone with which these transgressions are treated in literary works. Let us take as an example the cases of the violation of marital loyalty and family duty. In the writings of even so late a date as the middle of the nineteenth century (*e.g.*, Flaubert's *Madame Bovary*, or Leo Tolstoi's *Anna Karenina*, or Dumas fils's *La Dame aux camélias*, or Constant's *Adolphe*, or others), the breach of duty is almost invariably depicted as a tragedy, and in most cases the violators pay for it very dearly, often with their life. At the end of the nineteenth and the beginning of the twentieth century, such violations become rather common, the heroes marry and remarry, change their bed partners easily and cheerfully and, as it were, with the blessing of the author.

The other side of this situation is the *increasing frequency with which heroes in literature revolt against any duty, any inconvenient bond, obligation, or, as they liberally style it, "social convention."* They become more and more "revolters," whether conscious or unconscious, reasoning or unreasoning, in their actions. And many of the popular works of the period have been popular just because their heroes and heroines possessed this trait, of which authors approved. Revolters against God and religion, against "political tyranny," against economic oppression, against domestic slavery, against everything and everybody, have arisen in swarms. When, for some reason or other, an author could not find his rebel in the upper or the middle classes, or in the honest and respectable groups, he turned to robbers (Schiller and others), criminals (Hugo and others), prostitutes (Dostoevsky and others), or to plain housewives (Flaubert, Sudermann, and others), and skillfully dressed up these types and presented them in such a sympathetic and dazzling form that the public heartily approved him and his heroes — always in the name of "freedom," "the maximum happiness for the maximum number of people," and of similar slogans.

This increasing frequency of the breach of duty and of the revolt against all inconvenient conventions and values is certain evidence of a rising *individualism*, as opposed to the social or collective aspects of literature.

We have seen that individualism is something belonging organically to the Sensate art, culture, and mentality. We shall meet it in practically all compartments of the Sensate culture. Hence, the individualism, egotism, and eccentricity of the literature of the period is additional evidence of its predominantly Sensate character.

In painting, sculpture, and music the Ideational and Idealistic creations are calm, serene, and imperturbable, while the Sensate are *dynamic, passionate, pathetic, sensational, emotional.* The same is to be observed in literature. Even the lives of the saints, when they tell the most horrible or pathetic events, like tortures, recount them in a calm way, just as the Bible narrates the creation of the world or the passion of Christ in the same imperturbable manner. When we turn to literature after the fourteenth century, we find that calmness and serenity and imperturbability have vanished. It becomes more and more passionate; it begins to strive intentionally to be pathetic, emotional, to impress, to make a sensation, to "move," to "strike."

Every means is used to achieve that purpose. Hence, incidentally, the inevitable development of the mystery, detective, adventure, spook, horror stories, and novels, whether in the form of the Gothic tales of Walpole, Clara Reeve, Anna Radcliffe, "Monk" Lewis, and others of the eighteenth century, or in the form of the contemporary Sherlock Holmes crime stories and the innumerable detective-mystery-adventure stories, which provide a kind of "relaxation" for most of us. Hence also the "sentimental" literary works, whether in the form of the lachrymose *Pamela* of Richardson and novels of the type written by Sterne and Rousseau, or in the form of the "pastoral stories" of the seventeenth and eighteenth centuries, or in the form of the contemporary "weeping" novels which depict the sufferings of the poor, of noble but persecuted criminals, of the pure virgins who become prostitutes, of the great geniuses who become failures, of the saviors of mankind who turn into mere parlor socialists or first-class murderers or loafers of the type of Jean Christophe.

The literature of a Sensate culture and mentality must be dynamic and ever-changing. Perhaps investigators like Drommel and others, who claim that about every fifteen or thirty years there has been a change in the fundamental form of literature, stress unduly the periodicity and the regularity of the change. But they seem to be right in the contention that the literature of the last three centuries did indeed undergo rapid changes in fundamental forms. Even from the fifteenth to seventh centuries the main forms of literary works were changing in periods of some sixty to eighty years. This was the case with the blossoming of the heroic epic, of the chivalric romance, of the pastoral *roman*, of the picaresque story, of the heroic or classical drama and tragedy. Still shorter were the periods for the rise of the sentimental novel, the mystery story, and what not. At the present moment the tempo of change as well as the passion for variety is well shown by the kind of best sellers and books promoted by various "literary guilds," "Book of the Month

Clubs," and similar organizations for the spread of the standardized pabulum. They change in character with magic rapidity. Today *Trader Horn*, tomorrow Ludwig's intolerable concoction on Napoleon, the day after a psychoanalytical sex story, after that something romantic on China or India or Soviet Russia, and then . . . well, one cannot enumerate all the surprising "variety" and astounding contrasts presented by the ever-changing best sellers and "hits" of contemporary literature, which have their day and are forgotten within a few weeks.

Finally, the trait of *quantity and colossalism*, as against *quality*, is a typical sign of the Sensate culture and its art. This also is highly conspicuous in contemporary literature. One of its manifestations is the judgment of what work is good and what is poor. The most unquestionable contemporary criterion of this is the *number of copies sold*. If a work is a best seller, it is great. Its author is a genius; he becomes "famous." This is our main and almost only standard. Its very nature indicates the "colossalism" pervading our literature.

B. *External Traits*. The *Sensate literature is predominantly naturalistic and realistic*, like the Visual painting. Zola, as one of the most prominent exponents of the realistic or naturalistic style in literature, expressed well its essence: "Our quarrel with the idealists consists exclusively in the fact that we start with observation and experience while they start with absolutes."

Judged by the modern realistic and naturalistic literature "realism can then be defined as a system which reproduces from reality only that which impresses the senses most directly, that is, the external and the material aspect of human beings and objects."

This realistic style emerged, on the level of the major literature, only after the fourteenth century, in the form of the realistic novel, of the so-called *tableaux de moeurs*, and in part of the comedies. Afterwards it developed so greatly that in the nineteenth and twentieth centuries it has had a virtual monopoly.

An exception to this appears, at the very end of the nineteenth century and in the twentieth, in the work of such literary schools as the *symbolist*, *futurist*, *surrealist*, and others similar. But these have been, so far, minor rivulets. Moreover, like the anti-Visual painting and the anti-Sensate music, none of these currents is either Ideational or Idealistic; they are but a manifestation of reaction against realism and naturalism. In this respect they are important, but they have nothing in common with Ideational symbolism or Idealistic allegory, whether in their external form or in their inward nature. Like cubism, they are in several respects even more Sensate than the standard realistic literature of these centuries. They are simultaneously an extreme form of the Sensate and a revolt against it, and in this they are similar to corresponding currents in other contemporaneous fields of art. But they are not, as yet, the patterns of the coming Ideational or Idealistic literature.

C. *Criticism.* Finally, the art and literary criticism of that period also has all the earmarks of the Sensate type, already familiar to the reader from the discussion of the Graeco-Roman culture.

In the period from about 1530 to 1600

the extant critical writing, excluding mere rhetorical schoolbooks, probably exceeds, and very largely exceeds, the total of classical and mediaeval work on the subject which we possess, even inclusive of school books. . . . For the first time criticism . . . received a really large share of the intellectual attention of the period.

A great number of treatises on poetry (*Arte poetica, De poeta, Poetics, Versie regole*) appear. "In 1600 criticism is a classed and recognized department of literature."

With the advance of the seventeenth century the purely aesthetic standpoint crystallizes in the form of the codes and canons formulated by the Academies. It was a sensible, rationalistic, moderated, scientific, even mathematical Sensate criticism, free from vagaries, from any extreme and unbalanced radicalism and eccentricity, still slightly touched by the fading light of Idealism, and well protected from the vulgar, grossly hedonistic sensualism. And it reigned through the seventeenth century and in part in the eighteenth century.

The eighteenth century continued it by sheer inertia, but soon began to move in the Sensate direction.

Now the *professional critic* makes his big appearance, now the professional aesthetician, the professional theorizer on art and literature. More than that: he becomes a powerful figure not only in literature but in social life and politics. The critic becomes a kind of lawgiver and intellectual and social leader, often a figure with whom kings and prelates and magnates and powerful nobles have to reckon. He gets a big following among all sorts of people from clever politicians to hysterical females. Literary problems become one of the main topics of conversation in any gathering, from the tavern to the salon. Art and literary education begin to be one of the prerequisites of any "educated" man or woman. One can apply literally what Persius says of his Roman contemporaries: "*Ecce inter pocula quaerunt Romulidae satieri, quid dia poemata narrent.*" And the same, probably even greater, *ventosa et enormis loquacitas* on art and literary topics began among the upper and the middle classes. Such problems were discussed everywhere and by everyone. Concomitantly, critical journals, reviews, articles, pamphlets, essays, treatises, not to mention the number of critics and reviewers and "Book of the Month Clubs," increased and expanded greatly. In brief, the situation is an accurate example, on a large scale, of what usually takes place in such a phase of culture and of what took place in the history of the Graeco-Roman during an analogous period.

On the other hand, as in Rome, most of this criticism is empty, ignorant, thoughtless, negligible, so far as its inner content is concerned. It is, however, powerful in other respects: it determines the "best sellers" and thus the success or failure, the fame or tragedy, the victory or defeat, the poverty or fortune of the artists and writers. It also shapes the taste of the public itself toward good or bad. In these and other respects its influence is often in inverse proportion to its inner worth.

As it had once done in Rome, criticism also became commercialized through and through. As the level of the taste of the large masses is, in most cases, far from being very high, such production for a large market tends to lower the standard of both creative works and criticism. Hence the inner emptiness of both at the present day. We produce great quantities of literary and critical writings; and yet, most of the best sellers are forgotten within a few months or, at the best, a few years; and, in spite of the great number of the literary and art critics, there is hardly a single figure among them who is great.

Finally, a kind of anarchy in the field of criticism must be expected in such a phase; and we find this to be so indeed. Since most of the theories and principles are fragmentary, poorly thought out, every critic follows his own fancy or the fancy of the financial bosses of the papers and magazines for which he writes. The result is confusion, superficiality, bickering between factions and cliques, each trying to promulgate its own Lilliputian standard.

Under such conditions criticism is beginning to lose its prestige and influence. Even now best sellers are determined not so much by critics as by various business agencies and commercial techniques, like the group of persons upon whom depends the distribution of a given book throughout all the public libraries, like the amount of advertising done for the book, or like the success of the publisher in getting the book included among the monthly book selections of various "book clubs," and so on. Most of these agencies are practically anonymous and purely profit making, administered by men who make no claim to be connoisseurs of art or literature, or critics. This situation is a kind of Nemesis for the progressively declining criticism itself.

The emptiness of modern criticism explains also the emergence at the very end of the nineteenth and in the twentieth century of the *criticism of the critics*. It is a kind of revolt against Sensate judgments of whatever kind — a revolt similar to that against the Visual painting, and the Sensate music, architecture, and literature, such as has been marked above. It has manifested itself in various forms, from Leo Tolstoi's sarcastic castigation in his *What Is Art?* and in his attack on Shakespeare and contemporary literature and art and criticism, to the *manifestos* of mainly young and wild hotheads — futurists, symbolists, surrealists, and other "arch-modernists," who violently and quite disrespectfully assail the predominant Sensate critical currents, declare them to be outmoded, and reject them practically entire. In their negative reaction these revolutionaries are quite definite and are therefore a symptom of the crisis in the Sensate criticism. But in their positive program they have not yet found a new path leading to a new and great kingdom of art and literature and criticism.

Thus from the fifteenth century to the present time literature does indeed show all the characteristics of a predominantly Sensate mentality, whether it is considered from the standpoint of its inner properties, or its external forms, or of the nature of the art and literary criticism of the period.

VI. General Summary on Art Fluctuation

Our study of the fluctuation of the Ideational and Sensate forms of art in its main fields warrants the following conclusions.

A. The history of the Graeco-Roman and Western European art shows that the long-time fluctuation or alternation of the Sensate and Ideational forms really occurs in all fields of art: painting, sculpture, music, architecture, literature, and drama.

B. When one of these forms becomes dominant, various traits logically belonging to it begin in fact to infiltrate into the art and manifest themselves in all fields. These characteristics are at once logical elements of each of these forms and symptomatic of its presence. In other words, they are logically and in fact associated with each of these forms and with one another and should be expected, and can be foreseen, if we learn that the predominant art of such and such a period is either Sensate or Ideational or Idealistic, and if the art in question is indeed integrated. Most of these specific traits have been discussed above in some detail. Here, for the sake of clarity and conciseness, the most important of them are briefly repeated in the form of an inventory of the elements of each of the main styles.

Are the association of these traits in characteristic groups and the association of these groups each with its proper form of art something peculiar only to the Graeco-Roman and the Western arts, or can they pretend to the status of a uniformity of a general type, not only in time — that is, in the course of the Graeco-Roman and the Western culture — but also in space, in the sense that these specific traits can be expected to occur in any Ideational art no matter where and when the culture, the group, the personality, whether it concern the Hindu, the Tibetan,

ELEMENTS AND SPECIFIC CHARACTERISTICS OF THE MAIN STYLES OF ART

Ideational	*Idealistic*	*Sensate*
	A. Inner Traits	
1. Predominantly religious topics.	1. Religious-secular, heroic.	1. Secular predominantly.
2. Persons are God, deities, superhuman beings, saints. Mainly "otherworldly."	2. Semidivine and human heroic and positive types, noble, beautiful, virtuous. Abstract idealized types rather than individual persons.	2. Mortals, common type of people; at the later stages picturesque, picaresque, negative, pathological: rogues, urchins, insane, criminal, etc. Mainly individual persons with their purely individual traits and environment.
3. Events dealt with: transcendental events in the kingdom of the invisible, mainly; or the visible signs of such events.	3. Noble, heroic, positive, virtuous deeds and events, partly in the super-Sensate world, partly in the Sensate world.	3. Everyday events, deeds, actions, of a common character, or picturesque, amusing adventures of the same Sensate world.
4. Emotional tone: otherworldly, ascetic, antisensual: negative to the joys and pleasures of this world. Unquestioning faith.	4. Idealistic; partly otherworldly, partly earthly, but noble, sublime, pure, free from hedonistic emotionalism, from pathetic, macabre passions. Serene and calm. Faith in harmony with reason and the senses.	4. Emotional, sentimental, passionate, pathetic, often macabre, still more often sensual and sexual. Skepticism and cerebral intellectualism.
5. Little of nudity, and even then ascetic and nonfleshly.	5. Some nudity, but it is neither ascetic nor sensual. It is abstract in its idealized forms	5. A great deal of nudity. It is erotic, sensual, voluptuous, and fleshly.
6. Turned mainly to the super-Sensate world, it pays little attention to *paysage*, to concrete and real historical events, to earthly *genre*, to individual portraiture of real persons. It deals with the eternal world of Being, of God, wherein there is no change.	6. Concentrates upon the relatively durable and positive *types*, and not upon individual persons, events, nature, and other concrete traits of empirical reality. The types are invariably positive, ennobled, idealized.	6. Singularistic individualism: of persons — hence portraiture: of nature — hence *paysage;* of events — hence the daily *genre.*
7. No satire and caricature; in the Ideational mentality there is no place for that. No comedy, no operetta, no farce, no vaudeville.	7. Some satire but free from vulgarity, coarseness, and bitterness, and from serving daily purposes.	7. Development of satire, the debunking skeptical attitude. Great development of comic opera, of comedy, of farce, of vaudeville, and so on.

Ideational	*Idealistic*	*Sensate*
8. Transcendental anonymity and union in God.	8. Familistic and harmonious free collectivism.	8. Individualism and "professionalism."
9. Art is religion and inseparable from it. Therefore it is in a sense sacred and is service to God and to His kingdom.	9. Art is a great moral and civic and religious agent, serving man and the empirical world, and representing one of its semi-Ideational and semi-Sensate values.	9. Art is an instrument of a refined Sensate enjoyment: its function to give pleasure, joy, amusement, entertainment; to increase the sensate happiness of sensate human beings.
	B. External Traits	
1. Symbolic; "formal," "conventional."	1. Allegorical, typological.	1. Visual, sensual, realistic, naturalistic, impressionistic, singularistic.
2. Static: in its character as well as in its resistance to change.	2. Static-dynamic: in character and in the slow tempo of its change.	2. Dynamic: in character and in a progressively accelerating tempo of change.
3. Simplest means, instrumentalities, and technique. Simple and "archaic"; often intentionally stripped of all the beautifying trimmings and accessories.	3. Moderate but marvelously effective in its means, technique, and instrumentalities. Harmonious in its inner and external synthesis of Ideational and Sensate beauty.	3. Most complex. Colossal. Quantitative "bigness and betterness." Most complicated technique, artificially designed to sensually impress, to stun, to "hit." Enormous apparatus of instruments, means, accessories.
4. Art of performers concentrated on inner significance, rather than art for an audience.	4. Inner-external. Art of performers and audience, collectively participating, but in various degrees, in creation or performance.	4. All external; behavioristic, carried by professional performers or artists for passive audience (so far as participation in creativeness is concerned). "Showy" and designed to be "Hollywoody."
5. No professionals, as artists; division of functions mainly upon the basis of the religious and magical roles played by various individuals.	5. Professionals as *primus inter pares*.	5. Artist is professional.
6. No Sensate criticism, connoisseurism, aestheticism.	6. Emergence of criticism, but still in Mixed form: it is religio-ethico-aesthetical.	6. Sensate criticism and universal art education, discussion, estimation, from the standpoint of the Sensate delight.

the Chinese Taoist, or any other? In other words, do the associations which we have found occur in many cultures at various times? or are they to be considered a particular association applicable only to the cultures studied and to none outside of these?

In spite of my dislike for the sweeping generalizations for all times and societies, I am inclined to say that these associations are valid far beyond the periods of the Graeco-Roman and Western cultures which we have examined. This is not the place to enter into a detailed discussion of this problem, which in itself would provide the subject of a monograph. But on the basis of my study of the problem, I have come to the conclusion that practically all the associations and correlations established in the course of the preceding chapters are valid for at least several great cultures, and to many social groups and personalities. Here are some of the crucial cases.

We have seen that the Brahmanic-Hindu culture, the Buddhist, the Taoist, the Lamaist-Tibetan, the Jainist, are and have been throughout their long existence, predominantly Ideational (not, however, without some, though slight, fluctuations).

In preceding chapters we have shown, especially in regard to painting, that the pictorial art of the Taoist, Hindu, Buddhist Ideational cultures has been Ideational; that the pictorial art of the Mixed cultures, like the Egyptian or the Confucianist, was also Mixed; that finally, so far as we note the fluctuations of the Ideational and Sensate phases in these cultures, the forms of art fluctuate also with a corresponding rise and decline of the satellites of each form.

To repeat, this means that the associations and correlations established above go far beyond the Graeco-Roman and the Western Christian cultures. In other words, they recur in social space as well as in social time.

C. Generally speaking, the fluctuations from one main type to another go hand in hand in all fields of art. If we take fairly long periods, say not shorter than a century, then with very few exceptions all the arts — painting and sculpture, architecture and music, literature and drama — pass simultaneously from one, say Ideational, to another, say Idealistic or Sensate form. Only in the field of the European music was there a noticeable lag in its passing from the Ideational to the Idealistic and from that to the Sensate phase.

If shorter periods are taken and the smaller fluctuations are studied, a lack of simultaneity seems to occur somewhat more often, as was shown in part in Chapter Twelve and all the preceding chapters. But these short-time fluctuations are similar to ripplings upon great waves; they are neither deep nor fundamental. In these short-time and nonsynchronous fluctuations there is hardly any uniformity, in the sense that the change invariably takes place first in a certain field of art with a lag in some other. The reality is that at one time one art may be leading, another lagging; at another period, the situation may be reversed. This means that all the theories of the existence of a uniform sequence in the change of various arts, with a certain art always leading and others lagging in a uniform order — that all such theories are fallacious.

D. To the extent that the long-time changes in all the arts are parallel and more or less synchronous it is suggested that all the arts of the cultures studied have been integrated logically and causally to a high degree; that all the fine arts of these cultures are part of one living unity, the manifestation of one system; and that therefore when this culture begins to undergo the process of transformation, they all naturally follow the same path and change in the same direction.

Later on we shall see that not only the arts but practically all the main compartments of a culture: science and philosophy, law and ethics; forms of social, political, and economic organization — all change synchronously and in the same direction. This shows that in their mentality such cultures are living unities, real systems, though not quite rigid and closely knit; and not a mere agglomeration of various compartments accidentally placed side by side in time or in space — capable of change in quite divergent ways in its different parts.

E. Since, within the period of some twenty-five hundred years which we have studied, there have been several rising tides of each of the cultural forms, there is no foundation for claiming the existence of any perpetual linear tendency in this respect: in the course of time art has been moving neither steadily toward bigger and better Ideationalism nor in the opposite direction. It moves merely from one side to another in alternating fashion. When one of the forms has completed its immanent course and has lived the span of time destined to it, it decays and is replaced, after the proper intermediary stages, by the other form. So it has been in the past, and so probably it will continue to be. Since the dominant form of art for the last five centuries has been Sensate, when this has run its life course its place will be taken, in all probability after a Mixed phase of transition, by Ideational art. When that has lived its appointed span, the Sensate culture will recur again, and so it will go until integrated culture or mankind disappears.

In other words, here again we see the validity of the erratically or creatively recurrent conception of sociocultural processes.

F. I have pointed to many indications that at the end of the nineteenth and in the twentieth century there has appeared in all the fields of art a strong reaction against the dominant Sensate-Visual-naturalistic form. The revolt is clear, but its positive program is as yet confused, chaotic, incoherent, similar to that of the transitional period of the third and the fourth centuries A.D., when art began to pass from the overripe Sensate to the developing Ideational form. Whether this reaction is the first swallow of the coming Ideational spring or just a temporary reáction nobody can tell certainly. But considering the overripeness of our Sensate art and its other characteristics, which point to the possible exhaustion of a wave which has lasted from the fifteenth to the twentieth century, it is not improbable that this change is indeed the beginning of something new.

PART THREE

FLUCTUATION OF IDEATIONAL, IDEALISTIC AND SENSATE SYSTEMS OF TRUTH AND KNOWLEDGE

13

FLUCTUATION OF IDEATIONAL, IDEALISTIC, AND SENSATE SYSTEMS OF TRUTH AND KNOWLEDGE (QUANTITATIVE)

I. Ideational, Idealistic, and Sensate Systems of Truth

From Art we pass now to the next fundamental "compartment" of culture — to its *System of Truth and Knowledge.* This system, in integrated or unintegrated form, is embodied in what is loosely styled *Religious, Philosophical, and Scientific Thought* of a given culture.

In the study of the categories of Truth and Knowledge, we shall employ a method similar to that used in the study of the forms of art in Volume One. What are the main systems of truth and knowledge? Are the categories Ideational, Idealistic, and Sensate applicable to truth generally? If they are, what are the meanings of Ideational, Idealistic, and Sensate systems of truth and knowledge? What are the important characteristics of each of these systems of truth? Are such systems actually given in the historically existing cultures? Do they fluctuate in their domination in the life history of culture generally and of the cultures studied here specifically? If so, which have been the periods in the history of the Graeco-Roman and the Western cultures when each of these systems of truth dominated? How does the fluctuation of the system of truth reflect upon hundreds of various general and special theories?

In an Ideational culture, some system of truth based upon a criterion of validity different from the evidence of our senses has to be dominant. This dominant system of truth has to be either the system of *truth of faith* — based upon some kind of non- or superempirical source revealed by personal or impersonal God, deity, or mana — in the way of revelation, divine inspiration, intuition, mystic experience, and the like — or the system of *truth of reason and logic of human mind* viewed as a source independent of the organs of senses.

For a purely Ideational culture mentality, the truth of faith has to appear more infallible than human reason and logic. Therefore, we should expect that in predominantly Ideational culture the dominant system of truth must be mainly "revelation" (the religious or magical system of truth) in a supersensory and even superlogical way "revealed," "granted," "inspired" by superempirical agency or power or source, be it personal or impersonal. Based upon the revealed truth of God, absolute, perfect, and omniscient, the truth is also believed to be absolutely certain in its validity.

In a Sensate society and culture the Sensate system of truth based upon the testimony of the organs of senses has to be dominant. Since for the bearers of a Sensate mentality and culture there is no reality behind and except the sensory reality of Becoming; and since this sensory reality is "signaled" to us through our organs of senses, through what we see, touch, hear, etc., these senses must become the main and almost the only judges of what is true and what is false. If we see or hear a given empirical phenomenon in exactly the same way in which it is described by a given theory, the theory is valid and "scientific." If the testimony of these organs contradicts it, the theory is wrong and "unscientific."

If now we consider the Idealistic mentality and culture, its underlying system of truth must be one between the supersensory revelation and sensory evidence; one in which both these systems are organically united. The system of truth which meets these requirements is the truth of human reason and logic, the *idealistically rationalistic system of truth of the medieval Scholastics* of the twelfth to the fourteenth centuries. In that system the main judge is human reason and logic itself with its own laws of the true and false. This judge, however, is not reluctant to hear the testimony of the organs of senses and is willing to use their information to transform it and to sanction it as true, and is also not reluctant to accept the truth of revelation when it appears to be reasonable and reconcilable with the logical laws of the human mind which itself, in a sense, has a vein of divine nature.

The other "Mixed" mentalities and cultures require also a combination of truth of faith and of truth of senses, but the mixture is not necessarily a consistent synthesis, since these "mixed" mentalities are not integrated internally. The truth of faith and of senses may coexist mechanically, undigested and unintegrated. Finally, in the *passive and cynical forms of Sensate mentality*, the *system of skepticism*, *incapable of believing in any system of truth*, is by deduction the one most consistent with such a mentality and culture. Likewise, for the *Ideationalists of despair* the most consistent system of truth must be one "of a desperate will to believe" by those who, like Apostle Thomas, wish to but cannot believe without great difficulty.

From the very nature of each of these main systems of truth and knowledge several further characteristics follow. Their subject matter as well as the method of verification of any statement about the subject matter has to be profoundly different in each of these systems. In a concise way the following outline sums up the essentials of each of these systems as to the subject matter of their study as well as the method of proving the validity of each statement or theory about this subject matter.

SYSTEM OF IDEATIONAL TRUTH OF FAITH

Subject Matter

Mainly the supersensory, and superrational "subjects" and "realities." God, devil, angels, spirits; soul, immortality, salvation; sin; redemption; resurrection; paradise, purgatory, inferno; and so on, with an enormous number of other subproblems of the same kind, like St. Augustine's problem. Can angels use devils as their messengers? What is the estate of angels? Are the hellish pains proportional to crimes and so on?

The sensory and empirical phenomena are studied only incidentally and even then not for their own sake but merely as "visible signs of the invisible world," as symbols of the supersensory reality. The supreme discipline in such a system of truth is always theology as a science of the supersensory realities. The exposition of the truth is apodictic and symbolic.

SYSTEM OF IDEALISTIC TRUTH OF REASON

Subject Matter

Partly supersensory, partly sensory-empirical. Each for its own sake, but the value of the knowledge about the sensory phenomena is subordinated to that of the supersensory "realities."

The total system of knowledge here incorporates, usually in the form of idealistically rationalistic philosophy ("Scholasticism" of Plato and Aristotle, of Albertus Magnus and St. Thomas Aquinas; or "Scholasticism" of the Upanishads and other Idealistic philosophies based upon the Vedas in India), reasoning and empirical knowledge in the sense of the contemporary science. The ultimate reality is thought of as knowable. The exposition of the truth is dialectic and deductive.

SYSTEM OF SENSATE TRUTH OF SENSES

Subject Matter

Mainly the world of the sensory perception, like the phenomena studied in the natural sciences. When, for instance, in the field of psychology, culture, and "values," the phenomena seem to have an aspect not easily reducible to the sensory-material forms, science concentrates mainly at their sensory aspect and either disregards the "nonmaterial" aspect or treats it as a subsidiary and tries to "measure them" through the measurement of the sensory-external phenomenal forms. Hence, the tendency to "objectivism," "behaviorism," "quantitativism," "mechanisticism." The supersensory realities are declared either nonexistent, or irrelevant, or "unknowable" (critiism, agnosticism, positivism). The natural sciences become the leaders as the most perfect, exact sciences, and are copied by philosophy and by even abortive pseudotheology which tries in the period of domination of the truth of senses to create "scientific religion." Exposition of the truth is "inductive" and especially "experimental."

SYSTEM OF IDEATIONAL TRUTH OF FAITH

Method of Validation

Mainly reference to the Sacred Source, to the Scripture (revealed) in the form of quotations from it which would show that the statement perfectly agrees with the Scripture. If a new "truth" is claimed, the method of demonstration is to show that it is due to the same "divine inspiration" to which the Scripture is due. Purely logical reasoning and the testimony of the organs of senses have only a subsidiary role, and only in so far as they do not contradict the truth of the revealed Scripture. Otherwise they are unhesitatingly rejected as invalid or even inspired by the devil (heresy, blasphemy, black magic, etc.)

SYSTEM OF IDEALISTIC TRUTH OF REASON

Method of Validation

Intermediary between the methods of the other two systems. Mainly the method of logical reasoning ("Scholastic" method) but also reference to the testimony of the organs of senses. Both these methods are always "covered" and given an ultimate support by the proper reference to the Scripture and the revealed truth. Hence, concretely in the works which embody this system of truth one always finds the dialectical method, reference to the organs of senses and their data, and quotations from the Scripture or a source equivalent to it. All these references to the three sources of truth tend to show that their testimony is unanimous and that they do not contradict one another. It is the method in which the evidence of Scripture, of logic, and of the senses is perfectly harmonious.

SYSTEM OF SENSATE TRUTH OF SENSES

Method of Validation

Mainly the reference to the testimony of the organs of senses (often reinforced by their extensions — telescopes, microscopes, etc.), supplemented by the logical reasoning, especially in the form of the mathematical reasoning. But even the well-reasoned theory remains in the stage of pure hypothesis, unproved until it is tested by the sensory facts; and it is unhesitatingly rejected if these "facts" contradict it. The truth of faith and its "Scriptures" do not play any role in the system and are not regarded as "evidence." If anything they most often are regarded as mere "superstitions." In the cases where some pious or hypocritical reference to the Scripture is given (often merely for practical reasons) it usually does not play any important part and is mostly superfluous. The truth of faith has as little value by itself in this system of truth as the testimony of senses in the system of truth of faith.

This schematic characterization shows that each of these systems is quite consistent within itself and with the major premises of the respective mentality; that the character and "contents" of each of the systems of truth, from the standpoint of their subject matter, as well as the method of testing the truth, are profoundly different, and therefore the mentality incorporated in each of these systems differs again profoundly from that of any other.

Since Science and its system of truth are to be supreme in the Sensate and secondary in the Ideational society, it can be expected that Ideational cultures and periods are to be marked by fewer important scientific discoveries; and since the mentality of Ideational culture is turned away from the world of senses toward the ultimate reality of everlasting Being, it is neither interested in an investigation of this empirical world nor in making various scientific (that is empirico-Sensate) discoveries concerning it.

In Sensate periods the situation must be reversed for the same reasons. Sensate mentality turns to the Sensate reality and is eager to study it, and either does not recognize any other reality or is not interested in it. For these reasons it is to be expected that such periods and cultures are to be marked by comparatively greater progress in science, scientific discoveries, and technological inventions in the field of the natural and technological sciences.

If the last two expected regularities are valid, then not only the system of truth has to change with the change in the character of culture, particularly the relative position of "scientific system of truth" among other systems and its comparative blossoming, but even within the scientific system of truth several fundamental theories also have to change. General principles and categories of science — space, time, number, and the like; the cosmogony and theory of the universe; atomistic theory and theory of matter; mechanistic and vitalistic principles; theory of causation; fundamental principles of biology or evolution; and the like — also have to be expected to change when a given culture passes from one of its fundamental forms to another.

It can also be expected that even within the scientific system of truth of senses the main topics which would be worked out in Sensate and Ideational cultures would also considerably differ. The "scientists" of Ideational cultures are likely to concentrate their attention on one group of Sensate phenomena as the most important, while scientists of Sensate culture may find these problems unimportant and may concentrate on another class of phenomena having little interest for the scientists of Ideational culture.

The above expectations and inferences mean, if they are valid, that even such primordial values as truth and knowledge, so far as their content, criteria, and evidences are concerned, in sociocultural actuality (but not in Plato's world of ideas) depend greatly upon the type of culture of which they are a part. In other words, what appears to be true and what is not, what appears to be scientific and what is not, what is a valid criterion of truth and what is not, are, in the statistico-mathematical language, in a considerable degree a "function" of the sociocultural variable. If this be found valid, then the sociologist should have his say also in the problems of epistemology and logic, in so far as there is a place — and a large one — for what the Germans call *Wissenssoziologie*. Adequately understood, it composes one of the most important parts of sociology of culture.

Let us turn now to an empirical verification of these deductions. If the cultures studied are logically integrated, it will be found that these deductions are corroborated by the empirical data. Such a corroboration would demonstrate again, on the one hand, the heuristic value of the "logico-meaningful" method and, on the other, that within the "compartment of truth and knowledge" these cultures also are integrated "causally."

II. Fluctuation of the Main Systems of Truth: Empiricism, Religious and Idealistic Rationalism, Mysticism, Skepticism, Fideism in the Graeco-Roman and European Cultures from 580 B.C. to A.D. 1920

I. METHODOLOGICAL AND EXPLANATORY PRELIMINARIES

The purpose of the study of this fluctuation is not to discuss the truth or error of the main systems of truth, nor is it to take sides concerning them. My objective is very different. Assuming the position of a perfectly impartial observer, and taking the systems involved as the factual datum, I am going to inquire whether in the life history of the Graeco-Roman and Western cultures the comparative influence and popularity of each of these systems of truth have been constant or variable in the mentality of the *leading thinkers* in the field. If variable, has there been in the course of time a linear trend of continuous increase in the influence and acceptance of one of these systems at the expense of the others, or has such a trend been absent? If such a trend exists, then what is its nature or, to use favorite terms of the nineteenth century, what has been its line of "progress" or its "historical tendency"? Has its direction been one of greater and better truth of faith, of reason, or of senses? If there be no such linear trend, then how have the rise and fall of these currents fluctuated? Have there been definite "cycles" and "periodicities" in these fluctuations, or only nonperiodic "ups and downs" of each of these currents, without any uniform tempo and rhythm? If the same themes recur, but each time with new variations, then is it possible to indicate with reasonable accuracy at which periods from about 580 B.C. to A.D. 1920 each of these systems of truth rose and declined, and to what extent? Finally, if the preceding questions are answered, what are the reasons (or the "causes" and "factors") of such fluctuations?

II. RESERVATIONS AND QUALIFICATIONS

A. The fluctuations of the influence of the truth of faith, of reason, and of senses are studied only within the Graeco-Roman and Western cultures, from about 580 B.C. up to A.D. 1920.

B. The study roughly estimates the increase and decrease of the comparative acceptability and influence of each of these currents of thought, as they are represented, first, by the *number* of their partisans among the majority of prominent thinkers in the field, in each twenty-year period, and in each one-hundred-year period from 580 B.C. to A.D. 1920; second, by the comparative "weight" or influence of these partisans in each of these periods.

Practically all the names of the great thinkers in the field of this problem were selected. For the last three or four centuries, when the number of scholars increased greatly, only the names of the most prominent philosophers and scientists who contributed to the problem were included. But the samples are so large that in all probability they are representative for these centuries. In this way Tables 1 and 2 and Figure 1 are based upon material far larger than any study of this problem hitherto made.

Respectively, two sets of data were computed. First, for each period, was computed the number of partisans to each of these currents among the total number of thinkers in the field, in that period, whose names are preserved in the annals of history. Turned into percentages, these numbers indicate the main changes in the comparative strength of each current from period to period, as manifested by changes in the number and percentage of its partisans. Second, for each period, data are given concerning the *comparative weight or influence* of each current in each period among the same group of thinkers; whereas, from the point of view of the number of partisans in each period, each of the thinkers is assigned the same value of influence, namely, one. In the "weight" data each of them is assigned different values of influence on a scale of one to twelve. Those thinkers who, like Plato, Aristotle, Plotinus, St. Augustine, St. Thomas Aquinas, or Kant, obviously exerted much greater influence than many others, are given the highest weight of influence, namely twelve. Those whose influence seems to have been noticeable (or their names would not be preserved in the annals of history), but seemingly the smallest in comparison with the influence of the other thinkers, are given the value of one. The rest of the thinkers are assigned values intermediary between one and twelve proportionately to their appraised influence.

The assignment of these values to each thinker is a difficult but not an impossible problem, if it does not pretend to be more than roughly accurate, and if several conditions are present.

Guided by these considerations, and following the above conditions, Professors N. O. Lossky and I. I. Lapshin and I have assigned the appropriate value to each of the contributors (in their influence) in the following way.

As objective criteria of the comparative influence of each of the philosophers — the following data were selected:

(1) The number of special monographs devoted to a philosopher.

(2) The approximate frequency with which the philosopher's name has been mentioned, not only in the works of his contemporaries but also in those of the subsequent thinkers in this field.

(3) Whether he was a founder of a school of philosophic thought.

(4) Whether his name is mentioned even in the most elementary texts of history, epistemology, and theory of knowledge.

(5) The number of his avowed disciples and followers among the thinkers in the field.

(6) Whether his works have been translated into foreign languages.

(7) Whether his works have been republished again and again in spite of the length of time that had elapsed since his death.

(8) Whether he was a creator of an original and complete system of philosophy and epistemology.

From the above criteria one can see that almost all the relevant data have been considered. On the basis of these criteria the following number of units of influence and the corresponding scale of grades were constructed: We started with the number of special monographs devoted to the thinker and distributed them into twelve classes, from zero to 2560 and more monographic studies. Beginning with five the number doubles in each subsequent class. In the second row the value of influence assigned increases by one unit, giving a scale of values from one to twelve. Then the number of monographic studies has been corrected by other considerations mentioned previously. Weighting all these carefully, we assigned to each thinker in the field the value between one and twelve which appeared to be most adequate.

Number of Monographs on a Philosopher	*Units of Value Given*
0	1
1	2
5	3
10	4
20	5

Number of Monographs on a Philosopher	*Units of Value Given*
40	6
80	7
160	8
320	9
640	10
1280	11
2560 and more	12

In this way the elemental subjectivity in assigning the influence value to the thinkers has been reduced as much as it is humanly possible. The names of the thinkers and the values assigned to each one are given in the Appendix to this chapter. Any specialist in the field would probably give a similar weight to those values presented in the list. Even though a few discrepancies might occur, they would not change the result in any tangible degree when the total weight of all the partisans of each period has been grouped and summed up, providing the scale of values remains not very different from one to twelve. The weight of all the partisans of a given current in each period is summed up; from these figures percentages are computed which indicate roughly the main changes in the increase and decrease of the influence of each current from period to period. This is the rough but systematic method used to estimate the movement of each of the currents of thought, in the course of time, as embodied in Tables 1 and 2 and Figure 1.

As stated before, these results from the points of view of both number and weight cannot pretend to reflect the changes in the mentality of the whole population from period to period. But it is probable that, in both cases, they indicate, at least roughly, the main changes in the mentality of the leading thinkers. In so far as the totality of the leading thinkers in a given field of a given period embodies the mentality of a given culture in that field, *upon its highest, or leading, or logically integrated level, the above results possibly reflect the main changes of the respective mentality of the Graeco-Roman and the European cultures upon this level in each of the specified periods.*

The reasonableness of our scale is attested, among other things, by the fact that the curves constructed upon a basis of weight and the curves constructed upon the basis of number, in which an equal value of one is given to each thinker, agree in their essential movements. This means that, all in all, the scale conforms to the principle that the greater the influence of a thinker in any given period, the greater is the proportion of thinkers who followed the same stream of thought, and vice versa.

The empirical system of truth is the system of the natural sciences; if one grows, the other must grow; if one declines, the other must decline.

These curves are based upon radically different items and sources: one upon the *number of the discoveries and inventions in the natural sciences* computed from Darmstaedter's work; the other upon the systematic registration of all the known or all the important known thinkers who are mentioned in the histories of philosophy, epistemology, logic, and science. The items and the sources were entirely different and the computations were made by different persons who were not aware of the work of the other computers. (Professors Lossky and Lapshin had no knowledge of my study, and Dr. Merton, who made the computation of the scientific discoveries, was unaware not only of my study but also of the computations made by Professors Lossky and Lapshin.) Under the circumstances, the agreement between the curve of the scientific discoveries and inventions (Figure 3) and the curve of the fluctuations of the influence of the system of truth of senses (Figure 1) is particularly strong evidence that the results obtained in both cases are neither incidental nor misleading.

If it be maintained, especially by the historians, that no quantitative appraisal is possible in this field, and therefore any scale is inadmissible, the answer is simple: *Medice cura te ipsum.* The point is that there is scarcely any historical work, whether in this or in any other field, where, explicitly or implicitly, quantitative judgments are not given in verbal form. What historians of ideas, human thought, science, religion, art styles, political systems, or economic processes do not use quantitative expressions like the following: "The period was marked by an *increase* of riots, revolts, and disorders," "The period was marked by a *decline* of idealism and religion," "Kant was one of the *greatest* philosophers," "It was the epoch of the *rise and triumph* of materialism, nominalism, the Gothic style, or socialistic doctrine," and so on? Statements like these, in many forms, are met in practically all historical works. They are but a variety of quantitative statements aimed to measure a comparative influence, popularity, magnitude, value, size, frequency; or an increase or decrease, growth or decline, rise or fall, of this or that cultural phenomenon. It is scarcely necessary to add that such statements are quite unavoidable in most sociocultural, humanitarian, and historical studies.

The usual statements of historians and social scientists are quantitative and also *verbal quantitative.* The procedure used here is *numerical quantitative.* The first makes quantitative statements but in an indefinite verbal form without the use of figures or numerical indicators. The second describes the quantitative changes with the help of figures. Which method is preferable, verbal or numerically quantitative? That is the question.

In the first place, the numerical method proposed is much more concise and economical.

In the second place, verbal quantitativism has a very limited number of gradations: "bad," "worse," "the worst"; "good," "better," "the best"; "big," "bigger," "the biggest"; and so on. The reason is that language has normally only from three to six comparative terms. With such limited gradations verbal quantitativists cannot describe any curve of movement of a social process in its numerous increases and decreases, "ups" and "downs"; or any series of quantitative values far more numerous than six.

In the third place, the method proposed makes clear to any reader its foundation, its bases, and its measuring stick. The yardstick used is uniform for all the periods compared, and these periods are all systematically taken and studied from this same standpoint. This claim can hardly be made for "increase," "decrease," and their equivalents used in most quantitative verbal judgments, where the bases, the nature of the measuring stick and its application remain unknown, or are often the result of intuitive guesswork.

III. EMPIRICISM, RATIONALISM, MYSTICISM, SKEPTICISM, FIDEISM, CRITICISM

Let us now turn to our main task, *i.e.*, a study of the fluctuation of the main systems of truth in the life history of the Graeco-Roman and the Western cultures. The nature of the relevant material requires a slight modification of the three systems of truth. Instead of a direct study of the rise and decline of the truth of faith, of reason, and of senses, we shall follow the fluctuation of the influence of the six main epistemological currents in the mentality of the Graeco-Roman and European cultures; empiricism, religious or ideational rationalism and idealistic rationalism, mysticism, skepticism, fideism, and criticism. *Of these, ideational or religious rationalism, mysticism, and fideism incorporate mainly the truth of faith; the idealistic rationalism, mainly the truth of reason; empiricism, mainly the truth of senses.* Skepticism is a purely negative system of "cynical" and "passive" Sensate mentality; criticism a specific mixture of skepticism, empiricism, and rationalism. The last two are important symptoms of specific cultural conditions and are discussed below. Following the fluctuation of the influence of these currents of thought from 580 B.C. to A.D. 1920, we shall obtain the fluctuation of influence of the three main systems of truth, translated into the above epistemological currents. Before beginning the study of these fluctuations, however, we shall present a brief characterization of each of these currents which will give only a rough outline of each of these systems of truth.

A. *Empiricism.* This theory corresponds to the truth of senses. The only source of knowledge and truth, according to empiricism, is the sensory perception of the singular objects and events separated in time and space. It gives us our exterior or interior experience. Logical and a priori principles are but mere associations of these experiences, mere "routine of perceptions." In Tables 1 and 2 and Figure 1 the data on empiricism are fairly adequate measures of the movement — expansion and contraction — of the system of truth of senses.

B. *Rationalism.* This term covers two essentially different systems of truth which have a common generic trait but which are profoundly different in their *differentia specifica*, namely, the *ideational rationalism* and the *idealistic rationalism.* Both subclasses assert that truth is knowable and that the reality can be known with certitude because both of them give a more or less important role to the mind or thought and its nonsensory categories and concepts. Both regard the truth of reason, of logical and mathematical inferences, more valid than the truth of senses. Likewise they both give some place to the truth of faith and truth of senses.

(1) *The ideational* or *religious rationalism* in its extreme form is merely what is styled the *truth of faith.* Supersensory and sometimes superlogical revelation or its varieties is really its main truth. The truth of reason holds but a subsidiary role in the truth of faith and is entirely subordinated to it. It cannot independently disagree with the truth of faith. If it does it becomes invalid, even sinful, heretical, or blasphemous.

(2) *Idealistic Rationalism.* This second type of rationalism notably differs from the ideational rationalism. Its main difference is that idealistic rationalism gives (in fact, often contrary to the declarations of its authors) the main role to reason, to intellect, and to its categories as such. It also gives a more prominent role to the truth of senses than does religious rationalism. For these reasons idealistic rationalism is a blend of all the three forms of truth, each being given an important role, though the superior knowledge is still reserved for the truth of faith. While in religious rationalism the truth of faith plays an all-important — almost monopolistic — role, in idealistic rationalism all truths are harmoniously united into one and, factually, in spite of the declared supremacy of the truth of faith, the real power is the truth of reason. Dialectics and logic are used here to prove the validity and the possibility of the revealed truth.

C. *Mysticism.* Like religious rationalism, mysticism also contends that the supreme source of truth and real knowledge is supersensory and superlogical intuition or revelation. The truth of senses and that of reason as such can give but the pseudo knowledge of the surface or of mere appearance of the phenomena. They cannot penetrate to the ultimate reality and to the absolute truth. In this sense mysticism is also mainly the system of *truth of faith.* From religious rationalism it differs, however, by several secondary characteristics; such as stressing that the "mystic way" of obtaining truth almost always assumes a form of esoteric trances, and the like; that it requires a special training in that direction.

Mysticism has several forms. In a schematic way we shall distinguish two. First, the remotest from religious rationalism can be styled *mysticism of despair*. It is a mysticism par excellence. Visions, trances, ecstasies, and similar "pathologies" play a particularly conspicuous role in it. In hundreds of ways it shows its "antirationalism and irrationalism." This variety of mysticism prevailed in the fifteenth and subsequent centuries. Second, there is the type of mysticism which differs little from religious rationalism.

D. *Skepticism* is a systematic and methodical doubting of the possibility of valid knowledge. "We cannot know anything with certainty; if we can, we cannot express it adequately; if we can express it others cannot understand it; therefore abstain from any judgments." This is the motto of skepticism. A diluted variety of it is agnosticism: it also denies a possibility of knowledge of the ultimate reality. It even doubts its existence and is not interested in it but is different from a "straight skepticism" in that it believes in the possibility of knowing in the empirico-sensory world.

E. *Fideism* is logically connected with skepticism. Fideism, agreeing with skepticism that the truth of the most important principles and facts — like the existence of the external world, of God, of mind and psychical "self," psychical experiences of the others and so on — cannot be obtained through mere cognition, empirical or rational, believes further that the certainty of such most important truths can be obtained only through the act of volition, will to believe, or instinct, or natural suggestion, and the like. In this sense it stresses the element of volition and belief as noncognitive factors in obtaining and ascertaining the most important truths or fundamental knowledge. In this respect fideism is related in a sense to mysticism and often they merge imperceptibly into each other. If we view it as a positive system of truth, not merely a negative theory like skepticism, then fideism is mainly a desperate form of the truth of faith.

F. Finally, *criticism* or *agnosticism* is a theory which contends that only the phenomenal or empirical world is accessible to our knowledge, while the ultimate or transcendental reality — whether it exists or not — is inaccessible and does not need to be known. Differing from the other theories, it admits empiric as well as rationalistic elements in our cognitive activity and tries to tie them together and to make them corelated, codependent, and mutually conditioned. Criticism, therefore, occupies a somewhat middle position between empiricism, rationalism, and skepticism but more likely approximates empiricism.

Since we are mainly interested in the problem of fluctuation in the three systems of truth — of faith, of reason, and of senses — Tables 1 and 2 and Figure 1, given in the terms of these six systems of truth and knowledge, have to be translated into the terms of the truth of faith, of reason, and of senses according to the previous explanation or "legend." The results of the study of the fluctuation of the comparative influence of each of these epistemological currents during twenty-five hundred years are summed up in the two tables and the figure that follow.

Table 1 gives the numerical indicators of the comparative influence of each current by periods of twenty years from 580 B.C. to A.D. 1920.

Table 2 gives the numerical indicators of the influence of each current by periods of one hundred years with the different values of influence on the same scale.

Figure 1 delineates the fluctuation of the influence by one-hundred-year periods, as it is given by Table 2.

III. Main Results of the Study

The figures suggest the following conclusions.

A. *Trendless Fluctuation instead of Linear Trend.* A mere glance at Tables 1 and 2 and Figure 1 is sufficient to indicate that within the period of some twenty-five hundred years there has been no continuous linear trend of any kind. None of the main systems has tended steadily to increase or decrease or remain constant throughout all the period, but each system has fluctuated, now rising in its influence, now declining, or remaining for a time comparatively constant. The popular and almost commonly accepted opinion that there exists a linear trend in this field, and that the linear trend consists in a progressive increase of the empirical truth of senses at the expense of a progressively declining truth of faith (religious rationalism, mysticism, and fideism) or the truth of reason (idealistic rationalism) is contradicted by the data. During the last five centuries empiricism or the truth of senses has been rising very rapidly.

The creative recurrent conception of sociocultural processes and likewise my contention that there have been different systems of truth which have fluctuated without leading to the "final" predominance of any one of them are well corroborated by the data.

B. *No Spencerian Evolution.* There was no perpetual Spencerian "evolution" from the less differentiated and integrated to the more differentiated and integrated status.

C. *Fluctuation of the Truth of Senses* (*Empiricism*). Turning to the tables and the figure, we note the following fluctuations of the truth of senses in so far as it is embodied in empiricism. The period from 580 to 560 B.C. opens with the absolute domination of empiricism. This conclusion is not reliable, however, because it is based on the contributions of only

TABLE 1. INDICATORS OF FLUCTUATION OF THE INFLUENCE IN MAIN SYSTEMS OF TRUTH BY 20-YEAR PERIODS

(on the basis of *different values* of influence given from 1 to 12)

PERIOD	*Empiricism*		*Rationalism*		*Mysticism*		*Criticism*		*Skepticism*		*Fideism*		*Total*	
	No.	*Per cent*	*No.*	*Per cent*	*No.*	*Per cent*	*No.*	*Per cent*	*No.*	*Per cent*	*No.*	*Per cent*	*No.*	*Per cent*
580–560 B.C.	4	100	0	0	0	0	0	0	0	0	0	0	4	100
560–540	4	28.6	10	71.4	0	0	0	0	0	0	0	0	14	100
540–520	2	10.0	18	90.0	0	0	0	0	0	0	0	0	20	100
520–500	2	9.1	20	90.9	0	0	0	0	0	0	0	0	22	100
500–480	2	6.9	27	93.1	0	0	0	0	0	0	0	0	29	100
480–460	2	9.1	20	90.9	0	0	0	0	0	0	0	0	22	100
460–440	11	26.8	17	41.5	0	0	0	0	13	31.7	0	0	41	100
440–420	13	27.1	22	45.8	0	0	0	0	13	27.1	0	0	48	100
420–400	18	23.7	22	28.9	0	0	0	0	36	47.4	0	0	76	100
400–380	9	12.3	30	41.1	0	0	0	0	29	39.7	5	6.9	73	100
380–360	16	26.2	24	39.4	0	0	0	0	16	26.2	5	8.2	61	100
360–340	9	13.6	23	34.9	15	22.7	0	0	14	21.2	5	7.6	66	100
340–320	1	2.2	31	66.0	5	10.6	0	0	5	10.6	5	10.6	47	100
320–300	14	16.7	38	45.3	5	6.0	0	0	16	19.0	11	13.0	84	100
300–280	24	29.0	23	27.8	1	1.2	0	0	15	18.0	20	24.0	83	100
280–260	16	22.8	11	15.9	1	1.4	0	0	18	25.7	24	34.2	70	100
260–240	4	11.1	3	8.3	1	2.8	0	0	6	16.7	22	61.1	36	100
240–220	7	11.5	4	6.6	1	1.6	0	0	9	14.7	40	65.6	61	100
220–200	3	7.7	8	20.5	1	2.5	0	0	7	18.0	20	51.3	39	100
200–180	4	17.4	9	39.1	1	4.4	0	0	3	13.0	6	26.1	23	100
180–160	2	9.5	6	28.6	1	4.7	0	0	6	28.6	6	28.6	21	100
160–140	3	13.6	5	22.7	1	4.6	0	0	7	31.8	6	27.3	22	100
140–120	2	10.0	2	10.0	1	5.0	0	0	9	45.0	6	30.0	20	100
120–100	4	21.1	2	10.5	1	5.2	0	0	4	21.1	8	42.1	19	100
100–80	7	26.0	5	18.5	1	3.7	0	0	2	7.4	12	44.4	27	100
80–60	5	13.9	16	44.4	1	2.7	0	0	0	0	14	39.0	36	100
60–40	18	27.0	10	15.0	4	6.0	0	0	5	7.4	30	44.6	67	100
40–20	10	22.2	12	26.7	1	2.2	0	0	5	11.1	17	37.8	45	100
20–0	1	5.0	7	35.0	2	10.0	0	0	5	25.0	5	25.0	20	100
0–20 A.D.	1	4.4	9	39.1	8	34.8	0	0	0	0	5	21.7	23	100
20–40	1	4.4	5	21.8	11	47.8	0	0	0	0	6	26.0	23	100
40–60	1	3.3	2	6.7	11	36.7	0	0	0	0	16	53.3	30	100
60–80	1	2.6	2	5.3	8	21.0	0	0	0	0	27	71.1	38	100
80–100	1	2.7	2	5.4	16	43.2	0	0	0	0	18	48.7	37	100
100–120	1	2.3	12	27.9	16	37.2	0	0	2	4.7	12	27.9	43	100
120–140	2	3.1	8	12.3	32	49.2	0	0	6	9.2	17	26.2	65	100
140–160	3	4.4	14	20.6	31	45.6	0	0	6	8.8	14	20.6	68	100
160–180	10	13.7	15	20.6	31	42.5	0	0	6	8.2	11	15.0	73	100
180–200	12	12.8	26	27.6	42	44.7	0	0	6	6.4	8	8.5	94	100
200–220	20	27.4	13	17.8	33	45.2	0	0	6	8.2	1	1.4	73	100
220–240	12	23.5	9	17.6	29	56.9	0	0	0	0	1	2.0	51	100
240–260	11	21.6	3	5.9	36	70.6	0	0	0	0	1	1.9	51	100
260–280	13	32.5	3	7.5	23	57.5	0	0	0	0	1	2.5	40	100
280–300	9	34.6	2	7.7	15	57.7	0	0	0	0	0	0	26	100
300–320	7	26.9	4	15.4	15	57.7	0	0	0	0	0	0	26	100
320–340	9	21.4	16	38.1	17	40.5	0	0	0	0	0	0	42	100
340–360	6	20.7	12	41.4	11	37.9	0	0	0	0	0	0	29	100
360–380	3	5.1	16	27.1	40	67.8	0	0	0	0	0	0	59	100
380–400	9	16.4	16	29.1	30	54.5	0	0	0	0	0	0	55	100
400–420	8	16.0	20	40.0	22	44.0	0	0	0	0	0	0	50	100
420–440	6	13.1	22	47.8	18	39.1	0	0	0	0	0	0	46	100
440–460	4	12.9	14	45.2	13	41.9	0	0	0	0	0	0	31	100
460–480	4	14.3	11	39.3	13	46.4	0	0	0	0	0	0	28	100
480–500	1	3.9	11	42.3	14	53.8	0	0	0	0	0	0	26	100
500–520	1	3.2	16	51.6	14	45.2	0	0	0	0	0	0	31	100
520–540	1	2.6	24	61.5	14	35.9	0	0	0	0	0	0	39	100
540–560	0	0	17	73.9	6	26.1	0	0	0	0	0	0	23	100
560–580	0	0	6	85.7	1	14.3	0	0	0	0	0	0	7	100
580–600	0	0	8	100	0	0	0	0	0	0	0	0	8	100
600–620	0	0	10	90.9	1	9.1	0	0	0	0	0	0	11	100
620–640	0	0	6	50.0	6	50.0	0	0	0	0	0	0	12	100
640–660	0	0	3	33.3	6	66.7	0	0	0	0	0	0	9	100
660–680	0	0	2	25.0	6	75.0	0	0	0	0	0	0	8	100
680–700	0	0	2	100	0	0	0	0	0	0	0	0	2	100
700–720	0	0	3	100	0	0	0	0	0	0	0	0	3	100
720–740	0	0	8	100	0	0	0	0	0	0	0	0	8	100
740–760	0	0	5	100	0	0	0	0	0	0	0	0	5	100
760–780	0	0	1	100	0	0	0	0	0	0	0	0	1	100
780–800	0	0	4	100	0	0	0	0	0	0	0	0	4	100
800–820	0	0	6	100	0	0	0	0	0	0	0	0	6	100
820–840	0	0	8	100	0	0	0	0	0	0	0	0	8	100
840–860	0	0	8	50.0	8	50.0	0	0	0	0	0	0	16	100
860–880	0	0	9	52.9	8	47.1	0	0	0	0	0	0	17	100
880–900	0	0	3	60.0	2	40.0	0	0	0	0	0	0	5	100
900–920	0	0	2	50.0	2	50.0	0	0	0	0	0	0	4	100
920–940	0	0	2	100	0	0	0	0	0	0	0	0	2	100
940–960	0	0	1	100	0	0	0	0	0	0	0	0	1	100
960–980	0	0	1	100	0	0	0	0	0	0	0	0	1	100
980–1000	0	0	3	100	0	0	0	0	0	0	0	0	3	100

TABLE 1. — *continued*

1000–1020	0	0	6	100	0	0	0	0	0	0	0	0	6	100
1020–1040	0	0	3	100	0	0	0	0	0	0	0	0	3	100
1040–1060	0	0	8	61.5	0	0	0	0	0	0	5	38.5	13	100
1060–1080	0	0	11	40.7	11	40.7	0	0	0	0	5	18.6	27	100
1080–1100	3	11.5	9	34.7	11	42.3	0	0	0	0	3	11.5	26	100
1100–1120	3	15.0	7	35.0	7	35.0	0	0	0	0	3	15.0	20	100
1120–1140	3	9.4	17	53.1	12	37.5	0	0	0	0	0	0	32	100
1140–1160	3	7.5	21	52.5	16	40.0	0	0	0	0	0	0	40	100
1160–1180	3	10.7	17	60.7	8	28.6	0	0	0	0	0	0	28	100
1180–1200	7	30.4	6	26.1	10	43.5	0	0	0	0	0	0	23	100
1200–1220	4	13.8	15	51.7	10	34.5	0	0	0	0	0	0	29	100
1220–1240	4	17.4	17	73.9	2	8.7	0	0	0	0	0	0	23	100
1240–1260	4	11.8	29	85.3	1	2.9	0	0	0	0	0	0	34	100
1260–1280	10	16.1	44	71.0	8	12.9	0	0	0	0	0	0	62	100
1280–1300	9	12.5	56	77.8	7	9.7	0	0	0	0	0	0	72	100
1300–1320	5	6.9	53	72.6	12	16.4	0	0	3	4.1	0	0	73	100
1320–1340	12	20.3	30	50.8	10	17.0	0	0	7	11.9	0	0	59	100
1340–1360	16	27.6	13	22.4	25	43.1	0	0	4	6.9	0	0	58	100
1360–1380	7	18.9	4	10.8	26	70.3	0	0	0	0	0	0	37	100
1380–1400	4	20.0	4	20.0	8	40.0	0	0	0	0	4	20.0	20	100
1400–1420	0	0	2	20.0	4	40.0	0	0	0	0	4	40.0	10	100
1420–1440	0	0	9	53.0	4	23.5	0	0	0	0	4	23.5	17	100
1440–1460	0	0	9	42.9	12	57.1	0	0	0	0	0	0	21	100
1460–1480	3	13.6	3	13.6	16	72.8	0	0	0	0	0	0	22	100
1480–1500	3	50.0	3	50.0	0	0	0	0	0	0	0	0	6	100
1500–1520	3	20.0	4	26.8	6	40.0	0	0	1	6.6	1	6.6	15	100
1520–1540	8	27.6	4	13.8	11	37.9	0	0	4	13.8	2	6.9	29	100
1540–1560	8	21.6	4	10.8	13	35.2	0	0	2	5.4	10	27.0	37	100
1560–1580	8	13.3	14	23.4	22	36.7	0	0	8	13.3	8	13.3	60	100
1580–1600	9	14.5	20	32.3	24	38.7	0	0	8	12.9	1	1.6	62	100
1600–1620	18	21.7	39	47.0	17	20.5	0	0	8	9.6	1	1.2	83	100
1620–1640	24	31.2	39	50.6	12	15.6	0	0	1	1.3	1	1.3	77	100
1640–1660	31	31.6	42	42.9	17	17.3	0	0	1	1.0	7	7.2	98	100
1660–1680	32	20.4	74	47.2	42	26.7	0	0	2	1.3	7	4.4	157	100
1680–1700	50	26.3	84	44.2	44	23.2	0	0	11	5.8	1	0.5	190	100
1700–1720	35	24.1	63	43.4	39	27.0	0	0	7	4.8	1	0.7	145	100
1720–1740	30	35.7	35	41.7	16	19.0	0	0	1	1.2	2	2.4	84	100
1740–1760	65	37.8	73	42.4	14	8.2	0	0	19	11.0	1	0.6	172	100
1760–1780	80	43.5	53	28.8	26	14.1	0	0	19	10.3	6	3.3	184	100
1780–1800	79	29.9	68	25.7	58	22.0	41	15.5	2	0.8	16	6.1	264	100
1800–1820	58	21.9	78	29.4	61	23.0	36	13.6	3	1.1	29	11.0	265	100
1820–1840	64	29.0	78	35.3	65	29.4	8	3.6	1	0.4	5	2.3	221	100
1840–1860	102	31.4	97	29.9	93	28.6	11	3.4	18	5.5	4	1.2	325	100
1860–1880	187	46.0	80	19.6	74	18.2	25	6.1	20	4.9	21	5.2	407	100
1880–1900	304	47.1	90	13.9	94	14.6	100	15.5	21	3.2	37	5.7	646	100
1900–1920	439	53.0	107	12.9	101	12.2	121	14.6	36	4.4	24	2.9	828	100

TABLE 2. INDICATORS OF FLUCTUATION OF INFLUENCE IN MAIN SYSTEMS OF TRUTH BY CENTURY PERIODS

(on the basis of *different values* given from 1 to 12)

PERIOD	*Empiricism*		*Rationalism*		*Mysticism*		*Criticism*		*Skepticism*		*Fideism*		*Total*	
	No.	*Per cent*	*No.*	*Per cent*	*No.*	*Per cent*	*No.*	*Per cent*	*No.*	*Per cent*	*No.*	*Per cent*	*No.*	*Per cent*
600–500 B.C.	6	19.4	25	80.6	0	0	0	0	0	0	0	0	31	100
500–400	23	19.2	61	50.8	0	0	0	0	36	30.0	0	0	120	100
400–300	31	14.6	89	42.0	17	8.0	0	0	54	25.4	21	10.0	212	100
300–200	34	21.7	34	21.7	1	0.6	0	0	28	17.8	60	38.2	157	100
200–100	11	19.6	16	28.6	1	1.8	0	0	12	21.4	16	28.6	56	100
100–0	26	24.3	26	24.3	7	6.5	0	0	7	6.5	41	38.4	107	100
0–100 A.D.	2	2.3	13	14.6	27	30.3	0	0	0	0	47	52.8	89	100
100–200	13	6.7	45	23.0	90	46.0	0	0	16	8.0	32	16.3	196	100
200–300	33	24.8	17	12.8	76	57.1	0	0	6	4.5	1	0.8	133	100
300–400	19	15.2	43	34.4	63	50.4	0	0	0	0	0	0	125	100
400–500	11	11.7	42	44.7	41	43.6	0	0	0	0	0	0	94	100
500–600	1	1.6	45	72.6	16	25.8	0	0	0	0	0	0	62	100
600–700	0	0	13	65.0	7	35.0	0	0	0	0	0	0	20	100
700–800	0	0	13	100	0	0	0	0	0	0	0	0	13	100
800–900	0	0	21	67.7	10	32.3	0	0	0	0	0	0	31	100
900–1000	0	0	6	75.0	2	25.0	0	0	0	0	0	0	8	100
1000–1100	3	7.7	17	43.6	11	28.2	0	0	0	0	8	20.5	39	100
1100–1200	13	14.3	38	41.8	37	40.7	0	0	0	0	3	3.2	91	100
1200–1300	21	12.8	117	71.4	26	15.8	0	0	0	0	0	0	164	100
1300–1400	28	17.2	83	51.3	40	24.7	0	0	7	4.3	4	2.5	162	100
1400–1500	3	7.2	15	35.7	20	47.6	0	0	0	0	4	9.5	42	100
1500–1600	24	15.8	44	29.0	51	33.6	0	0	21	13.8	12	7.8	152	100
1600–1700	132	29.6	179	40.1	104	23.3	0	0	21	4.7	10	2.3	446	100
1700–1800	260	37.5	212	30.6	131	18.9	41	6.0	29	4.0	20	3.0	693	100
1800–1900	644	42.6	320	21.1	261	17.2	156	10.3	42	2.8	90	6.0	1513	100

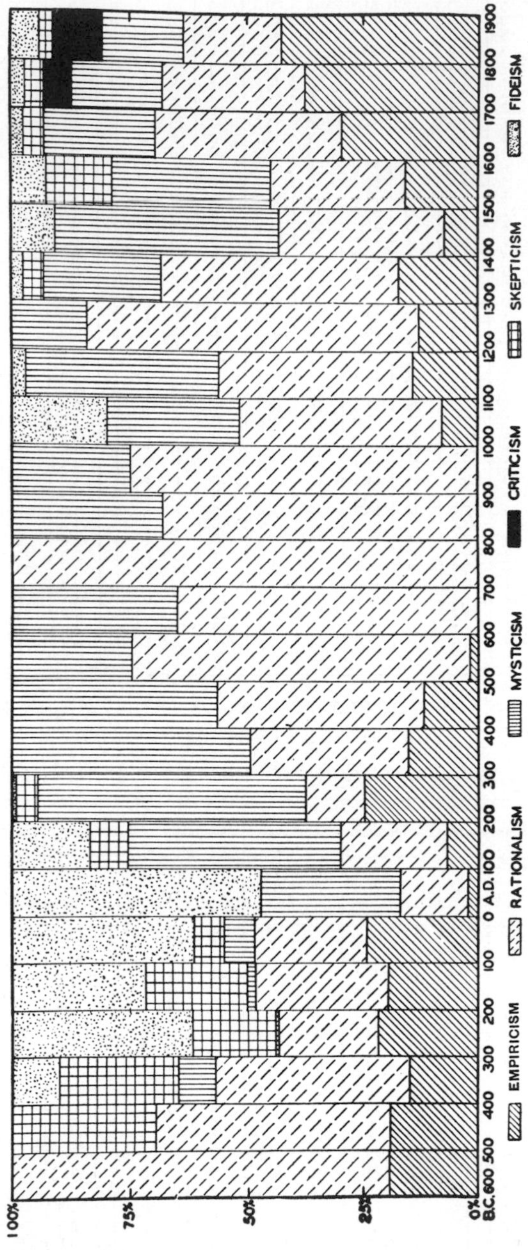

FIG. 1. FLUCTUATION OF THE INFLUENCE IN SYSTEMS OF TRUTH BY CENTURY PERIODS

one man, Thales, whose theories were mildly empirical and who is known to us only through insignificant fragments.

Other evidences we have clearly indicate that the dominant mentality at that time was strongly religious and was permeated by the *truth of faith* and by religious and magical revelations which dominated the empirical evidence and distorted its meaning according to its own nature. For these reasons the percentage of one hundred allocated to empiricism for the years 580–560 B.C. has to be discounted. This is justified by the data of the next period, 560–540 B.C., when empiricism falls sharply to 28.6 per cent and continues its decline in the subsequent period, 540 to 480 B.C., when it reaches a low of 6 per cent. This means practically that up to *the beginning of the* fifth century B.C. the predominant mentality was not empiricism but mainly religious rationalism.

The truth of faith, represented by the ideational or religious rationalism, until about 460 B.C. amounted in our system of indicators to about 90 per cent of all the systems of truth. It was only after 460 B.C. that the truth of senses (empiricism) began notably to rise and grow with minor fluctuations. It remained comparatively strong until 20 B.C., when it weakened again, and was low up to about A.D. 160, when it flared up again and stayed comparatively high until about A.D. 480. After that date it sharply declined and after A.D. 540 disappeared from the "highway" of the thought, being submerged by the rising truth of faith of Christianity. It remained hidden until about 1100, roughly some six centuries, then emerged again and began, with minor fluctuations, to climb; and in the twelfth, thirteenth, and the fourteenth centuries again attained considerable influence, notable but not dominant, somewhat approaching its influence in the fifth and the fourth centuries B.C. in Greece. In the fifteenth century, for some sixty years it disappeared again (1400–1460), then re-emerged and rose rapidly, and with minor fluctuations grew steadily up to the present time, reaching in the nineteenth century the extraordinary and unique indicator of 42 per cent (for the whole century) and foı the twentieth century a still higher indicator of some 53 per cent! For the last four centuries we have thus had a rising tide of the truth of senses, the contemporary scientific truth. This extraordinary domination of this system of truth at the present time explains why we are inclined to identify truth generally with the truth of senses, why other truths appear to us as "superstitions," why we believe that from now on the truth of senses is destined to grow further and further until it will eliminate forever all the other systems of truth. Such a mentality is but natural for this period.

D. *Movements of Truth of Senses and of Discoveries and Inventions in the Natural and Technological Sciences.* Previously it was mentioned that an additional criterion of the approximate validity of the quantita-

TABLE 3

CENTURY	NO. OF SCIENTIFIC DISCOVERIES AND INVENTIONS			INDICATORS OF EMPIRICISM	
				WEIGHT (ABSOLUTE FIGURES)	PERCENTAGE OF THE INFLUENCE OF EMPIRICISM AMONG ALL SYSTEMS OF TRUTH
	Greece	*Rome*	*Greece and Rome*	*Greece*	*Greece*
8 B.C.	6	0	6	0	0
7	3	2	5	?	?
6	26	5	31	6	19.4
5	39	1	40	23	19.2
4	52	5	57	31	14.6
3	42	3	45	34	21.7
2	14	3	17	11	19.6
				Greece and Rome	*Greece and Rome*
1	12	20	32	26	24.3
1 A.D.	25	35	60	2	2.3
2	5	13	18	13	6.7
3	0	6	6	33	24.8
4	1	15	16	19	15.2
5	0	4	4	11	11.7
6	3	1	4	1	1.6
	Western Christian Europe			*Western Christian Europe*	
7	4			0	0
8	4			0	0
9	6			0	0
10	7			0	0
11	8			3	7.7
12	12			13	14.3
13	53			21	12.8
14	65			28	17.2
15	127			3	7.2
16	429			24	14.8
17	691			132	29.6
18	1574			260	37.5
19	8527			644	42.6

tive indicators of the absolute and relative changes in the expansion and contraction of the systems of truth in the course of time is the essential agreement of the curve of the discoveries in the natural sciences and technological inventions with the curve of empiricism. Let us place the data and the curves of both movements side by side in order to verify this statement. The century indicators for both movements are shown in Table 3.

Although the data on empiricism and the scientific discoveries are not comparable because, on the one hand, we have the number of the discoveries, on the other, the percentage of the influence of empiricism among all the systems of truth or the weighted indicator of its representatives, nevertheless the three series are somewhat instructive. They show naturally many minor divergencies from century to century, and yet, when the most essential long-time waves of the discoveries and of the percentage of the influence of empiricism are taken, their remarkable agreement cannot fail to be noticed. Beginning with the twelfth century both grow from century to century. Through the period from the sixth to the twelfth century A.D. both are practically on zero line. In Greece both are comparatively high in the period from the sixth to the second century B.C.

E. *Fluctuation of the Truth of Faith. Ideational Rationalism, Mysticism, and Fideism.* The truth of faith is represented by religious or ideational rationalism, by mysticism, and by fideism. The latter two are esoteric and desperate forms of the truth of faith, while religious rationalism is the expression of a mentality free from any doubt or questioning of the truth of faith.

Understood, then, as an ensemble of religious rationalism, mysticism, and fideism, the truth of faith has had, within the period studied, the following periods of domination over the other two systems of truth.

(1) Before the fifth century B.C. in Greece, by one-hundred-year periods, religious rationalism was given a value of 80.6 per cent, and a value of 71 to 90.9 per cent in the indicators by twenty-year periods. The whole field of the systems of truth was held by religious rationalism and by a minor stream of empiricism.

(2) The period from the beginning of our era to the end of the fifth century A.D., when these three currents of the truth of faith give the indicators: 97.7 per cent for the first century; 85.3 per cent for the second; 70.7 per cent for the third; 84.8 per cent for the fourth; 88.3 per cent for the fifth. But qualitatively this period was very different from that before the fifth century B.C. because mysticism and fideism were most powerful and dominated the truth of faith. This means it was not a period of a serene faith, untroubled by doubt, but it was a period of a desperate "will to believe" assailed and attacked by empiricism and skepticism.

(3) The centuries from the sixth to the twelfth. These centuries were periods of monopolistic domination of the truth of faith over the truth of senses and the truth of reason. The truth of faith occupied 100 per cent of the field.

(4) The fifteenth century. All the three systems of truth of faith were given a total value of 92.8 per cent. Here again the main currents of the truth of faith are represented mainly by the desperate forms of mysticism and fideism, but not by religious rationalism.

It impresses us as being the last desperate effort of the truth of faith to maintain its influence before its inexorable decline for several subsequent centuries up to the present time. This decline is shown in Tables 1 and 2 by the indicators of hundred- as well as of twenty-year periods. Beginning with the sixteenth century the truth of faith in all its forms declined more and more, giving the dominant position to other systems of truth, particularly to that of truth of senses.

The following periods of the minor upward movements of each of these two currents of the truth of faith can be noted.

For Mysticism: (1) At the debut of mysticism, about the middle of the fourth century B.C. (Plato after 385, Xenocrates, and others). (2) Around the beginning of the Christian era (Philo, Thrasyllus, and others). (3) With slight oscillations it rose from the second to the end of the fourth centuries (up to A.D. 370); remained generally high throughout the fifth, sixth, and seventh centuries; and then disappeared, being merged into religious rationalism. It appeared again in the ninth and reached a high point in the twelfth century (Erigena, Maximus, Confessor, and others). (4) In the thirteenth it was low. It rose again in the fourteenth and reached its climax in the fifteenth century. In the sixteenth century it stayed high, though much lower than in the fifteenth. (5) There were slight crescendos from 1660 to 1720 and from 1780 to 1840. Since 1840 it has steadily declined up to recent times.

Fideism's highs have been: 280–240 B.C.; the first century B.C.; the first and second centuries A.D.; from the third to the eleventh centuries it was submerged, emerged for a brief period, disappeared again until the fourteenth century. Since that time, however, it has continually existed but as a current of even less importance than skepticism. Immediately after the French and other revolutions at the end of the eighteenth century it jumped up temporarily, but it soon receded and has remained at this low level up to the present time.

F. *Inverse Movement of Truth of Faith and Atheism.* It is to be logically expected that the essential movement of the curve of the truth of faith goes on inversely with the curve of the rise and decline of atheism, as the denial of God (or gods) and supersensory and superhuman intelligence, and that atheism's curve runs parallel with the truth of senses (empiricism and its allies: materialism, ethics of happiness, nominalism, temporalism, etc.). A. B. Drachmann in *Atheism in Pagan Antiquity* studies its rise and fall; his results follow inversely our curve of the movement of truth of faith and other curves (idealism, eternalism, ethics of the absolute principles, ontological realism) associated with it. Up to the fifth century B.C. we scarcely have a single case of atheism among the known thinkers, and no criminal prosecution of it. In the second part of the fifth century a decline of religion becomes noticeable and atheism as well as criminal condemnation for impiety appear (Anaxagoras, Diogenes of Apollonia, Hippo of Rhegium, Protagoras, Critias, even Socrates, and others). These streams grow in the fourth, in the third, and partly in the second centuries B.C. With the beginning of the second century A.D., if not earlier, we witness definite signs of a decrease of atheism and an increase of religiosity in the sense of a system of beliefs and practices posited in a supersensory world; beginning with God (or gods) and other transcendental values. During subsequent centuries — the third and the fourth — atheism declined and practically disappeared during all the centuries of the Middle Ages. Thus, this "variable" — a mere detail of the main variables dealt with in my work — moves in the way which can easily be deduced from the essentials of the theory of Ideational and Sensate cultures.

It is hardly needed to add that parallel with the decline of truth of faith at the end of the Middle Ages, atheism in various forms has been rising up to the present time, with minor setbacks.

G. *Fluctuation of the Truth of Reason. Idealistic Rationalism.* In the sense of the harmonious synthesis of the truth of reason, of faith, and of senses, with the truth of independent reason dominant (if not *de jure* then *de facto*), there were, so far, only two periods when this system of truth of Scholastic intellectualism was dominant. The first of these periods was about the fifth and the fourth centuries B.C. in Greece, and the second period was from the end of the twelfth to the second part of the fourteenth century with the thirteenth century as the climax. The rationalism of these periods (qualitatively not separated in Tables 1 and 2 from the religious rationalism) was idealistic rationalism. In the next chapter the qualitative analysis of the systems of truth will be given.

The upward movements of idealistic rationalism during the following periods may be mentioned.

(1) 540–450 B.C.: Pythagoreanism, Herakleitos, the Eleatian School.

(2) Second half of the fifth and the first half of the fourth century B.C. (its climax in Greece). Socrates, Plato, Aristotle, the Meharians, and others.

(3) About 200 B.C.

(4) About 80 B.C.

(5) The twelfth, the thirteenth, and the first half of the fourteenth centuries (its climax in the history of the Western culture).

(6) The first half of the fifteenth century.

(7) The sixteenth and the first half of the seventeenth centuries.

(8) The end of the eighteenth and the beginning of the nineteenth centuries. After which time the trend has been downward.

H. *Pulsation of Skepticism and Criticism.* Skepticism, as a denial of possibility of any truth, emerged rather late in the history of the Greek mentality (about the middle of the fifth century B.C.). The late appearance of this stream of thought as well as its comparatively lesser power is comprehensible.

Skepticism reached its high points in the periods from 460 to 380 B.C., 180–120 B.C., about 20 B.C., and then in the second century A.D. when it flared up for the last time in the Graeco-Roman world. After the third century A.D., when the era of the truth of faith was ushered in, there was no place for skepticism and it disappeared until the fourteenth century, when it emerged for a short time. Disappearing again in the fifteenth century (the century of mysticism and fideism), it reappeared in the sixteenth century and since that time has existed only as a minor stream of thought. Since the sixteenth century the periods 1520–1540, 1560–1600, 1740–1780 were marked by increases in the influence of skepticism.

By examining its trends it can be observed that skepticism emerges usually when the truth of faith declines and when truth of reason and especially truth of senses begin to grow. In this sense it is a satellite of the first phases of growth of empiricism because of its relativistic and agnostic tendencies. However, when empiricism triumphs, skepticism retreats, although it does not disappear as it does in the periods when truth of faith dominates.

It can be observed, also, that the periods of a flaring up of skepticism have usually been those either immediately preceding or coinciding with the periods in which great social upheavals and calamities occurred: the Peloponnesian War and subsequent calamities; the great civil wars in Rome of the first and the second triumvirates; the Black Plague; the emergence of Christianity; the Reformation; the religious wars of the Reformation and of the League; and the great French Revolution.

The third fact to be noted is that as soon as skepticism rises its emergence or rise is almost immediately followed by emergence and rise of fideism as a desperate reaction against it.

Finally, *criticism* (in a specific sense a critical philosophy) is a special rivulet which emerged at the end of the eighteenth century mainly through the works of Hume and Kant. It appeared comparatively strong at once. After about 1810, however, it experienced, like several currents of thought, a sharp decline in strength as a result of the reaction against the ideologies of the Revolution. After 1860 it reassumed its growth, and at the end of the nineteenth century and at the present time has become, next to empiricism, the most powerful current. From the figures one can see that its movements are almost opposite to that of skepticism. This suggests that in a sense it is a diluted form of it and fulfills in a much milder way the functions of skepticism which in a pure form cannot function under the given psychosocial conditions.

I. *Total Mental Spectrum of the Main Periods*. We shall now concentrate on the total mentality of the main parts of the period under investigation. The following inferences are warranted by the character of the "mental spectrum" of these parts.

(1) The total spectrum of mentality (in the field studied) of Greece before the fifth century B.C. appeared to be predominantly Ideational. The system of the religious rationalism was overwhelmingly dominant, and empiricism only as a minor force was present; neither skepticism, mysticism, fideism, criticism, nor even idealistic rationalism existed. It was the period of certitude in the Greek mentality, the age of the certitude of faith; the age of calm serenity and untroubled simplicity.

(2) The fifth century, especially its second part and also the first two-thirds of the fourth century B.C. were marked by the domination of the *idealistic rationalism* or the *truth of reason.* The system of truth of "scholastic intellectualism" (the truth of the autonomous and dialectic reason in contradistinction to religious rationalism) occupied about 40 per cent of the field; truth of faith was still recognized in the form of Plato's "divine madness" or Aristotle's theology; empiricism was not only present but was also comparatively strong; even skepticism, mysticism, and fideism existed, although each was comparatively weak.

All the three truths harmoniously coexisted, and more than that, all were organically blended into one system of truth; namely, idealistic rationalism, giving *suum cuique* to the truth of faith, of reason, of senses. The main governor, if not *de jure* then *de facto,* was dialectics, through which and upon which was based the evidential power of even the truth of faith. The mental spectrum was marvelously balanced and free from any extremism. None of the negative or desperate current (skepticism, fideism, mysticism) tended to be dominant. All these characteristics are evidences of the domination of truth of reason in that period.

In the light of such a spectrum of the Idealistic system of truth, and in the light of the data concerning all the main branches of art of the fifth and fourth centuries, their culture and mentality appear to be idealistic. This means that the contended correlation between the main types of cultures and the respective main types of the dominant systems of truth (Ideational culture and truth of faith; Idealistic, and the truth of reason; Sensate and the empirical system of truth) is so far well supported by the data.

(3) In the subsequent centuries — the third, the second, and the first B.C. — the tide of empiricism grew and became as strong as rationalism. Rationalism of both types greatly declined and the negative and desperate forms of truth flourished. The above correlations indicated a rising tide of the Sensate culture and a decline of the Ideational and the Idealistic cultures in their strong and balanced forms; and a growth of the esoteric, exotic, and desperate mentality in the field; or a great mental disturbance, disorganization, and upheaval. Subsequent centuries —

from the first B.C. to the third A.D. — were stamped by the entrance of the Romans in the field. In the first and second centuries A.D. Christianity with its thinkers appeared. The spectrum of the mentality in the field of truth in these centuries is very interesting and peculiar. In reference to the Pagan mentality (data have been computed separately for the Christian and for the Pagan thinkers of these centuries) empiricism and rationalism (in the sense of the truth of reason) declined; in their places, skepticism, mysticism, and fideism grew, indicating a disturbed mentality and a great transition from one form of culture and truth to another fundamentally different. The dominant system of the period is either cynical skepticism, purely negative in its cynicism, or esoteric and desperate systems of mysticism and fideism. In a sense such a mentality is a mixture of Ideationalism, partly Idealism and partly Sensate truth. It bears some resemblance to Idealism but merely imitates it because the real Idealism is harmonious idealistic rationalism. From the analysis of the forms of art we have seen that the period was indeed pseudo Idealistic, on the one hand, and cynically Sensate, on the other. It bears the marks of the confused mixture of artificial pseudo Idealism with cynicism, so typical for the periods foreboding a decline of a Sensate form of culture and a transition to the Ideational form.

The Christian mentality represented, since the second century, only two currents: desperate and militant mysticism and religious rationalism. Mysticism, however, was about twice as powerful as religious rationalism (the indicators of religious rationalism being thirty-two for the second century, and that of mysticism sixty-one for the Christian thinkers). This means that the Christian thinkers rejected entirely the empirico-Sensate (scientific) system of truth, and embraced mainly an admixture of the truth of faith and the truth of subservient reason.

The total indicators of Tables 1 and 2 for these two centuries thus represent a mixture of these two widely different mentalities of the Pagan thought with a very dissimilar Christian truth of faith. The Pagan thought was thrown out of balance by the tragic circumstances of the preceding period and somewhat lost its faith in the truth of the senses as well as in that of independent reason and turned, instead, either to cynicism and skepticism or to fideism, as the artificial will to believe, and to mysticism, as the desperate truth of faith. The Christian thought broke completely with the truth of senses and turned to a belief in the truth of the Gospel, in revelation, and in mystical experience, slightly supported by the truth of logic in so far as it did not contradict the creed and could be used for its purpose. Here, then, was a great shattering of the empirical and idealistically rationalistic systems of truth which were dominant before.

(4) When the indicators of the spectrum of mentality of the next

two centuries — the third and the fourth — are examined, the first impression is that the mental balance shattered previously has been somewhat regained; skepticism and fideism practically disappeared; among the Pagans empiricism had a revival (even a few Christian thinkers shared it); rationalism grew also, mainly among the Christian thinkers; but mysticism gained especially great influence with the Pagan as well as with the Christian contributors.

(5) We are at the end of the empirico-rationalistic system of truth and at the beginning of the domination of the truth of faith, with the truth of reason assuming a subsidiary role. Within one century or a little more this became clear; empiricism declined and disappeared. The truth of faith became dominant and clothed itself in the solid and confident form of the religious rationalism; as such it was stabilized and from that time needed no extreme and desperate forms, like fideism or esoteric mysticism. We are ushered into the age of faith which questioned nothing in the Gospel and in God's truth. We are in the age of a new great ideationalism of the Middle Ages, in the monopolistic domination of the truth of faith with its "handmaid" human reason (not questioning but only justifying and serving faith). The indicators show that such a situation continued for about six centuries.

This is certainly an Ideational age, not only on the basis of the dominant truth of faith, of the dominant Ideational art, but also upon the basis of data given subsequently. If at any period in the history of the Western mentality the philosophers and the people as a whole felt that they were in the possession of truth, the whole truth, and nothing but truth, it was in these centuries. There was no skepticism, no questioning, no doubt, no relativity, no hesitation, no reservation.

(6) Then in the eleventh century empiricism reappeared after many centuries. Weak at the beginning, it doubled its strength in the twelfth century, especially at its end, and stabilized itself in the thirteenth and fourteenth centuries. Thus in these centuries the monopolistic domination of the truth of faith with its subordinate, the truth of reason, was ended. The mental spectrum changed; it became a harmonious blending of empiricism and of mysticism with the dominant truth of independent rationalism different from religious rationalism of the previous period.

The harmonious blending of the truths of faith, of senses (empiricism), and of reason gave the idealistic rationalism of the great Scholastics of the twelfth and the thirteenth centuries the dominant position in that period. In it *suum cuique* is given to all these sources and to all the criteria of truth and knowledge. It united them all harmoniously into one organic unity where faith, senses, and reason did not fight one another, but all were co-operating in the great service to God, to truth, and to man's real happiness, in building the full and complete truth, real wisdom and knowledge not narrowed to one vista and not reduced to one source. A wonderful and happy age! An age in which science did not fight religion, and vice versa; in which the organs of senses did not disdainfully reason: "*Nihil esse in intellectu quod non fuerit prius in sensu*," or reason did not consider the senses as the foolish and incompetent registers of the shadows of reality, but respected them and accepted their testimony within certain limits in the fields where they were thought to be competent. The age of Idealistic system of truth. It was the European replica of the Greek Idealistic mentality of the fifth and fourth centuries B.C.

In the second part of the fourteenth and in the fifteenth centuries the Idealistic system was shattered and a desperate and esoteric kind of mysticism prevailed. Its wave swept over Western society. During the second part of the sixteenth century, and especially in the seventeenth, however, mysticism subsided, and empiricism gained in strength, which with very slight fluctuations has persisted up to the present time. The system of faith, as well as rationalism, and the truth of reason also lost ground and the truth of senses became triumphant. At the end of the nineteenth and in the twentieth century (at least up to the prewar time) its influence has grown to unprecedented heights. Verily we are living in the age of scientism! This means our culture is Sensate culture par excellence! As a result, the other systems of truth have been constantly degraded to a lower level of sterile speculation, fantastic and unscientific and unverified purely logical derivations — in regard to the truth of reason; and to mere superstition and ignorance so far as the truth of faith is concerned. Discord between these systems of truth marks this period. Scientific truth leads the offensive in an effort to exterminate entirely the other systems of truth, and they in turn are fighting for their existence. So far the offensive of the empirical system of truth has been successful and has driven the other systems from the vast territory which they occupied before the seventeenth and especially the fourteenth centuries. It has weakened also their inner strength and confidence in themselves and their validity. It has forced them to imitate — even in the question of pure theology and logic — the weapons, the tactics, and the strategy of the triumphant scientific truth of senses. Hence scientism as a cult; hence the commonly accepted opinion that there is only one truth and knowledge — the scientific; hence the belief that in the future these other systems of truth will be entirely eliminated from human mentality as useless survivals of ignorance and superstition; hence all the other similar phenomena and beliefs of that kind. On the other hand, our age being resplendent in the variety of its scintillating colors has, at the same time, something of "the devil's spectrum," if one may say so figuratively. Its spectrum is exceedingly complex. *It believes less than almost any other age in reason, in nonsensory sources of truth, in thought itself;* in anything and anybody that cannot be seen, heard, tasted, smelled, touched, and sensed generally. In this sense it is the age which looks for truth only in "the empirical bank" of senses, investing a greater part of its mental capital in it (in contradistinction to the Middle Ages particularly). As this bank has had many difficulties, however, investors cannot have complete confidence in its integrity or in the safety of their too little diversified investments. For these reasons the undercurrents of skepticism and criticism flow unhindered and destroy the serenity, faith, and sense of security in the truth of senses. We try to convince ourselves that our investments are safe and that we are happy, but only for a moment, as our feeling of insecurity never vanishes but tends rather to grow more and more. Skepticism and criticism compose about 20 per cent (for the years 1880–1900 and 1900–1920) of all systems of truth — an unusually high percentage, indicating a growing crisis of our Bank of the Truth of Senses!

This and other symptoms make the future of the "Bank of Empirical Truth" uncertain. There are already many indications of the coming crisis of the scientific system of truth (as the truth of senses) and of its decline. Any system of truth that is dominant begins to be undermined from within the system itself. The feeling of confidence in science has begun to wane as it waned in the system of faith at the end of the Middle Ages. There are many symptoms examined elsewhere in this work. For these and many other reasons it appears improbable to me that the trend of growth of empiricism and scientism will continue, but sooner or later the trend will probably change and possibly even be reversed. As a matter of fact, many empirical truths of the social sciences and humanities, sufficiently corroborated by empirical data, have already been declared untrue, treasonable, and heretical, and have been replaced by the truths, faiths, credos, dogmas, and revelations of the Communist, Hitlerite, Mussolinian, or democratic bosses. The words on the wall are beginning to be written; and they forebode the coming decline (perhaps temporarily, perhaps for a long time) of the triumphant empiricism.

During some twenty years that elapsed after the publication of the *Dynamics*, the prognosis has been well corroborated. First, through the discovery of the nuclear and bacteriological means of destruction, science and its empirism threaten now the very future of mankind, and the future of science itself. If a new world war explodes, it is likely to stop for a long time scientific creativity itself through destruction of civilization and a considerable part of the human population.

Then during these twenty years science and its empirical system of truth have undergone a substantial change. This change has already made today's science less empiricistic, materialistic, mechanistic and deterministic — less sensate — than it was during the preceding centuries. For this modern science, matter has become but a condensed form of energy which dematerializes into radiation. The material atom is already dissolved into more than thirty non-material, "cryptic, arcane, enigmatic and inscrutable" elementary particles: electron and anti-electron, proton and anti-proton, photon, meson, etc., or into "the image of waves which turn into the waves of probability, waves of consciousness, which our thought projects afar. . . ." These waves, like those associated with the propagation of light quanta, need no substratum in order to propagate in space-time; they undulate neither in fluid, nor in solid, nor yet in a gas. . . ." Around a bend of quantum mechanics and in a subatomic world the basic notions of materialistic, mechanistic, and empiricistic science such as: matter, objective reality, time, space, causality, are no longer applicable and the testimony of our senses largely is already replaced in the modern science by Heisenberg's principle of uncertainty, by fanciful "quanta jumps", by a mere chance relationship or — in psychosocial phenomena — by "voluntaristic," "free-willing, law of direction" free from causality and chance.

Similar transformations have taken place in biological, psychological and social sciences. All this means that science itself has already become much less sensate and empiristic than it was in the nineteenth century.

Likewise, almost all newly emerging systems of philosophy, like Existentialism, Intuitivism, Integralism, Neo-Mysticism, Neo-Realism, Neo-Thomism, New-Vendantism, are essentially different from all forms of empiricism, materialism, "positivism" and other Sensate systems of philosophy.

These changes excellently corroborate the *Dynamics*' prognosis of the coming decline of the domination of empirical, Sensate system of truth and science.

J. *Principle of Limit and of Self-regulation of Sociocultural Processes.* If the closest rivals among these systems are selected and studied for three separate periods, and also for the entire period, the total sums of the indicators of each of the rival currents are shown in Table 4.

TABLE 4. SUMS OF THE INDICATORS OF SOCIOCULTURAL PROCESSES

Periods	*Fideism*	*Skepticism*	*Empiricism*	*Rationalism*
580 B.C. to A.D. 100	185	137	133	264
100 to 1500	52	29	145	515
1500 to 1900	132	113	1060	755
Total	369	279	1338	1534

No arithmetical and mechanical balances are sought in this or in any other social process; nevertheless, considering the fact that the length of the total period studied is about twenty-five hundred years, and that all these indices have been made without any idea of an arithmetical balance, one must confess that the sums of the indices for fideism-skepticism and empiricism-rationalism are strikingly close. It suggests that in the sociocultural life and sociomental processes there seems to be present some factor which, in the long run, does not permit any single or extreme current to absorb all the other systems for any length of time and thus to narrow the richness and many-colored completeness of truth.

These figures give a concrete idea of the principle of immanent self-regulation of sociocultural processes. This immanent self-regulation is manifested, however, by our data in a different form.

The unfolding of the course of the currents studied starts with a mild empiricism which almost simultaneously is balanced by a mild rationalism. Action of empiricism, so to speak, is followed almost immediately by counterreaction of rationalism. When one is moderate the other is moderate also.

Then, in the process of differentiation, skepticism appears; and almost immediately it is counterbalanced by the appearance of fideism and partly by mysticism. Again action is followed by counterreaction. Those who know the character of the philosophies of each of the periods can scarcely fail to see that if one current becomes more extreme in its accentuation of its own truth and in its denial of the truth of its rival, the competing philosophies usually become also more sharp and extreme.

Further on, it can be seen again that when skepticism disappears from the highway of thc philosophical mentality, fideism, as its closest rival, disappears also, and later on when one reappears the other soon reappears.

Empiricism and rationalism, selected as closest rivals, show considerable deviations from the line of balance, especially during the Middle Ages. Yet, the data show that all in all even these great deviations are but temporary phenomena and over a longer period of time seem to be corrected, if not quantitatively then quantitatively-qualitatively.

For the whole period considered the total sums of the indicators for each of these currents and the respective systems of truth are as follows:

Fideism	369	*Truth of faith*	1650
Skepticism	279	*Truth of reason*	1292
Mysticism	1039	*Truth of senses*	1338
Criticism	197	*Skepticism and Criticism*	476
Empiricism	1338		
Rationalism	1534		

These figures show that in the cultures studied the religious and the idealistic rationalism has been so far the most powerful system of truth. Then next in importance was empiricism, then mysticism, then fideism, then skepticism and criticism. Interpreted in another way, in reference to the system of truth, the total sums of the indicators of power of all the systems of truth are fairly close, giving a slight edge to the truth of faith. This demonstrates once more the principle of immanent self-regulation of sociocultural processes and their autonomous tendency to balance one another, sometimes quantitatively, sometimes qualitatively, sometimes quantitatively and qualitatively. The data suggest, also, that possibly each form of truth has its own important function in the psychosocial life of mankind and is equally necessary. Otherwise this unexpected balance would hardly have been possible. Perhaps, indeed, the devil in one of Anatole France's novels was after all not so wrong in saying that the absolute and whole truth is "white," meaning by white a color which represents a blending of all the colors of the spectrum. Perhaps the whole and absolute truth is indeed the truth which embraces in some way all the three forms of truth, each of which is therefore only a "partial truth."

14

QUALITATIVE CLARIFICATION OF THE FLUCTUATION OF THE SYSTEMS OF TRUTH AND KNOWLEDGE

For many readers who are not familiar with epistemology, philosophy, and the theory of science, the data as well as the conclusions of the previous chapter may appear less significant and convincing than they are. Partly for this reason and partly as a further substantiation and corroboration of the theory set forth previously, it is advisable to show, as concisely as possible, that a shift from one system of truth to another means the greatest revolution of human mentality and culture, and that these revolutions have occurred several times during the periods and centuries marked by the above tables.

I. Ideational Phase of Greek Mentality

Before the fifth century B.C., the theory of truth which dominated in Greece was the religious and magical truth of faith, supplemented by subservient reason, and by the truth of senses. Such was the truth mentality of Homeric Greece, of the Hesiodic *Theogony* and *Work and Days;* and, as was shown, by the Greek religion of the period; by many "truth institutions" of Greece, such as the oracles, prophets, seers, priests; by many religious and magic practices, agencies, and institutions as the mouthpieces of the divinely inspired and revealed truth which was unconcerned with the testimony of the organs of senses.

II. Idealistic Phase of Greek Thought

The indicators for the fifth and fourth centuries B.C. show a considerable change in the spectrum of the epistemological mentality which is now the spectrum of the Idealistic theory of truth.

If rationalism, the most powerful of all the currents of the period, is considered separately, it can be seen that it preserves all the earmarks of the Idealistic system of truth. The systems of truth of Anaximendros, Pythagoras, Xenophanes, Herakleitos, Parmenides, Hippasos, Zenon, Anaxagoras, Archytas, Archelaos, Philolaos, Aeschines, Kratilos, Melissos, Eukleidos, and others have these earmarks. Naturally this comes in a most perfect form in the systems of truth of the greatest leaders of the period, namely, Socrates (469–399 B.C.) and his greatest pupil, Plato (427–347 B.C.).

What are its essential traits from the standpoint of our problem? Reduced to a brief formula they are as follows: There are three degrees of knowledge and truth, three sources and ways of cognition: first, through the organs of senses is obtained a knowledge of the ever-changing empirical world and phenomena which gives a very uncertain truth. All the empirical sciences based on observation through organs of senses give this inferior and unlasting truth. Plato disdainfully terms such a knowledge mere "opinion." The second form or degree of knowledge is based partly upon the data of the organs of senses and partly upon the logical laws of human intelligence which uses and fashions the raw material of the organs of senses according to its own laws; for example, mathematics, geometry, and human logic itself. Their verities are mainly those of the human mind or intelligence, and their certainties are much greater than those of the truths of senses. Finally, the third and the most sublime form of knowledge is "divine intuition," or "divine contemplation," or "divine madness," which in an act of pure and sublime contemplation, divine inspiration, or mystic experience and revelation, goes beyond the empirical appearances, beyond even human logic, to the everlasting ultimate reality — the eternal Being — identifies itself with it and merges into it, not only from without but from within, and thus achieves complete, eternal, and certain knowledge — the supreme and absolute truth. This sublime, divine, or mystic form of truth cannot be imparted by teaching or training because it is the gift of the gods, and only those who have this spark can grasp it.

It is not incidental also that for an allusion of the most sublime verities, Plato uses — and is forced to use, as an Ideationalist — a poetic-symbolic language, images, and terms. The Platonic system of truth and knowledge, then, embraces all the three main forms of truth — the truth of "divine madness or revelation," the truth of reason or intelligence, and the truth of senses. It also combines them, giving *suum quique*, into one coherent whole, in which empiricism is assigned an unimportant but a real place and divine contemplation is given the highest place. All this is shaped through and by the finest dialectic of human mind. Such a system is *idealistically rationalistic*, par excellence.

Besides Plato and the Platonic school, not to mention other rationalists of the period studied, idealistic rationalism was professed also by the other powerful school, the Peripatetic, whose great leader was Aristotle (384–322 B.C.). In spite of the fact that the elements of the truth of senses played a much larger part in the Aristotelian theory of truth than in the Platonic (that is also significant as an expression of the further increase of scientific discoveries and inventions and of a growing "sensualization" of the Greek culture as we pass from the fifth to the fourth centuries B.C. and from the first part of the fourth century to its second part), as a whole the Aristotelian theory of truth is a variety of the same idealistic rationalism, embracing in its organic synthesis the elements of all the three systems of truth. The truth of the senses is given much more importance than in Plato's system; the truth of reason or logic, with its categories and the Νοῦς (though here lies one of the dark points of the Aristotelian logics), is not derived from perceptions but organizes perceptions of the senses into knowledge; and finally, the truth of theology or metaphysics is the ultimate and supreme knowledge with God, to which it leads and whose existence it states.

These two schools were the great schools of the time and as such typify the dominant system of truth of that period.

In the field of the thought they both can be styled the Phidias and the Praxiteles. They possess the same traits, play the same role, and give the same type of creations as Phidias and Praxiteles in sculpture; as Polygnotus in drawing; as Pindar, Aeschylus, and Sophocles in literature and music.

Let us glance at the subsequent "confused" period.

What spectrum of mentality is shown by the third and the second century B.C.? We have a great decline of idealistic rationalism; a comparative increase of empiricism; and especially a great growth of fideism and skepticism. Thus a situation existed very similar to that which was encountered in the field of Hellenistic art.

During the entire third century Hellenistic Greece continued successfully its scientific work, as shown by the number of discoveries and inventions. Likewise, the mature Sensate culture continued to scintillate, spreading far and wide. Hence, a comparatively high level of empiricism. And yet at the same time shadows of the coming decline of this culture and empiricism quickly grew. After the Peloponnesian War (431–404 B.C.)

Greece was in all respects in a hopeless state of decline. . . . The old morality and propriety of conduct disappeared. . . . The old belief in the Gods was gone. Art could no longer compare with the excellence of the strictly classic period. The government became more ineffectual.

Each party as it gained the supremacy, in turn massacred the prominent members of the opposition. Tyrants in name or in reality; foreign adventurers in search of power or pleasure; mercenary troops with no national ties and respect for law, morality, or religion; exiles saturated with the gathered hatred of the years. These and similar inflammable conditions throughout Greece made the life of a peaceful inhabitant impossible. With no security for life and property, poverty and lawlessness spread apace; and the young not infrequently grew up indifferent to their country, sceptical of their religion, bent upon enjoyment, and seasoning sensuality with a dash of literary or philosophic cultivation. . . . Such was Greece in the beginning of the third century.

About one hundred and thirty-five years elapsed from the time of Pericles to the organization of the Stoic school. During this period occurred the Peloponnesian War (431–404) which ruined Greece; the collapse of Sparta before the Thebans at Leuctra (371); the subjection of Greece to Macedonia after Chaeronea (338).

Whatever were the reasons, one thing is clear, that adaptation through a successful alteration of the exterior (social, biological, and cosmic) world became more and more difficult for Greek society after the end of the fourth century and especially after the third century B.C.

In spite of their difficulties, all the main currents have one trait in common; namely, a tendency to turn away from the sensate reality — imperturbability (ataraxia) of Pyrrho and other Skeptics; freedom of body from pain and of mind from disturbance achieved through inner tranquillity of the Epicureans; a complete contempt for external environment by the Cynics; and the apathy and concentration on the inner self of many of the Stoics. They all are similar and all advocate the achievement of happiness, equilibrium, peace of mind, even partly truth, or physical and mental adaptation, not so much through modification of the external environment as through modification of man himself and his mind.

Hence fideism and skepticism increased during this period. As a result the spectrum of mentality is one of overripe Sensate culture whose zenith is over.

III. Mixed Phase of Graeco-Roman Mentality

Let us pass now to the mental spectrum of the next centuries. Beginning with the first century B.C. the Romans — meaning by the Romans not only the Romans by nationality but all the thinkers in the orbit of the Roman Empire — entered the field. Many of these were of Egyptian, Syrian, or of other Oriental extraction. The mental spectrum of these centuries was not a natural development of the previous Roman mentality but a violent transformation of it through the most effective influence of Hellenistic mentality complicated further by Oriental influences.

An examination of the diagram will show that in the first century B.C. almost all the field is occupied by a somewhat reinforced Epicurean empiricism, fideism, skepticism, mysticism, and a still less influential idealistic rationalism.

The total sociocultural constellation of the first centuries B.C. and A.D., with their tragic events, prevented such a development and resulted in the most *desperate and tragic spectrum of the Roman truth mentality of the first century* A.D.

Of the twenty-five centuries it had the smallest percentage of idealistic rationalism; the lowest percentage of empiricism (with the exception of the medieval centuries), and more than 80 per cent of it was taken up by fideism and mysticism. Tragic and desperate spectrum indeed! And, yet, when the relevant factors are considered, such a spectrum is but natural. Why?

It is enough to point out the main tragedies of the centuries considered in order to comprehend the inevitability of this.

Roughly, from the end of the second century B.C., the first signs of a decline of the successful Sensate adaptation appeared. Outwardly Rome was still victorious and continued to mold the other societies into its own body, and it continued to grow. Inwardly conditions changed. Inner class struggles started and resulted in a series of riots, revolts, and the great civil wars of the first and the second triumvirates, which lasted, with short intervals of interruption, about one century.

During this period (the end of the second and the first centuries B.C.) life became exceedingly difficult. First, security of life was gone. Mass terror and mass slaughtering of the opponents of the temporarily victorious faction made security of life impossible. Incessant mass confiscations of property of the defeated faction reduced to zero the sacred right of property and material security. Farmers and peasants were dispossessed of their land and were turned into the urban proletariat. The proletariat itself — mental and intellectual — was placed in the position of a homeless, lawless, and propertyless parasite, poorly fed and poorly amused at the cost of the state. It became the bearer of the spirit of restlessness and destruction at the hands of the demagogues and politicians. Previous prosperity led to a development of sensuality and materialism; traditional rustic mores vanished. The result was a general demoralization.

The time of Augustus and a few other periods showed temporary improvement, but even then "a nameless unease, amounting to fear, sometimes assailed men. . . . A mist of unshed tears seems to haunt the stream of Virgil's genius . . . majestic in its sadness at the doubtful doom of human kind." Similar presentiment is noticeable in Lucretius. Among the masses the idea of the end of the world began to spread.

After the first century, with a few breathing spells, the decline of the Roman Sensate culture, with its economic comfort, security, sentient pleasures, and so on, resumed its course and led to the so-called "Fall of the Roman Empire."

The mental effects of such a desperate situation are almost always an enormous growth of the apocalyptic fideism and mysticism on the one hand and, on the other, cynical and nihilistic skepticism and *Carpe diem* sensualism. This is what is reflected in our tables.

Since the active Sensate adaptation through change and improvement of the external world proved itself more and more helpless, a part of the people and thinkers began to turn more and more to the Ideational world in their ethical mentality as well as in their quest for truth and knowledge. The turning, however, was made in despair. Therefore, it assumed not the form of calm and serene Ideational rationalism but that of fideism and mysticism — desperate and militant.

Under these conditions the catastrophic and apocalyptic mentality was natural. Inevitable, also, was the firm belief in the approaching end of the world. We have more than enough evidence showing the widespread belief in this end by Christians, Jews, Gnostics, Roman Stoics, Neo-Platonists, Neo-Pythagoreanists.

This belief persisted during the next centuries as the calamities continued:

they regarded the end of the world as quite near. And these beliefs continued to grow toward the fifth century amidst the calamities which accompanied the invasions of the barbarians and the collapse of the Empire.

Relaxation of the mores at the beginning of the Christian Era has often been exaggerated, but it was real. Many unsound symptoms testify to a profound moral anarchy. As the end of the Empire approached the wills of the people seem to have been softened and the temperaments enervated. There was less and less of the robust soundness of character; greater became the diffusion of degeneration and deterioration which follow the orgies of the passions; the same weakness which led to crime was responsible for the attempts to find absolution in the practice of asceticism and the people went to the priests of the oriental religions, as to the physicians of soul, demanding spiritual remedies.

It would be a miracle if in such an atmosphere mysticism and fideism would not develop.

On the other hand, such a catastrophic constellation favored also a development of nihilism, cynical skepticism, or passive and cynical Epicureanism.

Later on, and with the great masses of people, it changed into the desperate tone of the *Carpe diem*, and bitter and cynical disappointment became extreme. This philosophy, during the period of Rome's decline, affected not only the uneducated but the intellectuals as well, like Lucian (A.D. 120–200), who wrote: "The altars of Zeus are as cold as Chrysippus. Religion is absurd, philosophy vacuous, therefore, let us enjoy the moment, eschewing enthusiasms." For a short time society can believe in such a *Carpe diem*, but it cannot continue to do so indefinitely. An examination of Tables 1 and 2 and Figure 1 discloses that after the third century this Epicurean skepticism and nihilism disappeared.

IV. The Rising Tide of Ideational Truth of Faith

Stoics, Neo-Platonists, Neo-Pythagoreans, and some others among the Pagans, all more and more began to subscribe to mysticism and fideism as the desperate forms of the rising Ideational system of truth. The partisans of various esoteric and mystic religions and sects, with which the Roman culture began to be flooded, did likewise. Finally, the Christians, who were destined to absorb all these rivulets, became the main bearers of the rising Ideational truth and the main destroyers of the truth of senses and even of pure reason (for these first centuries of the Christian era). Though during the second and especially the third centuries A.D. the empirical system of truth rose again — after its depression in the first century — and though scientific discoveries continued during these centuries, amounting to eighteen, six, sixteen in the Graeco-Roman world for the second, third, and fourth centuries respectively, the last flaring up of the Graeco-Roman empiricism and science before its long-time sleep took place. After the third century empiricism rapidly waned and in the sixth century disappeared; likewise, the number of scientific discoveries decreased to only four in the fifth, sixth, and seventh centuries. The Sensate culture mentality and system of truth declined and the new Ideational mentality and truth rose in influence. During the first centuries of its growth, Ideational truth assumed the desperate form of mysticism and fideism on account of sociocultural conditions and its struggle for existence and growth. After the fifth century A.D., when its victory was secured, mysticism and fideism gave place to Ideational rationalism as the serene and confident system of truth of faith.

In the light of the preceding conditions it must be obvious that the *first five or six centuries of the Christian era were periods in which one of the greatest mental revolutions occurred.* During these centuries the Graeco-Roman and then the Western mentality changed from the predominant system of truth of senses to that of truth of faith. It was accomplished, as is any great mental revolution, not without bitter mental and moral clashes of the radically different systems of truth. The partisans (the Christians) of the rising Ideational truth realized fully its incompatibility with the truth of senses and of reason and were fully aware of what they were doing when they pitilessly attacked the truth of senses and the truth of reason. The partisans (the scholars, intellectuals, scientists, and philosophers) of the declining truth of senses and of reason seem not to have understood, especially at the beginning of the struggle, the gravity of the situation and the mortal danger in which their system of truth and knowledge was placed. Like many contemporary scientists and scholars, they regarded the Christian, as well as other Ideational systems of truth, as mere superstition or ignorance.

And yet, contrary to their firm belief, the truth of an unquestioning and professedly illogical, irrational, un-Sensate, or, to use the current jargon, "an unscientific, blind, superstitious," truth of faith came and was monopolistic for almost nine centuries in the form of the system of truth of the Christian Faith.

One of the greatest and deepest mental transformations in the history of mankind — the revolution in the very foundations of truth, knowledge, wisdom, upon which depend and by which are conditioned all the superstructures of all the theories and opinions about everything, in any field of culture and in any compartment of the mental activity, in the sciences, in the arts, in philosophy, in ethics and law, and what not — took place.

Its essence was a complete shift from the truth of senses and that of the reason, and from the vagaries of skepticism, fideism, and other systems of mental weariness, and of disillusionment, to the dogmatic, superrational, supersensible, superskeptical, superfideistic *truth of pure faith*, openly negligent and disdainful of all other sources of truth and knowledge *except faith and divine revelation.*

Already the Apostles, who had absolute confidence in the truth of the Gospel, revelation, and prophetic gift, clearly and unequivocally expressed this negative attitude toward empirical science, the empirical system of truth, and logical reason.

Likewise the Gospel itself, as *the glad tidings* about Jesus, does not pretend to prove its truths by empirical tests, but by faith and creed. The Apostles, including St. Paul, do not teach the gospel of empirical experience but the "Gospel of God," "the word of the Lord," "the word of faith," or "the truth."

"We preach not ourselves, but Christ Jesus," says St. Paul. And in the Epistle to the Galatians he definitely states that he received this Gospel or the word of faith not from man but through direct revelation from Christ.

Quite consistently, therefore, the early Christian thinkers unequivocally rejected *expressis verbis* the empirico-Sensate and even rationalistic systems of truth.

> Paul has a profound contempt for Philosophy [and still greater for the empirical science, one can add] or "the wisdom of this world," "the wisdom of men," as he calls it.

From this standpoint "the wisdom of this world is foolishness with God." Similar, perhaps even more forceful, language is used by the early Christian thinkers and Church Fathers in their radical rejection of the testimony of the organs of senses or of reason (respectively empirical and rationalistic systems of truth) as the criteria of truth.

In the *Legatio pro Christianis* of Athenagoras (*c.* A.D. 177) we read:

Poets and philosophers . . . have not been found competent fully to apprehend the truth, because they thought fit to learn, not from God concerning God, but each one from himself.

When we pass to the writings of Irenaeus (*Adv. haereses*, *c.* 185), of Clement of Alexandria (*Stromateis*, *c.* 200), of Origen (185–254), (*Philocalia*), especially of Tertullian (*Apology*, *c.* 197), then of St. Jerome (*Epistles*, *c.* 384), of Athanasius (*Ad monachos*, *c.* 358–360); of St. Basil of Caesarea (*Epistles*, *c.* 370–379), of Gregory of Nazianus (*Orations*, *d.* 390), and, omitting other names, of St. Augustine, the same motives and statements are reiterated still more powerfully and the negatively contemptuous estimation of human knowledge — empirical or rational — becomes still sharper and still more emphatic.

St. Augustine, who like St. Jerome and St. Basil before him, was before his conversion one of the leading intellectuals of his age, well versed in Graeco-Roman science and philosophy, expressed all this in a still more emphatic and temperamental form, similar to the "bolshevistic" denunciation of all Human Wisdom and all systems of Truth, except that of the Gospel, by Tertullian.

After St. Augustine's conversion to Christianity his attitude toward the whole Graeco-Roman culture and social world was purely "bolshevistic." Rhetoricians, scientists, and philosophers are for him "the buyers and sellers of grammar rules," "the deceivers and babblers," "full of deceits and tricks"; Roman history and culture are nothing but a tale of "slaughtering, bloodshed, inhumanity, riot, rapine," and so on; the Roman religion and others are but vile inventions of "the unjust and devil-like princes" for the exploitation of the people; Homer and the whole art and literature are "immodest fables"; law is but the art of deception and injustice.

Augustine's positive program is the pure truth of the Christian faith, divinely revealed, and as such, being supersensible, superrational, superlogical, is directed toward the ultimate reality which is God. *Deum et animam scire cupio. Nihilne plus? Nihil omnino*, such is his motto.

Such a mental revolution, as mentioned, was not limited to the Christian thinkers of the period. A similar trend toward rejection of empirical and rationalistic systems of truth prevailed also among the Pagan thinkers, which was shown previously by my indicators. Qualitatively the main currents of the period like Neo-Platonism, Gnosticism, Donatism, Neo-Pythagoreanism, Pythagorean Platonism, Graeco-Judaic philosophy (Philo and others), not to mention other currents, shared with Christianity a negative attitude toward the empirical and purely rationalistic systems of truth and knowledge.

All these systems became theurgic and religious.

Plotinus, the greatest thinker of the period, had the same negative and contemptuous attitude toward empirical and rationalized knowledge as did the Christian Church Fathers.

Thus, during these six centuries from the beginning of our era this supposedly superstitious and ignorant system of truth of faith emerged and grew, and, contrary to the expectations and beliefs of many intellectuals of these first few centuries of our era, the empirical and rationalistic systems of truth were conquered and driven out, with all the infinitely great and numerous changes of mentality which such a transformation involved.

V. Truth of Faith Triumphant

As my tables show, after the sixth century the victory of the truth of faith was complete and during the next six or seven centuries it dominated the mentality. (See Tables 1 and 2 and Figure 1.) The truth of reason as such ceased to exist; the logic of reason was, of course, employed to some extent, but only in a subservient role of a "handmaid" to theology and only in so far as it could serve without the slightest contradiction to the truth of faith. *Credo ut intellegam* and *intelligo ut credam*, such is its essence.

"There were theologians who would not be philosophers; so far as we know, there were no philosophers who were not theologians." "The thought of the Middle Ages was essentially theocentric and the great Medieval thinkers were one and all of them theologians; as soon as this ceased to be, the Renaissance may be said to have begun."

The medieval thinking is marked, first, by a great *development of theological dialectics* at the cost of observation and of independent logic unrestrained by creed.

Hence, when even some information about the external world (physics, geometry, mathematics, astronomy, which composed the so-called *Quadrivium* or the second part of the teaching, the main part being composed of the *Trivium* — grammar, dialectics, and rhetoric) was touched or given, it always represented "the intermixture of matters and arguments in philosophy with theological questions and arguments."

This is equally true of the texts like *The Lay Folk's Mass*, the *Primer*, the *Psalter*, Isidore of Seville's *Encyclopedia; De Mirabilibus* of Augustine of Hibernia; *De ordine*, of pseudo Isidore; Bede's *History; De Universo* of Rabanus Maurus; Strabo's *Glossary;* Honorius's *De imagine mundi;* the *Summulae of Petrius Hispanus*, *Nuptials of Philology and Mercury*, Donatus's text, *Sentences* of Peter Lombardus, the *Consolations* of Boethius, several grammars and other texts widely used, many for several centuries without any change, like those of Isidore of Seville.

In a logical consistency with the dominant truth of faith stands the *exceedingly small number of discoveries in the natural sciences and of technological inventions*. For the seventh, eighth, ninth, tenth, and eleventh centuries, the total number of the discoveries and inventions was respectively only four, four, six, seven, eight. As the mentality turned to the supersensory world little interest was shown in the study of the sensory world — physicochemical and biological sciences. Hence little progress was made by the natural sciences during these centuries of domination of the Ideational truth.

Another trait of this medieval mentality was its *symbolism*, already pointed out. It is enough to add here in this connection that its symbolism was not incidental. Since the reality (God) is supersensible and immaterial, it cannot be described otherwise but through use of symbols as "the sensible or visible signs of the invisible and supersensible world." Hence it is inevitable that any system of knowledge based upon the truth of faith has to be symbolic.

Thus the truth of faith reigned supreme for about six or seven centuries. When in the fifth and sixth centuries it became dominant, empiricism, skepticism, and fideism were almost entirely eliminated. Now that this truth became triumphant and unquestionable, there was no need for them. The truth of faith was now firmly entrenched and was certain, absolute.

In contradistinction to the "mysticism of despair," the mysticism of the early Middle Ages was so balanced, moderate, and normal that without any particular difficulty these mystics could be put into the main current of the theological rationalism of the Middle Ages. In which case, mysticism would be almost nonexistent in that period.

When these qualifications are considered, the monolithic unanimity and uniformity of the system of truth and of the mentality of the period from the sixth to the twelfth centuries stand out particularly clearly. It was indeed the age of unshakable, unquestioning, absolutely confident faith. There was no doubt, no uncertainty, no inner disharmony, and no mental conflict. There was no dualism between religion, science, and philosophy, because science and philosophy were banished and faith reigned supreme.

The same period from the sixth to the twelfth centuries shows itself in the compartment of art as predominantly Ideational; thus art and truth compartments here are again logically and factually integrated: both are Ideational.

Further, my second proposition is again well corroborated: that in the period of domination of the Ideational truth of faith, when the truth of senses is low or nonexistent, the progress of scientific discoveries and inventions becomes either much slower, or stops, or even regresses.

VI. The Idealistic Phase: the End of the Eleventh, Twelfth, and Thirteenth Centuries

At the end of the eleventh century, the empirical system of truth reappears and begins to rise also; religious rationalism declines and fideism reappears. This means first the reawakening of the spirit of empiricism — a datum which is in complete agreement with what is shown by the curve of the scientific discoveries and is therefore hardly misleading; it means also that some new and important change took place in the system of truth and also in the whole mentality of the period, compared with the preceding one. From the standpoint of our present problem, in what did this change consist?

The years from the end of the eleventh to the fourteenth centuries are the Age of the Idealistic Rationalism, quite similar to that of the age in Greece of the fifth and the fourth centuries, but not a continuation of the preceding system of the truth of faith with mere subservient truth of reason. We are now in a very different mental atmosphere and this atmosphere is that of the idealistic rationalism in the sense given to that term above. The *Scholastic philosophy of these centuries with its climax in the thirteenth is not a system of truth of faith but that of idealistic rationalism as a harmonious blending together, into one system, of the truths of faith, of reason, and of senses.* It is similar in that respect to the idealistic rationalism of Plato and Aristotle. Such is the thesis contended.

What are its evidences? The curves of the movement of scientific discoveries and of empiricism show that they reappeared again and began to grow. Since the truth of faith and that of reason are present also, all the three systems are now on the stage, functioning together.

Furthermore, it can be clearly seen from Tables 1 and 2, and from Figure 1, that the curve of the truth of faith began to descend while the curve of the truth of senses began to ascend. Moving so, they had to meet, so to speak, and blend together in some system similar to idealistic rationalism.

These considerations are sufficient to indicate why this age is a new and different phase in the movement of the systems of truth, as is shown by the quantitative data.

Are these contentions corroborated by the qualitative examination of the dominant systems of truth of the period?

Everyone who is acquainted with the Scholastic philosophy of the period, as it is given by its greatest creators like Albertus Magnus (*c.* 1193–1280) and his still greater disciple St. Thomas Aquinas (1225–1274) cannot fail to observe that the Scholastic system of truth was exactly the system of idealistic rationalism. Its essential tenets are: there are practically the three kinds of knowledge — sensory, intellectual, and superintellectual or divine. Any cognition begins with the sensory perception (as with Aristotle), but to become knowledge and truth as *adequatio rei et intellectus* the sensory data are, so to speak, transformed by the intellect, which has a power to render a material object immaterial, and especially by the active intellect which brings out the universal or the intelligible in the object or thing perceived. Thus (omitting many details already presented) the co-operation of both sources and forms of truth — the sensory and the intellectual — is evident. For a knowledge of most of the empirical phenomena these two forms of truth and of sources are sufficient. But there are the superempirical phenomena which cannot be perceived either by the senses directly or cannot be apprehended by human reason and logic. They can be known only by the grace of God, who reveals such truths to mankind through prophets and in other ways. This form of truth is the most supreme and sublime of all forms of knowledge.

> The sense always apprehends the thing as it is, except there be an impediment in the organ or in the medium. [It can do so because] sensible objects exist actually outside the soul.
>
> Sensory cognition is occupied with external, sensible qualities, but intellectual knowledge penetrates to the very essence of the things.
>
> Certitude of knowledge varies in various natures. . . . Because man forms a sure judgment about a truth by the discursive process of his reason: and so human knowledge is acquired by means of demonstrative reasoning. . . .

As to the divine knowledge or the truth of faith, practically almost the whole of the *Summa contra Gentiles* and also many parts of the *Summa theologica* — particularly the latter section of the second part devoted to Faith, and to the Gratuitous Graces as well as the many other parts — are but a systematic development of the theory of the existence of such a truth. Here is its essence.

> In the things which we hold about God there is truth in two ways. For certain things that are true about God wholly surpass the capability of human reason; for instance that God is three and one; while there are certain things to which even natural reason can attain, for instance, that God is, that God is one, and others like these, which even the philosophers proved demonstratively of God, being guided by the light of natural reason. . . . That certain divine truths wholly surpass the capability of human reason is most clearly evident . . . since our intellect's knowledge originates from the senses: so that things which are not objects of sense cannot be comprehended by the human intellect, except in so far as knowledge of them is gathered from sensibles. . . . Accordingly some divine truths are attainable by human reason, while others altogether surpass the power of human reason.

In the next chapters St. Thomas demonstrates

that those things which cannot be investigated by reason are fittingly proposed to man as an object of faith. Divine Wisdom Himself, Who knows all things most fully, deigned to reveal to man the *secrets of God's wisdom* . . . the truth of His doctrine and inspiration, [foretold by] the manifold oracles of the prophets.

In the *Summa theologica* this truth of faith he styles exactly by this term "truth of faith"; and under the name "wisdom" separates it from intellectual-sensible knowledge, indicating again and again that this "divine wisdom" or "truth of faith" has much greater certitude than knowledge of intellect and is supreme in comparison with it.

From the foregoing discussion, the skeleton of St. Thomas's theory of knowledge is clear and there is no doubt but that it is idealistic rationalism in my meaning of the term. The three forms of truth are all harmoniously blended. Not to leave any uncertainty, St. Thomas again and again stresses that this "truth of faith" in no way contradicts the sensory-intellectual truth but supplements it and leads it to the higher level of the divine wisdom.

It is impossible for the aforesaid truth of faith to be contrary to those principles which reason knows naturally.

And vice versa:

Those things which are naturally instilled in human reason cannot be opposed to this truth [of Christian faith]. The truth of reason is not in opposition to the truth of the Christian Faith.

Such is this system of the idealistic rationalism. It is a European variety of the system of the Platonic-Aristotelian idealistic rationalism.

Thus, this concise examination of the greatest and also most influential theory of truth of the period under consideration well corroborates the expectation and thereby the propositions which are set forth at the beginning of this part of the work.

VII. The Crisis of the Fourteenth and the Fifteenth Centuries and the Crescendo, Forte, and Fortissimo of the Empirical System of Truth from the Sixteenth to the Twentieth Century

The Idealistic culture, with the Idealistic forms of its main aspects, comes usually when the Sensate culture begins to rise and the Ideational culture begins to decline.

Emerging in such circumstances, Idealistic culture is, therefore, by its nature, transitory and as a point of "equilibrium" can hardly last for any length of time in the incessantly fluctuating forces of Ideational and Sensate culture.

This was true in the Greek culture, and also in the history of the Western culture, when the Idealistic phase lasted hardly more than about one hundred and fifty years. Toward the second part of the fourteenth century, in most of its main compartments it was already broken and, since the new Sensate culture was only in the state of potential shaping, and not as yet established, the result was confusion — mental, moral, and social.

Such seems to have been the period which we enter, as it is shown, in the field of the system of truth and mentality generally, by Tables 1 and 2 and Figure 1. A glance at these shows at once the essential traits of the mental conditions of the second part of the fourteenth, and the fifteenth centuries. Its spectrum is decidedly that of sharp instability, profound confusion, mental crisis, and extremism, not unlike the spectrum of the after-Idealistic centuries, third and later in the Graeco-Roman culture. Indeed the indicators show that all in all the line of idealistic rationalism sharply declines (as usual with minor fluctuations); likewise even the line of empiricism temporarily drops also at the end of the fourteenth and at the beginning of the fifteenth centuries; thus these two most balanced forms of truth greatly weaken. On the other hand, the "exotic" and "extreme" systems — fideism and skepticism — reappear again while mysticism grows enormously.

Any investigator of the mentality of that period knows how the high tide of mysticism swept over the whole European culture at that time. We met it in the field of art. It was indeed a "Time of Trouble" and, in a sense, of despair; wars, the Black Death, and hundreds of other most tragic events battered the population.

What is still more important is that the mysticism of that period is very different from that of the Ideational medieval period. There, as mentioned, it was free from any desperate sensitivity, and, if I am permitted to say, emotional and pathetic exhibitionism.

Here mysticism is conspicuously different. It is pathetic; it is empirically oversentimental and oversensitive; it is macabre, as we saw already in the field of art; it broods and centers on such images as death, as the wounds of Christ, as corpses, as tortures, Hell, and other most terrifying events and objects. Through all this it shows that it could not reach the sublime ataraxia in regard to the empirical reality.

The same characteristics have to be attributed to fideism. Finally there reappeared the usual satellite of any crisis of the truth of faith — the demon of skepticism — the *alter ego* of mysticism and fideism of despair, the phantom of the lost certitude. Skepticism has a cynical mask; the others (mysticism and fideism), a pathetic one; but all three are the creatures which appear in periods of deep mental crisis. They now become more powerful than the more balanced rationalism and empiricism.

Toward the end of the fifteenth and the beginning of the sixteenth centuries, the fruits of empirical science and of scientific discoveries grew to such an extent that in the debris of the previous crumbling systems of truth, the truth of senses became the only possible foundation upon which a new house of truth could be built. Discoveries and also empiricism now begin to increase very rapidly. We are at the beginning of the age of domination of the truth of senses; in an era of scientism and empiricism; at a stage of vigorous growth of the greatest Sensate culture the world has ever known.

To the leading minds — both scientific and philosophical — this rise became evident in the sixteenth century; in the great seventeenth century it reached such a level that even the "blind" had to reckon with it.

Such a situation naturally called forth several consequences in the mentality concerned with truth. It had to, and did indeed, inspire the thinkers with pride, enthusiasm, and confidence in the truth of senses and the truth of science. *Since that time it has been less and less an age of the co-operation of science, religion, and philosophy than an age of their warfare — explicit and implicit.* When we have truce, it is like that of two belligerent states: not cordial, nor permanent.

Side by side with these tendencies other ones had to appear, only slightly at the beginning, but later more and more clearly. The point is that empiricism and the truth of senses by its very nature, and on testimony of the senses themselves, cannot have a certitude of the truth of faith or of idealistic rationalism. The testimony of the organs of senses is conditioned by their anatomy and their functions: for the blind in the empirical world there are practically no colors; for the deaf, no sounds; the perception of the same object by the senses of man and of ant are probably different. The real nature of the empirical world, therefore, *as it is, für und an sich,* is practically inaccessible or at least not certain in its adequate knowableness; hence the doubt, skepticism, relativism, criticism, conditionality, conventionality, and general uncertainty — at the best only a conditional probability of the verity of the truths of science and of organs of senses. At the "springtime" of rising empiricism in the period considered, these motives were not particularly strong, but their seeds were there and they had to grow.

A few quotations from the prominent leaders of thought of the period will show clearly these tendencies. Pride, confidence, and intoxication with the progress of science and empirical truth were shared by many thinkers. Here are a few examples.

Campanella (1568–1639):

Our century has more history in its hundred years than had the whole world in the previous four thousand years; more books have been published in the last century than in the five thousand years before it; for it has profited by the recent inventions of typography, cannon, and the marine's compass.

Leibnitz (1646–1716):

We have raised up a truly philosophical age, in which the deepest recesses of nature are laid open, in which splendid arts, noble aids to convenient living, a supply of innumerable instruments and machines, and even the hidden secrets of our bodies are discovered; not to mention the new light daily thrown upon antiquity.

Francis Bacon (1561–1626):

No age hath been more happy in liberty of enquiry than this.

Even Luther (1483–1546) in 1521:

Whoever reads these chronicles will find that from the birth of Christ on, the whole history of the world in these hundreds of years is unparalleled, in every way.

And so on. We hear and read these statements every day in almost any newspaper, in any address of a politician, lecture of a professor, or sermon of a minister, and practically everywhere.

The following excerpts give a typical picture of the superior attitude of the scientific truths to other truths, their mutual tacit or open animosity, their explicit or implicit warfare.

Descartes (1596–1650) who is far from being extreme or atheistic:

And although religion teaches us much on this subject (the nature of our souls and their immortality), nevertheless I confess in myself an infirmity which seems to be common to the greater part of mankind; namely that though we wish to believe and even think we believe strongly all that religion teaches us, yet are we not usually so touched by it as by what has been brought home to us by natural and clear reason.

The testimony of such witnesses (biased, but in this instance, just because of the bias, it is particularly trustworthy) as Bossuet (1627–1704) gives the picture of the objective results of the scientific truth upon the religious truth of faith. The scientists factually were

denying the work of creation and that of redemption, annihilating hell, abolishing immortality, stripping Christianity of all its mysteries and changing it into a philosophical sect agreeable to sense, by which all religions are made the same. The foundation of faith attacked, Scripture directly assailed, and the path opened to Deism, which is disguised Atheism.

In brief now from the victor (empiricism) the truth of faith began to receive "the rough treatment" which it itself gave to the truth of senses at the moment of its victory from the period of early Christianity to that of idealistic rationalism.

There is no doubt that many scientists like Kepler, Newton, and others were religious, but the objective results of their scientific works often proved detrimental themselves or were used by others injuriously against the truth of faith and of reason, contrary to the desire of the scientists, as was the case with Newton (who wrote his great *Principia*, on which is based the "classical mechanics and physics," and *Commentary on Apocalypse*).

As to doubts and skepticisms, their germs reappeared simultaneously with the beginning of the decline of the idealistic rationalism, and then, after a brief disappearance, they emerged almost simultaneously with a big upward swing of empiricism around the beginning of the sixteenth century. Since that time they have been with us up to the present moment. The inner reason for the lack of certitude in empiricism was mentioned previously.

This reason, as well as the uncertainties and doubts, was felt and understood fully by the delicate and refined minds of the sixteenth and the seventeenth centuries. Pascal (1623–1662) can serve as an example of that.

> I look on all sides and I find everywhere nothing but obscurity. Nature offers nothing which is not a subject of doubt and disquietude.

A little later, thinkers like Montaigne (1533–1592) and Peter Bayle (1647–1706) developed this seed of skepticism much further and tried to show that though neither religious nor scientific truth is certain, it is unimportant because from the practical standpoint the certain truth is not more useful than error.

Having started with the burning of the truth of religion, skepticism could not stop there but tended to burn science and everything which was taken as a new refuge of certainty. This is exactly what happened. After religion, the certainty of the reason and science itself was also doubted. "Men have tried everything and sounded everything, but have found in this mass of science . . . nothing solid and firm, but all variety," is the motto of Michel de Montaigne. Religion is uncertain; our reason is uncertain; science as well as philosophy is full of fantastic follies which come and go as fashion; truth is a neighbor of falsehood; even probability is hard to obtain in knowledge.

Then Kant (1724–1804) with his criticism contributed something to its further development in so far, at least, as he demonstrated that the true reality in itself and for itself was unknowable, was even somewhat uncertain whether or not it existed, and in this way prepared the ground for agnosticism, positivism, "fictitionism" ("as if," *als ob*), conventionalism (the framework of science is conditional and conventional), relativism, and finally for pragmatism and illusionism.

Such a stream had to call its "counterpoison," *fideism*, and it can be seen that it appeared only a short time after the reappearance of skepticism, and since that time has remained in the open, being almost equal in power to skepticism, its *alter ego*, and has repeated fairly regularly, with a slight lag, the fluctuations of skepticism as its "counteraction."

VIII. Truth of Senses Triumphant

These tendencies, however, have been secondary. The main trend has been the rising tide of empiricism quite parallel to the rising tide of the scientific discoveries. There have been some minor fluctuations in this ascendance: temporary declines at the end of the sixteenth and at the beginning of the seventeenth centuries (the period of the Counter-Reformation and of Ascetic Protestantism); at the beginning of the eighteenth and of the nineteenth centuries (reaction against the mentality of the Enlightened Philosophy and the Revolution, at the beginning of the nineteenth century), but these down-swings were secondary and temporary. The trend for the last four centuries has been for empiricism to rise steadily until, at the beginning of the twentieth century, it reached a unique, unprecedented level, making about 53 per cent of all the systems of truth. There was also a unique and unprecedented multiplication and increase of important discoveries and inventions in the sciences. Thus we truly live in the age of the truth of senses, of a magnitude, depth, and brilliancy hardly witnessed in other cultures and periods. Scientism is in truth the most prominent and most important mark of our mentality.

In the light of that it is comprehensible why we are prone to think that there is only one system of truth, the scientific truth; and that everything outside it, particularly the truth of faith or of reason, is either "superstition" or "baseless speculation"; why many ministers of God now try to make "scientific religion" and to remodel their nominally Christian creed along the lines of science — so much so, that in their "scientific religion" or "liberal Christianity" there often remains little if anything from Christianity and its dogmas; why the center of the intellectual life shifted from the church pulpit to the university laboratory or classroom; why we look mainly and often exclusively to science as the only agency to solve our individual and social difficulties; and why science is regarded by many as powerful a panacea as God in the eyes of the believers. Just as in the age of the truth of faith God's name was everywhere, so in our time Science is on everyone's mind and lips, from quacks and salesmen to scientists and scholars themselves. If something is qualified "scientific," even soap, face powder, car grease, or dog biscuits, it sounds to us as great as the word "orthodox" in an age of faith. "Unscientific," on the contrary, sounds as bad as the words "heretic," "sacrilegious," and "blasphemous" in the period of the early Middle Ages.

Many other traits follow from, and are indeed mere logical elements of, this dominant system of truth. Just as the mentality dominated by faith feels and views the sensory world as a kind of illusion, so the empirical mentality views and feels the supersensory world as a mere delusion. Just as the mentality of the *truth of faith spiritualizes everything*, even the inorganic material phenomena and their motions or happenings, so the mentality of the truth of senses, which by definition perceives and can perceive only the material phenomena, *materializes everything, even the spiritual phenomena*, like the human soul. Empiricism, materialism, mechanisticism, and determinism are positively associated and go together, while the truth of faith, idealism, indeterminism, and nonmechanisticism go together.

This explains why, in a period when empiricism dominates, there is a tendency even to interpret man's mind, psychology, ideas, feelings, beliefs, and likewise the immaterial culture itself "mechanistically," "materialistically," "deterministically," "behavioristically," "physiologically," "reflexologically," "endocrinologically," "psychoanalytically," and why all such "mechanistic" interpretations of man and culture, which leave in man nothing divine or spiritual, or non-reflexo-animal, prosper in such an age and are viewed as particularly, and the only, "scientific."

Not all these traits only, but also hundreds and hundreds of others of our mentality, are easily apprehended in the light of the present dominating system of truth. In the discovery of truth itself and the scientific methodology such conspicuous characteristics of the "scientific method," as *quantitative approach and measurement* of everything, including even what cannot be measured: intelligence, mind, qualitative values, and so on. It was not incidental that the seventeenth century created "social physics," wherein all the spiritual, cultural, and other immaterial phenomena were studied *modo mathematico sive geometrico* in exactly the same manner and with the same principles with which physics studied matter.

Since that time *the transportation of the methods of the physicochemical and mathematical sciences into* the field of psychology, sociology, history, religion, culture, art, and so on, has been incessant and indefatigable and has continued up to this day. For a scientific study of anything and the discovery of truth, the role of thought as such has been considered less and less important. Instead, the *role of "technique" is regarded paramount.* If the "technique" applied is right, even an idiot can make a contribution; such is the situation suggested by the incessant talk of scientific and other technique which is going on now and has been going on for these four centuries. Respectively, the role of "speculation," in the sense of the analytical and synthesizing work of thought as such, has fallen into disrepute.

In other fields of social life the satellites of such a mentality have been multitudinous, as indicated by the enormous expenditures of money for schools, universities, laboratories, and research; by the elevated position of scientists and researchers, up to the countless "experts" and "brain trusters" as the real power in political, social, or any other control.

IX. Movement of Scientific Discoveries and Technological Inventions

It was stated in the preceding sections that the movement of scientific discoveries and inventions is associated with the type of culture and its prevalent system of truth. The rate of scientific development tends to become slow, stationary, even regressive in Ideational cultures (in which there is a complete domination of the truth of faith), becoming rapid and growing apace in Sensate cultures (wherein the truth of senses dominates).

In the original four-volume edition there is a detailed study of this proposition through an analysis of the development and fluctuations of the natural sciences and technology. The important evidence is summed up in Table 5, which is here given. The significant results of that analysis may be briefly summarized. (1) The cultivation of natural sciences seems indeed to be associated positively with the truth of senses and negatively with that of faith, the neutral position being occupied by the truth of reason. (2) The development of the natural sciences, like the empirical system of truth, is subject to fluctuations, at times manifesting rapid advance, at others stagnating. No linear trend is noticeable either in the life history of single cultures or in the life history of mankind generally. (3) The empirical system of truth and the natural sciences have both had an unprecedented growth during the last four or five centuries. This development is at present continuing vigorously in both fields. (4) However, scrutiny of the recent development of the natural sciences discloses a slowing up in the rate of progress and signs of "fatigue." At this juncture it cannot be said whether it is a purely temporary and short-time "relaxation" or the beginning of a long-time decline. (5) Moreover, this "fatigue" at the close of the nineteenth and the twentieth century accords with similar departures from the overripe Sensate culture, which our culture displays in most of its compartments. To this extent it is not an isolated "sign" but merely one of the many mutually related symptoms of a — short-time or long-time — transformation experienced by our culture in this period. (6) As the direction of movement in this field is likewise away from the reality of the senses, this means that even in this most recent period our culture shows itself not only logically but also causally integrated.

TABLE 5. WESTERN WORLD OUTPUT OF NATURAL SCIENCE, TECHNOLOGICAL, AND GEOGRAPHICAL DISCOVERIES AND INVENTIONS, BY 100-, 50-, AND 25-YEAR PERIODS

Period	*Mathematics*	*Astronomy*	*Biology*	*Medical Science*	*Chemistry*	*Physics*	*Geology*	*Total (Science)*	*Technology*	*Geographical Discoveries*	*Grand Total*	*Boldyreff's Geometric Averages*
3500–801 B.C.	1	2	—	—	2	—	—	5	17	—	22	—
800–701	—	3	—	—	—	—	—	3	6	—	9	—
700–601	—	—	—	—	1	1	—	2	5	—	7	—
600–501	2	7	2	3	3	2	1	20	10	1	31	—
500–401	3	8	2	8	4	8	1	34	5	1	40	17.9
400–301	8	5	14	8	5	6	—	46	12	2	60	14.7
300–201	7	9	2	4	—	11	—	33	12	—	45	64.5
200–101	2	5	4	2	—	1	—	14	2	1	17	12.9
100–0	—	2	1	6	1	4	—	14	17	1	32	30.7
1–100 A.D.	1	2	6	15	5	10	—	39	21	1	61	22.5
101–200	2	7	3	9	—	2	—	23	4	—	27	49.0
201–300	2	—	—	2	—	1	—	5	3	—	8	4.3
301–400	—	—	1	4	—	3	—	8	8	—	16	24.4
401–500	—	—	—	1	1	—	—	2	2	—	4	0.0
501–600	—	2	1	4	—	1	—	8	5	—	13	12.1
601–700	—	—	—	2	—	—	—	2	2	—	4	4.1
701–800	—	2	1	—	—	—	—	3	1	—	4	0.0 [2]
801–900	—	—	—	—	—	—	—	—	5	1	6	0.0 [2]
901–1000	—	—	—	—	—	—	—	—	5	2	7	0.0 [2]
1001–1050	—	—	—	—	1	—	—	1	3	1	5	0.0 [2]
1051–1100	—	—	—	—	—	—	1	1	2	—	3	0.0 [2]
1101–1150	1	—	—	2	—	—	—	3	5	—	8	0.0 [2]
1151–1200	—	—	—	3	—	1	—	4	—	—	4	0.0 [2]
1201–1250	2	—	5	4	3	1	—	15	3	2	20	12.2 [2]
1251–1300	1	—	2	3	12	6	—	24	6	3	33	13.2 [2]
1301–1350	3	7	3	5	1	—	1	20	12	4	36	8.8 [2]
1351–1400	—	1	3	2	2	1	2	11	13	5	29	5.8 [2]
1401–1450	1	2	1	1 (2)[1]	3	3	1	12	17	10	39	0.0 [2]
1451–1500	10	4	2	5 (29)[1]	4	1	7	33	32	23	88	12.1

1501–1525	3	3	1	7	48[1]	3	7	—	24	27	26	77	96.3
1526–1550	7	5	4	40		10	4	6	76	28	17	121	
1551–1575	3	13	10	25	68[1]	4	2	3	60	28	6	94	187.0
1576–1600	14	24	13	17		8	9	—	85	38	14	137	
1601–1625	14	31	3	13	66[1]	19	6	—	86	31	12	129	295.0
1626–1650	28	13	3	10		24	16	3	97	32	5	134	
1651–1675	23	24	16	56	112[1]	34	14	3	170	53	6	229	420.7
1676–1700	21	24	30	22		23	18	1	139	53	7	199	
1701–1725	12	19	9	16	107[1]	33	21	1	111	47	2	160	451.0
1726–1750	46	25	30	73		40	29	6	249	90	1	340	
1751–1775	21	20	32	58	165[1]	83	39	5	258	121	4	383	1318.0
1776–1800	24	26	37	64		191	67	7	416	261	14	691	
1801–1825	19	34	113	82	269[1]	307	110	21	686	378	26	1090	2042.2
1826–1850	22	42	231	137		478	242	39	1191	803	27	2021	
1851–1875	19	37	382	178	455[1]	489	311	27	1443	1073	39	2555	
1876–1900	7	55	371	263		459	430	32	1617	1223	21	2861	
1901–1908	—	15	77	114		216	123	7	552	309	1	862	
Total	329	478	1415	1268		2469	1511	175	7645	4830	286	12,761	

[1] Figures taken from F. H. Garrison, *An Introduction to the History of Medicine* (1929).
[2] Without Arabia and Persia.

X. Forebodings

Such, then, is the system of truth which now dominates and with which we have breathed and lived since the beginning of our conscious life. What is the future? Shall we expect, as most of the scholars and scientists in these centuries and especially in the nineteenth century assured us, that this trend of bigger and better empiricism will continue forever and ever?

Forecasting of the future must of course be mere guess; but with this reservation one can say that this dominant belief is hardly probable. Since in the past there have occurred fluctuations from one system to another and from the empirical to the Ideational truth, there is no guarantee that such a shift cannot happen in the future. And in conformity with the principle of "immanent causation" empiricism in its development must have a limit after which it has to "turn its direction" from ascendance to stagnation or decline. Without interference from external factors, it bears, like any other system of truth, the germs of its self-destruction or decline for some time.

And an attentive observer of the modern times and the modern science can possibly already notice several signs of such a self-destruction.

Empiricism and empirical science in the process of its developments have quite unexpectedly themselves brought us to a strange result: to the illusionary and visionary nature of the "reality" with which they deal. Since they recognize only the sensory reality, logically, with the progress of their study of it, this reality has been found more and more conditional, subjective, refracted, diffracted, and modified by the organs of senses, their variety, their changes, their modifications by the environment, and respectively by the contradictory results given by persons and groups who either had sensory or cultural differences or differences in the instruments and in the technique of their empirical study. The result has been agnosticism, positivism, pragmatism (what is pleasant is true, what does not help eudaemonistically or hedonistically or pragmatically is untrue: if the idea of God helps one to enjoy life, God exists; if it does not help, He does not exist. Quite an elastic theory of truth!); relativism, *and illusionary impressionism in science — the mentality of "as if"* (formulated by Vaihinger and other Neo-Kantians).

The first and safe world of matter has already disappeared. It has become a mere "possibility of perception." Today, even atoms and solid matter, together with the solid laws of mechanics, are shattered. As a result the science itself in its immanent course has brought us to something very indefinite, very nebulous, quite uncertain, conditional, relativistic, and illusionistic. A similar illusionism we met in the modern art. We shall see that in other compartments of the present-day culture a similar illusionism is also paramount.

Not only illusion but science also in the process of its development, especially in the last fifty years, has been bringing more and more uncertainty. More and more discrepancies between various hypotheses began to become apparent. Faster and faster the fundamental, basic principles and theories began to change and today's "generally accepted" theory will be found inadequate tomorrow and will be replaced by a new order (only new the day after tomorrow), which in turn will be replaced by a "new new" theory, and so on. Such a rapid change robs man more and more of his certitudes. Factually we are already living in the Age of Incertitude. Nowadays, in any science scarcely a fundamental principle exists concerning the empirical world, as well as the laws of logic, which is uncontested and "universally accepted."

If such a situation continues — and empiricism, as long as it is dominant, cannot help continuing it — the incertitude will increase. In such circumstances, the truth of senses can easily give way to a truth of faith.

Then we must not forget the "*primum vivere deinde philosophare.*" Life, in order to be decently possible, needs many other values besides science: for instance, the decent behavior of its members; several virtues, beginning with a readiness to make sacrifices; some altruism, willingness to perform duty, and many other values. Now, by its very nature the standpoint of empirical science is totally amoral, areligious, asocial. Good and bad, sacred and profane, sinful and virtuous, harmful and beneficial, these and similar categories are perfectly heterogeneous to it and are outside of it. It studies with "the same objectivity" the saint and the criminal, the moral and unmoral, the sacred and the vulgar phenomena. If and when, therefore, science drives out the other truths within which such categories are natural, the result may be amoralism, asociality, and similar phenomena which make decent social life impossible. Suppose someone should discover a simple but terrific explosive which could easily destroy a considerable part of our planet. Scientifically, it would be the greatest discovery, but socially the most dangerous for the very existence of mankind, because out of 1,800,000,000 human beings there certainly would be a few individuals who, being "scientifically minded," would like to test the explosive and as a result would destroy our planet. Such an explosion would be a great triumph of science, but it would lead to the destruction of mankind. This half-fantastic example shows that there must be limitations of science imposed by the reasons which are outside it, and these reasons usually come from the truth of faith and that of reason. This possibility has actually been realized now in the invention and use of nuclear weapons. Morally irresponsible science threatens the very future of mankind.

In conclusion, the above gives an allusion to the immanent consequences of science itself, which come with its excessive development and begin to inhibit it in its further progress and in its excessive domination over the other truths. Regardless of any exterior factors, these immanent consequences are sufficient to slow down or even to stop for some time the growth of this domination and to call forth a revival of the other forms of truth. I have already noted that during the last few decades science itself already has changed and has become more ideational and idealistic and less sensate.

The truth of senses in this respect is not in an exclusive position. The same is true of the other forms of truth: their excessive domination is also followed by immanent consequences which inhibit internally their further development and lead to their decline for some time, regardless of the interference of the external factors. Thus the domination of the truth of faith slowed down and then declined not so much because of the interference of external factors but because of the internal development of this system of truth itself.

With the progress of Christian faith there began to appear one after another somewhat discordant but purely theological "interpretations" of the creed and dogmas. One kind of a divine revelation was followed by another divine revelation which was different from the first, and sometimes contrary to it. One interpretation of the words of the Scripture was followed by another, but different, interpretation. For instance, such discordant sects and factions appeared in Christianity very early, almost simultaneously with its emergence. In the fourth and the fifth centuries the theological discordance was already terrific and necessitated the all-Christian Councils of Nicaea and others with all the clash of the opinions and struggle of the factions (Arian, Monophysitic, Nestorian, and other "heresies"). No creed is exempt from the appearance of such conflicts of interpretations, dogmas, and principles, though they all claim to be the truths of faith. As a result, it is merely a matter of time before they begin their mutual struggle and are forced to resort to reason, logic, and sensory experience to prove the point of each faction.

These circumstances and tendencies show that the truth of faith has also a limit in its development and domination and immanently calls forth its own decline for some period of time. This is also true of idealistic rationalism. All the forms of truth are subject to this "dialectical destiny" and are hardly exempt from a self-preparation of their own decline in the course of their development.

In the light of these considerations it is probable that the present domination of the truth of senses will hardly continue forever. As mentioned, its domination is already greatly limited: today's science is already much less sensate than it was at the time of writing this work. Probably in some near or remote future its domination will decline also and after the transitory period of reorganization of the system of truth, the truth of faith — whatever is its form — will rise again and will again be dominant. Then again it will find its span of time at an end and will decline, giving place probably to some kind of idealistic rationalism; then the truth of senses will rise again and so on, forever and ever as long as the history of the *homo sapiens* is continued.

The sequential order of these alternations in most of the cases is probably such as described, but it is not to be assumed that in some cases the sequence cannot be different. However improbable it seems for the present domination of the truth of senses to be followed by that of the truth of reason, or the truth of faith to be followed directly by that of senses, I would not swear that it has never taken place and never will. Though the typical, or the most frequent, sequence is the one that I have described, exceptions are to be found in every rule of history, and they might be found in this instance also.

Whatever is going to be the future system of truth, the foregoing shows that the systems of truth truly fluctuate in their domination and in the increase and decrease of their power in the course of time. Perhaps the deepest reason for such a fluctuation is that none of these three systems contains the whole truth, the truth of a really omniscient mind. Each of them has, perhaps, only a part of truth and side by side with it a part of falsity. When falsity begins to take the upper hand over the truth which the system has, it begins to decline and the other form of truth accentuates that part of the Whole Truth which was deficient in the preceding system. Then in its turn it repeats the same "cycle." In these "accentuations" of different aspects of the Whole Truth its manifoldness, richness, inexhaustibility, and infinity are demonstrated. This Whole Truth of the Omniscient Mind seems to be far greater and deeper and many-sided than the narrow truth either of faith only, or of reason only, or of senses only.

15

FLUCTUATION OF "FIRST PRINCIPLES": I. FLUCTUATION OF IDEALISM AND MATERIALISM

I. Preliminaries

In this chapter and subsequent chapters an attempt will be made to indicate the changes in the general principles and basic ideas of reality which explicitly or implicitly underlie every philosophy, science, and important theory.

These principles relating to the nature of the ultimate reality are determinism and indeterminism, absolutism and relativism, eternalism and temporalism, and the like. In similar fashion, such categories and fundamental concepts as those of time, space, relation, causation, number, structure of matter, vitalism, mechanisticism, structure of the universe, and so on, have, in some form or other, comprised the basic framework of reference — a framework which served to put in order an immense number of "facts," and to organize all concrete data. Without such a framework no systematization, classification, or even apprehension of the facts would have been possible.

The nature of reality, particularly of the ultimate reality, has always constituted one of these first principles. Beginning with the earliest mythologies of preliterate and historical peoples and ending with contemporary science, philosophy, and religion, everywhere and always has this question been raised and, in some way, answered. These answers can be grouped into three main classes: Idealism, Materialism, and a Mixed class comprised by those theories which do not fall into either of the other classes.

It is not our intention to discuss the truth or error of these theories, nor to adopt any of them, but rather to study the rise and decline in influence of each of these three currents of thought in the life history of the Graeco-Roman and Western cultures.

II. Fluctuation in the Influence of Idealism, Materialism, and Mixed Theories

By *Idealism* as philosophy, metaphysics, or mentality is meant a system of ideology which maintains that the ultimate, or true, reality is spiritual, in the sense of God, of Platonic ideas, of immaterial spirit, of soul, or of psychical reality. The several varieties of Idealism can be

TABLE 14. INDICATORS OF FLUCTUATION OF IDEALISM, MATERIALISM, AND THE MIXED SYSTEMS,[1] BY 20-YEAR PERIODS, FROM 580 B.C. TO A.D. 1920

PERIOD	MATERIALISM						IDEALISM						MIXED		GRAND TOTAL	
	Pluralistic		*Monistic*		*Total*		*Hylozoistic*		*Mechanistic*		*Total*					
	No. of points of weight	*Per cent*	*No. of points of weight*	*Per cent*	*No. of points of weight*	*Per cent*	*No. of points of weight*	*Per cent*	*No. of points of weight*	*Per cent*	*No. of points of weight*	*Per cent*	*No. of points of weight*	*Per cent*	*No. of points of weight*	*Per cent*
580–560 B.C.	0	0	0	0	0	0	4	100.0	0	0	4	100.0	0	0	4	100
560–540	0	0	5	35.7	5	35.7	9	64.3	0	0	9	64.3	0	0	14	100
540–520	8	40.0	5	25.0	13	65.0	7	35.0	0	0	7	35.0	0	0	20	100
520–500	8	36.4	5	22.7	13	59.1	9	40.9	0	0	9	40.9	0	0	22	100
500–480	10	34.5	12	41.4	22	75.9	7	24.1	0	0	7	24.1	0	0	29	100
480–460	2	9.1	12	54.6	14	63.7	8	36.3	0	0	8	36.3	0	0	22	100
460–440	1	5.3	8	42.1	9	47.4	10	52.6	0	0	10	52.6	0	0	19	100
440–420	8	15.7	8	15.7	16	31.4	20	39.2	2	3.9	22	43.1	13	25.5	51	100
420–400	19	24.1	3	3.7	22	27.8	11	14.0	10	12.6	21	26.6	36	45.6	79	100
400–380	25	33.3	5	6.7	30	40.0	7	9.3	9	12.0	16	21.3	29	38.7	75	100
380–360	25	41.2	6	9.8	31	51.0	5	8.2	9	14.8	14	23.0	16	26.0	61	100
360–340	42	63.7	3	4.5	45	68.2	5	7.6	2	3.0	7	10.6	14	21.2	66	100
340–320	21	42.2	17	34.7	38	76.9	5	10.9	1	2.0	6	12.9	5	10.2	49	100
320–300	15	18.5	35	43.2	50	61.7	11	13.5	4	5.0	15	18.5	16	19.8	81	100
300–280	7	8.3	30	35.7	37	44.0	20	23.8	12	14.3	32	38.1	15	17.9	84	100
280–260	7	9.5	14	18.9	21	28.4	24	32.3	11	15.0	35	47.3	18	24.3	74	100
260–240	1	3.0	3	8.1	4	11.1	22	61.1	4	11.1	26	72.2	6	16.7	36	100
240–220	1	1.7	4	6.5	5	8.2	40	65.5	7	11.5	47	77.0	9	14.8	61	100
220–200	1	3.0	8	23.5	9	26.5	15	44.1	3	8.8	18	52.9	7	20.6	34	100
200–180	1	4.4	9	39.1	10	43.5	6	26.1	4	17.4	10	43.5	3	13.0	23	100
180–160	1	4.8	6	28.5	7	33.3	6	28.6	2	9.5	8	38.1	6	28.6	21	100
160–140	1	4.6	5	22.7	6	27.3	6	27.3	3	13.6	9	40.9	7	31.8	22	100
140–120	1	4.6	4	18.1	5	22.7	6	27.3	2	9.1	8	36.4	9	40.9	22	100
120–100	1	4.9	4	19.0	5	23.9	8	38.1	4	19.0	12	57.1	4	19.0	21	100
100–80	3	11.5	2	7.7	5	19.2	12	42.7	7	30.4	19	73.1	2	7.7	26	100
80–60	12	34.3	4	11.4	16	45.7	14	40.0	5	14.3	19	54.3	0	0	35	100
60–40	18	27.0	4	5.8	22	32.8	22	32.7	18	27.0	40	59.7	5	7.5	67	100
40–20	16	36.3	5	11.4	21	47.7	9	20.5	9	20.4	18	40.9	5	11.4	44	100
20–0	4	19.0	6	28.6	10	47.6	5	23.8	1	4.8	6	28.6	5	23.8	21	100
0–20 A.D.	8	33.3	10	41.7	18	75.0	5	20.8	1	4.2	6	25.0	0	0	24	100
20–40	11	45.8	6	25.0	17	70.8	6	25.0	1	4.2	7	29.2	0	0	24	100
40–60	11	36.7	2	6.7	13	43.4	16	53.3	1	3.3	17	56.6	0	0	30	100
60–80	8	21.1	2	5.3	10	26.4	27	71.0	1	2.6	28	73.6	0	0	38	100
80–100	16	43.3	2	5.4	18	48.7	18	48.6	1	2.7	19	51.3	0	0	37	100
100–120	19	43.2	10	22.7	29	65.9	12	27.2	1	2.3	13	29.5	2	4.6	44	100
120–140	31	47.0	10	15.1	41	62.1	17	25.8	2	3.0	19	28.8	6	9.1	66	100
140–160	35	49.3	13	18.3	48	67.6	14	19.8	3	4.2	17	24.0	6	8.4	71	100

[1] On the basis of different values given from 1 to 12.

TABLE 14. INDICATORS OF FLUCTUATION OF IDEALISM, MATERIALISM, AND THE MIXED SYSTEMS,[1] BY 20-YEAR PERIODS, FROM 580 B.C. TO A.D. 1920 — *continued*

PERIOD	IDEALISM						MATERIALISM						MIXED		GRAND TOTAL	
	Pluralistic		*Monistic*		*Total*		*Hylozoistic*		*Mechanistic*		*Total*					
	No. of points of weight	*Per cent*	*No. of points of weight*	*Per cent*	*No. of points of weight*	*Per cent*	*No. of points of weight*	*Per cent*	*No. of points of weight*	*Per cent*	*No. of points of weight*	*Per cent*	*No. of points of weight*	*Per cent*	*No. of points of weight*	*Per cent*
160–180 A.D.	42	53.2	17	21.5	59	74.7	11	13.9	3	3.8	14	17.7	6	7.6	79	100
180–200	58	58.0	23	23.0	81	81.0	8	8.0	5	5.0	13	13.0	6	6.0	100	100
200–220	41	56.2	16	21.9	57	78.1	7	9.6	3	4.1	10	13.7	6	8.2	73	100
220–240	35	66.0	10	18.9	45	84.9	7	13.2	1	1.9	8	15.1	0	0	53	100
240–260	44	80.0	5	9.1	49	89.1	5	9.1	1	1.8	6	10.9	0	0	55	100
260–280	32	75.4	5	11.6	37	86.0	5	11.7	1	2.3	6	14.0	0	0	43	100
280–300	19	76.0	1	4.0	20	80.0	4	16.0	1	4.0	5	20.0	0	0	25	100
300–320	24	92.3	0	0	24	91.3	1	3.8	1	3.9	2	7.7	0	0	26	100
320–340	37	88.1	0	0	37	88.1	4	9.5	1	2.4	5	11.9	0	0	42	100
340–360	26	78.8	0	0	26	78.8	6	18.2	1	3.0	7	21.2	0	0	33	100
360–380	59	90.8	0	0	59	90.8	6	9.2	0	0	6	9.2	0	0	65	100
380–400	52	88.0	0	0	52	88.0	7	12.0	0	0	7	12.0	0	0	59	100
400–420	45	84.9	0	0	45	84.9	8	15.1	0	0	8	15.1	0	0	53	100
420–440	43	82.7	0	0	43	82.7	9	17.3	0	0	9	17.3	0	0	52	100
440–460	32	97.0	0	0	32	97.0	1	3.0	0	0	1	3.0	0	0	33	100
460–480	27	90.0	0	0	27	90.0	3	10.0	0	0	3	10.0	0	0	30	100
480–500	24	88.9	0	0	24	88.9	3	11.1	0	0	3	11.1	0	0	27	100
500–520	30	97.0	0	0	30	97.0	1	3.0	0	0	1	3.0	0	0	31	100
520–540	38	97.4	0	0	38	97.4	1	2.6	0	0	1	2.6	0	0	39	100
540–560	25	100.0	0	0	25	100.0	0	0	0	0	0	0	0	0	25	100
560–580	8	100.0	0	0	8	100.0	0	0	0	0	0	0	0	0	8	100
580–600	8	100.0	0	0	8	100.0	0	0	0	0	0	0	0	0	8	100
600–620	12	100.0	0	0	12	100.0	0	0	0	0	0	0	0	0	12	100
620–640	14	100.0	0	0	14	100.0	0	0	0	0	0	0	0	0	14	100
640–660	9	100.0	0	0	9	100.0	0	0	0	0	0	0	0	0	9	100
660–680	8	100.0	0	0	8	100.0	0	0	0	0	0	0	0	0	8	100
680–700	2	100.0	0	0	2	100.0	0	0	0	0	0	0	0	0	2	100
700–720	3	100.0	0	0	3	100.0	0	0	0	0	0	0	0	0	3	100
720–740	8	100.0	0	0	8	100.0	0	0	0	0	0	0	0	0	8	100
740–760	6	100.0	0	0	6	100.0	0	0	0	0	0	0	0	0	6	100
760–780	1	100.0	0	0	1	100.0	0	0	0	0	0	0	0	0	1	100
780–800	4	100.0	0	0	4	100.0	0	0	0	0	0	0	0	0	4	100
800–820	6	100.0	0	0	6	100.0	0	0	0	0	0	0	0	0	6	100
820–840	10	100.0	0	0	10	100.0	0	0	0	0	0	0	0	0	10	100
840–860	18	100.0	0	0	18	100.0	0	0	0	0	0	0	0	0	18	100
860–880	21	100.0	0	0	21	100.0	0	0	0	0	0	0	0	0	21	100
880–900	9	100.0	0	0	9	100.0	0	0	0	0	0	0	0	0	9	100
900–920	4	100.0	0	0	4	100.0	0	0	0	0	0	0	0	0	4	100

920–940 A.D.	2	100.0	0	0	2	100.0	0	0	0	0	0	0	0	0	2	100
940–960	1	100.0	0	0	1	100.0	0	0	0	0	0	0	0	0	1	100
960–980	1	100.0	0	0	1	100.0	0	0	0	0	0	0	0	0	1	100
980–1000	3	100.0	0	0	3	100.0	0	0	0	0	0	0	0	0	3	100
1000–1020	8	100.0	0	0	8	100.0	0	0	0	0	0	0	0	0	8	100
1020–1040	5	100.0	0	0	5	100.0	0	0	0	0	0	0	0	0	5	100
1040–1060	13	100.0	0	0	13	100.0	0	0	0	0	0	0	0	0	13	100
1060–1080	31	100.0	0	0	31	100.0	0	0	0	0	0	0	0	0	31	100
1080–1100	32	100.0	0	0	32	100.0	0	0	0	0	0	0	0	0	32	100
1100–1120	22	100.0	0	0	22	100.0	0	0	0	0	0	0	0	0	22	100
1120–1140	36	100.0	0	0	36	100.0	0	0	0	0	0	0	0	0	36	100
1140–1160	42	100.0	0	0	42	100.0	0	0	0	0	0	0	0	0	42	100
1160–1180	28	100.0	0	0	28	100.0	0	0	0	0	0	0	0	0	28	100
1180–1200	25	100.0	0	0	25	100.0	0	0	0	0	0	0	0	0	25	100
1200–1220	24	80.0	6	20.0	30	100.0	0	0	0	0	0	0	0	0	30	100
1220–1240	24	100.0	0	0	24	100.0	0	0	0	0	0	0	0	0	24	100
1240–1260	42	100.0	0	0	42	100.0	0	0	0	0	0	0	0	0	42	100
1260–1280	64	91.4	6	8.6	70	100.0	0	0	0	0	0	0	0	0	70	100
1280–1300	74	92.5	6	7.5	80	100.0	0	0	0	0	0	0	0	0	80	100
1300–1320	83	95.5	1	1.1	84	96.6	0	0	0	0	0	0	3	3.4	87	100
1320–1340	52	75.3	2	3.0	54	78.3	8	11.6	0	0	8	11.6	7	10.1	69	100
1340–1360	49	71.0	3	4.3	52	75.3	13	18.8	0	0	13	18.8	4	5.9	69	100
1360–1380	41	87.3	1	2.1	42	89.4	5	10.6	0	0	5	10.6	0	0	47	100
1380–1400	19	79.3	1	4.1	20	83.4	0	0	0	0	0	0	4	16.6	24	100
1400–1420	8	80.0	2	20.0	10	100.0	0	0	0	0	0	0	0	0	10	100
1420–1440	15	88.2	2	11.8	17	100.0	0	0	0	0	0	0	0	0	17	100
1440–1460	19	90.5	2	9.5	21	100.0	0	0	0	0	0	0	0	0	21	100
1460–1480	20	90.9	2	9.1	2	100.0	0	0	0	0	0	0	0	0	22	100
1480–1500	5	62.5	3	37.5	28	100.0	0	0	0	0	0	0	0	0	8	100
1500–1520	15	62.5	6	25.0	21	87.5	1	4.2	1	4.1	2	8.3	1	4.2	24	100
1520–1540	34	63.0	8	14.8	42	77.8	1	1.9	1	1.9	2	3.7	10	18.5	54	100
1540–1560	36	63.0	11	19.0	47	82.0	1	2.0	1	2.0	2	4.0	8	14.0	57	100
1560–1580	49	69.0	6	8.5	55	77.5	1	1.4	1	1.4	2	2.8	14	19.7	71	100
1580–1600	72	73.0	10	10.0	82	83.0	1	1.0	4	4.0	5	5.0	12	12.0	99	100
1600–1620	86	69.0	13	10.4	99	79.4	6	4.8	1	0.8	7	5.6	19	15.0	125	100
1620–1640	118	82.5	1	0.7	119	83.2	8	5.6	1	0.7	9	6.3	15	10.5	143	100
1640–1660	90	69.7	8	6.2	98	75.9	10	7.8	13	10.1	23	17.9	8	6.2	129	100
1660–1680	107	69.0	15	9.6	122	78.6	13	8.0	11	7.0	24	15.0	10	6.4	156	100
1680–1700	128	61.5	19	9.1	147	70.6	5	2.4	11	5.3	16	7.7	45	21.6	208	100
1700–1720	98	65.2	10	6.7	108	71.9	1	0.7	4	2.7	5	3.5	37	24.7	150	100
1720–1740	62	59.6	12	11.5	74	71.1	1	1.0	7	6.7	8	7.7	22	21.2	104	100
1740–1760	93	51.0	5	3.0	98	54.0	21	11.5	17	9.2	38	20.7	46	25.3	182	100
1760–1780	75	44.0	5	3.0	80	47.0	16	9.2	37	21.6	53	30.9	38	22.2	171	100
1780–1800	90	42.0	14	6.5	104	48.4	9	4.0	30	14.1	39	18.1	72	33.5	215	100
1800–1820	122	48.6	38	15.2	160	63.8	1	0.4	11	4.4	12	5.5	79	31.4	251	100
1820–1840	170	63.2	26	9.7	196	72.9	6	2.2	4	1.5	10	3.7	63	23.4	269	100
1840–1860	205	58.9	21	6.0	226	64.9	1	0.3	31	8.9	32	9.2	90	25.9	348	100
1860–1880	207	42.7	46	9.5	253	52.2	17	3.5	66	13.6	83	17.1	149	30.7	485	100
1880–1900	284	36.3	98	12.5	382	48.8	95	12.2	45	5.7	140	17.9	261	33.3	783	100
1900–1920	253	28.1	110	12.2	363	40.3	100	11.1	110	12.2	210	23.3	328	36.4	901	100

[1] On the basis of different values given from 1 to 12.

TABLE 15. MOVEMENT OF IDEALISM, MATERIALISM, AND THE MIXED SYSTEMS, BY 100-YEAR PERIODS, FROM 600 B.C. TO A.D. 1900

PERIOD	IDEALISM						MATERIALISM						MIXED		GRAND TOTAL	
	Pluralistic		*Monistic*		*Total*		*Hylozoistic*		*Mechanistic*		*Total*					
	No. of points of weight	*Per cent*	*No. of points of weight*	*Per cent*	*No. of points of weight*	*Per cent*	*No. of points of weight*	*Per cent*	*No. of points of weight*	*Per cent*	*No. of points of weight*	*Per cent*	*No. of points of weight*	*Per cent*	*No. of points of weight*	*Per cent*
600–500 B.C.	8	25.8	5	16.1	13	41.9	18	58.1	0	0	18	58.1	0	0	31	100
500–400	30	25.4	20	17.0	50	42.4	28	23.7	10	8.5	38	32.2	30	25.4	118	100
400–300	67	34.9	41	21.4	108	56.3	23	12.0	14	7.3	37	19.3	47	24.4	192	100
300–200	8	4.1	41	24.3	49	28.4	61	36.7	24	14.2	85	50.9	35	20.7	169	100
200–100	1	1.4	18	25.4	19	26.8	21	29.6	11	15.5	32	45.1	20	28.1	71	100
100–0	30	27.3	12	10.9	42	38.2	32	29.1	26	23.6	58	52.7	10	9.1	110	100
0–100 A.D.	27	35.1	14	18.1	41	53.2	35	45.5	1	1.3	36	46.8	0	0	77	100
100–200	129	57.7	37	16.6	166	74.3	32	14.3	6	2.9	38	17.2	19	8.5	223	100
200–300	94	71.3	21	15.9	115	87.2	11	8.3	4	3.0	15	11.3	2	1.5	132	100
300–400	102	90.2	0	0	102	90.2	10	8.9	1	0.9	11	9.8	0	0	113	100
400–500	88	88.9	0	0	88	88.9	11	11.1	0	0	11	11.1	0	0	99	100
500–600	63	100	0	0	63	100	0	0	0	0	0	0	0	0	63	100
600–700	21	100	0	0	21	100	0	0	0	0	0	0	0	0	21	100
700–800	13	100	0	0	13	100	0	0	0	0	0	0	0	0	13	100
800–900	39	100	0	0	39	100	0	0	0	0	0	0	0	0	39	100
900–1000	9	100	0	0	9	100	0	0	0	0	0	0	0	0	9	100
1000–1100	47	100	0	0	47	100	0	0	0	0	0	0	0	0	47	100
1100–1200	93	100	0	0	93	100	0	0	0	0	0	0	0	0	93	100
1200–1300	171	93.4	12	6.6	183	100	0	0	0	0	0	0	0	0	183	100
1300–1400	155	81.5	5	2.7	160	84.2	18	9.5	0	0	18	9.5	12	6.3	190	100
1400–1500	37	84.1	7	15.9	44	100	0	0	0	0	0	0	0	0	44	100
1500–1600	159	67.4	35	14.8	194	82.2	5	2.1	8	3.4	13	5.5	29	12.3	236	100
1600–1700	385	71.7	37	6.9	422	78.6	28	5.2	15	2.8	43	8.0	72	13.4	537	100
1700–1800	309	53.0	35	6.0	344	59.0	25	4.3	58	9.9	83	14.2	156	26.8	583	100
1800–1900	715	45.3	167	10.6	882	55.9	102	6.5	98	6.2	200	12.7	496	31.4	1578	100

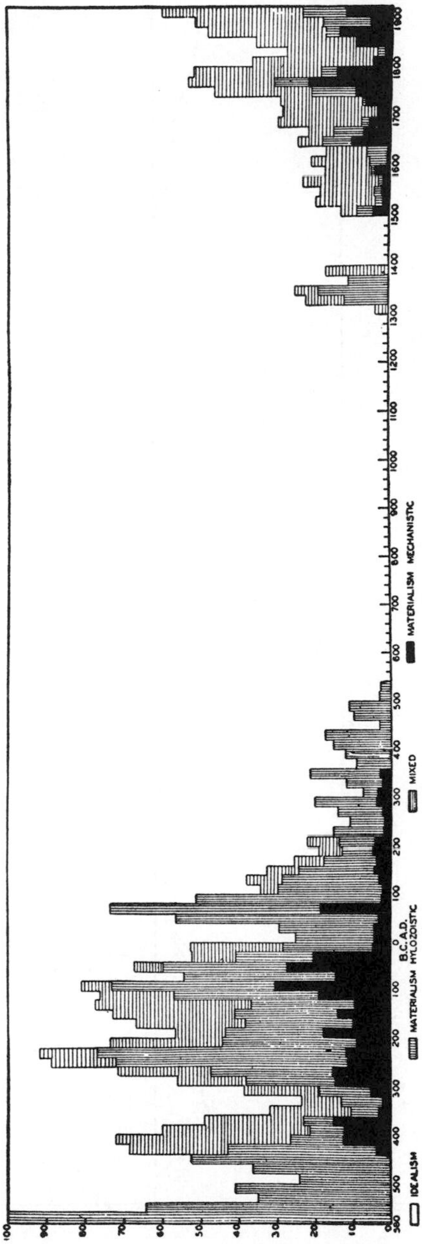

FIG. 10. FLUCTUATION OF THE MAIN SYSTEMS BY THEIR WEIGHT AND BY 20-YEAR PERIODS

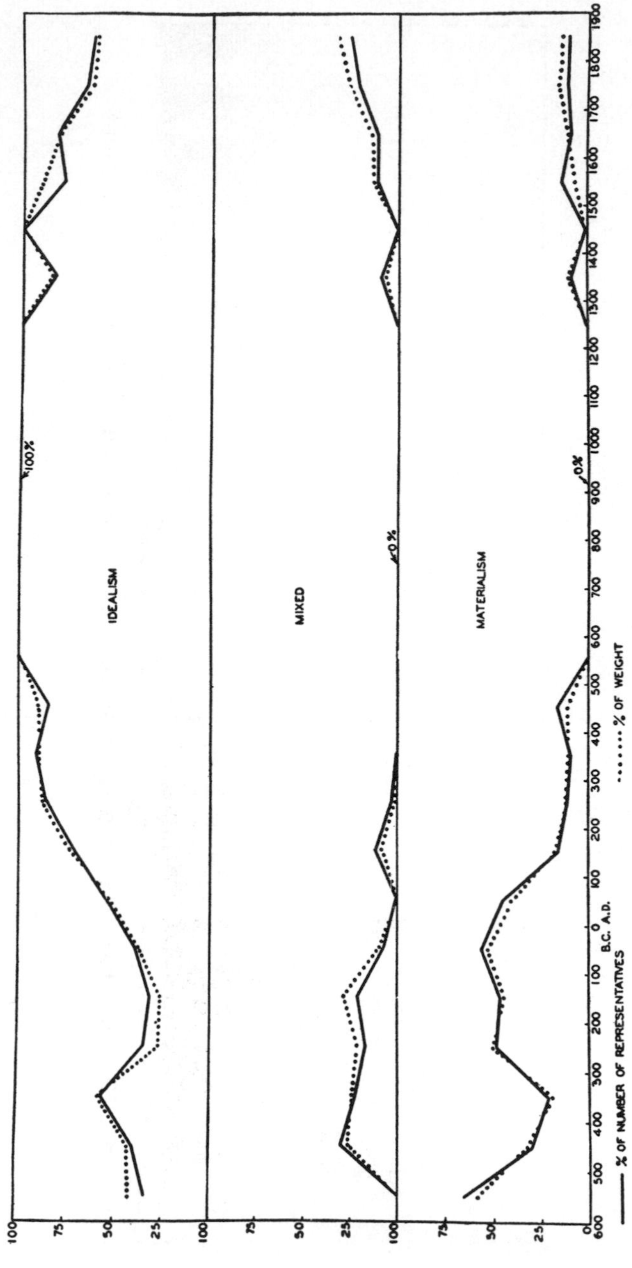

FIG. 11. FLUCTUATION OF THE THREE MAIN SYSTEMS BY THEIR WEIGHT AND BY CENTURIES

reduced to two fundamental classes: monistic and pluralistic Idealism. *Monistic* idealism holds that all the individual and separate systems of the immaterial, spiritual, and psychical reality are but temporary manifestations or emanations of One Principle or One Ultimate, All-Embracing, Spiritual Being, be it God, Absolute Idea, Absolute Mind, Absolute Spirit, or the like. In contradistinction to this, *pluralistic* idealism contends that there exists a multitude of independent centers or systems of spiritual and psychical realities — such as souls, spirits, monads, and other spiritual-immaterial entities — which constitute the ultimate reality.

By *Materialism* is meant that philosophy which holds that the ultimate reality is matter, and that spiritual or immaterial phenomena are but a manifestation of it, are simply the result of the motion of particles of matter. Of the many varieties of Materialism, there are two which are most important. *Hylozoistic* materialism ascribes a species of life to matter, and maintains that the ultimate reality is living matter which possesses sensation, conation, and, in a sense, consciousness. Materiality or corporeality and spirituality are inseparable. Hylozoism is similar to what is frequently termed "monism." *Mechanistic* materialism, on the other hand, is much more "materialistic" than hylozoism. While the latter is a sort of Pan-Somatism which does not radically deny the spiritual principle but claims that it is always incorporated corporeally or somatically, mechanistic materialism maintains that matter is the *only* reality and that spiritual or immaterial phenomena, if they exist, are nothing but a purely passive product of matter and of purely mechanistic motions of material particles.

Each of these forms of Idealism and Materialism has many varieties and shadings, but since we are concerned with the fluctuation of only the main forms of Idealistic and Materialistic mentality, these minor variations are not considered.

Idealism and Materialism constitute the major categories with which we are concerned. The third, the Mixed category, includes all those intermediary doctrines pertaining to the nature of the ultimate reality which cannot be classified as Idealistic or Materialistic; and also such systems as skepticism, agnosticism, critical philosophy, and the like.

III. Main Results

A. *Correlation with Ideational and Sensate Cultures.* Having outlined the main fluctuations of Materialism and Idealism, we may attempt to depict the spectrum of the whole mentality in this field during the various periods studied.

(1) We begin our analysis with the sixth century B.C. For the reasons mentioned above it is to be regarded, in spite of the formal

"hylozoistic" domination, as essentially monistic idealistic, where "nature" is inseparably united with the spiritual principle. It was the period of a simple, undifferentiated, and undivided mentality, without any clash of decidedly different streams of thought. Idealism and Materialism were very similar, and no Mixed theories are yet to be found.

(2) The fifth and the fourth centuries were predominantly Idealistic. Idealism became more pronounced and more conspicuous in its nature, as did *also* Materialism. In addition, several Mixed theories appeared. The whole period was one of differentiation of the previous undifferentiated and uniform mentality; each of the main streams began to separate from the preceding undifferentiated "oneness." But of these streams Idealism was the most powerful. In this sense the field under consideration is found to be similar to the other compartments of the culture during this period. Being idealistico-rationalistic in ontological mentality, the period is also found to be idealistico-rationalistic in its system of truth, in its art, and in other compartments of culture.

(3) Our indicators (by 20-year, as well as by 100-year periods) show further a decrease in Idealism, an increase in Materialism, and especially in mechanistic materialism, in the centuries from the third B.C. to the beginning of our era. This means that the increase in Materialism, and the decrease in Idealism proceeded hand in hand with an increase in the empirical system of truth (the truth of the senses), and a decrease in idealistic rationalism. Both of these factors mean an increase in Sensate culture.

(4) From the beginning of our era up to the sixth century A.D. may be observed (especially in the indicators by century periods) a new rising tide of Idealism (among the Christian as well as the Pagan thinkers). At the same time, however, the opposite current, and especially the extreme types of materialism, became even more extreme. In the process of their decline they showed temporary, short-lived flarings. For instance, mechanistic materialism, having fallen from 23.6 in the first century B.C., and to 1.3 in the first century A.D., then rose to 2.9 in the second and to 3 in the third century A.D. Idealism also became more extreme; in the main, extreme pluralistic idealism grew at the cost of Materialism as well as of monistic idealism. In brief, the data show that these centuries were the period of a sharp struggle between Materialistic and Idealistic mentalities, and though Idealism was progressing victoriously, its progress was not without desperate opposition by its chief opponent.

The spectrum of mentality in the field of the system of truth is in a sense highly consistent with the spectrum of mentality outlined above. In the systems of truth, the period was marked by a growing trend toward the truth of faith at the cost of the other truths (of reason and of the senses). But the truth of faith, as in the case of Idealistic philosophy, was growing mainly in its more extreme forms, the forms of mysticism and fideism (especially in the first, second, and the third centuries A.D.). With a temporary increase in empiricism in the third century A.D. there was even a corresponding increase in mechanistic materialism, though the amplitude of the increase in the latter was much more narrow than in the case of empiricism.

(5) The period from the sixth to the eleventh centuries A.D., in the field of the forms of truth, as well as in the field of the problem studied, again appears to be perfectly uniform and similar: monopolistic idealism in the latter case, and a monopolistic domination of the truth of faith in the former. Idealism and the truth of faith were again very closely related.

(6) The monopoly of the truth of faith ended in the twelfth century, whereas the monopoly of Idealism did not end until the fourteenth century, a lag of about two hundred years. However, if the Idealistic systems of the twelfth and thirteenth centuries be studied from a qualitative point of view, it will be seen that they began to differ from the simple, purely religious, idealism of the previous centuries. The idealism of the twelfth and the thirteenth centuries became more and more "intellectualistic" and "dialectical." This fact cannot be detected by the quantitative indicators, but is evident from a qualitative study. Therefore, here again we see a positive association of the truth of reason with dialectical idealism, a situation somewhat similar to that in the fifth and the fourth centuries B.C. in Greece.

(7) In the fourteenth century both the truth of senses and Materialism again increased in importance. During the fifteenth century they both underwent a marked diminution in influence; then, beginning with the sixteenth century, they have both been on the increase up to the present time (though Materialism gave an index for the nineteenth century slightly lower than for the eighteenth century, but the Mixed systems, some of which are but a diluted form of Materialism, grew systematically up to the twentieth century). Thus again we have positive association between the empirical system of truth and Materialism. On the other hand these four centuries have been marked by a decrease in the truths of faith and of reason, and by a systematic decrease in Idealism. These "variables," then, are positively associated and change in a parallel manner.

When these data are properly considered, they justify the following conclusions.

(a) If not in all the minor fluctuations, then at least in the main waves, the empirical system of truth of senses shows itself positively associated with Materialism, the truth of faith with Idealism, especially in its pluralistic form, and the truth of reason with less religious and more dialectical idealism, especially with monistic idealism. (Note that it reappears in the thirteenth century.)

(b) In so far as the empirical system of truth showed itself tangibly associated with the movement of scientific discoveries and inventions, the above proposition means that the empirical system of truth, Materialism, and scientific discoveries are tangibly associated with one another.

(c) In so far as the truth of faith showed itself negatively associated with the movement of scientific discoveries, this means that the truth of faith, and pluralistic idealism, on the one hand, and scientific discoveries and empirism on the other hand, are negatively related.

These propositions do not hold for all the minor fluctuations, but they do hold in regard to the main upward and downward long-time waves. Such associations are to be expected logically, from the very nature of Idealism and the truth of faith, Materialism and the truth of senses; logical expectations are indeed borne out by the factual data. Here again the logically expected integration is realized, to a tangible degree, by the causal-functional integration.

(d) In so far as Idealism is a trait of Ideational and of Idealistic culture (in accordance with the character of the Idealistic theory) and Materialism is a trait of Sensate culture, the above spectra of mentality in this field, as well as in the field of art, of systems of truth, and of the movement of the natural sciences, suggest the following inferences. The predominant form of culture in Greece in the sixth, fifth, and fourth centuries B.C. was mainly Ideational and Idealistic; in the centuries from the third to the beginning of our era it was mainly Sensate; from the first to the sixth centuries A.D. it was transitory, in the sense of a decline in the Sensate culture and a rise in the Ideational; from the sixth to the twelfth centuries it was monopolistically Ideational; the twelfth and the thirteenth and fourteenth centuries were mainly Idealistic, but with a rising tide of Sensate culture; in the fifteenth century there was a desperate reaction against this tide; but beginning with the sixteenth century, the rising tide of the Sensate culture was resumed and, with minor fluctuations, has been on the increase to the present time. We have seen and shall also see that similar "spectra of the forms of culture" will be given by data concerning other compartments of culture, and particularly by data in the field of art.

This discussion may now turn to a brief characterization of other "tales" told by Tables 14 and 15 and Figures 10 and 11.

B. *No Continuous Linear Trend.* The next, and hardly questionable, conclusion suggested by these tabulations is that, for this period of about twenty-five hundred years, there is no indication of any perpetual *linear* trend for any of these three main currents. From 580 B.C. to A.D. 1920 there is no tendency toward a continuous increase, decrease, or constancy of Idealism, Materialism, or the Mixed current. For a given period, any of these currents rises at the cost of the others, but sooner or later the ascent ceases, is replaced by a downward movement, and the other current begins its "crescendo." This does not exclude the possibility of a monopolistic domination for a time by one of these currents and sometimes even for a long period, as is witnessed by the interval of about seven hundred years of an exclusive domination of Idealism, about A.D. 540 to about 1280. All traces of Materialism and other currents seem to have disappeared during that period. And yet, this domination came to an end, the opposite currents of Materialism or Mixed ontologies again reappeared, developed, and during several periods even became dominant.

For those of us who are followers of Idealism, Materialism, or the Mixed philosophies, and therefore maintain, as some popular writers would have it, that "the opposite philosophy has been disproved once and forever" and that "the future belongs entirely to the philosophy we hold," these data should inspire a more cautious attitude. It is nothing but a mere wish, and it is by no means warranted by the facts.

C. *Principle of Limits and of Self-regulation.* Thirdly, these statistical data provide clear-cut illustrations of the "principle of limits" and the principle of the "immanent" or, as Professor I. Lapshin puts it, "dialectic" self-regulation of sociocultural processes. One of the ontological currents increases for a given period, attains its limit in this direction, changes its course, and reverses itself. This limit varies for the different periods: at times, the upper limit of a given current is but 30 per cent, sometimes as much as 80 or even 100 per cent. The reversion occurs in the form of a reappearance and reinforcement of the opposite current of thought.

D. *Comparative Strength of Each Current of Thought.* Which of the three currents has been most influential throughout the period studied? Which, during certain specific periods? Table 16 provides the answer to these queries.

TABLE 16. RELATIVE INFLUENCE OF THE THREE MAJOR SYSTEMS

Period	*All Idealisms* (weighted indices)	*All Materialisms* (weighted indices)	*The Mixed Theories* (weighted indices)
580 B.C.—A.D. 100	322	304	142
100–600	534	75	21
600–1500	609	18	12
1500–1900	1842	339	753
1900–1920	363	210	329
Total	3670	946	1257

The figures show that, by and large, the Idealistic theories have been most influential, with the Mixed less, and the Materialistic system least, influential. The prevalence of the Idealistic current has actually been about four times as marked as the Materialistic. This may perhaps be interpreted as an indication that, all in all, a certain predominance of Idealism over Materialism is necessary for the continued existence of human culture and society and that a balance of the Mixed-Idealistic-Materialistic systems is still more indispensable than pure, otherworldly Ideationalism and Idealism. It is hardly incidental that Materialism has been at all times a relatively insignificant philosophical system; there was not a single period within a span of twenty-five hundred years when it was monopolistic or even clearly dominant.

These facts make one ponder whether any culture can subsist with only materialism, and especially with mechanistic materialism! It seems that a considerable proportion of idealism is a prime requisite for the durable existence of society. This implication is reinforced by a study of the character of the periods in which the tide of materialism rose. It almost always occurred before or during crises, hard times, social disintegration, demoralization, and other phenomena of this kind.

However that may be, the data seem to show clearly that Materialistic mentality has been a much less influential current than the Idealistic or Mixed, in spite of the fact that hylozoism is also included in materialism. Table 16 also summarizes the specific spectrum of the mentality of each of the long periods. It indicates that the period from A.D. 100 to 1500 was characterized almost exclusively by Idealism and the Mixed mentality. The period from 1900 to 1920 was dominated by an excessive reinforcement of the Materialistic current in comparison with its strength in all other periods, save that from 580 B.C. to A.D. 100.

E. *No Mechanical Periodicity.* The fifth tale told by the data involves a repudiation of numerous mechanical theories which claim the occurrence of certain periodicities in many social processes and their fluctuations, in business cycles, political processes, etc. One of the recent theories in the field of philosophy which claims an approximate hundred-year periodicity in the pulsation of philosophical theories, particularly those of individualism and collectivism, "binding and loosening," is developed by Karl L. Joël in a thoughtful and excellent work. Without dealing specifically with Joël's theory, it suffices to indicate that our data concerning ontological mentality here, as well as those concerning science, art, and other compartments of culture, do not show this or any other regular periodicity. Rising and falling tides of any one of the main currents have occurred within very different spans of time, varying from some 20 and 40 years to almost 1000 years. Frequently, they evidence a duration of about 60 or 80, or even 100 years, but this is by no means an invariable or even a clearly predominant duration. Therefore, to insist upon the occurrence of any uniform mechanical periodicity in these crescendos and diminuendos is to impose upon reality a uniformity which it does not possess. History repeats itself, but its themes recur in variations ever new — with changes not only in content, but also in rhythm and tempo. As a great artist, history provides creative, not monotonously mechanical, variations.

F. *Variations in Patterns of Fluctuation.* The sixth tale told by the data is that the rise and fall of the tides of Materialism and Idealism have different patterns in different times. In some instances, the fluctuation is sharp; in others, constituting the more general pattern, the curves of rise and decline are more or less gradual and relatively smooth, but even in these cases there is considerable variation in period.

G. *Long- and Short-time Waves.* A glance at Figure 11 suffices to demonstrate that there are both small, short-time — in a sense incidental — oscillations, and large, long-time, secular trends; the former are ripples and wavelets, and the latter waves and tides. The manifest import of this is that a study of merely short-time fluctuations in any field of culture is insufficient. The longer trends, or tides, are of great importance, not only in and of themselves, but also for an adequate understanding of the shorter fluctuations.

Contemporary research in the various fields of social phenomena has been virtually restricted to relatively short trends; economics especially has been limited by the study of almost exclusively short-time business cycles. Only quite recently have appeared some scattered attempts to study somewhat longer fluctuations, but they are still very few and the periods rarely extend beyond some twenty-five to sixty years, periods of comparatively brief duration. Despite the difficulties inherent in the study of long-time trends, such research is indispensable, for otherwise even the most careful study of short-time fluctuations is likely to lead to many theoretical and practical blunders, as has often occurred, particularly within the last few years. The past few years have convincingly disproved the "business forecastings" presented prior to 1929, which were based on the study of short-time business fluctuations.

H. *Diversity of Rhythms and "Beats."* The data also lead to a correction of the Hegelian, or similar, "dialectical" formula, concerning the type of rhythm and the number of "beats" in recurring processes. The famous formula of a three-beat rhythm, "thesis-antithesis–synthesis," to which, it is maintained, all processes can be reduced, is not universally applicable. In its rigid sense, it is hardly applicable at all to the phenomena studied here. The point is that in most cases thesis and antithesis (Materialism and Idealism) exist contemporaneously in the same culture. Sometimes they are well balanced, in other cases one of them is now slightly, now greatly, predominant, or even monopolistic. Under such circumstances it is difficult to say where and when the thesis has ended, where and when the antithesis has begun, or finally where and when there is a synthesis. The formula oversimplifies the variety of the real processes and imposes upon them a nonexistent monotonous uniformity. Instead, an admission of plurality of the various phases, rhythms, and beats in each wave is much nearer to the truth, and once again supports the thesis of the "creative-erratic" nature of the whole historical process. Hegel's formula describes only one of many varieties of rhythms and the number and character of the beats constituting various waves. It exceeds legitimate generalization.

I. *Alternation of Periods of Complication-Differentiation and of Simplification-Uniformization.* Now let us glance at some of the psychosocial meanings of the data, and at their mutual relationships. Greek philosophy opened with a monolithic domination of hylozoism, or more properly, of monism. As a consequence, there was only one stream of thought with no dissension or difference — a serene and balanced idealistic naturalism, indicating a unanimity of ideology and mind. Soon, however, the unanimity was disrupted: in 560 B.C. the stream of philosophy was divided into two currents, Idealistic and Materialistic; in 540 B.C. Idealism itself split into two subcurrents, pluralistic and monistic; and in 440 B.C. we find not only that Materialism and Idealism split into their main subclasses, but also that several Mixed philosophies appeared and occupied an important place. Thus as time goes on, and the Greek culture develops, we witness an increasing differentiation, as Spencer would say. It means a division in the previous unanimity of philosophical thought and ideology, the growth of various schools and factions, and their mutual struggle and antagonism.

This differentiation, though not necessarily increasing in its complexity and sharpness, continued to exist. This was the case up to our era, especially from 80 B.C. to *anno Domini*. By the first century B.C. the Mixed theories had begun to show signs of recession, and by the beginning of our era they had disappeared. In this way a step toward unification was made — a step, note, quite opposite to the previous trend of differentiation. The Mixed theories reappeared, for but a century, as the last sigh of a dying movement. By A.D. 220 they had completely disappeared, not to return for a thousand years.

The fate of the Mixed theories was followed, with a lag, by Materialism. Materialism began to die about A.D. 100; the "agony" lasted for some four hundred years, after which Materialism was nonexistent on the "front page of culture" for almost eight hundred years. In this way the second fundamental step toward an involution, or decrease of differentiation and increase of unanimity, was made. Simultaneously with the decline of Materialism, Idealism itself showed in part the same tendency; by A.D. 300 the monistic stream of idealism had dried up, and only one, the pluralistic, stream remained. Toward the beginning of the sixth century of our era, there was again a monolithic unanimity of philosophical thought, as simple as at the beginning of its history in Greece. If its beginning corroborates Spencer's formula of progress-evolution, the subsequent development contradicts it utterly. Instead of ever-increasing differentiation and integration the Graeco-Roman philosophical thought, after its initial stages, began to fluctuate indefinitely in this respect, made a definite move toward a decreasing differentiation, and finally returned to its initial simplicity and monolithic unanimity. These ugly facts, like many others, serve to kill Spencer's beautiful generalization, as well as most of the linear conceptions of evolution in whatever form they be given.

The story discussed does not end here. Subsequent indices show that after a long, but happy, sleep during the Middle Ages — when the mentality was undivided, faith was firm and free from any deep uncertainties, and there was a wonderful age of unanimity of mind, soul, and conscience — the devil of diversity and differentiation reappeared. First he was modest and hesitant, even temporarily withdrawing; then he became more and more audacious, potent, and relentless. After 1500 the soul of our culture was again divided into various streams of different philosophical thought, each with its vanity and glory, its dissensions and creations. If we would judge the movement toward differentiation by the percentage of the Mixed theories, then the century from 1680 to 1780, the end of the nineteenth century, and the present day may be considered the times when unanimity of philosophical mind is particularly low, with, it may be said, "as many philosophies as philosophers." In brief, instead of a calm and serene unanimity, the philosophical soul of these times has been rent into many dissenting ideologies; differentiation, or even atomization, has been rampant. This is especially true of the twentieth century, a period of factions, of a multitude of various currents, each strong enough to leave its stamp upon the culture, but yet too weak to subsume and dominate the others, and to give the public an authoritative, unquestioned guidance.

Such is the tale told by the data in this respect. When the whole series for twenty-five hundred years is taken, it demonstrates the existence of long-time waves, or recurrences, of increasing differentiation and decreasing unanimity in the philosophical thought, and opposite waves of an increasing unanimity and decreasing diversity. Thus, quite unexpectedly, the long row of figures has disclosed to us a peculiar, though rarely mentioned or seriously studied, alternation of the trend to diversity with the trend to unanimity and similarity. The rhythm of these waves has a bearing on Spencer's formula, but in the sense of demonstrating its faultiness. After any differentiation and complication, sooner or later there come simplification and uniformization, and after any simplification sooner or later there comes the opposite trend toward differentiation.

Such is our formula. It tells a quite different story from Spencer's concept of linear evolution-progress. It again points to the validity of our *principle of limits* and of the immanent self-regulation of various trends, and their directions, in the field of philosophy (as in all the other sociocultural processes).

If these principles are valid it may be predicted that the present trend toward differentiation, in the field studied, cannot go on forever. Sooner or later it will be replaced by the opposite trend. One after another many of the existing currents are destined to dry up, and one of the main currents (who can say which?) is destined to grow and to dominate the others. And then, as at the beginning of the Middle Ages, it will become monopolistic; philosophical mind will become one and unanimous, calm, simple, serene, and believing, instead of being questioning, skeptical, sophistic, cynical, and disbelieving. Such a unanimous philosophy will be, at the same time, religion, as it was at the dawn of Greek philosophy and at the beginning of our culture. When its time elapses, it is destined to be rent in its turn into partial currents. The phases of differentiation and unanimity will continue to alternate as long as the culture itself exists.

J. *Contemporary Situation.* In some of the other compartments of culture studied — art, system of truth, and science — we discovered that at the end of the nineteenth and in the twentieth century there appeared the symptoms of revolt against the dominant tendencies of the overripe Sensate culture. In ontology we do not find a similar rebellion (just as we did not find it in the field of empiricism) during the period 1900–1920. But the previous period, 1880–1900, is also marked by a considerable decline of mechanistic materialism (from 13.6 in 1840–1860 to 5.7 in 1880–1900). Moreover, the indices of mechanistic materialism for the nineteenth century generally are lower than those for the eighteenth century. This decline should perhaps be taken as a manifestation of revolt against an overripe Sensatism, a revolt much more pronounced in other fields of culture (especially art). Though, in accordance with the previously established uniformity of increased Materialism during periods of sociocultural crisis, the indices of Materialism during 1900–1920 were higher than hitherto, the possibility that the twentieth century, regarded as a whole, may experience a recession of Materialism is not excluded. In a word, in this field, as in others, there are symptoms of revolt at the close of the nineteenth century, though they are neither pronounced nor definite.

K. *Rising Tide of Materialism and the Sensual Interpretation of Man and Culture.* It has been suggested in previous pages that the recent tendency in science to interpret man, culture, and history mechanistically, materialistically, "reflexologically," "endocrinologically," "behavioristically," "psychoanalytically," "economically," etc., is but a reflection of our overripe Sensate mentality. Here again, we find added verification of this proposition. Since scientists and scholars of the last four centuries have been living in an atmosphere of a rapid rise in Materialism, and decline in Idealism, their progressive inability to see "the idealistic," "divine," "spiritual" aspects and forces of man and culture becomes readily understandable. More and more they have been led to see there principally the material, sensory, external, mechanistic, and other sensual aspects and forces. Hence the increasing fashionableness of materialistic, reflexological, endocrinological, biological, psychoanalytic (man viewed as an entity of largely superphysiological sex), and other anti-idealistic interpretations of history, culture, and man. Such theories have been more and more popular; more and more accredited as "scientific"; more and more readily and widely adopted as the "last word of science." The continued successful diffusion of these doctrines among the lay public has developed to the point where, at the present moment, virtually every aspect of sociocultural reality is being interpreted almost exclusively in terms of these "sensual variables."

It is not my task to censure or praise this vogue. My function is to indicate that it stands in the closest relationship with the predominant system of truth and the swelling tide of Materialism, just as the predominantly Idealistic interpretation of man and culture in the Middle Ages, during the domination of the Ideational mentality, was clearly harmonious with that mentality. This observation should provide abundant warning to the partisans of the "sensual" or "idealistic" interpretation of man; it should lead these theorists to disavow the claim that their doctrines constitute "the last word of science," that they incorporate the whole truth, and only the truth. The data show that both "sensual" and "idealistic" positions are conditional and highly subject to fluctuation. Both positions probably contain a part of truth, but only a part. Either interpretation in extreme forms may involve more "un-truth" than truth. Consequently, these extreme views are bound to be confronted, sooner or later, with a reaction against their misleading pseudo truth.

It will not be surprising, then, if in the future this position is confronted with a rapidly and unexpectedly increasing reaction in the form of Idealistic interpretation. Whether this conjecture is fulfilled is of secondary importance. Such a reaction has already appeared in science and philosophy in the last three decades. Here we see once again how that which is accepted as truth and verity in a certain period is conditioned by the dominant mentality of the given culture.

IV. Corroboration in Social Space

The observed association of the truth of faith and partly of reason with Idealism and with a low productivity in the natural sciences, and of the truth of senses with Materialism and with a high level of science, is found also in several other great cultures. We have seen that the predominant system of truth in the Hindu culture was that of faith and partly of idealistic reason. The expectation, based on uniform associations in other instances, that Idealism would consequently have been the predominant system of ontology is well fulfilled indeed.

The overwhelmingly dominant metaphysics of India from the Vedic period up to the present has certainly been Idealism of various types. Detailed data concerning this subject were presented in Chapter One, where the role of Materialism in Hindu thought was concisely and adequately outlined. In that discussion, it was found that the domination of Idealism was so complete that only through a considerable amount of intensive research has it been possible to find any traces of Materialism in the higher levels of Indian thought. It is true that there are some slight traces in Vedic and post-Vedic India, but the very sparsity of Materialism suggests that it had virtually no influence. Moreover, materialistic allusions are found almost solely in the works of idealistic writers engaged in attempts to refute such ideas. Two Brihaspati and the school of Chārvākā and of Nastika are virtually the only materialists. But even these are mentioned mainly in the works of their idealistic critics — such as Krishna Misra's *Probodha Chandrodaya*, or *Rise of the Moon of Intellect* — or occasionally in the Brahmanic texts or in the essentially idealistic literary works (*e.g.*, *Vemana*, *c.* A.D. 1400) or in some political writings (*e.g.*, *Artha-Shastra*). Such facts are eloquent testimony to the pronounced dominance of Idealism in the Indian culture and furthermore verify the thesis that an Ideational culture comprises the truth of faith and Idealistic ontology and that these are associated with but slight developments in science and technology.

What has been said of India likewise applies not only to Buddhism, Jainism, etc., but also to the Taoist culture and its metaphysics. We have seen that its truth is principally that of faith and it may now be added that its ontology is predominantly Idealistic. Even a cursory examination of Taoist texts permits the conclusion that Materialism occupies little if any place in its philosophy. Moreover, in this instance as well, is found a close association of truth of faith, Idealism, and a low level of the natural sciences.

16

FLUCTUATION OF "FIRST PRINCIPLES": II. FLUCTUATION OF ETERNALISTIC AND TEMPORALISTIC MENTALITY

I. Eternalism, Temporalism, and Mixed Theories

A further general principle which underlies — implicitly or explicitly — many scientific, philosophical, religious, and ethical theories, and which likewise conditions a number of more special ideologies, beliefs, and convictions, is the principle of Eternalism as against Temporalism.

As to the classification of the main solutions of the problem, the three main classes into which all the solutions fall are: (1) The *ideology of Being*, or *eternalism*, which stresses that the true ultimate reality is an unchangeable super- or all-time Being. Any change or any Becoming is either pure illusion or something secondary. (2) The *ideology of Becoming*, or *temporalism*, according to which the true reality is an incessant change, a never-ceasing flux, where any moment differs from another, with its "earlier-later," "before-after," and other time references. (3) *Synthesis*, or *reconciliation of both eternalism and temporalism*, according to which the true reality has both these aspects. These are the main classes into which practically all the answers to, and theories in, the field of this vital problem fall. The reduction of change to Being has consisted in attempts to show that Becoming (or its equivalents) is either nonexistent or unreal, or represents nothing but a specific aspect of Being. The predominant thought of Brahmanic India, the Taoism of China, many a theological concept of God, many an "ultimate reality" of several philosophical systems, Parmenides's and Zeno's philosophies of the true reality, and Zeno's famous proofs of the nonexistence of movement — all these give an example of this philosophy. Here are a few typical formulas of it. "The really existing is neither this nor that, is neither effect nor cause; is neither past nor future." . . . "It is without sound, without touch, without form, without decay, without taste, without smell, without beginning, without end, eternal, beyond the Great and unchangeable." . . . "It sprang from nothing, nothing sprang from it." . . . "The ancient is unborn, eternal, everlasting." Such is one of the best formulas of Being ever offered in the history of human thought. Many centuries before our era it was formulated in Ancient India.

Along the same lines run other philosophies of Being. Here is the formula of Taoism, almost identical with the Hindu formula.

There was something, undifferentiated and yet perfect, before heaven and earth came into being. So still, so incorporeal! *It alone abides and changes not.* It pervades all, but is not endangered. It may be regarded as the mother of all things. I know not its name; if I must designate it, I call it Tao.

The Greek theories of Parmenides and Zeno are too well known to be quoted here extensively. We are familiar with the skillful and logical reasoning of Zeno and his four famous arguments, the Dichotomy, the Achilles, the Arrow, and the Stadium, in which he tried to prove that there is no movement or motion or change in this world. When, later on, other formulas of God or ultimate reality are given, they often present it as a form of Unchangeable Being. St. Augustine's formula may serve as an example: "*Quid es ergo, Deus meus?*" "Thou art truth indeed, *wherein no change, no shadow of alteration* . . . most constant and incomprehensible . . . immutable . . . never new and never old . . . still the same."

In many variations, this philosophy of Being, either in its application to true reality generally, or to the ultimate reality only, has been going on throughout the whole history of philosophy and human thought from the remotest past to the present time.

The opposite effort, to reduce the category of Being to that of Becoming, is represented by the philosophy of *Becoming*. It claims that everything is in the state of incessant Becoming, change, flux; that Becoming or process is the only reality, and there is no unchangeable and everlasting permanency whatsoever. At the best, a Being is nothing but a slow Becoming, viewed statically, and nonexistent in reality. This stream also flows throughout the whole history of human thought, from the remotest past to the present time. Herakleitos's famous: "All things are born through opposition and all are in flux like a river. . . . Reality is a condition of unrest" is one sample of this conception; Zend-Avesta's somewhat similar conception of reality as an incessant strife and change of the two opposite forces, Ahura-Mazda and Angra Mainyu, until the final victory of Ahura-Mazda is secured, is another.

Nearer to our time is the Hegelian conception of reality and, in our own day, that of A. N. Whitehead. Finally, we have the writings of a crowd of modern professors and journalists, who again and again stress—intentionally or not—that only process, change, Becoming are existing reality.

The third solution of the problem has been to give direct or indirect recognition to both categories, and an allotment of some room to each. The forms of this solution have been divers. *One* of them, connected with the names of Leukippos and Democritus, found it in an *atomistic* theory; the atoms or the last particles of the reality are unchangeable; they represent Being; their combinations are ever changing; they give process, Becoming. Replace the atoms by electrons, protons, or by the still smaller elements, and you will have arrived at most of the contemporary theories of reality of the same type. *Another form* of this solution is given by the theories of *aeternitas*, *aevum*, and *tempus* of Plato, the Neo-Platonists, partly of the Peripatetic School, by most of the medieval thinkers (from Augustine, St. Thomas, the Scholastics up to Spinoza) and by many others, where the realm of Being is allotted to the ultimate or supreme reality; the realm of Becoming to the empirical reality of our sense perception where "generation and corruption," change and process, the beginning and the end, reign supreme. In some of the theories there is a gradation of reality in three and four classes, with an increasing Being and a decreasing Becoming, as we pass from the lower to the higher forms of existence. A *third* variation of this solution is given by an enormous number of both the old and the modern theories which claim that the concrete things are changeable (are in process), but that the relationships between the things and the laws which govern the changes are constant and immutable. The former are in the realm of Becoming, the latter in that of Being. This idea is predominant in the nineteenth-century conception of "evolution," according to which everything incessantly changes, but the causal laws of this change are supposed to be constant and everlasting. The usual conception of the existence of invariable scientific laws and uniform relationships between the ever-changing phenomena; the very essence of a causal relationship according to which A is invariably connected with B in this ever-changing universe; the very essence of any scientifically true concept or definition which is supposed to be true forever (otherwise it is not true and not scientific, according to the prevalent opinion), but which describes ever-changing reality — these and dozens of similar theories and beliefs are all merely variations of this third solution. In one way or another, all of them — explicitly or implicitly — allot a place for Becoming and another for Being (sometimes contrary to their own contentions). The *fourth* variety is represented by those theories, in all fields of science and philosophy, which claim that the "form" of a class of phenomena is constant while the content is ever changing. Here the form is in the realm of Being, the content in that of Becoming. Still another diluted example of the same is given by the fundamental concepts of the natural sciences. Whether or not scientists want fixed and — hypothetically or factually — immovable points of reference in their study of phenomena in flux, they are forced to assume, to admit, to postulate, such fixed and for the time being invariable framework of reference.

In the Newtonian mechanics, absolute space is taken as ever identical with itself and immovable.

In the special field of human relations, there are hundreds of concrete examples of the same solution. The Greeks viewed "nature" as the realm of immutability, and man-made norm as that of change. When the Romans thought that the *jus civile, jus Quiritum*, and *jus honorarium* were all changeable, while *jus naturale* and *aequitas* were unchangeable, eternal, immutable, valid for all times and for all peoples, they again gave *suum cuique* to Being as well as to Becoming.

With a slight variation and under the name of either "the eternal law" (St. Thomas Aquinas and others) or "natural law" or "divine law," almost all theorizers about law and morals have admitted or stressed the unchangeable and everlasting Being in this field in contradistinction to the "positive law" and concrete codes of laws, mores, prescriptions, which are changing in time and in space.

The same concept has been given, in a slightly different form, as applied to all human relationships and institutions. As an example of this, the physiocratic concept of the natural order and natural law can well serve. While admitting that the concrete set of mores, laws, social relationships, and institutions is ever changing, François Quesnay and other leaders of the physiocrats claimed that side by side with these there exists an immutable "*l'ordre naturel*" and "*le droit naturel*" different from "*le droit légitime.*" This natural order and natural law are eternal, "immutable," everlasting, and unchangeable.

In a somewhat different form, essentially the same method of the reconciliation of the Being and Becoming in human affairs is presented by all the numerous theories which, admitting and stressing the ever-changing character of human behavior, relationships, laws, mores, institutions, historical destinies, and what not, at the same time claim that in all these changes there are the *uniformities, the regularities, the causal relationships, and the laws* according to which these changes proceed, and that these uniformities, regularities, and causal laws are themselves immutable, constant, unchangeable; and that the task of science consists essentially in the discovery and formulation of these immutable uniformities, causal laws, and regularities.

These examples give a sufficiently clear idea of the variety of the third solution where, explicitly or implicitly, neither of these categories is absorbed by the other.

Having outlined these solutions, I must note that all the attempts to reduce one of these categories to another, in the way of exclusion of the other category, have failed, with hardly any exception. This means that these theories in a disguised form have had to give place to the other principle, and in fact, though contrary to the claims of their authors, represent also a variation of the third solution. When a Hindu, Brahman, or Taoist, a Zeno or St. Augustine, or any other philosopher of Being, unchangeable, everlasting reality, has to give a meaning to the concept of Being, he can do it only by invoking Becoming and its equivalents. Only by contrasting their Being to Becoming, *aeternitas* to *tempus*, could they give to it any sense. More than that; the changeableness of the empirical reality is such an undeniable dictum that they could not deny its existence and had to recognize it. All that they could do was to qualify it as inferior, less real, more illusionary; or, having expelled it from the realm of reality, return it as one of its properties. We shall not quarrel with their evaluation of what is superior and what is inferior reality, it does not concern us here; what does concern us is that, whether in the form of inferior or superior reality, they have admitted it, and were unable to reduce it to nothing, or let it be merged into Being. That is exactly what they did. In other cases, after expelling it from the realm of reality, they put it back there secretly. What I mean by that is well shown by a continuation of the quotation from St. Augustine given above. Note it attentively. "Thou art truth indeed, wherein no change, no shadow of alteration; most constant and incomprehensible; *immutable, yet changing all things; never new and never old, yet renewing all things*" . . . and so on.

The italicized statements show how Becoming is clandestinely reintroduced into the realm of reality.

Mutatis mutandis, the same is to be said of the philosophers of Becoming. To make meaningful their concept of Process, they have to recur to that of Being. Having expelled Being from reality, they have to reintroduce it, either in the form of "the ultimate reality" (A. N. Whitehead), the transcendental, the *ding an sich und für sich*, matter, energy, cosmic rays, Universal Spirit, Will, Herakleitos's *One* or *Fire*, God, the Unknowable, "Conation," World's Mind, Brahma, or any other ultimate entity, which is in process, and which, in spite of that, has to remain identical with itself. Otherwise, there is no logical subject which is in process, and no possibility of talking of a process.

This difficulty of reduction of one of these categories to the other explains why the number of the pure eternalists and the pure temporalists has been small during the twenty-five hundred years studied. It makes it also advisable to differentiate our three classes a little more exactly, namely, to separate them into five different classes: (1) *pure eternalism;* (2) *eternalism-temporalism, where the aspect of Becoming is present but is greatly overshadowed by the aspect of permanent Being;* (3) *pure temporalism;* (4) *temporalism-eternalism, where the aspect of Becoming is much more stressed than that of Being;* (5) finally, the theories of *equilibrium of eternalism-temporalism, where are found only those concepts which give equal importance to both aspects and regard them as equally important modes of reality.* Subsequently this study is made along the line of this fivefold as well as the threefold classification. In the threefold classification are united pure and preponderant eternalism and pure and preponderant temporalism; the third section is made up of the "equilibrium" theories.

Table 17 shows by 20-year periods the main ups and downs of the influence of each of the five, as well as the three, main streams of thought in the field.

Table 18 gives the same by century periods. Figure 12 depicts the movement by century periods.

II. Main Results

A. As in all other similar tables, no perpetual linear trend and no increasing differentiation — complication or the opposite, simplification, uniformization — are shown by the data. Instead of any linear trend, the currents rise and fall, fluctuating without any continuous tendency in the course of time.

B. A glance through either the 20-year or 100-year periods shows at once that the *current of eternalism* (philosophy of Being) *is indeed closely associated with the Ideational culture and its various aspects, while the mentality of temporalism is allied with the Sensate culture and its variables.* The century-periods table shows:

(1) In the sixth century B.C. — the Ideational century according to the earmarks of other aspects of its culture — eternalism is the highest, comparatively; then it tends to decrease from the fifth to the first century B.C., the period of the rise of the Sensate culture, as is shown by the other aspects of that culture. On the other hand, during these centuries temporalism rises (from the sixth to the fifth B.C.) and stays up to the beginning of our era very high and powerful. Such a movement of these rivals is a direct corroboration of the expectation that follows from the very nature of the Ideational and Sensate cultures.

(2) After the first century A.D. temporalism begins to decline rapidly and disappears entirely after the fourth century A.D. — again a result in perfect agreement with the movement of the Ideational and Sensate curves in all the other compartments of culture. Thus throughout the Middle Ages, up to the fourteenth century, temporalism remains underground, as it were; materialism, empiricism, natural sciences, visual art, and, as we shall see, ethics of happiness, nominalism, singularism, and other variables of the culture studied here also remain underground, or of very low value. The Middle Ages emerge as the period of the monopolistic Ideationalism, with its mentality turned not to the temporal and fleeting aspects of reality, but to its eternal aspects; not to Becoming, process, change, progress, Evolution, but to Being, permanency, *aeternitas* and *aevum*. This medieval period is marked by a rise of eternalism and

TABLE 17. FLUCTUATION OF ETERNALISM AND TEMPORALISM FROM 560 B.C. TO A.D. 1920 BY 20-YEAR PERIODS

PERIOD	*Eternalism*			*Temporalism*			*Eternalism-Temporalism*			*Temporalism-Eternalism*			*Equilibrium of Both*			PERCENTAGE OF ALL ETERNALISM	PERCENTAGE OF ALL TEMPORALISM	PERCENTAGE OF THE EQUILIBRIUM OF BOTH
	Number of representatives	*Their weight*	*Percentage of the total*	*Number of representatives*	*Their weight*	*Percentage of the total*	*Number of representatives*	*Their weight*	*Percentage of the total*	*Number of representatives*	*Their weight*	*Percentage of the total*	*Number of representatives*	*Their weight*	*Percentage of the total*			
560–540 B.C.	0	0	0	0	0	0	2	10	100	0	0	0	0	0	0	100	0	0
540–520	0	0	0	0	0	0	2	10	50	1	2	10	1	8	40	50	10	40
520–500	0	0	0	1	7	32	1	5	23	1	2	9	1	8	36	23	41	36
500–480	1	7	24	1	7	24	1	5	17	1	2	7	1	8	28	41	31	28
480–460	2	12	50	1	7	29	1	1	4	2	3	13	1	1	4	54	42	4
460–440	2	8	38	1	1	5	1	1	5	4	10	47	1	1	5	43	52	5
440–420	2	8	18	2	10	22	1	1	2	7	20	45	2	6	13	20	67	13
420–400	1	3	4	8	29	40	1	1	1	4	18	25	6	21	29	5	65	29
400–380	1	3	4	7	27	39	1	2	3	3	11	16	9	26	38	7	55	38
380–360	1	3	6	3	15	28	2	14	26	3	16	30	3	5	10	32	58	10
360–340	0	0	0	6	18	29	4	20	33	5	15	25	6	8	13	33	54	13
340–320	0	0	0	5	9	20	4	10	22	5	10	22	6	17	36	22	42	36
320–300	0	0	0	8	17	24	3	6	8	7	13	18	11	35	50	8	42	50
300–280	0	0	0	9	18	26	4	9	13	6	17	24	6	26	37	13	50	37
280–260	0	0	0	7	16	26	3	7	12	4	13	21	7	25	41	12	47	41
260–240	0	0	0	4	14	40	0	0	0	2	4	11	7	17	49	0	51	49
240–220	0	0	0	8	27	45	0	0	0	4	7	12	10	26	43	0	57	43
220–200	0	0	0	5	14	42	0	0	0	2	3	9	6	16	49	0	51	49
200–180	0	0	0	2	3	14	0	0	0	3	4	18	7	15	68	0	32	68
180–160	0	0	0	2	6	30	0	0	0	2	2	10	5	12	60	0	40	60
160–140	0	0	0	2	7	33	0	0	0	2	3	14	5	11	53	0	47	53
140–120	0	0	0	3	9	43	0	0	0	1	2	10	5	10	47	0	53	47
120–100	0	0	0	2	4	20	0	0	0	2	4	20	7	12	60	0	40	60
100–80	0	0	0	2	4	15	0	0	0	4	7	27	7	15	58	0	42	58
80–60	0	0	0	1	2	6	0	0	0	3	5	14	10	28	80	0	20	80
60–40	0	0	0	1	5	7	1	4	6	4	18	27	17	40	60	6	34	60
40–20	0	0	0	1	5	11	1	2	5	3	10	23	11	27	61	5	34	61
20–0	0	0	0	1	5	24	2	4	19	2	2	10	5	10	47	19	34	47

TABLE 17. FLUCTUATION OF ETERNALISM AND TEMPORALISM BY 20-YEAR PERIODS — *continued*

PERIOD	*Eternalism*			*Temporalism*			*Eternalism-Temporalism*			*Temporalism-Eternalism*			*Equilibrium of Both*			PERCENTAGE OF ALL ETERNALISM	PERCENTAGE OF ALL TEMPORALISM	PERCENTAGE OF THE EQUILIBRIUM OF BOTH
	Number of representatives	*Their weight*	*Percentage of the total*	*Number of representatives*	*Their weight*	*Percentage of the total*	*Number of representatives*	*Their weight*	*Percentage of the total*	*Number of representatives*	*Their weight*	*Percentage of the Total*	*Number of representatives*	*Their weight*	*Percentage of the total*			
0–20 A.D.	0	0	0	1	1	4	1	8	32	2	2	8	9	14	56	32	12	56
20–40	0	0	0	1	1	5	1	8	40	1	1	5	7	10	50	40	10	50
40–60	0	0	0	2	2	8	1	8	31	1	1	4	4	15	57	31	12	57
60–80	0	0	0	2	2	5	2	8	21	1	1	3	7	28	71	21	8	71
80–100	0	0	0	2	7	19	2	8	22	1	1	3	4	21	56	22	22	56
100–120	0	0	0	2	8	20	2	6	15	1	1	2	7	26	63	15	22	63
120–140	0	0	0	3	7	12	6	17	28	1	1	2	12	35	58	28	14	58
140–160	0	0	0	3	7	12	8	21	35	2	2	3	14	30	50	35	15	50
160–180	0	0	0	3	12	15	8	23	28	2	2	2	14	45	55	28	17	55
180–200	0	0	0	3	12	12	9	21	21	2	4	4	17	63	63	21	16	63
200–220	0	0	0	1	6	10	6	22	37	1	3	5	8	29	48	37	15	48
220–240	0	0	0	0	0	0	4	20	51	1	1	3	4	18	46	51	3	46
240–260	0	0	0	0	0	0	4	15	33	1	1	2	7	30	65	33	2	65
260–280	0	0	0	0	0	0	3	10	29	1	1	3	6	24	68	29	3	68
280–300	0	0	0	0	0	0	3	13	69	1	1	5	3	5	26	69	5	26
300–320	0	0	0	0	0	0	3	15	63	1	1	4	4	8	33	63	4	33
320–340	0	0	0	0	0	0	6	18	49	1	1	2	6	18	49	49	2	49
340–360	0	0	0	0	0	0	7	14	48	1	1	4	4	14	48	48	4	48
360–380	0	0	0	0	0	0	9	20	32	0	0	0	10	42	68	32	0	68
380–400	0	0	0	0	0	0	7	22	37	0	0	0	9	37	63	37	0	63
400–420	0	0	0	0	0	0	5	16	33	0	0	0	12	33	67	33	0	67
420–440	0	0	0	0	0	0	5	16	37	0	0	0	11	27	63	37	0	63
440–460	0	0	0	0	0	0	3	12	52	0	0	0	4	11	48	52	0	48
460–480	0	0	0	0	0	0	3	12	48	0	0	0	7	13	52	48	0	52
480–500	0	0	0	0	0	0	3	12	55	0	0	0	7	10	45	55	0	45
500–520	0	0	0	0	0	0	4	14	50	0	0	0	6	14	50	50	0	50
520–540	0	0	0	0	0	0	4	14	38	0	0	0	6	23	62	38	0	62
540–560	0	0	0	0	0	0	2	5	23	0	0	0	5	17	77	23	0	77

560–580 A.D.	0	0	0	0	0	0	1	1	17	0	0	0	2	5	83	17	0	83
580–600	0	0	0	0	0	0	1	4	50	0	0	0	2	4	50	50	0	50
600–620	0	0	0	0	0	0	1	4	33	0	0	0	3	8	67	33	0	67
620–640	0	0	0	0	0	0	1	6	43	0	0	0	3	8	57	43	0	57
640–660	0	0	0	0	0	0	1	6	67	0	0	0	2	3	33	67	0	33
660–680	0	0	0	0	0	0	1	6	75	0	0	0	1	2	25	75	0	25
680–700	0	0	0	0	0	0	0	0	0	0	0	0	1	2	100	0	0	100
700–720	0	0	0	0	0	0	0	0	0	0	0	0	1	3	100	0	0	100
720–740	0	0	0	0	0	0	0	0	0	0	0	0	2	8	100	0	0	100
740–760	0	0	0	0	0	0	0	0	0	0	0	0	2	6	100	0	0	100
760–780	0	0	0	0	0	0	0	0	0	0	0	0	1	1	100	0	0	100
780–800	0	0	0	0	0	0	0	0	0	0	0	0	1	4	100	0	0	100
800–820	0	0	0	0	0	0	0	0	0	0	0	0	2	6	100	0	0	100
820–840	0	0	0	0	0	0	1	2	20	0	0	0	3	8	80	20	0	80
840–860	0	0	0	0	0	0	2	4	22	0	0	0	3	14	78	22	0	78
860–880	0	0	0	0	0	0	3	6	29	0	0	0	4	15	71	29	0	71
880–900	0	0	0	0	0	0	0	0	0	0	0	0	4	9	100	0	0	100
900–920	0	0	0	0	0	0	0	0	0	0	0	0	2	4	100	0	0	100
920–940	0	0	0	0	0	0	0	0	0	0	0	0	1	2	100	0	0	100
940–960	0	0	0	0	0	0	0	0	0	0	0	0	1	1	100	0	0	100
960–980	0	0	0	0	0	0	0	0	0	0	0	0	1	1	100	0	0	100
980–1000	0	0	0	0	0	0	0	0	0	0	0	0	1	3	100	0	0	100
1000–1020	0	0	0	0	0	0	0	0	0	0	0	0	3	8	100	0	0	100
1020–1040	0	0	0	0	0	0	0	0	0	0	0	0	2	5	100	0	0	100
1040–1060	0	0	0	0	0	0	2	5	38	0	0	0	3	8	62	38	0	62
1060–1080	0	0	0	0	0	0	4	16	52	0	0	0	6	15	48	52	0	48
1080–1100	0	0	0	0	0	0	3	14	44	0	0	0	7	18	56	44	0	56
1100–1120	0	0	0	0	0	0	5	15	65	0	0	0	4	8	35	65	0	35
1120–1140	0	0	0	0	0	0	7	21	58	0	0	0	6	15	42	58	0	42
1140–1160	0	0	0	0	0	0	7	25	61	0	0	0	7	16	39	61	0	39
1160–1180	0	0	0	0	0	0	7	19	73	0	0	0	4	7	27	70	0	27
1180–1200	0	0	0	0	0	0	6	14	64	0	0	0	4	8	36	64	0	36
1200–1220	0	0	0	0	0	0	9	17	55	0	0	0	6	14	45	55	0	45
1220–1240	0	0	0	0	0	0	8	16	67	0	0	0	3	8	33	67	0	33
1240–1260	0	0	0	0	0	0	9	18	55	0	0	0	4	15	45	55	0	45
1260–1280	0	0	0	0	0	0	11	37	58	0	0	0	8	26	42	58	0	42
1280–1300	0	0	0	0	0	0	15	36	50	0	0	0	11	36	50	50	0	50
1300–1320	0	0	0	0	0	0	13	30	37	0	0	0	15	50	63	37	0	63

TABLE 17. FLUCTUATION OF ETERNALISM AND TEMPORALISM BY 20-YEAR PERIODS — *continued*

PERIOD	*Eternalism*			*Temporalism*			*Eternalism-Temporalism*			*Temporalism-Eternalism*			*Equilibrium of Both*			PERCENTAGE OF ALL ETERNALISM	PERCENTAGE OF ALL TEMPORALISM	PERCENTAGE OF THE EQUILIBRIUM OF BOTH
	Number of representatives	*Their weight*	*Percentage of the total*	*Number of representatives*	*Their weight*	*Percentage of the total*	*Number of representatives*	*Their weight*	*Percentage of the total*	*Number of representatives*	*Their weight*	*Percentage of the total*	*Number of representatives*	*Their weight*	*Percentage of the total*			
1320–1340 A.D.	0	0	0	0	0	0	7	14	22	1	4	6	16	47	72	22	6	72
1340–1360	0	0	0	0	0	0	11	30	45	1	4	6	11	33	49	45	6	49
1360–1380	0	0	0	0	0	0	6	24	51	0	0	0	8	23	49	51	0	49
1380–1400	0	0	0	0	0	0	2	6	32	0	0	0	5	13	68	32	0	68
1400–1420	0	0	0	0	0	0	1	4	40	0	0	0	2	6	60	40	0	60
1420–1440	0	0	0	0	0	0	2	7	44	0	0	0	3	9	56	44	0	56
1440–1460	0	0	0	0	0	0	2	7	33	0	0	0	4	14	67	33	0	67
1460–1480	0	0	0	0	0	0	3	9	41	0	0	0	3	13	59	41	0	59
1480–1500	0	0	0	0	0	0	2	3	30	0	0	0	4	7	70	30	0	70
1500–1520	0	0	0	1	4	7	13	36	67	1	6	11	1	8	15	67	18	15
1520–1540	2	5	7	1	4	5	15	53	71	2	12	16	1	1	1	78	21	1
1540–1560	2	5	9	1	2	4	10	39	74	1	6	11	1	1	2	83	15	2
1560–1580	1	1	1	2	8	10	24	57	69	1	1	1	2	16	19	70	11	19
1580–1600	1	1	1	3	12	9	34	84	66	3	15	12	2	16	12	67	21	12
1600–1620	1	8	5	3	12	8	25	66	43	7	32	21	6	34	22	48	24	22
1620–1640	2	12	8	1	1	1	23	65	45	5	27	19	7	38	27	53	20	27
1640–1660	7	34	24	1	1	1	17	46	33	6	23	16	6	36	26	57	17	26
1660–1680	1	7	6	3	6	5	19	63	50	7	27	21	8	23	18	56	26	18
1680–1700	1	1	1	4	10	6	36	89	50	13	49	28	7	26	15	51	34	15
1700–1720	1	1	1	3	11	8	29	71	48	10	39	26	5	25	17	49	34	17
1720–1740	1	1	1	1	3	2	18	53	41	11	48	37	11	23	18	42	39	18
1740–1760	1	1	1	3	20	11	14	54	31	17	60	35	8	39	22	32	46	22
1760–1780	3	4	2	3	20	10	18	64	30	20	82	39	8	39	19	32	49	19
1780–1800	1	1	0.5	1	2	1	24	78	37	18	75	35.5	14	55	26	37.5	36.5	26
1800–1820	3	21	9	1	1	0.5	30	88	37	14	56	23.5	23	71	30	46	24	30
1820–1840	6	28	10	2	7	3	46	141	53	10	50	19	9	40	15	63	22	15
1840–1860	5	30	8	5	25	7	72	204	57	17	71	20	8	29	8	65	27	8
1860–1880	10	53	11	5	25	5	62	187	37	36	179	36	9	53	11	48	41	11
1880–1900	7	40	6	5	26	4	72	207	34	55	242	39	30	103	17	40	43	17
1900–1920	10	47	6	11	37	4	100	268	32	97	382	45	34	109	13	38	49	13

TABLE 18. FLUCTUATION OF ETERNALISM AND TEMPORALISM FROM 600 B.C. TO A.D. 1900 BY 100-YEAR PERIODS

PERIOD	*Eternalism*			*Temporalism*			*Eternalism-Temporalism*			*Temporalism-Eternalism*			*Equilibrium of Both*			PERCENTAGE OF ALL ETERNALISM	PERCENTAGE OF ALL TEMPORALISM	PERCENTAGE OF THE EQUILIBRIUM OF BOTH
	Number of representatives	*Their weight*	*Percentage of the total*	*Number of representatives*	*Their weight*	*Percentage of the total*	*Number of representatives*	*Their weight*	*Percentage of the total*	*Number of representatives*	*Their weight*	*Percentage of the total*	*Number of representatives*	*Their weight*	*Percentage of the total*			
600–500 B.C.	0	0	0	1	7	26	2	10	37	1	2	7	1	8	30	37	33	30
500–400	3	15	13	10	37	31	2	6	5	9	30	25	9	31	26	18	56	26
400–300	1	3	2	21	57	31	7	26	14	13	35	19	20	61	34	16	50	34
300–200	0	0	0	19	49	34	4	9	7	12	27	19	18	56	40	7	53	40
200–100	0	0	0	5	12	21	0	0	0	7	11	19	18	34	60	0	40	60
100–0	0	0	0	3	9	8	3	8	7	10	27	24	33	68	61	7	32	61
0–100 A.D.	0	0	0	3	8	9	3	16	18	4	4	5	20	59	68	18	14	68
100–200	0	0	0	6	23	12	19	49	25	4	6	3	35	115	60	25	15	60
200–300	0	0	0	1	6	5	11	41	36	2	4	3	18	64	56	36	8	56
300–400	0	0	0	0	0	0	18	53	42	1	1	1	20	71	57	42	1	57
400–500	0	0	0	0	0	0	9	31	36	0	0	0	25	55	64	36	0	64
500–600	0	0	0	0	0	0	7	20	36	0	0	0	13	36	64	36	0	64
600–700	0	0	0	0	0	0	2	10	48	0	0	0	5	11	52	48	0	52
700–800	0	0	0	0	0	0	0	0	0	0	0	0	4	13	100	0	0	100
800–900	0	0	0	0	0	0	4	8	21	0	0	0	10	31	79	21	0	79
900–1000	0	0	0	0	0	0	0	0	0	0	0	0	4	8	100	0	0	100
1000–1100	0	0	0	0	0	0	5	19	41	0	0	0	11	28	59	41	0	59
1100–1200	0	0	0	0	0	0	21	60	64	0	0	0	16	34	36	64	0	36
1200–1300	0	0	0	0	0	0	42	103	60	0	0	0	25	68	40	60	0	40
1300–1400	0	0	0	0	0	0	27	66	38	1	4	2	37	104	60	38	2	60
1400–1500	0	0	0	0	0	0	6	18	40	0	0	0	10	27	60	40	0	60
1500–1600	3	6	2	6	24	8	69	192	66	6	28	10	6	41	14	68	18	14
1600–1700	10	49	9	8	19	4	101	265	52	27	104	20	19	76	15	61	24	15
1700–1800	4	5	1	8	36	6	85	240	38	57	215	35	37	127	20	39	41	20
1800–1900	19	89	6	11	52	4	233	640	45	102	420	29	68	237	16	51	33	16

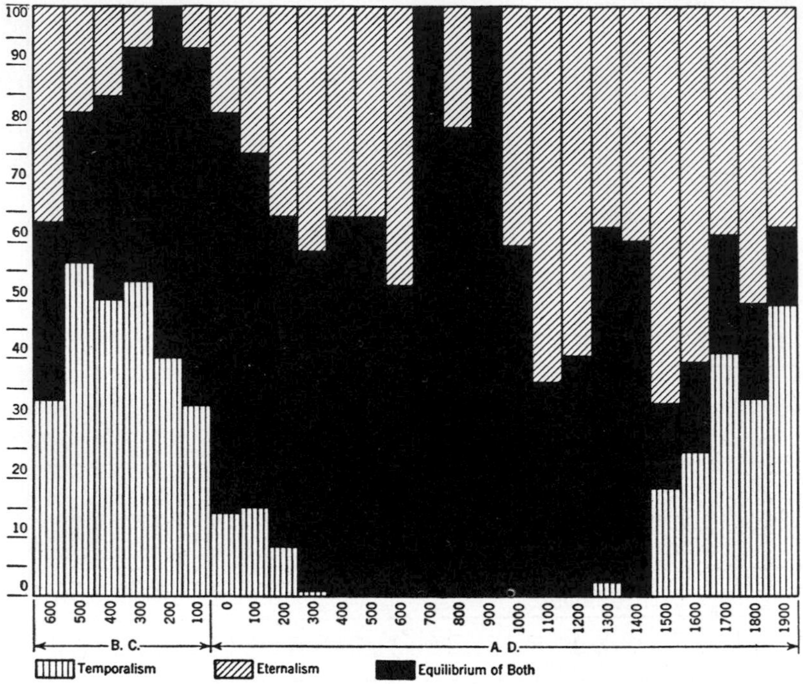

FIG. 12. TEMPORALISM, ETERNALISM, EQUILIBRIUM OF BOTH

by a high level of the synthetic current of the "equilibrium" permeated greatly by eternalistic elements (see further on the *aevum* of the medieval thinkers). These two currents share all the field.

(3) The fourteenth and fifteenth centuries are marked by a notable decline of eternalism and the re-emergence of temporalism, with the "equilibrium current" present. Thus this period appears again as "synthetic" or "idealistic" in the sense of a harmonious and partly eclectic mixture of all the currents, and with a particularly strong rise of the "equilibrium current." Though slightly later than painting and a few other variables of culture which gave the Idealistic phase in the thirteenth and fourteenth centuries, this period, from the thirteenth to the fifteenth century inclusive, stands out here also as a "mixture" or Idealistic phase.

(4) Having re-emerged in the fourteenth century, temporalism, with a short-time recess in the fifteenth century (again similar to many recesses met in other variables), rapidly and steadily grows from the fourteenth (only 2 per cent there) to the eighteenth century, where it reaches 41 per cent and then slightly recedes to 33 per cent in the nine-

teenth century and soars up again to 49 per cent in 1900–1920 (the last column in Table 17). Thus it grows in this period, as all the other curves of the Sensate culture in all its compartments have been growing during the centuries from the sixteenth to the twentieth.

C. The 20-year period data show several short-time flare-ups of pure eternalism and of pure temporalism. Studying the periods of the respective flare-ups, we notice that here again, as in the case of skepticism and fideism, *these extreme mentalities tend to flare up together*, the pure temporalism of the *Carpe diem* rising a little earlier and being followed by the extreme eternalism as its counterirritant. In this sense they counterbalance each other and show the phenomenon of "action reaction," and of self-regulation of sociocultural processes. Here we see a replica of the movement of skepticism and fideism. Looking at the periods of the short-time flares of these two extreme currents, we notice at once that they are the periods of short-time but sharp social crises; the Reformation, peasant, and other wars and revolutions; religious wars, including the Thirty Years' War; the prerevolutionary license, revolutionary crises, and postrevolutionary reactions. As in the flarings of skepticism, mysticism, fideism, and extreme ascetic and hedonistic mentalities, *such crises, with their insecurity, instability, anxiety, and sufferings, split human beings into the two opposite extreme types. Some of them are turned into pure eternalists* who try to *anchor human existence* to something solid, lasting, capable of withstanding all the storms of the empirical reality; *others are turned into the extreme sensual temporalists* of the *Carpe diem* type, with their tendency to catch the pleasure of the moment for "tomorrow is uncertain" ("*di doman no c'e certezza!*"). Which psychological types are turning into the one, and which into the other is unimportant just now. What is important is the fact of such a split, under catastrophic sociocultural conditions, into the extreme mentality of "eternalism, asceticism, and mysticism of despair," on the one hand, and into that of "temporalism, sensualism, and skepticism of despair," on the other. We have met and shall meet this law of polarization several times. It seems to be of fairly general nature.

D. In regard to the spectrum of the nineteenth and twentieth centuries in this respect, Table 17 tells us that since 1860 the mentality of our culture has been marked by a decline of eternalism — 65, 48, 40, 38, respectively, for each 20-year period from 1840 to 1920; by an increase of temporalism — 27, 41, 43, 49, respectively; and by a relatively small role played by the equilibrium theories — 8, 11, 17, 13 per cent, respectively. These dry figures tell in their own way several significant things. They show that *our mentality has been becoming more and more "temporalistic,"* seeing less and less the eternal or lasting aspect of the reality and more and more its fleeting and passing qualities. The first consequence of this has been an enormous growth of *dynamic viewpoint* in our mentality. All things began to be viewed more and more in their dynamic aspects, as something incessantly moving, changing, never being in the state of rest or unchangeableness. Everything is regarded as in a state of flux, of continuous change. The very terms "essence" and "unchangeable nature" are viewed suspiciously and branded as "scholastic" and "metaphysics." So-called "*Biologismus*" and "*Psychologismus*" invaded the field of epistemology, logic, philosophy, and attempted to destroy the category of immutable truth, with its absolute validity. An effort was made to reduce truth and validity to mere biological "reflexes," and useful "adaptation" (most of the biologists); to psychological "associations," "routine of perception," "conditioned responses," or "to the utility of the principle of the most economical line of least resistance" (E. Mach, K. Pearson, R. Avenarius, H. Poincaré, Maxwell, P. Duhem, W. James, and other pragmatists), and the like.

According to the theories of these scientists:

A scientist is never placed by nature in the presence of a decisive alternative between the true and the false. Consequently the very word "verity" — in the categorical meaning that hitherto made a value of it — tended to disappear from the scientific vocabulary and to be replaced by the terms of convention and convenience.

The validity of the laws of nature (in physics and mechanics and other branches of the natural sciences) was made more and more conditional and relativistic. If the Copernican system was regarded as more acceptable than the Ptolemaic, the reason was only that the first "is more convenient" or better fitted to the present convention.

Thus the 19th century, so famous as the century of science, ended in an unexpected crisis of scientific scepticism. The earlier physicist dreamed of basing the necessity of the causal relationship simultaneously upon the intelligible purity of the mathematical demonstrations that make its conclusion irrefutable for a mind; and upon the evidence of the facts which experimental demonstration imposes upon it. The two conditions of scientific necessity whose union was consecrated by the classical mechanics, resolved themselves finally into a double contingency. The principles of the rational deduction and the factual evidence supplied by the experimental technique, between which mechanics proposed to exercise mediating functions, became plastic in their own turn. The whole system of human knowledge began to be menaced, to liquefy and to slip from the hands that were believed to have grasped it.

In such temporalistic "truths" there remains nothing of the absolute ever-valid truth. It is replaced by fleeting, conventional, relativistic shadows and phantoms. The whole world, including the world of our mentality, with its categories, becomes an eerie and phantasmagoric complex (I cannot even say "space," or "realm," or "universe") of ever-fleeting, ever-changing, ever-passing shadows of events, objects, persons, values, and what not. There remains nothing "firm," no "fixed point of reference," no eternal and absolute boundary line between the true and untrue, right and wrong, and so forth.

And indeed, what happened to truth and validity happened still more to "the right and wrong," "good and bad," "beautiful and ugly," "great and small," "positive and negative value." "Right and wrong" became mere species of "mores" and "conventions." We literally returned to the dynamic quality of the sophists — Protagoras, Kritias, Thrasymachos, and others — with their "everything is relative in the world; man (the singularistic individual) is the measure of all things"; truth and right and beauty are mere conventions invented by the minority for the exploitation of the majority. They change, as everything changes in this world.

Another aspect of this temporalistic and dynamic viewpoint was *an extraordinary rise, especially since the end of the eighteenth and the beginning of the nineteenth century, of various theories of Becoming, from the theory of the biological evolution of Lamarck-Spencer-Darwin-Huxley-Heckel and the biologists, to the theories of social dynamics, social evolution, cultural change, social progress of Turgot-Condorcet-August Comte, and a vast legion of sociologists, anthropologists, historians, economists, political and social scientists generally.*

The category of Becoming — of change, of process, of evolution, of flux, of transformation, of mutation, of revolution — has become the fundamental category of our mentality, the specific glass through which more and more the Western society has been seeing the reality. It has been becoming blinder and blinder to the eternal or lasting aspects of it.

Of religion, God, philosophical truth, art, mores, ethical values — including the law, the family, property, the political organization — in brief, of anything and everything we say, as a mere matter of fact: "Well, they change; and there is no reason to deplore it. What was sacred yesterday is today profane. Our task consists in moving and changing as times change. We must make the necessary 'adjustment of the maladjustments' caused by this change." In millions of forms we repeat: "*tempora mutantur, et nos mutamur in illis*" and *tempus fugit* and *tempus edax rerum* — statements coined also in the period of a high level of temporal mentality.

From the nature of the temporalistic mentality, it follows that astronomical or watch time plays a particularly great role in it. Time is the basic category of any Becoming. And Becoming is a succession of stages in time. Such a succession is *history*. Hence, the development of historical-mentality in our culture. It is in this sense evolutionary-historical mentality par excellence. *Historismus* is a category of the Sensate-temporalistic mentality, while it plays only a modest role in the Ideational-eternalistic mentality.

It has been pointed out that the Middle Ages had a blurred sense of time. In the literature of the Middle Ages the past, present, and future were hopelessly mixed. Likewise, no real history and no successful development of history should be expected or could occur. For the Ideational-eternalistic mentality, the empirical time as a marking system separating one empirical event from another is perfectly superfluous, because these events are superfluous. A. A. Macdonell puts the idea clearly in application to the Hindu Ideational mentality:

> The Brahmins . . . had early embraced the doctrine that all actions and existence are positive evil, and could therefore have felt but little inclination to chronicle historical events. . . . Nothing can be more confused, nothing more imperfect than the chronology of the Indians; no people which has attained to culture in astronomy, mathematics, is as incapable of history; in it they have neither stability nor coherence.

"The historical sense being lacking, the difference between reality and mythology became obliterated. So history became mythologised."

In contradistinction to this, the Sensate-temporalistic mentality is immersed in the time sequence of events, and has to mark it and chronicle it. Hence, development of history, historical bent of mind, and historical — that is time-sequential — narrative of events. For these reasons, it is not incidental that in Greece the history as history (Herodotus, Thucydides, and others) did not emerge until the fifth century. It is not incidental that in European culture history emerged only in the fourteenth or thirteenth century (Joinville, Froissart, and a few others), and reached its climax in the nineteenth century. In a larger sense, *Historismus* permeates our mentality, beginning with endless genealogical histories of this or that family, memoirs, personal diaries, biographies, reporters' narratives of events and scandals in the newspapers, and ending with tremendous archives, collections of documents, multitudes of courses in history, and an unembraceable literature of history. We cannot help viewing everything historically. The standpoint of "origin and development and evolution" is our main standpoint in studying anything, from religion to the stock market.

Another aspect of this supreme role of time category in our mentality is the *mechanistic timing of everything*, the use of time units as the marking system for the punctuation of events, phenomena, processes, and the subjecting of our whole life to time control. It is not incidental that the mechanical clock was invented in the early stages of the rising tide of the temporalistic mentality (in the fourteenth century), and with the progress of this rise, more and more perfected watches and watch time were developing in our culture. At the present, this wonderfully perfected watch time most tyrannically controls our whole existence. We cannot live without a watch. We go to bed winding it; we get up at the command of the hands or alarm of a clock; we move, work, act, eat, sleep, love, quarrel, study, pray, live, by a watch and controlled by watch time. Watch-time category is the supreme ruler of our mentality, action, life.

Therefore, it is not incidental that we coined our famous phrase, "*Time is money.*" Where the reality is viewed temporally, the reality of our own existence is so viewed also. As such it is short and is limited in the span of its existence. Time becomes a precious commodity which, like anything scarce, becomes valuable. Another aspect of it is the *particular stress upon the present moment* in contradistinction to the past and the future. By definition, temporalism is centered in the present. Remote past is over; remote future is uncertain. Only the present moment of the endless flux is real, only it exists and only it has value. Hence our stress of the present. We are unwilling to sacrifice it for a remote future. If we are forced to make a concession in regard to the near future, we require some compensation for such a sacrifice, be it interest on our savings, be it "profit" on our invested capital.

We live in and appreciate mainly the present. In the field of our practical activity this temporalism manifests itself in hundreds of different ways, so familiar to us and so strange to an Ideational mentality, from "get rich quick" (no matter how: through the stock market, kidnaping, racketeering, or any productive activity); "wine, women, and song"; from the "maximum of happiness" in a given moment; from thrills and pleasures, to our politics and our policies — financial, social, and otherwise — that look for immediate effects and care little for the long-time consequences.

The "short-time" attitude prevails and permeates our mentality in all fields. To make a "sensation," to "create a hit," to have an "instantaneous success" — in movies, in music, in literature, in science, in business, in politics — that is our motto, our supreme ambition, our paramount dream. "Time is money" is indeed one of the most characteristic formulas of our time.

The next consequence of the temporalism discussed is the *ever-quickening tempo of our life and the ever-faster rhythm of social change.* Tempo of change has increased already to a maddening speed in the turnover of all our values, from the changing models of our cars, radios, clothing, buildings, to the turnover in husbands and wives, mores, best sellers, art styles, scientific theories, philosophies, beliefs, and economic and political structures. In this rush our temporalistic time begins to devour its own children. Before a new "model" has time to settle and become rooted, it is swept away or torn down by a still newer "model," or "fashion," or "pattern." Not incidental, therefore, is the discovery of the sociologists of the nineteenth century that the "mode" and "fashion" are the lawgivers of our culture. *Fashion is indeed the most intimate child of our temporalistic mentality, while the "lasting tradition" is the child of the more eternalistic culture.* Who does not know that "fashion" and "mode" rule our life? And who does not know that the tempo of their change is ever increasing? We are already half crazy in our desire to be "most modern," to have "the newest and the latest" model of everything. These are for us the best, regardless of whether they are rotten or good.

Nothing has sufficient time to crystallize. Everything is in a liquid state. Nothing has a chance to be tested for its good or bad qualities. We really do not know which of the incessantly changing "models" and values are good and which are poor. Therefore *the whole social life and the whole mentality are also in a liquid state, formless, shapeless, foggy, like a primeval protoplasm or a crowd of fleeting shadows.* One would look in vain, in this fog of shadows, for clear-cut boundary lines between the sinister and the benevolent, the good and bad, the true and false, the beautiful and ugly, the wholesome and harmful, right and wrong. The shadow values are so crowded, so foggy, they come and go so fast, that no such lines can be established. Hence the supreme reign of relativism in our mentality and culture — relativism of everything. *Hence a lack of any certainty, stability, and security in our mental and social life.* In this atmosphere of queer, dancing shadow values nobody can feel secure; nobody can have firm ground under his feet. We try our best to "adjust" ourselves to this continuous change. A hopeless task, more hopeless than that of Sisyphus. The only result of this desperate "adjustment of maladjustments" is exhaustion, fatigue, and the senseless state of "being busy doing nothing."

The high tide of wars and revolutions of our time, of the multitude of internal and external disturbances that overcrowd it is but one of the numerous manifestations of this instability, inseparable from temporalistic culture. Since we indefatigably build and tear down our steel and concrete skyscrapers, why not do the same to any social structure? Hence, one social shock follows another; one explosion after another occurs before our eyes. The result is instability, a fleeting change of regimes, gluttonous competition, forever new and ever bolder social "experiments," with inevitable anarchy on the one hand and a rule of the boldest coercion on the other. The experimenters are permeated by the same temporalistic mentality: "Though short, my hour of triumph!" "Though short-lived, what an adventure and what a thrill!"

And all this is accompanied by the "*for tomorrow is uncertain*" creed. Yes, almost everybody now feels that in various forms. Certainty and certitude, the safety which is based upon it, the security which demands it — all is evaporating. Hardly anyone nowadays, from the dictator to the unemployed, feels any certainty of the morrow. No new scientific theory is expected to live for long; even when it appears, it does not claim either certainty or certitude; it is regarded as "the first approximation," "a mere hypothesis," and any cautious scientist and scholar expects, of course, that soon it will be blasted by a still newer theory. Science has also become "fleeting" and is changing more and more rapidly. Still less certainty exists in the philosophical and religious beliefs. Relativity of the ethical values is triumphant. They are expected to change, as a mere matter of fact, and any moral command is expected to be reversed. There is still less certainty in economic life; from the rich to the poor, nobody feels sure that tomorrow they will not be confronted with ruin or unemployment, or some other catastrophe. Still less does one feel secure of the safety of his life from dictators, racketeers, and other vicious forces, and of the inviolability of his "inalienable rights as man and citizen." Friends are not certain of the everlasting continuation of their friendships. Instead of one "sweetheart," lovers expect to have dozens. Among wives and husbands divorce becomes more and more fashionable. Like a branch in a wild torrent each of us is carried on by the whirlpool of social life, knocked about, tossed and thrown, regardless of our wishes and efforts. We have little chance of being left quietly on the shore to take a breath and to take stock of where and what we are, what we are doing, and where we want to go. Instead, we are more and more "busy," more and more in a rush, more and more greedy to live faster and faster, "for tomorrow is uncertain." We forget entirely the wisdom that "doing nothing is better than to be busy doing nothing." "Business" — in both the narrow and wide meaning of this term — is our motto; and it means but an incessant Sisyphean "reconstruction," "readjustment," "change," "remodeling," tearing down and building up, no matter whether in the field of industry, of education, or in science, religion, art, philosophy, law, or what not.

We are prisoners of this curse of temporalism where, using Maltus's terminology, maladjustments grow in geometric ratio while our adjustments grow only in arithmetical ratio.

Thus our temporalistic culture grinds its values into a more and more relativistic dust; robs them of their lasting nature; reduces them constantly to the decreasing value of the ever-shorter "present moment." In this way it depreciates them, immanently, by its own hand and by its own destiny. Likewise, by its own immanent development — through its increasing tempo of change — it devours itself and prepares its own destruction. Steadily it makes itself more and more impossible, poisonous, deadly. In this way it paves the way for its own decline and for an ascendance of the eternalistic mentality, with its unhurried life, its rest, quiet repose, and static contemplation of eternal verities, or what is believed to be such.

E. If we glance at the spectrum of the mentality in the field by long periods, and attempt to ascertain the comparative strength of each of the five groups generally, and in each of the long periods, an answer is given by Table 19.

TABLE 19. COMPARATIVE STRENGTH OF ALL ETERNALISMS AND ALL TEMPORALISMS

PERIOD	*Eternalisms*		*Temporalisms*		EQUILIBRIUMS
	Pure	*Mixed*	*Pure*	*Mixed*	
600 B.C.–A.D. 100	18	75	179	136	317
100–600	0	194	29	11	341
600–1500	0	284	0	4	324
1500–1900	149	1337	131	767	481
1900–1920	47	268	37	382	109
Total	214	2158	376	1300	1572

All eternalisms, 2372 *All temporalisms*, 1676 *Equilibriums*, 1572

A glance at these figures shows that of the five currents of thought, mixed eternalism has been the most influential; next in order come the equilibrium current, mixed temporalism, and then pure temporalism and pure eternalism. Glancing at the totals of each of the three united currents, we see that the *eternalistic current has been the strongest throughout the whole period studied; then comes temporalistic and close to it the equilibrium current.* However, the comparative strength of the rivals is not strikingly different; with some preponderance of eternalism, their strength has been fairly close to one another. Even the totals for pure temporalism and pure eternalism are not far different from each other. Considered that the periods studied are, in a sense, taken incidentally, such an approach of the total points of each of the three currents to one another is again suggestive of the principle of self-regulation of cultural processes and changes. Just as in the study of idealism and of materialism we found out that idealism prevails over materialism, and that such a prevalence is perhaps necessary for the lasting existence of a creative culture, a phenomenon of the same kind seems to be met here.

When we take the figures for the specific periods, we find deep contrasts and differences from period to period. The spectrum of the period A.D. 600 to 1500 and then from A.D. 100 to 600 is decidedly eternalistic; the spectrum of the periods 440 B.C. to A.D. 100, 1900 to 1920, and then 1500 to 1900 is either predominantly temporalistic or temporalistic in a degree much greater than the spectrum of the first groups of the periods.

F. Finally, the preceding data and comments teach us again that what appears to be truth fluctuates; in the predominantly eternalistic times the eternalistic theories receive the credit of being truth, and are believed in; in the temporalistic mentality the theories of change-evolution-progress acquire an infective and convincing power. Studying these fluctuations, we see again that they have been going on hand in hand with those of the three main systems of truth, which in their turn are but one of the elements or aspects of the rise and fall of the Ideational, Idealistic, and Sensate cultures.

As a practical moral to be drawn from that, the following words can be addressed to the partisans of eternalism, temporalism, and equilibrium: If the temporalists are now in the saddle, they have reason to rejoice; their creed is dominant, and any domination is inducive to rejoicing. But let their joy, as well as the regret of the eternalists, be not too great; sooner or later, temporalism will decline and eternalism will become triumphant again. If eternalism today is subdued, this means that it will be dominant tomorrow. So it has been, and so it probably will be in the future. For this reason the factions should not necessarily war with each other and should perhaps be inclined to believe that not all the truth is in their own credo and not all the credo of their adversary is error and blunder. The pure truth and the whole truth is possibly "white" and contains in itself the eternal as well as the temporal aspects: Being and Becoming, permanence and flux, eternity and moment. This, however, is only my personal credo and metaphysics; therefore it is not obligatory for anybody else to accept it. What may be obligatory is the fact of the fluctuation of these mentalities and their logical and functional integration with Ideational and Sensate cultures.

G. That this association is not limited to the Graeco-Roman and the Western cultures has briefly been shown already. The Ideational mentality of the Hindu, the Taoist, the Tibetan cultures has certainly been predominantly eternalistic in its conception of the true reality; of the true value — ethical, intellectual, and any other; of slow tempo in the change of their cultures and in all the other earmarks of these cultures. This statement appears to be so obvious and certain that there is hardly any need for its detailed corroboration. When the comparative decline of the Ideational mentality occurred, it led also to the decline of the eternalistic mentality; in this sense their fluctuation seems to show the same association.

17

FLUCTUATION OF "FIRST PRINCIPLES": III. FLUCTUATION OF THE INFLUENCE OF REALISM, CONCEPTUALISM, AND NOMINALISM

I. Preliminaries

Like idealism-materialism, like empiricism-rationalism-mysticism, like determinism-indeterminism, and a few other principles, the theory of realism-nominalism is one of the most general and contains fundamental principles which compose a framework for the system of truth and knowledge of a given period. More than that. Many an actual problem of the social sciences, especially such as individualism-collectivism, society and the individual, universalism and singularism, are most closely tied up with this problem and can hardly be studied fruitfully without its preliminary investigation.

By *logico-ontological realism* is meant a system of thought which claims that in all singularistic objects or subjects of the same class, which exist singularistically at different points of space — for instance, horses or dogs or stars — there is, besides their specifically individual differences, some essence or element which is common to all of them and which composes, so to speak, their essence or their *universalia*. Horse A may be white, horse B brown, but besides this and other differences, A and B have an element, say "horsiness," which is the same in both and in all horses, and without which A and B cannot exist; neither could we style A and B as "horses," put them into one class, and have a concept or definition of a horse generally if they lacked this element. Just because such an identical, generic element or, better, a superspatial and supertimely essence universal to all horses exists objectively outside our minds, we are able to create a general concept of a horse, and this concept is not something which exists only in our minds but is something that corresponds to the transsubjective reality, be it transcendental or immanent. In this sense, such generic concepts, such *universalia*, are neither a mere fiction nor a mere idea of our minds, but in a sense they are the "holy of holies," the very essence of reality itself, not to mention the fact that they are the heart and soul of our knowledge. In brief, logico-ontological realism insists that the generic concept — be it of a triangle generally, a man generally, a horse, atom, number, society, organism, a social class generally — exists really in our mind as well as outside of it in the transsubjective world, in the forms of the *universalia*.

The consequence is that the system of realism contends that the *identity* of the essence of all the singular phenomena of the same class is embraced by the same generic or general concept. Plato's *idea*, Aristotle's *form*, Christianity's concept of the identity of the members of the Holy Trinity (the Father, the Son, the Holy Spirit), Plotinus's *Logos* (Νοῦς), the ultimate realities of many philosophers, are examples of such a realism. In this, as well as in many other respects, it has several variations. Logico-ontological realism may be, for instance, *transcendental or immanent* or *transcendental-immanent*. When a realist claims that ideas which exist in the Divine Mind and compose the Kingdom of Ideas are transcendental to the objects learned through experience, we have *transcendental realism*. In this sense, many a philosopher has interpreted, for instance, the philosophy of Plato.

For a transcendental realism, the abstract generic concepts exist *ante rem* only, but neither *in re* nor *post rem*. The immanent realism contends that the ideas in the sense of the realistic *universalia* are immanent to the phenomenal world of the singular objects. It claims that the *universalia* exist *in re*. Aristotle's theory is an example of such an immanent realism. Others, like Plotinus, teach that the *universalia* exist in the mind of God (Νοῦς) as well as *in re;* that is, they are, at the same time, immanent to the empirical world of singular objects. In other words, they claim that the *universalia* exist *ante rem* and *in re*. Such a theory is a synthesis of *transcendental as well as immanent realism.*

These and other secondary differences among the realists do not, however, play any role in our classification and computation. The extreme as well as the moderate, the transcendental as well as the immanent and mixed realists, all are put into the class of the realists and computed as such.

The second fundamental current in this field is *conceptualism*. In contradistinction to realism, it states that in the transsubjective world there exist only singular or individual objects — horse A, horse B, horse S, each occupying a different position in space and time. They may be similar in regard to various properties, but they are neither identical nor quantitatively the same. In other words, in the transsubjective world there is no "horsiness." The cognizant subject perceives only the singular and individual impressions of things and objects and cannot perceive any *universalia*. However, in our mind these impressions and perceptions of the singular objects undergo a process of transformation into the general and generic concepts, the *universalia*. Out of similar traits we create the generic concept, which becomes in our mind a substitute for each of the singular objects compared.

These concepts exist in our mind as concepts; we think with them; we operate with them. Thus conceptualism occupies an intermediary position between realism and nominalism. With realism it agrees in that the general concepts exist in our mind, but disagrees in that the *universalia* exist in the *transsubjective* world. With nominalism it agrees in that there are no *universalia* in the transsubjective world, but disagrees in admission of the reality of the *universalia* in our mind — which is denied by nominalism.

Finally *nominalism* is the opposite pole to realism. It contends that there are no *universalia* either in the transsubjective or subjective worlds. In *rerum natura, extra nos et praeter nos* there exists nothing which corresponds to any concept or *universalia.* Outside us only the singular objects are given. In our mind also there are only singular images and impressions, but no real concepts. What is regarded as concept is practically a mere word or symbol which we use, but, using it, we always think in terms of a singular object — horse A or horse B, in our case. We do not and cannot think about any "horsiness" or "horse generally." Thus it claims that the generic essences are nonexistent in the transsubjective as well as subjective worlds. A simulacrum of a concept in our mind is a kind of illusion, due to a mere association of various singular impressions with the same *word or symbol.* Using the word "horse" for A, B, C, we are prone to believe that the identity of the word in all such cases means the existence of the identity of the objects compared, or the concept. Meanwhile, it is mainly an identity of the word used, and nothing more. From this it is comprehensible why the current is styled by the name of nominalism (*universalia sunt nomina*).

Such are the main currents in the field of this fundamental problem. As mentioned before, its fundamentality must be obvious to every person who is not a total stranger either to science or to thought generally. What are all the concepts and definitions and generalizations of science, from mathematics to sociology? Are they mere fictions or artificial images in our mind to which nothing corresponds in the *rerum natura?* Are they, in this sense, a kind of illusion with which we build an illusionary world which may last for somé time but which sooner or later is bound to vanish and disappear? Or are they something which exists in our mind as well as in the reality outside it? As soon as the question is put in that form, it becomes axiomatic that the problem of nominalism-realism did not originate in the Middle Ages (though the terms did) but began with the conscientious thought of man, and continues to this day. It exists today and will exist as long as human thought. And indeed, from the earliest date at which our quantitative study begins it is present, is discussed, and answered. On the other hand, when a contemporary physicist or chemist or mathematician — not to mention the social scientist — creates his definition of number, space, time, force, matter, atom, "species" (in taxonomy), religion, social class, demand and supply, economic phenomenon, State, law, culture, cause and effect, and so on, any such scientist or scholar is confronted with the problem; he cannot escape it and gives — explicitly or implicitly, conscientiously or not — his answer to it. More than that: giving the answer, he gives it along one of the currents outlined here.

The problem is inescapable at any time, regardless of whether we want to solve it or not. A study of the fluctuation of thought in that field is a study of one of the most fundamental and eternal problems of human thought, human science, and system of truth.

The next question to be asked is: What relationship does it bear to the main systems of truth and to the Ideational and Sensate types of culture respectively?

Deductively, we seem to be justified in expecting a certain relationship. Logically, *domination of the system of the truth of faith has to be followed by that of realism, the system of truth of senses by that of nominalism; and the system of truth of reason by that of conceptualism, followed by the currents of diluted realism as well as diluted nominalism.* The reasons for such an association are: since the truth of faith aims at eternal reality and since it is meant to be supersensory, the *universalia* of realism are the eternal reality sought for by the truth of faith. Also the world of Plato's ideas, Aristotle's forms, and the ultimate realities of various thinkers are the reality sought for by the truth of faith. Likewise, even in this phenomenal or empirical world, the reality of the generic "essences" or "concepts" or "*universalia*" is more important to the truth of faith than the reality of the singularistic empirical phenomena. In brief, logico-ontological realism and truth of faith are logically consistent and congenial; therefore, if human mentality in history is logical to some extent, it has to show this correlation and association. Similarly, truth of the senses (empiricism) and nominalism are twins in their logical nature. Both claim that we can know only the world of the senses. Both contend that in the world of the senses only singular objects can be perceived and no *universalia* are given. For both, *nihil esse in intellectu quod non fuerit prius in sensu.*

Finally, so far as the truth of reason is in a sense a blending of both extreme systems of truth, and so far as conceptualism occupies also an intermediary position between nominalism and realism and is in this sense their blend also, some association between the two has to be expected.

II. Main Results

The main results given by Tables 20 and 21 can be summed up as follows.

A. If the whole period from 540 B.C. to A.D. 1920 is taken, there is no perpetual trend of a continuous increase or decrease of any of these

TABLE 20. MOVEMENT OF NOMINALISM, CONCEPTUALISM, AND REALISM FROM 540 B.C. TO A.D. 1920 BY 20-YEAR PERIODS

PERIOD	*Number of Representatives*			*Indicators of Weight*			*Comparative Weight in Percentages*		
	Nominalism	*Conceptualism*	*Realism*	*Nominalism*	*Conceptualism*	*Realism*	*Nominalism*	*Conceptualism*	*Realism*
540–520 B.C.	0	0	1	0	0	8	0	0	100
520–500	0	0	1	0	0	8	0	0	100
500–480	0	0	2	0	0	15	0	0	100
480–460	0	0	3	0	0	13	0	0	100
460–440	0	1	3	0	5	9	0	36	64
440–420	1	2	4	8	11	14	24	33	42
420–400	7	2	4	27	14	21	43.5	22.5	34
400–380	6	1	7	25	8	27	42	13	45
380–360	3	1	5	15	8	21	34	18	48
360–340	7	1	5	19	1	23	44	2	54
340–320	6	1	3	10	1	18	34	3	62
320–300	8	1	6	15	1	29	33	2	64
300–280	9	1	6	23	8	19	46	16	38
280–260	7	2	3	23	13	7	54	30	16
260–240	5	1	1	17	5	1	74	22	4
240–220	9	3	2	28	13	2	65	30	5
220–200	3	2	2	8	8	4	40	40	20
200–180	3	3	1	4	6	3	31	46	23
180–160	2	2	1	2	6	2	20	60	20
160–140	2	2	1	3	6	2	27	55	18
140–120	1	2	1	2	6	1	22	67	11
120–100	1	4	1	2	8	1	18	73	9
100–80	5	4	1	9	10	1	45	50	5
80–60	4	4	2	7	12	9	25	43	32
60–40	4	11	3	18	22	17	31.5	38.5	30
40–20	2	6	2	9	9	13	29	29	42
20–0	1	3	3	1	6	5	8	50	42
0–20 A.D.	1	2	3	1	3	11	7	20	73
20–40	1	1	2	1	1	10	8	8	84
40–60	1	2	2	1	12	10	4	52	44
60–80	1	4	2	1	19	5	4	76	20
80–100	2	2	2	7	11	11	24	38	38
100–120	1	1	7	6	6	21	18	18	64
120–140	3	4	8	6	12	25	14	28	58
140–160	4	3	12	7	6	32	15	13	71
160–180	3	1	12	4	6	36	9	13	78
180–200	3	2	15	6	12	48	9	18	72
200–220	2	2	8	9	7	32	19	15	66
220–240	2	2	4	7	7	21	20	20	60
240–260	2	1	8	2	1	37	5	2.5	92.5
260–280	3	1	6	4	1	22	15	4	81
280–300	3	0	3	5	0	10	33	0	67
300–320	2	0	4	3	0	18	14	0	86
320–340	5	0	5	13	0	19	41	0	59
340–360	2	0	4	5	0	12	29	0	71
360–380	2	0	6	2	0	34	6	0	94
380–400	2	0	5	6	0	28	18	0	82
400–420	1	0	5	5	0	19	21	0	79
420–440	1	0	5	3	0	20	13	0	87
440–460	2	0	3	6	0	13	32	0	68
460–480	1	0	3	3	0	14	18	0	82

TABLE 20. MOVEMENT OF NOMINALISM, CONCEPTUALISM, AND REALISM FROM 540 B.C. TO A.D. 1920 BY 20-YEAR PERIODS — *continued*

PERIOD	*Number of Representatives*			*Indicators of Weight*			*Comparative Weight in Percentages*		
	Nominalism	*Conceptualism*	*Realism*	*Nominalism*	*Conceptualism*	*Realism*	*Nominalism*	*Conceptualism*	*Realism*
480–500 A.D.	1	0	3	1	0	13	7	0	93
500–520	1	0	6	1	0	21	5	0	95
520–540	2	0	6	5	0	28	15	0	85
540–560	1	0	5	4	0	16	20	0	80
560–580	0	0	1	0	0	2	0	0	100
580–600	0	0	1	0	0	4	0	0	100
600–620	0	0	1	0	0	4	0	0	100
620–640	0	0	1	0	0	6	0	0	100
640–660	0	0	1	0	0	6	0	0	100
660–680	0	0	2	0	0	8	0	0	100
680–700	0	0	1	0	0	2	0	0	100
700–720	0	0	1	0	0	3	0	0	100
720–740	0	0	2	0	0	8	0	0	100
740–760	0	0	1	0	0	5	0	0	100
760–780	0	0	1	0	0	1	0	0	100
780–800	0	0	1	0	0	4	0	0	100
800–820	0	0	2	0	0	6	0	0	100
820–840	0	0	2	0	0	6	0	0	100
840–860	0	0	2	0	0	12	0	0	100
860–880	0	0	2	0	0	11	0	0	100
880–900	0	0	2	0	0	5	0	0	100
900–920	0	0	2	0	0	4	0	0	100
920–940	0	0	1	0	0	2	0	0	100
940–960	0	0	1	0	0	1	0	0	100
960–980	0	0	1	0	0	1	0	0	100
980–1000	0	0	1	0	0	3	0	0	100
1000–1020	0	0	2	0	0	5	0	0	100
1020–1040	0	0	1	0	0	2	0	0	100
1040–1060	0	0	2	0	0	5	0	0	100
1060–1080	0	0	5	0	0	19	0	0	100
1080–1100	1	0	4	3	0	17	15	0	85
1100–1120	2	0	5	4	0	14	22	0	78
1120–1140	2	0	10	7	0	27	21	0	79
1140–1160	1	0	13	4	0	34	10.5	0	89.5
1160–1180	0	0	7	0	0	15	0	0	100
1180–1200	0	0	6	0	0	12	0	0	100
1200–1220	0	0	12	0	0	24	0	0	100
1220–1240	0	0	8	0	0	19	0	0	100
1240–1260	0	0	11	0	0	30	0	0	100
1260–1280	1	0	14	6	0	52	10	0	90
1280–1300	1	0	19	9	0	52	15	0	85
1300–1320	1	0	17	3	0	51	6	0	94
1320–1340	4	0	14	16	0	32	33	0	67
1340–1360	8	0	8	22	0	18	55	0	45
1360–1380	7	0	2	13	0	8	62	0	38
1380–1400	4	0	1	10	0	3	77	0	23
1400–1420	1	0	1	4	0	4	50	0	50
1420–1440	1	0	4	4	0	11	27	0	73
1440–1460	1	0	5	1	0	19	5	0	95
1460–1480	1	0	3	3	0	13	19	0	81
1480–1500	1	0	2	3	0	2	60	0	40

TABLE 20. MOVEMENT OF NOMINALISM, CONCEPTUALISM, AND REALISM FROM 540 B.C. TO A.D. 1920 BY 20-YEAR PERIODS — *continued*

PERIOD	*Number of Representatives*				*Indicators of Weight*				*Comparative Weight in Percentages*			
	Nominalism	*Conceptualism*	*Realism*		*Nominalism*	*Conceptualism*	*Realism*		*Nominalism*	*Conceptualism*	*Realism*	
			Secular	*Secular and Religious*			*Secular*	*Secular and Religious*			*Secular*	*Secular and Religious*
1500–1520	1	3	6	10	6	10	16	26	14	24	38	62
1520–1540	3	2	10	15	18	11	34	46	24	15	45	61
1540–1560	1	3	5	10	2	15	15	35	4	29	29	67
1560–1580	2	1	16	25	8	4	43	70	10	5	52	85
1580–1600	6	1	23	38	28	4	61	108	20	3	43.5	77
1600–1620	9	1	14	31	32	1	45	95	25	1	35	74
1620–1640	5	3	13	31	27	19	50	99	19	13	34	68
1640–1660	6	4	11	22	23	26	39	68	20	22	33	58
1660–1680	10	9	15	26	36	39	47	85	22	24	29	53
1680–1700	19	3	29	48	69	15	87	133	32	7	40	61
1700–1720	14	4	19	39	54	29	51	94	31	16	29	53
1720–1740	12	12	7	18	51	26	26	50	40	20	20	39
1740–1760	20	10	8	12	82	45	34	46	47	26	20	27
1760–1780	24	12	5	12	106	57	22	38	53	28	11	19
1780–1800	21	19	14	22	83	69	53	70	37	31	24	32
1800–1820	17	30	28	36	55	88	90	112	22	34	35	44
1820–1840	17	15	32	52	69	55	120	167	24	19	41	57
1840–1860	29	9	55	78	117	31	175	227	31	8	47	61
1860–1880	49	17	36	57	239	68	142	186	49	14	29	37
1880–1900	66	43	37	82	275	157	160	254	40	23	23	37
1900–1920	80	46	44	90	322	173	186	276	42	22	24	36

currents in the course of time, whether by 20-year or 100-year periods. Instead, we have trendless fluctuation, increase and decrease of each of these currents. The same is true in regard to either Graeco-Roman or Western culture, taken separately.

B. Measured by the presence or absence of each of these currents there is no progress of Spencerian differentiation and integration in this field of thought in the course of time. The series opens with a monopolistic domination of realism. Subsequently conceptualism (460–440 B.C.) and then nominalism appear. The field becomes thus progressively differentiated. But beginning with A.D. 280–300, one of the streams, conceptualism, disappears, and then, after A.D. 560, nominalism disappears also. Thus, instead of further differentiation, we have the opposite movement, from the more to the less differentiated and a return to the initial simplicity. After A.D. 1080 the opposite direction — toward increasing differentiation — again appears and continues practically up to the present time. Here again, then, we have a result similar to those obtained in many fields before.

C. Studying the ups and downs of each of the currents, we see a tangible, factual corroboration of the logical deductions concerning the

TABLE 21. MOVEMENT OF NOMINALISM, CONCEPTUALISM, AND REALISM FROM 600 B.C. TO A.D. 1900 BY 100-YEAR PERIODS

PERIOD	*Number of Representatives*			*Indicators of Weight*			*Comparative Weight in Percentages*		
	Nominalism	*Conceptualism*	*Realism*	*Nominalism*	*Conceptualism*	*Realism*	*Nominalism*	*Conceptualism*	*Realism*
600–500 B.C.	0	0	1	0	0	8	0	0	100
500–400	7	3	8	27	19	42	31	22	47
400–300	20	2	15	53	9	71	40	7	53
300–200	19	4	9	56	21	24	55	21	24
200–100	6	8	3	9	16	6	29	52	19
100–0	10	18	8	28	32	27	32	37	31
0–100 A.D.	3	8	6	8	29	24	13	48	39
100–200	6	6	29	17	24	90	13	18	69
200–300	6	2	18	15	7	72	16	7	77
300–400	9	0	13	22	0	62	26	0	74
400–500	4	0	11	12	0	40	23	0	77
500–600	2	0	11	5	0	38	12	0	88
600–700	0	0	3	0	0	12	0	0	100
700–800	0	0	3	0	0	12	0	0	100
800–900	0	0	6	0	0	23	0	0	100
900–1000	0	0	3	0	0	7	0	0	100
1000–1100	1	0	7	3	0	24	11	0	89
1100–1200	3	0	27	8	0	66	11	0	89
1200–1300	2	0	50	9	0	131	6	0	94
1300–1400	15	0	29	39	0	82	32	0	68
1400–1500	3	0	9	8	0	26	24	0	76

PERIOD	*Nominalism*	*Conceptualism*	*Realism*		*Nominalism*	*Conceptualism*	*Realism*		*Nominalism*	*Conceptualism*	*Realism*	
			Secular	*Secular and Religious*			*Secular*	*Secular and Religious*			*Secular*	*Secular and Religious*
1500–1600	11	5	44	74	54	20	127	215	19	7	44	74
1600–1700	35	13	59	128	120	54	173	364	22	10	32	68
1700–1800	67	43	46	92	258	158	156	256	38	24	23	38
1800–1900	137	91	144	244	531	301	376	577	38	21	27	41

correlation of realism with the truth of faith and Ideational culture; of nominalism with the truth of the senses and Sensate culture; and, to a less degree, of conceptualism with the truth of reason and Idealistic culture. The sixth century B.C. — the period of the domination of the truth of faith and Ideational culture — appears monopolistically realistic. The fifth and fourth centuries represent a balance of realism and nominalism, about fifty-fifty, with an admixture of conceptualism. Though the fourth century gives the per cent of realism as slightly higher than that of the fifth (53 and 47 per cent respectively), in the fourth century B.C. the nominalism is also reinforced at the cost of the milder conceptualism, and gained even more than did realism. Subsequent centuries, the third and the second B.C., give a decisive decrease of realism in

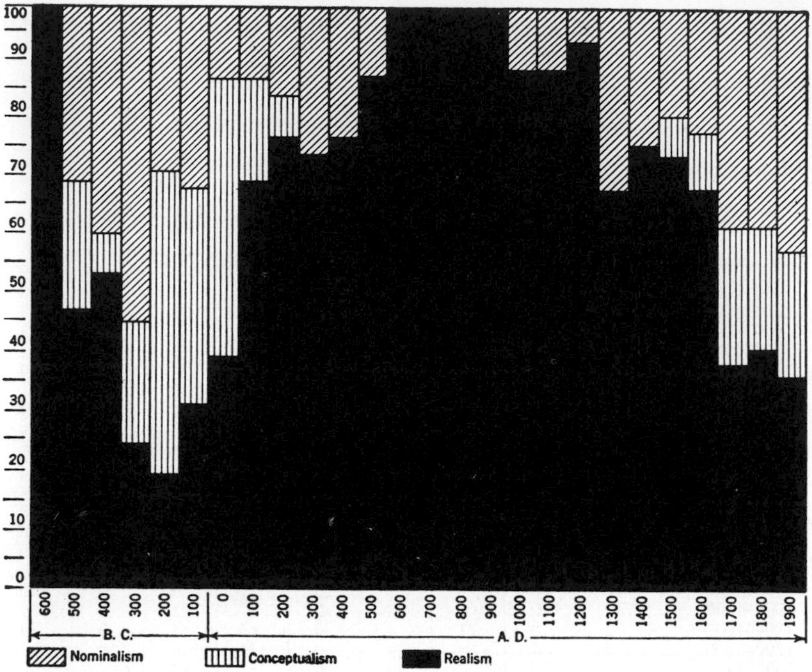

FIG. 13. MOVEMENTS OF NOMINALISM, CONCEPTUALISM, AND REALISM

favor of nominalism and conceptualism. Thus, in the history of Greek and Hellenistic culture we see a quite unmistakable association of the movement of these currents with their logical "partners." The same result is obtained if one takes 20-year periods instead of century periods.

Association continues to be quite tangible in the subsequent period. Beginning with the second century A.D., realism starts to grow again and its rivals begin to decline. After the fifth century A.D., realism, like the truth of faith and other earmarks of the Ideational culture, becomes monopolistic and reigns supreme up to the twelfth century. Then nominalism emerges again, but during the first few centuries remains a small rivulet. We saw the same change occur in regard to the re-emergence of the truth of reason and the senses, and the other earmarks of the Idealistic and Sensate cultures. The parallelism is not exactly perfect, but quite evident.

Finally, after the thirteenth century, notwithstanding these minor reactions, we witness a steady trend of a rising tide of nominalism, and especially of conceptualism, at the cost of the retreating tide of realism. So far we have again a complete agreement of the logical expectations and the actual data.

When the Sensate culture rises, nominalism seems more and more "scientific" and "true" to the leading minds and thinkers of the period. When the Ideational tide is rising, realism appears to be more and more "scientifically valid." In this sense, "validity" of each of these currents is a function of the type of culture. That is, human truth is a sociological, category, in a great degree, and cannot be understood without a consideration of the culture in which it lives and functions. As stressed, this does not make illogical any of these cultures. By the same logic, they all are logical within their major premises, but their premises are different. Such a difference in premises does not prevent me from being an absolutist in the field of the complete truth. But such a whole truth is never given in full to our minds and exists only in the Divine Mind or is a goal toward which mankind eternally strives; at any given moment one grasps some part or aspect or approximation of it, but never the whole truth and the only truth.

D. Coming to the time we live in, we see that the eighteenth, nineteenth, and twentieth centuries have been the period when realism has been at its lowest. One has to retreat to the third, second, and first centuries B.C. to find as low an influence of realism. These centuries were the period of the domination of nominalism and especially conceptualism. However, beginning with about 1860, the further decline of realism is practically halted; likewise a further rise of nominalism (after 1880) and conceptualism is stopped. Whether this fact is one of the numerous short-time "flurries," after which the trend of the decline of realism is to be continued, or whether it is the beginning of the coming trend of rising realism, nobody can tell. What is important is that this symptom agrees with many similar "twists and turns" and "revolts" in most of the compartments of culture which we see at the end of the nineteenth and in the twentieth century Here again our data are in agreement with the others and once more testify to the integrated character of our culture.

E. However high is the correlation outlined, it is not absolute. The movements of the curves of the systems of truth and of the currents studied are not identical. There are numerous secondary deviations, as can be seen from the curves of Figures 19 and 20. Similar secondary discrepancies we have seen in the relationship of the other sociocultural variables studied here. This fact means two things important to us.

(1) In the integrated cultures, the sociocultural mentality is *logical* to a very considerable degree; facts as they stand in our study are indeed close to the logical deductions from the nature of each of the variables considered. The thinkers who stress particularly the illogicality of human mentality are somewhat overshooting the mark, so far as the mentality of the cultures studied is concerned.

(2) The deviations signify that the mentality of the cultures and of the thinkers who embody it is not entirely logical; if the deviations were absent, it would have been; since the deviations are given, their existence and the degree of the discrepancy between the perfect correlation which logically follows and the tangible but imperfect association factually given, between the cultural variables studied, is an evidence and, in a sense, a measure of the amount of the illogicality of the mentality of the integrated cultures. Even the integrated cultures, in the field of their mentality, are in a degree illogical. So far as we deal with the logical integration, even within the compartments of various forms of social thought, the integration logically due is not perfectly followed by the causal one. The main reason for this, as explained above, is the margin of immunity and autonomy which every system, including the system of thought, has. It permits it to live its own life, within a certain margin of autonomy. Incompleteness of data may be responsible for that also.

F. Of the other results given by the data, few deserve to be mentioned. In the courses on history of philosophy and science, it is customary to read that nominalism was started by W. Ockham; that it is, in contradistinction to realism, the only scientific standpoint in the field of the problem; that with the progress of science, nominalism has also been progressing; that the whole problem was started by the medieval Scholastics and represents a purely medieval phenomenon. In the light of the data given, we see that the problem is eternal, existed long before the Middle Ages, has existed in modern times, and will exist in the future. Next, we see that the nominalistic current re-emerged much earlier than is usually supposed: already in 1080–1100 nominalism composed 15 per cent of the total 100 per cent of all the three currents. Later, the data show that nominalism, empiricism, and scientific discoveries have advanced together, though the connection is far from being perfect. And what is still more important is that after the fifteenth century conceptualism grew much faster than nominalism and represented a current notably more powerful than it is customary to admit.

G. Finally, if we sum up the number of the representatives, as well as the weight of each current, for the whole period studied, as well as for its main parts, we obtain the results shown in Table 22.

These figures are interesting in several respects. We see that of the three currents, the most powerful has been realism, whether we take the number or the weight. This is a good warning to the too ardent partisans of nominalism not to overestimate it. If, however, we unite nominalism and conceptualism, then we get a curious equilibrium of the two currents for the whole period; by the number, nominalism and conceptualism taken together give 695 and realism 851; by the weight, the first two give

TABLE 22. CURRENTS IN NOMINALISM, CONCEPTUALISM, AND REALISM

PERIOD	NUMBER OF REPRESENTATIVES			INDICATORS OF WEIGHT		
	Nominalism	*Conceptualism*	*Realism*	*Nominalism*	*Conceptualism*	*Realism*
540 B.C.–A.D. 100	65	43	50	181	126	202
100–600	27	8	82	71	31	302
600–1500	24	0	137	67	0	383
1500–1900	250	152	538[1]	963	533	1412[1]
1900–1920	80	46	44	322	173	276
Total	446	249	851	1604	863	2575

[1] Both secular and religious realism.

2467, while realism gives 2575. In both cases, we have a curious equality or a counterbalancing of each of the currents by the other. Such a balance suggests that each current embodies in itself a part of the truth and represents an aspect of the true reality; as such, each seems to perform an important function in the mental life of a culture, and as such is immortal in the history of human thought. It points again to what is styled here the principle of limit and a kind of an autonomous self-regulation of sociocultural processes in the field of the mentality of a given culture.

Another service of Table 22 is that in a concise way it gives the mental spectrum of each of the periods in regard to the problem studied. We see that the most even distribution of all of the three currents occurred in the periods 540 B.C. to A.D. 100 and 1900 to 1920; the most realistic period was 600 to A.D. 1500. So much for main conclusions. Now we can pass to a specific aspect of the problem of realism-nominalism in its sociological application. This problem has never been abstract and "academic" and has always been very concrete and important, though many a social thinker has not been aware of that. One of the purposes of the next chapter is to show that fact convincingly.

18

FLUCTUATION OF "FIRST PRINCIPLES": IV. FLUCTUATION OF THE INFLUENCE OF SOCIOLOGICAL UNIVERSALISM AND SINGULARISM

I. Main Currents in the Field

That the problem of realism-nominalism has a direct bearing upon many a practical question is evidenced by the movements of such basic social problems as that of sociological universalism and singularism, society and the individual, collectivism and individualism, and still more by the fluctuation of the purely juridical conceptions of juridical personality, corporation, and the like. The problems: What is society? Is it a reality that exists per se as a true reality, different from the mere sum of its members (sociological realism), or is it a mere fiction, to which nothing corresponds in the transsubjective or in the subjective world of mind, and which is no more than a mere word, mere phantasma (sociological nominalism)? Or is it something that does not exist as reality in the transsubjective world but exists as a real concept in our mind (sociological conceptualism)? Similar questions arise in regard to "social group," "real collectivity," "juridical personality," "corporation," "the State," and the like. These problems of *the ontological social reality are closely connected with the socioethical aspect of these problems.*

Shall social and political order be organized in such a way that the individual and his values — life, liberty, creativeness, comfort, and the like — be dominant and not restrained by any social considerations; or, on the contrary, shall the *salus populi* be the *suprema lex*, and, for the sake of the welfare of society, is the individual to be sacrificed and restrained as much as the considerations of the *salus populi* may demand?

The purpose of this chapter is not to take sides with one of these solutions, but, as before, to classify numerous solutions and theories into a few main classes; then to inquire how, in the history of the Graeco-Roman and the Western cultures, each of these classes fared; which of them has been dominant in its influence, and during which period. Finally, what has been the reason for the fluctuations, and have they been tangibly connected with the fluctuations of the main types of culture studied here?

When one considers the respective theories, one can see at once that they present the problem mainly in two aspects: *the ontological and the ethical.*

The ontological setting consists of an inquiry as to which of the two — the individual or society — is the true reality. When the problem is taken ethically, it presents the question: Which of the two is the supreme value?

Subsequently, all the theories in the field are classified into the following classes: (1) sociological singularism; (2) sociological universalism; (3) sociological mystic unity of individuals. A few commentaries follow to clear the meaning of each class.

A. *Sociological Singularism.* By this is meant any theory which claims that ontologically any society is a mere sum of its members and, apart from that, does not have any true reality per se. It is a sociological variety of nominalism. Like the latter, it contends that in the trans-subjective social world there exist only individuals.

It is an atomistic conception of society as an aggregate of singularistic individuals, behind and beyond which there is no ontological entity called society. Such being the general characteristics of sociological singularism, it gives further several varieties, due especially to the combination of the ontological with the ethical principles. Main subclasses of it are as follows.

(1) *Extreme or Consistent Sociological Singularism.* This states that the individual is the only social reality ontologically, and also that he is the supreme ethical value. It is atomistic-singularistic, not only in its sociological ontology, but also in its system of values; all its primary values are those of singularistic existence; security and safety of the individual, his happiness, pleasures, comfort, liberty, etc. The super-individual and supersingularistic or social values are, in this system, at the best purely derivative and aimed to be the means to the singularistic values: society is of value only in so far as it serves the purpose of securing the life and happiness of the individual. In such a setting, the ethical system of the extreme singularism is almost always a system of the ethics of happiness in its hedonistic or eudaemonistic or utilitarian variety (see Chapter Thirteen). It is natural, therefore, that the curves of the extreme singularism and the ethics of happiness should go hand in hand to quite a perceptible degree. This current embraces a large variety of the thinkers, from the extreme hedonists of the *Carpe diem*, or the *après moi le deluge* types, up to the anarchists and moral individualists of the kind of Stirner and many others. It is ontological as well as ethical singularism or sociological nominalism.

(2) *Moderate Sociological Singularism.* Like the extreme form of singularism, it assumes the ontological reality of the singularistic individuals; but in its ethical aspect it insists that for any given individual not only he himself is the supreme value, but all the other individuals and society, as a sum of the individuals, are also the supreme values.

So far, on its ethical side it is a deviation from the singularistic ethics to the social or universalistic ethics, interpreted atomistically as the sum of individuals or, in the familiar motto of utilitarianism, "the maximum of happiness for the maximum of the individuals." Ethically it is also connected with the moderate and sensible-eudaemonistic or utilitarian-ethical systems. The liberalism of the nineteenth century, with its rights of man and citizen, with its maximum of happiness and liberty, and its rugged or soft individualism moderated by the equal interests of other individuals, is one of the best examples of this moderate singularism.

(3) *Collectivistic Sociological Singularism.* In its ontological aspect that society is a sum of the individuals, it has the same singularistic position as singularism generally, but in its ethical aspect it claims the priority and superiority of the value of the collectivity compared with that of the individual. It contends, therefore, that the individual and his interests should be subordinated to the social welfare and interests of the collectivity, that the individual should be dissolved, so to speak, in the collectivity. This is a peculiar combination of ontological singularism with ethical "regimentation" of the individual to the proletarian class; the Communist Party; the Fascist or Hitlerite group; the nobility; the religious collectivity, the given state, and so on. Hence, their collectivistic singularism: the *salus populi* (of the group which they extol) becomes the *suprema lex.* All the individuals that oppose it can and should be subordinated, restrained, muzzled, even exterminated, if necessary; but being collectivistic in this sense, they remain ontologically singularists: all this subordination and extermination is done for the glory of their collectivity, which is still an aggregate of the interacting individuals, each existentially separate from the others and each representing an atom beyond whose aggregation there is no social reality and no other entity. Ethically again, it is connected with one of the varieties of the ethics of happiness, often with the rudest, purely materialistically hedonistic form of it.

These three branches embrace almost all the varieties of the sociological singularism.

B. *Sociological Universalism.* In contradistinction to the sociological singularism, the sociological universalism states that society is much more than a mere number of individuals — interacting or not; that ontologically, like the claim of realism in regard to the *universalia* and concepts, there is an ontological social entity which embraces all the individuals externally as well as permeates them internally.

This social reality is sociological *universalia* which exists in the trans-subjective social world as well as in our mind. From these premises it naturally follows that society is a superindividual and supersingularistic system, which lives its own organic (but not organismic) life and has its own existential modus, irreducible to the existence of the individuals.

From this ontological position of sociological universalism it logically follows that ethically society is of neither secondary nor derivative value, but a supreme value which — regardless of the singularistic values — should be guarded, cared for, and promoted. The main varieties of sociological universalism can be divided into two classes.

(1) *Extreme Sociological Universalism.* It regards the individual as a mere part, a toe of a foot, so to speak, of the societal whole; as a mere organ or even as a part of an organ which, as such, does not have any ontological autonomous existence. Ethically, it considers him as a value of a mere part much inferior to the value of society as a whole.

(2) *Moderate Sociological Universalism.* Sharing in the fundamental principles of universalism, it concedes some independent reality to the individual as well as his value. Sometimes, some of the representatives of this branch treat the reality and value of the individual as equal to that of society. Such representatives imperceptibly merge with the group of the partisans of the mystic unity of individuals.

It is to be expected, and the expectation is well corroborated by the facts, that most of the universalists are in agreement, ethically, with the ethics of the absolute principles (see further on). For a justification of a given political or religious or social order, and of the restraint of an individual, they usually refer to the absolute principles — religious, moral, philosophical, and others — and on this basis demand a subordination of the individual, limitation of his appetites and liberties, and sacrifice of his life. Often they declare that the singularistic values, including the life of the individual, matter little in comparison with the demand and the imperatives of the absolute ethical principles enacted by God, or government, or dictator, or Pope, or any other authority. On this point they often meet closely with the partisans of the collectivistic singularism. Both are not opposed to the regimentation imposed by their authority. Both cling to the *salus populi suprema lex*, whether they are members of the Communist Party, of the Inquisition, of theocracy, of the autocratic dictators, or what not.

C. *Sociological Mystic Integralism.* The third current in the field is mystic integralism. In many respects it is near to a moderate form of universalism as well as of singularism. Nevertheless, it does not coincide with either one and has several specific accents which entitle it to be regarded as the third current of *sui generis.* It attempts to give a harmonious synthesis of individualistic singularism with universalism. Ontologically, it thinks that society and the individual both are real; the individual is the singularistic incarnation of the societal reality;

TABLE 23. MOVEMENT OF SINGULARISM, UNIVERSALISM, AND MYSTIC UNITY BY 20-YEAR PERIODS, 580 B.C.—A.D. 1920

PERIOD	*Extreme Singularism-Individualism*			*Singularism-Universalism*			*Universalism-Singularism*			*Universalism*			*Mystic Unity of Singularistic Persons*			*All Varieties of Singularism*			*All Varieties of Universalism*			*Mystic Unity*		
	Number of representatives	*Their weight*	*Percentage of the total*	*Number of representatives*	*Their weight*	*Percentage of the total*	*Number of representatives*	*Their weight*	*Percentage of the total*	*Number of representatives*	*Their weight*	*Percentage of the total*	*Number of representatives*	*Their weight*	*Percentage of the total*	*Number of representatives*	*Their weight*	*Percentage of the total*	*Number of representatives*	*Their weight*	*Percentage of the total*	*Number of representatives*	*Their weight*	*Percentage of the total*
580–560 B.C.	0	0	0	0	0	0	0	0	0	0	0	0	0	0	0	0	0	0	0	0	0	0	0	0
560–540	0	0	0	0	0	0	0	0	0	1	5	100	0	0	0	0	0	0	1	5	100	0	0	0
540–520	0	0	0	0	0	0	1	8	62	1	5	38	0	0	0	0	0	0	2	13	100	0	0	0
520–500	0	0	0	0	0	0	2	15	94	1	1	6	0	0	0	0	0	0	3	16	100	0	0	0
500–480	0	0	0	0	0	0	2	15	68	1	7	32	0	0	0	0	0	0	3	22	100	0	0	0
480–460	0	0	0	0	0	0	1	7	37	2	12	63	0	0	0	0	0	0	3	19	100	0	0	0
460–440	0	0	0	1	5	26	1	6	32	2	8	42	0	0	0	1	5	26	3	14	74	0	0	0
440–420	0	0	0	3	19	47.5	2	11	27.5	3	10	25	0	0	0	3	19	48	5	21	52	0	0	0
420–400	4	10	14	7	48	66.5	2	9	12.5	2	5	7	0	0	0	11	58	81	4	14	19	0	0	0
400–380	3	11	17	7	42	65	3	10	15	1	2	3	0	0	0	10	53	82	4	12	18	0	0	0
380–360	1	6	13	4	23	50	2	5	11	1	12	26	0	0	0	5	29	63	3	17	37	0	0	0
360–340	4	9	17	4	19	37	3	10	19	2	14	27	0	0	0	8	28	54	5	24	46	0	0	0
340–320	4	4	11	3	10	26	4	22	58	1	2	5	0	0	0	7	14	37	5	24	63	0	0	0
320–300	2	4	8	7	14	28	7	32	64	0	0	0	0	0	0	9	18	36	7	32	64	0	0	0
300–280	3	12	21	7	14	25	8	30	54	0	0	0	0	0	0	10	26	46	8	30	54	0	0	0
280–260	4	15	32.5	2	3	6.5	7	28	61	0	0	0	0	0	0	6	18	40	7	28	60	0	0	0
260–240	4	12	50	1	2	8	2	10	42	0	0	0	0	0	0	5	14	58	2	10	42	0	0	0
240–220	8	23	51	2	4	9	4	18	40	0	0	0	0	0	0	10	27	60	4	18	40	0	0	0
220–200	3	8	38	1	2	10	3	11	52	0	0	0	0	0	0	4	10	48	3	11	52	0	0	0
200–180	3	4	28	1	1	7	4	9	64	0	0	0	0	0	0	4	5	35	4	9	65	0	0	0
180–160	2	2	13	1	5	33	3	8	53	0	0	0	0	0	0	3	7	47	3	8	53	0	0	0
160–140	2	3	13.5	2	7	31.5	4	12	55	0	0	0	0	0	0	4	10	45	4	12	55	0	0	0
140–120	1	2	10	2	7	33	4	12	57	0	0	0	0	0	0	3	9	43	4	12	57	0	0	0
120–100	2	4	20	1	2	10	6	14	70	0	0	0	0	0	0	3	6	30	6	14	70	0	0	0
100–80	4	7	32	2	5	23	4	10	45	0	0	0	0	0	0	6	12	55	4	10	45	0	0	0
80–60	3	5	16	2	5	16	6	21	68	0	0	0	0	0	0	7	10	32	6	21	68	0	0	0
60–40	4	18	28	1	1	2	14	37	58	0	0	0	1	8	12	5	19	30	14	37	58	1	8	12
40–20	2	9	17	2	8	15	9	28	53	0	0	0	1	8	15	4	17	32	9	28	53	1	8	15
20–0	1	½	1	4	15	44	5	19	56	0	0	0	0	0	0	5	15½	45	5	19	56	0	0	0
0–20 A.D.	1	½	1	3	9	35	4	17	65	0	0	0	0	0	0	4	9½	35	4	17	65	0	0	0
20–40	1	½	1	1	2	12.5	4	14	87.5	0	0	0	0	0	0	2	2½	13	4	14	87	0	0	0
40–60	1	½	1	1	1	4	5	17	65	0	0	0	1	8	31	2	1½	4	5	17	65	1	8	31
60–80	1	½	1	1	1	4	5	16	64	0	0	0	1	8	32	2	1½	4	5	16	64	1	8	32
80–100	1	½	1	2	7	24	2	8	28	0	0	0	2	14	48	3	7½	24	2	8	28	2	14	48
100–120	1	½	1	1	6	19	3	10	32	1	1	3	2	14	45	2	6½	19	4	11	36	2	14	45
120–140	1	1	2	2	5	10	8	21	44	2	5	10	3	16	33	3	6	12	10	26	54	3	16	33

140–160 A.D.	2	2	5	2	5	12	11	27	64	3	6	14	1	2	5	4	7	17	14	33	78	1	2	5
160–180	3	6	11	1	2	4	10	31	56	1	1	2	3	15	27	4	8	15	11	32	58	3	15	27
180–200	3	8	11	2	8	11	16	49	64	1	1	1	2	10	13	10	16	22	17	50	65	2	10	13
200–220	1	3	6	1	6	11.5	10	32	61	1	6	11.5	1	5	10	2	9	17.5	11	38	72.5	1	5	10
220–240	1	½	1	1	6	17	3	11	30	1	6	17	2	13	36	2	6½	17	4	17	47	2	13	36
240–260	1	½	1	0	0	0	4	13	30	2	8	19	3	22	51	1	½	1	6	21	49	3	22	51
260–280	1	½	1	0	0	0	4	9	29	2	8	26	2	14	45	1	½	1	6	17	55	2	14	45
280–300	1	½	1	0	0	0	3	6	33	1	4	22	2	8	44	1	½	1	4	10	56	2	8	44
300–320	1	½	1	0	0	0	2	4	17	1	1	4	4	18	78	1	½	1	3	5	21	4	18	78
320–340	1	½	1	0	0	0	4	11	39	1	1	4	4	16	57	1	½	1	5	12	43	4	16	57
340–360	1	½	1	0	0	0	3	9	50	2	4	22	2	5	28	1	½	1	5	13	72	2	5	28
360–380	0	0	0	0	0	0	4	13	28	2	4	8	5	30	64	0	0	0	6	17	36	5	30	64
380–400	0	0	0	0	0	0	2	6	13	2	11	24	5	28	62	0	0	0	4	17	37	5	28	62
400–420	0	0	0	0	0	0	4	10	31	2	11	34	3	11	34	0	0	0	6	21	65	3	11	34
420–440	0	0	0	0	0	0	5	12	40	2	11	37	2	7	23	0	0	0	7	23	77	2	7	23
440–460	0	0	0	0	0	0	2	5	29	1	1	6	2	11	64	0	0	0	3	6	35	2	11	64
460–480	0	0	0	0	0	0	2	6	33	1	1	6	2	11	61	0	0	0	3	7	39	2	11	61
480–500	0	0	0	0	0	0	2	4	27	1	1	7	2	10	66	0	0	0	3	5	34	2	10	66
500–520	0	0	0	0	0	0	4	17	71	1	1	4	2	6	25	0	0	0	5	18	75	2	6	25
520–540	0	0	0	0	0	0	5	21	62	1	1	3	3	12	35	0	0	0	6	22	65	3	12	35
540–560	0	0	0	0	0	0	4	14	67	0	0	0	2	7	33	0	0	0	4	14	67	2	7	33
560–580	0	0	0	0	0	0	2	5	50	0	0	0	2	5	50	0	0	0	2	5	50	2	5	50
580–600	0	0	0	0	0	0	2	6	75	0	0	0	1	2	25	0	0	0	2	6	75	1	2	25
600–620	0	0	0	0	0	0	2	8	100	0	0	0	0	0	0	0	0	0	2	8	100	0	0	0
620–640	0	0	0	0	0	0	1	4	40	0	0	0	1	6	60	0	0	0	1	4	40	1	6	60
640–660	0	0	0	0	0	0	1	1	14	0	0	0	1	6	86	0	0	0	1	1	14	1	6	86
660–680	0	0	0	0	0	0	1	2	25	0	0	0	1	6	75	0	0	0	1	2	25	1	6	75
680–700	0	0	0	0	0	0	1	2	100	0	0	0	0	0	0	0	0	0	1	2	100	0	0	0
700–720	0	0	0	0	0	0	1	3	100	0	0	0	0	0	0	0	0	0	1	3	100	0	0	0
720–740	0	0	0	0	0	0	1	3	37.5	0	0	0	1	5	62.5	0	0	0	1	3	37.5	1	5	62.5
740–760	0	0	0	0	0	0	1	1	17	0	0	0	1	5	83	0	0	0	1	1	17	1	5	83
760–780	0	0	0	0	0	0	1	1	100	0	0	0	0	0	0	0	0	0	1	1	100	0	0	0
780–800	0	0	0	0	0	0	1	4	100	0	0	0	0	0	0	0	0	0	1	4	100	0	0	0
800–820	0	0	0	0	0	0	2	5	100	0	0	0	0	0	0	0	0	0	2	5	100	0	0	0
820–840	0	0	0	0	0	0	3	6	100	0	0	0	0	0	0	0	0	0	3	6	100	0	0	0
840–860	0	0	0	0	0	0	3	6	43	0	0	0	1	8	57	0	0	0	3	6	43	1	8	57
860–880	0	0	0	0	0	0	2	4	25	2	4	25	1	8	50	0	0	0	4	8	50	1	8	50
880–900	0	0	0	0	0	0	1	3	60	1	2	40	0	0	0	0	0	0	2	5	100	0	0	0
900–920	0	0	0	0	0	0	1	2	100	0	0	0	0	0	0	0	0	0	1	2	100	0	0	0
920–940	0	0	0	0	0	0	1	2	100	0	0	0	0	0	0	0	0	0	1	2	100	0	0	0
940–960	0	0	0	0	0	0	1	2	100	0	0	0	0	0	0	0	0	0	1	2	100	0	0	0
960–980	0	0	0	0	0	0	1	2	100	0	0	0	0	0	0	0	0	0	1	2	100	0	0	0
980–1000	0	0	0	0	0	0	1	3	100	0	0	0	0	0	0	0	0	0	1	3	100	0	0	0
1000–1020	0	0	0	0	0	0	2	5	83	1	1	17	0	0	0	0	0	0	3	6	100	0	0	0
1020–1040	0	0	0	0	0	0	1	2	100	0	0	0	0	0	0	0	0	0	1	2	100	0	0	0
1040–1060	0	0	0	0	0	0	1	3	37.5	2	5	62.5	0	0	0	0	0	0	3	8	100	0	0	0
1060–1080	0	0	0	0	0	0	2	6	27	3	12	55	1	4	18	0	0	0	5	18	82	1	4	18
1080–1100	0	0	0	0	0	0	3	8	27	4	18	60	1	4	13	0	0	0	7	26	87	1	4	13
1100–1120	0	0	0	0	0	0	2	4	22	4	14	78	0	0	0	0	0	0	6	18	100	0	0	0
1120–1140	0	0	0	0	0	0	5	12	50	2	7	29	1	5	21	0	0	0	7	19	79	1	5	21
1140–1160	0	0	0	0	0	0	5	12	40	3	13	43	1	5	17	0	0	0	8	25	83	1	5	17
1160–1180	0	0	0	0	0	0	2	4	16	7	21	84	0	0	0	0	0	0	9	25	100	0	0	0

TABLE 23. MOVEMENT OF SINGULARISM, UNIVERSALISM, AND MYSTIC UNITY BY 20-YEAR PERIODS — *continued*

PERIOD	*Extreme Singularism-Individualism*			*Singularism-Universalism*			*Universalism-Singularism*			*Universalism*			*Mystic Unity of Singularistic Persons*			*All Varieties of Singularism*			*All Varieties of Universalism*			*Mystic Unity*		
	Number of representatives	*Their weight*	*Percentage of the total*	*Number of representatives*	*Their weight*	*Percentage of the total*	*Number of representatives*	*Their weight*	*Percentage of the total*	*Number of representatives*	*Their weight*	*Percentage of the total*	*Number of representatives*	*Their weight*	*Percentage of the total*	*Number of representatives*	*Their weight*	*Percentage of the total*	*Number of representatives*	*Their weight*	*Percentage of the total*	*Number of representatives*	*Their weight*	*Percentage of the total*
1180–1200 A.D.	0	0	0	0	0	0	2	3	15	6	14	70	1	3	15	0	0	0	8	17	85	1	3	15
1200–1220	0	0	0	0	0	0	3	5	26	3	11	58	1	3	16	0	0	0	6	16	84	1	3	16
1220–1240	0	0	0	0	0	0	2	4	21	3	9	47	1	6	32	0	0	0	5	13	68	1	6	32
1240–1260	0	0	0	0	0	0	2	4	15	6	22	85	0	0	0	0	0	0	8	26	100	0	0	0
1260–1280	0	0	0	0	0	0	2	8	19	7	35	81	0	0	0	0	0	0	9	43	100	0	0	0
1280–1300	0	0	0	0	0	0	3	11	29	9	27	71	0	0	0	0	0	0	12	38	100	0	0	0
1300–1320	0	0	0	1	3	5	6	19	31	10	31	51	1	8	13	1	3	5	16	50	82	1	8	13
1320–1340	0	0	0	3	11	19	6	18	31	8	21	36	1	8	14	3	11	19	14	39	67	1	8	14
1340–1360	0	0	0	2	8	14	8	22	39	4	7	13	4	19	34	2	8	14	12	29	52	4	19	34
1360–1380	0	0	0	0	0	0	7	16	41	2	4	10	4	19	49	0	0	0	9	20	51	4	19	49
1380–1400	0	0	0	0	0	0	6	15	71	1	2	10	1	4	19	0	0	0	7	17	81	1	4	19
1400–1420	0	0	0	0	0	0	4	11	69	1	2	12.5	1	3	18.5	0	0	0	5	13	81.5	1	3	18.5
1420–1440	0	0	0	0	0	0	4	12	63	3	7	37	0	0	0	0	0	0	7	19	100	0	0	0
1440–1460	0	0	0	1	2	8	4	10	38	2	6	23	1	8	31	1	2	8	6	16	61	1	8	31
1460–1480	0	0	0	0	0	0	7	15	55.5	3	4	15	1	8	29.5	0	0	0	10	19	70.5	1	8	29.5
1480–1500	0	0	0	0	0	0	6	12	63	2	3	16	1	4	21	0	0	0	8	15	79	1	4	21

PERIOD	Extreme Singularism-Individualism			Singularistic Collectivism			Singularism Universalism			Universalism-Singularism			Universalism			Mystic Unity of Singularistic Persons			All Varieties of Singularism			All Varieties of Universalism			Mystic Unity		
	Number of representatives	*Their weight*	*Percentage of the total*	*Number of representatives*	*Their weight*	*Percentage of the total*	*Number of representatives*	*Their weight*	*Percentage of the total*	*Number of representatives*	*Their weight*	*Percentage of the total*	*Number of representatives*	*Their weight*	*Percentage of the total*	*Number of representatives*	*Their weight*	*Percentage of the total*	*Number of representatives*	*Their weight*	*Percentage of the total*	*Number of representatives*	*Their weight*	*Percentage of the total*	*Number of representatives*	*Their weight*	*Percentage of the total*
1500–1520 A.D.	1	4	9	1	6	14	1	1	2	3	10	23	2	12	28	2	10	23	3	11	25	5	22	51	2	10	23
1520–1540	2	6	10	2	8	14	1	6	10	2	10	17	5	25	42	1	4	7	5	20	34	7	35	59	1	4	7
1540–1560	1	2	5	2	2	5	0	0	0	3	14	35	3	21	54	0	0	0	3	4	10	6	35	90	0	0	0
1560–1580	2	3	6	1	1	2	1	1	2	8	25	51	5	19	39	0	0	0	4	5	10	13	44	90	0	0	0
1580–1600	1	2	3.4	1	1	1.4	1	1	1.4	5	22	31.4	9	36	51.4	1	8	11	3	4	6.2	14	58	82.8	1	8	11
1600–1620	1	4	6	3	6	8	1	1	1	4	18	25	10	42	59	0	0	0	5	11	15	14	60	84	0	0	0
1620–1640	1	1	2	1	7	13	1	1	2	3	17	32	4	20	38	1	7	13	3	9	17	7	37	70	1	7	13
1640–1660	1	1	1	3	4	6	2	2	3	9	35	51	3	14	20	2	13	19	6	7	10	12	49	71	2	13	19
1660–1680	1	1	2	1	2	3	1	8	13	3	13	21	8	31	50	1	7	11	3	11	18	11	44	71	1	7	11
1680–1700	1	1	1	1	6	7	3	16	20	3	24	17	12	45	55	0	0	0	5	23	28	15	59	72	0	0	0
1700–1720	2	8	9	1	6	7	3	16	18	4	17	20	8	35	40	1	5	6	6	30	34	12	52	60	1	5	6
1720–1740	1	2	4	1	1	2	4	19	35	2	8	15	6	24	44	0	0	0	6	22	41	8	32	59	0	0	0
1740–1760	3	19	16	2	7	6	9	47	41	2	12	10	5	23	20	1	8	7	14	73	63	7	35	30	1	8	7
1760–1780	2	10	6	2	6	4	20	91	54	6	24	14	8	17	10	2	20	12	24	107	64	14	41	24	2	20	12
1780–1800	2	12	8	3	8	5	11	47	32	7	38	25	9	23	16	2	20	13	16	67	45	16	61	42	2	20	13
1800–1820	1	4	2	1	8	4	9	39	22	8	46	25	24	71	39	1	12	7	11	51	28	32	117	65	1	12	7
1820–1840	1	4	2	1	4	2	15	70	33	11	43	21	21	83	40	1	5	2	17	78	37	32	126	61	1	5	2
1840–1860	7	33	12	5	23	8	16	64	22	12	55	19	29	107	37	1	5	2	28	120	42	41	162	56	1	5	2
1860–1880	5	29	8.5	9	33	10	16	80	24	24	103	30	22	83	24	2	12	3.5	30	142	42.5	46	186	54	2	12	3.5
1880–1900	10	37	9	22	75	19	37	139	36	22	89	23	9	42	11	1	7	2	69	251	64	31	131	34	1	7	2
1900–1920	8	37	9	31	80	19	31	111	27	33	134	33	15	50	12	0	0	0	70	228	55	48	184	45	0	0	0

TABLE 24. MOVEMENT OF SINGULARISM, UNIVERSALISM, AND MYSTIC UNITY BY CENTURY PERIODS

PERIOD	*Extreme Singularism-Individualism*			*Singularistic Collectivism*			*Singularism-Universalism*			*Universalism-Singularism*			*Universalism*			*Mystic Unity of Singularistic Persons*			*All Varieties of Singularism*			*All Varieties of Universalism*			*Mystic Unity*		
	Number of representatives	*Their weight*	*Percentage of the total*	*Number of representatives*	*Their weight*	*Percentage of the total*	*Number of representatives*	*Their weight*	*Percentage of the total*	*Number of representatives*	*Their weight*	*Percentage of the total*	*Number of representatives*	*Their weight*	*Percentage of the total*	*Number of representatives*	*Their weight*	*Percentage of the total*	*Number of representatives*	*Their weight*	*Percentage of the total*	*Number of representatives*	*Their weight*	*Percentage of the total*	*Number of representatives*	*Their weight*	*Percentage of the total*
600–500 B.C.	0	0	0	0	0	0	0	0	0	2	15	71	2	6	29	0	0	0	0	0	0	4	21	100	0	0	0
500–400	4	10	9	0	0	0	8	53	48	5	30	27	4	17	16	0	0	0	12	63	57	9	47	43	0	0	0
400–300	9	19	12	0	0	0	17	72	46	12	49	31	3	16	11	0	0	0	26	91	58	15	65	42	0	0	0
300–200	11	35	34	0	0	0	9	18	17	13	51	49	0	0	0	0	0	0	20	53	51	13	51	49	0	0	0
200–100	7	11	24	0	0	0	3	8	17	12	27	59	0	0	0	0	0	0	10	19	41	12	27	59	0	0	0
100–0	8	25	22	0	0	0	6	20	17	23	63	54	0	0	0	1	8	7	14	45	39	23	63	54	1	8	7
0–100 A.D.	1	1	1	0	0	0	5	16	21	11	36	48	0	0	0	3	22	30	6	17	22	11	36	48	3	22	30
100–200	6	10	7	0	0	0	4	17	11	28	83	57	4	7	4	6	31	21	10	27	18	32	90	61	6	31	21
200–300	2	3½	3	0	0	0	1	6	6	18	51	47	3	14	12	6	35	32	3	9½	9	21	65	59	6	35	32
300–400	1	½	1	0	0	0	0	0	0	9	25	25	4	15	15	12	59	59	1	½	1	13	40	40	12	59	59
400–500	0	0	0	0	0	0	0	0	0	9	22	39	2	11	19	6	24	42	0	0	0	11	33	58	6	24	42
500–600	0	0	0	0	0	0	0	0	0	9	24	57	1	1	2	5	17	41	0	0	0	10	25	59	5	17	41
600–700	0	0	0	0	0	0	0	0	0	4	11	65	0	0	0	1	6	35	0	0	0	4	11	65	1	6	35
700–800	0	0	0	0	0	0	0	0	0	3	8	61	0	0	0	1	5	39	0	0	0	3	8	61	1	5	39
800–900	0	0	0	0	0	0	0	0	0	6	14	50	3	6	21	1	8	29	0	0	0	9	20	71	1	8	29
900–1000	0	0	0	0	0	0	0	0	0	3	7	100	0	0	0	0	0	0	0	0	0	3	7	100	0	0	0
1000–1100	0	0	0	0	0	0	0	0	0	5	13	32	7	24	58	1	4	10	0	0	0	12	37	90	1	4	10
1100–1200	0	0	0	0	0	0	0	0	0	11	23	30	15	45	59	2	8	11	0	0	0	26	68	89	2	8	11
1200–1300	0	0	0	0	0	0	0	0	0	8	20	19	21	75	72	2	9	9	0	0	0	29	95	91	2	9	9
1300–1400	0	0	0	0	0	0	3	11	8	21	57	40	19	46	33	5	27	19	3	11	8	40	103	73	5	27	19
1400–1500	0	0	0	0	0	0	1	2	3	16	36	53	8	15	22	3	15	22	1	2	3	24	51	75	3	13	22
1500–1600	5	12	7	5	11	6	3	8	5	17	61	33	15	67	37	4	22	12	13	31	18	32	128	70	4	22	12
1600–1700	2	5	2	9	25	11	5	18	8	18	76	32	27	101	42	2	13	5	16	48	21	45	177	74	2	15	5
1700–1800	9	44	11	7	20	5	32	144	36	16	77	19	23	86	21	4	33	8	48	208	52	39	163	40	4	33	8
1800–1900	17	68	6	33	111	10	74	300	29	57	246	24	70	288	28	4	29	3	124	479	45	127	534	52	4	29	3

society is the *universalia* of all the individuals, permeating all of them; it is the condition without which the individual is impossible. Like entelechy it permeates all of them and is the generic essence of every individual. Therefore the synthesis of individualism and universalism is achieved by this current, not mechanically, not through addition of the value or reality of the individual to that of society, but intimately, mystically, internally, in the sense that the genuine realization of the individuality of every singular person is obtained through free creative effort of the person, the effort which aims to realize the absolute and universal values for their own sake, for the pure love of them. Since these absolute and universal values are incorporated in superindividual culture and society, their realization is at the same time realization of the aims of society and of its values. When the individual makes such an effort, he expresses through it the societal *universalia* and objectivizes the reality as well as the value of society. Such a harmony or coexistence of the individual and societal reality is somewhat mystic in its nature. It mystically pre-exists the individual as a singularistic person. Such is the essence of the ontological position of the mystic integralism. Ethically, it logically claims that both the societal and the individual values are inseparable; that they are the same but represent two different aspects of the same value; that, consequently, both the individual and society are the absolute value and this value is the same; therefore neither the individual nor society can be relegated to a secondary or derivative value, and neither of them can be used as the mere means for some other purpose.

In this harmonious and ideal form, the mystic integralism attempts to solve the problem. In view of the specific difficult traits and mentality of this integralism — which, like mysticism generally, is accessible only to a relatively few persons — its representatives have been less numerous and the current less ample than those of its two other rivals.

II. Main Results

A. Whether we take the fivefold division of the main currents in the field or the unified threefold division, we do not find any continuous trend during the whole period studied, by 20-year or by the 100-year period. Instead, we see a trendless fluctuation, now one of the currents rising, now the others. This result is similar to those found in other fields.

B. The rise and fall of the main rival currents, universalism and singularism in all their varieties, show again a quite tangible correlation with the rise and fall of realism and nominalism; with the system of truth of faith and of the senses; with eternalism and temporalism; Ideational and visual art; and, finally, with the main waves of the Ideational and Sensate cultures.

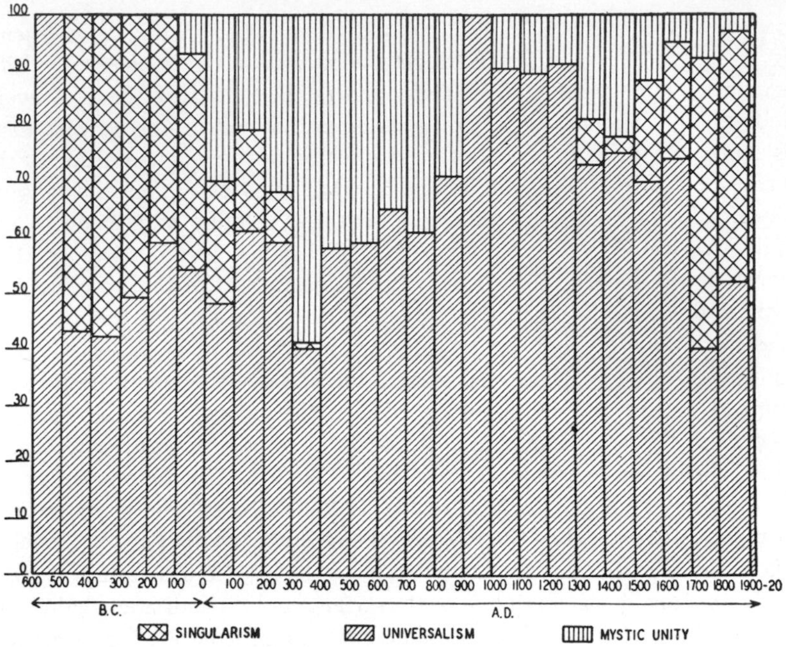

FIG. 14. MOVEMENT OF SINGULARISM, UNIVERSALISM, AND MYSTIC UNITY

(1) The sixth century appears to be the period of decisive domination of universalism.

(2) Beginning with the fifth century B.C., the monopolistic domination of universalism is broken, and singularism emerges in its extreme form. In so far we have coexistence of both main currents almost equally balanced, with a slight predomination of both forms of singularism over universalism, giving respectively 57 and 43 as the comparative weight of the currents. Considering, however, that the extreme universalism is almost twice as strong as the extreme singularism, this decreases the slight domination of singularism and makes the period almost ideally balanced in this respect. This is a direct evidence of the idealistic character of the century, according to the meaning of the term in this work, and supports the idealistic earmarks of it found in other compartments of this century.

(3) The fourth, the third, and the second centuries B.C. are marked, in spite of minor fluctuations, by a decided recession of extreme universalism, which disappears after the fourth century, and by a notable rise of extreme singularism (with a rivulet of the collectivistic singularism not given in Table 24). This, again, well supports the rising tide of the Sensate culture in this period, evidenced by the rise of the Sensate forms

in other compartments of the Greek culture.

The great tide of singularism in the period from 420 to 380 B.C. called forth a temporary reaction against it, led by the standard-bearers of universalism: Plato and Aristotle, with their followers. Plato's universalism, like that of Xenophanes, is colored by Spartan sympathies; Aristotelian universalism is more abstract; but both schools were universalistic, in spite of their other differences.

These two powerful schools are responsible for the temporary recession of singularism in its mainly moderate form in the second and the third quarters of the fourth century B.C. But even they were unable to check the extreme singularism and to reduce the moderate singularism to a small rivulet.

(4) Beginning with the end of the first century B.C., and then with the first century A.D., the tide turns in the opposite direction: singularism, especially its extreme form, begins to recede, followed by a rise of universalism. If the latter rises more slowly than singularism recedes, the reason is the emergence and then the rapid rise of mystic integralism, which is nearer to universalism than to singularism. Antisingularistic reaction thus assumes two forms: universalism and its, so to speak, desperate form, mystic integralism. This trend continues up to the fifth century A.D. In that century it reaches the point of the disappearance of singularism entirely from the "highway" of the mentality of the culture of the period.

This trend in the period studied is manifest among the Christian as well as the Pagan thinkers. Except for several external points of difference, the mentality of the Christian and the Pagan universalists and of the Christian and the Pagan integralists is similar in many essential points. It is different from the preceding universalism of either the sixth century B.C. or of even Plato and Aristotle. There the empirical universalist State was at the same time the reality permeated by the divine or sublime value: the supreme good. No dualism, in the form of aspiring to the universalist ideal City of God or the ideal State, and at the same time despising or considering the real State as the least of the evils, existed there. Now this dualism appeared and assumed a conspicuous form. The empirical bodies social were regarded at the best as the least of the evils, though the ideal State or "the City of God" was blessed and aspired to.

In such a setting as this one, the fundamental problem of singularism and universalism was complicated by the intrusion of this dualism and assumed specific forms of mystic integralism, which now emerged and became practically the most powerful current. Its peculiarity consisted not in the mere attempt to harmonize society and the individual — but in the manner in which the solution of the task was sought. It did not assume the form of the so familiar and somewhat flat discussion that the individual and society were two inseparable aspects of the same reality; that the individual could become a personality only through society, and society could exist only through the individuals; that, therefore, what was good for the one was good for the other, and so forth — the discussions given and repeated in almost any elementary text on sociology. The solution of the mystic integralism and of the transcendental universalism (Christian and Pagan) of the period consisted, on the one hand, in treating the empirical bodies social as something of low order; in toleration of them as the least of the evils; in estimation of the empirical, political, and social activities as something of low order also. On the other hand, in the positive assertion that the supreme goodness is union with God (or with some other transcendental absolute value); that, respectively, the peak of human existence is the state of ecstasy in which man frees himself from the tenets of the empirical world and enters into union with the infinitive Divine. In such a union there is no individuality, no singularity; all become dissolved in God and God's kingdom, and all are united into oneness in the City of God.

It sharply separated the realm of the empirical reality from that of the transcendental kingdom; it "invested" all the universalism in this transcendental universe of God as the Supreme Love, and as a real *coincidentia oppositorum*, in which the singular is dissolved in the infinity. In this love of God and of every neighbor, the individualism dissolves entirely and becomes an absolute transcendental universalism or integralism. Through this transcendental medium of unification, each individual Christian is entirely fused with all the others, with "neighbors." The singular empirical individual is turned into the "soul" as a ray of God or of the same absolute and infinite value.

(5) After the legalization of the Christian Church and subsequent "institutionalization" of it, the "desperate" mood and the firm conviction in the end of this world begin to pass. This expresses itself in a liquidation of singularism in the fifth century A.D. and in an increase of more balanced and less desperate universalism at the cost of mystic integralism.

The centuries from the fifth to the thirteenth appear as the period of ideational or transcendental universalism and of mystic integralism without any sign of singularism whatsoever. In this respect, the result is strikingly similar to those obtained in other compartments of culture studied. We are in an age of all-powerful Ideationalism.

In the first centuries of Christianity the Christian Church seems to have been thought not so much an institution (*Anstalt*) as a purely spiritual community of souls united in God — a kind of "pneumatic or charismatic democracy," as Harnack puts it. Subsequently, after its legalization, it became more and more institutionalized.

This process of the empirical institutionalization of the Church has been followed by the growth of universalism, at the cost of mystic integralism, after the fifth century A.D. In the subsequent centuries the latter flares up only sporadically and convulsively, while universalism becomes the main and almost monopolistic ideology up to the re-emergence of singularism in the fourteenth century. This universalism remains still transcendental, but it is more and more permeated by the worldly empirical motives, and the individual is required now to submit himself to the Church in its visible form, as an empirical or worldly institution.

We are in an age of a *theocratic universalism*, so far as its specific nature is concerned.

(6) The early years of the fourteenth century were marked by the re-emergence of singularism, and this was followed by its rapid growth during the subsequent centuries. For this reason, its movement during these centuries, followed by a recession of universalism and mystic integralism, is in complete accordance with the rising tide of the Sensate culture and all its cultural variables. By the century period, the highest level of singularism is given in the eighteenth and nineteenth centuries. This shows again that these centuries were indeed the period of the triumphant individualism and singularism, as is shown by other compartments of the culture of these centuries. Especially high was singularism in 1880–1900 (64 per cent) and in 1900–1920 (55 per cent), though in this period it slightly receded. The end of the nineteenth and the first twenty years of the twentieth centuries were further marked by a rapid rise of the singularistic collectivism which has been during the last sixty or seventy years the main gainer of all the five currents.

Thus, here again the essential movements of the main currents are in tangible agreement with those of practically all the variables or components of the Ideational and Sensate cultures. This shows once more the integrated character of the culture studied, as well as the validity of the theory developed here that when the integrated culture passes from one form — Ideational or Sensate — to the other, all its main compartments change also.

It is needless to add that the movement of universalism and singularism shows close association with that of realism and nominalism, with the respective system of truth, with eternalism and temporalism, idealism and materialism, Ideational and Sensate art, and so on.

So far as the qualitative transformations of each of the three main currents during these centuries from the fourteenth to the twentieth are concerned, they have been considerable. Each of the currents has experienced, as in the preceding centuries, several modifications of form and shading. It is superfluous here to try to characterize all these perambulations. It is enough to say that the main trend of the qualitative transformation of universalism during this period consisted, a few short-time flarings excepted, in a further weakening of its previous transcendental character and in its secularization. As we approach our own time, the transcendental universalism, in the sense of subordination of the singular to the transcendental, God or the like, more and more evaporated. Its place has been increasingly occupied by empirical universalism, which maintains the inferiority or derivativeness of the singular in regard to the *empirical* universals: the State, the class, the order, the family, the union, the party, and so on, and for empirical reasons. The place of the Church or the *corpus mysticum* began more and more to be occupied by the State, by mankind, by class (proletarian and others), by syndicate, by association generally, and by other bodies social viewed not transcendentally but empirically.

Similarly, the re-emerged singularism has undergone several changes during these centuries and has consisted of diverse rivulets of different colors: singularism spiritual, singularism liberal, singularism anarchistic, singularism of the Stirner type, of the Ibsen type, of the "bourgeois type," with its rights of man and citizen, and prosaic "live and let live." The general trend of singularism for the centuries has possibly consisted of an evaporation of the transcendental motives of the Christian singularism of man as a pure soul, and in its progressive replacement by the "behavioristic individual," consisting of "anatomy and physiology," plus "reflexes and habits," psychoanalytical "libido" and similar "complexes," with ever more doubted "mind" and "soul," "conscience and consciousness." Ontologically and ethically singularism tended to become more and more eudaemonistic, hedonistic, utilitarian, and behavioristic. Not the salvation or damnation of his "soul" but "the greatest happiness" of the individual — of myself only or of the "greatest number" of the individuals — becomes now the goal of singularism.

As mentioned, of various rivulets of singularism, the particular growth of the collectivistic singularism or singularistic collectivism, has been an especially conspicuous trait of these centuries.

Thus the above data show clearly that the fluctuation of universalism and singularism is indeed connected with that of the Ideational and Sensate cultures and is one of its components as well as its signs.

C. A glance at these minor fluctuations in the short periods shows that the extreme and moderate universalism tended to flare up, in minor fluctuations, besides its general connection with the rise and the domination of the Ideational culture, in *the periods either of the existence of strongly integrated*, powerful groups, like tribes and other — mainly kinship — groups, as in Greece before the fifth century; or in the period of building the vast bodies social, like the State and the Church, the crystallization of their organization, the concentration of their power, and the expansion of their controlling functions.

The latest example of this is given by the slight but unmistakable rise of universalism in the period from 1900 to 1920, and up to the present time. This is the period of a sharp absolutization of the State and the state dictators; of extension of the regulative and regimentative functions of the State in almost all countries of Europe. It is enough to be lightly acquainted with the Fascist and pro-Fascist, with the Communist and the pro-Communist, with the Hitlerite and the pro-Hitlerite regimes, with the growing totalitarian trends in democracies, with laws enacted and doctrines taught, in order to see an enormous swing toward, if not a pure and consistent universalism, then at least a rude form of it as opposed to singularism in all its forms, except, perhaps, the collectivistic one. This "turn" is again a variety of the "revolt against the Sensate culture at the end of the nineteenth and the beginning of the twentieth century that we met in art and in most of the other compartments of our culture. Its consistency with the anti-Sensate revolts in other fields deserves to be mentioned. Taken together, they show that this "revolt" is real indeed, and is spread over almost all the compartments of our culture.

Logically, such a hypothesis is easily comprehensible. When vast bodies social emerge with their powerful and all-controlling government, the factual power of individuals as individuals and of their free and voluntary association decreases. If they are opposed to the Leviathan and to its government, they are pitilessly crushed. If they support it, their support increases the power and the authority of the autocrat. In both cases, the individual becomes a *quantité negligeable* in the social reality.

As to the periods of ascendancy of mystical integralism, it seems to tend to rise, besides its fundamental connection with the domination of Ideational culture, in the periods of great social calamities and catastrophes, and generally in the periods when the existing sociocultural system was upset — when its shattering, its decline, preceded the establishment of a new and solid sociocultural order. At least, its prolonged blossoming in the first six centuries of our era generally and its minor rises during this and subsequent periods well agree with that hypothesis.

Finally, as to the minor or short-time ups and downs of singularism (its major movements being the "function" of the type of the dominant culture), their main "factors" or causes are generally opposite to those of universalism and mystic integralism, though in the ups and downs of extreme singularism the factors of "despair" and calamity may also play some part. As we saw, such calamities tend to make some persons "stoics" and "mystics"; others "epicureans" of a vulgar type of the hedonistic *Carpe diem* (the law of polarization). When the dominant culture is of the Sensate type, calamities of the sociocultural and political order tend to reinforce the motives of extreme singularism in sensate persons and groups: since the State, or the society, or culture, or any superindividual order and body and value are at a crisis and do not secure or supply the maximum of pleasure, away with them; let them go to the devil. And let the clever or wise persons center their lives around themselves and the individual generally.

Extreme singularism may be bred also by a prolonged, comfortable epicurean prosperity. In their search for excitement and thrill, the people, bored with their quiet existence in the confines of the state or other social body, can easily be induced to fancy singularism as one of the unusual forms of thrill.

As to the moderate forms of singularism, they are satellites of the comparatively prosperous and comfortable and balanced Sensate culture, before its disintegration and sensualization, or of the Idealistic culture where it shares and mixes with the forms of the moderate universalism.

Finally the *minor flare-ups of the collectivistic singularism* also seem to occur more frequently in the periods of crises, especially of crises of a deeper kind, when the previously existing culture and orde rapidly declines. At least, the periods 1500–1540 and 1880–1920 fit this theory. Historical knowledge testifies also that in the history of Greece and Rome, the flare-ups of this current occurred mainly in such periods.

Likewise in the Middle Ages, in the centuries twelfth to fifteenth, before 1500, the occurrences of the diluted collectivistic singularism-mysticism represented by various sects, like some of the Arnoldists, the Poor Brethren of Lyon, the Utraquists, the Patarini, the Catharists, the Valdenses, the "Spirituals," the Bohemian Brethren, the "Flagellants," the Taborites, the "Millenarians," "Conventuals," "Brothers of Free Spirits," and others, took place in the transitory period from the Ideational to the Sensate culture, not to mention that some of these sects and their "ideology" were born in the years and in the circumstances of a catastrophic and calamitous character. In this sense the collectivistic singularism-mysticism, like the mystic integralism and partly the extreme singularism, is a "desperate form" of singularism, which tries to pull itself out of the difficulties through resorting to a simulacrum of universalism or mystic unity, but without its inner content and value. The catastrophic nature of the period after 1914 is largely responsible for the present flare-up of collectivistic singularism. It is almost always the phenomena of crisis and transition, but rarely, if ever, the constructive current which builds a new social body, united inwardly, and a new social order which stands by the virtue of its inner value, without a superabundant use of the cement of a rudest coercion and force. However, as a sign of "revolt" against Sensate culture, it is symptomatic and, through its destruction, it possibly paves the way for the advent of a real universalism with not external but inner — "familistic" — fusion and unification of individuals into real unity approaching that of good members of a strong family. This role it possibly plays at the present time of dissolution of the singularistic contractual ties in our society.

So much for the minor fluctuations of the currents studied and their causes (factors).

D. The movement of the currents shows again that there is no trend to a continuous increase of differentiation and heterogeneity at the cost of homogeneity.

E. If we inquire which of these currents has been more powerful generally, and what has been the "spectrum" of the main periods in regard to the respective mentality, the answer is given by the summary of the weight points for the whole period studied as well as for the main subperiods (see Table 25).

TABLE 25. CURRENTS IN SINGULARISM, UNIVERSALISM, AND INTEGRALISM

Period	*All Singularisms*	*All Universalisms*	*Mystic Integralism*
600 B.C.–100 A.D.	288	300	30
100–600	37	253	166
600–1500	13	400	82
1500–1900	766	1002	97
1900–1920	228	184	0
Total	1332	2139	375

The figures show that the most powerful current throughout the whole period has been universalism. It is almost twice as powerful as singularism. Only in the period 1900–1920 was singularism slightly more powerful than universalism, and both were about equal in the period from 600 B.C. to A.D. 100. Especially universalistic was the period from A.D. 100 to 1500. These figures give a concise spectrum of the mentality of each period; at the same time they suggest that both of these currents seem to reflect two different aspects of the transsubjective reality; that probably neither one of them is totally wrong or totally right, totally true or totally false; therefore, it is not likely that one of them can drive out the other forever.

The data seem to suggest again that for a lasting culture and social system the universalist current has to be stronger than the singularist one. The possible reason for this requirement is somewhat similar to that in the case of idealism and materialism, namely, that the universalist ideology and mentality are necessary, to a degree, for the maintenance of social cohesion and solidarity. As a cohesive agent they are more needed than the singularist ideology, which fosters the centrifugal forces of society and, if much more powerful than the universalist, leads, in conjunction with other factors, to the disruption of social ties, and makes social life, with its authority and government, with its free or forced sacrifices of the individual, impossible.

The figures which are given in Table 25 also show the "proportionate balance" of the main rival currents and therefore the spontaneous self-regulation of sociocultural processes. In this sense, they exhibit once more the validity of the "principle of limit" and other principles emphasized in this work.

F. The above results, together with the next chapter, have an important bearing upon the theories of many sociologists and social scientists busy with a study and definition of such terms as society, group, social phenomenon, and the like. The data show that the period from 1880 to 1920 was one of the few periods when the singularist stream was more powerful than the universalist one. Confront this datum with the dominant definition of society in sociology or in social-science treatises of democratic countries of that period, and the result is interesting in a number of ways. The definitions of society or group or collective unity given in a great majority of sociology courses and in other texts for the period 1880–1920 are almost invariably singularistic, either in the form of the extreme or — more often — a moderate singularism. No social *corpus mysticum*, no society as the primary reality, no social entity as fundamentally irreducible and inexpressible in the terms of the individuals — interesting or not — is admitted. Similarly in socioethical valuation of culture and the individual, the individual is made the measure of all things, no matter whether the smaller or the greater collection of them. Hedonism, utilitarianism, eudaemonism, dominant to recent times, are all more or less singularistic and can hardly help being so.

I mention this situation, however, in order to emphasize once more the principle carried through this work and in this part particularly, namely, that what appears to be true or scientific — and most of the social scientists of this period regarded their standpoint as scientific and the universalistic standpoint as metaphysical — is in a greater part, for each given period, a reflection of the nature of the culture then predominant. The domination of the Sensate culture favors sociological singularism appearing and being considered "scientific"; while the domination of the Ideational or Idealistic culture leads to the universalistic or mystic integralist ideology being credited as true or "scientific." Here again social conditions interfere with human epistemology, methodology, logics, and observation of the "facts." They "fool" the scientists and scholars in what appears to them scientific or true and what is not. The scientific nature of the modern singularism in sociology and social sciences generally is, from this standpoint, neither more nor less scientific than the nature of the universalistic theories.

The complete and absolute and eternal truth in this field is also "white" in a sense of being a synthesis of both and of something else. So much about this aspect of the "sociology of sociology texts and treatises."

For the present these conclusions suffice. Some others are to be added in the next chapter, where the same topic is taken up but in the still more specific and narrow form.

Starting with nominalism and realism, we narrowed the topic to singularism and universalism as its social forms; and now we are going to narrow it still more, to a study of the juridico-analytical conceptions of the juridical personality, throughout the same period of the same cultures.

19

FLUCTUATION OF "FIRST PRINCIPLES": V. FLUCTUATION OF REALISTIC, NOMINALISTIC, AND MIXED CONCEPTIONS OF THE REALITY OF THE JURIDICAL PERSONALITY: CORPORATIONS (*Universitas Personarum* or *Collegia Personalia*) AND INSTITUTIONS (*Universitas Bonorum* or *Collegia Realia*).

I. Main Types of Conceptions

In this chapter I shall show that the Ideational or Sensate culture mentality determines the dominant theories or ideologies, even in such a specific field as the problem of the reality of so-called juridical personality. Upon this or that solution of this problem have depended often the life, property, and liberty of thousands of persons. This means that the problem has not only a theoretical but also a paramount, practical importance.

In the period of the domination of the Ideational mentality, the theories or beliefs in the true reality of the juridical personality tend to dominate and to be considered "true" or "scientific," while in the period of domination of the Sensate and nominalistic-singularistic mentalities the nominalistic theories are likely to be believed to be "true" and "scientific."

By juridical personality in law is meant *any body consisting of one or more individuals treated by the law as a unit, and usually endowed with the right to perpetual succession and to act as a single person.* Since the Roman Law, two main forms of the juridical personality have been distinguished: (1) Corporations (*universitas personarum*, or the medieval *collegia personalia*), where the union of the members as persons is stressed — such are most of the various corporations, incorporated societies, firms, etc. (2) Institutions (*universitas bonorum* or the medieval *collegia realia*) as a complex of property with a specific purpose, endowed by the law to act as a single person, such as various universities, asylums, etc. (3) Mixed juridical personalities, intermediary between the two (*collegia mixta*).

If the general juridical concept of the juridical personality seems to be clear and simple (though in fact it is not; see especially Petrajitsky's criticism of it), the problem of its nature and its reality has caused unspeakable difficulties and hardships to the jurists. What is the juridical personality: is it a true reality of the transsubjective social world, different from that of its individual members, or is it a mere fiction, which does not have any transsubjective reality beyond that of its members, but which, for practical purposes, may artificially be treated as if it had a reality similar to that of a single person? (Note here this famous "as if," *als ob*). Such, in brief, is the crux of the problem.

An enormous number of theories have attempted to solve it in a simple or complicated, flat or ingenious manner, with hundreds of thinkers and jurists and lawyers exerting their imagination, logic, observation, intuition in any way they could. Omitting secondary differences, these theories can easily be classed in three main groups: Realistic, Nominalistic, and Mixed, with several subdivisions within each of the groups.

A. *Realistic Conception.* According to it, juridical personality is a transsubjective and superindividual reality, which truly exists in the social world. This reality is neither secondary to nor derivative from the reality of its members, nor coincides with it. It exists side by side and above it. It is neither fiction, nor mere artificial device, intentionally set forth for practical convenience. In no way is it less real than the singular individual. Such being the general conception of realism in the field, in other — more specific — details, realistic theories differ from one another. Some of the more important subclasses of realism are as follows.

(1) *Transcendental realism* of juridical personality sees its reality in some supersensory or transcendental "essence" or "entity." An example of it is given, for instance, in the "charismatic conception" of the early Christian Church, where all and everything Christian is united and dissolved in God. Instead of God, any other transcendental reality may serve.

(2) *Empirico-organismic realism*, which views the juridical personality as a real organism of superindividual character, with its own body and its own system, partly corporeal, partly psychological. Such are, for example, the conceptions of many of the eminent representatives of the Germanic School in Jurisprudence, like Beseler, Bluntschli, Gierke (partly), and of a few even of the Romance School of Law, like Baron, Regelsberger, and others.

(3) *Psychological realism*, whose partisans see the reality of the juridical personality mainly in some superindividual psychological essence or substratum, like "public opinion," "group mind," "common will," and so on. In the juridical literature specifically, the detailed theory of "will," "corporeal and uncorporeal," was developed, especially by Zitelmann. Other theorizers use "group interest," "group aims," and so on, instead of the "will."

(4) *Functional or naïve realism* bases its belief in the reality of the juridical personality upon its functional unity, which sensorily appears as a reality of *sui generis*, different from that of its members. Such a theory may be more or less sophisticated, more or less extreme, the moderate forms merging imperceptibly into the kind of theories inter-

mediary between realism and nominalism.

B. *Nominalistic Conception.* It is opposite to the realistic. For its partisans there is no reality of the juridical personality different from that of its members, either in the transsubjective social world or even in our thought. The only real elements in it are its individual members and various sensory objects attached to it artificially. The juridical personality is a *fiction* created artificially for specific practical needs and conditionally treated "as if" (*als ob!*) it were a unity or reality, though in fact it is not. It is merely convenient and serviceable fiction. Again the nominalist conception of the juridical personality has several varieties, ranging from the extreme nominalism which sees in it a pure fiction to which nothing corresponds in reality and which is nothing more than the mere sum of the individuals — its members and the singularistic complexes of material objects — up to the moderate nominalism, which is ready to admit that though the juridical personality does not have any reality independent and different from that of its singularistic members, the specific combination of these members creates a reality different from what they possess as a mere collection of individuals not united by juridical and other interrelationships.

C. *Mixed Conception.* Between the realistic and nominalistic conceptions there are many intermediary conceptions which are composed of eclectic, sometimes inconsistent, sometimes systematic, combinations of various characteristics of both conceptions. One of the important forms of these intermediary theories is the conceptual. Like the conceptualism in ontology, it contends that in the transsubjective social world there is no reality of *sui generis* of the juridical personality which is not derived from that of its individuals and their possessions. In this sense, it is near to nominalistic conception. But to our mind, there is a concept of the juridical personality which is different from the mere sum of its members; which has its own existence as a conceptual reality; is different from the concept of the mere collection of its members. According to the conceptual theory, the juridical personality exists as a reality of *sui generis* in our mind, though it does not exist in the outside social world. In this it is near to the realistic conception of the juridical personality. This theory has again several shadings, some of which imperceptibly pass into the moderate forms of the realistic, others into those of the nominalistic conceptions.

Such are the main types of the conceptions of the nature and reality of the juridical personality and collective unity generally. As we see, they represent but a special case of the problem of realism, conceptualism, and nominalism generally and of universalism and singularism specifically.

II. Main Conclusions

A. No perpetual trend, only short and long-time fluctuations.

B. Ups and downs of the realistic conception of the juridical person go tangibly together with those of the general philosophical realism, with sociological universalism — mystic unity — with the truth of faith, and, partly, of reason, with eternalism and generally with the rise and decline of the Ideational culture. Ups and downs of juristic nominalism move with philosophic nominalism, sociological singularism, the truth of the senses, temporalism, and of the Sensate culture generally.

Finally, mixed, eclectic, and conceptualistic theories crop out and dominate in the period of the mixed, partly Idealistic, culture and its respective variables.

C. This association means also that even such seemingly special problems as that of the juridical person enter as an organic component into an integrated culture and live and change as such a culture changes.

D. It means, further, that the rise and decline of the main conceptions in the field are, like all the other special phenomena studied, incomprehensible without considering them in the light of the much larger perspective and much broader and more embracing "variable" — the culture — of which it is a part. Without such a setting, one can hardly account intelligently for the fluctuations and would have either to take them as a mere riddle, or tie them to some special variable (economic factor, religion, science, or what not, up to sunspots) which can hardly yield any valid result. Here, then, once more we find a reason for the use of the larger perspectives and "totalitarian" approach. Too narrow a specialization and perspective can never grasp the logic of these changes nor even the mere fact of the long-time fluctuations. Like a microscope it may show well many details of an infinitesimally small particle of reality; but the whole wide world is infinitely larger and richer and more colorful than this particle, and to know something of the universe we need a telescope no less than a miscroscope. *Sapienti sat!*

E. The above gives additional support to the conditioning by the type of culture of what appears to be true and "scientific." A nominalistic theory in the field cannot be dominant and believed to be "true" and "scientific" in a blooming Ideational culture; and vice versa, a realistic, especially a transcendentally realistic — theory has little chance of being accepted as "scientific" and "true" by the majority of the leading scientists in a period of the blooming of the Sensate culture. The above shows that. Therefore, in the light of this result, I can but humorously take the most enthusiastic defense, or a criticism by a sociologist, social scientist, or anybody, of one of these theories as perfectly "scientific," "true," "observational," "logico-experimental," "proved forever," while other theories may be styled "unscientific," "meaningless," "metaphysical," false, and so on.

Such overenthusiastic and not too well-informed debaters may be reasonably assured that, even if their theory is generally accepted today, tomorrow, if another type of culture comes, it will be generally rejected. These "ricorsi" have been repeated many times and will probably be repeated many times more in the future.

20

FLUCTUATION OF "FIRST PRINCIPLES": VI. FLUCTUATION OF THE INFLUENCE OF DETERMINISTIC AND INDETERMINISTIC MENTALITIES

I. Determinism and Indeterminism

The next general principles underlying most of the scientific and philosophical and ethical theories are the principles of indeterminism and determinism. Again, explicitly or implicitly, theoretically or practically, they lie at the basis of most of such theories. In this sense one of them is a basic principle of science, philosophy, religion, ethics, politics, and practical activity. All the respective theories in the field represent either a deterministic or an indeterminate or a mixed standpoint. By *determinism* in a broad sense is meant a theory that everything in the world, including man and his mind and actions, are causally conditioned, subject to the principle of the uniform and necessary relationship, and that each cause A has invariably the same effect B and therefore is invariably connected with it. More specifically, it contends that no free will exists as a factor in human behavior. Man is determined as rigidly as any other phenomenon.

Indeterminism is a theory opposite to determinism, especially in application to man. Generally, it denies the existence of invariable causal relationship between the phenomena; it admits a potentiality of variation there: either through the will of God or Providence, or any supreme intelligent power; or through "incidental" or "creative" variations; or as a possibility of several and diverse effects, B, C, D, of the same cause, or variable, A. In brief, it denies the category of the uniform and specific and invariable necessary relationship between the phenomena generally. In regard to man, it contends for the existence of either free will, or free choice, or, in a diluted form, several diverse potentialities in steering his behavior and mind. Here particularly it denies the rigid and invariable and imposed conditioning of his behavior in the same fixed course as that of the motion of inorganic bodies.

Such being the general characteristics of determinism and indeterminism, each of them has an enormous variety of concrete forms and shadings. There is a whole gradation of more or less rigid determinisms and more or less free indeterminisms, as they have been given in various theories. In some of the deterministic theories man's behavior is consid-

TABLE 26. INDICATORS OF THE FLUCTUATION OF DETERMINISM AND INDETERMINISM FROM 540 B.C. TO A.D. 1920 BY 20-YEAR PERIODS
(on the basis of different values given from 1 to 12)

PERIOD	*Determinism*		*Mixed*		*Indeterminism*		*Total*	
	No.	*Per cent*	*No.*	*Per cent*	*No.*	*Per cent*	*No.*	*Per cent*
540–520 B.C.			8	100			8	100
520–500			15	100			15	100
500–480			15	100			15	100
480–460			7	100			7	100
460–440			1	100			1	100
440–420			9	100			9	100
420–400			29	100			29	100
400–380			41	100			41	100
380–360			42	100			42	100
360–340			47	100			47	100
340–320	30	71.0			12	29.0	42	100
320–300	34	62.0			21	38.0	55	100
300–280	37	69.0			17	31.0	54	100
280–260	37	77.0			11	23.0	48	100
260–240	22	76.0			7	24.0	29	100
240–220	40	78.0			11	22.0	51	100
220–200	20	65.0			11	35.0	31	100
200–180	6	68.0			13	32.0	19	100
180–160	6	43.0			8	57.0	14	100
160–140	6	46.0			7	54.0	13	100
140–120	8	67.0			4	33.0	12	100
120–100	10	62.0			6	38.0	16	100
100–80	12	57.0			9	43.0	21	100
80–60	23	72.0			9	28.0	32	100
60–40	40	65.0			22	35.0	62	100
40–20	24	67.0			12	33.0	36	100
20–0	10	91.0			1	9.0	11	100
0–20 A.D.	12	57.0			9	43.0	21	100
20–40	15	65.0			8	35.0	23	100
40–60	19	66.0			10	34.0	29	100
60–80	27	93.0			2	7.0	29	100
80–100	26	93.0			2	7.0	28	100
100–120	23	64.0			13	36.0	36	100
120–140	47	78.0			13	22.0	60	100
140–160	38	63.0			22	37.0	60	100
160–180	31	46.0			36	54.0	67	100
180–200	34	40.0			50	60.0	84	100
200–220	9	18.0			40	82.0	49	100
220–240	5	16.0			27	84.0	32	100
240–260	15	37.0			25	63.0	40	100
260–280	13	37.0			22	63.0	35	100
280–300	4	33.3			8	66.7	12	100
300–320	1	12.0			22	88.0	23	100
320–340	1	4.0			27	96.0	28	100
340–360	2	9.0			20	91.0	22	100
360–380	2	5.0			36	95.0	38	100
380–400	3	7.0			41	93.0	44	100
400–420	3	8.0			33	92.0	36	100
420–440	3	7.9			35	92.1	38	100
440–460	1	4.0			24	96.0	25	100
460–480	1	5.0			18	95.0	19	100
480–500	1	8.0			12	92.0	13	100
500–520	1	13.0			7	87.0	8	100

TABLE 26. INDICATORS OF THE FLUCTUATION OF DETERMINISM AND INDETERMINISM FROM 540 B.C. TO A.D. 1920 BY 20-YEAR PERIODS — *continued*

(on the basis of different values given from 1 to 12)

PERIOD	*Determinism*		*Mixed*		*Indeterminism*		*Total*	
	No.	*Per cent*	*No.*	*Per cent*	*No.*	*Per cent*	*No.*	*Per cent*
520–540 A.D.	1	6.0			16	94.0	17	100
540–560	0	0			11	100.0	11	100
560–580	0	0			3	100.0	3	100
580–600	0	0			4	100.0	4	100
600–620	0	0			4	100.0	4	100
620–640	0	0			6	100.0	6	100
640–660	0	0			6	100.0	6	100
660–680	0	0			8	100.0	8	100
680–700	0	0			2	100.0	2	100
700–720	0	0			1	100.0	1	100
720–740	0	0			5	100.0	5	100
740–760	0	0			5	100.0	5	100
760–780	0	0			0	0	0	0
780–800	0	0			4	100.0	4	100
800–820	0	0			4	100.0	4	100
820–840	0	0			4	100.0	4	100
840–860	0	0			14	100.0	14	100
860–880	0	0			15	100.0	15	100
880–900	0	0			5	100.0	5	100
900–920	0	0			2	100.0	2	100
920–940	0	0			2	100.0	2	100
940–960	0	0			0	0	0	0
960–980	0	0			0	0	0	0
980–1000	0	0			0	0	0	0
1000–1020	0	0			0	0	0	0
1020–1040	0	0			0	0	0	0
1040–1060	0	0			0	0	0	0
1060–1080	0	0			14	100.0	14	100
1080–1100	0	0			21	100.0	21	100
1100–1120	0	0			12	100.0	12	100
1120–1140	0	0			21	100.0	21	100
1140–1160	0	0			27	100.0	27	100
1160–1180	0	0			19	100.0	19	100
1180–1200	0	0			16	100.0	16	100
1200–1220	0	0			13	100.0	13	100
1220–1240	3	18.0			14	82.0	17	100
1240–1260	3	15.0			17	85.0	20	100
1260–1280	6	16.0			31	84.0	37	100
1280–1300	9	19.0			39	81.0	48	100
1300–1320	6	10.0			54	90.0	60	100
1320–1340	8	18.0			36	82.0	44	100
1340–1360	12	37.0			20	63.0	32	100
1360–1380	6	30.0			14	70.0	20	100
1380–1400	5	71.0			2	29.0	7	100
1400–1420	2	33.0			4	67.0	6	100
1420–1440	2	15.0			11	85.0	13	100
1440–1460	2	12.0			14	88.0	16	100
1460–1480	2	15.0			11	85.0	13	100
1480–1500	7	64.0			4	36.0	11	100
1500–1520	8	40.0			12	60.0	20	100
1520–1540	19	54.0			16	46.0	35	100
1540–1560	38	66.0			20	34.0	58	100
1560–1580	22	44.0			28	56.0	50	100

TABLE 26. INDICATORS OF THE FLUCTUATION OF DETERMINISM AND INDETERMINISM FROM 540 B.C. TO A.D. 1920 BY 20-YEAR PERIODS — *continued*

(on the basis of different values given from 1 to 12)

PERIOD	*Determinism*		*Mixed*		*Indeterminism*		*Total*	
	No.	*Per cent*	*No.*	*Per cent*	*No.*	*Per cent*	*No.*	*Per cent*
1580–1600 A.D.	24	39.0			37	61.0	61	100
1600–1620	27	47.0			30	53.0	57	100
1620–1640	30	52.0			28	48.0	58	100
1640–1660	42	61.0			27	39.0	69	100
1660–1680	38	43.0			51	57.0	89	100
1680–1700	36	33.0			73	67.0	109	100
1700–1720	31	35.0			57	65.0	88	100
1720–1740	27	40.0			42	60.0	69	100
1740–1760	40	40.0			60	60.0	100	100
1760–1780	59	56.0			47	44.0	106	100
1780–1800	52	39.0			80	61.0	132	100
1800–1820	79	47.0			90	53.0	169	100
1820–1840	76	49.0			80	51.0	156	100
1840–1860	100	47.0			114	53.0	214	100
1860–1880	163	61.0			105	39.0	268	100
1880–1900	186	54.0			157	46.0	343	100
1900–1920	205	53.0			185	47.0	390	100

TABLE 27. INDICATORS OF THE FLUCTUATION OF DETERMINISM AND INDETERMINISM FROM 600 B.C. TO A.D. 1900 BY CENTURY PERIODS

(on the basis of different values given from 1 to 12)

PERIOD	*Determinism*		*Mixed*		*Indeterminism*		*Total*	
	No.	*Per cent*	*No.*	*Per cent*	*No.*	*Per cent*	*No.*	*Per cent*
600–500 B.C.			15	100			15	100
500–400			44	100			44	100
400–300	110	84.0			21	16.0	131	100
300–200	75	66.4			38	33.6	113	100
200–100	18	41.9			25	58.1	43	100
100–0	60	62.5			36	37.5	96	100
0–100 A.D.	65	83.3			13	16.7	78	100
100–200	96	55.2			78	44.8	174	100
200–300	25	24.8			76	75.2	101	100
300–400	6	6.5			86	93.5	92	100
400–500	4	6.3			59	93.7	63	100
500–600	1	4.2			23	95.8	24	100
600–700	0	0			12	100.0	12	100
700–800	0	0			10	100.0	10	100
800–900	0	0			23	100.0	23	100
900–1000	0	0			2	100.0	2	100
1000–1100	0	0			21	100.0	21	100
1100–1200	0	0			61	100.0	61	100
1200–1300	12	12.6			83	87.4	95	100
1300–1400	22	19.3			92	80.7	114	100
1400–1500	11	32.3			23	67.7	34	100
1500–1600	75	45.5			90	54.5	165	100
1600–1700	89	35.7			160	64.3	249	100
1700–1800	137	41.5			193	58.5	330	100
1800–1900	395	48.3			423	51.7	818	100

ered as rigidly conditioned as is the motion of a stone falling. In others its conditioned character is qualified by so many reservations, exemptions, and limitations that such a deterministic theory almost imperceptibly merges into indeterminism. *Mutatis mutandis*, the same can be said of various conceptions of indeterminism, which range from almost absolute freedom of man, or anything else from any external conditioning except man's free will, to such diluted indeterminisms as are on the border line between determinism and indeterminism.

By dozens of other characteristics, the theories in the field differ from one another in their conceptions. Some philosophers, like Kant, contend that man's behavior in this phenomenal world is absolutely determined, and if we knew all the circumstances, it could be predicted as accurately as an eclipse of the sun or the moon; on the other hand, as an "intelligible" and "noumenal" being (in contradistinction to man as an empirical phenomenon) he is quite free from any external conditioning. In other theories determinism amounts almost to fatalism; in several theories the clear-cutness of the concepts is complicated by the introduction of such factors as destiny, Providence, predestination, God's will; by consideration of the moral responsibility of man for his actions; by distinction between actual and potential freedom, between absolute and relative freedom; by the introduction of a gradation of forms of conditioning and of freedom, and by hundreds of other circumstances. There are few problems in which so many of the most vital interests of man are involved. Theologians, educators, lawyers, moralizers, politicians, statesmen, scientists, teachers, social reformers, and even the "forgotten man" — each one and everybody is confronted with it, theoretically or practically, and has to give to it some theoretical or practical solution. As their needs and interests are different, each, so to speak, has to cut it to fit his own particular requirements. Therefore an enormous variety of forms, shadings, accentuations, reservations, and qualifications have been injected into the problem and have resulted in a most intricate diversity of concepts of determinism and indeterminism.

I mention all these complexities in order to indicate that this study is made with a full awareness of them and confronts them at its very beginning in its work of classifying the thinkers under one head or another.

The indicators of Tables 26 and 27 and Figure 15 give only quantitative fluctuations of the influence of the currents. For an adequate knowledge of the real situation, these indicators need to be supplemented by at least a qualitative study of the theories involved. This study is naturally omitted here. Such a qualitative shading is especially important for some of the periods like 540–320 B.C., or A.D. 1900–1920 and others. When it is done, the meaning of the figures in Tables 26 to 28, and of Figure 15 would change somewhat.

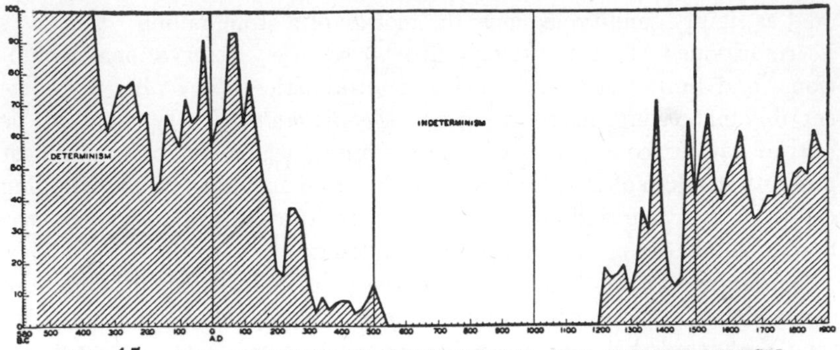

FIG. 15. FLUCTUATION OF DETERMINISM AND INDETERMINISM

II. Main Results

After the commentaries on the tables in preceding chapters, it is unnecessary to comment at length on Tables 26 and 27 and Figure 15. It is enough to say that all the conclusions suggested and warranted by them are sustained by these: fallacy of the linear conception of historical processes; fallacy of an existence of evolutionary linear tendency; fallacy of the Spencerian formula of evolution; fallacy of the belief of the partisans of determinism and indeterminism that their case is "finally and irrevocably" proved, that the fallacy of the rival theory "once and forever" is exposed, that the future is insured for their theory and theirs only. Tables 26 and 27 and the reality they represent can but furnish a laugh at these "ever-recurrent" naïve beliefs.

The next point which needs to be mentioned is the bearing which Table 28 has on the problem of the immanent self-regulation of the currents in the course of time. The total sum of the indices for each of the currents for the total and the specified periods is given in Table 28.

TABLE 28. INDICES FOR DETERMINISM AND INDETERMINISM

Period	*Determinism*	*Indeterminism*
580 B.C.–A.D. 100	678	212
100–540	239	557
540–1500	73	519
1500–1920	1302	1339
Total	2292	2627

Again it is worthy of mention that in spite of a long course of time — 2500 years — and in spite of the fact that the indices are made regardless of their possible quantitative balance, this balance is there, and all in all is rather surprisingly close. For each short period, or even for the longer periods given in the above figures, there is a considerable quantitative difference in the strength of the rival currents; but for the total period, or even for the period of the last 420 years, they fairly closely balance each other. In the light of this, the "ever-recurrent" foolish assurances that one of the currents would disappear forever becomes particularly childish as a scientific statement.

So far as the highs and lows of each of the currents in Figure 15 are concerned, the most conspicuous periods in these respects are as follows.

The period from 540 to 380 B.C. is that of the domination of a kind of Mixed form represented by a belief in Destiny, God, *Fatum*, Μοῖρα, and εἱμαρ μένη, the Pythagorean belief in the mystic, quantitative relationship between phenomena, etc. In a sense, it is a kind of determinism, but a determinism very different from the purely mechanical determinism of the later period. No less can it be styled indeterminism, because the determination here is near to "God's will," or *logos*, indeterministic in its nature. The period is a mixture of both, so typical of the Idealistic culture. A similar situation was met before in the systems of Truth and of Idealism-Materialism. The real blossoming of determinism in Greece and Rome is the period beginning with the second half of the fourth century B.C. and ending with the first century A.D., with its climaxes in the fourth century B.C. and the first century A.D. Since the second century A.D. it has rapidly declined and after the sixth century it becomes "unnoticeable."

Now comes the turn of the domination of indeterminism. It becomes monopolistic from the sixth to the thirteenth century. In the thirteenth century (note again, the century of the Idealistic culture), determinism reappears and rapidly grows, reaching a climax in the sixteenth century; then it recedes slightly in the seventeenth and resumes its rise in the eighteenth and nineteenth centuries.

During the last four centuries both streams have been almost equal in their strength.

The next point to be mentioned is that when the Graeco-Roman culture split into the Pagan and the Christian streams — approximately from A.D. 100 to the sixth century when the Christian stream absorbed the Pagan — the Pagan as well as the Christian philosophical thought had in this (as well as in other respects considered above) practically the same course of direction. We find the Pagan as well as Christian thinkers split between these two currents; in both groups, after the second century, appeared almost simultaneously the trend of reinforcement of indeterminism, and after the third century a rapid weakening of determinism. Thus, the "turn of the direction" which appears in a given culture involves equally all the sects or factions of that culture, in spite of all their dissensions, and each of them contributes to that pending "turn," even though its members do not want to facilitate it. A similar thing has been shown by preceding tables.

A glance at the figures shows, further, that the patterns of the fluctuations are neither uniform nor periodical in time. They exhibit a wonderful diversity in both respects.

As to the why of these crescendoes and diminuendoes, generally determinism fluctuates parallel with the variables of the Sensate culture (truth of senses, materialism, increase of discoveries, temporalism, nominalism, visual art, and so on); indeterminism with those of the Ideational culture (truth of faith, ideational art, realism, idealism, and so on).

Finally, the Mixed indeterminism-determinism — mixed in the theories and mixed in the sense of a coexistence of both currents — seems to be typical of the Idealistic culture.

The dominant current in the field in Greece of the fifth and of the first half of the fourth century B.C., as well as in the Western culture of the thirteenth and fourteenth centuries, was "indeterministic determinism" in the sense of God or Destiny or some other superempirical power running the universe, but running it along "orderly lines," like a clock made and started by power. Such is the dominant conception of the Schoolmen of the thirteenth and fourteenth centuries, as well as of the Greek thinkers of the centuries mentioned. And such a parallelism is not incidental. We have seen that these periods resemble one another in the systems of truth, in idealism-materialism, in their art styles, and now they show similarity in this point also.

Concerning the recent period, 1880–1920, we see a slight recession of determinism (quantitatively). It seems to have been followed by a qualitative recession. The period from 1920 to 1957 has witnessed a further quantitative and qualitative decline of determinism. If, around the middle of the nineteenth century, the scientists and thinkers believed in a kind of "iron determinism," inexorable, invariable, rigid, and unavoidable in its necessity, in the twentieth century such an "iron determinism" has greatly softened: the inexorable, invariable, and necessary relationships have been more and more replaced by the standpoint of a mere probability that implies little, if any, "necessity," "inexorability," or even invariability. "Uniformity of relationship" between A and B, viewed from the standpoint of probability, is an enormous shift from the "rugged determinism" to its very liberal brand, which is quite close to a "conservative indeterminism." Causality is already largely replaced by: (a) Heisenberg's "principle of uncertainty"; (b) by chance or probabilistic uniformities in macrophysical world; (c) by fanciful "quanta jumps" in sub-atomic world; (d) by "free will," "voluntaristic decision," and "immanent self-direction" free from causality and chance in a large portion of psychosocial, human world. That is the standpoint of the majority of the leading scientists and thinkers of the present time.

This quantitative recession and qualitative softening of determinism is a sure sign of a "reaction" against the rugged determinism of the Sensate culture. It is a variety of revolt against the Sensate forms and variables, which we have met in practically all the variables studied at the end of the nineteenth and in the twentieth century. It reinforces the reality of the revolt in other compartments of culture and is sustained by these revolts in its own reality.

21

FLUCTUATION OF "FIRST PRINCIPLES": VII. FLUCTUATION OF THE LINEAR, CYCLICAL, AND MIXED CONCEPTIONS OF THE COSMIC, BIOLOGICAL, AND SOCIOCULTURAL PROCESSES

1. Introductory

"Whither Mankind?" and "Whither the World?" Whence did they start and where are they going? These questions have also been among the oldest and most basic problems of human thought. Many answers have been given. As shown in Chapter Four of Volume One, all these answers, from the standpoint of the problem, "whence and whither," can be grouped into the classes: (1) Linear, (2) Cyclical, and (3) Mixed, including in the Mixed also the erratically or variationally recurring conception. An explicit or implicit answer to these questions conditions the nature of thousands of theories in the more specific problems of science and human knowledge is one of the "First Principles" of science and human knowledge.

The appearance and success of the Darwinian and general linear theory of evolution in biology quite definitely determined the trend, the character, the solutions, and the whole orientation of the research and theories in thousands of very specific biological problems. Likewise, the similar success of the linear theory of social evolution and progress, especially after its formulation by Auguste Comte and Herbert Spencer, stamped quite definitely the whole field of the social sciences, oriented uncounted special theories along the linear principles of social evolution and progress, conditioned their nature and their application, and at one time threatened to reduce almost all sociology and most of the social sciences to an endless variation of the same theme of social evolution and progress, its stages, its trend, the traits of each stage, the level reached by this or that people, and so on, with the monotonous refrain: Glory to evolution and progress that leads mankind to never-ceasing betterment and perfection. If we imagine for a moment that such a conception had not risen, or had not been successful, we can rest assured that three quarters of the works, problems, and theories produced in the social sciences after Auguste Comte would never have appeared.

It is not my purpose to give in this chapter a detailed history of the fluctuation of the influence of each of the three main conceptions in this field. Space and time do not permit it, however fascinating the subject is, and however much I should like to do the work. Instead, in a very succinct form, I shall draw the most important lines of the "distribution in space," as well as swings in time, of each of the main conceptions. The main propositions relevant to the main topic of this work can be summed up as follows.

A. The linear, the cyclical, and the mixed conceptions fluctuate in their influence in the course of existence of the Graeco-Roman and the Western cultures.

B. These fluctuations are dependent, in a tangible degree, upon the fluctuation of the Ideational, Idealistic, and Sensate types of culture.

(1) The progressively linear conception of the course of the world, and especially of mankind, tends to rise with the rise of the Sensate culture. When it begins to be overripe and to decline, the progressively linear conception tends to be replaced by partly regressively linear or cyclical or trendlessly undulating, or various mixed theories.

(2) Certain types of cyclical, trendlessly undulating, and eschatological conceptions, with two or one "terminal" points of perfection, tend to be dominant in the periods and cultures of the mainly Ideational type. Namely, the types where the cycles and fluctuations are viewed not mechanically but as manifestations of the inner transformations experienced by the ultimate or true spiritual reality (God, Brahma, Providence, Tao, and the like). This means that not all the cyclical and undulating conceptions are claimed to have such an association. The theories that claim cycles and revolutions to be purely mechanical uniformities, similar to the revolutions of a motor, are not necessarily to be associated with the Ideational culture. Such theories are congenial either to the declining phase of Sensate culture or to the Mixed cultures generally.

(3) Finally, in the periods and culture of predominantly mixed type, all these theories, as well as theories mixed in their character, coexist and tend to be dominant.

Interpreted not too rigidly, with a number of exceptions admitted, these propositions seem to describe the "laws" of the distribution in social space and of pulsation in time of the conceptions discussed with rough accuracy. The minimum of commentaries and references to the relevant data follow.

II. Domination of the Cyclical and Trendlessly Undulating Theories in the Hindu and Chinese (and Babylonian) Cultures

A. *Hindu Culture Mentality.* Hindu culture has been predominantly Ideational, as we have seen. Whatever have been the streams of the linear conception of the course of the universe and mankind in Hindu thought, the dominant conception has been mainly cyclical or recurring. More than that. These cycles and recurrences are the manifestations of the transformations which the ultimate — spiritual — reality, say, Brahma or Vishnu, endlessly undergoes. In accordance with the nature of the transformation of the Ideational ultimate reality, the empirical cycles have a respective duration and character. In this characteristic the connection of the Ideational mentality with the cyclical-undulating conceptions comes out with particular clearness. There are several variations of this conception in various Hindu sources; but the above general character is found in all of them.

A typical and one of the most developed variants is given in the *Vishnu Puránâ.* Here are a few excerpts from it.

> Time effects the production and dissolution of all creatures. . . . At the period of creation, the god of gods creates; in that of duration, he preserves; and at the end (of all) he is mighty to annihilate.

> This creation and dissolution is incessantly repeated.

> The dissolution of everything is of four kinds: "occasional" (Naimittika); "elemental" (Prakritika); "absolute" (Atyantika); "perpetual" (Nitya). The first occurs when the sovereign of the world (Brahma) reclines in sleep. In the second, the mundane egg resolves into the primary elements whence it was derived. "Absolute" nonexistence of the world is the absorption of the sage (Yogin), through knowledge, into supreme spirit. "Perpetual" destruction is the constant disappearance, day and night, of all that are born.

More specifically: "Occasional" destruction takes place endlessly at the end of Brahma's day; it is the destruction of singularistic forms and creatures, but not of the substance of the world. "Elemental" means a periodic general resolution of the elements into their primary source or prakriti, and occurs at the end of Brahma's life. "Perpetual" is the imperceptible change that all things suffer in the various stages of growth and decay, life and death, produced by the irresistible stream of time taking everything away. Finally, the "absolute" destruction concerns the individual and his annihilation in the form of dissolution of the individual stage in the supreme spirit or ultimate reality. It is Moksha, exemption forever from future existence. "Occasional" dissolution occurs at the end of every Kalpa or Brahma's day. It is equal to 4,320,000,000 mortal years.

> At the end [of Kalpa] the earth is exhausted. A total dearth then ensues . . . and all beings perish. [The whole world in its concrete or sensory forms is also destroyed.] The world is now enveloped in darkness; and all things — animate and inanimate — having perished, the clouds continue to pour down their water for more than a hundred years. . . . When the universal spirit wakes [after its slumber], the world revives.

The "elemental" dissolution or cycle occurs at the end of Brahma's life. In it every element of the world — space, smell, color, form, flavor, sound, ether, matter, and all its properties; self, consciousness, mind, and all its properties — all is resolved. The true reality becomes Pure Supreme Spirit, "that spirit which is other than embodied spirit, in which there are no attributes of name, species or like, which is one with all wisdom, and is to be understood as sole existence."

It occurs once in 311,040,000,000,000 mortal years.

After this period of dissolution, The Pure Spirit again creates and incarnates itself into the material form, and so the cycles go on.

As to the course of mankind within these large periodicities of world cycles, it has shorter periodicities and cycles that endlessly continue. Within the shortest time span in the world pulsation, 4,320,000 mortal years, there are four ages that incessantly repeat themselves in the same sequence: the Krita Yuga (1,728,000 mortal years); the Treta Yuga (1,296,000 mortal years); the Dwapara Yuga (864,000 years); and the Kali Yuga (432,000 years).

The creation of the world takes place always in the Krita age, while its dissolution comes in the Kali age. The worst of these ages — the age of decline — is the Kali age. According to the *Vishnu Purâná*, beginning with about the fourteenth century B.C. the history of mankind entered the Kali age.

Here are a few characteristics of this age, so far as human culture is concerned.

The observance of caste, order, and institutes will not prevail in the Kali age [that is everything that is inconvenient and uncomfortable to the sensate individual] nor will that of the ceremonies [of religion]. Marriages, in this age will not be conformable to the ritual. . . . The laws that regulate the conduct of husband and wife will be disregarded; and oblations to the gods with fire no longer be offered. In whatever family he may be born, a powerful and rich man will be held entitled to espouse maidens of every tribe. [Religion will be disregarded.] Every text will be scripture, that people choose to think so . . . all gods will be gods to them that would like to worship them; and all orders of life will be common alike to all persons. . . . Wives will desert their husbands when they lose their property; and they only who are wealthy will be considered by women as their lords. He who gives away much money will be master of men; and family descent will no longer be a title of supremacy. . . . Accumulated treasures will be expended on ostentatious dwellings. The mind of men will be wholly occupied in acquiring wealth; and wealth will be spent solely on selfish gratifications. Women will follow their inclinations, and be ever fond of pleasures. Men will fix their desires upon riches, even though dishonestly acquired.

[The rulers will be] of churlish spirit, violent temper, and ever addicted to falsehood and wickedness. They will inflict death on women, children, and cows; they will seize the property of their subjects; they will be of limited power and will rapidly rise and fall . . . their lives will be short; their desires insatiable; and they will display but little piety. Earth will be venerated but for its mineral treasures. . . . Dishonesty will be the universal means of subsistence . . . menace and presumption will be substituted for learning . . . mutual assent will be marriage. . . . . Thus, in the Kali age, shall decay constantly proceed, until the human race approaches its annihilation. . . .

At its end there will appear a Brahman with superhuman faculties. He will destroy "all thieves and all those whose minds are devoted to iniquity. He will then reestablish righteousness upon earth." Then purified and awakened men "shall give birth to a race who shall follow the laws of the Krita age (or age of purity)." In this way the cycle returns again to the Krita age and then it is revolved again and again. Finally the sources indicate a short-time — five-year — period in which various political and religious events are repeated.

With some variations, this conception of the direction of the world's history, as well as of human history, goes, from the earliest to the later times, throughout the history of Hindu thought.

The whole conception is cyclical. Only within the long-time cycles there are shorter phases (like the four ages) during which there is a temporary linear trend, like the trend of creation and purity in the age of Krita, or degeneration and decline in the age of Kali. But these are temporary phases of the ever-repeated larger cycles, ending with the largest "elemental" cycle of dissolution of the whole material world into the immaterial spirit, the rematerialization of the spirit into the sensate form.

So far then, in the case of the Hindu (and also of the Buddhist and Jainist) culture, the formulated association of the Ideational culture mentality with the domination of the cyclical or endlessly undulating conception of the course of the world and mankind's history is well corroborated.

B. *Chinese Culture Mentality*. This, being partly Ideational (the ancient Chinese and the Taoist stream) and partly Mixed (the Confucianist stream), presents us with the coexistence of the cyclical or trendlessly recurrent and undulating conception with one partly linear and even progressively linear. The cyclical and endlessly undulating conception of the world course as well as of human history is represented, first of all, in the most basic theory of *eternal rhythm of the Yin and Yang*, and then in the prevalent, almost habitual, "cyclical" standpoint of Chinese traditional history in regard to the rise and fall of its various dynastics; the rhythm of integration and disintegration of China; the rise and decline of its prosperity and depression, its blossoming and decay, order and disorder, peace and war, and so on. All these and many other fluctuating processes are, after all, but special varieties of the eternal rhythm of the Yin and Yang. It stamps the Chinese historiography, philosophy of history, cosmogony, and all the relevant fields of Chinese thought: science, philosophy, religion, and ethics.

It would be superfluous to attempt to characterize here the complex and manifold meaning of the Yin and the Yang and of their rhythm.

The antithesis of the Yin and the Yang is neither that of two opposed Substances, nor two Forces, nor two Principles. It is simply the antithesis of two Emblems, more rich in their suggestive power than all of these.

Being such, they are opposed to and, at the same time, inseparable from one another. One calls forth, immanently, the other; engenders it.

The absolute moves and engenders Yang [fire, the sun disk, and other symbols]. The movement having reached its climax, rest ensues. From rest springs Yin [coiling clouds over the sun, water, and other symbols]; and when rest has reached its utmost limit, again movement follows. Thus we have alternately now movement, now rest.

The Ultimate Principle has operated through all eternity.

Cyclical also are all social processes. "Dynasties are founded, attain their zenith, decline, disappear . . . History assigns the same causes to the same effects." Parallel with this cycle of a dynasty, the people are virtuous and happy when the dynasty is rising and attaining its zenith; and they become violent and degenerated when it declines. And so does the whole culture and sociocultural life. The conception is but a special case of the general principle of endless alternation of the Yin and Yang. It corroborates the expectation that follows from the general diagnosis of Chinese culture as partly Ideational, partly Mixed, in our terms.

The expectation seems to be sustained also in regard to the Linear and Mixed conceptions that are to be expected from the Confucianist and other more Sensate streams in Chinese culture. The Confucianist theory of the three stages in the interpretation of many is indeed the linear theory of progressive evolution. According to it, mankind passes through three main stages in the course of time: the *Disorderly Stage*, with its anarchy, continuous warfare, primitive conditions, lack of efficient social control and other traits of a "primitive society"; the *Stage of Small Tranquillity*, characterized by the institutions of the family, private property, egotism, social instability, and other traits of a "capitalist society"; the *Stage of Great Similarity*, marked by social order, almost common property, mutual benevolence, and reverence.

Thus our expectation is well corroborated, considering the power of the stream of Confucianist thought in the cultural history of China and in Chinese mentality.

C. *Babylonian Culture Mentality.* The history and the nature of the Babylonian culture mentality is too little known for us to venture to apply this hypothesis to it. With this reservation, it is possible to note the fact that the cyclical conception of the course of world history seems to have been dominant there also. The fact itself being reasonably assured, it is somewhat uncertain as to whether these cycles were viewed mechanically, as a mere uniformity of the astrologico-astronomical nature (Sensates), or were regarded also as the manifestation of the spiritual ultimate reality. The first of these alternatives seems to be more probable than the alternative of an interpretation of the Babylonian cyclic theories in the Ideational sense. This conclusion is supported also by the nature of the theories which are based mainly upon purely astrological-astronomical foundations and depict the cycles (so far as the sources permit that to be said) as an immanent uniformity of the heavenly bodies and of the Sensate world as such.

The essentials of the old Babylonian cyclical conceptions concerning the course of the world in its existence are known to us mainly from Graeco-Roman sources, through the work of Berosos.

Main theories set forth by the old Babylonians in the field studied are as follows: First of all the theory of *annus magnus*, "the world's year" cycle in the life of the universe as well as of mankind. Its essence is thus described by F. Cumont.

> The existence of the universe is formed out of a series of "the great years," each having its summer and winter. Their summer comes when all the planets are in conjunction in the same point of Cancer, and it leads to a general conflagration; their winter arrives when all the planets are reunited in Capricornus, and it results in a universal flood. Each of these cosmic cycles, whose duration, according to the most authoritative computation, has been 432,000 years, is an exact reproduction of the preceding ones.
>
> The stars reassuming the same position must act in the same way. This Babylonian theory being an anticipation of that of "the eternal return of the things," whose discovery Nietzsche was so proud of, enjoyed a durable favor in antiquity and was transmitted in various forms up to the time of the Renaissance.

Since these conceptions assumed the dependence of human affairs upon the movement of stars and constellations, it follows that each of these cycles marks also a cycle in the course of mankind. The Mixed and largely Sensate character of the Babylonian culture mentality is associated with the "mechanico-astrological" cyclical conceptions of the direction of the world processes, and possibly of the processes of mankind's existence. With these reservations, the case of this culture seemingly does not contradict the propositions of this chapter.

III. Fluctuation of the Main Conceptions in Graeco-Roman and Western Cultures

A. The earliest Greek conception in the field known to us is Hesiod's regressively linear (though not quite that) theory of the succession of the Golden, the Silver, the Bronze, the Heroic, and the Iron ages.

Likewise, in Homer, there is a passage that depicts the past as better than the present.

Since the exact time when either Homer or Hesiod lived is unknown; and since the exact relationship between the Creto-Mycenaean and the Greek culture is also not quite certain, it is not possible to say anything definite about the relationship of these theories and the types of culture in which they (especially Hesiod's theory) were produced. If, however, Hesiod's time is somewhere between the eleventh and eighth centuries B.C., and if that period was the transitional period from the "overripe Sensate Creto-Mycenaean" to the Ideational culture of the centuries from the eighth to the sixth, then the regressive linear theory of Hesiod fits well the proposition made at the beginning of this chapter about some congeniality between such a transitory stage from the Sensate to the Ideational culture and the regressive linear conception of historical process.

B. The theories of the sixth and the first part of the fifth centuries are almost uniformly "cyclical" and most of them not only mechanically but "ideationally cyclical," viewing the endless rhythm behind these cycles as a manifestation of either spiritual or animated ultimate reality in the Sensate world and Sensate human history.

Such are the conceptions of Pythagoras and the Pythagoreans; of Alcmeon of Crotona, Oenopides of Chio, Philolaos, and others; of Herakleitos, Empedocles, Anaximander, Anaximenes, and practically almost all the theorists of the period in the field discussed. Almost no linear theory (except the repetition of Hesiod's theory) is known in that period. The idea of periodicity, long- and short-time cycles in which identically the same world and any element in it recurs ("numerically" or quite identical to it, if not exactly the same), seems to have been quite dominant. There is hardly any single fragment from that period that pleads the cause of the linear progressive conception. So far as the sixth and the beginning of the fifth centuries were predominantly Ideational (in the compartments we examined), the association of the Ideational mentality with the cyclical (nonmechanical) conception seems to be well sustained. Giving different formulation to the cyclical conceptions, the thinkers also give different numerical lengths for the span of various cycles, beginning with the longest (*annus magnus*) and ending with the shorter one. According to Censorinus's *De Die Natali* (probably in the third century A.D.) and the *Placita* of pseudo Plutarch, the great cycle of the *annus magnus* was, according to Aretas, 5552 years; Herakleitos, 18,000 years; Dion of Naples, 10,884 years; Orpheus, 100,020 years; according to others either of shorter or much longer periods.

C. As we proceed along the fifth and then to the fourth century, the cyclical conceptions still are prominent. Plato and Aristotle and their followers are still the bearers, in spite of the somewhat complicated character of the theories of both, and especially of Plato. Some change, however, is taking place. First, the regressive linear conceptions of Hesiodic type seem to have lost their prestige.

On the other hand, the progressively linear conceptions or, perhaps, motives, begin to make their appearance. In various forms, then, these "progressive" motives are found in the funeral oration of Pericles, in some of the tragedies of Aeschylus, in Euripides, in the fragments of Anaxagoras, in the Hippocratic writings, in Archelaus, Democritus, Protagoras, Critias, Timotheus, Philemon, and others. The outlook on human history becomes somewhat more optimistic and more "progressively linear," at least so far as comparison of the present with the past is concerned.

So far, in these centuries of the prevalent Idealistic culture, we see coexistence of the cyclical with the undeveloped (as yet) progressively linear, and with the remnants of the regressively linear beliefs. Such a mixture, together with the inner mixture of the elements of these conceptions in several theories, seems to agree with the statement made at the beginning of this chapter.

D. The third and the subsequent centuries B.C. and the first three centuries A.D. give here, as in other compartments of culture, a checkered picture, due partly to the rise of the Hellenistic centers, with Alexandria as the scientific one, the decline of Continental Greece and then the entrance of the Roman stream into the picture. As a result, we have a continuation of the undeveloped "progressively linear" conceptions and a revival of the cyclical or trendlessly undulating theories by the Stoics, Neo-Platonists, and others. At the same time, partly regressive, partly catastrophic theories of the end of the world began to emerge. Finally the Christian conception complicated the picture still more. Among the Greeks, the "eclectic progressively linear" statements continued to circulate (Philemon, Moschion, Athenio, Polybius, Diodorus Siculus, and others). Among the Romans rose the somewhat similar eclectic theories of Lucretius, Cicero, Varro, Virgil (partly), Horace, Cratius Faliscus, Vitruvius, Manilius, Pliny the Elder, Galenus, Celsus, and others. With the exception of Pliny the Elder, who expressed the linear progressive theory clearly by his famous: "Let no one lose hope that the ages will always grow better," none of these thinkers developed any consistent theory of progressive linearism. All were eclectic and in a sense inconsistent. The course of many social processes they viewed cyclically, like Polybius's cycle of the forms of government. This stream continued to flow after the beginning of our era, up to at least the fourth century A.D. (Macrobius and others). It seems to have been an expression of the optimistically Sensate mentality of the period.

The second stream that ran side by side with it was the revived (not without a diffusion of the astrology of the Orient), and step-by-step spiritualized, cyclical conception. It found its partisans among the Stoics and Neo-Platonists, the Neo-Pythagoreans, and some of the Gnostics (Zeno, Cleanthes, Chrysippus, Posidonius, Seneca, and later Stoics; Plutarch, Plotinus, Porphyry, Nigidius, Apuleus, Proclus, Asclepius, Nemesius, Manilius, Censorinus, Celsus, Philo, Claudius Ptolemy, Galenus, Julius Firmicus Maternus, Timon Magnus, Bardesanes, and others). All of these believed also in the existence of the Grand Year Cycle, as well as several shorter cycles. It is to be noted, however, that as we pass from the third century B.C. to the first centuries of our era, the cyclical conception tends to assume more and more spiritual forms until in the theories of Plotinus and other Neo-Platonists and Gnostics, the cycles of the sensory universe become mere manifestations of the Soul of the World, or its Intelligence.

The third current, not very noticeable in the third and second centuries B.C., was an "eclectic regressive" theory of the pending or actual decay of mankind. It assumed mainly the form of an unfavorable comparison of the present with the past, particularly with the remotest past, viewing the road taken by mankind as a downward one. Some admitted the hope of a future upgrade movement; but this was a secondary theme in their "music." Hyginus, Ovid, Tibullus, Statius, the Hermetic Corpus, Asclepius, and others are the representatives of this theory.

The early Christians, with their Apocalyptic and catastrophic beliefs in the end of the world, and an unbearable present, were perhaps the extreme upholders of this conception, with the difference that they added to it their eschatological belief in the coming of Christ and Christ's City of God.

Thus, in the transitory centuries, especially from the second B.C. to the fourth A.D., we find the coexistence of these three currents: one expressing the still lingering optimism of the decaying Sensate culture, especially from the third century B.C. to the first A.D., when the decay had progressed little as yet; another, the premonition and pessimism of its decline; the third — the cyclical — the generation and growth of the coming Ideational culture.

E. With the triumph of Christianity, we enter, after the fourth century A.D., the Ideational phase of European culture. The main changes in the field studied are: (1) *the rise of a specific eschatological conception of the world's and mankind's history;* (2) *the disappearance almost entirely of the linear — regressive as well as progressive — conception;* (3) *the domination of cyclical concepts of the course of mundane affairs between the two terminal points of the world's and mankind's existence, marked by the eschatological conception.* So far as the complete history of the world and of mankind is concerned, the Christian conception of it assumed a specific form. First, the empirical world and its duration in time, as well as time itself, was regarded as finite, having a beginning (Tertullian's *natum et factum*) and destined to have an end. Second, the initial point of this history and the final terminal point were both viewed as perfect: the Eden of Adam and Eve at the beginning and the City of God at the end, after the Last Judgment. The intermediate link, that is, practically the whole of human history, that lasts between the Fall and the Last Judgment, was viewed as something infinitely more degraded than the initial and the final terminal points. In this sinful and degraded *continuum*, there were admitted to be relative ups and downs, certain decisive and "progressive" points; nevertheless, no linear trend — progressive or regressive — that persists throughout all this period between the terminal points was contended or claimed.

This whole history of "the City of Man" is purely temporary. It "totters through the one transitory instability." "*All earthly things have their changes, revolutions, and dissolutions.*" No happiness is possible in their pursuit. Wealth does not give it. "He that is good is free, though he be a slave, and he that is evil, a slave though he be a king." Earthly kingdoms are "but fair thievish purchases"; great empires are but a piracy on a large scale; kings are but pirates and sword players. True Christians in this world are but pilgrims. Their permanent place is "the City of God."

> That city is eternal: no man is born in it because no man dies in it. Felicity is there fully, but no goddess, but a god's gift; of this habitation have we promise by faith, as long as we are here in pilgrimage on earth, and long for that rest above. The sun arises not there both upon good and bad, but the Sun of righteousness shines only over the good. . . .

This is "the end without end. For what other thing is our end, but to come to that kingdom of which there is no end. Amen."

Such is the main conception of Christianity that persisted throughout the Middle Ages. To such an eschatological mentality the whole empirical history of mankind and of the world was of comparatively little importance, as a passing, purely temporary thing.

Side by side and partly combined with it, so far as the empirical history between the terminal points is concerned, there flowed another current which interpreted the course of the mundane world as mainly cyclical or as trendlessly undulating. In a sense it continued the old astrological and cyclical conceptions.

The early Church Fathers well understood the incompatibility of the Christian *credo* with the eternal return of things, the eternal dissolution and rebirth of the universe and of everything in it, claimed by the theories of the *annus magnus.* They also understood well the incompatibility of astrology, with its absolute determination of man's conduct and all human history. Therefore, whether St. Basil, or Origen, or St. Gregory, or St. Augustine, they all were opposed to both, and took great pains to refute the cyclical theory of the Grand Year, as well as the astrological claim of the absolute dependence of man upon the heavenly bodies and their constellations.

And yet, even St. Augustine admitted the influence of the sun and the heavenly bodies upon the bodily aspects of men. Furthermore, some of the Church Fathers, like St. Clement of Alexandria, Minucius Felix, Arnobius, even Origen (partly), Bishop Theodoret, and a few others seem to have accepted from the previous astrological cyclical conceptions even more than this. Subsequently this stream continued, partly in the form of the nonastrological conception of cycles and periodicities; partly associated with it and tangibly permeated by the astrological theories of the *annus magnus* and other — shorter — periodicities.

The *Pseudo Clementines* and its Latin version the *Recognitiones; De mirabilibus Sacrae Scripturae* of Augustine of Hibernia (*c.* A.D. 660); John Chrysostom, Peter Abelard, Erigena (partly), Hugh of St. Victor, Roger Bacon, Adelard of Bath, William of Conches, Bernard Sylvester, Daniel of Morley, Roger of Hereford, Alexander Neckam (with his *annus magnus* of 36,000 years), the influential spurious works like *Theology, Book of Judgment*, and one of the "best sellers" of the Middle Ages, the *Secret of Secrets*, and many others shared this cyclical astrological conception.

As we come to the scholars of the thirteenth and the next two or three centuries, the astrologico-cyclical theories, influenced by the theories of some of the Arabian thinkers, tend to become more and more elaborated, and attempts are made to establish more and more correlations of human affairs with the cosmic and geographic (astrologico-astronomical) factors and respective periodicities along the lines not unlike the theories set forth by C. Ptolemy in his famous *Tetrabiblos* (in the second century A.D.). Scholars like Michael Scot, William of Auvergne, Thomas of Cantimpré, Bartholomew of England, Robert Grossteste, Gilbert, Albertus Magnus, Dante (in his *Convivio*), St. Thomas Aquinas, Roger Bacon, Siger of Brabant, Peter of Abano, William Ockham, Nicolas of Bonet, and many others, in various ways subscribed to the theory that these cycles and periodicities in the history of the world, as well as in human history, were caused by the influence of the heavenly bodies and their conjunctions, operating either as the instruments of God's will or — and this tendency becomes more and more prominent — immanently, at the virtue of their own uniformities.

In this way, a number of periodicities and fluctuations were set forth in the movement of vital processes (births, deaths, marriages, epidemics, health), forms of government, war and peace, catastrophes and happy periods, prosperity and depression, revolutions, and other social processes.

Thus, summing up the main features of the Ideational medieval period, we see that the eschatological (with the two "terminal perfect points") conception and the cyclical or endlessly undulating conceptions occupied the field. Little, if any, attention was paid to the linear conception, of either regressive or progressive variety. So far, the propositions set forth seem to be corroborated by this period also.

F. As we move from the thirteenth to the next three centuries, these two streams — the eschatological and the cyclical or trendlessly undulating — continue to occupy almost the whole field. There appear, however, several changes, slight and not spectacular, but nevertheless quite tangible. First, no clear-cut linear theory appeared; none the less, the linear — progressive — motive, especially in regard to the progress of arts and sciences and technique, began to sound more distinctly and more frequently, beginning with the twelfth century. In the works of Hugh St. Victor, then St. Thomas and Albertus Magnus, Joachim de Floris, Roger Bacon, Vincent de Beauvais, and several others, these motives are already quite noticeable. Some of them were like Joachim's; he set forth in his theory of the Eternal Gospel, something like a progressively linear law of the "three stages of Humanity": the stage of the Old Testament, of the New, and of the Eternal Gospel, each stage being more perfect than the preceding one: the first being the stage of law and fear or intimidation; the second that of grace and faith; the third that of love.

This fact is important for us because it shows once more the Idealistic character of the mentality of these centuries which we have met several times in other compartments of its culture. The progressively linear ideas, as an ingredient of the Sensate mentality, appear here and give to it Idealistic color.

The next change is in the internal character of these eschatological and cyclical conceptions, compared with that of the earlier period. The eschatological theories began to decrease in popularity, while the factual course of human history and that of the world began to attract greater attention. The cyclical and trendlessly undulating theories tended to be elaborated more and more, and, as mentioned, the cycles, the periodicities, the fluctuations and recurrences began to be interpreted more and more "immanently"; as a manifestation of the properties of the universe and heavenly bodies as such, or of that of the empirical qualities of man and society.

Now treatises on astrology — enormous volumes — were flourishing and being published in great numbers. Their authors — usually "teachers of mathematiks and astrology" — explained all "mutations" of social life — political, religious, literary, scientific, etc. — as occurring mainly through the influence of the heavenly bodies. They repeated the earlier theories of periodicities in human history; computed and forecasted them; predicted the future of an individual and group; in brief, with slight variation and with indefatigable energy, they repeated what had been said many times before and is known to us from the above. As is well known, among these astrologers there were several great scientists, like Tycho Brahe, Kepler, Cardanus, not to mention other names.

When we approach the end of the fifteenth and enter the sixteenth century, we notice that the cyclical and trendlessly undulating theories continue to have the front-stage position, some of them detached from the astrological basis; at the same time, new progressively linear motives begin to be heard in crescendo, continuing and enlarging their beginnings of the twelfth and thirteenth, and their stream of the fourteenth and fifteenth century.

G. Beginning with the seventeenth century, we are in a rapidly rising tide of the progressively linear conception of human history — Fontenelle, L'abbé de Saint-Pierre, Montesquieu, Voltaire, Turgo, Shaftesbury, Mandeville, G. P. Turnbull, D. Hartley, Hume, A. Ferguson, A. Smith, Price, Priestley, Paley, the Encyclopedists, Condorcet, Lessing, Herder, Kant, and others. In hundreds of forms this conception begins to rise: in literature, science, philosophy, political writings, social theories. A few, and perhaps the greatest voices, still continue to advocate the cyclical conceptions, like G. B. Vico and some others; nevertheless, the day of cyclical, trendlessly undulating, regressive linear theories, and of Christian eschatological conceptions, was over. These concepts all begin the course of decline. The rising sun is the sun of progressive linearism.

After Turgot, Lamarck, Condorcet, and then Saint-Simon and Auguste Comte in France; Lessing, Kant, and Herder in Germany; the English Deists, Spencer, Darwin, and other prominent thinkers, the idea of linear evolution progress (or uniform sequence of stages arranged linearly) was the dominant category in the mentality of the eighteenth and especially of the nineteenth century.

This conception became especially dominant in the field of biological and social and humanistic sciences and theories. In biology, after Lamarck, Milne, Edwards, Spencer, and Darwin, the linear conception of the direction of the life process in unilinear, fluctuating, spiral, or branching varieties became almost unanimously accepted, under the name of evolution of life or biological evolution. It continues to be dominant up to the present time.

Similar linear conceptions have been dominant also in the field of the social, humanistic, and other sciences dealing with man and his culture. Sociologists, historians, economists, political scientists, and even theologians of the eighteenth and nineteenth and twentieth centuries, have indefatigably been manufacturing by dozens these theories of progress "from caveman or ape or even amoeba to modern man," seeing it as a progress from ignorance to science; instinct to reason; disorderliness to order; wretchedness to the "three-car-per-family" standard of living; fetishism to monotheism; promiscuity to monogamy (or vice versa, according to the preferences of an author); despotism to liberty; the *Gemeinschaft* to *Gesellschaft;* "mechanical to organic solidarity"; from imperfectly revealed religion to more fully revealed; inequality to equality; and so on and so forth. Or in the form of various "laws of stages": three, four, five, six, seven, or more, through which mankind as a whole, or its knowledge, or its economic organization, or its family, or its art or what not, have supposedly been passing and are destined to pass. These linear — and mostly progressively linear — conceptions flooded the social and humanitarian sciences; became their chief topic, their main ordering principle; the main perspective in which everything else and all the "facts" have been viewed. "Progress" and its derivatives became the main category of these sciences in the nineteenth century particularly.

All this is so well known and is so unquestionable that there is no need to give quotations and references.

To sum up, *in so far as the period from the fifteenth to the twentieth century has been that of the rise and triumph of the Sensate mentality and culture, the parallel rise and triumph of the progressively linear conception in the evolution of life and mankind well supports the proposition as to the association of progressive linearism with rising Sensate culture.*

IV. The Beginning of Reaction

As we approach the end of the nineteenth and pass into the twentieth century, we notice a slight, perhaps, but hardly doubtful, tendency of re-emergence and then growth of the cyclical and trendlessly undulating conceptions, partly in regard to the direction of the life processes, and especially in regard to that of sociocultural processes. In the field of biology, the tendency manifested itself in an increasing criticism and rejection of many previously unquestioned traits of the Darwinian evolution theory, meaning by this not only Darwin's, but that of the powerful current that made Darwinism its flag and symbol. Survival of the "fittest" began to be interpreted more and more critically in the sense that those who survive are not necessarily the best and fittest; that therefore the line of evolution is not necessarily so linear, especially the progress line; that there are many reversals, deviations, and other byways that make the linear route not so certain; that the whole theory has many points that are not so settled as they first appeared to be; that even the ancestral line and "tree of life evolution" is a conjecture rather than an ascertained fact, and so on. Likewise, the basic points of the theory began to be more and more questioned: the role of the struggle for life; the mechanical ways of variation; their fixation by heredity; the role of heredity and environment; and hundreds of other points. To sum up: the net results have been, so far, an increasing criticism of an ever-growing number of the facets of the theory of evolution; an increasing questioning of its linearity and its identification with progress. Parallel with that, an interest began to grow in the theory of short- and long-time cycles in the diverse vital processes, beginning with the "cycles of epidemics" and "latent and kinetic" stages of various micro-organisms, and ending with the life cycles of vital processes among many species. In other words, in the biology of the end of the nineteenth and of the early twentieth centuries, there seems to have appeared a slight tendency toward the weakening of the previous linear conception of life evolution and an increase of interest toward the recurrent, cyclical, and trendlessly undulating pulsations of life phenomena.

In the field of the social and humanitarian sciences, this tendency has expressed itself more clearly and conspicuously than in biology. The end of the nineteenth and the beginning of the twentieth centuries are marked by a *definite decline of the theories of the uniform sequences of stages through which various societies pass in their life process.* This theory at the present moment is practically dead; neither sociologists nor anthropologists nor respectable social scientists of the present moment, in an overwhelming majority, subscribe to this variety of the linear conception, so popular in the nineteenth century (it probably had its zenith around 1860–1900). Its decline means the decline of various linear conceptions.

The second symptom of the same decline is the progressively increasing attention of the social scientists to the "cyclical," "recurrent," "fluctuating," and "undulating" aspects of the sociocultural processes. If the economists of the nineteenth century were very busy with the "economic stages of development" (Roscher, Hildebrand, Bücher, Schmoller, and others), at the present time economists are mainly busy with business "cycles, fluctuations, oscillations," and recurrences. The situation is similar in almost all the social and humanitarian sciences. At the present moment there are few, if any, of the leading specialists in anthropology, sociology, law, ethics, political science, psychology, history, social philosophy, or history of religion who are devoting their main time and energy to works in which they aim to formulate the respective "uniform sequence of stages" through which, by the order of evolution progress, all societies and cultures supposedly pass in the course of time. That was the main business of the scholars and scientists busy with "social dynamics and progress" in the nineteenth century. Instead, the "cyclical" or "fluctuating" aspect of these processes is beginning to attract their attention more and more. In brief, linearism in this form is also fading.

The third symptom is *the emergence and rapid growth of the literature and theories that try to formulate the nonlinear conceptions of sociocultural processes and, what is still more important, the success which such theories are beginning to have.*

The meaning of the second part of this statement is illustrated by the attention which Nietzsche's enunciation of the theory of the eternal cycles at the end of the nineteenth century received, and by the success which works like Spengler's *Decline of the West* had, as well as by the impression it made. Hardly any single work along the lines of the linear evolution-progress theory published after 1914, or even perhaps in the twentieth century, has had as much influence.

As to the increase of the literature that stands for the cyclical, or trendlessly undulating, and generally nonlinear conception of the course of sociocultural processes, this is hardly questionable. As a matter of fact, beginning with the second half of the nineteenth century, it has already grown to such an extent that a special monograph is needed to enumerate it and to give a brief account of the theories involved.

When all this is considered, the statement about the growth of the cyclical literature at the end of the nineteenth and in the twentieth centuries, and especially in the postwar period, would be acceptable. These three symptoms are sufficient to warrant a decline of the linear conceptions in the cultural and social sciences at this time.

This again is a variety of the revolt against the overripe Sensate culture we met in other compartments of this period. Its fact is reinforced by the other facts of the revolt, and it reinforces them in its turn.

V. Conclusion

The above sketch is very concise but I hope it is roughly accurate in tracing the main swings and distributions in the field of this "First Principle." It makes reasonably certain three conclusions: (1) that the comparative influence of each of the main conceptions is different in different cultures; (2) that in the life history of the same culture this influence fluctuates; (3) that the influence or acceptability or creditability of each conception depends greatly upon the character of the dominant mentality of a given culture at a given period. Less certain, but hardly misleading, is the fourth proposition, namely, the tentative correlations established between the Ideational and Sensate cultures and between the types of the conceptions favored by each of these types of cultures, and therefore, tending to become influential in it. The factual study along the lines briefly outlined in this chapter plus several logical considerations seem to make these propositions probable. Thus validity or invalidity of each of these conceptions is, like the other First Principles mentioned above, a matter of the predominant type of culture. All the conclusions made in preceding chapters apply also to this "category" of human thought.

22

FLUCTUATION OF THE BASIC CATEGORIES OF HUMAN THOUGHT: CAUSALITY, TIME, SPACE, NUMBER

I. Introductory

Preceding chapters have shown that with the change of the main types of culture and their systems of truth, the "First Principles" of human thought — scientific and philosophical — change also in their influence, acceptability, and verity and prestige. In this chapter I am going to pursue this idea further. With the change of the type of culture, not only do the first principles change, but a deep transformation of their meaning is experienced also by the *basic categories of human thought* such as *time, space, number, causality*, that are indispensable for any cognition of any phenomena. Some of these transformations possibly are independent of our main variables — the types of culture and their systems of truth. Some others seem to have a tangible connection with the rise and fall of each type of culture and are, therefore, included in the thousands of details that undergo modification with the respective modification of the dominant type of culture.

II. Fluctuation of Ideational and Sensate Conceptions of Causality

Contrary to the prevalent opinion, the terms *Time*, *Space*, *Number*, *Causation*, and their derivatives, do not have the same meaning in different cultures. The "time" of the Ideational mentality is profoundly different from that of the Sensate; though Ideational and Sensate time both belong to the Category of Time. The same is true of Ideational and Sensate space, number, causality, and several other categories.

Ideational as well as Sensate mentality admits that *each fact or phenomenon has a cause or reason* for its existence. But as to what this cause is, and where, in the field of the supersensory or sensory phenomena, it is to be looked for, these mentalities differ greatly. Logically it is to be expected that the Ideational mentality will look for the cause or reason (*causa sive ratio*, as Descartes and others used to put it) in the Ideational world that lies behind or above the illusionary world of the senses, while the Sensate mentality has to seek the cause in the field of the sensory phenomena and nowhere else. Logically it is to be expected, further, that for the Sensate mentality the second principle of causation — "the same causes are followed by the same effects" — is in a sense inevitable; otherwise the causal relationship itself would be imperceptible and undistinguishable from the incidental *post hoc ergo propter hoc* or mere spatial or temporal contiguity and succession of the respective facts.

Different is the situation in regard to the Ideational mentality. The supersensory nature of its cause (God, devil, Providence, Brahma, etc.) makes it unnecessary to claim that the same cause is to be followed by the same effects. "The will of the God is inscrutable"; the spiritual, creative, and free nature of the supersensory causative agent permits it to create an effect A and B and C and N — in brief, any effect.

If, then, the first principle of causality that everything has a cause or reason is acceptable to both the Ideational and Sensate mentality, the second principle of causality, invariability of the causal relationship between the cause and effect, is almost unavoidable for the Sensate and unnecessary for the Ideational conception of causality.

When the problem of causality is studied from this standpoint, the essential results may be summed up in the form of the following propositions.

(1) *There have been two profoundly different conceptions of causality, Ideational and Sensate, with several intermediary types.* The Ideational mentality looks for the cause in the supersensory world; the Sensate in the Sensate world; the Idealistic and the Mixed mentalities look for it in both the Ideational and Sensate domains.

(2) *These two different conceptions (plus the Intermediary ones) have been struggling with each other for domination in various cultures and in various periods of the life process of the same culture mentality.*

(3) *In essentials, in the dominant Ideational culture mentality, the Ideational conception of causality tends to be dominant; in the dominant Sensate culture mentality, the Sensate conceptions prevail; the dominant Idealistic mentality is marked by an intermediary or Mixed conception of causality.*

These deductions follow logically from the nature of the main types of mentality. Are they corroborated factually? An attentive study of the problem seems to answer the question positively. A brief résumé of the relevant facts follows.

A. *Mixed Idea of Causality among Primitive Peoples.* The works of anthropologists and sociologists, and especially of L. Lévy-Bruhl, have made it clear that a kind of Ideational conception of causality is widespread among them. On the other hand, contrary to the one-sided claim of Lévy-Bruhl, the idea of the Sensate causality is also not absent among them. Ideational conceptions come out in many forms, like the following:

Often in the primitive societies the deaths, most "natural" in our eyes, are accounted for by mystic causes. . . . Thus . . . death by a poisonous snake's bite is generally considered due to the snake being influenced by a sorcerer. . . .

[In these and numerous facts of this type] the mentality does not consent to be satisfied on the plan of the (sensory) experience. It goes beyond it in establishing the liaison between the visible (sensory) effect and invisible (supersensory) cause, rightly says Brunschvicg.

The very existence of magic and supersensory religion among the "primitive" and "prehistorical" peoples, in the form of belief in this or that deity, or in the supersensory power; in ceremonies of religious and magical character; in forms of sorcery; in shamanism; even in such a specific system of evidences as ordeals in deciding the question of guilt and innocence; in divination; and in hundreds of similar mores, institutions, and customs widely diffused among practically all the "primitive," "prehistorical," and earlier stages of the "historical" peoples — all this is an incontestable evidence of the existence of a variety of the Ideational conception of causality.

On the other hand, it is erroneous to think that only this conception is known to these peoples, and that all of them are equally Ideational in this respect. However little the question is studied, two things seem to be clear: first, that all or most of these primitive and prehistoric peoples have also a Sensate form of causality applied to many daily experiences where the connection between the phenomena is explained sensately and "experientially" as a result of the "natural" properties of the "variables" involved; second, that the relative influence of Ideational and Sensate conceptions varies from people to people and is not constant among all the groups.

B. *Chinese Mixed Causality.* Diagnosing Chinese culture mentality several times, we have diagnosed it as Mixed in the sense that it includes the two mentalities: Taoist (Ideational) and Confucianist (Mixed); and in the sense of the existence of theories and conceptions wherein Ideational and Sensate elements are mixed. The same is the conclusion to which we must arrive in the question of causality conception.

Mythical thought, and with it, the different techniques that are used for an appropriate control of the World, are penetrated by a belief that the realities are influenced (*suscitées*) by emblems. Viewing Tao as the Principle of Order that rules equally the mental activity as well as the life of the World, they admit uniformly that the changes in the course of the realities (*choses*) are identical with the substitutions of symbols in the course of thought. This axiom once admitted, neither the principles of causality nor that of contradiction can be invoked to take the role of the directive principles. This is not because the

Chinese thought enjoys confusion, but, on the contrary, because the idea of Order — and of the Order that is efficacious and totalitarian — dominates it, engulfing in itself the notion of causality and of class. . . . Instead of registering the succession of the phenomena, they register the alternations of aspects. If two aspects appear to them related it is not a relation of cause and effect; they appear to them to be like the two sides of cloth; or sound and echo; or shadow and light. . . . What they like to notice are not the causes and effects but (the order of the apparition being unimportant) the singular manifestations that are offshoots of the same root. Equally symptomatic, these manifestations appear to be substitutive (for one another). River that dries up; mountain that slides down; man that changes into woman — these announce the approaching end of a dynasty. Here we have four aspects of the same phenomenon: an order destined to disappear, giving place to a new order. Each aspect deserves to be noted as the premonitory sign or a confirmation of a sign (or of a series of signs), but nothing invites us to seek for an efficient cause. . . .

All the changes of the emblems and realities are accounted for, not by causality or causes, but by Tao, and then by the derivative principles of the Yin and Yang.

These lines show a peculiarly Mixed conception of what serves in lieu of causality. This conception has a large part of the Ideational elements: mental emblems influencing or being in a mystical *rapport* with things and events; premonitory signs — mostly rare, queer, and physically unrelated to the phenomena — viewed, as related, most intimately; the supersensory Tao and the Yin and Yang as the responsible Total, whose expressions are these signs. These elements by their very nature are outside of the Sensate world in the proper sense of this term. On the other hand, we are told that:

These dispositions of their thought have not hindered the ancient Chinese from manifesting their great mechanical aptitudes. . . . The perfection of their arcs and their carriages is an evidence of that. . . . In its other aspect their thought is animated by a passion of empiricism which predisposes it to the minutest observation of the concrete that has led it to such fruitful results [discoveries in pharmacopoeia, chemistry, agriculture, etc.]

Without continuing this characterization, the above shows well two elements — Ideational and Sensate — in the Chinese conception of causality, Mixed in the sense of coexistence of both in their culture, and Mixed in a peculiar combination within the same theory or conception. So far the proposition seems to be not contradicted by the data.

C. *Hindu Ideational Conception of Causality.* Being predominantly Ideational in all other compartments, the Hindu mentality is also predominantly Ideational in the field of the present problem. The character of the Vedas, other sacred sources, and the dominant philosophy of India, beginning with the Upanishads and ending with other main currents of the philosophical thought, make this hardly questionable. Real cause in all these sources is supersensory. Even the course of nature, of the world, and of its great and small cycles are but manifestations of the supersensory power, be it Brahma or other such agency. The rites and religious and magic ceremonies testify to the same. Behind the illusionary appearance of the Sensate phenomena, there operate non-Sensate forces, whatever their names. They are the reality and the real causes or forces that rule the phenomenal world and control it.

D. *Fluctuation of the Conception of Causality in the Graeco-Roman and Western Thought.* The main phases through which the conception passed may be summed up as follows.

(1) The Greek thought before the fifth century B.C. was dominated by a kind of Ideational conception of causality. Destiny, and the gods, and other supersensory agencies determined and controlled the fate of men and groups, and the course of events of the phenomenal world.

(2) Beginning with the second half of the sixth, and throughout the fifth and the fourth centuries B.C., the Greek conception of causality becomes less Ideational, more Sensate, and assumes the form of the Mixed conception; and among the Mixed, the Idealistic conception of causality becomes paramount.

This conclusion follows from the study of the causality or its substitutes in the Pythagorean stream of thought, in the works of Empedocles, Pindar, Aeschylus, Euripides, Aristophanes, Herodotus, Thucydides, and several other prominent thinkers of the period, and culminates in the Idealistic conception of Plato and Aristotle and their schools.

E. *From the End of the Fourth Century* B.C. *to the Beginning of Our Era.* This period is marked by the Stoic and Epicurean schools which represented the most powerful currents of the philosophico-scientific thought (philosophy for that period still embraced in itself science). The Cynics, the Skeptics, and a few other groups were present; but they were either secondary in influence or, like the Skeptics, occupied a "nihilistic" position toward science generally and causality in particular; therefore they can be passed by. So far as the causality of the Stoics and Epicureans is concerned, they took from the two streams of Platonian-Aristotelian thought, Sensate and Ideational — mainly the first.

This Sensate trend is still more noticeable in the conception of causality by the Epicurean school.

In brief, the period is marked, in this special field, by some increase of the Sensate mentality. It also agrees with the proposition that the dominant conception of causality is conditioned by the dominant type of culture mentality of the period.

F. *From the Beginning of the First to the Fourth Century* A.D. The period from the beginning of our era up to the fourth century A.D. was here, as in other compartments of culture, transitory: most diverse conceptions — Ideational and Sensate and Mixed — existed side by side in the Stoic, Epicurean, Neo-Platonic, Neo-Pythagorean, and Christian currents of thought. The trend, however, was toward a rise of the Ideational causality, not only in the Christian but in Neo-Platonic (Plotinus, Jamblichus, Proclus, and others) and other currents.

G. *From the Beginning of the Fifth to the End of the Twelfth Century* A.D. Around the fifth century A.D. this rise ended in a complete victory of the Christian Ideational conception of causality that continued to dominate almost up to the end of the twelfth century. The essentials of this conception can be summed up in the following propositions.

(1) The first and the last, the final and the efficient, in brief, the only real cause of anything is God. Everything that happens or does not happen, exists or does not exist, is God's will, created by him, and controlled by him.

(2) God's will is, in application to man, to grant him free will and make him responsible for himself and his conduct.

(3) A number of nonmaterial and spiritual agencies, like angels and the like, are participating in the production and change of the phenomenal world, but as the agencies of God.

(4) The omnipotence of God precludes an impossibility of "miracles" or the necessity of achieving the same effects through the same causes. Though He may will to establish an order in the phenomenal world and "natural laws" and "uniformities," they can be removed or replaced by quite different relationships if the inscrutable ways of God find it advisable. Respectively, the very contrast between the "natural" and "the miracle" did not appear to that mentality as great a contrast as it did to the Sensate mentality.

H. *From the End of the Twelfth to the Fourteenth Century.* When we approach the end of the twelfth, and then pass to the thirteenth and the fourteenth centuries, a tangible change becomes noticeable. The penetration of the influence of Arabian thinkers, plus the translation and circulation of many works of Aristotle previously little known, undoubtedly contributed to it, though they were neither the only nor the main reason. In few words, this change can be accurately characterized *as a replacement of the Ideational conception of causality by the Mixed and, particularly, Idealistic idea.* This follows merely from the fact that the dominant conception now became the Aristotelian conception of the fourfold causality, and partly the Platonic twofold conception of it. These two conceptions, with some variations, came to be shared by almost all the thinkers of this period.

In brief, here again we meet the same situation which we met in the theory of truth: the thirteenth and the fourteenth centuries reproduce here, as in many other fields, the Greek thought of the fifth and fourth centuries B.C. Both periods appear Idealistically minded.

I. *From the Fifteenth to the Twentieth Century.* When we come to the subsequent centuries, we find that their trend consists of a further decline of the Ideational conception of causality and a rise of Sensate conceptions. This trend realized itself in many ways. First, scientists began to press more and more the Sensate causality. Through the works of Galileo, Gassendi, Pascal, Kepler, Newton, and other great scientists of the sixteenth, the seventeenth, and the subsequent centuries, the triumph of the Sensate causality was greatly facilitated.

Secondly, the thinkers and philosophers moved in similar directions. The problem of the First Cause and transcendental causality generally began to receive less and less attention; while the study of the empirical causality of the empirical phenomena began to acquire progressively increasing importance. God as a final cause was left only in the respectable position of a nominal ruler.

> We must examine not the final but the efficient causes of created things. . . . We will not seek reasons for natural things from the end which God or nature proposed to himself in the creation [of the world, and we will entirely reject from our philosophy the search of final causes], for we ought not to presume so far as to think that we are sharers in the counsels of Deity; but, considering him as the efficient cause of all things, let us endeavor to discover by the natural light [faculty of reasoning] . . . what must be concluded regarding those effects we perceive by our senses . . .

Thus, in most polite form, the whole transcendental or Ideational causality was dismissed and replaced by a purely Sensate one: the necessary relationship between the empirical phenomena "perceived by our senses."

However different in several points are the theories of Malebranche, Berkeley, or Leibnitz from Descartes's conception, and from one another's, in this main point — respectful retirement of the Ideational cause to the position of an "Emeritus" and enthronement in its place of the Sensate causality — they all share equally.

Thus the empirical world was not only freed from any interference of any superempirical agency but was even declared to be subjected to purely mechanical laws.

Finally, when Kant produced his cleansing criticism, his relegation of the category of causality to the class of "forms of our mind" represented a dilution of the transcendentalism of the "retired Emeritus" (before it was God and the like), and a complete justification of the purely empirical, purely Sensate causality.

In these ways the tide of the Sensate causality was rapidly rising, especially after the sixteenth century; and at the end of the eighteenth century there was little left of the Ideational causality. In the nineteenth century it almost drove it entirely from the highway of scientific and philosophical thought.

The general notion of the Sensate causality of the period studied is contained in the statement that always and everywhere, where A is given, B is given — either coexisting with A or following A. If the relationship of A and B is one-sided (A always precedes B) the causal relationship is one-sided; A is the cause and B the effect. If it is two-sided, A and B always are given together, but we cannot say which is the cause and which is the effect, the causal relationship there is two-sided; or, as they say, functional, meaning by this the causal relationship of a two-sided character.

The formulas that discover and describe such relationships are called the causal or functional formulas or causal and functional laws. Montesquieu's definition that "Laws, in their most general signification, are the necessary relations arising from the nature of the things" or Auguste Comte's definition of laws as "the invariable relations of succession and resemblance" discovered through reasoning and observation, or the still more current formula of laws as "the uniformities," are samples of what is meant by causal-functional laws and relationships.

In other respects, various factions of Sensate causality have, however, differed greatly. First, *the nature of the causal bond has been represented differently*. By some, like Lagrange, Joseph Fourier, D. Bernoulli, Maxwell, K. Pearson, and most of the statisticians, it is considered purely *functionally or mathematically*, as probablistic relationship or chance uniformity, without any further inquiry as to why it is so or what lies behind this purely quantitative uniform relationship.

Some, like the Cartesian school, Fresnel, and others, represented it purely *mechanistically* as a bond due to the *continuity of motion* resulting in a uniform relationship between cause and effect. Still others represented it *dynamically*, where the causal liaison implies the existence of forces which bind the cause and effect into a uniform unity.

As we move from the seventeenth to the twentieth century, *the functional-mathematical interpretation has tended to increase at the cost of the mechanistic or dynamic*. Due to development of positivism, agnosticism, criticism, empiricism, the problem of what lies behind the quantitative uniformity has been regarded as more and more "metaphysical," and the mere quantitative description of the relationship as probablistic has been thought of as the only task of science and the only aspect having scientific value.

In connection with other tendencies mentioned further on, this has resulted in the contemporary reduction of the causality to probability, and to the mathematical calculation of it, from the loose "correlational" associations with the low coefficients of the correlations, up to the formulas with the high coefficient of probability and therefore more perfect association of the variables. Why the association is loose or close — this question is not set forth, no attempt is made to answer it, and it is regarded as "metaphysical."

The Sensate conceptions of causality differ also in regard to the assumption or nonassumption of the category of *necessity* as an element of the causal relationship. For many, beginning with Descartes, Newton, Leibnitz, and most of the thinkers of the seventeenth, eighteenth, and of the first part of the nineteenth centuries, including even such "occasionalists, solipsists, and associationalists" as Malebranche and Hume, as well as Kant and the Kantian criticism, mere "association" or "correlation" or, in the excellent terms of Hume, mere "contiguity and succession" of A and B is not enough to elevate such an association into the causal relationship. In addition, this association has to be a *necessary* connection. Without it, every *post hoc* would be *propter hoc*, the causal relations would be undistinguishable from incidental associations.

Others — and such are many of the functional-mathematical interpreters and, of course, most of the contemporary statisticians and most of the pure "empiricists" and "positivists" — do not demand the category of necessity as an element of causal relationship. For these such a category is also bad metaphysics, not given in our sensory experience, unobservable, and introducing only a speculative entity into the "scientific concepts." Remaining on the plane of probability, they distinguish only the uniformities with a high and low degree of probability; and respectively, express it through the value of the coefficient of probability or correlation on a scale from 0 to 1, one being the highest probability, zero being an index of the lack of any association between the variables. The reasons for such a position are different with different partisans of this faction, but the trait is common to many. As a matter of fact, *as we move from the seventeenth to the twentieth century, this second conception of causality, devoid of an implication of necessity and reduced to high probability association, has been more and more driving out the first one, especially beginning with the second half of the nineteenth century.*

In the chapter on the fluctuation of determinism and indeterminism, the great contrast between the causal conception of the eighteenth century and that of the end of the nineteenth was pointed out. Then, as the formula of Montesquieu shows, even the civil laws were considered as "the necessary relations arising from the nature of things"; now even the laws of nature are considered as mere associations. There is a great difference between the causal relationship and causal law understood as *necessary* and the causal relationship and law understood as a mere association with higher and lower probability, more or less frequently met, but devoid of anything related to the idea of necessity. In subatomic world even the chance uniformities are declared to be doubtful and are replaced by fanciful "quanta jumps." For these reasons our age is declared to be the age of "Causal Catastrophy" in modern physics. This is reinforced by the contention that in the field of "ego" and psycho-social phenomena the voluntaristic principle of self-direction — free from chance and causality — is the law.

All this means that at the present time we have a successful revolt against classical sensate causality and the first symptoms of a new Ideational or Idealistic conception. Here again we meet the revolt against the sensate order observed before in other problems discussed.

The foregoing concise sketch of the main transformations of the conception of causality and of the rise and fall of the influence of the Ideational and Sensate forms of it, shows that such fluctuation has indeed been going on; that the predominantly Ideational cultures and periods create Ideational causality; in the predominantly Sensate, the Sensate conception becomes dominant; while in the Mixed and Idealistic mentalities, the Mixed and Idealistic causality rises. So far the propositions of this chapter as well as of the preceding chapters are corroborated by the facts.

III. Fluctuation of Ideational and Sensate Conceptions of Time, Space and Number

What is said of causality can be said of another category of our thought, *time.* In regard to it we all can repeat St. Augustine's: *Quid est ergo tempus? Si nemo ex me querat, scio; si quaerenti explicare velim, nescio.* "What then is time? If no one asks me, I know; if I wish to explain it to one that asketh, I know not." For my purposes, however, it is enough to indicate that *there have been two different conceptions of time: Ideational and Sensate; that their comparative influence fluctuated; and that the Ideational conception of time tends to dominate in the cultures and periods mainly Ideational, while the Sensate conception does so in the cultures and periods mainly Sensate.*

To many of my contemporaries who have been reared in an atmosphere of Sensate space; who are even unaware of the existence of Ideational space conception; and who try to locate everything — even mind, and thought, and sociocultural values like Plato's system of thought, a Beethoven symphony, Homer's *Iliad,* Euclid's geometry — in some sensory *locus,* in some Sensate place — be it the nervous system, or the symphony score, or the hall where the symphony is given, or the book in which the *Iliad* is printed, and other similar "places" — to these contemporaries with these hopeless and perfectly absurd attempts at "objective location" of these values, the very idea of Ideational space appears something strange and queer. And yet, after the above remarks, even they have to admit that such strange conceptions have existed. More than that. If they would try to acquaint themselves more seriously with a few conceptions of space in various cultures, say, ancient Chinese, they would see that these strange conceptions not only existed, but they were elaborated in great detail and appeared to the respective people or thinkers as clear and definite as our sensory three-dimensional space of the classical mechanics, with all its specific properties.

Contemporary Sensate conceptions of the spatial structure of the universe do not speak of the Soul of the World, or God, or the Central Fire (the Mind of the World), or Demiurge, or Jupiter, or any other supersensory agency as the center of the world, as the inalienable, nay, central part of the spatial structure of the universe. Likewise, they do not talk of special regions reserved for angels, saints, sinners, and various categories of such supersensory "population." Neither do we find in these theories a classification and division of the universe into regions of paradise, or purgatory, or inferno. They are free from all such supersensory "additions"; they talk and discuss the spatial aspect of the Universe without anything supersensory, no matter whether they claim finite or infinite space; empty or filled with ether or atoms or anything else — again sensory. Turn from these theories to the cosmogonic pictures of the universe, whether of Hesiod, Homer, Pythagoras, Philolaos, Plato, or even Aristotle. What a contrast! The "supersensory" elements of the spatial structure of the Universe not only are there but they are the central — absolutely inalienable — part of it, be it the Soul of the Universe and its *locus* in it; be it Jupiter; be it "the center of the Necessity"; be it the spiritualized Central Fire; or the like. So also almost all Greek cosmogenic theories before the third century. The same is true of the medieval cosmogonic theories of the universe, preoccupied with the regions of souls, angels, saints, sinners, devils, and the like; with the qualitative properties of each respective region; with their "spatial relation"; with the most exacting attempts to give a picture of the universe and its space structure which will be in agreement with the Scripture and with some of its embarrassing statements, like the region of the "supercelestial waters." When one passes, after a study of the cosmogonic theories of the Greeks and the Romans, like Aristarchos of Samos or Claudius Ptolemy, to the study of the cosmogonies of the Church Fathers and the medieval cosmogonists (Isidore of Seville, Bede, Rhabanus, Walafrid Strabo, Honorius, Hugo St. Victor, Petrus Lombardus, and others), one cannot help being bewildered, even stunned with the change in this field. The whole mentality is altered and we are moved from one — considerably Sensate — atmosphere to something radically different — to the Ideational conception of space and the Universe.

Enormous also is the contrast in many details of the spatial image of the universe in the theories of the cosmogonists who lived in predominantly Ideational and predominantly Sensate periods.

These lines give an idea of the profound difference between Ideational and Sensate conceptions. They also indicate that, when studied, the rise and decline of these conceptions agree with the respective rise and decline of Ideational and Sensate mentalities.

IV. Ideational and Sensate Conceptions of Number

Without attempting to outline a history of the conceptions of number here, I want merely to indicate that this term has covered conceptions which are fundamentally different from one another. Here also one can distinguish Ideational and Sensate conceptions. At the present time most of us think of number as a result of counting or of comparison of quantities with a standard unit. Number and quantity, number and magnitude, appear to us as inseparable from one another. Number as a number appears to us quantitative only and devoid of any qualities except the quantitative quality of the number itself (odd and even, rational and irrational, prime and composite, and so on). Comparative magnitude again appears to us to be decided by the numerical magnitude of the numbers themselves: 6 as containing six units is greater than 4 or 5. These and others characteristics to which we are accustomed appear to us so clear and definite that no fundamentally different conception of number seems possible. Especially any conception where number is quality, rather than quantity, in which 4 may be greater than 6; where number functions not for a comparison of magnitude but for radically different purposes. To give an idea of one fundamentally different conception of number, however, let me quote again the case given by M. Granet.

The *Tso tchouan* tells of the debate of the (Chinese) council of war: Should they attack the enemy? The Chief is inclined to the idea of attack, but it is necessary that he should engage the responsibility of his subordinates and take their advice. Twelve generals, including himself, participate in the Council. The opinions are divided. Three generals refuse to engage in the battle; eight want to go to it. These eight are thus *majority* and they proclaim it. However, the opinion that unites 8 votes does not carry the opinion that unites 3 votes: 3 is [for the Chinese] almost *unanimity*, which is quite a different thing from a mere *majority*. The Chief will not fight. He changes his opinion. The opinion to which he adds his *unique* vote becomes the *unanimous* opinion.

Here we have an example of how 3 may be greater than 8 and how a number may function not for a comparison of quantitative magnitudes but for making up *qualities and values* (unanimity and majority) and their hierarchical scale. It shows also that number may be viewed as containing in itself qualities and properties that have nothing to do with number as a quantitative category. After this the subsequent statements of M. Granet are comprehensible and introduce us more fully into what I style the Ideational or Mixed conception of number.

Idea of quantity does not play any role in the philosophical speculations of the Chinese. Numbers, however, passionately interest the sages of the ancient China. . . .

Knowing, for instance, that for human species embryonic life lasts about ten months a philosopher reasons as follows. The Heaven signifies 1; the Earth, 2; Man, 3. 3 times 3 makes 9; 9 times 9 makes 81 [octant and 1]; 1 rules the Sun; the number of the Sun is [1 (ten)] 10; the Sun controls man; therefore man is born in the tenth month. [From this can be seen on the one hand a *symbolic equivalent* of *81* and *10*; *72* and *12*, while *63* and *54* signify *3* and *4*.] . . .

Numerical symbols command every sort of reality and symbol.

Side by side with their quantitative value they possess much more interesting symbolic value. . . . Numbers permit one to classify the things but not in a merely simple numerical order. . . . Chinese use numbers for the expression of the *qualities* of certain groupings, or for indication of a hierarchical scale.

Numbers do not function to express magnitudes; they serve to adjust the concrete dimensions to the proportions of the Universe.

The quotations give an allusion to a conception of number fundamentally different from what we are used to. The Ideationally Mixed nature and functions of numbers in this case are clear.

Does this Chinese case represent something unique? By no means. The spread and persistence of the Ideational "numerology," to use E. T. Bell's expression, is infinitely greater than in the Chinese case. Who, for instance, does not know about the Pythagorean numerological mysticism? In its nature, as Chavannes rightly remarks, Chinese numerology is a variety of Pythagorean numerology. For the Pythagoreans (including Philolaos), according to the preserved statement of Jamblichos, "numbers are permanent causes of everything that occurs in the Universe. . . . Unity is the principle of numbers and of everything that exists and that is identical with God."

Similarly, to certain numbers, 10, 3, 7, and some others, are ascribed a mystical significance and power. In their qualitative functions the different numbers may be equivalent, quantitatively smaller numbers may be greater, and equal numbers (say 72 made by 8 multiplied by 9, and 72 made by 12 multiplied by 6) may be quite unequal.

This Ideational conception was the dominant conception in Greece before the fourth century; it is found developed in the Hesiodic calendar of the lucky and unlucky days: in every month the sixth day is unpropitious for the birth of a female; the thirteenth, for sowing; the sixteenth, for planting; likewise the fifth, the fifteenth, the twenty-fifth are generally bad days; on the contrary, the fourth day is good for marriage; the ninth for begetting or birth of a child; and so on. It permeates the whole Pythagorean conception of number: beginning with the special numbers, like 10, endowed with a specific power, and ending with the mystical conception of number, the mystical relationship between numbers, music, and the harmony of the Universe. We all know the large part which a similar Ideational conception of number plays in Plato's philosophy, beginning with Plato's "perfect number" and ending with numerous similar discussions of numbers. The Pythagoreans and the Platonists followed this path. Other Greek thinkers of the sixth and the fifth centuries shared in that Ideational conception. It played a role in astrological numerology throughout the Middle Ages.

It is manifested *urbi et orbi* in the universal belief in the specific importance and mysterious power of certain numbers, like 3, 7, 9, 13, 81, and many others: in the Hebrew, the Hindu, the Mohammedan, the Christian, the Graeco-Roman, the Chinese, the Babylonian, and other culture mentalities. All this shows that such a conception of number has been something not exceptionally rare but something as diffused as the Sensate and "scientific" treatment of numbers.

These remarks are possibly sufficient to show that there has been and indeed exist Ideational and Sensate conceptions of number most profoundly different from one another. This primary difference manifests itself in many derivative uses, computations, numerical manipulations, measurements, and other procedures where numbers are involved. Quantitativism or, more accurately, numerology and mathematics of the Ideational and Sensate conceptions are fundamentally different numerologies, mathematics, computations, and quantitativisms.

It is out of place here to give an outline of the rise and decline of the Ideational and Sensate conceptions of number from the sixth century B.C. up to the present time. So far as my preliminary study shows, each of these conceptions seem to have fluctuated tangibly parallel with the rise and decline of Ideational and Sensate mentalities.

However brief and sketchy is the analysis and historical outline of the Ideational and Sensate fluctuations of the conception of causality, time, space, and number — as the fundamental categories of our thought — the above seems to be sufficient to demonstrate that each of these categories has indeed Ideational and Sensate forms; and that each of these forms rises and declines with the rise and decline of the respective culture

23

FLUCTUATION OF GENERAL AND SPECIAL SCIENTIFIC THEORIES

Not only do the first principles and the categories of human thought fluctuate, but also almost all of the scientific theories of a more or less general nature. Some of these fluctuations probably proceed independently from our main variables. The others seem to be connected with the rise and decline of our main types of culture mentality.

Perhaps only so-called facts remain unchanged, but any fact as a "routine of sense perception" is meaningless per se, if it is not put in some conceptual reference system or — what is the same — if it is not embraced by some kind of theory. Without this, no "fact" can exist as a relevant fact or can constitute knowledge in any sense.

As examples of the fluctuation discussed, I am taking cosmogonic theories, the atomistic theory, the mechanistic and vitalistic interpretation of life phenomena, the theory of light, and a few others. In this abridged edition, I am giving only the conclusions of a more substantial study of fluctuation of these theories published in the full text of the *Dynamics.*

I. Fluctuation of Atomistic Theories

The fluctuation of atomistic theories seems to have been tangibly associated with that of the main systems of truth. In so far as atomism is connected with materialism, according to the opinion of the competent investigators of its history, and in so far as materialism is associated with the truth of the senses, it follows that we should expect the curve of atomistic theories in its main upward and downward movements to go somewhat parallel with that of the empirical system of truth, and with mechanistic materialism. The survey of its main "ups and downs" corroborates this expectation.

In Greece, the first widespread promulgation of the atomic theory comes in the fifth century, with the establishment by Leukippos at Abdera of the so-called Atomistic school, which was later consolidated by Democritus, one of the disciples, about 420 B.C. However, thirty years after Democritus there remained almost no trace of his doctrine. At the close of the fourth and the opening of the third century, Epicurus revived the outcast theory with but few changes. But this revival was comparatively short-lived in Greece and, with the solitary exception of Asclepiades (the Greek physician who was the teacher of Lucretius) in the first century B.C., atomism was once again left to perish.

But, when the Greek ideas found their way to Rome, atomistic theory had its rebirth in the poem of T. Lucretius Carus (99–55 B.C.). However, around 200 A.D. atomism again disappeared in the Western world for approximately a thousand years.

Although the atomic theory did not find any significant degree of credence until its revival by Galileo and Gassendi in the seventeenth century, it reappeared on the scene in the twelfth century, and since that time has remained there, with slow — at the beginning — and then faster rising trend (after the sixteenth century). With the opening of the seventeenth century, atomic theories begin to come into their own. In the eighteenth century the atomic idea underwent a twofold change: it acquired forces, and these were conceived to be inherent in the atom. The nineteenth century was a peculiar compound of alternate acceptance and rejection of Atomism, in part and *in plenum*. Toward the end of the century, the rejection of the atom led to the positing of nonmaterial energy as the ultimate "reality" by Ostwald, Tait, and others.

In the twentieth century the atom has undergone the following transformations: first, it has been split into more than thirty "elementary" particles — electron, anti-electron, proton, meson, and others which are essentially non-material; second, it has been declared to be a mere concentrated form of energy; third, the motion of a single atom or of a small aggregation of atoms has been declared to be indeterminate, and uncertain (Heisenberg's principle of uncertainty and quanta jumps) and largely unpredictable; fourth, some scientists declared it to be a mere "symbolic conception" or "a schedule of pointer readings."

All in all, the material atom of the preceding centuries has been largely immaterialized, broken into many "cryptic, arcane, perplexing, and enigmatic," largely non-material elementary particles, to which the concepts of time, space, mass, matter, and causality are hardly applicable.

This change is but a radical revolt against the Sensate conception of matter and atom of the preceding centuries. Like many similar revolts we met in other fields of our culture, it may be a symptom of the decline of our Sensate order and a precursor of a new Idealistic or Ideational order.

Conclusions. First, atomic theories have fluctuated. At some periods they rose and gathered a power impressive enough to be accepted as the "last word" of science by the leading scientists and thinkers of the period. At other times they declined, and sometimes practically disappeared. Second, one can note that, all in all, atomism appeared in the periods of the Idealistic culture (fifth century B.C.; thirteenth century A.D.); it grew in the period of Sensate culture (third and first centuries B.C. and first two centuries A.D.; then the centuries from the sixteenth to the twentieth); and disappeared almost completely in the periods of domination of the Ideational culture (before the fifth century B.C. and from the fourth to the twelfth centuries A.D.). In Greece atomism gathered its greatest momentum possibly in the third century B.C. (Epicurus and the Epicureans); in Rome, in the first century B.C., and the first A.D., that is, in the periods when the Greek and the Roman cultures were Sensate par excellence; while in the Western culture it has been rapidly growing, beginning especially with the sixteenth century, up to the end of the nineteenth century. These fluctuations show that atomism is positively associated with the empirical system of truth and the Sensate culture. In the twentieth century, the atom is de-atomized, de-materialized, and undeterminized.

II. Fluctuation of Vitalism and Mechanism in Biology

The next example of the fluctuation of scientific theories is given by the increase and decrease of the "scientific" prestige, and acceptance of the rival theories of mechanism and vitalism, in the field of biology. This case also shows that these fluctuations have a tangible association with the ups and downs of the respective systems of truth and the types of cultures to which each of these systems belongs.

Mechanistic theories maintain that life is a special phenomena of matter, so that the organism is merely a dynamic structure which is subject to physicochemical principles without the significant intervention of any force or action which is not appropriate data for the investigations of physics and chemistry. The vitalistic doctrines, be they concerned with entelechy or holism or *anima sensitiva*, all possess one common characteristic: they state or imply that living matter entails some unique, inherently different principle from that of inanimate matter, which principle affects some or all of the activities of the organism in such fashion that the living body is not subject to the exclusive operation of physicochemical forces. The organism is thus, in varying degrees, differentiated from nonliving matter.

Our study of mechanism and vitalism shows in its movements the curve of vitalism goes with that of idealism and the truth of faith and partly that of reason, while the curve of mechanism goes with that of materialism, atomism, and the truth of senses. Indeed, we do not meet mechanism before the end of the sixth century B.C. It appears in the fifth century, but in the whole configuration of the mentality of the period is neither dominant nor exclusive. It is a part of the Mixed Idealistic mentality of the period. After the fourth century it grows, reaching its climax in the third, for Greek thought, in the first century B.C. for the Roman; that is, in the periods of domination of the Sensate cultures in these countries. After the first century A.D. it weakens and then disappears until the thirteenth century, when it emerges again and becomes a constituent element of the Mixed mentality in the field which corresponds to the Idealistic type of culture. After that century it begins to crystallize more and more and in the sixteenth century becomes powerful, in the seventeenth dominant. Then, with secondary and temporary setbacks, it steadily grows up to the end of the nineteenth century, parallel with the growth of the Sensate culture. In the twentieth century vitalism revives and mechanism comparatively weakens. Thus in these essential movements the ups and downs of these rivals run closely parallel with the main rising and receding tides of the types of the cultures and of the respective systems of truth to which each of them logically and — after the above — factually belongs. Scientific theory thus is but an opinion made "creditable" and "fashionable" by the type of the prevalent culture.

Revival of vitalism in our time may be a temporary reaction, like several reactions before. But it may also be a symptom of the beginning of the decline of the Sensate mentality. Whichever of these possibilities is true it is to be said that we find again a "revolt" here, similar to the "revolts" against overripe Sensate culture at the end of the nineteenth and in the twentieth century in other compartments of culture. For this reason, it deserves to be noted.

III. Some General Remarks on the Long- and Short-time Fluctuations of Prestige of the Natural-science Theories

The above examples, taken from the domain of the natural sciences, show that the scientific theories, like those in philosophy, and in other fields of thought have indeed fluctuated. They show also that the upward and downward movement of rival theories of a relatively broader character have been tangibly connected with the respective oscillations of the main systems of truth, and of the types of culture corresponding to each of them.

There is hardly any doubt that, as far as mere oscillation is concerned, there probably has been no scientific theory which has not undergone it, and, like a fashion, now has been heralded as the last word of science and now has fallen into disrepute. At least, for me it is exceedingly difficult, indeed practically impossible, to indicate any single comparatively broad theory in the whole field of natural sciences which has been free from such a vicissitude. I do not know of any single general theory which after being formulated has remained an unchanged truth in subsequent time, if that time has been sufficiently long. Some of the theories need a span of several centuries before being recognized as "the last word of science," or being discredited as erroneous and inadequate. Others require a much shorter time to undergo the cycle.

IV. Fluctuation of Theories in the Social Sciences and Humanities

If the "First Principles," "categories of human thought," and the natural-science theories rise and decline in their acceptability, this is equally true of all the theories concerning man, culture, and social phenomena that compose the social sciences — including history, psychology, and anthropology — and the humanities, including philosophy, ethics, and law. The content, the subject matter, the internal structure, the methodology of these sciences are conditioned by the type of the dominant culture probably even more than are those of the natural sciences. Therefore, they fluctuate in all their essential traits possibly even more than do those theories dealing with inanimate and organic phenomena. As a matter of fact, the long-time, and especially the short-time, transformation of these theories is almost spectacular. Their whole "style" or "physiognomy" changes notably even within a few decades. Still more pronounced are their long-time transformations.

We have already seen the latter. The fluctuations of the First Principles studied are but the first corroboration of that. It must be evident that the social sciences and humanities of the predominantly Ideational or Idealistic period have to be and are, in fact, fundamentally different from those of the predominantly materialistic mentality. In the periods when rationalistic mentality is dominant, the social sciences and humanities are profoundly different from the aspect they present in the periods when empiricism is dominant. This point has been illustrated at some length by a study of the movements and relationship of general nominalism and realism and of sociological universalism and singularism and the conceptions of the juridical personality. We have seen that during the domination of ontological realism, the sociological and social theories acquire a universalistic character profoundly different from the singularistic character which they acquire in the periods of dominant nominalism. Even the current definition of what is "society" is entirely different in these two periods.

The same has been shown in regard to the theories of juridical personality and the linear and cyclical conceptions of sociocultural and historical processes. Likewise it has been shown that during the domination of materialism and Sensate mentality, the social sciences and humanities also become materialistic in their choice of subjects studied, in their content, and in their method. Man, the sociocultural world, and the world of values become in such times mainly "materialistic," "physiologic," "reflexo-logical," "endocrinological," "economical," "psychoanalytical," "behavioristic." Social sciences become blind toward almost anything in man and the sociocultural world that is a manifestation of "divineness," "idealism," "nonmaterial values," and the like. Instead, they concentrate mainly upon the material and half-animal aspects of humanity and its world; try to interpret everything through such factors, and causes and forces as instincts, reflexes, prepotent drives, sex, hunger, economic conditions, "residues," and other sensory-corporeal conditions, be they the density of the population, intensity of interaction, ecological area, heredity, struggle for existence, or so on. The nobler, higher, less material and less tangible forces, aspects, and agencies are disregarded, are ridiculed as "back numbers" and "ignorance." The whole world of the sociocultural values is dragged down to the level of the reflexes and pure physiology. Heroes as values are similarly "primitivized." The heroes of the social sciences and humanities of the Ideational periods are gods, saints, angels, and other supersensory and divine creatures. The heroes of the Idealistic social sciences are noble and great men and demigods. In a prevalently Sensate period the heroes are the "common people," "the labor classes," and especially the "negative" types: criminals, prostitutes, the mentally abnormal, social derelicts, and the like. Here we have an exact replica of what we have met in the field of art, particularly in the field of portraiture and *genre*. There we have seen that with the progress of Sensate mentality, the "heroes" of painting and sculpture and literature become more and more "common people," the mediocrity, labor classes, and especially the socially pathological types. Professor W. C. Abbott excellently puts this condition in his brilliant characterization of the "new history."

On every hand we have a multitude of books endeavoring to depict for us not the great figures and events and movements of the past but the way the ordinary man lived, what he did for a living, what he ate and drank and wore, how much of various commodities he produced, what he did for his amusement, and what things attracted his attention as he went his daily round. Whether it calls itself "social," or is concerned with "civilization," it has chiefly to do with what it describes as the "common man," that heir of the ages once called the "average man," one of whose incarnations Ricardo christened "economic man," the French revolutionaries "the man and citizen"; he whom Sinclair Lewis named "Babbitt," and the author of the morality play called "Everyman." He now replaces Caesar and Alexander and Shakespeare and George Washington as the hero of the "new" history. . . .

In addition, this "new" history centers on social service, statistics of production, immorality, insane asylums, sex problems, and political corruption. . . ."

So it is with other social sciences and sociology and anthropology. They study "culture and civilization," not in the works of Homer, Plato, Aristotle, Phidias, Dante, Newton, Augustine, Bach, Beethoven, Kant, and Charlemagne; not in the finest creations of human genius; but mainly among the Ashantis and Trobrians, the Zulu and other primitive peoples; in the world of slums and gangs, in the "Middletowns" and prisons, and in the autobiographies of notorious criminals and the like, whose writings become more and more popular as treatises on sociology, criminology, psychology, anthropology, and political science. All heroes tend to disappear from the social literature of the Sensate period.

And even when such a hero is considered, be he Washington or Lincoln, Napoleon or Goethe, Christ or Mohammed, Caesar or Dante, by the biographers (all the Ludwigs and the Stracheys and other Sensate writers) they are so psychoanalyzed and "reflexologized" and sexualized and "physiologized" that the poor hero is stripped of anything heroic and debunked to the level of a mere physiological incarnation of sex or some similar complex.

This is only one of the innumerable traits in which the social sciences and the humanities of the predominant types of culture mentality profoundly differ from one another. In the preceding chapters many other differences have been pointed out. Generally, considered from the standpoint of the phenomena on which these sciences concentrate, their interrelation, their explanations (especially "factorial and causal analysis"), their methodology, the social sciences and humanities of the predominantly Ideational, Sensate, and Mixed periods differ from one another as much as can be. They look upon one another almost as strangers and are hardly on speaking terms. To the social sciences and humanities of the Ideational period, the social sciences of the Sensate period are the perverse disciplines, specializing in the reviling of God, man, and the world; a pitiful blasphemy; heresy; demoralizing and degrading instruments of deviltry. To the social sciences and humanities of the Sensate period, their counterparts of the Ideational period are but the eerie, queer, ignorant superstitions and phantasmas of the "uneducated and unillumined and unconditioned central nervous system of their bearers." They are so different that for Sensate social scientists the social sciences and humanities of the Ideational periods appear to be nonexistent. This is the reason why, for instance, in our courses and books on the history of social, political, economic, psychological, anthropological, and other theories, the Middle Ages are either barely mentioned, or only a few pages are devoted to several centuries, with the implicit or explicit assumption that there is nothing worth looking for along these lines, and that no social science existed then. All this is so unquestionable and has been and will be factually indicated so many times on so many concrete points that it is unnecessary to discuss it further.

Side by side with the great transformations of these social and humanistic disciplines in connection with the rise and decline of the main types of culture mentality, each of them and their theories undergo almost incessant short-time transformations. Almost continually, a number of the theories or interpretations commonly accepted at a certain period are discarded and replaced by different ones.

The political science, or economics, of the Middle Ages has little in common with those of the eighteenth and nineteenth centuries, while these latter are declared outdated by the political science and economics of the twentieth century, especially in the Communistic, Fascistic and Hitlerite countries, and also in the New Deal regimes. The science of psychology of Albertus Magnus or St. Thomas Aquinas is profoundly different from that of the seventeenth century, be it a Descartian, a Hobbesian or a Lockian psychology; and these, in turn, are again quite different from the psychologies of the eighteenth and nineteenth centuries. Even those of the second part of the nineteenth century differ widely from those of the twentieth. Nay, even prewar psychologies are vastly unlike the postwar ones. Within the last ten years, several fashions (behaviorism, reflexology, psychoanalysis, mental tests, Gestaltism, and other brands) came, blossomed, and are already gone. Not different is the story with anthropology, theories of language, religion, art, law, the mores, and philosophical systems. Still more true is this "throbbing" in the field of sociology. Within some seventy years after August Comte, dozens and dozens of different theories and approaches and systems rushed into the field of sociology, had their heyday, and dwindled. Today's commonly accepted theory is discarded tomorrow.

These remarks suffice for the present. Whether we like it or not, the long- and short-time fluctuations in the social and humanitarian sciences, as well as the connection of their deep transformations with the rise and decline of the main types of culture mentalities can hardly be questioned.

V. Concluding Remarks

Since I am not writing a history of scientific theories, the above examples are sufficient to show the relative validity of my first claim that in science, as in any other field of sociocultural mentality, the fact of oscillation of the acceptability and prestige of the theories cannot be questioned.

Also the above examples substantiate my second claim that even in the field of the natural sciences many of their broad and leading theories fluctuate in their prestige and acceptability in a tangible connection with the fluctuations of the systems of truth and the main types of culture. As mentioned, it is not claimed that all scientific theories show, or must show such a connection; many of them can fluctuate independently of our main variables, within their limited sphere of autonomy and the immediate mental atmosphere of their compartment. But many other theories and probably all of the "First Principles," "categories," and general principles of philosophy and science are conditioned in their credibility and scientific acceptability by the dominant system of truth and dominant system of culture.

A theory harmonious with the given dominant system of truth is likely to be proclaimed by the scientists and philosophers as the last word of science. And the same theory, under a different system of truth dominant, is likely to be declared an error or mere superstition.

Insistence on such a relativity of scientific theories does not mean skepticism on my part. It simply means that the full and complete truth is "white" and is possibly accessible only to the Divine Mind. We can grasp but its approximation. Our efforts in this direction seem in most of the cases to go beyond the proper limit when we accept this or that theory as radically true and reject other theories as radically wrong. According to the principles of limit and immanent self-regulation of the sociocultural processes, when, in our eagerness, we go too far beyond the legitimate limit of a given theory, a reaction sets in and leads to its decline. But the new theory also goes too far, denying to its predecessor not only its value, but often the germ of truth which it contains. Hence, in its turn, it is destined also, after its period of domination, to be discarded for a new theory, which often is a modification of the one previously overthrown. And so it goes.

In these eternal oscillations there is a great value, a great fascination, and a great optimism. They mean that we are almost always in close touch with the ultimate reality, in spite of our inability to grasp it fully. This is something quite different from skepticism or its allies. It means also that the whole truth is infinite in its aspects and unfathomable in its depth. It is more worth our while to be in real touch with, and in partial possession of, such an infinite value than to be in complete possession of something which is entirely graspable, and therefore is limited and finite. At least, such is the preference of the writer. However, this is a matter of taste, and is not obligatory for anybody. What is obligatory is to realize that the fact of the oscillations discussed seems to be without doubt.

We have traversed a long and arduous road to this part of the work.

Now we can look back and take stock of what we have seen.

(1) All four of the propositions with which this part is concerned and which follow logically from the nature of each of the main culture mentalities are corroborated inductively.

(2) The logically expected "integrations" happened to be integrated factually or causally. So far, the culture mentalities studied show themselves mainly logical, and not illogical or alogical as many claim. It is true that the causal and logical integrations are not perfect, but they are quite tangible. Due to the *Principle of Autonomy* of any really integrated system, each of the integrated currents of culture mentality studied should be expected to have some margin of this autonomy; therefore it should have some margin of an "independent movement" not completely related to the other currents and compartments of culture.

(3) The above shows also that our "main variables" or our key principles for a logical comprehension of the perceptional chaos of sociocultural phenomena work well. They work well, not only as the "heuristic principles" that help to look for functional connections where otherwise the connections cannot even be suspected of existing, but as the principles analogous to "causal laws" which order the chaos of the millions of fragmentary phenomena into a system; which give a sense to what otherwise is meaningless; which put in their proper places thousands of fragments and make out of them a comprehensible whole. Yes, we see now the "hows and whys" of the rise and decline of all the "First Principles," "categories," theories studied; and the thousands of more detailed subcurrents embraced by each of these. In this sense, the theory of the Ideational, Idealistic, Sensate culture mentalities meets well the test of its validity; fits as well as any other theory this class of phenomena; explains them as well as any other heuristic concept does. Therefore it is entitled to claim as large a share of validity as any theory in the field studied.

PART FOUR

FLUCTUATION OF IDEATIONAL AND SENSATE FORMS OF ETHICAL AND JURIDICAL CULTURE MENTALITY

24

FLUCTUATION OF IDEATIONAL, SENSATE, AND MIXED SYSTEMS OF ETHICS IN THE GRAECO-ROMAN AND WESTERN CULTURES

I. Preliminaries

We can pass now to the next compartment of culture: ethicojuridical. In this vast and complicated field we shall discuss the same problems that have been studied in the preceding compartments. A few introductory statements follow.

Every organized group and its culture has a set of ethical values. Even among the most primitive tribes or criminal gangs we invariably find it in the form of taboos of certain forms of conduct and objects and events, and in the permission or glorification of others as sacred, good, and recommended. In some form an ethical evaluation of "the right and wrong" is present in any culture and in any organized social group. In this sense the ethical mentality is a universal and permanent component of any culture mentality. The content of this mentality differs from society to society, from period to period, but its ethical forms are perennial.

Some of the cultures and their mentality may not develop this ethical mentality up to the level of the integrated ethicophilosophical systems. Other more integrated cultures develop it. In the case of the Graeco-Roman and the Western society, such systems are present.

For a sociologist and social psychologist, these ethicophilosophical systems have a specific interest. They are possibly the best manifestation of the ethical ideals of a given culture, the sublime peaks of its ethical mentality. Therefore, a study of these systems is necessary in order to grasp the character of this mentality at its best and noblest, without any inference as to whether the *real* actions of the members correspond to it or not.

It goes without saying that the real behavior of the respective society, and even of the creator of a given ethical system, does not always coincide with the predominant ethical ideal accepted. Factually, as we shall see further on, there must always be some discrepancy. For this reason one cannot infer from the dominant ethical ideal of a given society that the conduct of its members corresponds to it. On the other hand, some "affinity" between the ideal and certain aspects of behavior seems to exist. Many aspects of the actual conduct seem to be colored or permeated somehow by the predominant ethical system.

Thus, if the predominant ethical system is utilitarianism, the atmosphere of utilitarian principles permeates the conduct and moral mentality of the members of the society, in spite of the fact that they fail to carry out its supreme prescriptions. If the predominant system is the System of Love, it again reflects itself in the actual conduct of such a society, and especially in its moral mentality, though the actual conduct may violate the command of such a system.

II. Ideational, Idealistic, and Sensate Systems of Ethics

A. From the nature of the Ideational mentality, the following characteristics of the Ideational ethical system follow.

(1) It is not and cannot be intended merely to increase the sum of sensate happiness, comfort, pleasure, and utility. These are imaginary and therefore cannot be the end of the principles of Ideational ethics.

(2) The Ideational system of ethics must be and usually is absolute. Since it is intended to bring its followers into unity with the supreme and absolute value, its commands are also absolute. Therefore relativism, expediency, and anything that limits them is heterogeneous to such ethics.

(3) Its principles are considered as emanating from God or some other supersensory absolute value. In most cases, they are given as the Commandments of God (or gods).

B. The nature of the Sensate mentality determines the opposite characteristics of the Sensate ethical system.

(1) The aim of such a system of ethics can be only an increase of the total sum of a man's (or a group's) sensate happiness, comfort, utility, and pleasure. Since there is no reality except the sensory and no value except the sensory value, sensate happiness remains the only value which can be secured by Sensate ethics.

(2) Such a system can be but relativistic, because with the changing sensate conditions the ethical rules must change also; rules that serve the purpose in one set of conditions cease to serve it in different circumstances; therefore they can and should be replaced by rules that fit the new situation. Hence, relativism, expediency, and changeability of the rules of Sensate ethics.

(3) They always appear as man-made rules, having no other authority behind them. If they are reasonable and serve the purpose of happiness, they are useful. If they do not serve that purpose, they should be discarded.

C. Finally, the Idealistic ethical system occupies an intermediary position between these two systems.

(1) Its aims are simultaneously transcendental and earthly: service to God (the absolute ethical value), which leads, at the same time, to the real eudaemonistic happiness of those who do that.

(2) Its main principle is absolute; its subordinated commands are relative and therefore changeable.

(3) It gives its main principles as the commands of God or of some other supersensory supreme authority; its secondary principles as the commands of reason and of the human bearers of it.

Sensate ethics can be called the *ethics of happiness;* Ideational ethics, the system of *absolute principles.* Its specific variety, represented by the Christian ethical system, is *ethics of love.* It differs from other varieties of absolutistic ethics by several characteristics. Finally, Idealistic ethics is a class intermediary between these and is represented by the ethics of absolute principles somewhat diluted, mixed with the finest form of *eudaemonistic* ethics as a variety of the *ethics of happiness.* Let us clarify a little more each class of these three ethical systems.

To the Sensate ethics of happiness belong all hedonistic, utilitarian and eudaemonistic ethical systems which regard sensate happiness as the supreme value and make everything else a means for its achievement and quantitative and qualitative increase. All that leads to that is good; all that hinders it is evil; such is the criterion and the supreme value of such systems.

Though similar in this respect, various systems of ethics of happiness differ from one another in several secondary specifications. According to these specifications they can be divided into three principal subclasses. First is the *eudaemonistic* subclass which considers, as the supreme objective, happiness of the *whole system of life,* in which pleasure and joy shall outweigh pain, suffering, and grief. Not happiness as a mere *Carpe diem,* as merely grasping as many singular and fragmentary pleasures as possible. In accordance with that, eudaemonism means by happiness not merely the sum total of sensual pleasures but also — and rather — nonsensual pleasures, more refined, more noble, more lasting, and less fragile. In this sense it is neither mainly nor predominantly sensual and carnal, nor is it aimed at the passing moment only. It has a longer perspective of time in its evaluation of pleasure, and for this reason views happiness as a conscientious system of living and not as a mere hunt for transient enjoyment.

The *hedonistic* branch of the ethics of happiness differs from the eudaemonistic in that it views as the supreme objective of life separate or singular pleasures. The more such pleasures are caught, the greater the happiness, the greater the goodness of life. Accentuating these pleasures, hedonism has to be and in fact is more "sensual" and carnal than eudaemonism. The ideal of the "*Carpe diem*" or "Wine, women, and song," cannot be styled eudaemonistic, though it is in agreement with the principles of hedonism and is one of its forms. It does not stress the continuance of the pleasures and happiness, and does not give any premium to long-time values as compared with short-time ones, as does, in a sense, eudaemonism.

Finally, *utilitarianism* is also a form of ethics of happiness. Being nearer to the eudaemonistic system than to the hedonistic, especially in the works of the English utilitarianists, it differs from both in that it puts an emphasis on the *means* of obtaining happiness (on what is useful for the achievement of happiness) rather than on what the happiness itself is.

Eudaemonism, hedonism, and utilitarianism can be either individualistic or egotistic, when the happiness of only a given individual is considered, regardless of its effects upon the others; or social, when not so much the happiness of a given individual as that of a group is regarded as the supreme objective. The social forms of the ethics of happiness can have also various — more broad and less broad — forms, according to whether the happiness of the nearest group (for instance, of a certain family only) or a larger group (possibly the whole nation) or a still larger group (for instance, the whole of mankind) is the objective. Farther on, as mentioned, various systems of eudaemonism, hedonism, and utilitarianism can be and are more or less carnal and sensual. Between the extremes there is always a series of the intermediary forms. Such are the main forms of the Sensate ethics of happiness.

According to the Ideational *ethics of absolute principles*, the supreme objective of life is a realization of the highest value — for instance, union with God, salvation of soul, truth, goodness, beauty, for their own sake, regardless of whether or not such a realization leads to an increase of happiness.

Between the noblest systems of eudaemonism and that of the ethics of principles, the difference becomes often imperceptible. One is merged organically with the other, in the form of the Idealistic system of ethics, which is simultaneously absolutistic and — in part — relativistic, transcendental, and at the same time eudaemonistic.

Ethics of love, in a sense, is a variety of the *ethics of absolute principles*. Among and above all values it puts the value of infinite, unlimited, sacrificing love of God, and of all the concrete individual persons. Love in this sense includes all the other values. The genuine ethics of Jesus, St. Francis, and other Christians give examples of such ethics of love.

III. Fluctuation of Systems of Ethics

In the subsequent pages, the results of the study of the fluctuation of these systems in the history of the Graeco-Roman and the Western cultures, so far as they have been reflected in their ethicophilosophical thought, are given.

The Idealistic class is not specifically differentiated in Tables 29 and 30. These theories are put in the nearer of the two classes. However, further comments will show in which periods such a class was comparatively strong.

IV. Main Results

A. Table 29 and Figure 16 show that up to the second part of the fifth century B.C., the ethics of happiness did not play any role. The whole field was occupied by the ethics of principles: religious and moral commands were viewed as absolute, without any regard to their bearing upon sensate happiness. The moral values were held sacred, and their authority was transcendental gods, whose commands were neither doubted nor questioned. This was not only the standpoint of thinkers like Pythagoras and Hesiod, but also of the poets and literary oracles of the centuries preceding the fifth and of the first part of the fifth — Pindar, Aeschylus, Sophocles, Herodotus, and others. For all of these, moral commands are absolute commands of the gods. These commands are not questioned even when the gods punish men who seem to be not guilty at all from our standpoint.

TABLE 29. INDICATORS OF THE FLUCTUATION OF THE INFLUENCE OF ETHICAL SYSTEMS AND MENTALITY BY 20-YEAR PERIODS, 580 B.C.—A.D. 1920

(on the basis of different values given from 1 to 12)

PERIOD	*Ethics of Happiness (Eudaemonism, Hedonism, Utilitarianism)*		*Ethics of Principles*		*Ethics of Love*		*Total*	
	No.	*Per cent*	*No.*	*Per cent*	*No.*	*Per cent*	*No.*	*Per cent*
580–560 B.C.	0	0	0	0	0	0	0	0
560–540	0	0	0	0	0	0	0	0
540–520	0	0	8	100	0	0	8	100
520–500	0	0	15	100	0	0	15	100
500–480	0	0	15	100	0	0	15	100
480–460	0	0	7	100	0	0	7	100
460–440	0	0	1	100	0	0	1	100
440–420	13	52.0	12	48.0	0	0	25	100
420–400	53	79.1	14	20.9	0	0	67	100
400–380	49	73.1	18	26.9	0	0	67	100
380–360	29	56.9	22	43.1	0	0	51	100
360–340	22	44.0	28	56.0	0	0	50	100
340–320	8	20.0	32	80.0	0	0	40	100
320–300	17	27.0	46	73.0	0	0	63	100
300–280	24	38.7	38	61.3	0	0	62	100
280–260	35	53.8	30	46.2	0	0	65	100
260–240	21	61.8	13	38.2	0	0	34	100
240–220	32	58.2	23	41.8	0	0	55	100
220–200	8	38.1	13	61.9	0	0	21	100

TABLE 29. INDICATORS OF THE FLUCTUATION OF THE INFLUENCE OF ETHICAL SYSTEMS AND MENTALITY BY 20-YEAR PERIODS — *continued*
(on the basis of different values given from 1 to 12)

PERIOD	Ethics of Happiness (Eudaemonism, Hedonism, Utilitarianism)		Ethics of Principles		Ethics of Love		Total	
	No.	Per cent	No.	Per cent	No.	Per cent	No.	Per cent
200–180 B.C.	4	30.8	9	69.2	0	0	13	100
180–160	7	46.7	8	53.3	0	0	15	100
160–140	10	55.6	8	44.4	0	0	18	100
140–120	9	50.0	9	50.0	0	0	18	100
120–100	6	35.3	11	64.7	0	0	17	100
100–80	7	30.4	16	69.6	0	0	23	100
80–60	5	15.1	28	84.9	0	0	33	100
60–40	23	38.3	37	61.7	0	0	60	100
40–20	14	48.3	15	51.7	0	0	29	100
20–0	6	37.5	10	62.5	0	0	16	100
0–20 A.D.	1	4.8	20	95.2	0	0	21	100
20–40	1	7.7	12	92.3	0	0	13	100
40–60	1	4.3	22	95.7	0	0	23	100
60–80	1	2.8	35	97.2	0	0	36	100
80–100	1	2.9	34	97.1	0	0	35	100
100–120	1	2.4	38	90.5	3	7.1	42	100
120–140	2	3.3	56	91.8	3	4.9	61	100
140–160	3	4.8	54	85.7	6	9.5	63	100
160–180	9	12.5	57	79.2	6	8.3	72	100
180–200	11	12.3	68	76.5	10	11.2	89	100
200–220	9	13.2	49	72.0	10	14.8	68	100
220–240	1	2.2	36	80.0	8	17.8	45	100
240–260	1	2.4	31	73.8	10	23.8	42	100
260–280	1	3.3	27	90.0	2	6.7	30	100
280–300	1	5.9	15	88.2	1	5.9	17	100
300–320	1	5.25	17	89.5	1	5.25	19	100
320–340	1	5.0	15	75.0	4	20.0	20	100
340–360	1	6.7	6	40.0	8	53.3	15	100
360–380	5	9.6	21	40.4	26	50.0	52	100
380–400	5	9.6	15	28.9	32	61.5	52	100
400–420	0	0	12	37.5	20	62.5	32	100
420–440	0	0	13	41.9	18	58.1	31	100
440–460	0	0	17	68.0	8	32.0	25	100
460–480	0	0	12	70.6	5	29.4	17	100
480–500	0	0	12	85.7	2	14.3	14	100
500–520	0	0	18	64.3	10	35.7	28	100
520–540	0	0	17	63.0	10	37.0	27	100
540–560	0	0	14	87.5	2	12.5	16	100
560–580	0	0	5	71.4	2	28.6	7	100
580–600	0	0	2	33.3	4	66.7	6	100
600–620	0	0	4	50.0	4	50.0	8	100
620–640	0	0	4	40.0	6	60.0	10	100
640–660	0	0	1	14.3	6	85.7	7	100
660–680	0	0	1	14.3	6	85.7	7	100
680–700	0	0	1	50.0	1	50.0	2	100
700–720	0	0	1	50.0	1	50.0	2	100
720–740	0	0	1	16.7	5	83.3	6	100
740–760	0	0	1	16.7	5	83.3	6	100
760–780	0	0	0.5	50.0	0.5	50.0	1	100
780–800	0	0	1	33.3	2	66.7	3	100
800–820	0	0	1	33.3	2	66.7	3	100
820–840	0	0	6	85.7	1	14.3	7	100
840–860	0	0	6	42.9	8	57.1	14	100

TABLE 29. INDICATORS OF THE FLUCTUATION OF THE INFLUENCE OF ETHICAL SYSTEMS AND MENTALITY BY 20-YEAR PERIODS — *continued*
(on the basis of different values given from 1 to 12)

PERIOD	*Ethics of Happiness (Eudaemonism, Hedonism, Utilitarianism)*		*Ethics of Principles*		*Ethics of Love*		*Total*	
	No.	*Per cent*	*No.*	*Per cent*	*No.*	*Per cent*	*No.*	*Per cent*
860–880 A.D.	0	0	2	15.4	11	84.6	13	100
880–900	0	0	1	16.7	5	83.3	6	100
900–920	0	0	1	33.3	2	66.7	3	100
920–940	0	0	1	50.0	1	50.0	2	100
940–960	0	0	0.5	50.0	0.5	50.0	1	100
960–980	0	0	0.5	50.0	0.5	50.0	1	100
980–1000	0	0	1	50.0	1	50.0	2	100
1000–1020	0	0	1	33.3	2	66.7	3	100
1020–1040	0	0	1	33.3	2	66.7	3	100
1040–1060	0	0	5	62.5	3	37.5	8	100
1060–1080	0	0	5	22.7	17	77.3	22	100
1080–1100	0	0	6	26.1	17	73.9	23	100
1100–1120	0	0	3	20.0	12	80.0	15	100
1120–1140	0	0	5	21.7	18	78.3	23	100
1140–1160	0	0	2	9.1	20	90.9	22	100
1160–1180	0	0	2	16.7	10	83.3	12	100
1180–1200	0	0	2	16.7	10	83.3	12	100
1200–1220	0	0	2	20.0	8	80.0	10	100
1220–1240	0	0	4	44.4	5	55.6	9	100
1240–1260	0	0	4	26.8	11	73.2	15	100
1260–1280	0	0	10	26.3	28	73.7	38	100
1280–1300	0	0	12	21.1	45	78.9	57	100
1300–1320	0	0	3	4.9	58	95.1	61	100
1320–1340	0	0	4	11.8	30	88.2	34	100
1340–1360	0	0	9	24.3	28	75.7	37	100
1360–1380	0	0	6	18.8	26	81.2	32	100
1380–1400	0	0	1	11.1	8	88.9	9	100
1400–1420	0	0	2	33.3	4	66.7	6	100
1420–1440	0	0	2	15.4	11	84.6	13	100
1440–1460	3	13	2	8.7	18	78.3	23	100
1460–1480	0	0	2	10.5	17	89.5	19	100
1480–1500	0	0	1	33.3	2	66.7	3	100
1500–1520	10	23.3	32	74.4	1	2.3	43	100
1520–1540	17	18.3	45	80.6	1	1.1	63	100
1540–1560	16	33.3	31	64.6	1	2.1	48	100
1560–1580	28	41.8	35	52.2	4	6.0	67	100
1580–1600	45	52.3	27	31.4	14	16.3	86	100
1600–1620	56	48.4	48	41.3	12	10.3	116	100
1620–1640	35	35.7	54	55.1	9	9.2	98	100
1640–1660	34	39.1	46	52.9	7	8.0	87	100
1660–1680	32	29.1	71	64.5	7	6.4	110	100
1680–1700	30	23.2	94	72.9	5	3.9	129	100
1700–1720	33	28.4	78	67.3	5	4.3	116	100
1720–1740	35	34.0	64	62.1	4	3.9	103	100
1740–1760	56	35.9	88	56.4	12	7.7	156	100
1760–1780	82	52.6	60	38.5	14	8.9	156	100
1780–1800	61	35.0	93	53.5	20	11.5	174	100
1800–1820	54	28.5	102	54.0	33	17.5	189	100
1820–1840	60	29.4	108	52.9	36	17.7	204	100
1840–1860	127	40.3	150	47.6	38	12.1	315	100
1860–1880	138	38.3	166	46.1	56	15.6	360	100
1880–1900	188	42.8	187	42.6	64	14.6	439	100
1900–1920	200	43.0	191	41.0	74	16.0	465	100

TABLE 30. INDICATORS OF THE FLUCTUATION OF THE INFLUENCE OF ETHICAL SYSTEMS AND MENTALITY BY CENTURY PERIODS, 600 B.C.—A.D. 1900

(on the basis of different values given from 1 to 12)

PERIOD	*Ethics of Happiness (Eudaemonism, Hedonism, Utilitarianism)*		*Ethics of Principles*		*Ethics of Love*		*Total*	
	No.	*Per cent*	*No.*	*Per cent*	*No.*	*Per cent*	*No.*	*Per cent*
600–500 B.C.	0	0	15	100	0	0	15	100
500–400	53	63.9	30	36.1	0	0	83	100
400–300	72	46.2	84	53.8	0	0	156	100
300–200	64	50.0	64	50.0	0	0	128	100
200–100	18	42.9	24	57.1	0	0	42	100
100–0	31	33.0	63	67.0	0	0	94	100
0–100 A.D.	1	1.3	76	98.7	0	0	77	100
100–200	12	6.8	143	82.2	19	11.0	174	100
200–300	10	8.8	83	72.8	21	18.4	114	100
300–400	6	9.1	23	34.8	37	56.1	66	100
400–500	0	0	31	53.4	27	46.6	58	100
500–600	0	0	25	61.0	16	39.0	41	100
600–700	0	0	5	31.3	11	68.7	16	100
700–800	0	0	1.5	15.0	8.5	85.0	10	100
800–900	0	0	9	36.0	16	64.0	25	100
900–1000	0	0	1.5	30.0	3.5	70.0	5	100
1000–1100	0	0	9	29.0	22	71.0	31	100
1100–1200	0	0	7	13.2	46	86.8	53	100
1200–1300	0	0	18	18.9	77	81.1	95	100
1300–1400	0	0	15	13.8	94	86.2	109	100
1400–1500	3	8.7	5	13.5	29	77.8	37	100
1500–1600	100	43.5	109	47.4	21	9.1	230	100
1600–1700	129	38.4	181	53.9	26	7.7	336	100
1700–1800	175	36.3	272	56.4	35	7.3	482	100
1800–1900	395	38.0	499	48.0	146	14.0	1040	100

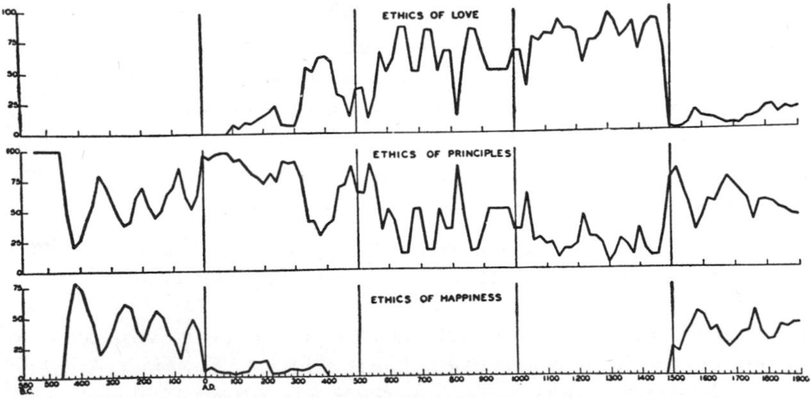

FIG. 16. FLUCTUATION OF ETHICAL CURRENTS

The real reason for it is the absolutistic conception of moral values and moral order. Since it is absolute and since it can be violated, it must be sustained; violated justice must be restored; the violation must not pass unpunished, no matter whether the violation was intentional or not; no matter whether we understand or not the will of the gods. It is assumed to be absolute and always right, even when we do not comprehend it. For any absolutistic system of ethics, any transgression of the absolute moral order cannot pass without its expiation, and without a restoration of the moral value itself. Such, in brief, is the moral mentality of Greek thinkers before and at the beginning of the fifth century B.C. It shows itself exceedingly Ideational — and in this respect happens to be in harmony with the Ideationalism dominant in other compartments of Greek culture of that period.

B. When we pass to the middle and then to the second half of the fifth and then to the fourth century B.C., the spectrum of the moral mentality changes — and changes greatly. First, the system of ethics of happiness emerges and rapidly grows, mainly in a noble eudaemonistic form. Second, more extreme Sensate systems of ethics of some of the Sophists appear. Third, the main theories of ethics, namely, of Plato and Aristotle and their followers, appear to be nearest to the Idealistic system. Such a spectrum means that the second half of the fifth and the fourth centuries show themselves here partly Mixed but mainly Idealistic. Plato's system is antihedonistic and antiutilitarian; it is not quite Ideational. It is Idealistic, with eudaemonism whose one foot is in the supersensory world of absolute values, the other in the noblest field of the sensory world — eudaemonistic happiness — as a consequence of the other aspect of the service to the gods, to the soul, or to the absolute moral value.

Idealistic also, though more "earthly," is Aristotle's system of ethics. His supreme *summum bonum*, the supreme end, is self-sufficiency, which is neither hedonistic nor utilitarian; it is again eudaemonistic and absolute. Concretely, it is described as a wise, contemplative life of the mind or soul which partakes of "the divine Principle." The eudaemonistic happiness follows, as a by-product, from such a *summum bonum*. But sensate happiness is neither the self-value, nor do sensate pleasures play an important part in such a happiness. A self-sufficient and perfectly happy life in the Aristotelian sense

> will be higher than mere human nature, because a man will live thus, not in so far as he is man but in so far as there is in him a divine Principle.

Idealistic also is the position of the great writers of the second part of the fifth and of the first part of the fourth century: Euripides, Aristophanes (partly), Thucydides. Their moral systems are still rooted in the transcendental world of gods. But now their will is scrutinized, sometimes questioned, sometimes protested on the basis and for the sake of the eudaemonistic sensate values of man's life. Eudaemonistic and utilitarian principles enter as components of their moral standpoint.

C. At the end of the fifth and the beginning of the fourth century B.C. (420 to 380), there is a great quantitative flaring of the ethics of happiness. It becomes dominant. It stays high throughout the fourth, the third, the second, and the first centuries B.C. So far it bears witness to the Sensate character of this period. Qualitatively, the moral mentality undergoes a still more important change. The noble eudaemonistic theories were more and more replaced by more primitive hedonistic and utilitarian branches of the Sensate ethics of happiness.

D. With the beginning of our era, it begins to decline, and after the fourth century A.D. it goes underground. Here again its movement is similar to that of all the other Sensate variables of Graeco-Roman culture.

E. The period from the fifth century A.D. to the end of the fifteenth century appears again monolithic, entirely dominated by the ethics of principles. This period, up to at least the thirteenth century, appears to be Ideational here also, similar to its Ideationalism in all the other fields of Western culture. The ethical mentality of it was in a perfect agreement with the other variables of the culture studied. The perfectly Ideational, even ascetically Ideational character of the medieval moral mentality is well known. Moral commands are those of God. They are absolute. They are the supreme value. They do not have any regard for the value of sensate happiness at all. If anything, they are inimical to it.

> Fear not them that kill the body.
>
> *Memento, homo, quia pulvis es et in pulverem revertis.*
>
> *Quisquic amat Christum, mundum non diligit istum*

These are the mottoes, in millions of variations, that dominated the medieval moral mentality. The emergence and growth of monasticism testify to the same contempt toward all the earthly values. This ideational mentality permeated the whole of life.

It is not surprising, therefore, that among the thinkers of these centuries from the fifth to the thirteenth, practically no name can be found that expounded a Sensate system of ethics.

F. In Table 29 we do not find any representative of such a system up to the fifteenth century. This does not mean, however, that *qualitatively* the ethical systems for all these centuries did not experience any change from the standpoint of our main categories. Formally, the ethical systems of these centuries are still religious, transcendental, and absolutistic. And yet, new notes begin to sound in them — a note of a sublime eudaemonism; a note somewhat reluctant to the previous monastic asceticism and torture of the body; a note of admissibility and justification of the supreme eudaemonistic happiness in so far and inasmuch as it does not contradict the commands of God. These new notes sound in the works of the great scholastics of the period as well as in those of the minor thinkers.

Peter Abelard, Hugo de St. Victor, Albertus Magnus, St. Thomas Aquinas, Walter of Brugges, Alexander of Halle, Roscelinus, Roger Bacon, Siger of Brabant, Dante, and others, not mentioning even such names as Petrarch; all these thinkers to some degree and in some forms introduced these "new notes" in their ethical systems. For this reason, the period appears not very unlike that of the fifth century B.C. in Greece. It is not incidental that the Platonized Aristotelian system of ethics is the ethics of St. Thomas, Albertus Magnus, Dante, and of many other Scholastics marked by the Idealistic stamp rather than by the purely Ideational form of the preceding centuries. The values of Sensate world "got some footing" in the ethical systems of these centuries and were now not regarded as absolutely valueless or negative. In this sense, the period was Mixed and Idealistic in its ethical mentality.

G. The growth of Sensate elements continues within the absolute systems of ethics of the next centuries, and culminates in an emergence of Sensate systems of ethics at the end of the fifteenth century, and their sudden enormous increase in the sixteenth century, up to 43 per cent of all the systems of ethics. Sensate (not Idealistic) eudaemonism, then hedonism, and utilitarianism re-emerge on the highway of the ethical thought of the Western society, and after that, with temporary fluctuations, rapidly grow. The expansion of this stream, or the trend toward the sensualization of ethics during the centuries from the sixteenth to the twentieth has proceeded in three ways: first, quantitatively, the ethics of happiness in all its three forms held during the last four centuries about 40 per cent of influence compared with 60 per cent of that held by the ethics of absolute principles. In the sixteenth century — the time of the Renaissance and the Reformation — quantitatively, Sensate ethics was the highest (43 per cent). In the next two centuries it fell slightly, but in the nineteenth and the twentieth century has rebounded. The second form of the expansion of this stream manifested itself in a greater growth of its hedonistic and utilitarian branches at the cost of eudaemonistic variety. Finally, the growth of the current manifested itself also in a greater and greater contamination by Sensate elements of the systems of the ethics of principles of these centuries. Formally many of these appear absolutistic and Ideational; factually, when one analyzes their content, one sees that many of them are rather Sensate than Ideational.

Notwithstanding their apparent ethical absolutism, the content and the role of these currents consisted indeed in undermining the real Ideational ethics and in justifying, beautifying, and sanctifying the utilitarian sensate mode of life. Max Weber, R. H. Tawney, E. Troeltsch, and many other investigators of these movements claim that in a way they were the godfathers of the contemporary capitalism, pecuniarism, economism, utilitarianism, or the rationalistic worldly epicureanism. Their works permit me to be brief and to use their studies for corroboration of the above claim. To put concisely what I mean by this, it is enough to compare the medieval attitude toward economic interests and values. In the moral theory as well as, to a considerable degree, in the practice of the Middle Ages, the economic conditions of life were regarded as entirely subordinated to the religious and moral values; the wealth as such was viewed, especially in the early Middle Ages, negatively, as a source of perdition, and the rich as the group for which it was more difficult to save their souls than for a camel to pass through a needle's eye.

Later on, after the twelfth and thirteenth centuries, this attitude began to be changed and, from being merely "soft-pedaled" at the beginning, was given a more and more "tolerant" interpretation, until after approximately the sixteenth and the seventeenth centuries it was forsaken, and the economic interests and values were raised to the level of the self-sufficing and almost the main value, to which all the others should be subordinated.

Here we have one of the immanent transformations of a social process. Just as the ascetic medieval Church, due to its asceticism, attracted wealth more and more and was changed, becoming the richest institution, so the commercial devotion of the ascetic Puritanism with its "limitation of consumption, its release of acquisitive activity led through this compulsory saving to accumulation of capital. And the greater it was, the greater became its grip and the more strongly it embraced Puritans in its tentacles," and dried out even those Ideational and noncommercial values which it had at the moment of its inception.

In the seventeenth and the eighteenth centuries, economic interest and expediency became the supreme value and the criterion for evaluation of all the other (especially the noneconomic) values, including the religious and moral ones.

> Honesty is useful because it assures credit; so are punctuality, industry, frugality, and that is the reason they are virtues. . . . Remember that time is money. . . . Remember that credit is money. . . . Remember that money is of prolific, generating nature.

These statements of Benjamin Franklin in Weber's interpretation show as great a revolution in the moral values as there could be. From being censored, branded, punished, and persecuted in the Middle Ages, the economic values and interests now became the king and queen of all the other values. Both utilitarianism and hedonism, along with their derivatives, also grew enormously and covered with their shadows the whole horizon of the social and moral world, and molded it according to their own ideals.

In a concrete, different form, the same transformation took place within the Catholic doctrines and moral teachings of these centuries.

H. During these four centuries, the ethics of happiness had its highs in the periods 1560–1620; then around 1760–1780; and finally, since 1880 up to the present time. We are living at the age of its high tide. Most of the Sensate systems have become more sensual, more relative, more earthly, and more carnal than, for instance, they were during the greater part of their Graeco-Roman history. This "carnalization" of all the ethical values in the public mentality of the present time has gone exceedingly far and has reduced almost all the ethical values to those of mere bodily comfort and enjoyment; these have become the measuring sticks for the evaluation of ethical as well as other values.

I. These dry figures reveal a number of the dominant characteristics of the contemporary mentality.

(1) Its predominantly utilitarian and hedonistic nature. *"Utility" in the Sensate meaning is the dominant trait of our moral mentality.* From science to religion we demand that everything be materially useful and profitable. If A is useful, A is good. If not, then it is not good. "Science is the most economic adaptation of man to environment, his thoughts to facts, and facts to one another."

Truth is the most economical and convenient mode of thinking, and science is the most economic form of adaptation of man.

"If belief in God is useful, God exists; if not, He does not."

"What is the truth's cash value in the experiential terms?"

These and dozens of other definitions of truth and science — "operational criteria of truth," "survival value of science," "science as the most efficient instrument for survival" — reflect this all-pervading utilitarian principle of our mentality. With proper modifications, the same is thought, asserted, and heralded in regard to any value. If God himself should come to us, His acceptance or rejection would depend upon whether He appears to us to be useful or not. If useful, we accept anything as God; if not, we reject Him.

(2) *Its second fundamental category is hedonism.* Whether in its sensible or reckless form, it again pervades our moral mentality, from the daily, "Unhappy? Buy a New Car," "Want to Be Happy? Buy A Brand Ham or Refrigerator," or to our "We immensely *enjoyed* the Sunday sermon" or "the lecture" or anything else. The term "enjoyment" bears the Sensate connotation, and we do not even notice how

awkward it is in its application to the values that do not need, and do not seek, "enjoyment" in order to be values. Everything is viewed by us from this hedonistic standpoint. It is demanded that sermons, lectures, philanthropic actions, even execution and murder be enjoyable and entertaining. Anything that does not contain in itself at least a promise of sensate pleasure has little chance of being appreciated in our times.

(3) The third category, derivative from that, is *our money madness*. It manifests itself in thousands of forms. Nowadays we strive to turn almost anything into a profit-making business. Titles, religious preaching, quintuplets, quadruplets, notoriety received at a kidnaping trial, participation in a murder case, fame in the scientific field, in a war, in a baseball game, in politics — all is sought to be turned into profit. Almost all such "heroes" sooner or later land either on the vaudeville stage, or on a Hollywood stage, or in the pages of a sensational paper, or on the board of directors of a bank or insurance company, turning their reputation into money.

(4) Its next form is *the contemporary leadership*. Who are our leaders? First of all, successful money-makers. It matters little how the money is made. With few exceptions, they are at the top of "society"; they are granted scientific degrees, with all their alphabets; they are trustees of everything; they are political leaders; they control this, that, and the other. Some of them, no doubt, deserve such prominence. The others — and they are the majority — hardly. Some certainly not. The money-makers are our heroes, from the Rothschilds to the lucky "wolf of Wall Street." Shall it be added that, in harmony with this, almost everything is for sale in our culture? Money buys all, from saintliness to "beauty." Old Jugurtha's *urbem venalem* is as applicable to us as it was to the culture of Sensate Rome. The main desire, ambition, dream, of most of our contemporaries is to be rich; to have "all that money can buy."

(5) Its fifth trait is "*moral atomism, relativism, nihilism.*" We hardly have any moral value now that is absolute or sacred. By the way of hypocritical inertia, individuals and groups, when they try to defend their existence, or their robbery of existence from others, continue to issue appeals "in the name of humanity," "to the public opinion," "to the sense of justice," and the like; but few except the hopelessly naïve people believe in these appeals and these so-called principles and values. There is no absolute categorical imperative binding upon communists and their victims, Hitlerites and Jews, Italians and Ethiopians, atheists and believers, the "moderns" and the "old fashioned," rich and poor, the oppressed and the oppressors, and the like! The result is moral anarchy; moral atomism. Everyone is — and under these conditions is entitled

to be — his own moral legislator. And many of us factually are that. Such an *anomie*, to use Durkheim's term, is inevitable when the absolute standards are rejected. It is a mere matter of time when the relativistic ethics of happiness, in the immanent process of its development, comes to this *anomie*. Our culture seems to have reached it.

The next consequence of it is the *rule of force and coercion* in our social life, in interindividual as well as intergroup relationships. When there are no absolute moral standards, the only guarantee for everybody is either hypocrisy and profit or force. As the profit is desired by all, force becomes the only means of self-protection or of coercion of the others to comply with our demands. Postwar periods have demonstrated clearly that international treaties and obligations do not mean anything; they are just scraps of papers aimed to deceive the naïve. Therefore, at the present moment nobody but the naïve believes in them; any statesman who is not hopelessly stupid does not rely, and cannot rely, upon contracts and treaties. The only means of reliance is force. Hence an enormous increase of its role in international and intergroup relationships. Since neither God, nor moral values, nor promises, nor contracts, can be relied upon, one is forced to rely upon his own rude force or that of his own group. Hence, use of force by every state that feels it can use it safely, be it Japan, Italy, Germany, Russia, or any other country. Hence, an enormous increase of armaments; military budgets; more and more destructive inventions as means to international, interclass, intergroup, interindividual wars. Hence the extraordinary explosions of World Wars, local wars, and revolutions that have made this century one of the bloodiest of all centuries of civilization. Force has become the supreme arbiter. We have approached very near to the Hobbesian hypothetical "war of everybody with everybody."

Such a rise of force to the position of the supreme moral arbiter is but an immanent result of the excessive development of the hedonistic and utilitarian moral mentality of our days. If this mentality is going to progress further, the role of force will be still more increased until it makes a social life impossible. Then the reaction is to be expected. And this reaction would mean, even has to be preceded by, a decline of the Sensate morality and rise of the ethics of absolute principles. Signs of such a reaction are absent, as yet. But we all feel sharply enough the "carnal inconveniency" of overripe Sensate morality: it has robbed us of our security of life, of our comfort, of our sensate well-being, of our position, of our self-respect, of our dignity, of almost everything. With a further movement in this direction, this "uncomfortable feeling" is likely to increase until it reaches the stage when a shift to the absolute moral standard becomes unavoidable, and with it, the reaction to these "constituents" of the overdeveloped ethics of happiness will set in. Then the curve of the ethics of principles will rise again while that of the Sensate ethics will decline once more. So it has been, and so it will go.

K. The data support all the main conclusions derived from Tables 29 and 30 as to the invalidity of any linear conception in this field; as to the principle of limits; Spencer's formula of evolution; the childish character of belief in a final victory of one of the systems over all the others and so on.

L. As to the comparative quantitative strength and balance of these systems, the picture at various periods and for the total period considered is given in Table 31.

TABLE 31. SUM OF INDICES FOR EACH SYSTEM FOR THE SPECIFIED PERIOD

Periods	*Ethics of Happiness*	*Ethics of Principles*	*Ethics of Love*
540 B.C.–A.D. 100	239	356	—
100–600	28	305	120
600–1500	3	71	307
1500–1900	799	1061	228
Total	1069	1793	655

Thus the first period was that of relatively close balance between the ethics of happiness and that of principles. In the second and third periods the balance was entirely broken and the ethics of principles prevailed almost absolutely. The fourth period is again a period of somewhat closer balance between the ethics of happiness and that of principles and of love. When the totals of both of these systems of ethics of principles and of love is taken for the whole period, the sum is 2448, which is more than twice as great as the total sum for the ethics of happiness. This may be interpreted in the sense that, all in all, social existence of man requires that in the relationship between the ethics of principles and that of happiness, the former must be generally much stronger than the latter. And perhaps such a conclusion would not appear strange to anyone who realizes that some degree of sacrifice and altruism is always necessary, and that the ethics of principles stimulates these forms of relationship much more than the ethics of happiness.

Another thing revealed by the figures in Table 31 is that these numerous "modern" writers on ethics, who assure us that the days of any authoritative system of ethics are over, and that from now on the future belongs entirely to the "scientifically calculated" moral engineering of a purely utilitarian or eudaemonistic or hedonistic type, are but poor victims of their flat imagination and limited knowledge.

25

FLUCTUATION OF ETHICOJURIDICAL MENTALITY IN CRIMINAL LAW

The best source or "social mirror" of the ethical mentality and respective forms of conduct, or of the mores, is usually given by the totality of the "official" laws of a given group, plus its "official" moral prescriptions. Any enforced and functioning code of "official" law is the most authoritative, the most (comparatively) accurate, and most reliable reflection of the ethical mentality and ethical differentiation of the actions in the above classes. There is no doubt that such an "official code" does not reflect the totality of the real imperative-attributive convictions of the members of the society perfectly. There always is some discrepancy between the situation as it is depicted in the "official law" and in the psychosocial mentality of the members of the society. And the discrepancy is the greater, the quicker the socioethical life of the society changes. As the official laws cannot be changed incessantly, so to speak, while the social life is changing constantly, the discrepancy is inevitable. However, the discrepancy should not be exaggerated, especially for the earlier centuries, when the tempo of the change of the ethicojuridical mentality, and of the respective forms of conduct, was slow. All in all, any functioning code of law which existed and was enforced for decades or centuries, and which has been the foundation for the activities of the courts and of the agencies of justice, does reflect the reality in essential parts fairly accurately, anyhow better than any other source. If in this or that special field it shows a discrepancy with the ethical mentality of the members, it does not do so in the greater part of the conduct covered by it. When the discrepancy becomes indeed considerable, such a code is revised or replaced by a new "official" code.

Having taken note of these generalities, we can turn now to the problem of our study. It consists of an elucidation of whether or not the ethicojuridical mentality on the level of the "daily routine conduct" fluctuates in the course of time. If so, how and what are some characteristics of this fluctuation? Do, for instance, the ethicojuridical rules and norms all change together, or do they change in one field of conduct independently of changes in other fields of action specified in the juridical official law and moral codes? In other words, is the totality of such norms and "laws" a unified organic system where a change in onc field leads to that in the whole system, or is it a conglomeration of several clusters of norms, each of which has its own existence and therefore changes independently? Finally, are the changes in the field of the juridicoethical mentality, as it is reflected in the "official law" and moral norms, associated in a tangible way with the alternation of the Ideational and Sensate cultures, and if so, in what way and how?

In this abridged edition, I am giving only the conclusions of a more substantial study of the codes of law — the criminal, the civil, and others — published in the full text of the *Dynamics*.

(1) Though the quantitative-qualitative fluctuation of punishment in reality is not identical with the curve of punishment in the subsequent criminal codes, nevertheless, in a more conservative and limited way, the codes as a whole reflect the main ups and downs of the curve of severity (but not of amount) of punishment in real social life. Aside from the short-lived codes, like those enacted in the time of revolution which sometimes do not last even long enough to be included and enforced in the functioning of criminal courts and justice; or are neglected in the time of revolution, when justice functions through other channels — with the exceptions of such codes and laws, the long-time functioning criminal codes reflect the main changes of the ethicojuridical mentality and of the penal system. But the fluctuation of the composition of the actions of criminal class, as well as of the amount and severity of punishment, is narrower in the codes than it is in reality. Codes in this respect remind us of an even and "averaged" curve from which the numerous erratic and wide fluctuations are eliminated. The fluctuations of crime and punishment in social reality are likely to be much more violent and irregular. Besides, the codes do not show all the fluctuations, sometimes enormous, which take place between two codes, especially when one of these codes is separated from its successor by decades and even centuries. Long-time functioning codes are enacted in normal times and intended for a long existence under normal conditions; the periods of abnormal crises and their systems of "justice" and punishment are not reflected in them, and when a "crisis code" is enacted, it usually reflects the reality in this field quite incorrectly.

With these reservations, codes, then, are roughly accurate indicators of the changes in the criminal and penal fields which take place in the course of time in the life history of a given social body.

(2) In the comparatively integrated cultures, the criminal and penal law also reflects the substantial changes in the inner nature of a given culture. So far as we are following the fluctuation of Ideational and Sensate types of culture, we see that the codes reflect this fluctuation in the criminal as well as penal parts. When a culture passes from the Sensate or even subcultural form to the Ideational form, the transformation manifests itself in the field of crime:

(a) by an increase of the actions qualified as criminal in the sense that a series of actions which were not regarded as criminal in Sensate or subcultural periods are now included in the criminal class;

(b) most of such newly created crimes are of Ideational nature, representing actions violating Ideational values. Of these especially are the religious values. Hence most of such newly created crimes represent, in usual terminology, crimes against religion and absolute moral principles. The consideration of mere individual or social utilitarianism, hedonism, eudaemonism, play little part in the creation of these new types of crimes;

(c) in the field of punishment, in the introduction of forms of punishment which have also a somewhat Ideational nature, like the deprivation of Christian burial, imposition of anathema, interdiction, and so on. In Ideational crimes against religion there is a tendency to punish with particular severity in the criminal law of the Ideational culture.

(3) Passage from the Ideational to the Sensate form of culture is marked by opposite characteristics in the Sensate criminal law, namely, by exclusion of almost all Ideational crimes from the class of criminal actions. This means the elimination of almost all the crimes against religion and Ideational values as such. If a few of them remain in the criminal class, they remain mainly because of some utilitarian effects which their perpetration may endanger. Otherwise, almost all the actions considered criminal in such Sensate criminal codes are those which are thought of as socially dangerous, or dangerous to the governing part of the society, from the utilitarian, hedonistic, or eudaemonistic standpoints. If such dangers are not involved, the codes tend to regard all the actions which do not have such effects as normal and permitted, though from the Ideational standpoint many of them would appear as great crimes as the "unforgivable sin," "blasphemy," "sacrilege," "most outrageous profanity," and so on. On the other hand, such codes make a revaluation of the gravity of crimes, tending to regard as the gravest those actions which from the same hedonistic-utilitarian standpoint endanger the hedonistic-utilitarian values of a given society and especially of its commanding and controlling groups.

In accordance with this principle, the crimes against property values and against bodily comfort tend to increase in such codes.

As to the changes in the penal part, they consist in elimination of penalty for most Ideational crimes; in an enormous mitigation for the few Ideational actions that remain punishable; in the elimination of most of the punishments of purely Ideational nature, like anathema, deprivation of Christian burial, etc.

As to the comparative severity and amount of punishment in the Ideational and Sensate codes, there is hardly any ground to contend that, per se, one of these types is correlated with much greater or less punishment.

With some reservation, the comparative severity and amount of penalty depend not so much upon the predominant type of culture in which the code is enacted as upon how deeply it is rooted, settled, crystallized, and engrafted. When either one of these types is deeply rooted and settled, the punishment tends to be mild and moderate. When either one of them is in a state of transition, just being introduced or beginning to disintegrate, then the curve of penalty tends to go up, and the sharper the transition, the more pronounced the curve. This explains why the curve of penalty rose in the periods of transition from the Sensate to the Ideational form (in the centuries beginning with the third A.D., and following); or from the Ideational to the Sensate in the centuries beginning with the thirteenth, up to the seventeenth. If other disturbing factors are not present, each of these cultures, as it progresses in the crystallization of its network of social relationships and systems of values, tends to have a lesser and lesser penalty, quantitatively and qualitatively. An example of this is given by the centuries from the seventeenth to the beginning of the twentieth, when, short-time fluctuations excluded, the curve tended to decline.

Such is the general answer to this question. One reservation, however, should be made. All in all, it is possible that the Ideational Criminal Law tends generally to be somewhat more severe and stern than the normal Sensate criminal law (but not the Sensate law of the period of crisis, which tends to be outrageously rude, cruel, stern, and almost bestial in its real form in social life). There are several reasons for that first, the requirements of Ideational culture, and its laws as to man's conduct, are generally more exacting and less loose and lenient than those of the Sensate law. The first aspires to a higher level of moral conduct, admits less opportunism, inhibits a greater number of the natural proclivities of sensate man than the opportunistic-utilitarian law. Therefore, the penal pressure of the Ideational criminal law should be, and is, somewhat greater than that of the purely Sensate criminal law. Without such pressure it can hardly reach even the minimum of its objective. Second, Ideational culture and law come usually after the disintegration of overripe Sensate culture and man, with appetites let loose, with hedonism, skepticism, sensualism rampant; with the human personality deeply demoralized and disorderly. Under such circumstances, in order to discipline such a man and such a society; in order successfully to bridle the rampant sensual appetites and passions, and engraft new forms of conduct inhibiting these tendencies, a culture and law cannot be too soft. One does not educate tigers not to touch a lamb by mere sermons and similar means. One needs a cage, sometimes a whip; sometimes something still more severe and materially efficient. It is not my intention to claim that these rude and material ways and means have been the main and the most efficient means with which the newly coming Ideational culture disciplines man; its other ways and means, of a nobler, more ingenuous, more "spiritual" nature, are certainly as efficient — nevertheless their work, especially in the initial stages of Ideational culture, has to be reinforced and supported by the ruder means of physical coercion and severe penalty. For these reasons, the average level of the Ideational penal system is likely to be more severe than that of the Sensate. This we see in the great expansion of punishable actions, as well as in an increase of penalty of the medieval codes in comparison with the Barbaric; of the penal system of Rome in the centuries beginning with the third with that of preceding eras. As explained, the increase of punishment in these periods was due not only to the growth of Ideational culture, but also to the growth of the ethicojuridical heterogeneity of the population.

A further reservation to this reservation is that though Sensate law in normal society tends to be somewhat milder in its penal system than the Ideational penal system, nevertheless in the period of crisis, like revolution, when not only religious and inner moral control, generally weak in such a culture, ceases to regulate human behavior, but all the other inner — and often external — inhibitive factors cease to work, and man becomes like a little boat tossed aimlessly by the stormy passions of sensual nature — in such cases the real penal system of such a culture (not the fictitious one of the "revolutionary code") usually is incomparably more severe and cruel and blind than the system of Ideational culture. For in the Ideational culture, even in emergency crises, the inner inhibitions continue to work; therefore they do not permit a purely cynical butchering and torturing of all the enemies of the ruling group, as is the case in the disintegrated Sensate culture in the periods of crisis.

PART FIVE

TYPES AND FLUCTUATION OF THE SYSTEMS OF SOCIAL RELATIONSHIPS

26

FAMILISTIC, CONTRACTUAL, AND COMPULSORY RELATIONSHIPS AND SYSTEMS OF INTERACTION (GROUPS)

I. Introductory

From the study of the forms and fluctuations of aesthetic, scientific, philosophical, religious, and moral culture mentality, we now pass to the study of the *social* phase of the sociocultural phenomena. The preceding parts dealt mainly with what are often styled culture and cultural values; all the parts of this section will deal mainly with what are called "*social* phenomena," in the sense of the interindividual and intergroup relationships of which any social system or group, any organization or institution, is made up, which compose their "texture" and their "structure." The difference between the categories "cultural" and "social" is very conditional and relative: any culture exists through and is objectivized by some social group; and any social group has this or that kind of culture. Nevertheless, technically they can be studied separately, and for the sake of analysis can be isolated from each other, as different aspects of the same one and indivisible "sociocultural world." This conditional "social world" embraces what the partisans of the Formal School in Sociology (Tönnies, Simmel, L. von Wiese, A. Vierkandt, and others) call "the forms of social relationships," interindividual and intergroup. This class of sociocultural phenomena is again double in its nature: on the one hand it consists of the "objectively" existing network of social relationships among the interacting and contacting individuals and groups; on the other, the nature of these relationships, their "color," "qualification," and "evaluation," depends most closely upon the mentality of those who are involved in them or who deal with them (observers, investigators, etc.).

Without this mentality these relationships do not and cannot have any social meaning or sense. Without it the relationships between the patient and the surgeon operating on him and between a knifer and his victim look alike. In their sociocultural sense, these two relationships are as different as they can be. "Pure behavior" divorced from the mentality becomes a mere "reaction" or "motion," devoid of any sociocultural meaning. The same can be said of all social relationships. For this evident reason, the phenomena of social relationships are always the phenomena of "mentality." They cannot be studied apart from it, whether it be the mentality of the persons involved in the relationship —

what they think and how they qualify the social relationships — or the mentality of other persons — observers, onlookers, investigators — and their qualifications of the phenomena. Therefore, we shall study the world of social relationships and their fluctuations as the phenomena of culture mentality also. On the other hand, we all know that the mentality of this or that person (whether involved in the relationships or outside them) qualifies the given relationship in one way; meanwhile the "objective nature" of the relationship viewed from the standpoint of the logico-meaningful mentality contradicts this qualification most sharply. Who does not know of many a master who considered the relationship of slave and master as most sacred and beneficial, not only to the master but to the slave also? Who does not know of various religious or political fanatics who have sent to death thousands, either *ad majorem gloriam Dei* or for the glory of the "Proletariat," or "Communism," or "Nationalism," or any other purpose? We may grant their sincerity; but in many cases we may question the identity of their qualifications of the relationship with its nature, considered impartially, from the logico-meaningful standpoint. These two aspects often contradict each other. Hence the necessity of keeping in mind these two aspects of the social relationship: the aspect of the mentality of the persons who qualify them; and the objective logico-meaningful aspect inherent in the nature of the relationships themselves. This aspect is also the aspect of mentality; but it is logico-meaningful mentality in contradistinction to the mere factual psychology — with its biases, emotions, passions, "residues," "derivations," and the like — of the persons swayed by their qualifications. A dictator may sincerely think he is doing everything for the benefit of mankind; a serious and competent investigator, after having examined the logico-meaningful nature and "causal" effects of his activities, may qualify them differently.

These remarks show that the nature of all social relationships has two aspects, psychological and logico-meaningful (including the "causal-functional" traits). Any social relationship has to be studied from both standpoints.

After these introductory remarks we can start with our study of the world of social relationships, their forms, and their fluctuations. By definition, the study will be also a study of the texture and structure of the main types of social systems of interaction, or groups. Let us begin with the study of the most general and most fundamental forms of social relationship.

II. Social Interaction and Its Modalities

Any real social group differs from a mere nominal conglomeration of individuals by the fact that its members are in the process of interaction, in the sense that the behavior and psychological status of a member are conditioned by the activities or even by the mere existence of other members to a tangible degree. Without such a tangible interdependence of the existence, behavior, and psychology of the members, there is no real social group. What exists instead is a merely "statistical" or nominal or fictitious collection of individuals.

This tangible interdependence of the actions and psychology of individuals is the *conditio sine qua non* of any real social group or socially interactive system.

A. *Modalities of Social Systems of Interaction.* Such being the general basis of a real social unity, the modalities of the interdependence lead to various forms of social groups or social systems of interaction. Of these modalities the following are important: *one- or two-sidedness of interaction; its extensity, intensity, duration, and continuity; its direction and its organization.*

(1) *One-sidedness and Two-sidedness of Interaction.* First of all, the interdependence of the parties in the process of interaction — and for the sake of simplicity of analysis let us take only two parties — may be more or less equal or it may be such that one party strongly conditions the other. The executioner conditions the behavior of the victim much more than the victim affects the executioner. A person who has another person in his complete power can condition his behavior and psychology more than the controlled person can influence his master. From this standpoint, in a relative way, we may talk of *two-sided* or *mutual*, and *one-sided conditioning.* The first type is what can properly be styled "interaction" or "interdependence," while the second is one-sided dependence or one-sided conditioning. Both forms, however, are varieties of the real social group.

(2) *Extensity of Interaction.* Second, we must distinguish the extensity of interaction.

By extensity of interaction is meant *the proportion of the activities and psychological experiences involved in interaction out of the total sum of the activities and psychological experiences of which the person's whole life process consists.* Let us say that 100, or a circle, is the symbol of the total sum of activities and psychological experiences which compose the whole life process of a given person. Theoretically we can imagine so complete an interaction that it would condition to some extent all the 100 activities and psychological experiences of that person. In the circle there is no sector exempt from conditioning by interaction. This means that none of a person's activities and psychological experiences is independent of the other person; that the whole life of the person, without any exception whatsoever, is conditioned by the process of interaction and is fused with the life of the other person. He cannot do anything without influencing and being influenced by the interacting party. Interaction covers all the fields of his existence and experiences. The extensity of the interaction is complete, unlimited, universal, or *totalitarian.*

In the real processes of interaction hardly a case can be given coinciding with this supposititious case of absolutely unlimited — *totalitarian* — *extensity* of the interaction, but various forms of interdependence give an imperfect approach to it. The interaction of a baby and his mother, who alone takes care of the child, is an approximation to that kind of interaction: sleep, feeding, clothing, bedding, most of the baby's actions and feelings, are dependent upon the mother. Interaction of the members of the closely integrated family is another approach to it: most of their important activities throughout every twenty-four hours are conditioned by the existence and activities of the other members: the time of their rising, the time and the character of their breakfast; what they do, how much, where, and when; their dinner and evening recreation; their tastes, their beliefs, their political attitudes, their occupations, their visits, their clothing; and so on. The joy or sorrow of one member influences the psychology of the others; a change in the activity or psychology of one member reflects upon those of the others. None of their spheres of activity and experience is exempt from conditioning by the others.

If not 100 but only a part of it is conditioned by the interaction with another person, we have a *limited — not universal, not complete — extensity of interaction.* Not the whole circle but only a sector may be involved in the interaction, and is dependent upon the other party. And the less the figure, in comparison with 100, or the narrower the sector, the more limited is the extensity of the interaction, the less universal and complete it is in covering the total field of man's activities and experiences. This means that the remainder of them are independent and unconditioned tangibly by a given process of interaction. Most of the contemporary interaction processes between employer and employee, housewife and grocer, house owner and plumber or carpenter, even a contemporary teacher and pupil, minister and parishioner, doctor and patient, political boss and his henchman, owner and tenant, and so on, are cases of such a *limited extensity* of interaction. In all of these the interacting parties have a specific sector of life, and sometimes — for instance, in purchasing a package of favorite cigarettes at a drugstore — a very narrow, small, and limited one. Interaction between the house owner and plumber concerns only the matter of plumbing and nothing else. The employee-employer interaction concerns only the matter of doing stipulated work for so many hours for such and such remuneration, and that is all. All the other infinitely great number of life activities and experiences of one party — religion, political activity, family, education; aesthetic, scientific, moral, and other activities; opinions, convictions, experiences — normally do not concern the other party. "They are not his business." Thus, from the standpoint of the extensity of the interaction, it may range from 100 — the total circle of human activities and experiences — down to 0.0000001 or the smallest line of the circle; *from an unlimited and universal or all-embracing totalitarian extensity, to the most narrowly specified and limited.*

(3) *Intensity of Interaction.* Quite different from that is *the intensity* of the interaction process. Within the same "sector" of interaction — for instance, in the interaction between the religious teacher and the religious pupil — the intensity may be such that every word of the teacher will be accepted as the Gospel, and everything that he advises will be followed by the pupil. In other cases, the words and teachings of the preacher will be of little influence; most of them will be given no attention and will be ignored in practice. The intensities may vary greatly from the possible maximum to the possible minimum.

The same is true of the intensity of an interaction involving not one but many sectors of activity and experience. The parent-child or husband-wife interaction in some cases displays an unlimited devotion, love, affection, so that anything happening to one party is reflected upon the other: the slightest joy or sorrow of one becomes a joy or sorrow of the other; and so with other experiences. In other cases only the most important actions and happenings that affect one party influence the other, and even then the influence is less deep and less intense. Theoretically, combining the extensity and intensity of the interaction, we can say that *the more extensive it is and the more intensive are the sectors of the interaction, the more conditioned and bound together (for good or bad) are the life, behavior, and psychology of the interacting parties.*

(4) *Duration and Continuity of Interaction.* Each of us knows that some of the interactions arise, exist a few moments, and end. Others are continued for years, or even for life. A tourist steps into a drugstore on the road, buys a few things, pays for them, says "Good-by" and is gone, forgetting the druggist as the druggist forgets the tourist. *Duration* of the interaction existed a few moments only. On the other hand are the interactions of parents and children, of husband and wife, which are continued — even now when the family ties are broken more often — for life, unto death, and even beyond it, because the memory of the dead and the social conditions which often perpetuate this memory (a prohibition to remarry, or a transmission of the rights and the liability of the deceased to the consort or children, and so on) affect the behavior and experience of the surviving party even after the death of the other. In such cases the duration of the interaction is a life duration, and sometimes lasts even beyond death.

(5) *Direction of Interaction.* As to *the direction* of the interacting process, it may be either *solidary* or *antagonistic* or *mixed.* The interaction is *solidary* when the aspirations and respective efforts of one party concur with the aspirations and efforts of the other party. In such cases the direction of the aspirations and efforts of both parties is the same or similar. When the desires and efforts of one party clash with those of the other party and meet resistance or hindrance from it, the interaction is mutually *antagonistic.* The direction of aspirations and efforts of the two parties is contrary.

Finally, there may be an interaction in which the parties concur in only part of their aspirations and efforts, while in another part they are antagonistic to each other. Such direction of the interaction is styled *mixed,* partly antagonistic and partly solidary. Such are the main types of interaction from the standpoint of its direction.

Since the interaction may be either all-embracing or limited and specific, from the standpoint of the extensity; more or less intensive, from the standpoint of intensity; more or less durable and continuous, from the standpoint of duration and continuity, *the antagonisms and solidarities of the interacting parties may be either universal and all-embracing or only limited by the specific "sector" of interaction relationship; more or less intensive; more or less durable and continuous.*

Assuming for a moment that all the other conditions of intensity, duration, etc., are equal, we have the following scale of antagonistic and solidary interrelations of the interacting parties:

The maximum solidarity is given when the interaction is all-embracing and all its numerous sections are solidary. This means that the lives of the two parties are completely fused into one unity in all the fields of life and experience.

As the sectors of the interaction field become more and more narrow, the solidarities among the interacting parties become also more and more limited.

The maximum of antagonism is given when (other conditions being equal) the interaction between the parties is all-embracing and universal, and all its sectors are antagonistic. It means that the life and all the actions of the interacting parties are an incessant mutual struggle.

With the narrowing of the sectors of interaction, the purely antagonistic interactions of the parties become also narrower and narrower until they come to a superficial and unimportant antagonism of two stranger-tourists who at an oil station begin mildly to argue as to which of two varieties of oil or gas is better. With "You are wrong," they depart, each in the opposite direction. Their antagonism covers only a negligible part of their life activities and does not mean anything.

Finally, between these purely solidary and purely antagonistic interactions there lie the "mixed" interactions, some of which are nearer to solidary, others to antagonistic.

(6) *Organized and Unorganized Interaction.* Finally we must distinguish the *organized and unorganized* forms of interaction, as the last modality important for our purposes. The interaction is *organized* when the relationship of the parties, their actions and functions, are *crystallized* into certain patterns and have as a basis a certain *crystallized* system of values. It is *unorganized* when the relationships and values are in an amorphous state, having no crystallization and no established patterns. This is an important point and therefore needs at least a brief commentary.

(*a*) A crystallized system of social relationships and values means that within an interacting group, or between interacting parties, there is a *definite system of distribution of the rights and duties, functions (conduct), and social position for each member.* The system defines pointedly what are the rights and duties of each member; what, under what conditions, when, and how much each member is entitled to do or not to do, to tolerate, or not to tolerate in regard to each member and outsider. Such a clear distribution of rights and duties means a definite assignment of the *functions* (and *conduct*) to each member of the system of interaction. The clear-cut delineation of the rights, duties, and functions of each member perfectly defines his *social status* or *social position* within the system of interaction. X, assigned the rights, duties, and functions of a slave or of the president of a state, has respectively the social position of a slave or of the president.

(*b*) As a result, the crystallized system of social relationships and values means further that such an interacting group has a definite system of values divided into three classes: *lawful, recommended,* and *prohibited.* When each member's conduct corresponds to the sum total of the specific rights, duties, and functions assigned to him by the crystallized system, his conduct is regarded as lawful. When he transgresses the norms he commits a sin, a crime, or some other action which violates the system. In this way, the class of negative values is always present in any organized group, whether it is styled by the term sin, sacrilege, crime, unlawful action, or "maladjustment." When, finally, a member discharges not alone his duty, but something above and beyond it, he is performing a "heroic," "saintly," "virtuous" action, far above the minimum prescribed for him by the system of rights and duties. In this way the category of the recommended actions is given in any organized group, no matter what its concrete content is.

(*c*) As a mere consequence of the above, the crystallized system of social relationship in a group or between the interacting parties means further the existence of *social differentiation and stratification* in any organized group or system of interaction. The fact of a definite distribution of the rights, duties, functions, and social positions among the members of a group (or interacting parties) means that the functions of each are specified, therefore differentiated. Even in such a small group as the family, the rights, duties, and functions of the father, the mother, the younger child, and the older child are not the same and cannot be the same on account of the age, sex, and other biosocial differences: they are specified sharply even in the most democratic and equalitarian and contractual family. This means also that such a group is *stratified*, because in any organized group there are the governing and the governed members. As soon as this is given, no matter whether in its most democratic form where the boss or the manager is just *primus inter pares*, or in an autocratic form, social stratification is given. It is an inseparable part, inalienable from the very concept of social organization.

The unorganized system of interaction does not have these characteristics. It is amorphous in all these respects: the rights, duties, functions, social position of its members are undetermined and undefined either in broad outlines or in meticulous details; so are its categories of the lawful, recommended, and prohibited forms of conduct and relationship; so its structure of social differentiation and stratification. They all remain respectively uncrystallized. The whole system of social relationships and values is confused and vague.

No doubt that the passage from the absolutely unorganized to the perfectly organized groups or social systems of interaction in reality is gradual.

The organized and unorganized modality of a system of interaction should not be mixed with the solidary and antagonistic modality. A model prison can serve as an example of that: it is an organized system of interaction, with a clearly defined system of the rights, duties, functions, social positions of each prisoner and each member of the guard. And yet, in most cases, we can hardly qualify the relationship between the prisoners and the guard as solidary: the first party endeavours to escape; the other hinders it. In many other respects their relationship is antagonistic.

There are many systems of interaction with the solidary good will of the parties involved, yet remaining often unorganized. This means that combining the organized-unorganized and antagonistic-solidary modalities, we can have the following types of social systems of interaction:

(i) *Organized-antagonistic System of interaction based on Coercion and Compulsion.* The prison system gives an example of that type. The systems of interaction imposed by conquerors upon the conquered; by masters upon slaves and serfs; and hundreds of other —

interindividual and intergroup — systems of interaction belong to this type.

(ii) *Organized-solidary System of Interaction.* It has all the earmarks of the organized system and of the solidary direction of the efforts and wishes of the parties involved. Many free associations, with voluntary membership; a good family; devoted religious, political, economic, and other co-operative associations belong to this type.

(iii) *Organized Mixed: Solidary-antagonistic System of Interaction.* It is maintained partly by compulsory enforcement, partly by voluntary support of the crystallized system of relationships and values, with its rights, duties, functions, social positions, assigned to each member. Probably most of the organized social systems of interaction, from the family to the Church, the State, the occupational union, and so on, belong to this type, some having the compulsory factor more greatly developed, some less. Most of the citizens of a given state would probably wish to belong to it voluntarily and voluntarily would support many of its laws. And yet, many of these same citizens would hardly pay their taxes, go into battle, or perform many other disagreeable duties if they were not forced to do so. Such "burdensome" duties exist in almost all organized systems of interaction, even in the universities and colleges: numbers of professors would prefer to be free from too many lectures, recitations, blue-book readings, if the choice depended entirely upon them, and if such omissions would not lead to a loss of their positions.

The same varieties exist among the unorganized groups: (1) *Unorganized-antagonistic*, (2) *Unorganized-solidary*, (3) *Unorganized-mixed.* So much about this modality.

B. *Social Groups or Systems of Interaction.* These range as follows.

(1) From the standpoint of the extensity of the interaction process, they range from the all-embracing unlimited totalitarian (maximally cumulative) to the slightest, where the interacting relationship is limited to one unimportant "interest."

(2) From the standpoint of intensity, from the most intensive to the barely tangible.

(3) From the standpoint of duration, from the most durable and continuous to the groups existing only a short moment, sometimes a few seconds.

(4) From the standpoint of the direction of the interaction, from the maximally and relatively solidary through the mixed groups, to the limited and all-embracingly antagonistic.

(5) From the standpoint of organization, from the highly organized to the barely organized and unorganized groups.

III. Familistic, Contractual, and Compulsory Types of Social Relationships

The above modalities, or types of social relationships, in the organized systems of interaction also rarely exist in an isolated form, but ordinarily are combined with one another, thus producing a few types of social groups or systems of interaction, which occur frequently and are met in any human universe. Of these "combined" types, three appear to me particularly important from many standpoints. They are met in almost any human universe, past, present, and probably future; primitive and modern; Oriental and Occidental. They are the Familistic, the Contractual, and the Compulsory types.

A. *The Familistic Type.* If we select from the above modalities of social relationships in the interaction system the following ones: (1) *universal totalitarian or all-embracing in extensity*, (2) *high in intensity*, (3) *purely solidary in direction*, (4) *durable* — then a combination of all the four modalities gives us what I style the familistic system of interaction or social relationship. Such is its "chemical formula."

A concrete example of this is given by the relationship between a loving mother and her baby; between the mutually devoted members of the family; between true friends, in the Aristotelian sense of real friendship. In these systems of interaction almost the whole circle of life activities of the parties is involved in the process of interaction, and certainly all the most important life relationships. In this sense, their whole lives are thrown together and organically united into one "we." There is almost nothing of the "it does not concern me," "it is none of my business," "mind your own affairs" attitude. On the contrary, what concerns one party concerns the other: joy and sorrow; failure and success; sickness and recovery; food, clothing, shelter; comfort, mental peace, beliefs, convictions, tastes of one party — all these concern most vitally the other, and meet concurrence, care, approval, aid, and sympathy.

It is as though they are bound by so short a rope that one party cannot make a step without pulling the other. Not only is the interaction all-embracingly extensive and highly intensive, but it is solidary par excellence. This solidarity comes out in millions of forms and continuously. It is as close as, sometimes even closer than, the mutual well-being of the various parts of one organism. The sorrow, joy, misfortune, success, of one becomes that of the other party. Their lives are fused together; their personalities are merged into one "we." The individuals here need one another, seek one another, and are bound into one unity, neither by compulsion, nor by considerations of profit, nor by contract; but spontaneously, for the sake of "being together," for the sake of the other party itself, regardless of pleasure, profit, compulsion, or contract.

Coercion is necessary here not to keep them together but to keep them apart. Likewise the bond is not a contract or a covenant. Most mothers want to be with their children spontaneously, organically, regardless of any contract or duty. The same is true of real friends. If a man is a "friend" of another man by mere contract, this means he is a pseudo friend. The real friend is, as Aristotle says rightly, "one who intends and does what is good (or what he believes to be good) to another for that other's sake; or one who wishes his friend to be and to live for that friend's own sake." Such a relationship among friends may give and usually results in some utility or pleasure for the parties, but neither one of these factors is the reason for the existence of such a tie; on the contrary, it is a mere result or by-product. Side by side with pleasure and utility, there is also sorrow and sacrifice in such a relationship, because any sorrow of one party becomes that of the other; the oneness of the parties leads each of them to offer or to render — again spontaneously — to the other any service or any sacrifice that is needed.

The contractual principle and psychology are heterogeneous to the familistic. In a collective oneness of the "we" of the familistic group, there is no place for a contractualism with its "so much, no more and no less." Any "no more and no less" is superfluous for a unity of the "we," where each individual, like an organ in a body, is a part of the whole, and as such spontaneously does and is expected to do his best, up to the ultimate sacrifice of his life for the "we" or its parts. "Sacrifice" here is felt as a privilege of free gift of a part to the whole. And the more is given, the more sublime is the "gladness" that flows from it.

As a consequence of that, no detailed *external* delineation of the duties and rights, of the "how much" and "under which circumstances," and other specifications and limitations of an *external* nature imposed by society are necessary for that kind of relationship. They become superfluous too.

The next point to be mentioned in regard to these relationships is the specific coexistence of *internal freedom of individuals with the external appearance of its limitation.* Considered outwardly, from a behavioristic standpoint, the familistic relationship may often appear as a great limitation of the freedom of the parties. From the standpoint of a contractual "flapper," the fact that the mother stays with the children, instead of going places and having parties, passes many a sleepless night instead of comfortably resting, spends her money buying necessities instead of purchasing a new dress for herself; for such a "flapper" all this is a "frightful" slavery or serfdom, a great limitation of freedom. However, when one puts himself in the position of the familistic party, most of these "limitations of freedom" of an individual arc not such at all. The mother or the father does not feel that "slaving" for the children is a limitation of freedom; on the contrary, they are glad to do it and prefer it to the freedom of the flapper. In brief, the familistic relationship permits us to reconcile duty and discipline with freedom; sacrifice with liberty.

Such in the ideal form is the nature of the familistic relationship or social bond. I style it familistic because most often, and in the purest form, it is met in the relationship between the members of the good and harmonious family. In a more diluted form it exists, of course, in many other nonfamilistic groups: between devoted and close friends; between the members of a religious organization; even between the members of the State, and of many other groups, as will be shown further. On the other hand, the term familistic must not lead to the conclusion that all or even the majority of the social relationships among members of the family are familistic. We shall see that it is not so, especially in application to the modern family, where, besides the familistic, the contractual form composes a considerable part of its total system of relationship. Such is the first fundamental form of social relationship and of the social bond in the organized groups.

B. *The Contractual Type.* In the terms of the modalities, its "chemical formula" is as follows.

(1) *It is limited definitely in the extensity* of the life activities involved in the interaction.

(2) *As to the intensity*, it may be high or low, depending upon the nature of the "contracted sector" of activities, but this sector is always limited; therefore the high intensity is limited by this sector and never extends over the whole life circle.

(3) It is limited in its duration; even when it is durable, the duration is again specified by the contract.

(4) Within the contract sector it is *solidary* (in a contract which the parties freely enter into and which fairly distributes their rights and duties). But this solidarity is in a sense egotistic, directed to getting either mutually some pleasure or service or profit or utility from the other party, or even to getting "as much as possible for as little as possible." It is egotistic-bargaining solidarity of rationalistically computed profit. The other party is important, not so much as an associate, and is not sought for itself, but as an agency or instrumentality which may render some service, enjoyment, utility, or profit. Besides the limited sector of the contracted interaction, the parties may remain either total strangers to one another in their "private life," or even be inimical and antagonistic to one another. Such, in brief, is the formula of the contractual relationship in the terms of the above modalities. On this skeleton framework we can now paint the living picture of contractual relationship. It is a well-known picture. "I agree to do so and so for you, and you agree to do

so and so for me. If you do not discharge your obligation, I am freed from mine and, besides, you will have to bear some unpleasant consequences of your breaking the contract." The parties may agree according to the classic Roman formula: "*Do ut does, facie ut facies, do ut facies, facie ut does*" ("Give to be given, serve to be served, give to be served, serve to be given.") Here parties do not merge into one "we," but each feels and acts as an independent party not concerned with any interests but its own. In this sense, the contractual group is more nominalistic and singularistic and less universalistic than the familistic group. Respectively, the place of sacrifice or dissolving of the individual interests in the collective "we" in contractual relationship is taken by the bond of mutual *bargaining*.

This means that the explicit or implicit attitude of the contracting parties toward each other is a *sensible egotism*, moderate or extreme, reasonable or unreasonable.

As a result of such an egotism, *the real contractual relationship cannot be blank, unlimited, or undefined meticulously*. As each party is pursuing in it its own interests, there cannot be, as a rule, a faith, a confidence, or a trust that one party will not try to take advantage of the other if their covenant is not specified and definitely agreed upon. More than that: there is often even no confidence that the other party will not try to twist the contract to the disadvantage of his partner. Therefore, a fixed or written contract, witnesses, and the notary to certify to its authenticity are a usual part of such an agreement. Since a definite distrust in regard to the sincerity and honesty of the other party is inherent in it, experts or experienced lawyers are hired to make the agreement clear and to leave no loophole through which the interests of a given party may be harmed by the other. Contractual relationship is the lawyers' paradise, their "bread and butter," while the familistic relationships do not need them, or a public notary, or even a judge.

Therefore, the members of the contractual group *always remain to a considerable degree strangers and outsiders in regard to one another*. They are contracted, or bound together, only in that specific respect which is covered by the contract. In all other respects, they do not concern one another; do not know one another; and do not want to be known. One calls his plumber, carpenter, or painter; agrees about the job to be done and the price to be paid for it — so far the parties cease to be complete strangers. But in all other aspects of which the life relationships are made up, they remain strangers.

It follows from the above that, compared with the familistic relationships, the contractual relationships bind the party not only by fewer bonds (only by those which constitute the contract), but these bonds are, as a rule, also shorter, so far as their duration in time is concerned. Most contracts have a definite time limit — a day, a week, a month, a year, and so on.

In contrast to that, most of the familistic relationships are more durable; the real familistic relationships are for life, even beyond it.

Finally, it follows that *the contractual relationship is inseparable from a great degree of freedom of each party from the other.* Since to enter or not to enter the contract (in real contractual relationships — not in pseudo-contractual, which are but a variety of the compulsory relationships) depends upon the choice of an individual; since the conditions upon which he enters depend upon him also, he is free to a great degree, at least outwardly. And since in the real contracts his precontractual position is such that he can afford to choose, the individual in a contractual group is indeed given a large opportunity for display of his singularistic freedom.

Again, in various forms and proportions, *the contractual relationships compose a considerable part of the network of the social relationships of many and various social groups, beginning with the "employers and the employees," "buyers and sellers," "owners and tenants," and ending with many a religious, political, state, occupational, educational, artistic, scientific, and even family groups and associations.* So it was in the past and so it is in the present.

C. *The Compulsory Type.* Its main trait is that it is *antagonistic* in its nature. Being such, it gives many varieties. It may be most intensive, seeking extermination of the party, and less intensive, seeking to inflict some pain, damage, or fines upon it. Again, its area can cover the whole circle of life or only a small sector. Respectively, there may be, like the familistic relationship, an all-embracing compulsory relationship, and one very limited, confined to one narrow sector of the interacting activities. The living picture of the compulsory relationship can be drawn up as follows.

When one of the interacting parties imposes upon the other certain forms of conduct, certain duties and functions — *contrary to the desire and inclination of that party*, and subjectively and objectively not for its welfare — and forces their realization exclusively by application of various forms of physical and psychophysical coercion, the social interrelation is compulsory in its nature. The bond which unites the parties and hinders its rupture is this coercion. It may have various forms, from a purely physical compulsion, infliction of various physical harms, tortures, and pains, up to the more complex psychosocial coercion, assuming now the form of depriving the party of necessities, like food, shelter, freedom of movement, and so on; now the form of threat to inflict injury upon other persons dear to the party: wife, husband, children, friends, and so forth.

The relationships of the master and slave or serf; of the executioner and the executed; of the conqueror and the conquered; of the despotic government and the governed; of the extortionist and the victim; of the ravisher and the ravished, are rich in this type of relationship. As a specific case come the pseudo-familistic and the pseudo-contractual relationships. By pseudo-familistic is meant a relationship where the stronger party takes over the similitude of the familistic relationship — its terminology, its "clothing," as "this is done with fatherly feelings," "for your own good," and so on — while factually the interests and the welfare of the weaker party under coercion are not considered at all, and the compulsion or pains imposed do not serve its welfare in any way. By the pseudo-contractual is meant a relationship where the weaker party enters into the contract seemingly by its own will, but in fact does not have any choice, and the "free agreement" is but a simulacrum of a really free decision.

In contradistinction to the familistic and contractual relationships, the compulsory relationships are marked by the following traits.

(1) They are internally *antagonistic.*

(2) *It does not give any freedom to the coerced party, while to the coercing party it gives a freedom* (in the sense of doing what one pleases) sometimes much greater than that *given by the contractual relationships to both parties.*

(3) Respectively, in the *pure compulsory* relationship, the parties remain to each other total strangers and outsiders. much more so than in any of the preceding relationships. And not only a stranger and outsider, but often a negative value, worse than a mere stranger. A slave to a cruel master is but a mere instrument, something even more "unhuman" than his cattle; at the best, he is but a species of animal. On the other hand, the coercing party remains also a stranger to the coerced. It is felt and perceived not as a human personality capable of understanding, feeling, being united by a psychosocial *rapport;* it is perceived merely as an instrument of oppression — cruel, inhuman, perverse, unjust, a kind of "whip" which only hurts, tortures, and oppresses. There is no bridge of real mutual understanding between the parties as human beings and personalities; there is no mutual fusion and no "we" feeling except the purely external, mechanical, like that between a cruel driver and his horse. The inner world of each party is mutually closed to the other; often there is not even a desire to open it.

D. *Mixed Forms.* These three forms seem to embrace almost all the pure forms of social relationship. The numerous concrete forms represent mostly their combination. Through a combination of various modifications of each of these three forms, it is possible to obtain most of the forms of social relationship given in the interaction of individuals and groups. As a matter of fact, the totality of interrelations within practically all the social groups represents usually a combination of these main forms: they are partly familistic, partly contractual, and partly compulsory. But the proportion of each type in the totality of the network of social relationships of various groups is not the same. It varies from group to group; and, in the course of time, changes even within the same group.

(1) If we select various social groups, we can easily see that some of them at all times have had *one of these types more predominant than the others*. If we take such groups as *the family, the Church, the association of real friends*, we find they almost always had an abundant portion of the familistic relationship in their relationship system. The ratio of this "familism" certainly varies from family to family; but as a rule it is considerable and in most cases is the dominant form of relationship. The others, the compulsory and the contractual relationships, are certainly present but, with few exceptions, they are hardly the main forms. Likewise, the *religious groups* have nearly always been built along the pattern of the familistic group. This is shown clearly in the terminology of such a group. "Our Father" (God), "we are children, sons and daughters of God," "God the Father," "God the Son," "Mother of God," "Mother Church," "Holy Father," "Sisters in Christ," "Brethren," "Spouse of Christ," and so on.

The same is true of real friends. Here again, as indicated, the relationship by definition is familistic and always assumes this type. This is shown again by such terms and "rites of passage" as mixing of blood, as drinking *Bruderschaft*, and the like.

If now we take such groups as the compulsory military group — the army as such (with the exception of groups like early medieval "companions in arms," which were modeled along the familistic pattern) — there compulsory relationships are always present to a considerable degree, especially where the army is large and recruited from all kinds of people. Likewise, in the state network of social relationships, especially in a despotic, dictatorial, or tyrannic State, a great portion of relationship is compulsory, as is manifest in the mechanism of the coercion of the State: its police, its army, its jails, its courts, its punishments, and other coercive forces.

Finally, when we turn to the commercial and trade organizations, they always had, to a considerable degree, a developed system of contractual relationship. Trade is ordinarily a "bargaining," the exchange of something for something.

These examples give an idea that some of the organized groups by their very nature are "destined" to have one of the main types more preponderant than the others and that there are several types of social groups which at all times have tended to build their network of social relationships predominantly either out of the familistic, or the contractual, or the compulsory relationships.

(2) *Warning: Do not confuse the existing nature of the relationship with how it originated or was established.* One must not mix these two different things. A given interaction and relationship may originate in a contractual form — for instance, the relationship between married parties or the relationship of the *fidelitas* in the Middle Ages. But in the course of time it may turn into either the familistic or compulsory type. The marriage contract even nowadays often turns into a real and pure familistic relationship between the husband and wife, parents and children. A business contract and subsequent meetings of the parties often lead to an establishment of true friendship between the contracting parties. Even many relationships compulsory in their origin turn into the familistic (for instance, in the past, in many marriages imposed upon one or both parties by others) or contractual form. On the other hand, a diluted familistic relationship, in the course of time, sometimes degenerates either into a contractual or even a compulsory one; or a contractual relationship degenerates into a compulsory one. In other words, one thing is *the way in which the relationship originated* (contractually or compulsorily or familistically); and quite another thing is *what it is in its nature* (familistic or contractual or compulsory). A certain form of origin does not always mean that its nature is the same as the form of origin, and vice versa.

The above concise but sufficiently precise characterization of the process of social interactions, of the modalities, of the types of social systems of interaction, and then of the familistic, contractual, and compulsory relationships with the respective systems of interactions, is sufficient to permit us to pass to a study of the fluctuation of the proportion and the quality of each of these relationships in the main social systems of the European population, from the beginning of the Middle Ages up to the present time. The subsequent chapters give mainly the conclusions of a much more detailed study of these fluctuations published in the full text of the *Dynamics*.

FLUCTUATION OF THE FAMILISTIC, CONTRACTUAL, AND COMPULSORY RELATIONSHIPS IN THE LIFE PROCESS OF THE MAIN EUROPEAN SOCIAL GROUPS

I. Introductory Remarks

The direct object of this part is: first, to find out whether, in the course of existence of the main social groups of the European population, the proportion of the relationship of each type within the structure of the same group, as well as the totality of these groups, has been fluctuating, and if so, how and when; second, to inquire whether these fluctuations have been correlated with those of the main types of cultures studied (Ideational and Sensate), and if so, which of these types of social relationship is positively associated with each type of culture and what are the reasons for such an association. Such are the main problems to be studied now. For a thoughtful person the importance of the inquiry is evident. For a less thoughtful reader it is enough to say that a change in the proportions of the familistic, contractual, and compulsory relationships that make up the "texture" of a group or social system of interaction is much more important, and indicates a much greater revolution, than any change of its political or economic structure. The first is fundamental and alters the very nature of the group; the second is only a partial and much more superficial change. Even this can amount to something only when it involves a quantitative-qualitative alteration of the main forms of social relationship. A political or economic revolution that does not involve a change of the proportions and quality of the familistic-contractual-compulsory relationship in a group amounts only to a change in the positions of its members, without any serious effect on the constitution or structure of the society itself. The so-called "Industrial Revolution" was an important change only because it meant a serious decrease of the familistic and compulsory relationships in the structure of Western society in favor of the contractual relationship. The so-called "Overripe Capitalist Regime," as an economic regime, means mainly a social structure composed primarily of contractual relationships. These taken away, the capitalist regime is destroyed. The contemporary crisis of capitalism is first of all the crisis of the contractual relations. The "to be or not to be" of the capitalist regime means the "to be or not to be" of the contractual society. If contractual relations continue to decrease quantitatively and degenerate qualitatively, the days of the capitalist regime are numbered. If the former are going to exist and grow, capitalism will become bigger and stronger. These remarks are sufficient, for the present, to enable us to understand the fundamental importance of the change in the proportions and quality of the main social relationships in the structure of any group.

A systematic study of the problem meets enormous difficulties. Without entering into their discussion, it is enough to say that the most careful study can yield, at the best, only roughly reliable results. But such rough approximation seems to be possible.

The study of the problem can be carried on in two different ways: the simpler and the more complex. By the simpler way I mean a study of the fluctuation of the proportions of each of these types in the total network of only *one* important organized social system in the history of one or more European country, such as the State or the Church or the family, or some other important group. Such a method is simpler, permits us to study the fluctuations more carefully, and has several other advantages. The fallacy and the shortcoming of such an approach as this must be evident, however, to everybody who has studied the problems of social structure and social organization. The point is that the state group or the religious organization or the family or the political party or the labor union or the "language-grouping" (nationality) — each of these groups is only one among many into which the population of a given territory or nation is differentiated and integrated. The line of social differentiation and integration of a given population into a social organized group is not unilinear and monistic but multilinear and pluralistic. Therefore, what happens in one of the systems into which a part of the population of a given area is integrated — for instance, in the State — does not necessarily happen in the other groups (the family, the Church, the labor union, etc.) which include a part of the same population. The structure of the state network of relationship may change from the familistic to the contractual; that of the religious association from the contractual to the familistic; and so on.

For this reason the more complex method is much more adequate, the more so that it gives all that the simpler method does. The essence of this more complex method in the study of our problem lies in the fact that we shall take at least most, if not all, of the diverse and important organized social groups into which the population of the given territory was integrated at a given period, and study what changes in regard to the proportions and the quality of the main types of social relationship have taken place within each of them in the course of time; and then within their totality. Knowing that, we can grasp, at least roughly, which of the types of bonds studied in the total population has been growing at a given period and which declining. Such a knowledge concerning most of the important social groups guarantees us against the mistake of generalization upon the basis of only one group.

The main groups whose structural changes, from the standpoint of the kind and the proportion of their social "fibers," are to be studied here, mainly within the French and the Germanic areas of Europe from the Carolingian even to the present time, are as follows: *the State*, *the Church*, *the occupational groups* (the guilds, labor unions, etc.), *the family*, *the military groups*, *the communes*, plus the *main organized social classes* (the orders, the seigniors, vassals, serfs) which united the free or unfree population into real collective bodies. To be sure, these do not exhaust all the important groupings into which the population of this main area of Europe was integrated in the course of the centuries studied; but they embrace at least the majority of them. For this reason, the results obtained in regard to all these groups are indicative of the main changes which have been occurring in the total social organization of the population.

If by the term *sociorelational "spectrum"* we style the predominant nature of the social relationships (bonds) in a given group — predominantly familistic, or contractual, or compulsory, or mixed — the problem studied can be set forth in the following way: What was the predominant spectrum of each of the important groups and of the totality of such groups in the French and Germanic population during the centuries from about the eighth to the present? Has the spectrum of each of these groups been changing, or has it remained constant? If changing, how, from which spectrum to which, and when? Do we move, in the course of time, more and more to the contractual, or to the familistic, or to the compulsory type; or is no such trend shown and, instead, do the types of these bonds just fluctuate, now giving victory to one, now to the other? The main results of a detailed study of these problems given in the full text of the *Dynamics* and omitted in this abridged edition are as follows.

II. Fluctuations of the Forms of Social Relationships in Western Societies

A. *From the Eighth to the Fourteenth Century*. The results of a concise analysis of the spectrum of social relationships and bonds of all the most important groups of the Middle Ages, from about the seventh and eighth centuries to the thirteenth and fourteenth, can be summed up in the following propositions.

(1) The predominant type of social relationships and bonds which shot through all the important groups of medieval society, and out of which the texture of their social life is woven, is familistic, of various degrees of intensity and purity. It is the main thread running through all the social relationships of the Church, of the family, of the guilds, the corporations, the fraternal associations. It is also the main fiber in

the texture of the system of state relationships — of the king and the *fideles* (subjects); of the king and his officials; and, to a smaller degree, of the military forces of the State. Likewise, the familistic is the predominant pattern among the members of the village community and the city communes. Finally, the feudal *fidelitas*, as the most general bond which binds together the free men and the free classes or strata of medieval society, is also predominantly familistic in its inner nature, in spite of the semicontractual form of the establishment of this bond in certain given cases. When properly analyzed, the *fidelitas* can be taken as the most common and universal form of social relationship in the Middle Ages. All this means that the "style" of the society considered is conspicuously familistic, or, as it sometimes used to be called, patriarchal. The last term is quite accurate, though many of those who used it were not aware of its deep meaning.

(2) Side by side with this predominant type, the other main forms are also present. The contractual type of bond is evident in almost all the groups. It plays a particularly important part in the initiation and establishment of relationships between the members of each of these groups, as well as between the groups themselves. The *fidelitas* almost always originated in the contractual solemn form. If one pays attention not to the inner nature of the bonds established but to the *mode* of their establishment, then the medieval society is to be regarded as predominantly contractual. But for reasons given above, we must clearly distinguish between two things: the manner in which this or that bond is established and the nature of the relationship itself. When this latter aspect is considered, there can hardly be a doubt that the main fiber of the texture of medieval society was familistic.

Likewise, the compulsory relations had their share in the structure of the social life of the period. They seem to have formed the main "rope" with which the upper, free strata of society were bound to the semifree and unfree classes. The "junction" where these two great sections of medieval society touch each other consists mainly of this kind of bond. The familistic and contractual "ropes" are also noticeable, binding together the foundation and the upper stories of the medieval building, but their role at this specific junction is quite secondary. On the other hand, it is to be emphasized that in cementing together the sections, either of the "foundation" or the "upper floors," the familistic rope plays a more important part than the compulsory one; as we have seen, the relationships of the members of the semifree and unfree classes toward one another were built mainly on the familistic pattern.

Besides the specific "junction" mentioned, the compulsory relationship played an important part in the binding together of various groups and persons around the *military* activity. It was also present — but in a secondary role — in the texture of all the medieval organizations. Such is the brief characterization of the "social texture" of medieval society.

(3) Passing from the earliest period of the Middle Ages to the twelfth and thirteenth centuries, we notice changes in this social texture. The main one seems to be that the threads of the contractual type become more and more frequent, more and more used in making the texture of this social fabric. Roughly, beginning with the end of the eleventh and with the twelfth century, the contractual character enters more and more the feudal relationships of *fidelitas*, the state system, the family system, the guilds and corporations and brotherhood systems, the urban communes, the military groups, even the bonds between the free and unfree classes. The familistic relationship begins to weaken slightly — quantitatively and qualitatively. The same is perhaps true also of the compulsory relationship. In other words, the *medieval society begins to move toward the contractual type of society.* The move is only in its initial stages, but it is tangible and fairly certain.

Such is the net result of the preceding analysis. Its meaning for our main topic, its relationship to the Ideational and Sensate cultures, will be discussed later. Here it is only to be noted that the period of the domination of the Ideational culture coincides with that of the familistic type of social texture. The period of the domination of the Idealistic culture (twelfth and thirteenth centuries) is marked by some weakening of the familistic and, partly, of the compulsory, and by reinforcement of the contractual relationships. This is shown here by a sort of synthesis and a more even distribution of all the main forms of social bonds, under the domination of the familistic type. It represents an interesting replica of the very essence of the Idealistic culture as an "organic culture" uniting the purely Ideational and Sensate elements under the domination of the Ideational form.

B. *From the Fourteenth to the Sixteenth Century.* Considering the changes in the main organized social groups of France and Germany during this time, we have to conclude that the main change consisted in *a weakening of the familistic bond in favor of partly the compulsory and partly contractual relationship.* Both of these seem to have grown in practically all the important horizontal and vertical intragroup and intergroup bonds except only (in France) the bond which roped together the free and unfree classes: here in France the compulsory threads were replaced in a notable degree by the contractual ones.

In passing, it is interesting to note that the centuries from the twelfth to the sixteenth inclusive appear in many other respects as the centuries of transition from the Ideational to the Sensate culture. In a very erratic way, the elements of the Ideational culture tended, with most irregular fluctuations, to decrease; those of the Sensate, to increase.

We see that such a transition in the culture is followed by a decrease of the familistic relationships and by an increase, also erratic, of the compulsory and contractual relationships. Such a "correlation" may be incidental; it may also be, as we shall show later, not incidental, but organically connected with these types of culture.

Another thing to be noted is this. A study of the movement of the internal disturbances given further on in this volume shows that the twelfth, thirteenth, fourteenth, and fifteenth centuries give the peak of the disturbances. So far as they are conditioned greatly by the strong or disorganized system of the social relationships, the above suggests that these centuries were indeed the period of a deep transformation with an unsettled condition in the social relationships which existed before: the waning and weakening of the familistic relationships of the previous period resulted in the disintegration, unsettling, and shattering of the whole system of social relationships. Hence, the amorphic status of the network and hence the growth of the disturbances of the period. Thus one part supports the other. One induction corroborates the others. Such a corroboration is a sign of some validity of each and of all the conclusions reached.

C. *From the Sixteenth to the Second Part of the Eighteenth Century.* This period is especially complex and contradictory, full of the most whimsical short-time turns of the most contrasting nature. When, however, all the secondary short-time turns and swings are disregarded, its main feature, from the standpoint of this inquiry, stands out as a *notable increase of the compulsory relationships at the cost of the familistic and partly even contractual forms of the previous period.* Compulsory relationships increased in the State, in the corporations and the guilds, in municipalities and village communities, in the French church organization, and in the military groups. *A secondary feature of this era is the maintenance of their position by the contractual relationships; if they were driven by the compulsory from many places, they obtained new ones, snatched from the familistic bonds. The net loser here, as in the previous period, happened to be again the familistic bond of social relationship.*

D. *From the End of the Eighteenth to the Twentieth Century.* The changes in the texture of the social relationships of various organizations of the French and German populations during this period were so numerous, so complex, so fanciful, so contrasting, that it is absolutely impossible to analyze them in a brief chapter. All that can be done is to point out that these centuries, up to the First World War, were marked by a decrease of the compulsory relationship and an enormous increase of the contractual relationship in the totality of the organized social groups of the period, as well as in most of the groups taken separately. The familistic relationship possibly also lost to some extent to the contractual. This form was the main gainer, during the period; it was the most important characteristic of the social texture of the nineteenth century — its mark, its pride, its vice, and its source of "perdition." Such an element stamped with itself the entire social network; manifested itself in millions of daily phenomena; permeated the mentality and culture of the people. And when, as any other form, it began to degenerate and decline internally, its "pathologic transformation" conditioned a decline and transformation of the social and political organizations of European society, its mentality and its culture.

E. *The Period Following World War I.* In France, in Germany, in Italy, in Poland, in Austria, in Yugoslavia, and especially in Russia, the post-war period is marked by decisive and violent changes of the spectrum of the totality of social relationships. The essence of the change can be formulated as follows: a violent decrease of the contractual relationships in favor of compulsory (mainly) and (to a less degree) familistic forms. The contractual relationships, so successfully functioning in the preceding era, in the postwar period show themselves in a decisive and rapid decline. They begin to realize their own nemesis. Whether the decline is temporary or for a long time, its very fact can hardly be questioned in all of the above and in practically all other Western countries. It follows from a conspicuous growth of state interference, which is transforming the state systems from the contractual-democratic form into the authoritarian, totalitarian state of the Communist, Fascist, Hitlerite, Socialist, Military, "New Deal," and other varieties. Such an authoritarian and totalitarian state greatly limits most of the previous contractual liberties, or destroys practically all of them, as does the Soviet State which declares they are mere "*bourgeois* prejudices," or partly eliminates them. (The "new" Soviet Constitution of 1936 changes the situation mainly in phraseology and little, if at all, in reality.) The elimination or abrogation of liberties means an enormous blow to contractualism. The State unhesitatingly imposes its own rules upon all its subjects, regardless of whether or not they are liked, approved, or disapproved. Contractualism is cut also by limitation or abrogation of the universal suffrage (*de facto*, at least) in many of these states, and it is limited further by the very increase of the state — and authoritative — regulation of an excessive number of the various relationships hitherto left to the parties. The Communist State prescribes and controls almost all important social relationships in all the significant fields of social life and culture. In other states the compulsory prescription is more limited and administered somewhat more cautiously, but it also has increased astoundingly. The press, the associations, the meetings, the strikes, the lockouts, the religion, the education, the work, the salaries, the wages, the prices, the profits — all and everything no longer are left to the contractual decision of the parties involved; to their own agreement or to their mutual choice; it is authoritatively regulated, prescribed, imposed, under the severest penalty for disobedience. The sphere of liberty or choice or agreement in the lives of the subjects of these states is terrifically narrowed; in the Communist State almost eliminated entirely. An enormous number of relationships are "regimented," "coded," "ordered." And this trend is universal in all the Western countries, no matter what concrete form it assumes in each — Communist, Fascist, Hitlerite, Labor Government, Socialist, Rooseveltian, Eisenhower's, or other. It enormously increased during the World Wars and has continued up to the present time in all countries.

The result of such a change in the state system means a similar change in almost all the nonstate organizations. Through the imposition of the obligatory state rules, the contractual fibers are decreased in the municipalities and village communities, in the trade unions and corporations, guilds and associations (which in many states are transformed into the state or prescribed or governmental unions, guilds, associations). Likewise, the entrepreneurs' and the employers' organizations have suffered the same decrease of contractualism in their systems and in their relationships to the outside world; the control of their business is taken largely out of their own hands and contractual bargaining is notably reduced. In many states a similar atrophy of the contractual fibers has taken place in the religious organizations, where some forms of religion are proscribed under the penalty of death or imprisonment or fines (as in the Soviet State), or some types of religious organizations and their functions are persecuted and other types imposed. The same is true of the family to a lesser extent; and especially applies to the majority of contractual associations — political, scientific, philosophic, economic, philanthropic, artistic, and others. In many of the states, numbers of them have been disbanded; others are prohibited; some are forced to modify their organization and activities.

The fact of this sudden and enormous decline of contractualism throughout the Western World is so evident and so unquestionable that there is no need to insist upon it.

It is less certain which of the other two main forms — familism or coercion — of the social bond has profited at the expense of the declining contractualism. There is no doubt that in all these States a certain part of the population whole-heartedly approves of the elimination of contractualism and the establishment of authoritative regulation by the dictatorial State. For such a part, these measures will be familistic rather than compulsory. There is also no doubt that there is another part among the citizens or subjects of these states to whom all these measures of a dictatorial state are merely coercion and often of the rudest, most painful, and least excusable type. Which of these groups is the larger? One can hardly answer the question by a general formula. In all probability, the situation is different in different countries.

The dictatorial government may for a time find an emotional echo in that part of the population which sees its enemies attacked; but that is not enough for the establishment of the real familistic relationship. When all relevant conditions have been considered, it becomes rather probable that the gainer from the contractual decline has been principally a rude sort of compulsion, a coercion of the new dictators and governments, but not a real familistic system.

This is corroborated by the general fact that compulsory relationships are usually the gainers during the periods of deep transition. We seem to be living in such a period now. Therefore, the new relationships can hardly be regarded as a further step toward higher and loftier forms of social relationships, or as the foundation of the new, large, and constructive civilization, in which to live humanly for a long time. They are the measures of a wrecking company, rather, which artlessly but energetically clears the ground of tumbledown, decaying, and more and more dangerous contractual buildings, beautiful in the past, but now rotten. The destruction of the contractual relationships being carried on by governmental and dictatorial "wrecking companies" is a manifestation of such a situation. They are not the builders of the future, but the grave-diggers of the past. Such is the time in which we live. Why and how this degeneration of the contractual relationships has occurred, I shall discuss further on.

III. Main Results

The fluctuation of the forms of social relationships in Western society may be pictured in summary form as follows:

(1) The social texture of relationships in the period from the eighth to the twelfth centuries appears to have been woven mainly out of *familistic and in a smaller degree compulsory* fibers. The contractual relationship played a relatively small role. The establishment of many familistic and compulsory relationships had a contractual form; but, as has been explained, the nature of the relationship was not contractual but familistic. It is a familistic and patriarchal society in the first place; compulsory in the second; and contractual in the third.

(2) Toward the thirteenth century the familistic forms show indications of decline; the contractual and the compulsory begin to multiply in their place. This trend continues throughout the centuries from the thirteenth to the sixteenth. It is a *period of a mixture of all three, with a slight domi-*

nation of the familistic, and with the other two playing a more or less equal role.

(3) The centuries from the sixteenth to the middle of the eighteenth are marked by a notable growth of the compulsory relationships at the cost of the familistic — mainly — and the contractual — partly. Up to perhaps the postwar twentieth century, we have hardly a period in which compulsory fibers were so many and so strong in the total social texture of the societies studied.

(4) Beginning with the last part of the eighteenth century, the compulsory relationships rapidly decrease and the contractual relationships increase throughout the nineteenth and the prewar twentieth century to a proportion unknown before in the history of the Western society. Contractualism is the most typical mark of the European and the Western society of the nineteenth century.

(5) The postwar period marks a rapid decline of contractual relationships in favor of mainly compulsory ones.

Thus the forms and combinations of the types fluctuate. Each form has had its heyday, and each has then declined. We see from this sequence that within the centuries studied there is no evidence that in the course of time one of these forms tends to grow steadily at the cost of others. Instead, they just fluctuate, without any clear indication that mankind proceeds steadily toward bigger and better familistic relationships, or toward bigger and better contractual relationships. Many theories which claim the existence of a certain perpetual trend of progress toward bigger and better sociality, solidarity, altruism (familism), or to the opposite, ever-increasing compulsoriness and antagonisms seem to be as unwarranted in this field as in many others.

This raises three important problems. What is the reason of this fluctuation? Why does not the texture of social systems remain constant, "eternally standardized" as to the quality and the proportion of the fibers from which it is woven? The second problem is: To what extent is the sequence of the domination of the forms of social relationship universal? Is this sequence something "incidental," in the sense that it happened thus in Western society but may be quite different in other societies? Or is the sequence typical and universal for all societies in the course of their existence? Is it something similar to what, for instance, Polybius claimed in regard to the sequence of the political regimes? The third problem is: Can these forms of social relationship be regarded as associated positively or negatively with the Ideational, Idealistic, and the Sensate types of culture?

Let us briefly take the problems. The general answer to the first problem is given by the "principle of limit" and "immanent changeability" of any empirico-sensory object or process ("immanent causation"). The forms of social relationship are a part of the sensory world. If everything in it belongs to the world of Becoming, they have to belong to it too. More specifically, not only in a vast social system composed of a multitude of individuals, each of whom changes incessantly, but even in the much simpler case of two individuals, the relationship alters all the time. Each of these individuals incessantly changes — biologically, psychologically, and culturally; the concrete conditions in which they live, act, and feel also change continually; therefore their moods, emotions, feelings, ideas, desires, volitions generally, and in regard to one another, change all the time. As a result, their relationship cannot help changing incessantly also. In some cases the amplitude of the change may be enormous, thus transforming friendship into hatred, affection into distaste, devotion into contempt, familism into contractualism or tyrannical compulsory exploitation. In other cases, the amplitude may be much narrower, changing, so to speak, not the nature of the relationship but just its shadings and modalities. Even most devoted and true friends, even the most mutually loving mother and child do not sustain the same intensity, tone, and timbre of their familistic bond all the time: it has its moments of highest pitch and its moments of weakened intensity. The same is true of the tempo of the change. Sometimes it is sudden, explosive, and surprises the parties themselves. Sometimes it is gradual and slow, imperceptibly growing for a long time before the parties become aware of the change.

Since such is the situation in the case of the social relationship of any two individuals, there is no doubt as well as no surprise that the relationships change in the vaster and more complex universe of large groups of individuals, with its everchanging intergroup and external conditions. It would be a real miracle if a social relationship remained constant and unchangeable. Such a constancy would indeed be contradictory to logic, and to observation, and to common sense. So much as to "why the social relationships change in their nature in the course of time in any social group."

Putting the same in more concrete form, I can say that in the course of time none of these forms of social relationship can really stay unchanged. Taking first the familistic and the contractual relationships and using Aristotelian-Polybian terminology, I can say that each of them is liable to degenerate into something which preserves only the external shell of the relationship without its inner content or with a content quite different from what it should be. Whether in the relationship of man to man, or of group to group, the initial form of the relationship — say familistic — established between a certain family A and the group of the families B, C, D, E, F, represents a real resultant of the qualities of A and of those of B, C, D, E, F. A consists of individuals highly gifted, strong in body and mind, capable of rendering important service to B, C, D, E, F. In this service A displays a real care of B, C, D, E, F, unselfish, paternal, wise, and felt respectively by B, C, D, E, F.

Suppose the next generation of group A to be quite different from the founders of group A. Suppose the members of A group now are stupid, weak, spoiled, in brief, devoid of the leadership qualities of the previous generation. If we even grant that the next generation of B, C, D, E, F is exactly the same as the preceding one, the mere change in A group is sufficient to lead to a deep inner transformation of the nature of the familistic relationship.

External or objectivized relationships founded by the initial A and B C, D, E, F cannot be changed as quickly as the internal nature of the relationship. Many long-time obligations were made by the initial families; many other "shells" came into existence, which cannot be either destroyed at once or changed rapidly, or generally modified to conform to the new inner nature of the relationship. Hence, the phenomenon of the existence of the "shells" of the relationship for some time, while the inner content becomes empty or different. Hence, the degeneration of the familistic into a pseudo-familistic, with the external "shell" which looks like the previous one but with the content very different from familism.

The same is true of the contractual relationship. Real contractual relationship presupposes equally free parties with an equal freedom to "bargain" and to choose in accepting or not accepting the conditions of the other party. It presupposes also that a choice is generally possible. In these circumstances the contractual relationship seems to deserve all the praise that has been lavished upon it. It is a free bond willingly chosen by a free man for the mutual benefit of himself as well as of his free party. When, after the elimination of serfdom and unfree forms of relationship, such a freedom (if not absolutely, then at least relatively) was given to the previously unfree groups, the change was certainly great and noble: no wonder that it went to the heads of many of them like a wonderful wine. In this sense replacement of the previous compulsory relationships of the sixteenth to the eighteenth centuries by contractual ones was a great achievement. But now suppose that this freedom of bargaining and choice is greatly narrowed or eliminated. Suppose you have on the one side a hungry (but free!) worker with hungry members of his family; on the other a "capitalist" who does not starve and has no need unsatisfied and no difficulty. In such a situation the freedom of one party is lacking. Therefore it is ready to accept any "contractual" condition which is offered: anything is better than nothing. The contractual form becomes compulsory in its nature. Suppose that the worker is glad to have any work on any conditions; but there is no work at all, as is the case with millions of the unemployed. Juridically, man is still free to accept the contract or not; but factually there is no contractualism any more; what exists is something even worse than the compulsorily imposed work with a small compulsory remuneration. The shell stays, the content is changed.

The same can be said of an enormous number of the important contractual relationships of European society of the nineteenth century. Toward the end of the nineteenth and the twentieth centuries many of them preserved only the shell while the content of a real contractual relationship was gone. Most of the liberties of speech, press, meetings, unions, and so on, continued to exist in law and on paper; but in fact they became inaccessible to an enormous section of the population: various private and public agencies monopolized them and created a situation in which the persons not belonging to the dominant factions, or unorganized, found themselves as speech-less, press-less, union-less, as the villeins and serfs of the previous period.

The universal suffrage was extended, and the governments became the mouthpiece of the people. But in fact the elections were monopolized by small factions, and the right of suffrage was reduced to the doubtful pleasure of checking on a piece of paper names chosen by one of the dominant parties regardless of whether the voter would have selected them personally or not. And so in almost any field.

Through a complex interplay of many factors the contractual relationships lost, in the twentieth century, in many fields, their real and vital content and became almost empty shells. As such they were deprived of a great deal of their value and service, and became in many cases mere "flattering and high-sounding" words without moral or material usefulness. As a result, we can hardly wonder that the masses ceased to appreciate them; that they showed a readiness to flock to the standards which openly slandered them and their liberties and their whole social system. Hence, the crises of parliamentarism, of democracy, of liberties, of liberalism, of democratic rugged individualism, of Adam Smith's "capitalism," of "liberal humanitarianism," and of hundreds of other manifestations of contractualism in the postwar period. Hence the ascendance of Communism, Hitlerism, Fascism, and of many other — anticontractual — regimes in political, economic, and social life.

An additional sign of the degeneration of contractualism has been particularly conspicuous in the postwar period. And, what is important, it has been displayed *urbi et orbi*, by the leading statesmen, financial and industrial leaders, and by moral, mental, religious, civic, and other leaders whose minds still run in the tenets of contractualism. Perhaps the most important condition of a real contractualism is the old Roman *pacta sunt servanda* — a contract should be fulfilled, and the duties taken discharged. Meanwhile, in our courts, through the intricate nature of contemporary laws and the overdevelopment of lawyers' ingenuity, many weaker parties cannot enforce the fulfillment of the contract duties of the stronger party: with the aid of first-class lawyers, the stronger party often finds a hole which invalidates the bona fide claims of the weaker party. The beginning of World War I saw the invasion of Belgium and the "scrapping of a mere piece of paper," on which was written the solemn promise of the invading party to keep the neutrality of Belgium. The later years were an almost incessant violation of the *pacta sunt servanda.* One after another the governments began to break their contracts, sometimes even before their signatures had time to dry. Almost immediately after the signing of the Versailles Treaty part of the signatories began to repudiate their signature and clamor for a revision of the treaty. Revisions started: the Dawes Plan, the Young Plan, the other plans; then followed one international conference after another, in which promises and previous contracts were broken, not two-sidedly but one-sidedly. The governments of the Western as well as the Eastern world (Russia, China, Japan, etc.) have mainly been busy with an incessant breach of their contracts of international character.

During and since World War II this trend has increased greatly. Not only treaties but also practically the whole of international law has been incessantly violated by all governments without exception. Democratic governments violate it not less than dictatorial ones.

In brief, the international relationships of recent years have mainly been a demonstration that any solemn contract is something less than a piece of paper; that it does not bind, or binds only up to the first convenient moment to break the agreement; that the high signatories do not intend to stick and are not believed by their party to have any intention of sticking to the contract. The contract — even a solemn international pact between members of the League or of the United Nations — has been reduced to precisely nothing. A similar violation of agreement has been shown by practically most of the governments in their internal activities. Beginning with breach of duty to pay in gold the bearers of gold certificates and ending with endless "reforms," most of which broke some governmental contractual obligations, the *pacta sunt servanda* and the similar *dura lex sed lex* (stern law but law) have been more and more replaced by "expediency." The expedient is a fine thing for the moment and from the standpoint of the moment (just as the sensual wine, women, and song), but in the long course of time it leads to nihilism and cynicism; to that "everything is permitted" for expediency, which ruins not only contractual duties but any duty, any obligation, any social and moral responsibility; and makes parties untrustworthy and faithless to one another. In such deep demoralization nothing except a rude force counts; neither the religious nor moral nor any other inhibitions and principles and values. If I have the power to impose my conditions upon all others, what shall stop me from this "expedient and profitable" operation! That is exactly the situation we are now in. Therefore, we should not wonder that the contractual relationships in internal and international affairs have declined and been replaced by a stern force and rude compulsion. They are mere fruits "dialectically following" from the seeds sown before. Any shell, including the contractual shell, can last for some time without its vital content; but not forever. The hour of reckoning always comes. And at the present time we are in such an hour, as far as contractual relationships are concerned. For the time being they have "immanently" outlived themselves.

This illustrates the meaning of the immanent change of each form of social relationship; and also the particular "why" of the present-day decline of contractualism.

With modifications, the same can be said of the respective familistic relationships in interindividual and intergroup action. Sooner or later they are bound to wither into either contractual or pseudo-familistic compulsory relationships, both on account of liability of internal change and of the play of external circumstances.

It is hardly probable that throughout the course of history there is a steady growth of familistic relationships at the cost of the others. However desirable and uplifting is such a belief, it is still mere belief and nothing more. The "ugly facts" contradict it.

Among the persons with whom each of us associates there are a few to whom we are bound familistically, usually the members of our own family and our closest friends. With the majority we are bound contractually. To some persons we are tied by the bond of coercion — psychologically we feel animosity, mild or sharp dislike, and sometimes even hatred. But in spite of that, many of us cannot sever the connection forced upon us by circumstances and have to endure the bond and relationship however antagonistic they are. So it is at the present; and so it was in the past.

Finally, the compulsory relationships are no exceptions to the above rule: they also cannot continue eternally without changing in their modality and without passing sooner or later into the contractual or even familistic form. Again in interindividual relationship, beginning with the old-fashioned compulsory marriages, where a party is married to the other, contrary to his or her will, by the coercion of parents or relatives or overlord, it has not been an exceedingly infrequent fact that the compulsory bond used to turn, after some time, into a real familistic or contractual one. Finally, in many cases, such relationships are ended by a disruption of the interaction and contact. The same can be said of the intergroup relationships. For some time a part of the members of one group may maintain a compulsory control over the other part, but not forever. Sooner or later the compulsory relationship will pass, at least in part, either into a contractual form, as we have seen in the case of the serfs liberated, or into the familistic; as we have seen in some cases, this has happened even in the relationships of masters and slaves, of conquerors and the conquered. Or, finally, the compulsory relationships, when they become too oppressive and too unbearable and when there is no other way out, lead either to disruption of the relationship and open conflict of the parties, or to the dying out of the oppressed party, or to some other form of their limitation, mitigation, termination, and transformation. No slavery is eternal; no serfdom; no tyrannical dictatorship; no other form of compulsion. For some time it may bind the group or groups together; but if, under this bondage, there is not forming a contractual or familistic bond to replace the chain of compulsion, the chain is bound to be rusted and decayed or violently broken, or it will kill the bearers of the chain and exhaust the masters who imposed it. In the next chapter we shall see in greater detail the reasons why some amount of freedom is biotically necessary and why if it is not given after a time the result is tragic: it kills the chained and it exhausts the chainers. For these reasons no compulsory tie is eternal; and it must pass, sooner or later, into a different form of bond, either contractual or even familistic.

So much about the first problem.

Passing to the second question, I do not think the sequence observed in the history of the Western society is universal or uniform for all societies and at all times.

First, there are no logical reasons why the observed sequence shall be universal and not merely one of those possible. Second, an observation of the simpler interindividual social relationships shows that in some cases a friendship turns in the course of time into a cold, bargaining contractualism, egotistic but reasonable; in other cases it turns into a hatred and antagonism, where the bonds and relationships are continued by the sheer coercion of one party by the other. The same is to be said of the change from the contractual to the other forms or from the compulsory to the other two. In other words, we do not observe a uniform and universal sequence in the transformation of a given form of social bond into the others, but a variation of different sequences. If such is the case in the interindividual relationships, there is still more reason to expect it in the intergroup relationships. And a slight observation of the alliances and animosities of two or more groups in the course of time supports the claim.

Turning finally to the third problem, the results show that at least empirically there is some — purely incidental or deeper — association of the main type of cultures with the domination of the forms of bond studied. From the above we see that the period of the domination of the

Ideational culture, from the eighth to the twelfth century, is marked by a domination of the familistic relationships, plus the compulsory relationship as subsidiary. The period of Idealistic culture — from the twelfth to the fifteenth centuries — is marked by a mixture of the familistic with a greater proportion of the contractual and the compulsory. The period of a rapid ascendance of the Sensate culture — the sixteenth, seventeenth, and the first part of the eighteenth centuries — by a proportionate rise of the compulsory relationship with some increase of the contractual ones, at the cost of the familistic. Finally, the period of the ripe and well-developed Sensate culture, the nineteenth century, is marked by an unusual increase of the contractual bonds. The twentieth century, which, as we have seen, is marked in many compartments of culture by a sudden revolt against the Sensate forms, is also marked by a sudden decline of contractualism.

How shall these "associations" be interpreted? As a mere coincidence in time and in space of the "relationship variables" and those of culture? Or has it either a functional or logical character? A definite answer is not possible. But with reservations, one seems to be entitled to claim that the "coincidence" is not purely incidental; that there are logico-functional reasons why Ideational culture would tend to be bound with the familistic (and compulsory for outsiders), and the rising Sensate with the compulsory; while the overripe Sensate culture coincides with the contractual form of relationships. What are these reasons? In concise form, they can be put in the following way.

Ideational culture has an affinity with the familistic type of social bonds first of all because it inhibits the sensual, carnal desires of its members; thus it makes them less egotistic and less prone to exploit their fellow men, or to bargain with another to obtain as much as possible for as little as possible. Whether the ideational man is an ascetic or an active ideationalist, he is much less interested in the acquisition and appropriation of the "commodities, wealths, and comforts of this world for himself at the cost of the others than a purely sensate man. The Ideational mentality is such that it does not value as highly as that of the sensatist the empirical values of this world. Therefore this mentality is reluctant to bargain in detail about the amount, the conditions, the proportions, the "no more and no less," so far as the empirical — especially the material and sensory — values are concerned.

The ideational man is a man with the psychology of the absolute and religious principles. These principles command a fraternal relationship to the members who are "brothers in God" or in Spirit. As these principles are much less "expedient," they do not admit egotistic "expediency" as much as the utilitarian, or hedonistic, and very relative principles of Sensate mentality and ethics.

In addition, the whole ideational psychology is such that there is a deep fusion of the individual "selves" into one "we." For an ideationalist, all the participants of the given system of Ideational culture are "one body and one mind." A kind of *corpus mysticum* is the only true reality.

Under such circumstances, with such a mentality, the relationships of the members of an Ideational culture tend to assume familistic character; sometimes, when the ideationalism is particularly intensive, as for instance among the early Christians, the familism is of the purest and all-embracing type. In other cases it is more diluted, but it still has much greater affinity to the familistic than to the compulsory or contractual form.

From this standpoint it is not a mere incident that the medieval Ideational culture coexisted with a domination of the familistic relationships. It is rather what should be expected in this as well as in almost all the cases of a real Ideational culture.

But how then to explain that side by side with familistic relationship the same medieval period witnessed a considerable development of the compulsory form? In a sense it is due to the inheritance of slavery and serfdom, from the Graeco-Roman and partly from the "Barbaric" cultures, where among several tribes the unfree groups existed. Christianity did not create these forms; neither did it aggravate them; if anything, it tended to mitigate and eliminate them. In the early Christian Church the slave members were not "slaves"; many early Christian leaders (preachers, priests, bishops) had been slaves. When the Church was legalized, the very entrance of a slave into the Christian Church often made him free. Subsequently, if the Christian Church did not eliminate serfdom entirely, it mitigated it and was the earliest and the main agent which fought for the freedom of slaves and their humane treatment. If it did not succeed entirely in that program, the fault was not with it but lay in the fact that the social and cultural world was not purely Ideational. The Sensate aspect of it weighed heavily and required its "pound of flesh."

This combination of circumstances was one of the reasons. The other reason may be inherent in Ideational mentality. In the preceding pages I have several times stressed the phrase "in regard to all the participants of a given Ideational culture." By this I meant that the ontological and sociological "realism" of Ideational mentality, and its psychological fusion of the individual "selves" into one real "we," is limited to the participants of the Ideational culture. Only such participants are a part of this "we"; only they are the empirical embodiment of the ideational entity (children of Jesus, brothers in God, etc.) which makes all of them one real collective unity, inseparable and nonexisting in separateness from one another. The situation becomes quite different in regard to all the outsiders who are not the participants in this "ideational entity." Since they are not bearers of this "grace," this "brotherhood in Christ," this ultimate and supreme value, they are neither "sacred" nor "brothers" nor "children of God." They are just strangers, heretics, Gentiles, or a mere empirical instrumentality which can be used as any instrumentality. Hence, in regard to such "outsiders" the Ideational mentality, unless it is really universalist and cosmopolitan, does not have any inhibition against treating them rudely, imposing all kind of coercions, sometimes being even more cruel than the purely Sensate mentality. This is one of the reasons why several Ideational cultures are followed by the coexistence of compulsory forms of social relationships in regard to the "outsiders" ("the outcasts, the Súdras, in India who were not "twice born"; the heretics and the pagans or "unbelievers," in other cases).

Such, in brief, are some of the reasons for a real affinity of Ideationalism with the familistic and partly the compulsory relationships.

Similar considerations explain the affinity of Sensate culture with the contractual and compulsory relationships. Sensate mentality is singularistic and individualistic. Only the separate individual is the true reality for it. Of these in the first place is "myself." Such a mentality has much greater difficulty in merging the "ego," the "self," into the "we" than the Ideational mentality. Either the contractual or the compulsory forms, with their "individual" centers as the "subjects" of agreement or coercion, are more congenial to such a mentality than familism.

Empirical mentality looks at man as a sensory creature. It sees mainly his bodily and sensate needs. Therefore it values the sensory and material values, commodities, objects, wealth. Sensate men thus strive to appropriate, each for himself, as much of these values as possible. They are more prone to "snatch" them from the others by force or acquire them from the others by a hard bargain. As most of these individuals have the same attitude, the result is a much more intense struggle for these values than in the society of ideationalists. Therefore, more antagonisms, more attempts either to "reasonably apportion the distribution to mutual benefit" through a fair or unfair contract, or to force the other party to concede them. When a contract fails, the Sensate mentality is ready to use force in order to "protect oneself" in the inexorable "struggle for existence." Here are no inherent inhibitions against using force as the *ultima ratio* of expediency. "Each man for himself," or "each sum of men, whose interests are the same, for themselves." Neither absolute religious or moral or any other principles hinder the use of force if such a use is possible and expedient. No *corpus mysticum* is hurt because no such *corpus* exists.

Finally, Idealistic culture, as a balanced synthesis of both, has to show, for reasons comprehensible from the above, a synthesis of the three forms, with some predominance of the familistic form.

It is thus comprehensible that the thirteenth, fourteenth, and fifteenth centuries show a mixture of all the three forms.

Toward the sixteenth century the Ideational culture declined still more and the Sensate made an enormous progress. Now sensate man appeared. But this man, having lost his ideational bearings, did not acquire at once the reasonable and balanced sensate outlook: "to live and to let others live." He was violent, emotional, greedy. Mere contractual and similar preachings were not strong enough to "order such a man." Hence the appearance of physical compulsion as the most convincing method of training him and the growth of compulsory relationships in the sixteenth, the seventeenth, and the eighteenth centuries.

Drilled by this method, the sensate man was tamed and began to realize step by step that contractualism is perhaps the best and most comfortable way to arrange things.

The wild youth of sensate man was over; he was becoming more and more balanced, reasonable, and ready to settle down. After the explosion of the Revolution, in the nineteenth century he became a solid contractual citizen, who wanted to bargain, instead of fight; who wanted to live and let others live. We are in an age of contractualism, the mature form of the mature and balanced Sensate culture.

However, as any other form, the Sensate culture and contractualism bear in themselves the seeds of their own destruction. In the nineteenth century these seeds grew; and in the twentieth century they led to the degeneration of contractualism itself. It turned more and more into a pseudo contractualism. Parallel with a revolt against the extreme forms of Sensate culture which we noticed in many compartments of the Western culture, beginning with the end of the nineteenth century, a revolt against the depreciated and defrauded contractualism took place also in the postwar period. So far it has manifested itself mainly in an ascendance of the compulsory forms. But there is hardly any doubt that sooner or later these forms will subside and either contractual or — what appears to me more probable — familistic forms will take its place. Hitlerism, Communism, Fascism, Socialism, and many other "isms" of our days are groping and looking for these forms. But unfortunately, like the cubists in art, they are strong in their revolt against contractualism but perfectly helpless in their attempt to establish a new "collective" or "familistic" form, because, like cubists, their eyes and mentality are materialistic and sensate par excellence, and their collectivism is a mere mechanical manipulation of men and social forces. The result is not so much a familism or altruism or anything like that, as it is the "collectivism" of the hard-labor prison, with its hatred and its coercion — the regime fundamentally opposite to familism and its allies. They successfully destroyed contractualism, but replaced it mainly by compulsory and mechanical slavery: soulless, mirthless, compassionless, largely devoid of real altruism, real familism, real solidarity. It has created so far only the pseudo solidarity of the executioners among themselves and the alliance of the victims. Since their mentality is anti-Ideational and Sensate through and through, nothing else can be expected. For the creation of really familistic, and in this sense really collectivistic, bonds, an Idealistic or Ideational mentality is necessary. As long as it is absent, the work of these "wrecking companies" will be very successful in destruction but of little value in the creation of the familistic relationship and a really collectivistic society.

28

FLUCTUATION OF THEOCRATIC (IDEATIONAL) AND SECULAR (SENSATE) FORMS OF GOVERNMENT AND LEADERSHIP

I. Preliminaries

In this and the following chapter I am taking into consideration the Ideational and Sensate forms of government and sociopolitical leadership; the Ideational and Sensate forms of freedom. They compose one of the central problems of the political and ethicojuridical disciplines. If in regard to them it can be shown that neither an adequate grasp of their main forms nor of the rise and decline of either of them is possible without a preliminary understanding of the main forms of culture and of social relationships, such a demonstration entitles us to conclude that still greater must be the dependence of many other sociopolitical phenomena upon our fundamental "variables." In this way their importance will be vindicated once more. We turn now to the problem of forms of government and leadership.

II. Pulsation of Ideational and Sensate Sociopolitical Regimes

The concept of Ideational culture implies logically that, if no external circumstances hinder, the government and the intellectual, moral, and social leadership (aristocracy) in such a culture must belong to the persons and groups that incarnate, or are supposed to incarnate, in themselves the Ideational values. Since the sensory-empirical values, whether wealth, physical might, sensory happiness, and the like, are only pseudo values to Ideational mentality, the rich, the physically mighty, the capable organizers of the economic, political, or other enterprises in such a society cannot be its recognized "aristocracy," its leaders, and its rulers, if they are not backed by the Ideational values, are not their upholders, or are not supported by the group that is thought to be the incarnation of these Ideational values par excellence. The supreme prestige and authority — and respectively the governmental influence — must belong in such a society to theocracy, be it the group of priests and the sacerdotal class generally, be it the caste of Brahmins, the lamas, the shamans, the "elders," or any other group which is believed to be in closest contact with the supersensory power and values, their manager and delegate in the sensory world.

And vice versa. In the Sensate culture, with its disbelief in Ideational reality and values, the leaders and rulers can be only those groups which are the bearers, the creators, the organizers, of the most important sensory values; physically powerful protectors of safety and security, organizers of prosperity of the given population. The aristocracy of such a society has to be, therefore, either the military class; or the rich class; or the group that physically dominates the society — various dictatorial factions and their leaders; or the clever politicians and machinators; or the organizers of new economic and other empires; or the inventors and scientists who deal with the "material forces of nature" and discover ever new sources of human, sensate well-being; or various manipulators and "bosses," down to the powerful leaders of criminal gangs.

Finally, the Mixed or Idealistic society is to be expected to have a political regime and leadership of a Mixed nature, partly theocratic, partly Sensate secular.

These deductions are corroborated by the data of history so well that it is hardly necessary to enter here into a detailed verification of them. A mere reminder of the fundamental facts in the field is sufficient.

A. First, *the proposition is well corroborated in social space.* The Brahmanic, Buddhist, Tibetan, and the Taoist part of the Chinese culture have been predominantly Ideational. Their aristocracy and their sociopolitical regime have been theocratic in their essentials. At least during two thousand years, the supremacy of the Brahman caste in India has never been questioned seriously. It is probably the longest-lived aristocracy in the world and less disputed in its superiority by the population of India than any other aristocracy. Even now, when the caste system seems to be weakened, the nearness of some three thousand other castes in India to the Brahmanic caste is the main criterion of their relative position in the hierarchical ladder of the social strata of India. Who are the Brahmans? Priests, without a church organization; religious and moral and spiritual leaders. What is the basis of their prestige? Only the belief that they are the bearers and representatives of the supersensory Ideational values. They are neither rich nor physically mighty; nor do they control the army; nor do they invent and create new sources of sensate well-being. They are nothing of the kind, and do not have any of these means for the maintenance of their prestige and superiority. They formally do not rule; the kings and the princes of India are the rulers. But if their power is not purely compulsory, its authority depends upon the attitude of the Brahmanic caste and its support. In brief, India is the country whose sociopolitical regime and aristocracy have been the decentralized theocracy par excellence, no matter whether the rulers have been the members of the Brahman or the Kshattrya caste.

The Tibetan regime is an explicit regime of the centralized theocracy.

The Dalai Lama is its supreme ruler and the head of its aristocracy, consisting of the multitude of lamas and monks who act as his agents. Similar has been the situation in the countries with a dominant Buddhist culture. The ruler himself may be the theocratic head of Buddhism, like the emperor Açoka, or he may not be such a head; but the power, the authority, the prestige of the government depends upon the approval of the theocratic authority. Often the government has been but an instrument of the theocratic group and values.

Similar has been the situation with the Taoist theocracy and the government of China, when and where (especially in southern China in some periods) the Taoist mentality was dominant.

In all these and similar cases the government has been an explicit or implicit, centralized or decentralized, theocracy, with its authority derived from the Ideational source; with its policy permeated by Ideational mentality; with its dependence based upon the explicit theocratic groups in the society.

The "objective fact" of such a situation is well reflected, in these cultures, in the respective sociopolitical and moral ideologies; in the social and political theories, opinions, convictions; in the literature and law of such cultures and periods. These ideologies and law provisions aimed to show the superiority of such an aristocracy, as well as the hierarchical rank of the main social classes on this Ideational scale. The Hindu ideology of the four castes can serve as an example of that. Here is one of its versions.

Now for the prosperity of the worlds, he (the self-existent Lord or Brahma) from his mouth, arms, thigh and feet, created the Brahman, Kṣatriya, Vaiçya, and Çūdra.

Now, for the sake of preserving all this creation, the most glorious (Being) ordained separate duties for those who sprang from (His) mouth, arm, thigh and feet.

For Brahmans he ordered teaching, study, sacrifice, and sacrificing (as priests); for others, also giving and receiving (gifts).

Defence of the people, giving alms, sacrifice, also study, and absence of attachment to objects of sense, in short, for Kṣatriya.

Tending cattle, giving alms, sacrifice, study, trade, usury, and also agriculture for a Vaiçya.

One duty the Lord assigned to a Çūdra — service to those (before mentioned) classes, without grudging.

Man is declared purer above the navel; therefore the purest part of him is said by the Self-Existent to be his mouth. Since he sprang from the most excellent part, since he was the first-born, and since he holds the Vedas, the Brahman is, by right, the lord of all this creation. What being is then superior to him, by whose mouth the gods eat oblations and the manes offerings? Of beings, the most excellent are said to be the animated; of the animated, those which subsist by intelligence; of the intelligent, men; of men, the Brahmans. . . . The birth of a Brahman is a perpetual incarnation of *dharma;* for he exists for the sake of *dharma*, and is for the existence of the Vedas.

These lines indicate clearly the Ideational basis of the superiority of the Brahman caste.

With many a concrete variation, the same principles will be found in all the ideologies of the theocratic-Ideational aristocracy and regime, be it the Buddhist (the Dalai Lama as an incarnated Buddha), the Taoist, or Egyptian, or Mohammedan, or the ancient Hebrew, or any other. In all such ideologies and provisions, the Ideational — and no other basis — is stressed as the source of this superiority. Any purely secular power, even that of the king, is declared to be subordinated to this ideational power and its bearers, if the king himself does not happen to be the head of this theocracy (as in Tibet, or in the early Mohammedan Caliphates, or in Ancient Egypt).

So far as contemporary knowledge concerning the "primitive peoples" is reliable, the proposition discussed seems to be supported also by these tribes. A study of the facts shows, first, that the culture of some primitive tribes, like the Zuñi and several Polynesian tribes, is more Ideational than the culture of many other primitive tribes; among the more Ideational tribes, the form of government and leadership respectively is much more theocratic than among the groups with a more Sensate culture. It is enough to study carefully the forms of government and leadership among the Zuñi to see that it is a conspicuous theocracy. Likewise theocratic is the regime and leadership of the Ideational tribes of Polynesia or Samoa. The ruling stratum, the aristocracy, and the chief there derive their power from "holiness" (*Heiligkeit*); are regarded as incarnated deities; are ascribed all the supersensory halo of power; in brief, the regime and leadership have the essential traits of theocracy. In other tribes with more developed elements of Sensate culture, the political regime, leadership, aristocracy, are also Sensate, and often are characterized as a "secular aristocracy" or even "plutocracy," and their authority is based either upon mere inheritance of position, or physical power, or utilitarian services to the tribe and the like.

Well corroborated by the data of various cultures and societies, the propositions are supported also by the historical data concerning the fluctuation of theocratic and secular (Sensate) political regimes and leadership, in time, in the history of the Graeco-Roman and the Western societies. Let us recall the main phases of this fluctuation.

In Greece, the earliest period was that of *sacerdotal monarchy*, with the king who was first of all and most of all the supreme priest, or *pontifex maximus*.

In the social system of the ancients, religion was absolute master; the State was a religious community, the king a pontiff, the magistrate a priest, and the law a sacred formula; patriotism was a piety; and exile, excommunication. This was before the sixth century, in the period which appeared in all the compartments of Greek culture as predominately Ideational.

B. Then, as we approach the sixth century, the theocratic Ideational source of the government and sociopolitical leadership seems to have greatly weakened. Already in the time before Solon (*c.* 639–559 B.C.) in Athens, at least, we find the leadership and the domination of the rich and the physically powerful. Respectively, during the sixth and the subsequent centuries, we notice in most of the Greek states (except, perhaps, Sparta) a progressive de-Ideationalization or secularization of the government and the sociopolitical aristocracy. Throughout all this period, from the sixth century to the end of Greek independence in the second century B.C., the religious-theocratic basis of the government, aristocracy, prestige, and leadership played a progressively decreasing role, and wealth, military power, physical force, political cunning, "intellectualism," and other factors played the decisive role in these matters and in numerous upheavals of sociopolitical regimes: in tyrannies, oligarchies, timocracies, democracies, and, finally, monarchies of the Greek states. So far, this trend was in agreement with the trend of progressive sensatization of the Greek culture during these centuries.

This trend was naturally reflected in the respective ideologies. If, in the poetry ascribed to Solon, the Ideational motives are still conspicuous, in the political theories of the fifth century B.C. they play either no part (as in the theories of the Sophists like Georgias or Thrasymachus, where law and government and leadership were reduced either to a kind of compact among the people to safeguard their sensate interests, or to the mere power of the mighty and the cunning of the clever to exploit for their own interests the people, without any trace of an Ideational reason or principle); or find only the Idealistic motives (in my sense of this term), as in the theories of Plato (with his Utopian kings-philosophers and aristocracy of the Idealistic philosophers and the guardians), or in the theories of Aristotle's three good forms of government (monarchy, aristocracy, and polity) in contradistinction to the three wrong or bad forms of government and leadership, where these Idealistic values are absent (tyranny, oligarchy, and mob rule). As we come to later centuries even these Idealistic motives are less and less noticeable. Their place is occupied by purely Sensate — eudaemonistic, utilitarian, hedonistic, or even cynical — considerations and justifications (or assailing) for wealth, might, physical power, organizing ability, and the like as the bases for leadership, superiority, and government.

C. The early — monarchical — period of Rome (before 510 B.C.) had also the regime of the sacerdotal government and aristocracy and leaders, where the king was simultaneously the secular ruler (*rex*) and the supreme priest (*pontifex maximus, rex sacrificulus*).

Even after the fall of the monarchy, in the early stages of the Republican regime, the sacral or Ideational elements were still strong in the Roman government, and in the leadership of the Roman aristocracy (the important roles of the *jus divinum, sacrum, fas,* sacral criminal law with its *sacer esto* and expiation; the religious form of marriage, *confarreatio;* the role of the *dies nefasti;* of *jus pontificum*; of augury; of the pontifical college, and so forth). However, the secularization of the government and of the aristocracy progressed in the subsequent centuries.

Toward the end of the Republic, there was little, if anything, left from the Ideational or theocratic bases in these fields. Only through that decay was it possible to proclaim the cult of the Caesars, where the Sensate man was elevated to the rank of the gods and demanded for himself the honor paid to deities (*divus, tamquam praesenti et corporali deo*). The incessant struggle for power, adventurers seizing the kingship when they can — all this shows the rule, "Might is right." So far as these centuries, from the second B.C. to the first centuries of our era, were Sensate in all the main compartments of Roman culture, this secular character of the government and of sociopolitical leadership is in harmony with the character of the culture.

D. With the growth of Christianity and its power, a new Ideational force entered the scene and toward the end of the fourth century turned the direction of the culture from the Sensate to an increasingly Ideational form in all the main compartments of Roman culture. This enormously increased power of Christian Ideationalism was one of the reasons for the acceptance of Christianity by Constantine and his legalization of the Christian Church. After that time the Ideational source and sanction of secular power became necessary. Leaders of Christianity, like St. Ambrose and many others, did not hesitate to censor, sometimes even to excommunicate, to guide, and to control the emperors and the subordinate secular rulers and leaders. During the subsequent centuries, especially after Leo the Great and then Gregory the Great, the government and sociopolitical leadership became again predominantly Ideational or theocratic. Either in the sense that the secular rulers were controlled by the Christian Church, and obliged to follow its guidance and to have its approval for obtaining and holding their positions, or in the sense that the spiritual power held the supremacy over the secular one, the doctrine and the reality lasted up to about the end of the thirteenth century. During these centuries Europe had a predominantly theocratic regime, with the Roman Catholic See as the supreme government and unquestioned power in spiritual matters, and as the great power in all secular matters, sometimes even greater than any secular king, and almost always indispensable for obtaining and holding power by any secular ruler. The doctrine that God is the only source of any government and the prevailing doctrine of explicit or implicit supremacy of the spiritual power over the secular one are the manifestation of this change. We know that the centuries from the fifth to the thirteenth were Ideational in the culture of Europe. At the end of the twelfth and in the thirteenth century, the objective historical reality and then the ideologies begin to show the first signs of the coming turn from the theocratic constitution to the secular, in the field discussed. Most of the political theories of the period try to reconcile the spiritual and secular power and in this way show their Idealistic character. But voices ascribing to the secular power supremacy over the spiritual appeared and began to multiply (John of Paris, Peter Flotte, W. Nogaret, Dante, Pierre du Bois, Marsilio of Padua, and others). The *Unam Sanctam* of Pope Boniface VIII, who in 1300 declared, "I am Caesar, I am Emperor," may be taken as a landmark of the beginning of the decline of theocracy and of the ascendance of secular power. The subsequent arrest of the pope by Guillaume de Nogaret, and the compulsory removal of the popes to Avignon, marked clearly this turn. In the political ideologies, the change was manifest in the ever-increasing theories which more and more clearly claimed the supremacy of the secular power over the spiritual. The center of the influence shifted to the emerging national monarchies and their new aristocracy and new leaders. The new aristocracy and leadership became more and more secular, nonreligious, sometimes antireligious. With minor fluctuations, the trend continued to grow up to the beginning of the twentieth century and in many Western countries resulted in the formal separation of the State and the Church, and into partly juridical — and especially factual — subordination of the Church to the State; of the spiritual power to the secular or sensate.

E. At the present time, most of the governments and the influential class of the people do not refer to God or to any other supersensory authority for "sanctification" of their power. An Ideational source is not mentioned. Instead, "the will of the people," or "of the proletarian class," or "of the nation," or of any other group, functions as the source of the power.

In the sociocultural reality, the power belongs either to the rich class, or to those groups which — no matter how — control the military and other physical forces by which they can rule and coerce society. At the top of the social leadership and aristocracy are "society" — that is, a group of the rich — or the "proletarian" — "the fascist," the "Nazi," the "socialist," the "liberal" factions, sprinkled with the Sensate aristocracy of the previous regimes and various sensate intellectuals. They base their authority upon the possession of the power itself, and do not try to refer to any Ideational reason or value for its sanctification. Again, to keep it, they rely only upon holding the physical power and its substitutes in their control, and try to feed their partisans and followers (at the cost of the others), to eliminate and, if necessary, to exterminate dangerous rivals; to prevent any organization of the rival forces and to disorganize such an organization by any accessible means, from killing, persecuting, imprisoning, banishing, up to bribery, propaganda, machinations, and manipulations of the most diverse character. Anything that hinders their objective is eliminated and brushed aside, without any hesitation, be it religion, be it science, be it art, be it ethics, or law. If they do not suit the objective, they are suppressed, eliminated, prohibited, no matter how great is their value per se. One of the first actions of almost every faction that seizes (obtains) the power is (1) to eliminate all the *laws* that are inconvenient to it (including often the faction's own promises); (2) to prohibit any *religious* or *moral* or *scientific* beliefs, theories, opinions, convictions, that contradict it; (3) to try to create their own "ideologies" — proletarian, fascist, racial, national, socialist, "New Deal type" — which aim to replace the values eliminated; (4) to forcibly teach the youth, in the schools and outside them, mainly — and only — their hurriedly tailored doctrines; (5) to silence all opponents through imposition of penalties, censorship, through depriving them of all the means of communication, from printing press to radio and school and meetings; (6) to seize all the means of communication and to use them exclusively for the propaganda of the governmental doctrine. Then come other, still more "material," means for maintenance of the power: creation of special guards (with their secret police and terroristic "committees," G P U, O G P U, Gestapo, etc.); the strategic disposition of these forces, especially in strategically important places; the physical extermination of opponents; and so on and so forth.

In some countries all this is done openly and without any ceremony; in other countries it is done more mildly, with decorum and decency, and supposedly in accordance with law. But everywhere the trend is the same. Law does not bind contemporary governments much if it is inconvenient; if the government's own contract and solemn promise become inconvenient to it, they are broken unhesitatingly, as "a scrap of paper." Likewise neither religion nor morals nor any other value — scientific, aesthetic, or cultural — binds the government. On the other hand, any theory, however silly it may be, is elevated to the rank of the eternal truth when it glorifies government. The same is true in regard to art. All the values that do not serve the narrowest, most immediate, utilitarian purpose of preservation and reinforcement of the power in the hands of the government are neglected and treated most unceremoniously. We have gone in this respect so far that this is true not only of the Ideational, but even of the general Sensate values themselves. Their value is narrowed to the smallest utilitarian demand of a given faction at a given moment. Utilitarianism here is suffocating itself through sacrificing the more general and durable utilitarian values in favor of the narrowest that serve the immediate purpose. Shall we wonder, therefore, that government and leadership have lost a great deal of their halo and are viewed as a game where one unceremonious faction tries to overcome another, as cynical and unscrupulous — just as in Sensate Hellenistic Greece and Sensate Rome, we observe endless riots, revolts, revolutions; most violent struggles for power among a multitude of factions, with a multitude of unceremonious adventurers trying to grab the power to which they have no right except the physical possibility of getting it through mere force? "Might again has become right." The whole matter is but a combat of physical force with physical force, without any Ideational or Idealistic or even decent Sensate reasons and justifications.

The political ideologies reflect this reality. Hypocrisy, lying, cynicism, partiality, factionalism, carelessness about the truth and the lasting values — these are the conspicuous traits of the present-day political ideologies, no matter whether they are communistic, socialistic, fascist, Nazistic, conservative, liberal, or democratic.

In different degree and proportion, the traits are present in them. All claim "open-mindedness," "impartiality," "scientific validity," and, of course, "justice"; and all break these claims on the first pretext. For persons and groups who indeed try to be impartial, the situation is particularly painful. Not identifying themselves with any of these factions, they are not helped by any and, at the same time, are the recipients of blows from all.

Other ideologies are "cynical." They openly admit that their ideologies are but a mere means — "derivations and rationalizations" — to help the respective practices of their creators.

Ideologies being "naked," the practices of the masters are also stripped of any decorum.

Rival factions do not make any secret of their preparation of physical force for their support. With a little modification, the Hobbesian motto can be used: faction to faction *lupus est* nowadays. As we have seen in preceding chapters, the compulsory relationships triumph everywhere, and particularly in this field. Here again we see the atomization of the values that finally grind them to dust.

It is hardly probable that such a trend and situation can continue forever or even for a long time. Sooner or later a reaction against this overripe Sensatism in government and leadership is bound to come. The reaction can only be a swing toward Ideationalism or Idealism. Signs of the revolt against this overripe and cynical regime are already noticeable. So far as the nineteenth century was the government of the rich (in alliance with Sensate aristocracy) this form of the overripe Sensate regime is already discredited and partly abolished. Then, especially in the immediate postwar period, came the so-called labor-socialist-radical variety of the Sensate regime. Within a short number of years it has lost its charm also, and in many countries is already superseded by either Communist, Fascist, or other totalitarian governments. These still exist, but in their existence, by the inexorable immanent development, they have either undermined themselves and lost any prestige except that of pure physical coercion, or are changing before our eyes, rejecting what they approved yesterday and approving what they rejected a short time ago. The cycle of the Sensate regime is approaching its end. One faction after another has been tried: radical and conservative; one class after another: rich and poor, aristocratic and democratic; business-labor, peasant-farmer — all have been tried and found wanting. We may continue for some time to drift in this Sensate current, changing one "sensate horse after another" And the more we change, the more we shall have to change, until all Sensate groups pass this cycle of "being tried and found wanting." The final result of this merry-go-round can be but Sensate dust: unrespected, incapable, impotent. With dust society cannot live for a long time. If it is going to live, it must begin to restore the sociopolitical values to their real level; to make them less and less relative, more and more universal. Their universalization will mean a shift toward Idealism or Ideationalism in some form and to some degree.

In the preceding chapters, we found that Ideational culture is connected with the familistic form of relationship; that the religious organizations are generally more familistic than many others; and that the present time is marked by a revival of the compulsory relationships. All this tallies well with the findings of this chapter: that Ideational periods are marked by an Ideational-theocratic regime; that theocracy is congenial to familism; that the rise of the secular-Sensate government and leadership proceeds hand in hand with that of the Sensate culture, with its contractual and compulsory relationships; that, finally, the present time is marked also by the coercive variety of the Sensate regime and leadership. The findings thus reinforce one another.

F. So far as the forms of government and leadership have theoretical and practical importance, the forms studied here are at least as important as any distinction of such forms of government as monarchy and republic, autocracy and democracy, and the like, given in most of the various treatises on Constitutional Law. When one fully understands that the sociopolitical regime of a given society is Ideational (or Sensate), from this major premise one can deduce, with a reasonable degree of certainty, a host of the characteristics that should be expected, and are usually contained, in such a regime. One can reasonably expect that the government of such an Ideational regime will be an implicit or explicit theocracy; that the laws will be regarded there as the absolute commandments or tabus of the supersensory power; that in the policy of the government and in the laws, the "supernatural sanctions" will play a considerable part (excommunication, *sacer esto*, deprivation of Christian burial, and the like); that as court evidence, various "supernatural techniques," like the ordeals and the "Judgment of God," will be used; that the government and the law will protect many Ideational values having no direct utilitarian or hedonistic value; that in the penal system the principle of "expiation of a sin or crime" will play a conspicuous role; that the system of education, so far as it is controlled by the leaders and the government, will be "theological" to a considerable degree; that some institutions of "oracles," "Pythias," "prophets," "saints and seers," will be a part of the political structure; that the rulers themselves will be closely connected with the performance of sacral duties; that the laws, beginning with the criminal laws, will be of absolutistic nature, with little room left for the principle of "relativity" and "expediency"; that, consequently, the contractual relationships will be little developed in the sociopolitical system of relationships; and hundreds of other traits and characteristics that give not only the external and formal silhouettes of the regime but its intimate and inner picture, its living portrait.

The same can be said of the Sensate or Idealistic sociopolitical regime. The validity of these "deductions" has been shown, to a considerable extent, in many previous chapters, particularly those that deal with ethical systems, with the criminal law, with the forms of social relationships. When one reads statements from the lawbooks like the following, one can be sure that they can be expected and found only in a society with a theocratic regime containing a great many of the Ideational elements.

> Now therefore hearken, O Israel, unto the statutes and unto the judgments, which I teach you, for to do them, that ye may live, and go in and possess the land which the Lord God of your fathers giveth you. Ye shall not add unto the word which I command, neither shall ye diminish ought from it, that ye may keep the commandments of the Lord your God which I command you.

Or

> If a man weave a spell and put a ban upon a man, and has not justified himself, he that wove the spell upon him shall be put to death. . . . If a man has put a spell upon a man . . . he upon whom the spell is laid shall go to the holy river, and the holy river overcome him, he who wove the spell upon him shall take to himself his house. If the holy river makes man to be innocent, and has

saved him, he who laid the spell upon him shall be put to death.
Or

Içvara created punishment, his son, as the protector of all beings, consisting of the glory of Brahma, criminal law. From fear of him, all beings, immovable and movable, are fit for enjoyment, and wander not from their law. . . . He, Punishment, is a royal person; he is a guide and ruler.

When properly understood, these and many similar statements are unthinkable and impossible for a Sensate regime and law; but they are in perfect accordance with the Ideational-theocratic regime and law.

This contrast and difference between these regimes comes out in thousands of other forms. Here, as in other divisions of culture, the categories of Ideational and Sensate political regimes and leadership are the "key principles"; once understood, they make comprehensible, even "predictable," many details of a given political regime, as soon as its Ideational or Sensate nature is defined.

G. The above means that again there is hardly any eternal trend toward a systematic growth of either Sensate or theocratic regimes and leadership in the course of time. Instead, each form grows, reaches its climax, and declines, giving way to the other form, which passes through the same cycle.

There is no proof for the theory of a historical trend from the sacral (Ideational) to the secular (Sensate) regimes and leaderships. Neither is there any basis to claim the opposite trend in the course of time. The nearest approximation to the reality is the theory that these regimes and forms of leadership fluctuate in time and in space. So much about this point.

Now the question arises: *Why these fluctuations?* The answer is the same that has been given many times — namely the principle of limit, of the immanent self-regulation of sociocultural processes, according to which any concrete cultural form sooner or later wears itself out (not to mention the influence of the factors external to it). More specifically, these regimes are connected with the respective Ideational and Sensate forms of culture. If these fluctuate, the political regime must fluctuate also.

III. Fluctuation of Other Forms of Sociopolitical Organizations and Processes

So far as other forms of the political regime are concerned, such as monarchy and republic; autocracy and democracy; or aristocracy, timocracy, oligarchy, tyranny, and the like, they all trendlessly fluctuate. The still popular belief that with the "progress of culture and civilization" the monarchy is driven out by the republic; autocracy by democracy; leadership of the military, or the rich, or the physically powerful tyrants is more and more disappearing, being replaced by the "self-government for the people, by the people, and of the people"; or by the guidance of the highly scientific, highly moral, and highly rational and just groups and persons — all these and a host of similar theories and beliefs, so far as they mean something definite by the terms used, are but *pia desideria* — noble and commendable — and nothing more. The historicosocial reality does not give any support to such claims. Much nearer to the reality are the ancient "cyclical" theories of Plato, Aristotle, Polybius, and many other thinkers of the past, who claimed that the main forms of government just fluctuate and immanently pass into one another without any perpetual trend whatsoever. The only questionable point in these theories, especially of the type of Polybius, is their contention that the sequence of the forms of the political regime is definite and uniform.

The same is to be said of other theories claiming a definite and universal succession of forms of a cycle. These theories — insofar as they claim a universal sequence of the order of the change of the forms of government and political regimes, or also the definite periodicity in these changes — can hardly be accepted. They fail through the elevation of a special and local case into a universal rule — the usual mistake of most generalizers.

FLUCTUATION OF IDEATIONAL AND SENSATE LIBERTY

I. Ideational, Mixed, and Sensate Liberty

Let us endeavor to define the elusive phenomenon of "liberty." In mechanics we read:

> When a particle is perfectly free to move in any direction whatever, it can move in three and only in three directions. . . . Like a particle, an unconstrained rigid body can have three possibilities, in the way of independent translation. But in addition to them, "the free rigid body has also three possibilities in the way of rotation, for it may be turned about any one of three rectangular axes. . . . A rigid body has therefore altogether six degrees of freedom, three of translation, and three of rotation; but by means of suitable constraint, the body may be deprived of any number of these six. [For instance, an elevator is deprived of five degrees (it can move in only one direction); a door swinging on its hinges is also robbed of five degrees of its freedom, though they are not the same as in the case of the elevator; a coin lying on the table has only three degrees of freedom: two of translation and one of rotation.]

Here we have a perfect "behavioristic" conception of freedom: no psychology, no inner subjective element, is involved in it. Human behaviorists can but envy such a definition.

However, even to the most enthusiastic behaviorists it must be evident that such a "perfectly behavioristic" definition of freedom is inapplicable to a human being. Whether his overt actions are free or not, the decisive criterion is the "subjective" experience of the individual: his wishes, desires, aspirations, wants, and the like. Generally, it can be said that a human being is *free when he can do whatever he pleases, need not do anything he does not wish to do, and does not have to tolerate what he does not want to tolerate. Consequently, his freedom becomes restricted when he cannot do what he would like to do; has to do what he would prefer not to do; and is obliged to tolerate what he would like not to endure.*

The definition introduces a new element nonexistent in the freedom of mechanics, namely, the inner, psychological experience described by the words "whatever he pleases," "would like," "prefers," or "wants" to do or not to do, to tolerate or not to tolerate. Without them, the concept becomes void, because a human being, as long as he lives, and whether he is free or not, would always be either doing or not doing, tolerating or not tolerating something.

Without a knowledge of the individual's desires, and observing his overt activities only, we cannot pass any judgment as to whether or not he is free. A person with a limited set of wishes can feel himself free in the narrow limits of the available possibilities of satisfaction of his needs (an ascetic, a fakir, a good mother tied to her child — in her time and activities). And vice versa, a person with a seemingly wide range of possibilities of satisfaction of his wishes can be quite unfree, if the number, intensity, and character of his desires exceeds the possibility of their gratification.

Hence the formula of Freedom of an individual $\frac{\text{Sum of the Available Means of possibilities of Gratification of Wishes}}{\text{Sum of Wishes}}$

In a short form it will be $\frac{\text{SM (means)}}{\text{SW (wishes)}}$

If the total "Sum of Wishes" is greater than the "Sum of Means" of their satisfaction, the individual is not free, and he is the less free the more the numerators exceeded the denominator. If the numerator (SM) is greater than the denominator (SW), or equal to it, the individual is free. Thus there are two forms of freedom, and two ways to preserve it, or even to increase it: first, the individual may minimize his wishes until they equal or are less than the available means of their gratification; or he may increase the available sum of the means of their satisfaction. The first is the inner Ideational way of being free; the second is the external Sensate way to be free. Thus, quite naturally, and somewhat unexpectedly, we are brought to two different (Ideational and Sensate) kinds of freedom. Both kinds are freedom in their generic trait (with SW not exceeding SM), but each is as different from the other as possible in their *differentia specifica*. One corresponds to our definition of Ideationalism; the other to that of Sensatism. Intermediary forms of freedom, where the SW is kept lower, or not greater, than the SM, partly through control of the wishes, partly through increase of the external means of their satisfaction, would fall into the Mixed type of freedom.

When this is understood, it becomes evident, first, that it is superficial to discuss freedom generally, without specifying the type involved (Ideational, Sensate, or Mixed); second, a usual mistake of all those who, consciously or not, assume there is only one kind of freedom, say, Sensate; and do not see any freedom where the SM is very modest, or the sum of wishes in regard to Sensate values is very limited. All such individuals or groups or cultures are identified by such Sensatists with the "unfree" conditions: slavery, serfdom, and the like. And vice versa; for a partisan of Ideational freedom, the Sensate freedom is but a most foolish imprisonment in the clutches of external material conditions, which rob the individual of every freedom and make him a plaything in the hands of blind material forces. The above formula of freedom permits one to see freedom of both types, providing that in both — Sensate and Ideational — situations the SW does not exceed the SM. The most sensate multimillionaire may be free or not, as he can or cannot gratify his every whim through the vast external means in his possession; and the sternest ascetic, with only bread and water barely sufficient to keep his body and soul together, is free if his wishes do not go beyond these means, and if his other wishes, including his aspiration for union with God, are satisfied. Finally, a well-balanced man, who does not give free rein to his wishes and who at the same time possesses the means to satisfy a great many of them, may also be free in the condition of Mixed freedom. In all such cases, the formula, freedom is $\frac{SM}{SW}$ where SW does not exceed SM, remains.

II. Fluctuation of Ideational, Mixed, and Sensate Forms of Freedom in Time and Space

One of the great marvels of a number of human beings is their ability to shift from one form of freedom to another, when such a shift is desirable or necessary. Through such a shift, they remain free, where otherwise they would be deprived of freedom and, as a result, would be miserable and unhappy. During the last few decades, many a person who had been rich and powerful was thrown into poverty and external dependence upon others. Not a few of these, deprived of the Sensate freedom which they had previously enjoyed, found, in their enormously reduced circumstances, an "inner" or Ideational freedom and remained in a sense happy and contented. On the other hand, almost everyone knows persons who had contentedly lived in modest material and social circumstances and then became rich and powerful and climbed the Sensate ladder fast and high. Parallel with their new opportunities they began to expand their wants, and shifted to more extensive Sensate forms of freedom. Some kept their balance and remained free in their new Mixed or Sensate freedom. Others expanded their desires faster than their means of satisfaction; therefore, they felt themselves no more, but less, free than before; the more they had the more they wanted to have. These individual cases are familiar enough and the shifts from one form of freedom to another are well known also. Likewise, the ability of some individuals to make such a shift successfully, and the inability of others to do it, are routine phenomena. On this individual scale, these phenomena of the fluctuations of the forms of freedom in the life history of individuals are the possession of every careful observer. Less known and less simple are the similar fluctuations that occur in the life history of an integrated culture mentality. As in other aspects of the culture mentality, such fluctuations do occur in social space, from society to society, and in time from period to period. Here and now Ideational freedom is dominant; there and at another period, the Sensate form was the main one.

Generally, in the predominant Ideational cultures, whether the Brahman, the Taoist, the Buddhist, the medieval Christian, or in the smaller Ideational cultural circles, like the Cynics, the Stoics, the Ascetics, Ideational freedom is the prevalent form, which is possessed, thought of, and aspired to; while in the predominantly Sensate culture, the Sensate form becomes prevalent, is sought for, praised, and paraded. In the Mixed culture mentality, the Mixed or balanced form of freedom tends to become dominant.

The following general remarks will elucidate the logical and factual connection of the respective forms of culture mentality with their forms of freedom.

(1) That a consistent Ideational mentality stands for the Ideational form of freedom, and a Sensate mentality for the Sensate, is axiomatic and self-evident. One follows from another logically.

(2) That factually, the predominant freedom is Ideational in the Hindu, the Taoist, the Buddhist, the early and medieval Christian, the Stoic, the Cynic, and in many other ascetic and Ideational mentalities, is also evident to everybody who has studied these currents of thought from this standpoint. None of them pleads for a maximum expansion of the sensate wishes; on the contrary, they preach their inhibition. None of them blesses a particular care for material values and external means in order to satisfy sensual needs. If anything, they damn it. All of them talk, preach, plead for, and extol only the inner freedom of soul, the inner "self-sufficiency," freedom in God, in Nirvana, in mystic union with the Absolute, and the like. All of them expose the frailty, the illusiveness, and the foolishness of any other freedom than the Ideational one.

With a slight modification, the subsequent formulas of the Ideational freedom of Epictetus, Marcus Aurelius, and Seneca are shared by all Ideational mentalities.

Seek not that the things which happen should happen as you wish, but wish the things which happen to be as they are, and you will have an even flow of life.

Is it not better to use what thou hast, like a free man, than to long, like a slave, for what is not in thy power?

Freedom is not gained by satisfying, but by restraining, our desires.

Not only ambition and avarice, but even desire of ease, of quiet, of travel, or of learning, may make us base, and take away our liberty.

Wherever I go, it will be well with me, as it has been here, and on account not of the place, but of the principles which I shall carry with me. They are all my property, and they will be all I shall need, wherever I may be.

Non qui parum habet, sed qui plus cupid, pauper est.

He is king who fears nothing and longs for nothing. Everyone may give himself the kingdom of noble thoughts.

He is free who rises above all injuries, and finds all his joys within himself.

Very little can satisfy our necessities, but nothing our desires.

The grandest of empires is to rule one's self.

Who has most? He who desires least.

And so on.

In a similar vein, Christianity extols the same form of inner freedom. So do Hinduism, Taoism, and other Ideational culture mentalities.

The bondage is of the mind; freedom is also of the mind. If thou shouldst say, "I am a free soul, I am the son of God; who can bind me?" free thou shalt be.

In the Sensate mentality, the concept of freedom would be and factually is Sensate. For all such mentalities and cultures the Ideational freedom is not freedom at all. Freedom to them is the right and possibility to do whatever one pleases sensately; and the more one expands his wishes and the more he can satisfy them, the greater the freedom.

The Ideational mentality is little interested in political and civil rights and declarations, in various political devices to guarantee the liberty of speech, press, convictions, meetings, and overt actions; in the constitution, in "free government," and the like. For it, in the terminology of Taoism, "the best government is that which governs least"; and "the more mandates and laws are enacted, the more thieves and robbers will there be." Or, "My kingdom is not of this world."

For the Sensate culture mentality, the Sensate freedom, with all these "guarantees," declarations, laws, and constitutions, the slogan "Give me liberty or give me death," is its heart and soul and "ethos." Sensate relativistic ethics of utilitarianism, hedonism, and eudaemonism also demand such a Sensate freedom. It is but natural that in all Sensate cultures or periods, that form of freedom should be dominant. A concrete case is furnished by the Western culture. Here the Sensate freedom emerged and has grown parallel with the emergence and growth of Sensate culture. The first theories of it, especially in the field of political freedom, appeared in the twelfth and thirteenth centuries. The first laws that were aimed to guarantee the political freedom of the upper classes were made about the same time. The Magna Charta of 1215 is a sample. Similar charters aimed at guaranteeing the political rights and privileges of the upper classes and then of the middle class (*bourgeoisie*) of the "free cities," and the political struggles for "liberties" on the part of these classes and cities date from about the same time, with particularly intensive fights and struggles on the part of the cities at the end of the twelfth and in the thirteenth and fourteenth centuries. These internal disturbances, with all the phraseology extolling freedom and liberty, constitute one of the most important processes in the sociopolitical life of the Western countries during these centuries.

Subsequently, with minor setbacks, this growth of Sensate freedom, with its political charters, laws, constitutions, with the accompanying political activities, struggles, uprisings, and so on, continued in Western society. After the nobility and aristocracy, the middle class clamored for this Sensate freedom; the lower classes followed in their footsteps, until, toward the end of the eighteenth century, the process became universal and led to an enormous number of constitutional and statutory provisions, declarations, laws, and charters, all with a view to guaranteeing the liberty of speech, press, religion, associations, meetings, etc. In France, the Declaration of 1789, the law of December 14, 1789, the Constitution of 1791, the Declaration of 1793, the Constitution of 1793 (a temporary reaction resulted from the Constitution of 1799 and the Napoleonic Code of 1810); then the charters of May 17, 1819, of July 18, 1828, those of 1830 and 1835; the Constitution of 1848; then the laws of September 5, 1870, June 30, 1881, March 28, 1907, July 1, 1901, and the laws of 1901, 1903, 1914, and 1916 — to mention the most important enactments — are the objective manifestation of this trend.

In Prussia and Germany, the *Allgemeines Landrecht* of 1794; the Constitution of July 8, 1815; the constitutions of 1848 and 1849 and 1850; the laws of May 7, 1874, December 11, 1899, April 19, 1908; and then the Weimar Constitution of 1919 are similar manifestations.

In Italy, the Statute of 1848 of Sardinia; the law of March 26, 1848; the laws of June 30, 1889, of 1906, and the others are landmarks of the growth of this trend.

A similar movement went on in other Western countries, in some at an earlier time, in others later; in some guaranteeing the greater, in others more modest liberties and "inalienable rights." Before the World War, there was not a single country on the European continent which was not involved in a similar movement toward a regime of Sensate liberty, with its satellites.

This brief sketch demonstrates the correlation of the movement of Sensate freedom with that of Sensate culture. The correlation holds, even for the postwar period. We have seen that the end of the nineteenth and the twentieth century are marked by a "revolt" against the overripe Sensate culture in almost all the other compartments of Western culture. We see the same here. The weakening of this culture is accompanied by a reaction against its Sensate sociopolitical liberties and laws. The Communist regime declared all these a mere "bourgeois prejudice" and abolished them entirely. Fascism, Hitlerism, and other dictatorial governments of the postwar period followed its example.

During and since the Second World War the trend has become universal for virtually all the Western countries ; it is quite the opposite of the trend that existed before the First World War.

Fighting the totalitarianism of the Communist bloc of nations, Western countries have increasingly become totalitarian also. And as long as the cold and hot wars between the two blocs continues, totalitarianism with its limitation of Sensate freedom is going to stay.

The revolt discussed is unquestioned. Its existence demonstrates the association claimed still more convincingly; we observe and feel it directly, from day to day, being its victims or its administrators. It may be a short-time flurry; it may be the beginning of a long-time trend; whatever its duration, the fact of the reaction is certain.

We are living, in this respect, in a definite period of limitation of Sensate freedom and liberty; in the period not of Sensate liberation, but of Sensate curbing of the individual. This does not mean that we are on an ascent to Ideational freedom. Here, as in other compartments of our culture, we are merely in a period of transition. From the shore of Sensate liberty we have departed; but we have not arrived at the Ideational port. As yet it is not even in sight. We are on a stormy sea, tossed aimlessly and roughly hither and thither; handled unceremoniously by the self-appointed, dictatorial "captains of the ship," suffering and stunned, demoralized and benumbed. A few of us perhaps have a glimmering of what is going to be the port of our destination. The majority, including the captains themselves, live from day to day, still permeated by the feelings of Sensate freedom only, but faded and superannuated, and therefore incapable of inspiring the old "Give me liberty or give me death" spirit. Hence all the unattractive characteristics of our times, in this field.

III. Why the Fluctuation of the Sensate and Ideational Forms of Freedom?

Why is either of the main forms of freedom not eternal, or why does not one perpetually grow at the cost of the other? One reason for minor, and so to speak "incidental short-time" fluctuations is the external factors which may reinforce one form of freedom and weaken the other. In hundreds of different forms, various external circumstances may help to lead to the decline of one form of freedom and to the rise of the other. However, the role of the external factors is, in a sense, incidental. Regardless of any external forces, each form of freedom is bound to rise and decline eventually, by virtue of its own development. In this development it generates the very forces that prepare its stagnation and decline. How and why? Suppose we take the Sensate freedom. Let us grant that it grows. Its growth means an expansion of wishes and an increase of the means of their satisfaction. In this double process sooner or later comes a point when something similar to the "law of diminishing returns," or to the so-called "Weber-Fechner law" takes place.

If old appetites are satisfied, a host of new ones appear, ravenously waiting for their satisfaction. The more a sensate man has, the more he desires to have, whether it be riches, popularity, or love experience; or fame or power or charm; or anything else. Meanwhile, in any given generation, there are always limits to the increase of the means for satisfying the ever-growing desires. Sooner or later there comes a moment when the expansion of the wishes outruns the available means for their satisfaction. In addition to this, sooner or later comes a moment when a further increase of means begins to give less and less complete satisfaction, or more and more diminishing returns. In the terminology of Weber-Fechner's proposition, the satisfaction increases only as a logarithm of the increase of the means of satisfaction. In both cases a discrepancy appears between the SW and the SM. The latter begins to be outdistanced more and more by the former. The result is dissatisfaction, a growing thirst for more and more freedom, which is unquenched. Eventually the dissatisfaction and misery lead to a devaluation of the less and less satisfying Sensate freedom; its charm fades; its value diminishes; it becomes little cared for or sought. People are ready to say "good-by" to it, as a pseudo value or of little account.

Overdevelopment of the Sensate freedom leads to the same result eventually through many other ways. One of these is its demoralizing, devitalizing, and disintegrating effects upon its partisans as well as upon society as a whole. The persons with an overdeveloped wish for Sensate freedom are likely to become the oversensual seekers for perverse pleasures that soon debilitate body and mind; or the egotists who do not want to reckon with or respect any value except their own fancy or volition. Through their scandals, indecencies, erratic exploits, and through the actions of robbery, murder, sacrilege, and the like, they ruin themselves and the society of which they are a part.

A society with a considerable proportion of these overfree members cannot exist for a long time, with such lunatics at large. It will either disintegrate, or must take measures to bridle them; bridling them means a limitation, sometimes even an elimination, of the greater part of Sensate liberty.

In a similar way, the Ideational freedom, pushed too far, unfailingly prepares its own decline. It generates the consequences which sooner or later begin to defeat Ideational freedom itself, and also become socially and even biologically dangerous for society. When such a stage of Ideational freedom is reached, it, in turn, loses its charm, prestige, fascination, holiness, and begins to be replaced more and more by Sensate freedom. Here is one of the methods of this self-destruction of Ideational freedom. In minimizing the wishes, even the carnal wishes, there is a physiological limit, even for ascetics. For the mass of people this limit is much higher. Respectively, they have to possess the minimum means for their satisfaction. If they do not have them, they will try to get them. If they cannot obtain them peacefully, they will attempt to get them by violence. If they cannot obtain this minimum of means in any way whatever, the people may begin to die out, in the strict sense of the term. The process of depopulation and devitalization is likely to be the result of such conditions. The society will become extinct, or weakened, or make a shift toward a greater Sensate freedom to save itself from the overstressed Ideational ascetic freedom of mortification.

This last point — the social and biological harmfulness of a too greatly overdeveloped Ideational freedom — deserves special comment. It is manifest in the fairly common phenomenon of self-destruction of many Ideational groups, which prefer their Ideational — inner — freedom to life without it.

More important are those more common facts which in various ways show that a too limited Sensate freedom becomes biologically harmful. Here are a few evidences of that.

Pavlov says that there exists a special freedom reflex.

> The freedom reflex is one of the most important reflexes, or, if we use a more general term, reactions, of living beings. . . . If the animal were not provided with the reflex of protest against boundaries set to its freedom, the smallest obstacle in its path would interfere with the proper fulfillment of its natural functions. Some animals, as we all know, have this freedom reflex to such a degree that when placed in captivity they refuse all food, sicken and die.

Whether or not such a reflex exists is unimportant. What is important is that for most of the people and races a minimum of Sensate liberty is a biological necessity, and when it is lacking, the people begin to dwindle biologically and even to die out entirely.

Many anthropologists have shown that most of the declining primitive races (either through high mortality or low birth rate, or both) have been those on which were imposed, to the very core of their lives, prohibition of many of their ways of living and enforcement of many ways which were new to them and which were contradictory to their inclinations and mores. The Melanesians, the Tasmanians, the Polynesians, the

Fijians, and other peoples of the Pacific give examples of this process. The rude exploitation is sometimes more healthy than the best-intentioned "reforming" coercively imposed.

An irreducible minimum of freedom to follow our own path, no matter how mistaken it may be, is as necessary to the health as it is to the happiness of mankind. This minimum doubtless varies as widely as education and experience among individuals and races. The consequences of an attempt, even by entirely wise and unselfish rulers, to uproot all our manifold deficiencies and force on us against our will a better way of life, might be as ruinous as the devastations of a Genghis Khan.

When, consequently, the restraint of the bodily needs and wishes and actions becomes too excessive, or lasts for some time, in severe forms, the vitality of the group tends to become impaired. A series of diseases, including possibly also neuroses, psychoses, and other mental ailments, begins to spread more and more widely. If the group can help it, it will try, consciously or not, to resist such effects and the excessive restraint. In other words, it will tend to fight the complete lack of freedom or the too severe Ideational freedom which, for the masses, often amounts to the same thing. If the resistance is successful, the group will shift toward Sensate freedom. In this way, Ideational freedom will be weakened and Sensate freedom reinforced. Hence the fluctuation.

The outlined way is but one of many which immanently generate from the overdeveloped Ideational freedom. Having once appeared, they begin to undermine it and prepare the way for Sensate freedom. Thus each form, when excessive, begins to destroy itself and to pave the way for the other. Hence their fluctuation and the alternation of their domination. Such, in brief, is the answer to the question: "Why the fluctuation of the forms of freedom?"

IV. Transition from One Form of Freedom to the Other, and the Movement of Internal Disturbances: Riots, Revolts, Revolutions

If the above theory of "Why the Fluctuation" be correct, we can expect that the periods of transition from one form of freedom to the other — the periods when a hitherto dominant form is on the eve of decline, and the other form on the eve of ascendance — will be marked by a notable increase of internal disturbances in the respective social system or society. In a society with an overdeveloped Sensate freedom they must increase, on account of the weakening and annulment of all the values that control, restrain, and inhibit its members from the unrestricted following of their own wishes.

Since, then, there is no other command than "Follow your desires," everything and anything can serve as a pretext for getting what one does not have and what others do have.

In the condition of such an overdeveloped thirst for Sensate freedom

> those who aim at equality will be ever ready for sedition, if they see those whom they esteem their equals possess more than they do, as well as those also who are not content with equality but aim at superiority; if they think that while they deserve more than, they have only equal with, or less than their inferior.

The same, with respective changes, can be said of the overdevelopment of Ideational freedom, when it is pressed upon the masses. Few ascetics and individuals can go along this path very far — much farther than most scholars think — and be perfectly satisfied with their inner freedom and self-sufficiency. But the masses of the people are not ascetics or excessive Ideationalists. When Ideational freedom is pressed upon them too strongly, and in too severe form, it amounts to them to a lack of any freedom. Styling it "tyranny," "despotism," "totalitarianism," "slavery," and the like, they cannot help but make efforts to free themselves from such intolerable and suffocating conditions. Hence revolts, riots, disorders — especially when the inner enthusiasms and *ethos* of Ideationalism are already spent, when it continues to exist merely by inertia, and mainly in its external form.

These considerations explain why, in the decaying period of each of these forms of freedom (and their respective cultures), the curve of internal disturbances should be expected to rise notably. Later in this work we shall see that the expectation is corroborated by the factual data: the tide of internal disturbances indeed rises greatly in the period of the transitions discussed.

V. General Conclusion on Qualitative Fluctuations of Social Relationships

The preceding chapters of this part have depicted the main qualitative forms of social relationships and respectively the main qualitative types of the network of social relationships of the social systems (organized social groups). Likewise, these chapters demonstrated the existence of the qualitative fluctuations of the social systems, so far as these qualitative types are concerned.

We turn our attention now to the quantitative aspects of the fluctuation of the network of social relationships and the respective social systems of interaction.

30

FLUCTUATION OF SYSTEMS OF SOCIAL RELATIONSHIPS IN THEIR QUANTITATIVE ASPECTS

("Rarefaction" and "Condensation" of the Network of Organized Social Groups. Their Oscillations between Totalitarianism and the *Laissez Faire*. Expansion and Contraction of Government Control and Regulation. Migration of Social Relationships.)

I. Preliminaries

In the preceding chapters the systems of social relationships have been dealt with almost exclusively from the qualitative standpoint. In this chapter attention is concentrated on the types of systems of social relationships (the network of organized groups) and their changes, viewed from the quantitative standpoint. By this is meant the *number of social relationships that serve as the "fibers" of any given network*. It has been pointed out that the *extensity* of interaction ranges from unlimited totalitarianism embracing all relationships between the parties, up to the most narrow, limited single link. This means that the number of social relationships that compose the "fibers" in a system's net work may range from the unlimited to one.

If a social system embraces all the relationships of its members, regulates their entire behavior and all their interrelations, the extensity of the social system is unlimited, or *totalitarian*. The number of social relationships involved in such a system is enormous. The network itself is thick and dense with its "wires." Almost any step of its member affects it and brings it into action. If its network is composed of only one relationship (say, the co-operative society of collectors of Nicaraguan stamps) the extensity of the network, or the number of the relationships that compose it, is only one. The "Association of the Collectors of the Nicaraguan Stamps" is a social system (group) that regulates only one relationship out of hundreds in the existence of its members. It covers such a small portion of their life and relationships that it amounts almost to the absolute *laissez-faire* system. The members can do anything, except co-operate in the collection of the stamps, without touching the network and its wires and bringing it into action. Viewed from this standpoint, the social systems range from those of only one relationship, or two, or three, up to those whose network is made up of thousands and tens of thousands of relationships. Other conditions being equal, the first type of social system influences, controls, and regulates very little the behavior and interrelationships of its members; the second, an enormous slice of them. This gives a preliminary idea of what is meant by the *quantitative* aspect of the social system of interaction, by the *number* of social relationships that compose the network of a group, and by the fluctuation of the *number* of the relationships in social systems.

Let us consider now the series of processes that recur in an organized social group in this quantitative aspect of their network of social relationships.

Even the ordinary man talks now of the increase of governmental control and regimentation in the postwar period. Intelligentsia use the term "totalitarian" to denote the Hitlerite, the Communist, the Fascist, and other state systems with an enormous expansion of governmental control and regimentation. Some are much worried about this contemporary expansion. Others welcome it, particularly the partisans of these governments. Most of the worried as well as of the welcoming groups assure us that such an expansion of government regimentation is a novelty of history and is happening for the first time. This is where they greatly err. Leaving the worries and cheers to the respective parties, one can say that the contemporary expansion of governmental regimentation is an old, old story: in various state groups it has occurred many times in the past, is occurring now, and will probably occur in the future. More than that: *the fluctuation of an increase of governmental regulation and its decrease is a process common to all organized groups in the process of their life history.*

Regulatory functions of government in any organized group are not constant in the course of time; but fluctuate, now expanding into greater numbers of relationships, now contracting. This is true of the family, of the religious group; the occupational union, political party, business corporation, and various educational, scientific, artistic, and other organizations. If they exist for any length of time, the regulatory and regimental functions of their respective governments (head, committee, bureau, chief, president, board of trustees, of directors, and what not) fluctuate, in some cases sharply, in others slightly.

Furthermore, every organized social group undergoes this process. Its network is experiencing almost all the time now inclusion of social relationships that before were outside it; now exclusion from its "wires" of some relationships that hitherto were its part; respectively, the functions of the social group increase or decrease in their *number* while its government's control and interference expand or contract in their extensity. The theoretical limits between which the process fluctuates are the absolute *totalitarianism*, where a given group and its government control and regulate all the behavior of its members, leaving nothing to their choice or to the regulation of other groups, and the absolute *laissez faire*, where the group does not regulate anything and its government's regulatory functions are at zero. Such a situation — an ideal anarchy — means practically the nonexistence of the group as well as of its government, while absolute totalitarianism of a group means that all its members belong only to that group and to none other and that this group absorbs and controls them completely, in all their relationships and behavior.

In actual reality there has hardly ever been a social group either of the absolutely totalitarian or absolutely *laissez-faire* type. But some of the real social groups in their system of social relationships have been nearer to the totalitarian, while some others have favored the "liberal" or "anarchistic" type. The same is true of the same group at different periods of its existence. At one period its network of social relationships swings toward the totalitarian pole, and the regulatory and regimental functions of its government increase and expand. At another period many "fibers" of its network drop from it; it tends to swing toward the liberal or anarchistic type, and its government's control and regulation decrease and contract in their extensity; its members now are given by the group government "liberty" and "choice" to manage the dropped relationships as they please (or their regulation is shifted to the government of different social groups, from the State to the Church; from the Church to the school; and so on).

This "swinging" between "totalitarianism" and the *laissez faire* may be styled as *the fluctuation of the quantitative aspect of the network of social relationships.*

This fluctuation is one of the processes that goes on *urbi et orbi* in the life history of any organized group. It has an important theoretical and practical significance.

Subsequently, we shall attempt to answer the following problems in this field, limiting our study to the state group (for the sake of brevity): (1) Has this quantitative fluctuation occurred in the history of the Western (and partly Graeco-Roman) state? (2) Which periods have been the periods of rarefaction and condensation of the network of social relationships and respectively of contraction and expansion of the governmental control in the state system? (3) What is the situation at the present moment in this respect? (4) What relationship has this fluctuation to that of the main types of culture and of social relationships? (5) What are its bearings upon the liberty of the individual? (6) Do social relations migrate from group to group?

II. Rhythm of Rarefaction and Condensation of the Network of the State System

A. *Long-time Waves.* That some of the state systems have been nearer to the totalitarian type than others and that the totalitarian type is not a novelty of modern times but has occurred many times in the past is beyond doubt. Totalitarian were the state systems of ancient Egypt, especially in some periods like the Ptolemaic Egypt; the state system of ancient Peru, under the Incas; that of ancient Mexico; of ancient China especially in periods like that under the leadership of Wang-an-Shi, in the eleventh century; that of Japan under the Tokugava shogunate; the state network of relationships of Ancient Sparta, Lipara, and some other Greek states; of ancient Rome, especially after Diocletian; of ancient Byzantium; the State of the Taborites, in Bohemia of the fifteenth century; several state systems of ancient India; that of ancient Persia; then many short-lived state systems in revolutionary periods in the Islamic Empire (during the revolutions of Haradgits, Alides, Karmats, Ishmaelites, Kopts, Babekists, Vakhabits), the Persian Empire (during the Mazdakist Revolution, and those under Kobad and Hormuz III); in the European Middle Ages (in Münzer and Mulhausen). These and several other state systems were as "totalitarian" as the contemporary Communist, Fascist, Hitlerite state systems. Likewise among some of the primitive tribes their state system is also "totalitarian," while in some tribes it is nearer to the *laissez-faire* type.

In the above totalitarian state systems the government control and regimentation was exceedingly large; it embraced the greater part of the lives of the subjects. The government managed almost the whole economic life: production, distribution, consumption; it controlled the family and the marriage relationships; the religious, educational, recreational, military, and other activities and relationships. The situation was factually not very different in all the essentials (except the phraseology) from that in the contemporary totalitarian state systems of Soviet Russia, Fascist Italy, or Nazi Germany. All the patterns in all the essential fields of their behavior and relationship were prescribed for the citizens or the subjects. What kind of occupation an individual may enter; what, where, and when to work; where to live; what to eat, to wear, to use; what to believe; what rank or position to hold; what to think and to say; what to approve or disapprove; what to learn; whether to marry or not, and if to marry, whom, where, and at what age; how many children to have; which of these children to allow to live and which to expose to death. Briefly, the network of the state system was so closely woven that an individual could hardly take any step without touching it and bringing it into action. From an *external* standpoint his liberty was almost nonexistent; he was a kind of puppet pulled by the government; and the government was a kind of central "power station" from which came all the "motor power" that moved the subjects. And for this reason any claim that the contemporary totalitarianism is something quite new in human history is utterly wrong: if anything, the past was more totalitarian than the Western state systems of the nineteenth century.

Thus the state systems of different but synchronously existing state groups differ from one another in this respect.

If we compare the state system of the *same state* at various periods of its existence, we can easily see that it fluctuates between totalitarianism and *laissez faire* in the course of time. In these fluctuations two kinds of "swings" are noticeable: long-time and short-time spasmodic fluctuations. The first proceed slowly and gradually and extend over a long period of time; the second come suddenly and quickly go. Let us take, in the first place, the long-time swings in the history of the Roman and the Western states, and note, at least, the most conspicuous moments of the comparative "totalitarianism" and *laissez faire* in their existence. Then we can briefly take the short-time fluctuations.

In the history of the Roman state system, at least one period of an enormous long-time swing toward "totalitarianism" stands out, namely, the period beginning with the end of the third century A.D., and especially with the time of Diocletian. Besides the short-time squalls there were probably other long-time waves of expansion and contraction of government regulation, but possibly none of them reached the degree of totalitarianism of the period mentioned.

The marks of this extraordinarily developed totalitarianism are (1) The Government becomes absolute: *Princeps legibus solutus est. Quod principi placuit — legis habet vigorem.* The emperor becomes a deity above the law; (2) complete centralization and all-embracing control by the state government of the population, in all its activities and relationships; (3) the centralized all-embracing planned economy of the State, which is now the exclusive and the main business corporation; (4) almost complete annihilation of private business and commerce; (5) complete loss of external freedom and self-government by the population; (6) degeneration of the money economy and replacement of money by "the natural" commodities and services: introduction of the "natural economy," ration system, with usual "ration cards" (*tesserae*); different rations given to different groups and strata of the population; (7) enormously increased army of the state officials and bureaucrats. Here we have on a large scale a well-developed state-socialist or totalitarian system. For those who know indeed the real character of the Soviet system in the period 1918–1922, its striking similarity to the totalitarian systems of Diocletian and the later Roman Empire needs no further evidence. Here is an abbreviated picture of the Roman state system of the period discussed.

All are regimented and controlled. For this purpose an enormous army of state officials is created. It robs and steals and aggravates the situation still more. The State needs gigantic financial means [to maintain the court, to feed the mob, army, officials, and to carry on wars]. . . . The work of the population and labor unions which before was free [unregimented by the State] now becomes regimented and hereditary. . . . . The empire is transformed into a huge factory where, under the supervision of the state officials, the population works for the emperor, the State, and private persons. Almost all industry is managed by the State. The State also distributes — very unequally — the produce. The members of the trade and labor unions are not free persons any more, that work freely for maintenance of their families; they are now the slaves of the State, that are supported, like the officials, by the State, but very poorly and inadequately. . . . Never was an administration as cruel and quarrelsome with the population, and as inefficient and unproductive for the country. The regime was based upon compulsion: everywhere the hand of the State; its tyranny. Everywhere coercion recruits and holds the workers. Nowhere do private initiative and free labor exist.

These lines give a most vivid idea of the situation. In this totalitarian form the Western Roman Empire dragged out its existence during the fourth and the fifth centuries until its fall. Likewise, in the Byzantine Empire the governmental regimentation was conspicuously high throughout its existence, rising still higher at some periods.

When the Merovingian and the Carolingian empires emerge, they start with a very considerable amount of governmental regulation and with a considerably "condensed" state system of social relationships. Nevertheless, it was far less totalitarian than the described Roman Empire. Then, with the development of feudalism, the medieval feudal State experiences an enormous "rarefaction" of its network and, respectively, an enormous decline of the regulatory, regimental, and controlling functions of its government. It is a clear case of dropping an enormous number of relationships from the state network and of the shrinking of state government interference. These dropped functions were taken over by other organizations.

Then, with the decline of feudalism and with the emergence of the so-called national state, the state system began again to "swell" and include an increasing number of social relationships. The process reached its culmination in the period of so-called "*Polizei-Staat*" or the absolutistic State of the seventeenth and eighteenth centuries. The state system of Louis XIV or Frederick the Great, or Maria Teresa and Joseph is the same system, with an enormous number of relationships included and quite compact with "relationship wires"; its government is absolutistic; its controlling and regimental functions are enormously expanded and concern almost all the important fields of the behavior of its subjects and their relationships: economic, religious, moral, educational, recreational, and so on. The swing toward totalitarianism was another long-time wave that in its rise and decline lasted about four centuries.

By the end of the eighteenth century it had spent itself, and its place was taken by the opposite swing toward *laissez faire* and liberalism and "individualism" and "contractualism." They reached high tide in the nineteenth century. Many relationships, such as liberty of speech, religion, the press, meetings, unionization, education, marriage (to a considerable degree); most of the economic activities, generally many relationships in "the pursuit of happiness and liberty" were dropped from the state network and left either to the free choice and contract of the individuals or were shifted to the networks of other social groups. The net result was, especially up to the last quarter of the nineteenth century, a conspicuous "rarefaction" of the state system of relationships, limitation of the government's power, control, and interference. The period was marked by the growth respectively of "democracy," "self-government," "liberty," "liberalism," "constitutional government," "contractual relationships," "rugged individualism," "private property," "private business," "private initiative," "equality of opportunity," "free associations," and other marks of the rarefied state system of relationships and of the limited amount of its regimental and regulatory functions. In the political and economic ideologies its reflections were the physiocratic, the free-trade, the liberal theories and philosophies.

With the end of the nineteenth century the signs of reaction against this comparatively *laissez-faire* state appeared and manifested themselves in the growing state regulation of labor, industry, business, and then of several other fields (a great number of measures aimed at the protection of child labor, the minimum wage, social insurance against sickness, old age, and the like; the regulation of commerce; interference into the relationship of the employer and employees; development of the state education system and compulsory laws concerning it; universal and obligatory military duty; interference in the family relationships; obligatory registration and regulation of marriages, births, divorces; an enormous number of measures concerning the public health and sanitation; and so on and so forth). Respectively governmental control and regulation started to expand again; at the beginning very slowly and gradually. With the World War, they made at once a tremendous jump; they soared into the stratosphere — due to the war factor (see further in this chapter). After its termination, in some countries in some fields, they slightly declined, but for a short time only. Soon they resumed their upward movement. At the present moment we are living in an age of an enormous swing toward state totalitarianism. The trend is common to practically all the Western (and also to some of the Eastern) countries. In some states, like Soviet Russia, Fascist Italy, Nazi Germany, the state totalitarianism has soared to "unbelievable" heights; in the United States of America, England, and a few other countries, it has grown also, though not to the same high level.

Its concrete forms and degrees vary from country to country; the trend itself is under way in all the Western countries. Here it takes the Soviet-Communist form; there, the Fascist; elsewhere the Hitlerite or New Deal form; in other countries the Pilsudsky-Horty-MacDonald-Baldwin-Blum forms. Whether we like it or not, we are living in an age of a sharp rise of "totalitarianism," of an enormous condensation of the Western state systems; of absolutization of the state power; and of an increasing interference of the state government in all affairs and matters which should and should not be its business.

During World War II the trend tremendously increased, and after a slight recession following the armistice, continues to remain at a very high level in all countries.

This brief outline gives an idea of at least the most conspicuous "highs and lows" of the totalitarian and the *laissez-faire* swings, the expansion and contraction of the Western state system and its government, from the Merovingian-Carolingian times to the present.

There is hardly any doubt that other state systems that existed for centuries experienced somewhat similar swings in their life history, as, for instance, the Chinese, Japanese, many Arabian caliphates, Ancient Egypt, several Hindu states, and some others.

The practical conclusion of this is that there is hardly any perpetual tendency in state history either toward bigger and better "totalitarianism" or toward the *laissez faire*. Neither the partisans of the totalitarian State — Socialist, Communist, Hitlerite, Fascist (the ideologists' absolutistic state, with its all-perfect bureaucratic guardian angels) nor the partisans of the absolute *laissez faire* or its diluted forms — anarchists, complete individualists (of the Stirner and Nietzsche type), liberal humanitarians, liberal democrats, with their "government of the people, by the people, and for the people," but not too much of it — none of these are supported by the sociohistorical reality in their contention that history steadily leads toward their favorite ideal. Here, as in most other fields, history fluctuates, now giving the upper hand to the totalitarian, now to the antitotalitarian swing.

What has been said of the long-time waves in this field of the state system can be said, with proper modifications, about any long-existing, organized, social system of relationship: the family, the Church, the guild, the trade union, the political party, and other organized groups. All of them experienced the pulsation of "rarefaction" and "condensation" of their networks; of the expansion and contraction of control of their governments. This "rhythm" is an immanent trait of all the long-living organized systems of social interaction.

Now for the short-time fluctuations in this field.

B. *Short-time Squalls and Ripples.* These occur in practically every organized group or social system, whether of the family, the religious body, or any other. As we shall see, these sudden short-time "convulsions" are, as a rule, the result of some sudden "emergency."

III. Reasons and Factors of the Long-time Fluctuations

As far as Ideational and Sensate cultures are concerned, logically no direct or very close relationship between these and the expansion or contraction of the state government interference is evident, with the following exceptions.

A. The ascetically Ideational culture (and its respective society) cares little for the State and its government; therefore, unless such a society becomes a prey to foreign invaders (as it does usually), no particularly "condensed" state system and totalitarian government should be expected in such a culture, society, or period.

B. The actively Ideational culture and society is likely to create a strong social body and a strong government. The body, however, is likely to be a religious organization, rather than the State, and the government accordingly would be that of the religious order rather than of the State. If the body in such a society happens to be the State, such a state and its government can be only the extreme theocracy.

C. Therefore, the totalitarian (and secular) state with an omni-managing government logically belongs mainly to the Sensate culture and society. Only in the Sensate societies and periods should it be expected to flourish; to rise with the rise of the Sensate culture and decline with its decline.

Such seem to be the possibilities that logically should be expected. Are the expectations sustained by the data of history? Not perfectly (for the reasons indicated further), but to a tangible extent. Here are a few broad classes of facts that seem to corroborate that.

(1) The predominantly Ideational Hindu culture rarely created for itself a powerful state, and the State has played in its life history a comparatively secondary role. The main role belonged to the Brahman caste, the caste of priests without church organization; teachers without state educational institutions; moral and social leaders without wealth, army, and support of state organization. India has known, of course,

many states, and some of them, like the Maurya and the Gupta empires, were very powerful. But these states were either theocratic or mostly organized by foreign invaders, or, in a few cases, by the Sensate Groups and in comparatively Sensate periods. As such, they remained social organizations which were foreign to the population, like British rule; they did not penetrate the heart and soul of India, and have always been something existing on the surface of its culture rather than as its organic and inner element. C. Bouglé well sums up the situation, stating:

In India there is no embryo of the State. The very idea of the state public power is entirely foreign to India. . . . All the state governments whatsoever seem to remain only on the surface of the Hindu world.

Il manque à l'Inde la Cité. Une organisation proprement politique n'a pas été donnée la société hindoue, et la tradition religieuse a pu la dominer tout entiére.

(2) If we turn to the verification of the propositions in time, in the life history of the Graeco-Roman and the Western cultures, they are not repudiated by the factual data. Indeed, if the early Greek and the Roman state were somewhat totalitarian in the period of domination of their Ideational culture, their totalitarianism was sacral and theocratic. With the progress of the sensatization of the Greek culture, the totalitarianism of the Greek States did not decrease, but rather increased, and became secular (after the fifth century B.C.). The role of the state in all matters became more important, and in Sparta and some other cities the State replaced and took upon itself many a function which hitherto had belonged to the nonstate groups (the family, the *phile*, the religious, and other social bodies). Likewise in Rome, with the progress of Sensatism, after the second century B.C., the totalitarianism of the state began to increase and become secular. Due to specific factors, the increase continued almost up to the "end" of the Western Roman Empire (in the fifth century A.D.). But in the fifth century and after — and please note that only in the fifth century and after did the Ideational culture of Christianity become dominant — the state system of the empire quickly began to fall to pieces and weakened to such an extent that the historians style it the "fall and the end of the Roman Empire." When we enter the Ideational Middle Ages, we are confronted with a very weak state, far indeed from any totalitarianism. Even when the Merovingian and Carolingian empires were created, they were still far from being "totalitarian." The place of the secular state was taken by the Christian Church and its organized system. The religious body became the most important and even the most powerful body social in the Ideational period, but not a secular totalitarian state. After the Carolingian Empire, the feudal state became something still less important; a rarefied, impotent, and insignificant social system of relationships, that played a very modest part

and in no way remind one of the Hobbesian Leviathan. Thus, here again we see a nonexistence of totalitarianism and the all-controlling State in the period of domination of Ideational culture.

(3) Further history is no less instructive. With the rise of the Sensate culture, the secular state, in the form of the newly formed national monarchies, began to rise also. Step by step it grew; absorbed into its system a greater and greater number of social relationships that were outside its reach in the Middle Ages. Parallel to that, the state government, the monarchs, began to expand their interference, control, regulation, and regimentation. Soon they challenged the Church theocracy in the form of the Papal See. Subsequently this trend continued with the progress of the Sensate culture and in the seventeenth and eighteenth centuries resulted in the creation of the absolute monarchies and the *Polizei-Staat* — the real Leviathans, with the monarchs *legibus solutus*, with enormously expanded government control and regimentation, and all the other signs of totalitarianism. Finally, the settled and prosperous Sensate culture of the nineteenth century produced a secular state, as the most important and powerful among other social systems, but "normalized" and "constitutionalized" within certain limits. This "limitation" was due, on the one hand, to the overripeness of that culture. Its bearers, these "men and citizens of the Declarations," had sowed their wild oats and now wanted to enjoy their liberty without any undue annoyance from the State or its government. On the other hand, as we shall see, it was due to the comparative security, prosperity, and peace of the European society of the nineteenth century.

With the World War I the factor of militarism appeared on the stage and led, as it regularly does (see later on), to a sudden flare-up of totalitarianism. Under its influence, and then that of its aftermaths (economic crises, insecurity, depression, and so on) the overripe Sensate man "went to pieces," lost his balance, went wild. Hence, the most violent and extremely totalitarian trend of the postwar period in which we live.

This sketch shows that the propositions offered have a serious basis and are borne out by the main swings of history rather well. It gives an additional proof of the dependence of this quantitative aspect of social systems upon the type of culture. But, as mentioned, the connection is not exceedingly close; all the time it is influenced by the interference of other, special factors that are responsible for "short-time and intermittent" swings in this field. Most of the deviations from the line of the propositions are due to the play and interference of these special factors.

Let us turn now to the special factors of the short-time and convulsive swings between totalitarianism and the *laissez-faire* poles of the state system and its government.

IV. Factors of Short-time Fluctuations

These factors are numerous. The most important are three: (1) *war or peace;* (2) *economic impoverishment or prosperity;* (3) *social emergency of any kind. Other conditions being equal, governmental control in a given social system tends to increase in periods of great social emergency; and of these emergency conditions, particularly in the times of strenuous war and in severe economic crises where there is a scarcity of the most important means of subsistence for a large part of the population.*

All emergency conditions call forth an extraordinary effort on the part of the state government, which leads naturally to expansion of its activity, control, and regulation.

The role of the military factor was well analyzed by Spencer. It goes without saying that as soon as a society enters war, the curve of government interference at once jumps and the state network of social relationships becomes more complicated. Instead of normal laws, martial law and a state of siege are introduced, which means an enormous expansion of government control. Many economic relationships heretofore uncontrolled by the State now become regimented by it: production, distribution, and consumption. Many other social relationships undergo a similar shift. The liberties and rights of the subjects or citizens are enormously curtailed. Military rule is absolute; it may concern anything that is urgent from a military standpoint; it imposes upon the population anything that is deemed necessary for military purposes. It may impose not only the draft into the army, but even mass execution of groups in the population. In a word, the fact of a sudden expansion of government control in time of war is unquestionable.

The main reasons for it are also axiomatic. Such a "totalitarian swing" is necessary for victory: of two nations equal in other respects, the nation that imposes a centralized and rigid discipline upon its population has more chances of being victorious than the nation whose efforts are not organized; which does not have a centralized system and strong discipline.

A second reason is that the military regime of life in barracks is in a sense "totalitarian" in its very nature. A soldier, especially during war, does not belong to himself. At any moment he can be sent to fight, to do whatever he is ordered, even to die. The commands are absolute and do not admit of any protest or discussion. The commanding officer, and especially the commander in chief, has the right of life and death over the army and even over the civilians. He is an absolute ruler. The regime of life in the military institutions is also "state communistic." The soldiers live in buildings not chosen by them; they eat whatever they are given, dress and do as they are ordered. Their time and activity, with the exception of a few hours, is most rigidly regimented.

In this sense, the army and the military regime have always been "totalitarian" par excellence. The best creators of totalitarianism, including the state socialism and state communism, have been not Marx or Engels or Lassalle or Lenin, but the greatest organizers of military forces and military empires: Jenghiz Khan, Tamerlane, Caesar, Napoleon, and the like.

If a country has long and frequent wars, such a regime becomes habitual for it. It extends beyond its army, over the whole country; as a result, the whole nation becomes "conditioned" to be totalitarian in the behavior and relationship of its members. There are other reasons, but these two are sufficient to explain why the factor of war and militarism facilitates the swing of the state system toward totalitarianism, while peace tends to work in the opposite way.

The whole matter is so clear and unquestionable, and is so well supported by the actual facts of history, that there is no need to go into its detailed corroboration. Every war exhibits the above regularities. The First World War as well as the smaller wars displayed them magnificently, even in the Anglo-Saxon countries of traditional liberalism. In subsequent pages devoted to the study of the movement of war, we shall see that the medieval centuries were comparatively peaceful; and these centuries had a State either very far from any totalitarianism, or of only a moderate degree of "condensation" and government interference. Then after the thirteenth century, the curve of war began to rise; and the state system and its government began to rise also. In the seventeenth and partly in the eighteenth centuries war reached its climax; and the state totalitarianism reached its climax also. The Revolutionary and Napoleonic periods were belligerent; and they were totalitarian in reality. The nineteenth century (after the Napoleonic Wars) was comparatively peaceful; and the state system and its government became moderate, contractual, and limited. The twentieth century, beginning with the World War, happened to be the most belligerent century so far; and the totalitarianism of the State and of its government soared into the "stratosphere." In brief, we find in the essentials the tangible parallel movement of the curve of totalitarianism and that of war.

Less known and evident is the "totalitarian" role of famine, impoverishment, and of severe economic crises of a given society. Therefore, a little greater space needs to be devoted to the establishment of this logical and factual association. Let us take the matter as concisely as possible. In a society where there exists a differentiation into poor and rich an extraordinary impoverishment facilitates an expansion of government interference in economic relations, and, through that, an increase of governmental control in other social areas. This is the second factor of fluctuation of the amount of governmental interference. From the standpoint of the proposition it does not matter whether an increase of the interference is made in a peaceful or revolutionary way, by a conservative or revolutionary government, under the name of socialism or absolutism. What matters is that in some way it takes place, regardless of these details.

The reason for this is at hand: abundance of a necessity makes unnecessary any governmental regulation. Since we have plenty of air to breathe, our need is satisfied without any compulsory regulation. If there is a scarcity of this necessity, the regulation appears unavoidable, as for instance in connection with our routes for airplanes. The same may be said of other necessities.

Whether we take the records concerning great famines in the history of ancient Egypt, or ancient Greece and Rome, or China and Persia, or Russia and many medieval societies, we can but notice an expansion of the economic control of the government at such a period.

An increase of governmental economic control in the periods of famine and impoverishment has been regularly manifest in the following phenomena: (1) in an establishment or reinforcement of governmental control oi exports and imports, which often amounted to governmental monopoly of foreign trade; (2) in an establishment of fixed prices on food and other necessities; (3) in governmental registration and tabulation of the entire amount of necessities in the country owned by its citizens; (4) in a complete control of purchase and sale of commodities, including amounts to be bought and conditions governing sales; (5) in governmental compulsion of private citizens' sending their commodities to market; (6) in requisition, to an extraordinarily large degree, of private necessities by the government; (7) in an establishment of numerous governmental agencies for the purpose of buying, producing, and distributing necessities among the population; (8) in the introduction of a ration system; (9) in an organization of public works on an extraordinarily large scale; (10) in a substitution of governmental control of production, distribution, and even consumption, of necessities for that by private individuals or corporations. All these and many similar phenomena have been regularly repeated in most dissimilar countries at most dissimilar times, as soon as famine and impoverishment have broken out. All this signifies great expansion of governmental interference in the economic relationships of the population and, through that, often in other fields of social interrelations. Here are a series of facts, a few out of many similar, which show this.

A. *Ancient Egypt.* The Bible gives us one of the oldest records which clearly shows the foregoing correlation. As a result of the great famine in the time of Joseph, the money, cattle, and land of the population of Ancient Egypt "became Pharaoh's." The people became the slaves of the government. The entire economic life began to be controlled by the government. In the modern terminology this means that everything was nationalized, and that the economic control of Pharaoh's government was expanded enormously at the expense of that of private individuals. Other Egyptian records show that this was repeated several times in the history of Ancient Egypt. Its pharaohs and officials often stress in their records that "in years of famine they plowed all the fields of the nome, preserving its people alive and furnishing its food." As war and famine, or danger of famine, were very frequent phenomena in Ancient Egypt, this accounts for a high level of governmental control throughout the history of Egypt. And yet, in the famine years and in periods of impoverishment, as the before-mentioned facts show, the control seems to have jumped still higher. The economic life of Egypt under the Ptolemy dynasty gives an additional example of this. Economic disorganization of this period was accompanied by an extraordinary growth of governmental control which led to a transformation of society into a universal state-socialist organization.

B. *China.* More abundant and conspicuous confirmation of the hypothesis is given by the history of China. It is the history of a society with very frequent famines and with a permanent danger of starvation. This accounts for an exclusively high level of governmental control in China throughout its history. The organization of Chinese society has been in essence an "economic state socialism," with "many governmental regulations to control consumption, production, and distribution." And yet, in the periods of great famine or impoverishment, governmental control expanded still more. This, according to the records, has invariably happened in the time of Yao, in the years of famine during the Yin, the Chow, the Hans, the T'ang, the Sung, and other dynasties. On the other hand, the attempts to introduce a real state-socialist organization, like the attempts of Wang Mang or Wang-an-Shih, regularly happened in the period of a great impoverishment of the country.

C. *Ancient Greece.* Aside from the factor of militarism, economic insecurity was responsible for a large degree of governmental control in Sparta, Athens, Lipara, and other Greek states. R. Pöhlmann says: "The products of the Spartan agriculture were not sufficient to satisfy the necessities of the population. The entire economic life was based on a very narrow and uncertain basis. Every economic crisis, every delay or interruption of imports of necessities was very dangerous. Shall we wonder that the strongest governmental control of economic life became inevitable?" In similar straits was Athens. In the periods of impoverishment and famine the governmental control intensified.
In the period of extreme impoverishment governmental control assumed

the forms of the present-day totalitarianism. The government confiscated private lands and wealth, distributed them in such a way as it found necessary, nationalized what it wanted; in brief, pushed its control up to possible limits. Such were, for example, the periods of impoverishment after the Messina War and in the times of Agis IV, Cleomenes III, and Nabis in Sparta; after the Peloponnesian War in Athens (the periods of the Thirty and the Ten Tyrants), and in some other periods. Either in a legal way or in the form of revolution, under conservative as well as revolutionary dictators, state interference in such periods grew to its limits and assumed the form of state totalitarianism.

D. *Ancient Rome*. Similar parallelism is given in the history of Rome. Here the years of famine, like the years A.D. 5, 8, 18, 52, were usually accompanied by a corresponding increase of the governmental control. Side by side with these small fluctuations we see that the periods of impoverishment of the masses were followed by an expansion of state interference which amounted sometimes to state socialism. It is well-known that in the period from the second half of the second century B.C. to the beginning of the first century A.D. there were many acute economic crises in Rome. The same period is marked by the Corn Laws of the Gracchi (123 B.C.); by the establishment of a special institution for prevention of famine and for control of the public supply (104 B.C.); by the introduction of a ration system and public supply free of charge; by many nationalizations and confiscations and restriction of private economic enterprise; by a great increase of economic functions of the government. Still more conspicuous was the discussed correlation in the period from the third century A.D. to the "end" of the Western Roman Empire. This was the time of economic decay of Rome. It was also the time of an establishment of a totalitarian economic organization in the Western Roman Empire. "The Empire was transformed into a big factory where, under the control of the officials, the population had to work. It was a real state-socialist organization of industry and labor. Almost all production and distribution of wealth was concentrated in the hands of the government." One who has observed the Soviet Communist system in the period from 1917 to 1922 can but notice the essential similarity of the Roman and the Soviet regimes.

E. *The Middle Ages*. Here the same correlation is repeated many times. In 792–793 the famine broke out. As a result, "Charles the Great introduced the first fixed prices under its influence." In 805 famine burst out again, and a decree was issued that "*ne foris imperium nostrum vendatur aliquid alimoniae*"; free trade was forbidden; fixed prices were reintroduced; the freedom of contracts was restricted; agriculture and industry began to be controlled more severely, and so forth. As in the Middle Ages famine was very frequent, this, besides the factor of war, seems to have been responsible for a relatively high State or Church government control of economic relations throughout the Middle Ages. It, however, jumped up in the years of famine. In the history of England such years were 1201–1202, 1315–1316, 1321, 1483, 1512, 1521, 1586, 1648–1649, and others. In the history of France such years were 1391, 1504–1505, 1565, 1567, 1577, 1591, 1635, 1662, 1684, 1693, 1709, to mention but a few cases. The same years were marked by an increase of government interference in economic relations. A historian of the food trade in France sums up his exhaustive study as follows: "As soon as famine was bursting out, governmental control became stronger; as soon as famine was weakening, the control weakened also."

The discussed correlation is still more conspicuously exhibited in the history of Russian famines. Each of the periods of famine or of great impoverishment has been invariably followed by an increase of governmental control.

In the light of this hypothesis it is comprehensible why governmental control in the form of the revolutionary or counterrevolutionary dictatorship usually increases in the periods of great revolutions. Such periods are marked by an extraordinary impoverishment and disorganization of economic life. Hence its result — an extraordinary increase of governmental control of the entire economic life of a revolutionary society. Sometimes it leads to an establishment of a "communist" or "state-socialist organization" in a revolutionary country, like the communist societies in Tabor (in revolutionary Bohemia), in Mühlhausen, in New Jerusalem, or in Paris in 1871, to mention but a few cases of that kind. In other cases it assumes other forms of totalitarianism: absolutism, dictatorship, fascism, Nazism, etc.

Finally, a striking confirmation of the hypothesis has been given by the expansion of governmental control during the two World Wars and after. During this period, not only in the belligerent, but in the neutral, countries, too, the control of economic life by the government increased enormously. In the belligerent countries it was due primarily to the factor of war, and secondarily to that of scarcity of food and other necessities. In the neutral countries the expansion of the interference was called forth principally by an increased scarcity of food and other necessities.

The same two factors have been responsible for the contemporary growth of the Communist, the Nazi, the military, and other totalitarian regimes in all countries. From this standpoint, the so-called "Communist" regime has represented the expansion of government control up to its limits. An annihilation of private property; a universal nationalization, beginning with factories and land and ending with the last silver teaspoon; a complete annihilation of private commerce and trade;

a regulation of the entire production, distribution, and even consumption of all products by the government; a complete substitution of governmental control for that of private individuals — such have been characteristics of the Communist regimes in Russia, in China, and in other countries.

What were the causes of this? Owing to the First World War, the lack of necessities began to be felt in Russia already in 1915. After the same period there appeared the tendency of the expansion of governmental control in the economic field. The decrees of August 15, 1915, and October 25, 1915, which gave the right to officials to search, to tabulate, to confiscate, to requisition all private food and necessities could be regarded as a beginning of what later on developed into "Communism." Owing to the growth of impoverishment, due to the war, this process necessarily grew also. As the revolution only aggravated the economic situation, governmental control continued to grow during the Provisional Government, whose policy in this respect only pushed further that of the Czarist Government. At the time of the overthrow of the Kerensky regime private trade and commerce were almost annihilated; private industry and agriculture were greatly restricted, state control was expanded enormously. Owing to the factors of the civil war and the growth of impoverishment the Bolsheviki pushed this process up to its possible limits. In this way appeared the so-called "Communist regime," which, in the present terminology of the Communists themselves, was nothing but "Military and Starving Communism." The continuation of this process is no less instructive.

In 1920 the civil war was finished. In this way one of the factors of "Communism" ceased to work. At the same time everyone, except a small group of Communists and swindlers, was ruined. Economic differentiation disappeared. An equality in poverty was established. If my hypothesis is true, under such conditions we should expect an opposite trend, toward a decrease of government control. This is what actually happened. In 1921 the Bolsheviki were forced to introduce the New Economic Policy. It meant a step toward the so-called "capitalist regime"; it represented a reduction of the governmental control of economic life and an increase of private control, initiative, and autonomy. With peace and improvement of economic conditions, this trend was continued up to the Second World War, when it was replaced by a new flare-up of totalitarianism.

For similar reasons, the Communists and other forms of totalitarian regimes have grown in all countries.

The foregoing series of facts, from ancient Egypt to A.D. 1937, a series which might be continued *ad libitum*, if there were need and space, seem to show clearly the logical and factual validity of the hypothesis discussed.

If the hypothesis is true, it gives a sufficient basis for the following tentative inferences.

(1) Since a considerable expansion of government control of economic relations has been a result of impoverishment or of a disproportionate economic contrast between the wealthy and the poor classes, it follows that the very fact of great expansion itself is a symptom of economic disorganization of society.

(2) From this standpoint, the Soviet Communism and other forms of contemporary totalitarianism have been but a form of an extraordinary expansion of governmental control due to wars and to an extreme impoverishment of the population caused by the war. In this sense, the totalitarianisms have been manifestations of a great social sickness, but not of a social improvement.

(3) Other conditions being equal, if in the near future an aggravation of the economic and war situation of a Western society takes place, or economic inequality within it grows, an increase of governmental control is to be expected.

(4) If there is peace and an improvement of the economic situation within such a society, or a diminution of economic inequality, a decrease of governmental control is likely to happen. It will probably manifest itself in the form of a decrease of popularity of totalitarianist demands for substitution of governmental control for that of private persons and corporations.

So much for this factor.

What has been said of war and impoverishment can be said of any social emergency that involves a considerable part of the population. Any such emergency tends to expand the regulative and controlling functions of the state (and other group) government, whether the emergency is an earthquake, a devastating tornado, a widespread epidemic, flood and inundation of a large area, or an extraordinary development of banditry and crime, or an explosion of ammunition warehouses, or a serious drought, or dust storms covering large areas, or something else. All these emergencies lead to an expansion of governmental activity; if the emergency is local, of the local agents of the government; if it is national, of the national agencies.

The proposition again is so self-evident and the facts of this association of emergency with the expansion of governmental functions are so numerous and have been recurring so regularly, from the remotest past up to this year's floods, droughts, earthquakes, tornadoes, and other — local and national — emergencies, that there is no reason to go into its detailed corroboration. From the oldest records of various emergencies up to this year's latest calamity, with the invariable indication of the increased activities of the government, of extraordinary measures taken, of the introduction even of martial law, the association has regularly recurred and is almost axiomatic.

If there were not a permanent — normal — emergency in any society, in the form of the maintenance of law and order, no government would be necessary in it. For the group of ideally perfect creatures — wise, moral, exceedingly social and altruistic; creatures of angelic nature — hardly any government with its compulsory nature and its regimentation would be necessary. They themselves, of their own will, would do all that was needed. Unfortunately such a society of human beings does not exist. Therefore some forms of government exist and must exist in any organized society. When an emergency grows, the government interference, compulsion, and regimentation grow. When the emergency declines, the latter decline also. Such is the factual and logical connection of these variables.

V. Liberty in Its Relationship to Totalitarianism and the Laissez Faire in the State System

Since Liberty's formula is $\frac{SM}{SW}$, an expansion of the government interference does not mean necessarily the limitation of liberty within either the state system or any other group. *If the expansion corresponds to the wishes of the members of the State* or other organized group, a totalitarian character of government is neither felt as a limitation of the liberty of the members, nor is it regarded as tyranny. It is estimated as a real social service, rather than an encroachment on the freedom and the rights of the members. In many religious sects, in many family groups, and generally in a group with a predominant familistic relationship, such a totalitarianism is welcomed and viewed as a positive value. Even in periods of war and emergency, dictatorship in a state and a swing to totalitarianism have often been willingly accepted.

On the other hand, if such an expansion of government regimentation is contrary to the wishes of the members, any step toward totalitarianism would mean a limitation of the liberty of the members, would be felt as such, and would be valued as tyranny, despotism, and the like. Such is the clear-cut, logical answer to the problem. It points out, first the one-sidedness of the contractual-liberal formula of liberty dominant in the nineteenth century. According to this, any expansion of government activity was viewed suspiciously as a potential limitation of the liberty of the citizens or members. Similar is the standpoint of anarchists. The above statement means that, contrary to these views, there are expansions of the government's activities which are not a limitation of the liberty of the members of the group. When in a group, especially in periods of calamity, the members wish the most vigorous action from the government, and the government fails to give it, such an abstention from expansion would be qualified by the members as a mere impotence and inefficiency of the government, and as a failure to render the social service expected. On the other hand, the policy of the government *laissez faire* in many cases is not a service to the liberty of the members of the group, but serves often the opposite purpose; it is like the noninterference on the part of an onlooker into the relationship where a cruel gangster tortures a child, or a physically powerful person coerces, without any just reason, the weaker party into an activity or conduct harmful to that party.

These considerations show why totalitarianism per se is not necessarily a limitation of the liberty of the members; and the *laissez faire* per se is not necessarily identical with the regime of freedom of the members. Everything depends upon the kind of totalitarianism and the kind of *laissez faire*. If the former is familistic, it is the best realization of the liberty of the group members. If it is compulsory, it is undoubtedly a limitation of their liberty. The same is true of the *laissez faire*. If it is in accordance with the wish of the members of the group and if the members are highly social and properly behave themselves in regard to one another, as "brothers," the *laissez faire* is a free regime. If the wish of the majority of the members suffering from the pseudo-contractual relationship is for a just and strong government that can help them and bridle the coercive section of the group, then the *laissez-faire* government is a shrine for a compulsory regime.

Does this mean that the contemporary totalitarianism is that of liberty? If it were familistic in its main nature, it would have been such. But, as we have seen, only in a small portion is it familistic; in its essentials it is mainly compulsory. The very presence of its harsh and severe coercive means used overliberally, without any restraint; its martial (juridically or factually) laws; the immense number of its victims and of its opponents; its reliance upon an unrestrained physical coercion — these and other symptoms are a fairly reliable barometer that it is not totalitarianism that is desired by all or even a large portion of the populations of the contemporary totalitarian countries. For them it is certainly not an enlargement of their liberty, but a radical limitation of it, even in comparison with the shadow of liberty they enjoyed under the pseudo-contractual regime at the beginning of this century.

Being such, present totalitarianism is the child of the transitory conditions. As such, it cannot exist in its present form for any length of time; it must turn either into familistic totalitarianism or into a regime of open and rude coercion which sooner or later will either be overthrown or curbed.

VI. Transfer and Migration of Social Relationships from One Social System to Others

Up to the present time, we have been studying the rarefaction and condensation of social relationships within one, the state social, system. Now let us glance at what is happening to the social relationships that drop from the state social system and cease to be regulated by its government. If the social systems were limited by the State, and if each individual belonged to one social system only, then any social relationship dropped from the state system would mean its transfer into the sphere of the free choice of an individual. We know, however, that the real situation is different. Within the same population there exists not only the state system but several other nonstate social systems that are different from it, such as the various religious organizations (the citizens of the same state often belong to different religious organizations; some are Catholics, some Protestants, some Hebrews, some Mohammedans, etc.; and, vice versa, members of the same religious organization — for instance, the Catholic — are citizens of different states), the occupational group, the "nationality" group, the political party, etc.

Each of us is a citizen of a state, belongs to some religious group (including the atheist societies); is a member of some occupational group; of some family; of a nationality; of a political party; of many associations and societies, each different from the state and from one another.

Under these conditions, inclusion of new relationships in the state system (expansion of its government control) or the exclusion from this system of some relationships that hitherto were a part of it, does not necessarily mean (respectively) a limitation of free choice or an increase of it for the individual, but in most cases it is a *transfer of the respective relationships from one social system to another*. If the feudal State lost some social relationships from its system, they were taken over by other social systems (particularly by the Church, by the feudal orders or estates, and the like) and began to be controlled and regulated by these nonstate organizations, instead of being left to the "free choice of the individual."

If the registration of marriages, births, deaths, and divorces was dropped in many cases from the network of the religious organizations (especially after the French Revolution), these relationships were not left uncontrolled by the social bodies, but were registered, regulated, and controlled by the State (in most of the Western countries). In other words, they were shifted from the regulative system of the religious group to the state group.

Such shifts, or "migrations," of social relationships from one social system to another are fairly frequent and normal phenomena. In moderate form, this movement goes on in any population, almost all the time. Now a certain relationship, say the prohibition of alcoholic beverages, which hitherto was regulated by the nonstate social groups, is included and begins to be regulated by the State; after some time, it is excluded, in its greater part, from the state system of relationships and begins to be regulated by other social groups (the family, the Church, the professional union, various prohibition societies, etc.). So it happens with a large number of social relationships. In some periods, such a "migration" assumes the mass character of a geologic earthquake; a large set of relationships is suddenly and en masse shifted from one social system to another — for instance, in the periods of the so-called "social revolutions." During the French, the Spanish, the Russian, or many other revolutions, most of the relationships that had been controlled by the Church before the revolution were suddenly shifted to the control of the Revolutionary state government. With the beginning of the Middle Ages, many relationships that were "fibers" of the Roman state system were dropped and taken over into the Christian Church social system. Social relationships in the field of marriage and divorce, and birth and death; of education, recreation, religion — in fact, practically all fields of social life — have frequently been shifted from one social system to another social system. Religion, during a certain period of the Middle Ages, and after the Augsburg Agreement, was included in the state system (*cuius regio*, *eius religio*); after the introduction of "freedom of religion," it was excluded from that control and migrated into the networks of other social systems. The relationship between a criminal and his victim was often not a part of the state system in the so-called tribal period. It was a matter of "self-redress" on the part of the victim, and of his family or clan. Then this relationship was transferred to the state system; self-redress was prohibited and the state government took upon itself the control and regulation of this relationship. In a so-called "capitalist society," most of the economic relationships between employers and employees in the field of production, distribution, and consumption are not a part of the state system; they are controlled by business corporations, associations, unions, including the family and the Church. The most essential traits of the socialist and communist and other totalitarian state systems at the present time is "nationalization" or "socialization" or "étatization" of most of the economic relationships. They are shifted into the state system and controlled by the state government either in all fields, as in the Soviet regime, or in most of the essential ones, as in other totalitarian systems of the present time. All the totalitarian governments control and regulate the main relationships in the field of production, distribution, consumption; in the field of interrelationships of employers and employees; in the field of prices, export, import, money, banking, and so on.

These examples give a sufficiently clear idea of the migration or transfer or shift or "mobility" of social relationships from social system to social system. It is one of the important and ever-present social processes.

(1) Assuming that the totality of social interrelationships between the units of a given population is constant, the greater is the part of the relationships that compose the fibers of the network of a given social system — for instance, of the State — the smaller is the part that makes up the fibers of the network of other social systems. If the State is totalitarian and the government tries to control most of the social relationships between its citizens, there remains little to be regulated by the other nonstate groups in the population. Their network will be thin and rarefied; they will have few matters to control and regulate.

(2) The network of the relationships of any organized social system does not remain constant, quantitatively or qualitatively, in the course of time.

(3) In regard to small social groups, sometimes their networks become so thin that there remain few, if any, social relationships in their system. Such a situation means the end of their existence as an organized social system.

(4) In the predominantly Ideational culture, the Ideational social systems, like the Church, "swell" quantitatively and include most of the qualitatively important relationships. In the predominantly Sensate culture, the Sensate social systems, like the state, the economic, and other organizations of a highly utilitarian nature, swell and involve in their systems most of the qualitatively important relationships.

(5) The above means that in the social life there is always present the process of migration of social relationships from one system to another.

(6) The intensity of this migration is not constant. There are periods when only a few social relationships shift; therefore the structure and configuration of the social systems remain in a universe of a given population almost unchanged. And there are periods when the migration of social relationships becomes rapid and on a large scale. Such sudden and mass migrations lead to: (*a*) a crumbling of many social systems; (*b*) a deep transformation of other social systems, due to the migration from their network of a series of relationships and to the inclusion of a series of new ones.

Such periods are marked by a substantial modification of the institutional and structural aspects of society. It experiences an earthquake which creates havoc with its previous order. The periods of so-called revolutions (social, political, economic, religious, and others) are examples of the periods of such mass migrations of the social relationships from social system to social system. We shall meet this phenomenon in a subsequent part of this work devoted to the movement of internal disturbances.

(7) In these fluctuations, so far as the large and fundamental social systems are concerned, like the big state, the world religion, the national the occupational, the family formation (not the single family, but the totality of the families of the same type), and others, there are limits; none of the groups can become absolutely totalitarian and drive all the other groups out of existence. In the process of the expansion of a given system there will always be a point of saturation beyond which the system cannot go, and if it tries, it soon fails.

This means that in the totality of the most powerful social systems (the Church, the State, the family, the occupational, the national, even the racial unions, the political parties, etc.) *the comparative power and totalitarianism of each group* has not been constant in the course of time, in the same society, and in different societies. It fluctuates. Now, as in the Middle Ages, the Church may be the most powerful group; then, as in modern times, its power and totalitarianism may decline, while that of the State rises. So it is with the occupational systems, whose role at the present time is especially important. In like manner has been changing the influence of the family formation, of kinship, of nationality organizations, and of other social systems. Thus in this field we see the existence of highly important migrations of social relationships; the quantitative-qualitative fluctuation of the network of social relationships of a given social system; and orderly and disturbing periods in the life of a given society. So much for this point.

The foregoing gives an idea of the qualitative and quantitative fluctuation of the systems of social relationships; of how much, in these fluctuations, they depend upon our main variables, and to what extent they are independent of them. The next chapter will add a little more to the picture.

31

FLUCTUATION OF ECONOMIC CONDITIONS

I. Preliminaries

Economic conditions do not remain constant in any social system but are subject to unceasing fluctuation. Some of the changes are slight, others great. Some are of short duration; others, especially the great fluctuations, manifest themselves completely only with the passage of decades or even centuries. Some come gradually, others with unexpected suddenness.

The purpose of this necessarily concise chapter is not a study of long-time trends, nor, contrariwise, of sudden catastrophic changes, in the economic history of the Graeco-Roman and Western cultures, but an elucidation of the relationship between the fluctuation of the Ideational and Sensate types of culture and that of economic conditions. Is there indeed any genuine relationship between them? If there is, what is it? Do the countries and periods of dominant Ideational culture tend to be associated with economic poverty or prosperity?

II. Relationship between the Main Types of Culture and Economic Conditions

If we mean by economic values the totality of the Sensate values concerned with the satisfaction mainly of bodily needs, and prized as the means of securing Sensate — that is, utilitarian, hedonistic, and eudaemonistic happiness and pleasure — it seems reasonable to expect that the predominantly Ideational cultures and periods must be less prosperous economically than are predominantly Sensate. In the completely Ideational mentality and culture the economic values logically occupy a much less important and less highly esteemed place than in the Sensate. Christ's statement that it is easier for a camel to pass through a needle's eye than for a rich man to enter into the Kingdom of God is a typical formulation of an attitude common to the Hindu, the Taoist, and other Ideational mentalities. Even, as in the Middle Ages, when economic values and the institutions associated with them are of necessity admitted into the system, they are regarded merely as the lesser evil, unavoidable since the Fall of Man. Similar is the attitude of the Hindu lawbooks and other Ideational sources, where the theory of the Fall also figures and is used to explain the toleration of this lesser evil.

We are all aware, on the other hand, of the positively exalted, sometimes the most exalted, position which the economic values have in a Sensate culture. The Sensate society is turned toward this world and, in this world, particularly toward the improvement of its economic condition as the main determinant of Sensate happiness. To this purpose it devotes its chief thought, attention, energy, and efforts. Therefore, it should be expected to be richer, more "prosperous," and more "comfortable" than the Ideational society.

Moreover, besides the difference in the *quantitative* economic achievements of the two opposed types of society, we must also expect a *qualitative* difference: a difference in the forms of economic organization — the character of the social relationships involved in production, distribution, and consumption — and in the theory of economic value, price, interest, profit, wage, and so on.

However, *such relationships are to be expected only if in a culture the mentality and the actual behavior of its members are closely integrated.*

We must not postulate, without a test, that mentality and actual behavior of human beings are always closely integrated and logically consistent. Who is not acquainted with persons whose words (or thoughts) and deeds are sorely contradictory?

Besides the existence within a system of fundamental discrepancies, *we must reckon with the possible interference of "accidental" and external conditions.* Suppose, for instance, a highly prosperous Sensate society is suddenly swept over by the black plague, or by some other "accident of history," like an earthquake, inundation, or drought on a large scale. Suppose, further, that it becomes involved in a disastrous war or a still more disastrous revolution. These external forces might easily ruin its prosperity, at least for a period.

Finally, the expected correlation of economic conditions with culture type may be upset by *the "immanent consequences" of the high development or even overdevelopment of the Sensate or Ideational culture itself.*

Some of these consequences may operate in the direction of weakening and destroying the culture that generates them. And, vice versa, some of the immanent consequences of Sensate culture may operate, in spite of the avowed positive attitude of the Sensate mentality toward economic values, in the direction of undermining its prosperity and eventually lead the Sensate society to impoverishment and a level of living below that of the Ideational society.

For instance, in an overdeveloped Sensate mentality, everybody begins to fight for a maximum share of happiness and prosperity. This leads often to conflicts between sects, classes, states, provinces, unions, etc., and often results in revolts, wars, class struggles, overtaxation, which ruin security and in the long run make economic prosperity impossible. As a consequence, the high level of economic conditions in such a society frequently declines.

Similarly, Ideational culture also generates forces that work against its negativistic or indifferent attitude toward the accumulation of wealth and the establishment of economic well-being. For example, the increasing prestige of saints, of ascetics, of spiritual leaders — such not infrequently has led the masses of the people, rich and poor, to flock to the abode of the saint, the hermit, the great bishop administrator; to flock and to bring their contributions; to intrust, to give, to bequeath their wealth to them, as the servants of God and disinterested servants of mankind. Such bearers of Ideationalism often find themselves eventually amidst wealth which they did not seek. A colony of the followers grows up near the place of the hermit; it soon expands into a monastery; the monastery becomes richer and richer.

Thus, despite its negative position regarding economic well-being and wealth, Ideationalism generates forces which often work toward an improvement of the economic situation, not only of Ideationalists themselves, but also of a much larger community. For example, such in fact was the history of the accumulation of wealth and the growth of economic functions in many a center of Ideational Christian, Buddhist, Taoist, Hindu religion. In this way, among several others, the otherworldly Christian Church became the richest property owner in the Middle Ages, deeply and inextricably involved in economic affairs, as organizer and manager of the economic and social life of medieval Europe. For the same reason other Ideational currents, like Taoism in China, have given rise to a large number of the cleverest statesmen and the greatest organizers of social and economic life. What Max Weber ascribes specifically to ascetic Protestantism is, in fact, an immanent consequence of the active Ideational mentality in general, at a certain phase of its development when the appropriate circumstances arise. The very fact of existence of theocratic political and economic regimes is another evidence of this.

Thus, one or more of the three sets of conditions that we have just considered — (1) the lack of a causal integration corresponding to the logical; (2) the influence of various external and "accidental" factors; and (3) the immanent consequences of each culture type operating against the very culture that generates them — may easily obliterate the relationships which should theoretically exist.

III. Main Conclusions

Omitting in this abridged edition the detailed analysis of economic conditions in the Graeco-Roman and Western cultures, we turn now to the main conclusions of that study:

A. Viewed from the Sensate standpoint, the economic situation (as this term is defined in the present work) of a country or nation, or of any other large or small social system, does not remain constant, nor does it show any perpetual trend toward improvement, but fluctuates, now rising, now declining.

B. There are short-time and long-time fluctuations.

C. So far as the long-time trends are concerned, they may be partly due to the interference of "accidental" factors external to the social system, but also they show a perceptible association with the rise and decline of the main kinds of integrated culture and with the immanent consequences generated by the development of each culture type.

D. All in all, and for the reasons mentioned above, the dominantly Ideational societies tend to exist in economic conditions which are on a lower level (judged from the Sensate standpoint) than those of primarily Sensate cultures. The periods when the Ideational culture begins to decline and the Sensate to rise are marked by the beginning of the improvement of the economic situation of the social system as a whole (though not necessarily of all its parts). The rise continues and reaches one of its high peaks in the period of the Idealistic or Mixed culture. The highest levels are attained, however, at the time of the fullest development of the Sensate culture, just before its subsequent decline. When the culture reaches this summit of ripeness, it begins to generate strongly certain conditions ("immanent consequences") which operate against the Sensate culture as a whole, as well as against the economic welfare as one of its main values. The operation of these forces, manifest even in the periods preceding the climax of development, works in the direction of Sensate cultural and economic decline. Such are the general trends in the field of the relationships between the fluctuations of the economic conditions and that of the main types of culture. These relationships do not appear where there is no integration of a culture as a whole, or where the culture is not integrated with its economic compartment. They may be temporarily, at least, obliterated by the intrusion of accidental external forces like plagues, famines, wars. They may be disturbed also by the operation of the immanent consequences of each culture. But in spite of all the influences of all these conditions, the associations postulated appear indeed to have existed, though not always fully or perfectly, in the history of Greece, Rome, and the West.

The associations are to be explained by the basic difference in mentality and even behavior of Sensate and Ideational man, a difference which is conditioned by the profound variance between the total system of Ideational and Sensate values, and especially of Ideational and Sensate economic values. In the Ideational culture the economic is viewed either negatively, or indifferently, or, at best, is admitted as the lesser evil within the limited range of necessity. In the Sensate system, it is either the main value by itself, or is included among the few main values. Therefore, the Ideational society devotes much less attention and energy to improving its economic well-being than does the Sensate society. The result is that the former does not attain such good results as the latter.

The reason for a comparatively high level of economic prosperity in a period of Idealistic culture seems to be comprehensible also. This is the period which to a notable extent enjoys the benefits of the increased economic efficiency of the Sensate mentality and efforts, and at the same time does not have, or has only in slight degree, the destructive immanent forces generated by the strongly developed and dominant Sensate culture. These forces are present only at their beginning stage and, in addition, are checked by the "inhibitions" (religious, moral, juridical, and others) of the Ideational culture which is still operative and still vital and as strong as the Sensate element.

E. As to the fluctuation of the economic condition of various classes of people in the same system, their economic curves do not all run parallel. While some classes are moving upward economically, others move downward. Even in the periods of rapid and great economic rise or decline, though most of the chief social classes move in one direction — hence the rapid increase or decrease of the prosperity of the social system as a whole — there always are one or more classes which are the losers or gainers.

F. Each of the main types of culture has one class or several classes which are its main bearers, agencies, and integrators. In the Ideational culture such classes seem to be mainly of two kinds: sacerdotal (the clergy, the priestly class, the Brahmans, the lamas, and so on), and the class of the religious landed aristocracy, which itself often discharges religious and sacerdotal functions and is always in close alliance with the sacerdotal class, as an allied companion, or as its secular instrumentality. In the Sensate culture, the main bearers are the capitalist-commercial bourgeoisie, the secular government, and the secular — independent free-thinking, "scientific," artistic, political — intelligentsia and the professional classes. The laboring classes, including the peasant and farmer, are rarely the main bearers and integrators of either type of culture. Their mentality, as a whole class, rarely reaches a high degree of integration.

G. All such integrating classes are immanently destined to elevate themselves socially and economically with the rise of their culture, and to decline with its decline. The sacerdotal class and the religiously minded groups of the landed aristocracy tend to become the organizing bodies and those most influential and economically most prosperous in the

Ideational culture, while the classes of the moneyed bourgeoisie, of the secular intelligentsia, and of the secular officialdom thrive in the dominantly Sensate culture.

The reasons for this are readily comprehensible as far as the Sensate integrating classes are concerned. They are eager to become rich and powerful by their Sensate nature and, when the opportunity comes, they seize it and elevate themselves, no matter by what means and at what cost. Less comprehensible is the economic elevation of the bearers of the Ideational culture, the sacerdotal group, and the religious landed aristocracy; less comprehensible because, by definition, they should be disdainful of, or at least indifferent to, wealth and economic values. And yet, directly or indirectly, they elevate themselves greatly, as was true, for instance, of the Christian clergy in the Middle Ages, or moderately, as with the lamas of Tibet or the Brahmans of India. Such a "paradox" is the result of the immanent consequences of certain sociocultural conditions: in these cases of the leading organizational position these classes assume in Ideational periods. As soon as they are placed in that position, often imposed upon them by circumstances; as soon as they become the builders of the Ideational culture and of its social, moral, mental, and economic order, they cannot help elevating themselves, no matter whether they wish it or not. Here we have a prime example of the working of the general principle of immanent consequences running counter to the nature of their parental culture.

H. The fact that the clergy and the religious landed aristocracy tend to become the leading and organizing classes in the Ideational, and the capitalistic bourgeoisie, intelligentsia, professionals, and secular officials in the Sensate culture, offers us unexpected corroboration of the theory of the theocratic and secular political regimes which was developed above. Quite independently of the considerations and evidences brought together in that chapter, our present study of the fluctuations of the economic conditions of the main classes indicates that in the periods of the domination of Ideational culture the theocratic groups become in fact the leading classes even economically, with the secular classes occupying this position in the Sensate culture.

I. The alliance of the sacerdotal groups with the religious landed aristocracy, on the one hand, and of the capitalist bourgeoisie with the secular, free-thinking intelligentsia and professionals and secular officialdom, on the other, suggests, among other things, *that the moneyed bourgeoisie and secular intelligentsia are twin children of the same parent culture, born from it, and reared by it, and bound together in their destiny, in their rise and decline.* The not infrequent quarrels between these brothers, and especially the frequent revolts of the free-minded intelligentsia against the "moneylenders," its denunciation of the "capitalist" regime, its attempts to discredit and to overthrow the "oppressor" — all of these actions and reactions occur usually and with increasing frequency, not when the Sensate culture rises, and with its rise elevates the classes of the capitalist bourgeoisie and of the secular intelligentsia, but after the climax of the Sensate culture is over and when it has begun to decline. The growth of the revolts of the intelligentsia contributes in this way to the decline of the Sensate culture itself. Regardless of, and contrary to, what the revolting intelligentsia thinks of its actions and its ends, the immanent logic of history makes it a mere instrument — and even a blind instrument — for the achievement of objectives fundamentally different from its "subjective purposes." *Volentem fata ducunt nolentem trahunt.* With proper modification the same may be said of the "elder brother" as well. As the declining stage of the Sensate culture, the capitalist class does its best to dynamite the ground upon which it stands. Its activities and policies also become more and more suicidal. It loses more and more energy, acumen, virility, determination, self-confidence, and especially self-respect. As a result, its social prestige and its power wane. In the postwar period we have witnessed a decline of both classes, the capitalists and the intelligentsia, in the revolt of the first against the second. The condition of the capitalist class and the intelligentsia of the declining Sensate is a sight as sore as that of the sacerdotal class and the landed aristocracy of the declining Ideational culture. The immanent logic of cultural and social processes makes all these classes a kind of plaything of history; elevates when the proper culture rises, and puts down when that culture declines, regardless of the ideologies and motives and "derivations" with which these classes amuse themselves.

J. The social and economic conditions of the "integrating classes" fluctuate within far wider limits than those of the laboring and agricultural (peasant) classes. As to the changes which we have noticed in the economic condition of the laboring classes — their rather low position in the dominantly Ideational periods, its improvement in the periods of Idealistic culture (as in Greece in the fifth and fourth century, in Europe in the thirteenth century), and in the West during the nineteenth century — the reasons for them have been indicated above. To recapitulate: their economic position is low in the Ideational culture because the economic level in such a culture is generally low. Their position is relatively high in the periods of Idealistic culture, because in such periods the restraining and controlling forces of Ideational culture are still operating, while the forces of the economic efficiency of the Sensate culture are already at work toward an improvement of the economic situation generally and of these classes especially. The destructive immanent consequences of the Sensate culture are, as yet, not released in any great degree. With the increase of the general wealth, these classes get, in such periods, a comparatively larger share of the total national income. Subsequently, as after the thirteenth century A.D., further improvement is hindered and every temporary regress takes place partly through the "accidental factors," partly through the destructive consequences of the developing Sensate culture. When, however, as in the nineteenth century, the upward movement of general economic conditions becomes unprecedently rapid and great, it becomes possible for these classes to benefit themselves and to improve their situation through that general enrichment of all society. In addition, the fully developed Sensate culture and mentality lead these submerged classes to a better Sensate organization in the fight for their share in the national income against the leading classes ; and this likewise procures for them a somewhat larger share in the total income.

K. Wars, revolts, revolutions, the increase of the class struggle, various political measures that not only take the eggs from the capitalist hen but often kill the hen itself — these and similar destructive consequences of the fully developed Sensate culture have overwhelmed us in the twentieth century. As a result, the general economic level has declined, and with this the position of the laboring classes has begun to decline.

We observe that the curve which was steadily and rapidly rising throughout the nineteenth century, first undergoes a decrease in its rate of rise, and then with the beginning of the First World War takes a downward direction. The Second World War still more aggravated the situation. Except the U.S.A., which prospered rather than suffered from these wars, in most of the other countries, despite an improvement in the period immediately following each war period, the general trend remains uncertain. If a new world war comes, it will go down.

Here, then, we have a change quite similar to those of almost all curves of the Western culture in the twentieth century. This economic fluctuation is additional evidence that a "turn" has indeed been experienced by Western culture. Whether it is one of the short-time and minor crises, or, what seems more probable, the beginning of a long-time decline of the Sensate culture itself, cannot be stated certainly. But the fact of a deep and general crisis is beyond serious doubt.

L. The conclusions of this chapter agree with the conclusions stated elsewhere in this work. Wars and revolutions happen in periods of impoverishment as well as enrichment. Therefore, economic factors per se are not the primary causes of these phenomena. Likewise, the data unexpectedly bear out our theory of the fluctuation of the theocratic and secular political regimes and social leadership. Directly or indirectly they give support to practically all the previous statements where the economic factors are involved.

M. What we have just said gives an answer to the problem: Is the economic class of the sociocultural phenomena integrated causally with the rest of the culture? So far as the Graeco-Roman and the Western cultures are concerned, we discover the *existence of a definite association between the rise and fall of economic well-being and the type of the dominant culture.* This means that our expectations on logical grounds are indeed realized by the actual causal and functional associations. Thus the answer to the problem is positive.

The association is, however, not close. It is definite, but it is frequently disturbed or partly dissolved by the intrusion of "accidental" forces of divers kinds, as well as by the complex set of the immanent consequences of the development of each type of culture. This means that our conclusions agree with those of the economic interpreters of history, as well as of the opposite type who claim that the economic section is integrated with the rest of the culture, including the ideological compartments. But in contradistinction to these theories, our conclusion is that the economic connection is rather loose as compared with the correlation of the other culture processes with one another. *Art and science, science and religion, ethical systems and law, law and religion and art — these and other especially "ideological" compartments of culture are interrelated and change in much closer unison than do, for instance, economic conditions and art, economic conditions and science, economic conditions and criminal codes, economic conditions and any other compartment of culture.*

Such are the main inferences from the study of the *quantitative aspect* of the fluctuation of economic conditions in the systems of integrated cultures.

N. Translated into terms of human behavior these conclusions mean that *there is a definite, though not close, association between the culture mentality and the actual behavior of individuals and groups.* The domination of the Ideational mentality manifests itself — even in the field of economic behavior — in a series of effects quite different from those upon the corresponding groups in the Sensate culture. The contemptuous or indifferent attitude toward all economic values dictated by the Ideational mentality results in the *nonperformance* of many activities aimed at an accumulation of wealth and the improvement of the economic conditions, on the one hand, and, on the other, in the *toleration* and *performance* of many acts which are not carried on by the Sensate man as being merely a waste of time and energy; as being senseless, "uneconomic," and "unprofitable." Among such acts may be, for instance, the investment of the economic resources in an "unprofitable," though magnificent, cathedral, or in a "useless" religious relic; or the bequeathing of all one's property to an "idle" monastery, or to a missionary enterprise to spread the Gospel; or the paying of a tenth or other portion of one's income to the priestly class; and the like. The Sensate mentality that makes economic value one of the greatest manifests itself behavioristically in the performance of many "economic" actions which Ideational man does not care to perform, and in the *nontoleration* and *nonperformance* of many acts which Ideational man does perform. Thus, we find here fairly general evidence of the existence of some degree of association between the type of mentality and the type of behavior. Mentality and behavior in the economic field do not remain isolated and independent of each other, but are bound together to a tangible degree. The causal association is not close, and leaves a considerable margin for the independent movement of the two variables, especially when various external and "accidental" forces interfere; nevertheless, it is quite clear and permits us to adhere to the above conclusion. Further on, the problem of the relationship between mentality and behavior will be taken up systematically, and we shall see that the conclusion reached here is sustained by other evidence.

O. This conclusion becomes still stronger if one examines not only the *quantitative fluctuations* of economic conditions in conjunction with the fluctuation of the types of culture, but the *qualitative forms* of economic organization and activities in each type of culture. Viewed from this qualitative standpoint, economic forms show thousands of differences in the Ideational and Sensate atmospheres. Beginning with the general attitude toward economic values or with the theories of capital; the place of wealth in the total system of values; the institutions of property and ownership, profit, interest, usury, price, alms, and bequests; theories of production and distribution and consumption, and ending with the forms of social relationships (familistic, or compulsory, or contractual) in the economic systems between their members and outsiders; and with the forms of use of the capital — in all these respects the economic forms and activities differ profoundly in Ideational, Idealistic, and Sensate cultures. This has been shown to some extent in the preceding parts of this work, especially in this part. Other investigators like Max Weber, F. de Coulanges, W. Sombart, A. Espinas, P. Huvelin, E. Durkheim, B. Malinowski, Hubert, Mauss, G. von Below, and many others, have also demonstrated it in many ways. The economics of an Ideational society are fundamentally different from those of the Sensate society. The economic theory applicable to one type of society would be inapplicable in many respects to the other.

PART SIX

FLUCTUATION OF WAR IN INTERGROUP RELATIONSHIPS

32

FLUCTUATION OF WAR IN THE HISTORY OF GREECE, ROME, AND EUROPE

I. Introduction

Any organized intragroup or intergroup system of social relationships experiences change in the process of its existence.

The change may be orderly, brought about by the constituted authorities of the group, according to its written or unwritten laws and constitution, or according to the desires and mores of its members.

In other cases, the change proceeds along different paths. The organized network of relationships of a given group, or the system of intergroup relationships, breaks down, contrary to, and regardless of, the laws, constitution, mores, and authorities.

When this crystallized system is broken, the organized group becomes disorganized, the organized relationships between the groups cease to be such. Order and peace (or equilibrium) disappear either in the life of the group, or in the relationship between interacting groups.

Such a confusion leads generally to a growth of conflicts between the members (in the group) and between the interacting groups. Increase of conflict means coercive antagonism in its open form, in the form of sheer violence applied by one party to another.

The outburst may then assume, in some cases, mild forms, in others the sharpest and rudest; in some cases the duration of disorder may be short — when the new crystallization takes place quickly — in others comparatively lasting. These variations occur, but an outburst of *confusion, conflict, overt violence* invariably follows any breakdown of the crystallized system of relationships.

When this process occurs within a group, we have the phenomenon of internal, or *intragroup, disturbance,* ranging from a little local confusion, disorder, riot, up to the greatest and bloodiest revolution possible, so far as the structure and functioning of its system of relationships is concerned.

When the process takes place in intergroup relationships, we have the phenomenon of the external or *intergroup disturbance,* ranging from a mild dispute, a straining and rupture of diplomatic relationships, army and navy preventive maneuvers, a few fights between a few members of the groups, and ending with the *ultima ratio* of solution of any conflict, external or intergroup: war, the sharpest outburst of violence in the breakdown of the system of intergroup relationships.

Thus internal and external disturbances — revolution and war — are but logical and factual consequences of the state of disintegration of the crystallized system of relationships.

Since that is so, a series of problems directly concerned with the study of sociocultural fluctuations arises, such as how often the breakdown of the crystallized system of relationships occurs in intragroup and intergroup relationships in the course of time; how great becomes the outburst of violence, quantitatively and qualitatively, in such breakdowns; how long these disturbances last; whether there is any trend in the course of time as to a decrease or increase of these external and internal disturbances; and a legion of other problems.

This part is devoted to the study of the fluctuations of war, as the vastest and sharpest form of external or intergroup disturbances. The next part deals with the fluctuation of the internal disturbances or revolutions in the field of the system of social relationships.

The phenomenon of the breakdown of the system, with ensuing war and internal disturbances, happens in the process of existence of the most diverse organized social groups; within and between families; within and between business organizations, criminal gangs, religious associations, trade unions, villages, educational institutions, political parties, and other social groups.

We shall limit our study here to the most important and historically registered disturbances that occur, on a large scale, in the vastest and most powerful systems of social interaction. The *interstate wars and intrastate disturbances satisfy this requirement.* They are not only the greatest and most influential, but they are to a considerable degree the resultant and the sum total of the most important internal and external disturbances within or between groups that live under the control of the state, or under that of the states involved in the war. If a disturbance inside a religious group, say, or between two religious sects, or two political parties, or two occupational unions, becomes considerable, it invariably involves the state where these groups live, and becomes also an internal or external disturbance to it.

Now let us turn to the study of the movement of war between states, as the vastest and bloodiest form of external or intergroup disturbance.

II. Methodological Explanations and Reservations

What has been the movement of war magnitude, measured either by strength of army or amount of casualties, in the life history of the Graeco-Roman and Western civilizations? Has it been decreasing, increasing, or fluctuating trendlessly? Has its movement been associated in some tangible way with the waves of the Ideational and Sensate cultures?

To all these questions contemporary social science gives no adequate answer. No doubt there are hundreds of different, seemingly cocksure theories which give very definite answers in a firm and unhesitating way, but among them there is hardly any which is based upon the necessary minimum of evidence.

The reason for such a situation is at hand, namely, the impossibility of a perfect or even satisfactory study of the problem. The difficulties which meet an investigator are so obvious and so insuperable that the problem cannot be studied and answered satisfactorily, no matter who studies it. A very brief survey of some of the difficulties shows this fact convincingly.

A. *Factual Difficulties.* (1) In many cases the *necessary data are lacking* concerning the size of the fighting forces, the number of human lives lost on each side, the proportion of the number of combatants to the total population of the countries involved in the war, etc. Up to the second half of the seventh century, and especially in the chronicles of Ancient Greece, Rome, and medieval times, a lack of even roughly accurate data is the rule; the presence of such data is the exception. This, then is the first source of error in our study.

(2) The next factual difficulty is the *unreliability and inaccuracy of much of the existing data.* Even in regard to the World War, 1914–1918, we do not have quite accurate figures for any of the belligerent countries. Even the official figures for that war show discrepancies, sometimes amounting to hundreds of thousands. How much more imperfect must be the data for the wars of previous centuries.

(3) The third factual difficulty is with the *wars that lasted for a number of years.* The intervals between the many battles in such wars varied from days to weeks, months, or even years.

(4) There is another great difficulty in these wars of *long duration.* Compare the World War of the present century with any long war of past centuries. The period from 1914 to 1918 was possibly the first period of relentless, almost incessant, warfare lasting for four years. Consider, on the other hand, the Hundred Years' War, the Wars of the Roses, the Thirty Years' War, or, in fact, any campaign lasting for more than a few days. Such wars were really a series of battles often separated by long intervals of time. During these intervals the fighting forces were out of contact, or in only passive contact.

The duration of wars being one of the variables of the magnitude of war, evidently two wars may be identical in their apparent duration (from the beginning to the peace) but quite different in actual length, and therefore quite different in magnitude. One can see how great this difficulty is and how easily it may lead to blunders.

(5) *Coalitional wars* cause further difficulty. Even if we know the size of the total army, we often do not know how large a share each of the

allied countries had in it.

(6) Similarly, how can we make comparable the study of *naval* and *territorial* wars? What can we take as a unit for the essentially different types of warfare carried on by sea and by land?

(7) The next difficulty, an appalling one, is presented by the fact that no country whose wars are studied has been quite uniform throughout the centuries in population, size, and extent of territory, but has varied considerably from period to period in these respects. Moreover, on a territory at one time occupied by one state several states has existed at other times, and vice versa.

(8) Finally, data are similarly lacking on *the exact size of the population of each country studied*, during each of its wars. Again we must make estimates and run all the risk of being inaccurate.

Not to continue this list of difficulties and obstacles, although there are many others besides the ones mentioned, the above gives an idea of how utterly impossible it is to study the problem "perfectly" and how great the danger is of making gross blunders in such a study, cautious as the investigator may be.

B. *Methodological Difficulty.* The main *methodological* difficulty, added to all these factual difficulties, is the impossibility of making a "perfect translation" into purely quantitative language of any phenomenon that is *qualitative-quantitative.* Most sociocultural phenomena, including the phenomena of war and revolutions, are of this nature. The most conscientiously made "translation" into indices can be only very imperfect and based on several arbitrary assumptions which may or may not be sound. Here is an additional source of errors.

In these conditions an investigator finds himself before an alternative. *Either he must pass the problem by, however important it be, in order not to take chances of making too many, or too great, blunders, or he must go ahead and take these chances. In this latter case the study would be of value only if he would try to be as careful and unbiased as possible in the study of the facts. The relevant facts he collects must be at least as complete as or more complete than in any other study hitherto made. He should not claim the privilege of infallibility or validity of his results. He must put "all his cards on the table," in the sense of stating his assumptions explicitly and making the nature of his procedure perfectly clear to the reader.*

Of these alternatives, I chose the second, with all its conditions. Some of the motives of this choice are obvious. The problem is too important to ignore it or to leave it to be handled "inspirationally." The tentative results based upon the available data are better than results based upon mere wishes or upon fragments of data.

Perhaps inexact in many details, it may yet not be misleading in its essential conclusions when an appropriate criterion of validity is applied to it. The point is that there are different criteria of adequacy for a general map of a whole continent and for an inch map of a given county. Judged by the inch map any general map is fallacious; it shows straight lines where the inch map shows fancifully curved lines; it fails to show many roads, streams, and lakes, and a thousand other things, shown on the county map. And vice versa, by the scale of reference of the general map the inch map is incorrect, too. Those critics, however, who can apply the proper criterion in each case will find each map correct in its own way and each as necessary for its own purpose as the other — one for planning a journey from the Pacific to the Atlantic, the other for detailed orientation on reaching a given street and house.

As the reader can see from the detailed list of the wars, most of the Greek and Roman war figures involve estimates concerning the strength of the army and the casualties. As such they are inaccurate from the standpoint of the inch map. However, from the standpoint of the continental map they are roughly representative. Most of the data of the medieval wars are estimates. And yet, we can be reasonably certain that the figures used are within the limits of the possible maximum and minimum of the forces and the losses for the respective periods.

For some of the wars we have a factual datum concerning the strength of the army and the losses in a certain battle. Therefore we are entitled to use these data, in many cases, as typical. For the wars of the seventeenth century and later, the situation is incomparably better because for these wars, in the majority of cases, we have roughly accurate data.

This study deals precisely with the three quantitative elements of war: *the strength of the army, the number of casualties (killed and wounded), and the duration of each of the wars studied.* No other aspect of the war phenomena is studied, not the economic losses, nor the morbidity and mortality of the civilian population, nor anything else. The conclusions reached are based upon the data of these three variables only, and concern these three aspects only, no more and no less.

III. The Materials of the Study

We have taken almost all the known wars of Greece, Rome, Austria, Germany, England, France, the Netherlands, Spain, Italy, Russia, and Poland and Lithuania from the periods indicated in the subsequent tables to the present time, or, in the case of Greece and Rome, to the loss of Greek independence and to the so-called "end of the Western Roman Empire," respectively. The existence of some roughly reliable data on war determines for each country the earliest period with which the study may start. The earlier periods, for which no data exist, have, of course, to be excluded.

In the way which has been outlined, we have studied 967 important wars (not battles) divided about as follows among the different countries: in Greek history, 24; in Roman, 81; in Austrian, 131; in German, 24; in English, 176; in French, 185; in Dutch, 23; in Spanish, 75; in Italian, 32; in Russian, 151; in Polish and Lithuanian, 65. Having obtained the data for the three variables for each of these wars, we then grouped these data by twenty-five-year periods for each of the variables, obtaining in this way three time series for each of these countries by twenty-five-year periods.

The figures given for each period are aimed not so much to lay down the actual number of the mobilized or killed and wounded as to obtain a rough measuring device to see the comparative increase or decrease of war from period to period. It is very important to keep this in mind.

The actual data are taken from authoritative historical sources, often ably summarized and elaborated by various special historical works like the often-quoted works of Delbruck, Bodart, and various encyclopedias of war and military science.

Such, in brief, is the material which has been used for making the three time series. Providing that the initial data and the estimates do not err fundamentally, it will probably be agreed that each of these time series is one of the important indicators of an increase or decrease of war activities. It is understood that the figures, whether for separate wars or for periods of a quarter century and century, are *absolute figures not corrected by the size of the population.* Taken as such without correction per unit of population, they are misleading. Whether the "burden of war" is decreasing or increasing, the figures can roughly answer only when they are turned into *relative indicators computed per unit of population.*

The last of the study deals with this problem and gives "*relative indicators*" of the army and casualty per unit of population in the history of Greece, Rome, and the whole of Europe from the twelfth to the twentieth century.

Concluding this "introductory-explanatory" part of the study, I can say that however great and numerous the shortcomings, the errors, the inadequacies, which I have frankly stressed and overstressed in the preceding remarks, may be, one thing seems very probable: such a study more nearly approaches the reality than mere guesses, than incidental and fragmentary statements, than theories made *ad hoc*, no matter by whom or with what intentions. We at least have now at our disposal as accurate an appraisal as possible of some one thousand wars "measured" uniformly by the same stick, and in as objective a way as I could design.

In Q. Wright's *A Study of War*, which appeared five years after the original publication of *Dynamics*, the results confirm the main movements of the curves and indicators here.

IV Figures for War Magnitudes in the History of Greece and Rome

Ancient Greece. Table 1 sums detailed figures for each quarter-century and century period. As mentioned, they are absolute figures not corrected by the size of the population — therefore, somewhat misleading. The corrected indicators follow in Table 2. The inter-Greek wars are regarded as internal and, as for all internal (civil) wars, their figures are doubled, because in such cases both adversaries are of the same country.

TABLE 1. TOTAL MEASURES OF WAR FOR ANCIENT GREECE FROM 500 TO 126 B.C. BY QUARTER CENTURIES AND CENTURIES

Century and Quarter Century	*Duration* (Years)	*Army's Strength* (Number)	*Casualties* (Number)
500–401 B.C.	**91**	**1,694,000**	**88,660**
500–476	25	500,000	25,000
475–451	34	752,000	42,600
450–426	8	64,000	3,200
425–401	24	378,000	17,860
400–301	**85**	**2,413,000**	**144,050**
400–376	19	489,000	47,850
375–351	18	720,000	36,000
350–326	25	698,000	34,900
325–301	23	506,000	25,300
300–201	**48**	**1,225,000**	**54,400**
300–276	18	360,000	14,400
275–251	15	250,000	10,000
250–226	2	120,000	6,000
225–201	13	495,000	24,000
200–126	**11**	**205,000**	**9,100**
200–176	5	115,000	5,600
175–151	4	60,000	3,000
150–126	2	30,000	1,500

These data suggest the following conclusions.

(1) The curves do not show any continuous trend toward either the increasing or the decreasing of war during the period studied, measured by the movement of any of the three variables.

(2) According to the variables, Army's Strength and Casualties, the maximum falls on the fourth century, the fifth century being next.

(3) Toward the end of independent Greece the curves tend to go down.

(4) There is no strict periodicity in the ups and downs of war, and no uniform rhythm.

(5) The data on the duration show that in the accepted system of computation of the duration of 375 years studied, 235 years (or about 63 percent) had an occurrence of war.

Many of these wars did not last through a whole year. If we inquire how many years of 375 studied had any occurrence of war and how many years did not (and were therefore peaceful), the answer is about 213 years were war years; that is, the per cent of the years with war (or wars) in that case is about 57 of the total number of Greek history studied. Both figures show that in the history of Greece frequency of war was much higher than many of us are wont to think.

(6) Although the data on the number of years with war in each twenty-five-year period, compared with the data of the other variables, are in some degree correlated, the association is remote and there is considerable discrepancy. The variables, Army's Strength and especially Casualties, seem to measure more adequately the magnitude or burden of war than mere duration of war and peace periods.

(7) The fifth and fourth centuries B.C. are generally accepted as the centuries of climax of Greek splendor, creativeness, and power. Scientific discoveries and technological inventions, used as criteria of scientific progress, numbered 26 in Greece in the sixth century, 39 in the fifth, 52 in the fourth, 42 in the third, and 14 in the second. The indicators of philosophical creativeness in Greece are: 38 for the sixth century; 99 for the fifth; 152 for the fourth; 98 for the third; and 47 for the second century. Thus the movement of the magnitude of war, as shown by our second and third variables, and that of the curve of scientific and philosophical creativeness run parallel in Greek history, giving the maximum in the fourth century, next in the fifth, and falling lowest in the second century. The third and second centuries are generally regarded as those of the decline of Greek culture, of Greek genius, and of an enormous decline of Greek political power, ending with a loss of the last simulacrum of Greek sovereignty and political independence. The same centuries show a decisive decline in war activities, which dwindled to a very low level.

Such are the results shown by the *absolute figures*. They are in a sense misleading. Therefore it is advisable to inquire what the results will be if we try to compute the war burden or war magnitude "per unit of population," say per 1,000,000. It goes without saying that exact statistics of the population of Greece for the various centuries studied do not exist. What do exist are the estimates given by the best historians on the basis of the totality of available data. As a basis for our computation we take, as mentioned above, Beloch's estimates. The estimates given by other specialists, like E. Meyer, R. Pöhlmann and others, deviate somewhat from the figures given by Beloch, but not so much as to make any essential difference in our results.

For the simplest form of relative indicators we can take the army's strength and casualty figures for each of the specified centuries, divide them by the estimated population of the corresponding century, and multiply by 1,000,000. The result will be the relative indicator of the losses of human life — or of the main form of war burden or war magnitude per 1,000,000 of population. Under these conditions the relative indicators of war-burden magnitude for specified centuries, per 1,000,000 of estimated population of Greece, will be as shown in Table 2.

TABLE 2. RELATIVE INDICATORS OF WAR MAGNITUDE FOR ANCIENT GREECE

Century	*Measured by the Casualties*	*Measured by the Army's Strength*
V B.C.	29,000 [1]	560,000
IV	from 48,016 to 36,012 [2]	804,333 to 603,250
III	from 18,170 to 13,600	408,333 to 306,250
II	from 3,033 to 3,640 [3]	82,000 to 68,333

[1] Assuming the population was 3,000,000, the estimate given by Beloch (3,051,000) for the period *c.* 432 B.C.
[2] Assuming the population was from about 3,000,000 to 4,000,000
[3] Assuming the population remained around 3,000,000 or even decreased to 2,500,000

From these rough and approximate figures one can see that the movement of the relative indicators is essentially the same as that of the absolute ones. The fourth century B.C. occupies the first place; next comes the fifth; and the least belligerent is the second century B.C. These results will remain if, instead of Beloch's estimates, any estimate of any of the greatest historians of Ancient Greece is taken. They will remain also if, instead of the assumptions made here, the figures for the population of these centuries are increased or decreased by 1,000,000 in either direction.

Figures 6 and 7 give an idea of the relative magnitude of war by casualties and by army's strength for the centuries mentioned.

Ancient Rome. The main results for Ancient Rome are given in Table 3. The table suggests the following conclusions:

(1) According to the number of casualties the most belligerent centuries in the history of Rome were: the third B.C., and the first, and then the second B.C.; then the third A.D. and the fifth A.D.; the most peaceful centuries were: the first A.D. and then the fourth B.C.

(2) Here also we do not find any continuous trend toward an increase or decrease of war; it just fluctuates up and down.

(3) According to the accepted system of computation of war duration, out of some 876 years studied, about 411 years or 47 per cent of the years had wars. If we count just the years with and without wars, regardless of how many wars occurred in the same year, then respectively 362 years, or a little more than 41 per cent, were years with war. Out of 35 quarter centuries studied, only 3 were free from serious wars.

(4) Table 3 shows further that though there is an association between the movement of the magnitude of war and that of the number of years with war and peace in the periods studied, the association is rather loose,

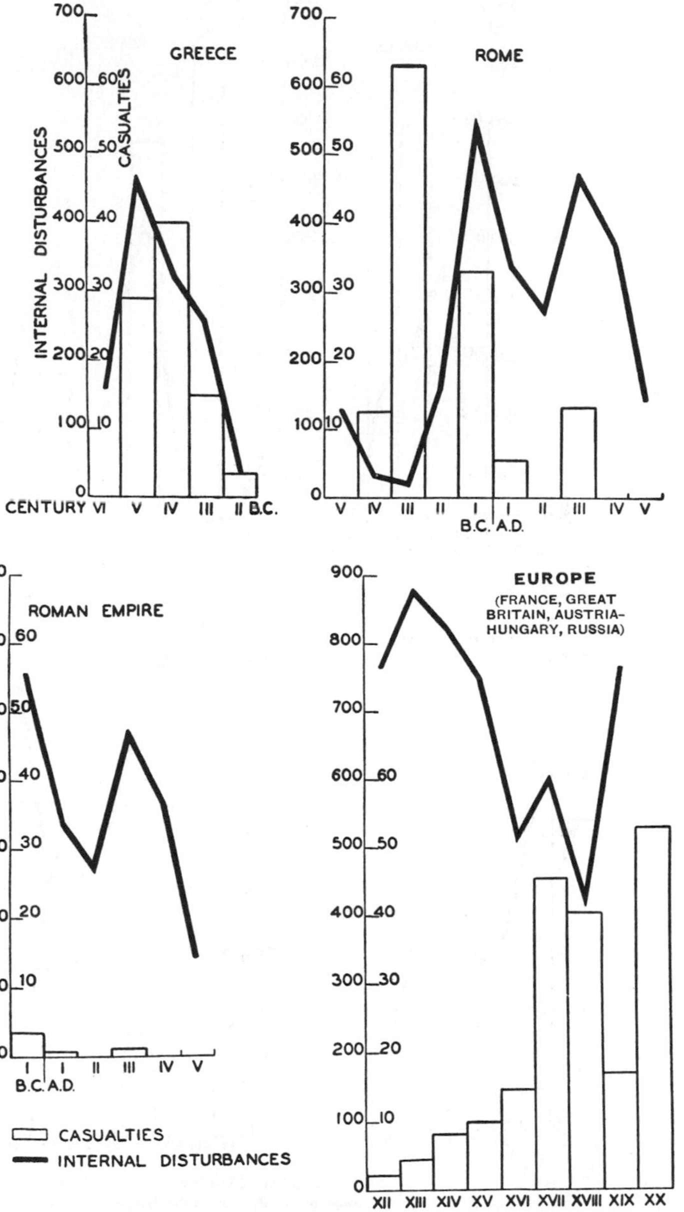

FIG. 6. RELATIVE WAR MAGNITUDE BY CASUALTIES AND INTERNAL DISTURBANCES

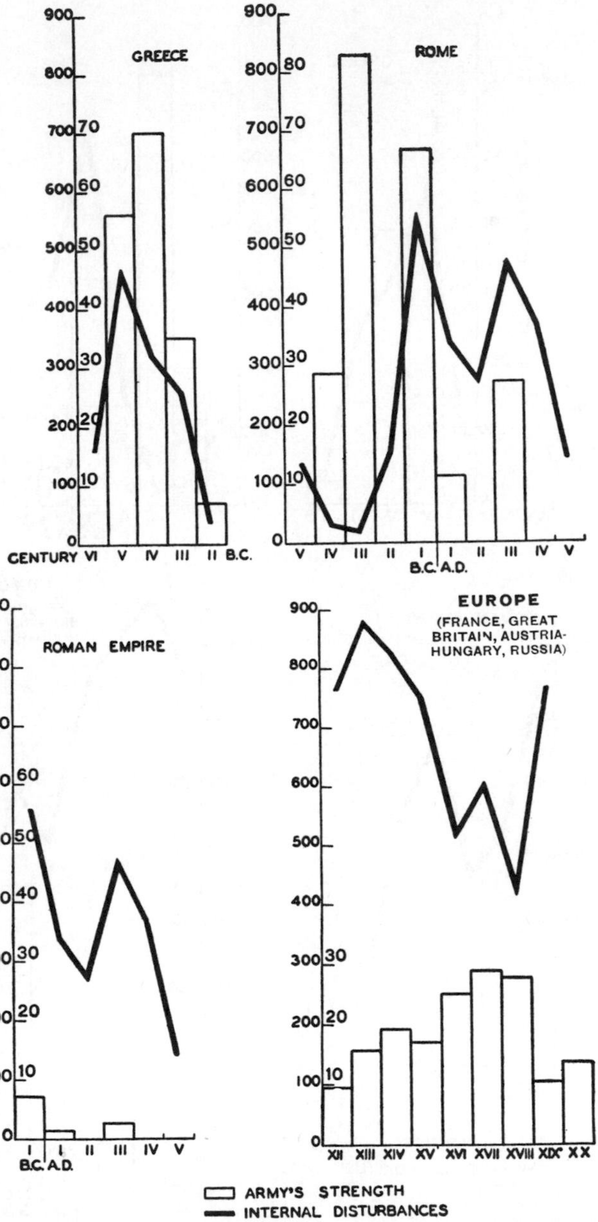

FIG. 7. RELATIVE WAR MAGNITUDE BY ARMY'S STRENGTH AND INTERNAL DISTURBANCES

TABLE 3. TOTAL MEASURES OF WAR FOR ANCIENT ROME FROM 400 B.C. TO A.D. 476 BY QUARTER CENTURIES AND CENTURIES

Century and Quarter Century	*Duration* (Years)	*Army's Strength* (Number)	*Casualties* (Number)
400–301 B.C.	**43**	**860,000**	**43,000**
400–376	2	40,000	2,000
375–351	11	220,000	11,000
350–326	7	140,000	7,000
325–301	23	460,000	23,000
300–201	**83**	**3,317,000**	**252,500**
300–276	21	581,000	44,100
275–251	18	732,000	45,200
250–226	12	440,000	22,000
225–201	32	1,564,000	141,200
200–101	**57**	**1,660,000**	**83,000**
200–176	8	240,000	12,000
175–151	4	80,000	4,000
150–126	24	560,000	28,000
125–101	21	780,000	39,000
100–1	**66**	**3,674,000**	**182,200**
100–76	20	1,200,000	60,000
75–51	30	1,734,000	86,700
50–26	10	620,000	29,500
25–1	6	120,000	6,000
1–100 A.D.	**29**	**784,000**	**38,800**
1–25	12	324,000	16,200
26–50	2	20,000	600
51–75	7	280,000	14,000
76–100	8	160,000	8,000
101–200	**28**	**1,120,000**	**56,000**
101–125	9	360,000	18,000
126–150	7	200,000	10,000
151–175	8	320,000	16,000
176–200	6	240,000	12,000
201–300	**42**	**1,620,000**	**80,600**
201–225	2	20,000	600
226–250	11	440,000	22,000
251–275	26	1,040,000	52,000
276–300	3	120,000	6,000
301–400	**26**	**1,235,000**	**61,450**
301–325	6	320,000	16,000
326–350	3	30,000	1,200
351–375	10	680,000	34,000
376–400	7	205,000	10,250
401–476	**37**	**1,400,000**	**70,000**
401–425	10	400,000	20,000
426–450	3	120,000	6,000
451–476	23	880,000	44,000

and the amplitude of the swings of the three sets of figures is quite different. This means again that the mere number of years with war and peace is an inadequate indicator of the war and peace movement.

(5) No definite periodicity and no uniform rhythm are noticeable in the "ups and downs" of war movement, whether by twenty-five- or one-hundred-year periods. It is a varying and shifting rhythm.

The *relative indicators* are given in Table 4. Relative indicator here means the number of casualties divided by population and multiplied by 1,000,000. Here again, as the basis for the size of the population of Italian Rome and of the Roman Empire we take the estimates of J. Beloch.

TABLE 4. RELATIVE INDICATORS OF WAR MAGNITUDE FOR ANCIENT ROME MEASURED BY CASUALTIES

Century	*Per 1,000,000 Population of Italy*	*Per 1,000,000 Population of the Empire*
IV B.C.	12,666 [1]	
III	63,125 [2]	
I	33,127 [3]	3644 [6]
I A.D.	5,543 [4]	712 [7]
III	13,433 [5]	1343 [8]

[1] Assuming the population of Italy *c.* 3,000,000.
[2] Assuming the population of Italy *c.* 4,000,000.
[3] Assuming the population of Italy *c.* 5,500,000.
[4] Assuming the population of Italy *c.* 7,000,000.
[5] Assuming the population of Italy *c.* 6,000,000.
[6] Assuming the population of the Empire *c.* 50,000,000.
[7] Assuming the population of the Empire *c.* 54,000,000.
[8] Assuming the population of the Empire *c.* 60,000,000.

If with the same assumptions concerning the size of the population we compute the relative indicators of the size of burden of the army "per 1,000,000," the results will be as shown in Table 5.

TABLE 5. RELATIVE INDICATORS OF WAR MAGNITUDE FOR ANCIENT ROME MEASURED BY ARMY'S STRENGTH

Century	*Per 1,000,000 Population of Italy*	*Per 1,000,000 Population of the Empire*
IV B.C.	286,666	
III	829,250	
I	668,000	73,480
I A.D.	112,000	14,519
III	270,000	27,000

Thus the movement of the relative indicators from century to century is similar to that of the absolute figures, with the exception of the relative positions of the fourth century B.C. and the third century A.D. Here the burden of war in the fourth century B.C. is greater than in the third century A.D. We see further that the relative indicators for Greece and Roman Italy are not greatly different from each other nor from those for the European countries which we see later. Their minima are near to the minima for the European countries; their maxima are near to European maxima.

Indicators for the whole Roman Empire are lower than they should be, because the losses of the "natives" of various conquered provinces are not computed. But if we increase them greatly, they still will remain probably comparatively low. One must marvel at the ability of the Romans to maintain the *pax romana* with slight military activities. The *pax romana* was indeed an exceptionally good organization of peace in the vast Roman Empire.

Similar detailed studies of wars of France, Russia, England, Austria, Hungary, Germany, Italy, Spain, Holland, Poland, and Lithuania are omitted in this abridged edition. We pass now to the main results concerning the whole of Europe. These results are greatly reinforced by the Second World War and the other wars from 1925 to the present.

33

SUMMARY AND MAIN RESULTS OF STUDY OF WAR IN THE HISTORY OF EUROPE

I. Absolute Figures

On the plan of absolute figures, for the armies' strength and the casualties, we can attempt to make a summary of their movement for four of the countries studied from the twelfth century to 1925. There are four countries which it is possible to study in this way, France, England, Austria-Hungary, and Russia. The remaining five countries, at least formally, enter the scene later, and therefore a summary for all nine countries would make comparison unfair, or even impossible, in regard to the later centuries. However considerable were the variations of the above four countries, they preserved essentially their continuity as well as the constancy of their territory and population. It is true that the total for these four countries is somewhat unfair in regard to the later centuries, because Germany before the sixteenth century figured in Austria-Hungary; and a considerable part of Italy, Holland, and Poland also entered the data for earlier centuries. For this reason, totals for the four countries from century to century tend to overestimate somewhat the figures for earlier centuries, before the seventeenth, and to underestimate somewhat the figures for the seventeenth and later centuries.

TABLE 15. SUMMARY FIGURES BY CENTURY PERIODS FOR FRANCE, ENGLAND, AUSTRIA-HUNGARY, AND RUSSIA FROM 1101 TO 1925

Century	*Army's Strength* (Number)	*Casualties* (Number)
1101–1200	1,161,000	29,940
1201–1300	2,372,000	68,440
1301–1400	3,867,000	166,729
1401–1500	5,000,000	285,000
1501–1600	9,758,000	573,020
1601–1700	15,865,000	2,497,170
1701–1800	24,849,000	3,622,140
1801–1900	17,869,800	2,912,771
1901–1925	41,465,000	16,147,550

Table 15 shows the summarized results by century periods of the movement of the army's strength and of casualties for France, England, Russia, Austria-Hungary, from the twelfth to the twentieth century.

Since the summary deals with the same four countries for the centuries compared, the figures, as absolute figures, are roughly comparable, though recognizing the slight overestimation for earlier centuries, explained above.

Before proceeding with the analysis of these figures, let us sum up the figures for all the nine countries, keeping in mind, however, that such a summary tends to inflate unduly the figures for the later centuries, for the reason just opposite to the one indicated in the preceding paragraph (see Table 16).

TABLE 16. SUMMARY FIGURES BY CENTURY PERIODS FOR NINE EUROPEAN COUNTRIES FROM 1101 TO 1925

Century	*Army's Strength* (Number)	*Casualties* (Number)
1101–1200	1,161,000	29,940 [1]
1201–1300	2,372,000	68,440 [2]
1301–1400	3,947,000	169,929 [3]
1401–1500	6,910,000	364,220 [4]
1501–1600	16,707,300	896,185 [5]
1601–1700	25,796,000	3,711,090 [6]
1701–1800	31,055,500	4,505,990 [7]
1801–1900	24,233,800	3,625,627 [8]
1901–1925	60,425,000	22,035,150 [9]

[1] Only Austria, England, France, Russia.
[2] Only Austria, England, France, Russia.
[3] Plus Poland for one quarter.
[4] Plus Spain.
[5] Plus Italy and the Netherlands.
[6] Plus Germany (all nine).
[7] All nine countries.
[8] All nine countries.
[9] All nine countries.

In Table 16 the data are comparable beginning with the second part of the seventeenth century, after which time all nine of the countries are present.

So far as the absolute figures are concerned, whether in Table 15 or in the comparable study (Table 16), they show a steady but uneven growth of the size of the army and the number of the casualties, from the twelfth to the eighteenth centuries inclusive, a notable decrease in the nineteenth century, and an unprecedented flare-up in the first quarter of the twentieth century. The casualty figure for that quarter exceeds the total casualty for all the preceding centuries taken together (in Tables 15 and 16). The figure for the army's strength is also exceptionally high (in both tables).

Although it is lower than the total for all of the previous centuries taken all together, nevertheless its stunning size, especially when it is remembered that it is only for one quarter century, is evident. The above means then, first, that *within the centuries studied there is no continuous trend, according to the tables; after an increase from the twelfth to the eighteenth centuries both figures are less in the nineteenth.* Second, as far as the absolute figures stand, *they do not warrant any claim for the existence of some continuous trend toward a disappearance or decrease of war.* Third, the figures for both variables show at the same time that the rate of increase of the size of the army and of the casualty has not been the same; all in all *the casualty rates increased faster than the strength of the army.* According to Table 15 (of the four countries), while the army's strength increased from the twelfth to the twentieth century by about 36 times, the rate of casualty increased by about 539 times; according to Table 16, the army increased by 52 times, the casualty by 748 times. In both cases the increase of the casualty is from 14 to 15 times greater than the increase of the army's strength.

This means that regardless of the size of the army, recent and modern wars have tended to become more devastating in their killing and wounding power, so far as such killing power is measured by the per cent of casualties in reference to the size of the "regular" fighting forces. This is shown more clearly by Table 17, which roughly estimates the casualties in each century as a per cent of the size of the army, for the four countries in Table 15.

TABLE 17. PERCENTAGE OF CASUALTIES IN FOUR COUNTRIES FROM THE TWELFTH TO THE TWENTIETH CENTURY

Century	*Casualties as Per Cent of Army's Strength*
XII	2.5
XIII	2.9
XIV	4.6
XV	5.7
XVI	5.9
XVII	15.7
XVIII	14.6
XIX	16.3
XX	38.9

With but slight differences the same results are given by Table 16. The invention and introduction of gunpowder in the fourteenth century, and the subsequent development of technology, physics, and chemistry, gave, by the progress of the technique of war, more destructive means of warfare. Especially great "progress" was shown in this respect by the wars of the seventeenth and then of the twentieth centuries when many new weapons were introduced, such as military airplanes, perfected machine guns, tanks, more powerful cannons, explosives, poisonous gas, and the like. The above percentages reflect in absolute figures the progressive perfecting of the means of exterminating human life in the wars of the last four centuries, especially the twentieth. One machine gun (not to mention poison gas, big Berthas, tanks, explosives) is more efficiently deadly than picks, spears, bows, arbalests, and swords of dozens of knights, the weapons of the twelfth century.

It is true in war, as in many other phenomena, that poison calls for counterpoison, new danger for new protection, action for reaction. Just as the weapons of the twelfth century led to the use of armor, high walls for the cities, and other means of protection, the deadly weapons of modern warfare called forth many means of protection against them. There is, however, one notable difference in the protective devices then and now. Formerly they aimed to protect human life by minimizing the deadliness of the danger; armor protected the body of the knight from many dangers and minimized the losses. Now the means of protection aim to protect both sides, not so much through various devices which minimize the total losses, as through infliction of the maximum losses upon the adversary. This modern protection in warfare is a mad race in the invention and use of ever stronger destructive means against the adversary. Explosives, guns, machine guns, airplanes, poison gas, plus the recent nuclear and bacteriological weapons, are not protection, like armor or the unassailable city wall, which reduced losses of both sizes, but are hellish means of mutual destruction. As both adversaries use them, the result is maximization of the losses on both sides.

When this factor alone is properly considered, it is comprehensible why the losses in the First World War amounted to 30 to 40 per cent of the armies, and in the Second World War up to 100 per cent, instead of the 1, 2, and 5 per cent as in the wars before them.

Another condition should be mentioned in connection with losses. As the armies of the medieval centuries were mainly armies of knights and nobility, with their code of chivalry and honor, a code which was enforced to a considerable extent, the losses were minimized. As soon as the adversary was wounded, taken, or overpowered, he was not necessarily killed; more often his life was spared for ransom, or by reason of the code. At the present time, poison gas, shell bullet, bomb, explosive, do not and cannot have any "code" of chivalry or honor; they strike anything and anybody that happens to be in their way. Besides, the "international laws of war" proved themselves during World War II to be noneffective. The adversaries on both sides by saturation bombing of the combattants and even more the noncombattants, including women and children broke all divine and human laws. This is another factor leading to greater losses now than in the wars of earlier centuries.

A still more important factor contributing to the high per cent of casualties in the twentieth century is the *real* duration of war. Here the World Wars and the other wars were unique. Our figure for its duration is computed on the usual basis, from the beginning of the war to the date of peace. This gives about four years for the first, and six years for the second, World War. The duration of wars in the past is computed upon the same purely "arithmetic" basis. However, as was explained above, four years' duration of the World War and four years' duration of the earlier, especially the medieval wars, are quite different quantities. The World War was filled with incessant warfare; every day, even every hour, the enemies faced and exterminated each other. These were, indeed, four years of continuous fighting, practically without interruption. A war four years long in past centuries was in fact mostly inaction, lacking much real fighting, interrupted only once in a while by this or that battle, skirmish, or engagement. The duration of real fighting in the Hundred Years' War was in fact many times shorter than in the World War. When this condition is considered in all its enormous importance it is understood why the number and the per cent of casualties in the twentieth century are so exceptionally high, and why the real magnitude of the World Wars was gigantic, actually greater than the figures show. In the light of these considerations Table 17 of the growing percentages of casualties with reference to strength of the army, as well as the exceptionally big figure of casualties for the twentieth century, appear to reflect the real changes in this field adequately, if not in details, then in essentials. So much for the absolute figures.

II. Relative Indicators of the Movement of War from the Twelfth to Twentieth Century

Multiplying the absolute figures for casualties and for army's strength for each century by 1,000,000 and dividing them by 90 per cent of the population for the middle of the respective century, or, in the case of the twentieth century, by the population of 1910 as the nearest date, we obtain the following relative indicators of the burden of the army and of the casualties for the seventeenth to the twentieth centuries, inclusive.

TABLE 18. RELATIVE INDICATORS OF WAR ACTIVITIES BY CENTURY PERIODS FOR NINE EUROPEAN COUNTRIES

Century	*Army's Absolute Strength*	*Casualties*	*90 Per Cent of Population*	*Relative Army*	*Magnitude of Casualty*
XX	60,425,000 [1]	22,035,150 [1]	401,000,000 [2]	150,685 [1]	54,955 [1]
XIX	24,333,800	3,645,627	238,000,000 [3]	101,823	15,234
XVIII	31,055,500	4,505,990	135,000,000 [3]	230,041	33,377
XVII	25,796,000	3,711,090	100,000,000 [3]	257,960	37,111

[1] For the first quarter only. As mentioned, the figure underestimates the indicator for the twentieth century.
[2] In 1910.
[3] About 1850, 1750, 1650.

As we shall see in Table 19, the relative indicators computed in the same way for the above four countries for these centuries give figures which, though slightly different, are identical to the above so far as the comparative position of the centuries is concerned, both in regard to the strength of the army and the casualties. From the seventeenth to the twentieth centuries, so far as the army's strength per population is concerned, the greatest burden of war was in the seventeenth century, then the eighteenth, and the lightest was in the nineteenth century. The twentieth century, in its one quarter, did not exceed the burden of the seventeenth and the eighteenth centuries, but exceeded the nineteenth century. Considering, however, that in one quarter it exceeded more than half of the indicators of the seventeenth and of the eighteenth century, the twentieth century is to be given, so far, first place in relative burden of the army per population. If the wars from 1925 to 1957 were included, the absolute and relative indicators for the first half of the twentieth century would be shown to greatly exceed those of preceding centuries. On the other hand, we must remember that it is also shown that war magnitude, measured by this criterion, has not been systematically increasing from the seventeenth century on but, on the contrary, was decreasing in the eighteenth and nineteenth centuries in comparison with the seventeenth century. The relative indicator shows also that though the army's strength per population in the twentieth century was exceptionally great, nevertheless it was not so bewilderingly great as is shown by the absolute figures. While the absolute figures of the army's strength for the first quarter of the twentieth century greatly exceed any two of the preceding centuries, the seventeenth, the eighteenth, and the nineteenth, taken together, the relative indicator shows quite a different picture. It only exceeds the indicator of the nineteenth century, but is almost twice as small as the indicators of the seventeenth and eighteenth centuries.

Thus the relative indicator greatly corrects the impression given by the absolute figures. To sum up, according to the relative indicator of the army's strength, the first place is to be given to the first half of the twentieth century, which exceed any of the preceding whole centuries, with second place to the seventeenth century, third to the eighteenth, and fourth to the nineteenth.

If now we take the relative indicators of the casualties, probably the most important criterion of war, they tell definitely and unequivocably that *the curse or privilege to be the most devastating or most bloody war century belongs to the twentieth; in one quarter century it imposed upon the population a "blood tribute" far greater than that imposed by any of the whole centuries compared. The next place belongs to the seventeenth, and then comes the eighteenth century; the nineteenth century appears to be the least bloody of all these centuries concerned.* But it is again necessary to stress the fact that the relative indicators of casualty of the twentieth century are much less bewildering than the absolute figures. Though it remains the highest even in this respect, yet its relative difference is not so astounding. Thus the conclusion given by the relative indicators of the army's size, as well as of casualties per population in the centuries compared, is that the *twentieth century, so far, was the most belligerent, then the seventeenth, eighteenth, and nineteenth respectively. The war burden imposed by the twentieth century is particularly great in the casualties or blood tribute, while in the size of the army it does not occupy a unique position.* We shall see that the same results are given by the relative indicators of the four countries mentioned for these centuries.

Much more doubtful becomes the situation when we try to compute the relative indicators for the centuries from the twelfth to the sixteenth, inclusive — not only because the absolute figures for the army's strength and the casualties for these centuries are mainly estimates, but also because the population of the countries studied for these centuries is unknown. *Only in regard to the above four countries may such a venture be attempted.* Considering that they embrace at least one-half of the European population, the results, if they be not misleading, may be typical for the whole of Europe, at least in their essentials.

Figures given in Table 19 for the population of these four countries in the centuries from the twelfth to the sixteenth inclusive, include practically all the estimates of competent historians. The computation of the relative indicators remains the same, and all the other qualifications mentioned above are applied here also. Now the table follows. (Figures 6 and 7, pages 297 and 298, give a pictorial idea of the movement, under the assumption of 40 per cent increase of the population from the twelfth to the seventeenth century, except the fourteenth with its decrease of the population.)

TABLE 19. RELATIVE INDICATORS OF WAR ACTIVITIES BY CENTURY PERIODS FOR FRANCE, GREAT BRITAIN, AUSTRIA-HUNGARY, AND RUSSIA

Century	*Total Population* [1]	*Relative Magnitude of Army's Strength*	*Relative Magnitude of Casualties*
XX [2]	305,000,000 [2]	136,278	52,943
XIX	171,530,000	104,179	17,034
XVIII	90,000,000	276,100	40,246
XVII	55,000,000	288,455	45,403

	Three Assumed Sizes.			*Relative Magnitude under the Specified Assumptions*					
	A	*B*	*C*	*A*	*B*	*C*	*A*	*B*	*C*
XVI	45 m.[3]	39 m.	35 m.	216,844	250,205	278,800	12,734	14,693	16,372
XV	35 m.	28 m.	25 m.	142,857	171,428	200,000	8,143	10,179	11,400
XIV	25 m.	20 m.	18 m.	154,680	193,350	214,833	6,669	8,336	9,263
XIII	18 m.	15 m.	13 m.	131,777	158,133	182,462	3,802	4,563	5,265
XII	13 m.	12 m.	10 m.	89,308	96,750	116,100	2,303	2,495	2,994

[1] In 1910, 1850, 1750, 1650, 1550, 1450, 1350, 1250, 1150. [2] One quarter century only. [3] m means million.

So far as the relative strength of the army is concerned, there is no clear-cut trend from the twelfth to the seventeenth century, or from the twelfth to the twentieth century. The indicators are the lowest for the twelfth century; then, under all three assumptions, they grow from the twelfth to the fourteenth century, inclusive; drop somewhat in the fifteenth century; then rise during the sixteenth and seventeenth centuries; drop in the nineteenth century; and rise again in the twentieth century. The maximum falls within the seventeenth century (with the exception of the twentieth, if the wars from 1925 to 1957 are included. Thus there is no continuous trend toward either an ever-increasing or decreasing size of the army in relation to the population. The burden of the army in the nineteenth century is lower than all the centuries with the exception of the twelfth.

Considerably different are the results given by the relative indicators of casualties per population. Under all three assumptions in regard to the size of the population, there is found a continuous trend toward an increase in this "blood tribute" for the wars from the twelfth to the seventeenth century, inclusive; after that they decline in the eighteenth and especially in the nineteenth centuries to reach a climax in the twentieth century. The minimum falls within the twelfth and the maximum within the twentieth century, in spite of the fact that the indicator for the twentieth century is only for one quarter.

The main results given by the relative indicators can now be summed up in a few statements.

(1) All in all, especially in regard to the casualties, the twelfth to the sixteenth centuries were much less bloody, and therefore much less belligerent than the seventeenth, eighteenth, and the twentieth centuries. In regard to the size of the army (per population) there is no such consistent difference.

(2) Of the later centuries, the nineteenth appears to have been, comparatively, very peaceful, especially in its last quarter.

(3) The twentieth century, so far, appears to be the most bloody within the period of European history studied, with respect to the relative casualties; the same century occupies an exceedingly high position with respect to the relative burden of the army.

(4) The study discloses a lack of any continuous trend (in relative indicators) during the centuries investigated.

(5) It is interesting to note that the relative indicators obtained for the European countries do not differ greatly from the relative indicators obtained for Greece and Rome. The maximums and minimums in casualties are very similar in both cases; in the strength of the army the difference in maximum is greater, but not incomparably so.

Such an outcome in this "guessy" adventure is one of the evidences that the results are not entirely misleading.

III. The Absolute and Relative Magnitude of War Activities of the Various Countries Studied

If we inquire which of the countries studied in their respective centuries has had the largest army and casualties (absolute figures), the answer is given by the following order of countries for each specified century.

It must be remembered that in the lists below the data for the twentieth century is based on the period 1900 to 1925.

In regard to the *army's strength* the order, beginning with the country with the largest army and ending with the smallest army, is as follows in each of the centuries studied (see Tables 6, 7, 8, 9, 10, 11, 12, 13, 14).

XII. Russia, England, France, Austria
XIII. Russia, England, France, Austria
XIV. England, France, Russia, Austria
XV. England, Poland, France, Russia, Austria, Spain
XVI. Spain, France, Austria, Poland, England, Russia, Holland, Italy
XVII. Austria, France, Spain, Poland, Holland, Russia, England, Italy
XVIII. Austria, France, Russia, England, Germany, Poland, Spain, Holland, Italy
XIX. France, Russia, Germany, Spain, Austria, England, Italy, Holland
XX. Russia, Germany, France, England, Austria, Italy, Spain, Holland

This list shows that so far as absolute figures of the size of the army are concerned, the comparative position of the countries is changing in the course of time, now one country occupying the first position, now some other one. Of course the small countries are not expected to hold a first position for obvious reasons. Nevertheless, we see that even their positions change greatly; Holland occupied fifth place in the seventeenth century, among the eight countries, while in the nineteenth and the twentieth it occupied last place.

A similar picture is given in regard to the *absolute* figures of the casualties in the centuries studied. In this respect the order of the countries is as follows, according to the century.

XII. Russia, Austria, England, France
XIII. Russia, England, France, Austria
XIV. England, France, Russia, Austria
XV. Austria, England, Poland, France, Russia
XVI. Austria, Spain, Russia, France, England, Poland, Holland, Italy
XVII. Austria, France, Spain, Poland, Holland, England, Russia, Italy
XVIII. Austria, France, Russia, Germany, England, Poland, Holland, Spain, Italy
XIX. France, Russia, Germany, Austria, Spain, England, Italv, Holland
XX. Russia, Germany, France, England, Austria, Italy, Spain, Holland

Thus in absolute figures Austria, Russia, and France have had the tragic privilege of bearing the greatest number of casualties in the centuries studied. Here again we see that, all in all, the place of various nations is shifting from century to century.

It goes without saying that the absolute figures do not give an idea as to the relative or real size of the army or of the casualties in relation to the size of the population. Such figures can be given only when the absolute figures are divided by the size of the population of the countries studied. Taking a rough estimate of the size of the population about the middle of the respective century and dividing by it the absolute figure of the casualties of that century, we obtain the rough relative indicators of the comparative burden of casualties borne by each specified country in the specified centuries. These relative indicators are given in Table 20.

TABLE 20. RELATIVE INDICATORS OF THE CASUALTY BURDEN OF THE SPECIFIED COUNTRY (PER UNIT OF POPULATION)

Country	XX	XIX	XVIII	XVII
Russia	41.1	11.1	21.5	7.9
Austria	48	5.8	94.0 [1]	130.0 [1]
England	66.5	5.0	30.1	20.0
France	92.0	51.0	45.8	36.6
Germany	94.7	13.1		
Italy	52.4			
Spain	2.2	11.0	11.8	
Holland	—	5.7	84.8 [1]	161.0 [1]

[1] This exceptionally high figure is due not only to the high casualty of the population of Austria and the Netherlands in the wars, but also to a large quota of foreign soldiers employed in the Austrian and the Netherlands' armies as well as participating in the battles. For this reason the figure notably exaggerates the real burden of the casualties borne by the population of Austria and the Netherlands. With this reservation, the figure is nevertheless symptomatic, showing the excessive burden of the wars of that century in the Netherlands and Austria. The figure for England in the twentieth century exaggerates the burden because a considerable part of her army and casualties were those of the Dominions. If the populations of the Dominions were included in the denominator, the figure would be notably lower.

These figures need correcting in the sense that in many countries these casualties were borne not only by their population, but also by soldiers who fought for the country but were "foreigners" to it. Even in the World War, and therefore in the twentieth century, in the armies of England, France, and to a much less extent in some others, there was a notable part of such foreign participation. As mentioned above, in the past, in the English, Dutch, French, Austrian, Spanish, and other armies there was always a considerable portion of such strangers. When this factor is considered, it leads to several corrections, sometimes of considerable importance.

Assuming that the populations of these countries for the seventeenth and the eighteenth centuries were near, or between, the two widely different estimates given for several countries, the data lead to the following

In the twentieth century (to 1925) the largest military burden per capita is carried by Germany, then by France, England, Italy, Austria, and Russia; the smallest is carried by Holland and Spain. In the nineteenth century, the first place is occupied by France; then come Germany, Russia, Spain, Austria, Holland, and England. For each and all the countries, with the exception of Holland and Spain, the burden in the nineteenth century is many times lighter than in the twentieth century. In the eighteenth century the first places are occupied by Austria-Hungary, Holland, and France; then come England and Russia. In the seventeenth century the greatest burden is carried by Holland and Austria-Hungary, the smallest by Russia.

All in all, a table made in this way confirms the conclusions reached above concerning the relative and absolute fluctuation of the magnitude of war from the seventeenth to the twentieth century. It confirms also the contention that the magnitude of "militarism" or "war effort" or "war burden" shifts from country to country in the course of time. Furthermore, Table 20 shows that there are no consistently peaceful and consistently militant countries. Although Holland has been peaceful during the last hundred years, it was particularly belligerent during the seventeenth and eighteenth centuries. *Mutatis mutandis*, the same can be said of all other countries. The popular opinion that democracies are much less belligerent than autocracies seems to be unwarranted by our data. In the twentieth century the relative magnitude of the war activities of democratic England (measured by casualties) was higher than of Spain; of France, higher than of Austria or Russia. In the nineteenth century democratic France was not more pacific than "autocratic" Germany, Russia, or Spain. During the seventeenth century, England did not occupy a lower position than Russia.

IV. The Percentages of Years with and without War

What is the comparative position of the countries in regard to the per cent of the total number of years studied, with war and with peace?

Table 21 answers this question.

TABLE 21. PERCENTAGE OF YEARS WITH WAR

Country	*Per Cent of Years with War of the Total Number of Years Studied*	*Country*	*Per Cent of Years with War of the Total Number of Years Studied*
Greece	57	*Italy*	36
Rome	41	*France*	50
Austria	40	*England*	56
Germany	28	*Russia*	46
Holland	44	*Poland and Lithuania*	58
Spain	67		

Table 21 shows that Germany has had the smallest (28) and Spain the largest (67) per cent of years with war, the other countries occupying various positions between the two. All in all, about 50 per cent of the years in these countries had an occurrence of war, and the difference between the maximal and the minimal figures is not excessively great. This does not mean that during 50 per cent of the time these countries have had war and during the remaining 50 per cent, peace. Many wars lasted much less than a whole year; therefore, the period of peace in the history of these countries is certainly larger than the per cent of years with peace according to the table. Even so, the per cent of years with war seems to have been much greater than is usually thought. So far, war phenomena seem to have been almost as common and "normal" as peace phenomena. The percentages given do not mean, of course, that the years of war and peace in the history of any one country have been evenly distributed; some periods have had uninterrupted war during two, five, ten, or thirty, and so on, years; other periods have had several years of undisturbed peace. But, as has been shown above, periods of peace as long as one quarter of a century have been exceedingly rare in the history of the countries, and a period up to 100 years or more of peace is almost unique, given in the history of Holland; in some of these countries such periods did not occur at all. Almost every generation (25 to 30 years) in the past, with very few exceptions, has been a witness of, or an actor in, war phenomena.

V. The Problem of Periodicity in the Fluctuation of War Magnitude

There have been several theories claiming that there exists a certain and definite periodicity in the rhythm of war and peace, in the comparative increase and decrease of war phenomena. As examples of such theories, two can be mentioned here. The first is the astrophysical, almost astrological, theory of R. Mewes. The essence of his theory is:

> The periods of war and peaceful culture blossoming are influenced mainly by the position of the three great planets: Jupiter, Saturn, and Uranus, in regard to the Sun. Upon this position depend the great periods of dryness and bareness and moisture and fertility of the Earth.

These periods in their turn determine — through climatic and similar influences, where the sun and the sunspots play a decisive part — human behavior and social events.

According to Mewes the above three planets recur in the same position in regard to the sun every 675.5 years. This period breaks up into six shorter periods of 111 to 112 years.

During this period of 111 or 112 years there are usually two periods of war and two periods of blossoming of arts and sciences, each period being about 27.8 years [on the average].

Mewes's arrangement is just "intuitional," where a few facts are picked up to suit the preconceived scheme. Not mentioning evident blunders and purely fantastic "history" in many parts of this long list of periods, the slightest test is sufficient to show that the periods of war and cultural blossoming (peace) are cut according to the wishes of the author, but contrary to the evident facts. In brief, Mewes's theory is untenable. Untenable are similar theories. Let us confront, for instance, a few of his periods of warfare and peace with our figures of casualties for these periods. Though the years of his periods do not coincide with ours, nevertheless they admit a confrontation. The comparison is given in Table 22.

Table 22 shows that several of the periods qualified by Mewes as peaceful were in fact belligerent, and several of his periods of war were in fact more peaceful.

TABLE 22. COMPARISON OF MEWES'S AND SOROKIN'S STUDIES

Mewes's Periods of War and Peace			*Our Absolute Casualty Figures for*	
			Austria	*France*
Peace	1487–1518	1500–1525	45,000	34,050
War	1518–1544	1526–1550	116,000	28,900
Peace	1544–1576	1551–1575	62,000	29,650
War	1576–1598	1576–1600	34,000	15,050
Peace	1598–1625	1601–1625	274,000	2,850
War	1625–1654	1626–1650	830,000	163,800
Peace	1765–1793	1776–1800	214,000	428,300

Discussing the question of periodicity in the figures of each country, we have seen that only in the history of Germany, Russia, and Italy for a few centuries are there noticeable periodicities of 25 or 50 years. That is all. In the other countries nothing like this or any other periodicity is noticeable. More than that, if one should take the chronology of wars in the history of any country studied, one would hardly find any kind of periodicity. As an example let us take the detailed chronology of the periods of peace and war in the history of France, year by year, the length of a given war followed by the length of the subsequent period of peace, and so on. The war periods are given in Roman, the peace periods in Arabic figures, expressing the duration of war or peace in units of one year. (In these symbols the actual duration of war-peace periods in the history of France is as follows. The year ending war and starting peace, or vice versa, is included in both periods.)

I–40, I–40, I–25, IV–7, XXIII–14, I–4, III–20, I–4, I–3, I–13, IV–3, VII–2, III–3, XXIV–2, II–8, IV–3, VIII–4, I–9, I–2, I–14, VIII–3, IV–2, IV–9, IV–11, and so on.

No regular periodicity is noticeable here, whether of 25, 27, 33, 50, or 56 years' duration. Instead, we find an enormous variety of rhythms. After prolonged wars several times there occur long periods of peace, but not always. In the earlier history the alternation of war-peace periods is slower and the peace periods longer than in later history. But again there are many exceptions to this rule.

To sum up, none of the periods claimed, whether the 27-year periods of Mewes, or the 10- to 12-year periods of Sasse, or the 30- to 33-year periods of several other "numerologists," or the 50-year period of Q. Wright, so far have been proven, and they can hardly be proven. The same is true of the much longer periods of 111, 300, 500, 600, 675 years, and so on, claimed by various authors. All that we can say is that the war-peace curve fluctuates, but in its fluctuations, with the exceptions mentioned, no regular periodicity or uniform rhythm is noticeable.

Considerably more interesting, and more factual, is the theory set forth by J. S. Lee concerning the periodicity of the internecine wars in the history of China (Figure 8). For the discovery of any long-time periodicity there is hardly any better country than China with its long history. Dr. Lee took the Chinese chronicles and computed almost all the occurrences of the internecine wars in the history of China from 221 B.C., the period with which the data become relatively complete and reliable, to the present time. He plotted the curve of their number by five-year periods for the 2150 years studied. The results of the computation and plotting have disclosed the existence of three long-time periods of about 810 to 780 years: the first from 221 B.C. to A.D. 589; the second from 589 to 1368; the third from 1368 up to the present time. Each of these long-time periods begins with a flaring up of civil war which is quickly ended, and the country enters a prolonged period of peace, marked by enormous technical and cultural achievements. After about the second half of the period of the curve, it begins to rise, showing shorter periods of peace, and a greater and greater number of wars. One period ends and a new period begins with a general internecine war and anarchy with their satellites. Then again the same phenomena are repeated. In each of these 800-year periods the curve of war has seven main waves; the smallest of these seven jumps is the fifth in each of the three periods. Such is the essence of this very laconic study.

It should be noted that the author plots, not the fluctuation of the magnitude of war in our sense, but merely the number of wars in each five-year period in the span of 2150 years. Putting aside many points which are not clear in the study, points concerning the sources, method,

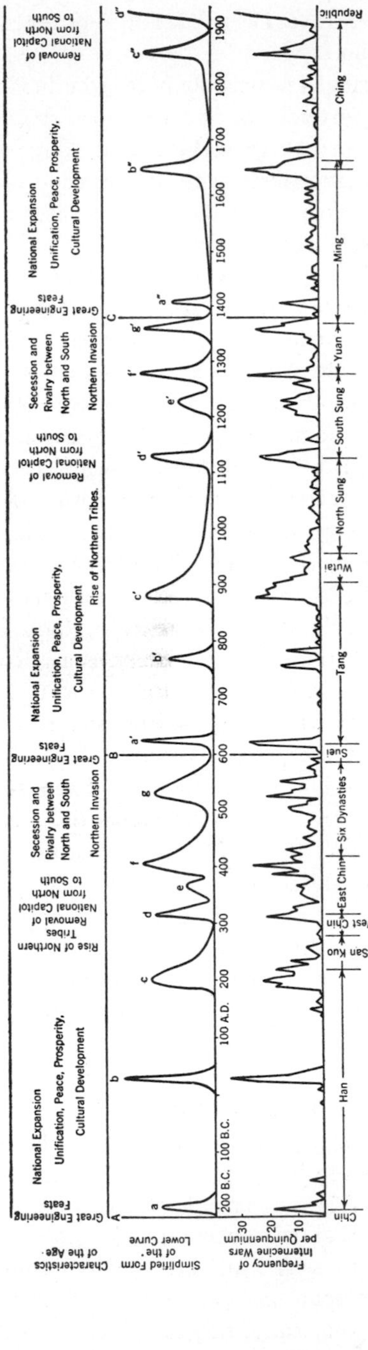

FIG. 8. J. S. LEE'S CURVE OF THE PERIODIC RECURRENCE OF INTERNAL DISTURBANCES IN CHINA

etc., and taking the study at its face value, one can say, however, that the conclusions of the author somewhat overshoot the data and the diagram which he gives. Studying them as they are given, especially the real, unsmoothed curve, one finds that the curve's configurations in each of the three long periods are far from being identical, similar, or, indeed, periodic. In the first period one finds from 10 to 12 main rises; in the second, 9; in the third, which seems to be incomplete, only from 4 to 5 as yet. And the length of time which separates the jumps in each of the three periods, as well as the height of the waves, is neither uniform nor equal, nor similar in general. In other words, the data of the author hardly give any real periodicity or uniform rhythm. What they give is a "trendless" shifting in the rhythm and in the number of recurring internecine wars. And that possibly is all that they entitle us to deduce.

In such an interpretation the results are similar to results obtained in our study of the movement of the magnitude of war in the history of Greece, Rome, and the other European countries. As has been mentioned, they do not show any real periodicity. History seems to be neither as monotonous and uninventive as the partisans of the strict periodicities and "iron laws" and "universal uniformities" think; nor so dull and mechanical as an engine, making the same number of revolutions in a unit of time. It repeats its "themes" but almost always with new variations. In this sense it is ever new, and ever old, so far as the ups and downs are repeated. So much for periodicity, rhythms, and uniformity.

VI. The "Evolution and Progress" of War Movements

A. *What Has Been in the Past?* If we could not accept the periodic and "cyclical" theories in the field studied, still more definitely must we reject all the "linear" theories here, which have been dominant since the end of the eighteenth century and throughout the nineteenth.

As we have already seen above, one of the most vital and important characteristics of the mentality of the nineteenth century was a belief in "bigger and better" progress and providential *de facto* evolution. The gods were dismissed, and their place taken by a real *deus ex machina*, blind, mechanical, or "emergent," which steers the course of the world and of mankind steadily to an ever "higher and better" level. This dogma was naturally applied also to war and to internal disorders. In the relatively peaceful international and internal conditions of the Victorian nineteenth century, it was quite natural to believe that a linear eternal trend must be found in the field of war, and that it could only be the trend of ever-decreasing war until its final disappearance; there would also be ever-decreasing violence in the sphere of the inner progress of societies.

It would be tedious and useless to reproduce these theories, or even the best among them. I have dealt with them rather extensively in one of my other works, *Contemporary Sociological Theories*, and those readers who wish further details may study them there.

What shall we say of all these theories, conceptions, and beliefs? Taken as a manifestation of wishes, they are very noble and commendable, and deserve every kind of success. Taken as a scientific description of reality and the real direction of social processes, they are nothing but beautiful beliefs, contradicted at almost every step by the "ugly facts." The above data do not support them at all.

As in the data presented there is nothing to support the claim of disappearance of war in the past, so is there nothing to support the claim, in spite of the exceptionally high figures for the twentieth century, that there has been (or will be) any steady trend toward increase of war. No, the curve just fluctuates, and that is all.

Such is the answer to this problem, however unpleasant it may be to many, including myself.

B. *What Is Going to Be in the Future?* Is the tragedy of war going to have a happy ending or is it going to continue in human history? Is war going to increase, decrease, or what will it do? My answer to that is, "I do not know." All that can be said is that, since no linear trend toward either a continued increase or decrease has been shown up to the present time, it is little probable that a trend would appear and go "forever" in the future. More probable is it that the curve of the magnitude of war will continue its "erratic" ups and downs in the future as it has done in the past. Though in the twentieth century, so far, it has flared up to an exceedingly high level, it is hardly probable that it will continue to rise forever; sooner or later it must reach its "saturation point," whatever it be, and then it must begin to fall.

Perhaps, as has already happened several times before, a relatively long peace will bless our generation after the extraordinary bloodshed of the World War. Perhaps a new conflagration will occur soon. We do not know, but whichever happens, neither war nor peace is likely to be eternal. The great tragedy, with its piano and forte, will probably be continued.

This does not exclude the possibility of a termination of creative history of mankind and the new nuclear wars, nor the establishment of a lasting peace, if mankind earnestly tries to reach it. Which of these alternatives will prevail remains unknown at this moment.

VII. The Curve of War in the Life History of a Nation

Since neither the cyclically periodical nor the linear theories of war evolution are valid, either in application to the history of mankind or to the history of any particular country, the question arises, Is there any other uniformity of war evolution, in the sense of its increase or decrease, in the life history of a nation? Can we say that wars are more frequent and greater at the earlier stages of such a history? Or does the magnitude of war tend to grow as we proceed from the earlier to the later stages of the existence of a nation?

It is hardly possible to answer these questions fully, because the vast realm of history of many nations, both past and present, has been studied too little from this standpoint. It is possible, however, to advance a tentative hypothesis, which can be phrased as follows: *In the life history of nations, the magnitude of war, absolute and relative, tends to grow in the periods of expansion — political, social, cultural, and territorial — of the nation at least as frequently as in the periods of decline. In such periods of blossoming the war activities tend to reach the highest points, probably more frequently than in the periods of decay, and vice versa.* Such seems to be one of the relatively valid but limited generalizations.

In the preceding chapter, this has been pointed out in regard to many countries. The fourth and fifth centuries B.C. give the highest figures, both absolute and relative, of war for Greece. And the same centuries were the climax of its expansion, growth, culture, and influence. The third and first centuries B.C. were similar periods in the history of Rome. Of the European countries, putting aside the twentieth century, Holland had its climax of war magnitude in the seventeenth and eighteenth centuries, Spain in the seventeenth and sixteenth centuries. These centuries in the history of these countries were again the period when the power, influence, and splendor of their cultures were at the peak. The role and influence of Holland and Spain during the nineteenth and twentieth centuries have been steadily declining: from great powers they slid down to be second- and third-class powers; and from being main cultural centers of Europe, the position they occupied during the previous "military" centuries, they have shifted to a much less important role, now transcended greatly by other countries. The Austria of the Hapsburgs has its highest indicators, absolute and relative, in the seventeenth, eighteenth, and sixteenth centuries, when it occupied the first place in the military scale. The same centuries were the climax of the international and cultural power of Austria. In the nineteenth century, in both military and cultural influence, its role was already more modest. Contrast with this the history of Germany. Its growth — cultural, economic, political, and international — was steadily progressing from the seventeenth to the twentieth century. Especially important were its power and influence in the eighteenth and nineteenth centuries. Correspondingly we see that its absolute indicators of war were steadily growing from the seventeenth to the twentieth century. France possibly had its greatest power and influence, military as well as cultural, in the seventeenth and eighteenth and nineteenth centuries. The same centuries give the highest indicators of war in its history. Russia has become an international power, and then a great power, since the time of Peter the Great (the end of the seventeenth and the beginning of the eighteenth century). The same centuries — the seventeenth, eighteenth, and nineteenth — give the highest absolute figures of its war magnitude. England shows the highest relative indicator of war in the sixteenth, seventeenth, eighteenth centuries; and in these centuries England emerged as a great empire and cultural center. Poland had its climax of warfare in the seventeenth century, and decline in the eighteenth.

These facts seem to support our proposition, to an extent. Logically it is easy to understand why it must be so. The expansion of any empire, if it does not take place in a sparsely populated area, like the American continent where the United States developed, can be made only at the cost of the territory of other nations. In order that this may be possible, these other nations must be conquered, because none is willing to present itself, its population, its territory, and its resources as a free gift to any other nations. Since the victim of the expansion must be subjugated and conquered, this means war, the only real instrument of subjugation. Hence war's increase in the period of expansion. Hence, for its increase to be possible, the conquering nation must be strong and resourceful. In order to be strong and resourceful in war, it must be strong in its population, in its economic resources, in its inner order, and its mental and moral qualities. These last are as important a factor of military victory as any other. Otherwise no military strength can be possible. This explains why the periods of expansion and growth of a given nation coincide frequently with the periods of the increase of war and of biosocial and cultural blooming of the country; why, on the other hand, a nation which is weak and secondary becomes often more peaceful. This latter may be true either because the nation is so small and weak that it dares not take the chance of assaulting any other nation, or even of resisting the claims of the others, however unjust they may be, or because such a nation is put into factual dependence upon a stronger nation and is relatively protected by its stronger boss and captor, or, finally, because such countries, by mutual agreement of the "strong dogs," are put in a "golden cage of neutrality" for some time unbroken by the stronger "dogs." The reasons for this coincidence are so clear and almost axiomatic that it is no wonder the facts support the proposition. It means a tragedy of human culture and history, but they have been tragic indeed.

All theories which claim that cultural effervescence is always incompatible with war, that the growth of war in the history of any nation is a sure sign of its decline, are one-sided. However commendable are the moral and other motives which are behind these sweet "theories," from the standpoint of facts and logic they are partly wrong. One-sided also are the opposite theories exemplified by the generalization of Joseph de Maistre. Following Machiavelli, he says:

> The best fruits of human nature, arts, sciences, great enterprises, great conceptions, and virile virtues, prosper especially in time of war. It is said that nations reach the peak of their grandeur only after long and bloody wars. The climax of Greek civilization was reached in the terrible epoch of the Peloponnesian War; the most brilliant period of Augustus followed immediately after the Roman civil wars and proscriptions. The French genius was bred by the wars of the League, and was polished by the war of the Fronde. All great men of the time of Queen Anne (1665–1714) were born amidst a great political commotion. In brief, they say that blood is a fertilizer of the plant called Genius. . . . I do not see anything less pacifistic than the periods of Alexander the Great and Pericles; the periods of Augustus, Leo X, François I, Louis XIV, and Queen Anne.

There is some truth contained in his statement, as well as in our above proposition, well warranted by a detailed study of the curve of war magnitude in the centuries investigated, and in the curves of the movement of scientific inventions, philosophical and musical creativeness (not to mention the movement of the social sciences and of the other arts). We have seen that the absolute and the relative curves of war magnitude in Europe, measured by casualty, have steadily been growing, from the twelfth to the seventeenth century, after which the relative indicators fall in the eighteenth and the nineteenth centuries while the absolute indicators continue to rise. The curve of inventions and discoveries in the natural sciences from the thirteenth to the twentieth century, also goes up, a growth which evidently could not have occurred if war were as destructive to science and art as is claimed by the above theories.

All this does not mean that war is the main or general cause of scientific progress. Here is the weakness of De Maistre's statement. This coincidence does not indicate that a great war is the cause of a great scientific blossoming or, vice versa, that a great scientific and cultural blossoming is the cause of a great war. But it means that both are manifestations of numerous still deeper forces which create, simultaneously with great military power and political influence, great scientific and cultural blooming.

Such is the meaning and reason for the first limitation of the proposition discussed. Its second limitation is more serious. *Not all wars and not all great wars are necessarily a manifestation of exuberance, or the biosocial and cultural effervescence of a given society.* Some, though seemingly the minority, may be the manifestation either of the decline and "old age" of a given society, or of the end of an epoch, in its sociocultural life history, and the transition to another epoch, one not necessarily better or more brilliant, but quite different from the preceding epoch of the society's culture. For instance, for Austria the war of 1914–1918 was hardly an effervescence of the superabundance of its energy and creative vitality. It was rather the final explosion of a brilliant torch which had burned magnificently during at least a thousand years. For all Europe the World War may also be a sign of the beginning of the end of the brilliant "Epicurean culture," which blossomed magnificently for some six hundred years from the period of the so-called Renaissance and the Reformation, and which possibly is coming to an end now, to be replaced by a new culture as different from the last as it was different from the medieval culture. Whether this allusion is valid or not, just now is unimportant. What is important is that such wars are shown to be manifestations of "old age," of the coming end of either the political or sociocultural body, or an end of an epoch in its life history. On the other hand, *there are peaceful periods marked by a notable blooming of arts and sciences and culture.*

For this reason the above proposition is not given as an absolute rule; it must have serious limitations and exceptions. But with those amendments it stands as a more valid generalization than most of the linear, cyclical, periodic, and other theories discussed. In the life history of a nation, in its occupied areas, most of the periods of its political, social, economic, moral, and mental effervescence, the most brilliant periods in its history, the period of the climax of its grandeur, power, magnificence, and genius are usually also the periods of its high militarism and warfare. The reverse, however, is less valid. *We cannot say that every period of warfare and great belligerency is necessarily a period of grandeur and blooming.*

These reservations make the proposition more accurate.

VIII War and Peace Factors

What are the reasons (causes and factors and independent variables) of the fluctuation of war? And is the fluctuation connected in some way with the rise and decline of the Ideational and Sensate types of culture?

As to the first question, it is enough to say that the prevalent theories that try to see the causes (factors and variables) either in climate and geographic conditions; or in instinct of pugnacity of the herd; or in human nature generally, and the struggle for existence particularly; or in race and heredity; or in this or that economic factor; or in this or that political regime; or in the size and the density of the population; or in a lack (or overabundance) of education; or in many other (biological or sociocultural) specific factors — all such theories can, at the best, account for only certain details of the curves of war fluctuation for this or that special war or some aspects of such a war; but they do not and cannot account for the greater part of the fluctuation curves of war in the countries studied, whether they are taken separately or together.

None of these factors can account for a greater part of the fluctuation of war magnitude. The above data on the movement of war show that wars happen in the periods of prosperity and depression; under both autocratic and democratic regimes; in the countries with prevalent illiteracy and literacy; in agricultural and industrial societies; in the "liberal" and "conservative" nations; among the peoples of different nationalities and races; in an international milieu comparatively simple and complex; in the societies with diverse religions, diverse density of the population; and so on and so forth. None of these and other factors taken separately can account for either the frequency and distribution of war in social space or for its increase and decrease in time. In a systematic analysis of "war causation," I would start my search with an investigation of the conditions that follow from the very definition of war as *a breakdown of the organized relationship between states. Such a breakdown or, if one prefers, disruption of the existing interstate equilibrium, is the absolute condition of possibility of any war.* By definition, and by fact, any war presupposes such a breakdown of the organized *status quo* relationship and comes as its resultant. Respectively *all the "factors" which facilitate this breakdown are the factors of war; all the factors that reinforce the organized relationships between the states are factors of peace, no matter whether these organized relationships between the states A and B are just or unjust, fair or unfair, or what not.*

The numerous and various attempts to see the cause of war in this or that *single* factor — and such is the enormous majority of the theories of war causation — are faulty at their very source. This means also that a further step along the study of the war causes should consist of an analysis and delineation of the few main and typical combinations of the factors that most frequently lead to the breakdown of organized relationships and then to war.

This means that on this point I am not going to explain the war-peace movement through our main factors: Ideational and Sensate culture. However large are these variables, even they, in my opinion, are insufficient to account directly for all the essential movements of the war-peace curve. What they seem to be able to account for are some of the specific traits of war and some of the movements of the above curves. In other words, I am not going to apply these "keys" directly to all the doors of war-peace. But some of these doors they seem to unlock satisfactorily. The main doors are as follows.

A. *Wars of the dominant Ideational culture (or period) tend to assume the form of religious or Ideational wars more frequently than the wars of the dominant Sensate culture (and period). These rarely have religious or Ideational color.* They are wars of economic, imperialistic, utilitarian, and other Sensate colors mainly: wars for "a place in the sun," for "white man's domination," for maintenance of high standards of living, for exploitation of the rich natural resources unexploited by the native savages, for political independence, and so on and so forth.

B. *Per se, possibly neither Ideational nor Sensate culture is more belligerent or peaceful than the other.* If Ideational society may not be anxious to start a war to obtain Sensate advantages, it may start a war to exterminate the infidels, the heretics, or to convert them to the true religion or to make it triumphal, *ad majorem gloriam Dei.* If Sensate society is not interested to fight for these values, it is highly interested to improve its Sensate welfare and standard of living, or to maintain them against encroachment through preventive and repressive wars. A well-ordered and crystallized Ideational society may be as peaceful or as militant as the well-ordered Sensate.

C. *The periods of transition from the Ideational to the Sensate, or from the Sensate to the Ideational, phase of culture are the periods of notable increase of war activities and war magnitude.* If crystallized and settled cultures of both types, Ideational and Sensate, tend to be comparatively peaceful (unless a strong external factor intervenes) when their system of values and their network of social relationship are firm and strong, *the periods of transition from one type of culture to another* must be logically the periods of comparative conflagration of war.

All in all, the movement of war by century periods agrees well with the hypothesis. In a modified form, it is also warranted by the movement of internal disturbances, as we shall see in the next part. Since the hypothesis is logically comprehensible, and since it accounts for almost all the major movements of war curves at hand, it seems to be entitled to claim a validity perhaps greater than any other hypothesis in the field.

Let us turn now to the next part, which deals with the fluctuation of the internal disturbances and their *ratio sive causa.*

PART SEVEN

FLUCTUATION OF INTERNAL DISTURBANCES IN INTRAGROUP RELATIONSHIPS

34

FLUCTUATION OF INTERNAL DISTURBANCES IN THE HISTORY OF GREECE, ROME, AND EUROPE

Tension and relaxation, sickness and health, crisis and repose, incessantly alternate in the life process of an individual. They usually coexist with one another, but now one alternative, now another, becomes dominant and colors the corresponding part of the life process. A similar pulsation seems to occur in the life process of a society. It also has its periods of tension and relaxation, stormy crisis and quiet order, or, to use Saint Simon's terms, its "organic and critical periods." The existence of this pulsation is well known and does not need to be discussed further. But its many aspects, and among them some important ones, are much less known.

In this study I am going to take several of these aspects and investigate them somewhat more systematically than has hitherto been done. Here are some of the problems. What is the general relationship between the "critical" and the "organic" periods in the life history of various societies when they are taken in a long-time perspective? Compared with the organic periods, are the periods of social storms something extraordinary and abnormal, as many seem to think? Are these conditions recurrent, and if so, is their recurrence periodical? Also, are there among the various countries some which are orderly and some which are stormy par excellence? Is there in the course of time a steady trend toward a progressive decrease of critical periods — decrease in their length, violence, frequency of occurrence, etc. — followed by a corresponding increase of periods of internal social peace, as we are assured by prevalent opinion? Are social disturbances indeed becoming more human, less bloody, less spasmodic? Finally, are they in some way associated with the pulsation of Ideational and Sensate cultures?

In regard to these and several other aspects of the pulsation discussed, our knowledge is limited indeed. A considerable number of theories in the field represent a farrago of beliefs and wishes rather than a carefully checked scientific theory. For this reason they do not fill the hiatus entirely. The subsequent pages attempt, if not to fill the gap, then at least to contribute something which will make it smaller and less "swampy" than it is at the present time.

Before passing to the study, let it be said here that *in an investigation of these problems the uncertainties, the possibilities of error, and all the other dangers, are probably even greater than in the study of war movement.*

For the sake of economizing time and space in this abridged edition, I shall not discuss these, nor all the methodological and technical problems involved in this study. Instead, the reader is referred to the full text of the four-volume edition.

Let us dispense with the technical preliminaries as briefly as possible.

The material of this study includes most of *the recorded internal disturbances of importance*, from the relatively small disorders to the biggest revolutions, which have taken place in the life history of Greece, Rome, France, Germany (Central Europe), England, Italy, Spain, the Netherlands, Byzantium, Poland, Lithuania, and Russia. The very fact of its mention in the annals of history is considered a sign of the importance of an internal disturbance. Quite insignificant disorders which do not affect the life of the country in any appreciable way usually pass by without leaving any traces in the records of history.

Each of the disturbances is studied in the four quantitative aspects that seem most important : (1) the proportional extent of the *social* (not merely geographical) area of the disturbance (social space) ; (2) the proportion of the population actively involved in the disturbance (for or against it) ; (3) the duration of the disturbance ; (4) the proportional intensity (the amount and sharpness of violence and the importance of effects) of the disturbance. Our concept of the magnitude of disturbance is composed as nearly as possible of the combination of these four variables. They do not embrace all the aspects of the disturbance, but they seem to embrace its most significant quantitative aspects. *Other conditions being equal, the greater the proportional extent of the social area of the disturbance, the greater the proportion of the population involved in it, the greater its intensity and the longer its duration, then the greater is the comparative magnitude of the disturbance.* As such, this magnitude aims to estimate, and does estimate, only those aspects which enter into it as an element or a variable; it does not aim to estimate other aspects of it, especially the qualitative one. A few comments on this magnitude follow.

I. As to the Social Area of the Disturbance

It goes without saying that the greater the social area involved in the disturbance, the greater is the disturbance, other conditions being equal. But social area is not the number of square miles over which the disturbance spreads : it may spread over thousands of miles of a little-inhabited subarctic region, and yet its weight and social effects may be much less than those of a disturbance in one big city occupying a few square miles. Generally, disturbances in the main cities of a given country, which are the centers of interaction and influence, are much more weighty than in small cities or in villages that lie upon the periphery of the nation's life and whose system of interaction is very small and limited.

Without developing in detail this line of thought, it is sufficient to note that this principle explains the subsequent grading of the disturbances from the standpoint of the social area where they happen and over which they are spread.

On the scale 1 to 100 the following values are given to the following disturbances so far as their social area is concerned:

1 to a disturbance of a local character in a rural county or similar limited area.

3 to a similar disturbance in several rural counties or in a small town.

5 to a disturbance in a larger town.

10 to a disturbance in several towns of medium size or in one important city or in a small feudal region or a small province.

20 to a disturbance in a larger feudal region or larger province or in a part of a capital city.

40 to a disturbance in several large provinces or in the whole capital city.

60 to a disturbance in the capital city and spread over several provinces.

80 to a disturbance where almost the whole country is involved.

100 to a disturbance in the entire country.

Such are the values given to different disturbances from the standpoint of the social area involved. The *proportional* nature of these gradations is clear from their scale evaluations. Arithmetically the one provincial city or rural district may be enormously different at two periods in the history of a given country, but proportionally they may be about the same.

II. As to the Duration of the Disturbance

Other conditions being equal, the longer the duration of a disturbance, the larger is its magnitude. Here, as with all other variables, several considerations have to be kept in mind. Usually a notable "explosion" is preceded and followed by several smaller disorders. In a single and short explosion such tremors possibly count for more than in a long-lasting disturbance. Other complicating circumstances are also to be considered in grading disturbances from the present aspect. Without enumerating them in detail, we have tried to give as much weight as possible to these complicating circumstances in the following value scale of disturbances considered from the standpoint of duration:

1 to a disturbance of momentary duration, where only one short-time shock is noticeable.

3 to a longer disturbance.

5 to a disturbance that lasted several months.

10 to a disturbance of the duration of about one year.

Then for every additional year up to five years' duration, the value 5 is added to 10; thus a disturbance of about five years gets a value of 30.

III–IV. As to the Intensity of the Disturbance and the Masses Actively Involved in It

The greater the amount of violence displayed and the larger the social classes involved actively in a disturbance, the greater the magnitude of the disturbance, other conditions being equal.

From the standpoint of the classes involved, the disturbances are arranged in the following five divisions: (1) disturbances actively engaging a few individuals (plots, murders, etc.); (2) those involving a small group; (3) those involving a large social class (extensive occupational, economic, racial, national groups, or a large political party, or a religious denomination, etc.); (4) those involving larger masses of the population (several extensive classes); (5) those involving practically all the active and adult population.

From the standpoint of the *amount of violence and the number of sociopolitical changes*, the disturbances are divided into five classes also: (1) those without violence; (2) those with slight violence; (3) those accompanied by destruction of life and property: murders, fights, arson, lootings, sackings, and other forms of violence on a considerable scale; (4) those accompanied by an even larger amount of violence and by the overthrow of the government in various centers, but without serious and lasting sociopolitical effects; (5) those involving violence on a still larger scale, followed by the irrevocable overthrow of the central government and by deep and lasting sociopolitical consequences.

Now disturbances of these five classes are given the values 1, 3, 5, 7, and 10 respectively, for each of the two variables, *i.e.*, for the masses involved and for the amount of violence. But in final grading both variables are combined and the values given to the disturbances from this combined standpoint are shown in Table 23.

TABLE 23. VALUES GIVEN TO INTERNAL DISTURBANCES

		By the Amount of Violence and Effects				
		I	II	III	IV	V
	I	1	3	5	7	10
By the	II	3	10	15	20	30
Masses	III	5	15	25	35	50
Involved	IV	7	20	35	50	70
	V	10	30	50	70	100

In this combined table, if a disturbance belongs according to one variable in the third class but according to the other in the fourth, it is given a value of 35; if it belongs both to the fifth and second classes it is given a value of 30; and so on.

Such are the four components of the magnitude of the disturbance, the scales for each component and the values of each scale given to specified classes of disturbances. *The magnitude of each disturbance is made up of the geometric average of the four values given to it with regard to its social area, duration, social masses involved, and the amount of violence and sociopolitical effects* — the values of the masses and of the violence being combined as explained above. By summing up the geometric averages of all the disturbances that occurred in a given twenty-five- and then a one-hundred-year period, we obtain the indicator of the magnitude of disturbances for such periods. By taking the figures for all such periods we obtain comparative indicators of the movement of the disturbances in the history of the given country from period to period.

Finally, so far as the movement of the disturbances for all these countries taken together is concerned, for almost the whole of Europe, the indicator of the movement of the magnitude of disturbances for each twenty-five-year period is made up of the indicators of the disturbances for this period of time in each country, multiplied by the weight of the country on a scale 1 to 5. The figures for all the countries studied are then summed up and the sum divided by the number of the countries for the given period. The result is made the indicator of the disturbance for all the countries during the time under investigation. A series of such indicators gives an idea of the increase and decrease of the disturbances from period to period.

As to the weight values given to each country on the scale 1 to 5, they are as follows:

Spain, up to the end of the fifteenth century (the time of political unification), 3; for the sixteenth and seventeenth centuries (the period of great power), 5; after the seventeenth century, 3.

France, throughout the whole period studied, 5.

England, up to the middle of the eleventh century (the Norman Conquest), 3; after that to the present, 5.

The Netherlands, to the end of the sixteenth century, 1; for the seventeenth century, 3; after that to the present, 1.

Germany, up to the end of the eighth century, 3; up to the present, 5.

Italy, throughout the whole period studied (especially in view of the location of the Roman Catholic See there), 5.

Byzantium, up to the middle of the seventh century (the period of the loss of most of its Asiatic possessions and of Egypt), 5; up to the end of the twelfth century (the conquest by the Crusaders in 1204), 3; after that, 1.

Poland and Lithuania, up to the end of the fourteenth century (the time of unification), 3; up to the middle of the seventeenth century (the period of great power), 5; after that up to the time of the division of Poland, 3.

Russia, up to the middle of the thirteenth century (when it falls into parts and is subjugated by the Tartars), 5; up to the end of the fifteenth century (when it is again united into a great power), 3; after that, 5.

Thus we have outlined all the necessary details for the construction of indicators of the magnitude of disturbances as well as for the estimation of the movement — increase and decrease — of the magnitude in the course of time for all the countries studied.

It is granted in advance that the method has many an important shortcoming. Thus, the whole attempt to estimate the magnitude of the disturbances introduces several assumptions which are arbitrary but unavoidable, no matter who the investigator, assumptions involving such matters as the scale, the assignment of the values on such a scale for each disturbance, the recourse to a geometric or any other average, and so on. All this is granted without question. From the standpoint of the Platonic absolute truth, the entire attempt is unsatisfactory. But Platonic absolute truth does not exist in this imperfect empirical world with its imperfect knowledge and truth, especially in the field of the social sciences; therefore, we have to apply relative criteria for the appraisal of the procedure. The whole problem can be put in the following way: Are the defects in this study so great as to vitiate hopelessly the result; are they greater than in other studies in the field; and is there any other way, free from these shortcomings, which can promise better and more reliable results? When the questions are so put — and only in such a way can they be asked by any intelligent critic or scholar — then the answer to them all can, in our opinion, only be in the negative.

As to the element of arbitrariness, it is per se neither a vice nor a virtue. There is no science, no theory, which is not based upon some arbitrary principles, from arithmetic, geometry, mechanics, and physics to economics and ethics. The point is whether the assumptions made are reasonable and sound, or, at last, as reasonable and sound as is possible within the field of the problem. The assumptions made in this study do not contain anything illogical or unsound per se. They are not perfect; but no perfect "translation" of the qualitative-quantitative sociocultural phenomena is generally possible, as mentioned above. In any case, in verbal form quantitative appraisals are made all the time by historians. If the shallow reader does not notice these quantitative appraisals, the reason is, besides the shallowness, the verbal but not numerical character of such statements. Who of the serious historians does not speak of "great revolutions," "small disorders," "considerable riots," "large sackings and lootings," "very violent," "comparatively bloodless," "long," "short living"; or of a "comparatively orderly (or disorderly) period," a "time of crisis," an "increase of disturbances," a "transition from a period of profound internal order to that of disorder and instability"?

In thousands of forms such quantitative statements are met with in almost any historical work. The above explains why they are unavoidable.

If such is the real situation, then the whole problem is narrowed to the question: Which is better scientifically, the indefinite and vague quantitativism of the above type, or a more definite numerical quantitativism of the kind used in this work? All in all, with some exceptions for specific conditions and problems, I prefer the quantitativism of the kind used here. It is more economical: in a few tables it permits one to cover enormous periods and to cover them more pointedly, accurately, and systematically than is possible in hundreds of pages of vague verbal quantitative descriptions. Such an economy is something by itself. In our study the basis, the assumptions, the measuring stick are placed clearly before the reader; nothing is left in the dark. The reader knows at once what he is dealing with, how the figures are obtained, what they mean. In most of the indefinite verbal quantitative judgments all this remains unknown: the judgments are a kind of mystical pronouncements of the scholar, whose bases, reasons, measuring stick, even exact meaning, remain hidden. They can be neither checked nor verified, rejected nor accepted. The verbal statement does not permit dealing with a large number of disturbances. Most languages have only six words for comparison: small, smaller, smallest; and great, greater, greatest. Therefore verbal quantitative specifications like great and small, more or less, increase and decrease, rise and decline, growth and decay, are limited in meaning and cannot be applied to even a series of a few dozens of disturbances with any exact power of expressing the magnitude of their movement and fluctuation. Similarly, a verbal quantitativist cannot uniformly apply his measuring stick, if he has any, to all the disturbances compared and cannot therefore even properly compare them. The numerical indicators, having no peculiar weakness in comparison with the verbal quantitative statements, do not have their limitations. This explains why generalizations and judgments made by many verbal quantitativists have, almost without exception, been based upon very few cases and have, therefore, had a very narrow and unstable factual basis. These considerations are sufficient to show why, not being an ardent quantitativist at all, I find that only some sort of system of numerical indicators can describe, more or less accurately, the movement of the phenomena studied, and why I use them and prefer them to the other verbalist procedure, so far as the quantitative aspect of the process is concerned. Whatever and however great are the weaknesses of this study, it is more systematic, more complete than, and as logical as any study of the subject hitherto made.

V. As to the Predominant Qualitative Nature and the Main Objective of the Disturbances

These are divided into five classes:

A, predominantly political disturbances, the main objective of which is a change of the existing political regime.

B, predominantly socioeconomic disturbances, directed toward a modification of the existing social and economic order.

C, national and separatistic disturbances, the main objective of which is national independence, or autonomy, or the elimination of disfranchisements, or the achievement of some other privileges and advantages.

D, religious disturbances.

F, disturbances with specific objectives — like some personal change in the government; resistance to a specific law, or tax, or other concrete measure — and disturbances without any single dominant objective but with two or more equally strong objectives.

These qualitative pigeonholings are to be regarded, of course, as very approximate. It can hardly be questioned that any social disturbance has several reasons and several objectives. On the other hand some movements are marked by the fact that they show one of these characteristics more conspicuously than the others. In many disturbances such "predominant color" is lacking; therefore they are lumped together into a group called "mixed."

Such is the system of classification and differentiation of disturbances. It is not exhaustive, but it gives a sufficiently detailed passport to each of them; it embraces most of the important characteristics — quantitative and partly qualitative — of the disturbances; takes into consideration most of their substantial traits; therefore, it grasps something of the real diversity of the processes studied. The organico-proportional nature of the variables, as well as of the total measure of the magnitude of a disturbance, is now clear. Such proportional units permit us to make rough comparisons between the magnitudes of the disturbances in a varying social body.

A few additional remarks are sufficient to dispense with the technical details of the construction of the indicators. As has been mentioned, all the disturbances of these countries which are recorded in substantial and competent standard texts are studied and "ranked." This means that no selection and no sampling is made by us, but all the recorded disturbances are taken.

The periods with which study of the disturbances begins and ends for each country are indicated in detail in the tables. For this reason they need not be specified here. Altogether there are 84 disturbances in the history of Greece; 170 in that of Rome; 49 for Byzantium; 173 for France; 150 for Germany; 162 for England; 251 for Italy; 235 or 242 (if seven disturbances which were wars rather than disturbances be included) for Spain; 103 for the Netherlands; 167 for Russia; 78 for Poland and Lithuania. A total of 1622 to 1629 disturbances is listed for all these countries.

Before passing to the study of the results, two other methodological details should be mentioned here. In the list of social disturbances are included only happenings which violated the existing social order and law of the period and of the society in which they occurred.

Similarly, social disturbances that were of purely or mainly international character (wars between various countries, the revolt of a conquered country against its victorious foreign invaders — as, for instance, the riots of the French communes against the English invaders during the Hundred Years' War, the wars of Louis XI with the dukes of Burgundy after the evaporation of the fealty, etc.), — were also excluded from the class of internal social disturbances. The reason is again evident: they are not symptoms of the inner tension and inner disturbance of one part of the same social system against another, but phenomena of international tension and disturbance, which are the objects of study in the previous treatment of war movement.

In the full text of the *Dynamics* the essential results of the study of the fluctuation of the magnitude of disturbances in the life history of the

TABLE 24. TOTAL OF THE GEOMETRIC AVERAGE OF INTERNAL DISTURBANCES OF ANCIENT GREECE FROM 600 TO 126 B.C. BY QUARTER CENTURIES

Quarter Century	*Number of Disturbances*	*Measure of Disturbances*	*Total for the Quarter*
600–576 B.C.	4	8.07	
		10.63	
		20.80	
		7.05	46.55
575–551	2	15.43	
		10.63	26.06
550–526	3	10.63	
		10.63	
		17.54	38.80
525–501	3	4.93	
		20.80	
		12.16	37.89
500–476	5	9.66	
		13.39	
		9.09	
		11.45	
		9.66	53.25
475–451	8	9.09	
		7.66	
		7.11	
		27.14	
		14.42	
		41.21	
		23.42	
		12.16	142.21

TABLE 24. TOTAL OF THE GEOMETRIC AVERAGE OF INTERNAL DISTURBANCES OF ANCIENT GREECE FROM 600 TO 126 B.C. BY QUARTER CENTURIES — *continued*

Quarter Century	*Number of Disturbances*	*Measure of Disturbances*	*Total for the Quarter*
450–426 B.C.	5	25.77	
		9.66	
		15.18	
		17.38	
		16.07	84.06
425–401	13	8.03	
		19.13	
		14.42	
		10.10	
		10.13	
		21.54	
		17.54	
		10.16	
		4.64	
		15.43	
		15.43	
		27.14	
		9.66	189.25
400–376	5	6.69	
		19.13	
		7.37	
		7.37	
		9.66	50.22
375–351	8	18.17	
		18.47	
		15.18	
		16.13	
		20.80	
		13.57	
		7.06	
		12.16	124.54
350–326	6	11.45	
		9.66	
		15.43	
		18.17	
		12.81	
		19.13	86.65
325–301	4	17.10	
		12.16	
		15.43	
		14.42	59.11
300–276	4	21.54	
		14.42	
		21.54	
		14.42	71.92
275–251	4	14.42	
		8.88	
		33.02	
		10.63	66.95

TABLE 24. TOTAL OF THE GEOMETRIC AVERAGE OF INTERNAL DISTURBANCES OF ANCIENT GREECE FROM 600 TO 126 B.C. BY QUARTER CENTURIES — *continued*

Quarter Century	*Number of Disturbances*	*Measure of Disturbances*	*Total for the Quarter*
250–226 B.C.	2	16.13	
		11.12	27.25
225–201	7	14.42	
		8.43	
		16.13	
		10.63	
		12.60	
		21.54	
		9.66	93.41
200–176	2	9.66	
		9.66	19.32
175–151	—	—	—
150–126	1	17.10	17.10

TABLE 25. TOTAL OF THE GEOMETRIC AVERAGE OF INTERNAL DISTURBANCES OF ANCIENT GREECE BY CENTURIES

Century	*Number of Disturbances*	*Number of Years with Disturbance*	*Total of the Geometric Averages for the Century*
VI B.C.	12	13	149.30
V	30	51	468.77
IV	23	23	320.52
III	17	22	259.53
II (first 3 quarters)	3	4	36.42

countries studied are given in tables and figures by quarter-century and century periods. In this abridged edition the tables and conclusions are given only for Ancient Greece, as an example of the similar tables and conclusions for other countries. We then turn to a summary of internal disturbances for Europe as a whole.

Ancient Greece. If we take century periods, whether we judge on the basis of the totals of the geometric averages, of the number of years with a disturbance, or of the frequency of disturbances, the most peaceful was the first half of the second century, then the sixth century, and near to it the third century B.C. The most disorderly were the fifth and the fourth centuries. Of the quarter centuries the periods 425–401 B.C. (with the magnitude 189.25); 475–451 (142.21); 375–351 (124.54); 225–201 (93.41); 450–426 (84.06); and 350–326 (86.65) were the most turbulent, while the periods 200–126, 575–551, and 250–226 were the most orderly. (See Figure 10.)

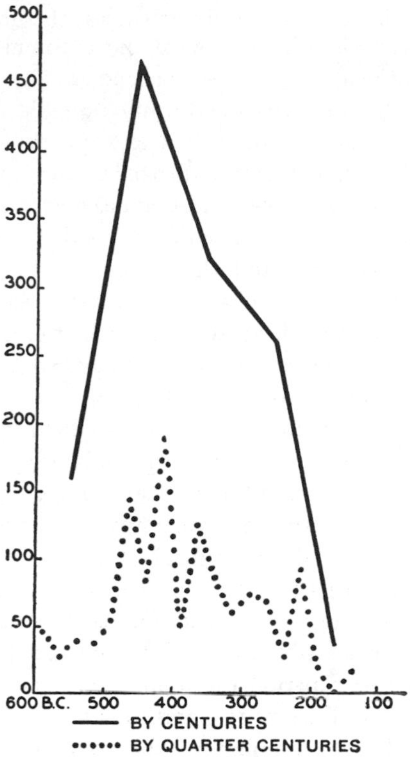

FIG. 10. MOVEMENT OF INTERNAL DISTURBANCES IN ANCIENT GREECE

If we inquire in which of these periods the greatest single revolutions happened, the answer is in the periods 460–440 (with the magnitude 49.19); 464–455 (41.21); 467 (37.14); 403 (27.14); 265–261 (33.02). (The detailed tables in the Appendix to this part show exactly what these disturbances were.)

On the basis of these data one is entitled to conclude that in the history of Greece the most turbulent centuries and periods were, like those periods of the maximum of war activities, not the periods of decline but of resplendence, when Greek culture reached its peak — the fifth and fourth centuries. In general, the curve of disturbances, judged by century periods, goes parallel with the curve of war. Here, then, we have a refutation of the claims that disturbances occur always in the period of decline. We shall see that some of them do occur in such periods, but not always, nor even as a general rule.

No continuous trend, no regular periodicity, and no uniformity in the amplitude of the ups and downs by quarter centuries, nor by century periods, are noticeable.

As to the characteristics of the disturbances, the data show that predominantly political disturbances were most common and frequent; then came the nationalistic and socioeconomic disturbances. Greece did not have religious disturbances in any tangible degree. The data show also that socioeconomic disturbances happened most often in the fifth century, while nationalistic disturbances were predominant in the fourth and partly in the third centuries, appearing at a later stage of the development of the Greek bodies politic. This does not mean that these reasons — the socioeconomic and the nationalistic — did not play any role in other periods; the socioeconomic played a very conspicuous role in the disturbances of the third and partly in the disturbances of the second century. But they were screened or cloaked in the exterior forms of disturbances of a political or a mixed nature.

Europe. When indicators for separate countries in the text are summed up by the quarter-century and century periods, they give the following picture of the movement of internal disturbances. The summing up, as mentioned, is done in the following way: the indicators of all the countries in a given period are multiplied by the comparative weight of the country among other countries in a period on a scale of 1 to 5; then these indicators are summed up and for each period divided by the number of the countries which enter into the summary of the period. Table 46 shows for each period the number of the countries, and then the total indicator for all countries, and the average indicator (the total indicator divided by the number of the countries) in each specified quarter-century and century period. (See also Figure 21.)

TABLE 46. TOTAL MEASURE OF INTERNAL DISTURBANCES OF EUROPE FROM 525 TO 1925 BY QUARTER CENTURIES

Period	*Total of the Indicators*	*Number of the Countries*	*Average*
525–550 A.D.	458.89	4	114.72
551–575	641.13		160.28
576–600	684.79		171.20
601–625	623.93		154.98
626–650	339.91		84.98
651–675	521.16	5	104.23
676–700	684.01	6	114.00
701–725	1507.40	7	215.34
726–750	1223.55		174.79
751–775	1294.82		184.97
776–800	1112.14		158.88
801–825	726.74		103.82
826–850	1763.45		251.92
851–875	667.41		95.34
876–900	969.95		138.57

TABLE 46. TOTAL MEASURE OF INTERNAL DISTURBANCES OF EUROPE FROM 525 TO 1925 BY QUARTER CENTURIES — *continued*

Period	*Total of the Indicators*	*Number of the Countries*	*Average*
901–925	782.69		111.78
926–950	1264.73	8	158.09
951–975	1112.55	9	123.62
976–1000	1295.44		143.94
1001–1025	1772.17		196.91
1026–1050	1478.97		164.33
1051–1075	1737.84		193.09
1076–1100	1256.18		139.57
1101–1125	1284.37		142.71
1126–1150	1734.30		192.70
1151–1175	1887.16		209.68
1176–1200	1963.97		218.22
1201–1225	2176.65		241.85
1226–1250	1648.26		183.14
1251–1275	2010.18		223.35
1276–1300	2111.01		234.56
1301–1325 A.D.	2100.43		233.37
1326–1350	1812.87		201.43
1351–1375	1283.90		142.66
1376–1400	2245.87		249.54
1401–1425	1297.70	8	162.21
1426–1450	1752.89		219.11
1451–1475	1549.73		193.72
1476–1500	1386.70		173.34
1501–1525	918.60		114.83
1526–1550	947.05		118.38
1551–1575	864.78		108.10
1576–1600	1349.67		168.71
1601–1625	1081.28		135.16
1626–1650	1808.24		226.03
1651–1675	1226.00		153.23
1676–1700	728.66		91.08
1701–1725	890.13		111.27
1726–1750	430.44		53.81
1751–1775	871.36		108.92
1776–1800	1132.69		141.56
1801–1825	1085.92	7	155.13
1826–1850	2703.23		386.18
1851–1875	979.91		139.99
1876–1900	599.37		85.61
1901–1925	2071.28		295.89

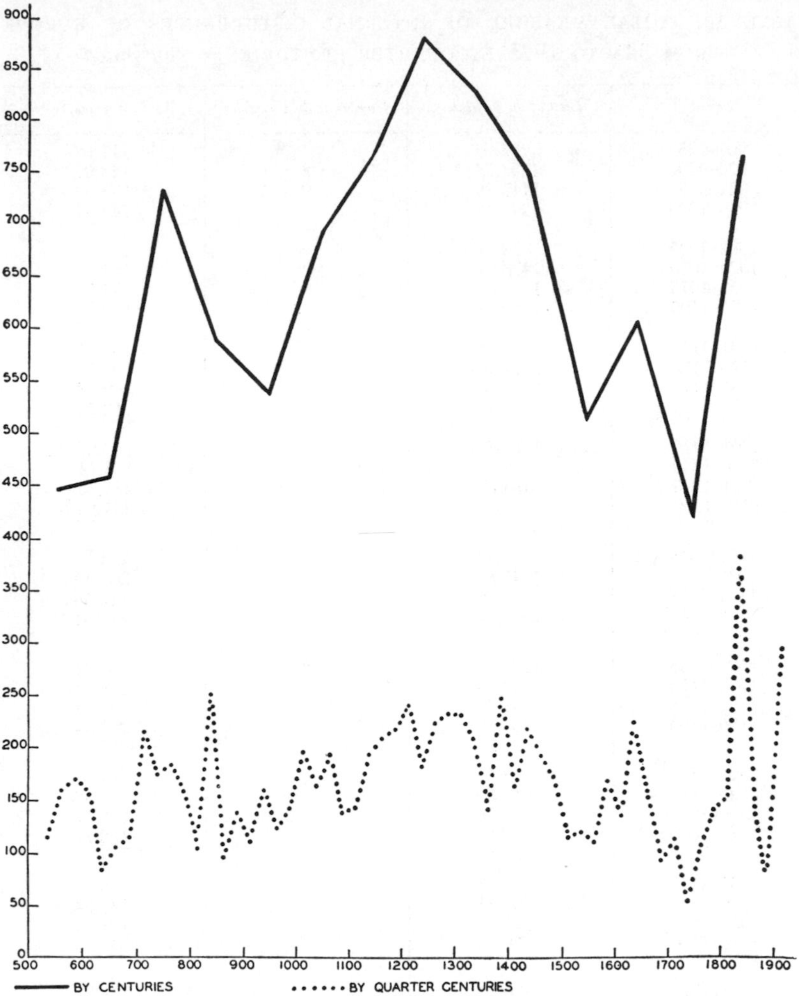

FIG. 21. MOVEMENT OF INTERNAL DISTURBANCES IN EUROPE

TABLE 47. TOTAL MEASURE OF INTERNAL DISTURBANCES OF EUROPE BY CENTURIES

Century	*Average*	*Century*	*Average*
VI[1]	446.20	XIII	882.90
VII	458.19	XIV	827.00
VIII	733.98	XV	748.38
IX	589.65	XVI	509.56
X	537.43	XVII	605.50
XI	693.90	XVIII	415.56
XII	763.31	XIX	766.91

[1] Three quarters only.

SUMMARY AND MAIN RESULTS OF STUDY OF INTERNAL DISTURBANCES

A. The first important conclusion concerns the *frequency of occurrence of important social disturbances in the life of social bodies.* Usually it is thought that they are fairly infrequent events. Meanwhile the data at hand show — and show consistently for all the countries studied — that on the average one notable social disturbance happens in about six years, for some countries in five years, for others in seventeen years. If, instead of taking the average time span per significant social disturbance, we ask ourselves what is the average number of years without a disturbance per years with a disturbance, then the results will be still more striking. They indicate that the relationship between the years with disturbances and those without them fluctuates between one to two and one to eight, depending upon the country. On the average in most of the countries studied, to one year with a significant social disturbance there have been only about five peaceful years, free from inner social tensions and storms. Table 48 gives more exact data in the field.

Even with the relatively wide deviation of Byzantium from the record of other countries (which is due in all probability to a less careful recording of the disturbances in the history of that country) the averages for the occurrence of disturbances (in years) and for the ratio of years without disturbance to years with disturbance are remarkably close. And this in spite of the enormous difference between countries and the times in which they have been making their history! The importance of these figures is that the occurrence of social disturbances is far from being so infrequent on the average as is usually thought. On the average, in about every six to eight years one social disturbance may be expected. In this sense disturbances are "normal" occurrences in the life process of social groups.

The following figures are, of course, averages. Such would be the average frequency of disturbances if they were distributed evenly in the course of time. But such evenness is lacking. Some periods have abundant disturbances, which sometimes continue for many years; other times are free from important social storms. Therefore, the actual distribution of disturbances in the course of time is somewhat different from those averages.

Once in a while, although only rarely, periods have occurred when there was no disturbance during the whole of a quarter century. In a few such periods — in all countries and for all the time studied, there are hardly more than ten cases — internal peace existed for about half a century. All in all, each generation is likely to have one or more important social disturbances during its life span.

TABLE 48. FREQUENCY OF IMPORTANT SOCIAL DISTURBANCES

Country	*Number of Years Studied*	*Number of Disturbances in Period*	*Average Occurrence of Disturbances (in Years)*	*Number of Years with Disturbance*	*Average Ratio of Years without to Years with Disturbances*
Ancient Greece (600 B.C. to 146 B.C.)	454	84	5.4	122	(2.7)
Rome (509 B.C. to A.D. 476)	985	170	5.8	219	(3.5)
Byzantium (532–1390)	858	49	17.5	89	(8.6)
France (531–1933)	1402	173	8.1	246	(4.7)
Germany and Austria (709–1933)	1124	150	7.5	204	(4.5)
England (656–1933)	1277	162	7.9	247	(4.2)
Italy (526–1933)	1407	251	5.6	365	(2.9)
Spain (467–1933)	1466	242	6.1	424	(2.4)
The Netherlands (678–1933)	1255	103	12.1	263	(3.8)
Russia (946–1933)	987	167	5.9	280	(2.6)
Poland and Lithuania (1031–1794)	763	78	9.8	146	(4.3)

B. Another suggestion follows from Table 48. It is a fairly common opinion that *there are nations "inherently" disorderly and inclined to anarchy and disturbances, and nations which are, by God's will or for racial or some other reasons, destined to be orderly and free from social convulsions.* Most of the conservative proponents of this theory include their own nation in the "orderly" class; most of the radicals, who are Don Quixotes of revolution, in the "revolutionary." During the last few years there have been not infrequent occasions for hearing that, for instance, "these Slavs and Russians are anarchists by nature, while we (the British, the French, the Americans, etc.), thank heaven! are an orderly nation." Variations on this theme have been numerous and ingenious. *A glance at Table 48 is sufficient to dissipate these theories. All nations are orderly and disorderly, according to the times.* At the best, some of them show somewhat less inclination to social disturbances than others. But the difference is not serious, and even this small discrepancy is likely to decrease if we should deal with their completed history, as for example with that of Greece and Rome.

This last means that, as we shall see, there is an observable tendency for a few of the countries (but not all) to have their disturbances decrease at the later stages of their history, after their climax is over, and the glory and the fame are in the past. For instance, the Netherlands show a low disturbancy during the last two or three centuries, and a high one during the time that they were engaged in making a place for themselves under the sun. Something similar we see in Greece, Rome, and Poland and Lithuania. This will be discussed later in more detail. For the present, the above data and these hints are sufficient to dissipate the myth of orderly and disorderly nations "by nature." The difference between peoples in this respect is small and does not warrant any such theory.

The partisans of orderly and disorderly nations may, however, find refuge in the contention that though the incidence of disturbances is common to all nations, they nevertheless differ radically in that revolutions proceed in the orderly nations without any, or with little, violence, while in the disorderly nations they are always violent, bloody, and cruel. During these last few years such arguments have been heard many times. Is such a claim valid? The answer is given by Table 49, which lists the percentages of the disturbances among the nations studied, according to the degree of their intensity and violence. From the standpoint of intensity all the revolutions are divided into five classes, beginning with Class I, the "pure and bloodless" disturbances, and passing in order to Class V, the most violent among the disturbances in both the quantitative and the qualitative aspects. In other words, our indicators of the intensity of disturbances are very near to being in fact what might be called the indicators of the violence, cruelty, and bloodiness of the disturbances. This is particularly true of the first three classes.

TABLE 49. INTENSITY OF REVOLUTIONS BY COUNTRIES — BY CLASS

COUNTRIES	I		II		III		IV		V		*Total*	
	No.	*Per Cent*	*No.*	*Per Cent*	*No.*	*Per Cent*	*No.*	*Per Cent*	*No.*	*Per Cent*	*No.*	*Per Cent*
Greece	1	1.2	11	3.1	30	**35.7**	24	28.5	18	21.4	84	100
Rome	2	1.2	49	28.8	79	**46.5**	19	11.2	21	12.5	170	100
Byzantium	2	4.0	1	2.0	10	20.4	36	**73.6**	0	0	49	100
France	17	9.9	43	24.5	74	**43.0**	33	19.2	6	3.4	173	100
Germany and Austria	12	8.0	24	16.0	73	**48.7**	39	26.0	2	1.3	150	100
England	15	9.2	41	25.3	51	31.5	52	**32.2**	3	1.8	162	100
Italy	13	5.1	35	13.9	88	35.1	112	**44.7**	3	1.2	251	100
Spain	4	1.7	46	19.5	132	**56.2**	43	18.3	10	4.2	235	100
The Netherlands	2	1.9	17	16.5	58	**56.4**	20	19.4	6	5.8	103	100
Russia	8	4.7	98	**59.0**	36	21.4	19	11.3	6	3.6	167	100
Poland and Lithuania	5	6.4	5	6.4	55	**70.5**	13	16.7	0	0	78	100
Total	81		370		686		410		75		1622	

Table 49 shows that there are some differences between the nations in this respect, but they are neither great nor consistent. This means that England and France, for instance, show the highest percentage of disturbances of those in Class I (the least violent) and in this point seem to be at the top of the list of the least violent countries. When, however, we find the predominant type of disturbances there, we see that their "mode" falls into Class IV and Class III, while the "mode" for all the other countries falls either into Class II, III, or IV. This means that all in all the English and French disturbances cannot be regarded in any way as less violent than, for instance, the Russian or German or Spanish or Dutch or the Roman.

On the basis of the data, first place in this respect seems to belong to Greece, whose percentage of Class V disturbances is excessive. However strange it may appear in the light of the contemporary Russian Revolution with its endless cruelties, so far the Russian disturbances seem not to have been more violent than those of other countries: 64 per cent of all the Russian disturbances fall into classes I and II, and only 36 per cent into the remaining more violent classes. Such an indicator is not shown by any other country among those studied. Other countries, generally speaking, occupy about the same position in this respect. All this means that the contention discussed is also a myth based on a mere wish and imagination. Together with the preceding data these results are enough to dissipate the legend of "orderly" and "disorderly" peoples.

Another conclusion suggested by Table 49 is that only about 5 per cent of all 1622 disturbances studied occurred without violence and about 23 per cent with slight violence. More than 70 per cent were accomplished and followed by violence and bloodshed on a considerable scale. This means that *those who dream of a "bloodless revolution" have little chance (some five chances out of one hundred) to accomplish their dream.* He who aspires for a disturbance must be ready to see violence and to be a witness or victim or perpetrator of it. This is true for all nations and groups.

C. The third item concerns the *duration* of the disturbances. From this standpoint there are ten different classes, beginning with the disturbances which lasted only a few days and ending with those which lasted for more than twenty-five years. The questions arise: What is the proportion of short and long disturbances? What is the predominant type of their duration? Are there appreciable differences in this respect between the disturbances of various countries?

These questions are answered by Table 50, which gives the actual and the per cent figures for the duration of the disturbances studied.

From these data it follows that for the majority of the countries taken separately *the predominant type of disturbance is of Class II, that is, of a*

TABLE 50. DURATION OF REVOLUTIONS BY COUNTRIES — BY CLASS

COUNTRIES	I		II		III		IV		V–VIII		IX–X		*Total*
	No.	*Per Cent*	*No.*	*Per Cent*	*No.*	*Per Cent*	*No.*	*Per Cent*	*No.*	*Per Cent*	*No.*	*Per Cent*	*No.*
Greece	22	26.2	36	**42.8**	12	14.3	3	3.6	10	11.9	1	1.2	84
Rome	42	24.7	88	**51.8**	21	12.3	9	5.3	10	5.9	0	0	170
Byzantium	8	16.3	22	**44.9**	7	14.3	1	2.0	11	22.5	0	0	49
France	28	16.3	69	**39.5**	34	19.8	10	5.9	32	18.6	0	0	173
Germany and Austria	20	13.4	40	26.6	53	35.4	10	6.6	26	17.4	1	0.6	150
England	28	17.3	67	**41.4**	33	20.4	8	4.9	25	15.4	1	0.6	162
Italy	85	33.7	67	26.5	44	17.7	17	6.9	37	14.8	1	0.4	251
Spain	45	19.1	108	**46.0**	23	9.8	22	9.3	36	15.3	1	0.4	235
The Netherlands	7	6.8	24	23.3	37	**35.9**	4	3.9	28	27.2	3	2.9	103
Russia	30	18.5	74	**44.0**	24	14.3	4	2.4	32	19.0	3	1.8	167
Total	315	20.4	595	**38.5**	288	18.6	88	5.6	247	15.2	11	0.7	1544

few weeks' duration. Only in Germany and Austria, and the Netherlands is the predominant type that with a duration of several months, while in Italy it is that of a few days. Next come the disturbances with durations of a few days and a few months (Classes I and II). Then the proportion of disturbances of longer duration decreases as the duration increases; disturbances with durations of above ten years are lacking altogether in the history of several countries, in others they are below 1 per cent of all the disturbances. Only in the Netherlands and in Russia are they above 1 per cent. In general, disturbances with a duration of less than one year compose about 80 per cent of all the disturbances. Disturbances with a duration of more than one year make about 15 per cent of the total. Thus *most of the internal crises in the life process of a social body* (like sicknesses in the life process of an individual) *come and pass their acute stage within a period of a few weeks.* Only a small proportion last for one year or more.

The same data show again that, although differences exist in regard to the duration of disturbances in various countries, they are not fundamental. On the contrary, the proportionate duration of the specified disturbances is closely similar in most of the countries studied, especially if disturbances with a duration of about one year or less are taken. The main deviations occur in the records of Byzantium and the Netherlands; but even they are not conspicuously great. This suggests again that there is no particularly strong basis for qualifying some nations as "bent to disorders," and some others as "bent to be orderly." This uniformity suggests also that the occurrence of the disturbances, their frequency, and their duration seem to be controlled by forces and conditions which lie very deep, far below the specific cultural and other circumstances, in which these countries differ markedly. What I imply by the phrase "deep factors" is that a social disturbance is perhaps an immanent trait of sociocultural life itself, and in this sense is inescapable and in its essentials is manifested similarly in all the social bodies. Here, probably, we meet again the same fact of the immanent self-regulation of social processes which any thoughtful investigator of such processes often comes across.

Finally, it is enough to glance at Greece, Rome, and Byzantium — the countries which existed a long time ago — and at those existing now, in order to see that there is no important difference between the duration of their disturbances. We cannot say that they were uniformly longer or shorter in the countries of the past compared with those of the present. Likewise, if the detailed data are examined for the duration of disturbances in the same country, beginning with the earliest and ending with the latest, they also show no uniform trend, in fact almost no trend at all. Here we strike, then, the first blow at the popular opinion that in the course of time disturbances tend to disappear, and to become shorter, less violent, and less inevitable. We find nothing corresponding to this pleasant view in the data of their duration.

D. In spite of all the vicissitudes and changing conditions within the system of the indicators accepted, the magnitude of the disturbances fluctuates from century to century much less than is usually expected. If we take all the European countries studied from the sixth to the twentieth century, the amplitude of fluctuation of the magnitude of the disturbances is between 414.65 and 882.90; that is, in the most turbulent century the disturbances are only a little more than twice greater than in the most orderly century.

If we take the indicators of the quarter centuries, the difference is naturally greater, the maximum figure being here 300.46 and the minimum figure 53.81, the maximum exceeding the minimum by five to six times. Such swings are not exceedingly wild. They indicate some permanently working forces, inherently connected with the essence of the social life itself, which do not permit either a complete elimination or the unlimited growth of disturbances. As soon as the curve of disturbances approaches either the minimum or the maximum level, a reaction sets in and sends its course in the opposite direction.

E. *In these "reactions" we observe several times, although not always, that when the curve approaches especially close to the minimum or maximum limits, the counteraction also becomes especially strong.*

We do not need a mystical or numerological interpretation when, as so often (though not always), we see that the further and the more sharply a curve swings in one direction the stronger is the reaction which sends it back again. It is simply that the swing from order to disorder, and the reverse, seems to have a limit, as do almost all sociocultural phenomena, and as physicochemical and biological processes apparently do. Besides indicating the comparatively narrow limits of the maximum and the minimum fluctuation of our indicators, the above suggests that deep within social life are forces, possibly two opposing sets, that manifest themselves in such pulsations. When one set of forces becomes too strong, other forces, in some way or for some reason, are set in motion in the opposite direction.

F. *The indicators for either quarter century or century periods show no continuous trend, either toward bigger and better "orderly progress" or toward ever-increasing disorderliness.* The curve fluctuates, that is all one can say. The popular theory that social change tends to become more and more orderly, more and more free from violence as "civilization progresses," is, then, nothing but a "pleasant myth." One reason why so utterly improbable a theory was accepted by so many scholars as well as by the public in general is shown by Table 46; the third quarter of the nineteenth century was more orderly than the three quarters preceding it; the fourth quarter (85.61) was more orderly than any of the preceding forty-three quarters from the sixth to the twentieth century, only two quarter centuries, 1726–1750 (53.81) and 626–650 (84.98), being slightly more orderly. Social conditions like these naturally are conducive to the popularity of such theories.

G. *According to Table 46, there is hardly any definite periodicity in the ups and downs of internal disturbances.* Their tempo, as well as their rhythm, is varied. From one period to the next *piano* or *pianissimo* replaces *forte*, and the reverse.

So all the fashionable theories which try to interpret sociocultural processes by a mechanistic principle and to ascribe a definite periodicity to these are wrong, in this field as well as in most others.

H. Tables 46 and 47 show which of the centuries and quarter centuries in the history of the greater part of the European continent have been particularly stormy and which particularly quiet. The turbulent centuries from the sixth to the twentieth were the thirteenth, fourteenth, twelfth, nineteenth, fifteenth, eighth, and eleventh. The maximum of disturbances fall within the thirteenth and then the fourteenth; the minimum fall within the eighteenth, seventh, sixth, and sixteenth centuries.

If quarter-century periods are taken, the most turbulent periods were: 1826–1850; 1901–1925; 826–850; 1201–1225; and 1301–1325. The most orderly periods were: 1726–1750; 1876–1900; 1676–1700; 851–875; 601–625. The most orderly and turbulent quarter-century periods for each of the seven countries separately studied were indicated above. Almost every country had one or more twenty-five-year periods with practically no important disturbances.

I. Table 46 shows, as mentioned, that the *last quarter of the nineteenth century was remarkably orderly;* of fifty-six quarter centuries from 525 to 1925 only two had a slightly lower figure of disturbances. Shall we wonder that in that orderly "capitalistic" milieu theories of assured "orderly progress" sprang up and were generally accepted? *At its height, therefore, the "capitalistic regime," which it is now the fashion to curse, was the most orderly of social systems and gave the greatest assurance of internal and external peace and of Sensate liberty and freedom for individuals.* In the light of this datum it is childish rather to ascribe to it all the vices of both anarchy and militarism and to strive to establish internal and external peace and the maximum of Sensate liberty by destroying capitalism and creating socialism, fascism, communism, Hitlerism, and other "isms" of today.

J. The data show, further, *where we now stand on the historical road.* The indicators are not carried beyond 1925. If they were, the data for the first half of the twentieth century would be still more conspicuous and definite. Even as it stands, the figures show that *after the very peaceful final quarter of the nineteenth century, Europe entered the stormy period of the twentieth.* The indicator for the first quarter of the twentieth century is exceptionally high. From 525 to 1925 only one quarter century shows itself more turbulent than the 1901–1925 period. We are in a rising tide of internal disturbances. Since 1925 there have been a large number of disturbances, and of great magnitude, in Germany and Austria, France, and Spain; and the number of smaller disturbances in England, Italy, and Russia is also great. *On its face value, as the figure shows, the first quarter of the twentieth century, 1901–1925, was not only the bloodiest period in the entire history of the international conflicts of mankind but also, when internal disturbances are considered, was one of the very turbulent periods.* Such is the unavoidable conclusion from our data on war and disturbances.

This, then, is the latest point of "social progress and evolution" to which we have come. This conclusion will certainly startle all the manufacturers and all the consumers of the "sweet" theories that civilization is progressive through a process of orderly change toward universal peace. They will undoubtedly ponder over it a little; and it would be very useful for them, no matter who they are — for the partisans of these theories are not, in the main, simple and ignorant people, but rather "highbrows and authorities" — to consider whether they have not been believing in their own wishes rather than heeding ugly facts, and whether they have not been too confident and too light-hearted in their theories and conclusions. *The twentieth century, so far, has been the bloodiest and the most turbulent period — and therefore one of the cruelest and least humanitarian — in the history of Western civilization and perhaps in the chronicles of mankind in general.*

K. If we inquire as to whether the movement of internal disturbances for the eight European countries studied is connected directly and synchronously with the movement of international war, the answer must be in the negative. Comparing the curve of war movement with the curve of the disturbances, both by century and quarter-century periods, we see that *so far as century periods are concerned, each process has had a course independent of the other, without either positive or negative association.* While war indicators increase by casualties and by army's strength from the twelfth to the seventeenth century inclusive (see Figures 6 and 7) the indicators of disturbances show no such tendency; they tend rather to decrease from the fourteenth to the nineteenth century. But while the indicator of war in the nineteenth century declines, the indicator of disturbances, on the contrary, rises greatly. Thus, their movements for these centuries were rather opposite or "compensatory." But for the centuries from the twelfth to the fourteenth and from the seventeenth to the eighteenth their course was parallel rather than compensatory.

Finally, both increase in the first quarter of the twentieth century. Thus, there is no evident consistency in the relation between the two indicators for the century period.

In a desire to elucidate the problem somewhat more, the annual and the quarter-century indicators of both processes in the history of Greece, Rome, and Russia were subjected to a detailed statistical analysis. No definitely consistent relationship between the two variables was found. There did seem to be a slight indication that *disturbances tend to occur more frequently during and around years of war, being more frequent in war years, and in the years immediately preceding and following wars, and becoming rarer as we move further in either direction from the years of war.* For instance, of all the 207 years with disturbances in Rome studied, 96, or 45 per cent, occurred during years of war, 19 within one year before or after a war, 11 within two years before or after a war, 9 within three years, 11 within four years, 7 within five years, 5 within six years, 4 within seven years, 3 within eight years, then 4, 3, 4, and 4 within 9, 10, 11, and 12 years, respectively, after a war; 180 disturbances out of 207 are distributed in this way, while the remaining 27 cases of disturbances occurred at a still greater distance from a war.

Considering, however, that war occurred in 41 per cent of the total number of years of Roman history, this result is less conclusive than may appear at first glance. In the history of Russia, 35 of the 70 disturbances from 1450 to 1925, or 50 per cent, occurred in years of war. War occurred, however, in about 46 per cent of all the years studied. The result is again very inconclusive, failing to show any definite and uniform association between the processes studied.

Such an ambiguous and indefinite result is perhaps due to the fact that in our analysis we did not divide the wars into victorious and unsuccessful. Mere common sense, together with slight historical observation, seems to suggest that victorious wars are much less likely than unsuccessful wars to be followed or preceded by internal disturbances. During and after World War I, revolutions took place in Bulgaria, Turkey, Germany, Austria, and Russia — that is, in the defeated countries — while England, France, Italy, and Serbia, or the United States of America, did not have any revolution or disturbance that led to the overthrow of the existing regime or was as great as those disturbances in the defeated countries. Likewise, Russia, after her defeat in the Russo-Japanese War of 1904–1905, had a revolution, during 1905–1906, while Japan had no disturbance. After being defeated in war in 1912, Turkey had a revolution and deposed Abdul-Hamid, while nothing like this happened in the victorious countries. Likewise, France had a revolution after being defeated in the Franco-Prussian War; and one might give a long list of such cases from recent as well as from remote periods.

If this consideration has any importance, then it is clear why our analysis showed no more definite relationship between the variables. We put together all the wars, successful as well as unsuccessful, and so, of course, obscured any consistent relationship which may have existed between them. It was advisable, therefore, to try to discover the connection between the movement of disturbances and the movement of successful and unsuccessful wars.

Such a study, however, proved very difficult. Many disturbances have been of a purely local nature, small in magnitude and somewhat undefined as to the exact time and duration of their occurrence. Many disturbances by peasants and workers have been a kind of unrest or milling around spread over a number of years, with only occasional outbursts here and there. Then there were several "palace revolutions" involving only a small faction without any active participation by the masses.

Finally, wars are often indefinite in result, without victor or vanquished. All this makes a comparison of all wars listed with disturbances impracticable and incapable of yielding definite results.

In view of this fact, another procedure seemed advisable, namely, to take only the biggest wars and biggest revolutions during recent centuries, for which data are comparatively accurate. However, even this method is not irreproachable; some of the biggest disturbances happened in time of war, and quite an insignificant war, while some of the biggest wars were synchronous with disturbances of a purely local character and insignificant magnitude. Even in the few cases when a defeat in war seemed to have been followed by a big disturbance, some specific circumstance, like the death of the king, occurred at the same time, making it impossible to decide whether the unsuccessful war or the death of the ruler was the really important factor in causing the disturbance. And there are dozens of such "obscuring" circumstances. All this material should be kept in mind.

There follow the approximate results of a study of several samples from several countries. In Russia since 1600 there have been 14 great disturbances. Of these 14, 4 occurred during or immediately after big and unsuccessful wars, 6 in a period of peace, and 1 during a successful war. Three others occurred in somewhat indefinite circumstances.

Thus the relationship is quite indefinite. If, on the other hand, we take the biggest wars for the same period, the results are about the same. Some of these big wars continued for a number of years, like the Napoleonic Wars, or the northern wars of Peter the Great. For a number of years they were unsuccessful, and for a number, successful; but in neither phase were they followed by any disturbance of importance. In the unsuccessful Crimean War of 1853–1856 there was only one, relatively very small, disturbance, in 1854–1855, among the soldiers. Another unsuccessful war, the Russo-Japanese, 1904–1905, was followed by a great revolution. The World War, 1914–1917, was followed by a great revolution. In brief, the results of the study are very indefinite.

The history of France from 1600 on gives similar results. From 1600 to 1925 we find 13 great disturbances. Seven of these 13 occurred in peaceful times when, except for two quite insignificant colonial expeditions, no war was going on. Among the 7 great disturbances were those of 1830 and 1848; 3 big disturbances definitely happened during or immediately after unsuccessful wars. The remaining 3 occurred in somewhat indefinite circumstances, during wartime, but when success or defeat was somewhat uncertain. When, on the other hand, we take all the big wars from 1600 to 1925, we find at least 25 wars of comparatively large magnitude. During 17 of these, at least, not less than 5 being unsuccessful, none of the great internal conflicts above mentioned occurred, either while hostilities continued or immediately after the close of the campaign. During each of the remaining 8 wars a big disturbance occurred, 4 of these disturbances being losing wars, 1 successful, and the remaining 3 only partially successful or of indefinite outcome.

These results seem to corroborate all the previous ones. Two other samples from two other countries lead to similar conclusions. On the basis of all these data, one must say that, *contrary to expectation, the data do not definitely show a positive association between unsuccessful wars and big disturbances nor between victorious wars and the absence of such. At best they yield only a very slight association between unsuccessful wars and disturbances.* As a study of the presence or absence of association between war in general and disturbances did not disclose any close uniform relationship between these, one has to conclude, at least until more refined analysis makes the question clear, *that the two processes proceed fairly independently of each other and that no direct nor quite tangible interdependence is shown.*

This means that the widely held opinion that there is a close dependence between these processes, and especially between unsuccessful wars and disturbances, needs some limitations, reservations, and toning down. The mere occurrence of an unsuccessful war as such is not sufficient to produce an important disturbance, if the country is not disorganized, mentally and morally, or otherwise. On the contrary, as has happened several times — to the Romans in the Punic Wars, the Russians in the "Fatherland War" with Napoleon, and to Belgium when invaded by the Germans — defeat, great danger, and privations, instead of demoralizing and disorganizing the invaded and defeated country, may make it strong as iron. Instead of an explosion of internal disturbances being caused by such conditions, these latter may decrease or entirely disappear. Only in a country with weak "nerves" and discipline and little solidarity may disturbances be started by successful or by unsuccessful wars or without any war whatsoever, by almost any incident or insignificant event.

Taking all this into consideration, it is clear that war, as such, no matter whether successful or not, is neither a necessary nor a sufficient condition for starting or reinforcing internal disturbances. Conversely, an important internal disturbance is neither necessary to start a war nor sufficient to start or greatly to increase one.

Data from various other countries studied corroborate this hypothesis. In Greece, for instance, the curves of war and disturbances are parallel for several periods, reach their maximum in the same centuries, the fourth and fifth, and then decline; but in Rome the direction of movement of one curve for several centuries is practically opposite to that of the other; the third century B.C. has the highest indicator of war and the lowest indicator of disturbances, while the first century A.D. has the lowest indicator of war and one of the highest of internal disturbances; a similar relationship is found in several other periods. Data for other countries also show the same contrast in the movement of the two curves, parallel during some periods, moving in opposite directions in others, and similarly with the total indicators of both processes, for all the European countries studied, as we have seen. So much for the direct relationship of the two processes to each other. *As we shall see, they are related to each other, but only in the identity of the main factor — the transition factor — that causes both processes.* But from the identity of their main cause, it docs not follow that they must be either synchronous or must be the direct cause of each other.

L. We must touch upon the problem already discussed when we traced the movement of the curve of the magnitude of war in relation to the periods of blossoming and decay in the history of the countries studied. Do internal disturbances tend to increase regularly in periods of bloom and well-being or of decay, or do they occur erratically, regardless of these periods? Taking the indicators of disturbances by centuries, the results can be summed up as follows.

In Greece the disturbances reached their peak mainly in the fifth and fourth centuries B.C., when the power, culture, and social life of Greece were at their summit. In Rome the peak of the disturbances occurred in the first century B.C., the second highest point in the third century A.D., and the third and fourth highest in the fourth and first centuries A.D. If the two centuries just before and after the birth of Christ can be regarded as the summit of Roman power and culture, these had already begun to decline by the third and fourth centuries A.D. On the other hand, the curve of disturbances is low in the fifth century A.D. and the third and fourth B.C., the fourth and third centuries B.C. being the periods of most vigorous growth, the fifth A.D. decidedly one of decline.

The data on Byzantium are likewise inconsistent. On the one hand resplendent periods of prosperity, when culture was at its height, have a low indicator of disturbances. Such are the "Golden Age" of the sixth century, especially the time of Justinian (527–565), and the period extending, roughly, from the beginning of the Macedonian dynasty in 867 to the end of the tenth century. On the other hand, centuries of decline like the thirteenth and, to some extent, the twelfth, have also low indicators, the thirteenth even much lower than the more flourishing tenth century. Then we find the highest indicators of disturbances in the seventh and eighth centuries, which were disastrous and agonizing, in spite of the activities and reforms of such rulers as Leo the Isaurian (717–741), and in the tenth, which all in all seems to have been a healthy and prosperous period. This means that here again we find no uniform and consistent relation between periods of decline and a decrease in disturbance.

We must conclude that *in periods either of blossoming or of decline, disturbances have sometimes increased in number and have sometimes decreased.*

If this conclusion is valid, there must be various kinds of disturbances. Some seem to be like the tensions of childbearing and of healthy growth, which are often associated with pain and with internal disturbances of the organism. Others are disturbances of illness or of senility. The former occur when the growth of the social group, the nation, is sound and rapid. The growing vital forces cannot be contained in the old network of social relations, and therefore disturb or disrupt it here and there.

Disturbances during social decline and disorganization result from the waning of the vital and creative forces of a given society or from some extraordinarily unfortunate combination of external circumstances, which makes an orderly life impossible for the group. Such disturbances are attempts, mostly blind and desperate, to "do something" to get rid of impossible conditions; and so occur during periods of decline and decay. A more detailed study of many great revolutions indicates that not all, nor perhaps even most, but at least many of them, occurred in just such periods of disorganization and decline.

M. Does the fact that disturbances occur in both periods really mean that no "uniformity" can be found in that "diversity"? Is it not possible to find in that diversity — almost opposition — of periods of bloom and decline something which belongs to both periods and in which both are similar? If so, might not this be the common factor "producing" disturbances in both periods?

With this idea in mind let us glance more attentively at the indicators, by centuries, of disturbances — first at the indicators for all the European countries studied and then at the indicators for separate countries. We find the following interesting phenomena. For the sixth and seventh centuries indicators are low (446.20 and 458.19). For the eighth century the indicator is very high (733.98); in the ninth, tenth, and eleventh centuries there is a considerable drop (589.65, 537.43, and 693.90 respectively); and it rises considerably in the twelfth century and reaches the highest points in the thirteenth and fourteenth centuries (882.90 and 827.00), followed by a decline in the fifteenth (748.38), during which century the curve is still high but notably lower than before; then they greatly decline in the sixteenth (509.56) and stay low in the seventeenth (605.50) and the eighteenth, when up to the last quarter of the eighteenth they give the lowest point (415.56). The curve then begins to rise and jumps greatly in the nineteenth century (766.91). Notwithstanding a temporary sharp decline in the last quarter of the nineteenth century, it flares up in the first half of the twentieth. Thus we have *three main peaks; in the eighth, in the thirteenth and fourteenth centuries, and in the nineteenth and twentieth. After each peak the wave of disturbances subsides and remains low till the next peak.*

Have these facts a meaning, and can an interpretation be found to fit them that will be satisfactory from a logical standpoint also? The answer is given by the whole character of this work, namely, all three peak periods are the periods of transition, either in the whole culture of Europe and in its system of social relationships, or in the system of social relationships only. We know already that the thirteenth and fourteenth centuries were those of the greatest transition of European culture and society from the Ideational to the Sensate form and from the feudal to the modern system of social relationships (from predominantly familistic to coercive-contractual; from theocracy to the secular regime, from Ideational freedom to Sensate; from the feudal regime to the national monarchies, and so on).

In all these respects, these centuries were the greatest turning point in all European history; with the greatest breakdown of the system of social values and of social relationships. Therefore the curve of the disturbances reaches the highest point during these centuries. They would be expected logically to be centuries of disturbances, and they were such in fact. The hypothesis of transition, with its breakdown of the system of values and relationships, as set forth in the preceding part in regard to war movement, accounts for this peak.

Can it account for the peaks of the eighth and the nineteenth and twentieth centuries? As for the nineteenth and especially the twentieth century, it accounts for it easily; we have seen that the twentieth century is transitional in all the compartments of European culture. As for the end of the eighteenth and the first part of the nineteenth century (which is responsible for the comparatively high indicator for the nineteenth century), we know also that this was the period of the "liquidation of the postmedieval relationships" in the system of social organization, and especially the period of transition from the predominantly compulsory to the predominantly contractual relationships. This shift was accomplished roughly in the period opened by the French Revolution in 1789 and the first few decades of the nineteenth century. Such a transition from one fundamental type of social relationship to another had to call forth, according to the hypothesis, a rise of the curve of disturbances; and this curve did indeed rise. Beginning roughly with the second part of the nineteenth century, Europe settled definitely into the comfortable new contractual house, and the fever of disturbances subsided. But toward the twentieth century, Sensate culture itself began to show signs of disintegration, and with it the contractual system of social relationships was disturbed. Both entered the sharp stage of transition. Hence the rapid rise of the curve in the twentieth century.

Finally, as to the eighth-century peak, it also agrees with the hypothesis. It was the period of the so-called Carolingian Renaissance. If it did not mean a fundamental change in the culture, which remained Ideational before and after it, it accomplished nevertheless some important modifications in it. Its transitional character was, however, mainly in the system of social relationships; in the forms of social, economic, and political organization or reorganization; and in this field it was a genuinely transitional period. As such, it had to give rise to disturbances; and it certainly did.

Thus all the three main peaks seem to be well accounted for by the hypothesis of transition. The same hypothesis accounts for the comparatively low level of disturbances in the other centuries: from the ninth to the twelfth; from the fifteenth to the eighteenth inclusive (except its last decade); and from the second part of the nineteenth to the beginning of the twentieth century. These were the settled periods in the type of dominant culture, as well as in that of the system of social relationships. Even a slight rise of the curve in the seventeenth century is accountable from this standpoint; it was the last stand of the Ideational culture and its satellites to regain its dominance. The effort failed, and the question was definitely settled.

Thus the hypothesis of the transition accounts for these tidal waves of disturbances. It means that, *other conditions being equal, during the periods when the existing culture, or the system of social relationships, or both, undergo a rapid transformation, the internal disturbances in the respective societies increase; when they are strong and crystallized, the internal disturbances tend to decrease and stay at a low level.* This proposition is but a different version of the statement regarding the main factor of war and peace given in a preceding chapter.

We have seen that disturbances occur in periods of bloom and of decline, in periods of prosperity and of poverty, and in periods when society moves upward with particular rapidity and during the phase of its rapid downward movement.

This "inconsistency" is quite consistent in the light of the above hypothesis. Indeed, the established social order and cultural system may be, and is, as easily unsettled in periods of rapid enrichment, vigorous blossoming, as in periods of catastrophe and decline.

Whatever factors lead to a rise and decline of each main form of culture and system of social relationship (and in passing I may say that the main factors calling forth change are "immanent" or "inherent" in cultural and social life itself, and that these factors in the course of time will bring any sociocultural order to confusion), *the main and the indispensable condition for an eruption of internal disturbances is that the social system or the cultural system or both shall be unsettled.* This datum seems to fit the facts much better than most of the popular theories. These theories, that ascribe internal disturbances either to growing poverty and "hard material conditions" or, on the contrary, to material progress, and that correlate them either with periods of decay or with periods of bloom, are sharply contradicted by relevant facts as well as by the bulk of the indicators. However hard living conditions may be in a given society, if the framework of its relationships and values is unshattered, no disturbances will be forthcoming. The members of such a society may be dying of starvation and yet not revolt; or, anyhow, make fewer attempts to revolt than members of a perfectly comfortable society in which the sociocultural system of values is loose. If one can imagine a society where everyone has the standard of living of a millionaire but sociocultural relationships are not crystallized and the main values are not compatible, such a society would be more turbulent and disorderly than one where even the main physiological needs are barely satisfied but where the sociocultural framework is strong and definite and the members of the society believe in the same values and live by them.

This hypothesis not only explains the movement of the indicators for the countries taken together, but also explains many of the ups and downs of the indicators for separate countries.

The reader may test its validity by indicators of disturbances and by the historical data on the conditions of the network of sociocultural values and relationships. *It is not my contention that the factor stressed explains all the ups and downs in the curves of disturbances.* But I do claim that the factor of the status of the sociocultural network of relationships and values is enough in itself to "explain" the main "ups and downs" of the curves in all the societies studied.

N. In view of all this it is easier to understand the facts emphasized in the previous chapters. Let us recall them.

The first is that inner tensions and disturbances seem to be phenomena inseparably connected with the existence and functioning of social bodies. These are no less "natural" and "common" than storms in ordinary weather conditions.

Second, disturbances occur much oftener than is usually realized. Only rarely does it happen that two or three decades in the life history of a vast social body pass without them. On the average of from four to seven years, as a rule, one considerable social disturbance may be expected. This fact confirms our conclusions that they are inseparable from the very existence and functioning of social bodies.

Their "causes" are as deep in social life as the "causes" of internal peace. A set of special conditions, like a poor government, a selfish aristocracy, stupid mob-mindedness, poverty and war, may play a secondary role in reinforcing or weakening, accelerating or retarding, disturbances, but these are only secondary factors. Even without them, disturbances, like storms, would frequently occur. They have occurred under stupid and under wise governments, under conditions of war and of peace, in monarchies and republics, in democracies and aristocracies, in prosperity and poverty, in ages of "enlightenment" and of "ignorance," in urbanized and industrial as well as in rural and nonindustrialized countries; and in other most diverse circumstances. To continue, therefore, to look upon them as something exceptional, abnormal, accidental, and incidental to social life itself is no more scientific than to look at indispositions, sicknesses, painful experiences, as incidental.

In stressing these facts before, I have indicated that they suggest that we must look far deeper for the "causes" of disturbances than is usually done. Now we have the deep, the inherent, causes before us. Since the main cause of these is the status of the sociocultural framework of relationships and of values, and since sooner or later, on account of immanent change inherent in any sociocultural system, such a system is bound to be unsettled, "withered," and broken, the sociocultural order of every society is bound to have periods of transition and with them rising tides of disturbances. On the other hand, any new system, if only it survives, will surely become crystallized and settled. This means that any society will also have periods when the wave of disturbances subsides, and hence the similarity of all societies in these respects, and the similarity of all the societies studied in the frequency and the magnitude of disturbances.

O. Another important problem in the field of internal disturbances, as of any other important social process, is to *what extent the direction, and particularly the quantitative direction, of the process is the same in various countries of the same "cultural continent" during the same period.* In other words, do disturbances, for instance, increase simultaneously in all the countries, or in several of these, or do they increase in some while decreasing in others? The answer, in the field studied, is given by the above figures.

All this means that the forces generating disturbances rarely, if ever, work in one country only. For good or bad, they seem to work in the areas of several countries simultaneously. Disturbances started in one country usually spread over or are independently originated in several others. So it was in the past and so it is in the present.

PART EIGHT

CULTURE, PERSONALITY AND CONDUCT

36

RELATIONSHIP BETWEEN TYPES OF CULTURE AND TYPES OF PERSONALITY AND BEHAVIOR

I. Preliminaries

That the dominant type of culture molds the type of mentality of human beings who are born and live in it, we conclude at once from the evidence of the preceding chapters. The scientific, philosophical, religious, aesthetic, moral, juridical, and other opinions, theories, beliefs, tastes, and convictions — in brief, the whole *Weltanschauung* — of human beings in an Ideational society are shaped to the Ideational pattern, while those of the persons living under the dominance of a Sensate culture are formed by the Sensate mold. Only those who have their physical being in the realm of a given culture, but are neither a part of it, nor come in psychosocial contact with it — only such persons and groups can escape this conditioning of their mentality by the culture of the physical space in which they live. With these exceptions, therefore, the mentality of every person is a microcosm that reflects the cultural microcosm of his social surroundings. This may be stated more specifically in the following fashion.

Other conditions being equal, (1) the mentality of a person will be clearly Ideational if he has had a contact only with the pure Ideational culture. The same is true with regard to the Sensate culture. (2) The mentality of a person will be Mixed if he has been in contact with different types of culture. The mixture will represent a combination of the elements of the various cultures involved. (3) The mentality of a person will be unintegrated, for instance, pseudo-Ideational, if he has been associated with only an unintegrated culture, or with a multitude of different cultures of contradictory character. An exception to the rule is provided by the comparatively rare case where a synthesis is achieved of various elements of different cultures in one integrated unity. The Idealistic culture is an example of this.

It is quite another matter with the problem of the *relationship between the dominant type of culture and the actual behavior or conduct* of the persons who are a part of it. The difference between the two problems is clear. To repeat Ribot, a person may know perfectly well Kant's *Critique of Practical Reason*, and may enthusiastically write a most scholarly commentary on it, and yet in his actions and behavior be at great variance with it and with his own mentality in this field. A man may agree with and extol the Christian principle of loving one's neighbor as oneself, and yet in his actual behavior be the most egotistic of individuals. Who does not know the type of persons who preach sincerely the virtues of honesty, altruism, chastity, moderation in drinking and eating, and so on, and who in their behavior quite frequently transgress in these respects? Still better known is the type of hypocrites whose speech reactions and actions are normally in contradiction. Similarly, we are quite familiar with our everyday practice of beautifying our often prosaic, selfish, even ugly actions by means of high-sounding, noble-appearing "motivations," "rationalizations," and "derivations." When a lion devours a lamb, he does not tell us that he does it for the sake of God, humanity, the proletariat, the nation, communism, fascism, international welfare, and so on. Among human beings it is not an infrequent occurrence that the worst actions, whether wholesale murder, or rape, or torture, or robbery (by criminals, by revolutionaries, by the powerful rich, and others), regularly find noble and often quite sincere justification on the part of their perpetrators. I stress the fact that such "beautification" is often quite sincere.

All this means that in contradistinction to the close connection between the dominant type of culture and mentality, the relationship between the dominant type of culture and conduct or behavior is likely to be loose, even perhaps imperceptible. Hence the necessity of a special study of this problem.

II. Main Propositions

A. *First Proposition. The relationship between the two variables — the character of the dominant culture and the character of the conduct of the persons that live in it — either cannot be very close or cannot be as close as the correlation between the dominant culture and the mentality of these persons.*

However different from each other are the Ideational and Sensate cultures, the societies that are the bearers of such cultures have of necessity a general fund of similar activities. This fund is composed in the first place of all those *acts necessary for the satisfaction of the elementary biological needs.* The members of the Ideational and Sensate societies must eat, drink, have shelter, sleep, work, reproduce their kind, defend themselves against agencies and forces menacing their existence, and so on. Though the extent to which these biological needs are satisfied and the forms which satisfaction takes may widely differ in such societies, there is a common minimum for all societies, whether Sensate or Ideational. *The existence of such a minimum lessens the contrast in behavior between the members of an Ideational and those of a Sensate culture. And the decrease in contrast points to diminution of the closeness of the relationship between culture and mentality.* This is the central reason for the hypothesis stated in the first proposition.

If this proposition be developed fully (and it is not the purpose of the present chapter to do so), it will explain why even in the conspicuously Ideational societies (say, in ascetic monasteries) the activities of their members are far from being entirely otherworldly; why they take the Sensate reality much more seriously in their behavior than in their mentality; why they satisfy many of their biological needs — say hunger or sex — much more fully than they profess to do; why so often they "sin" and fall victim to the "flesh"; why hypocrisy or cynical adaptation is so frequently met with among even the most Ideational of societies; why the discrepancy between ideologies and acts is such a common phenomenon; why "rationalization" and ennoblement, through "derivations" and ideologies of cruel, sometimes bestial, acts are a perennial trait of all societies; why crime, revolution, egotism, avidity, lust, and so on, are present, to some extent, in the Ideational as well as the Sensate groups. In spite of inhibitory cultural forces, the pressure of elementary biological needs is never reduced to zero.

All this explains why the relationship between the dominant culture and conduct cannot be very close; why in the field of conduct the difference between the members of the Ideational and Sensate societies is much less than in the field of culture mentality.

B. *Second Proposition.* If we should stop at this hypothesis, as many do, we should commit a great blunder. Having emphasized the fact that the relationship between culture and conduct is not always close, we are yet not entitled to conclude that there is no observable relationship whatever. The first proposition must, therefore, be supplemented by a second. It may be formulated thus: *Though the relationship between the dominant culture and the behavior of its bearers is not always close, nevertheless, it does exist. In application to the various types of culture, this means that the bearers of the Ideational and Sensate cultures differ from one another not only in their mentality (ideas, opinions, convictions, beliefs, tastes, moral and aesthetic standards, etc.) but also in their behavior and personality. All in all, the conduct of the Ideational man would be more Ideational than that of the Sensate man, and vice versa. Similarly the personality — understood here to mean the total mentality plus conduct of an individual — of the Ideationalist is also more Ideational than the personality of the member of a Sensate culture. The difference between the bearers of the Ideational and Sensate cultures is less great with respect to conduct and personality than to mentality; nevertheless, the difference exists and is quite readily perceptible.*

This second proposition follows, first of all, from the fact that there is hardly any clear-cut boundary line between mentality and behavior. They imperceptibly merge into each other, and many phenomena of mentality are at the same time phenomena of conduct and behavior, and vice versa. All the main compartments of culture mentality which have been analyzed previously in the present work — arts; systems of truth (science, philosophy, religion), moral systems, systems of law; forms of political, social, and economic organizations; and so on — are not only the phenomena of mentality, but also the phenomena of behavior in the most overt, "behavioristic" sense. Their creation and their existence and functioning in any culture presupposes an incessant stream of actions and reactions — that is, of behavior — on the part of the members of the culture. The creation of the Parthenon or the Chartres Cathedral involved the capital and labor (in the sense of the wealth and actions) of thousands of persons for a notable length of time. The creation and continuation of the activities of any institution, whether the Roman Catholic See; theater, law court, or moral sect; scientific, philosophical, religious, artistic, ethical, political, juridical, economic, or other social body, organization, or system — the creation, the existence, and the functioning of any of these are carried on through an incessant activity, *i.e.*, through the behavior, in the most overt sense of this term, of a few or of many human individuals. *Since, as we have seen, these activities assume one form in an Ideational and a quite different form in a Sensate society with respect to all the sociocultural compartments, this means that a very large part of the conduct and behavior of the members of an Ideational culture assumes Ideational forms, while those of the members of a Sensate society take on Sensate forms.* It is not a phenomenon of mentality only but of behavior also, that members of medieval society build a cathedral, whereas members of another society build Radio City; that A leaves his property to a monastery, B to a university, and C to a society of atheists; that Phidias creates the statue of Athena, an unknown artist the statue of Christ the Good, and Rodin or Canova molds a statue of Sensual Love. Likewise, it is not only mentality but also a long and complicated chain of overt actions that is embodied in preaching the New Testament or the gospel of communism. And so with all other phenomena of culture mentality. To the extent that this work has shown that Ideational, Idealistic, Mixed, and Sensate cultures have their own forms of mentality in all the main fields of sociocultural relationships; to the extent that any phenomenon of this culture mentality is at the same time a phenomenon of overt behavior — to these limits *the conduct and behavior of the members of any such culture is conditioned by it, and stands in a consistent and clear association with it.* These considerations are so self-evident that there is hardly any need to develop the argument further.

Placed on its inferences, this conclusion means (1) that the *forms* or *patterns* of almost all the overt actions and reactions (or conduct and behavior) of the members of each dominant type of culture are shaped and conditioned by it; (2) that each culture, to some extent, stimulates many activities and inhibits many others in conformity with its nature; (3) that only the actions and reactions that are most closely related to the elementary biological needs experience, in conformity with our first proposition, a comparatively mild conditioning by the dominant culture, *so far as the performance or nonperformance, the frequency, and the intensity of their satisfaction are concerned.* The forms in which these activities are discharged are also conditioned by the dominant culture: for instance, the forms of marriage, the forms of property, the forms of securing elementary safety.

If the second proposition is valid, then it follows that (*a*) in Ideational societies and periods the desire to satisfy biological needs and the level — the frequency, intensity, and in part, extensity — of their satisfaction, necessarily tend to be less high than in a predominantly Sensate society, the Idealistic and Mixed societies occupying an intermediate position. The chapter on the fluctuation of economic conditions further supports this inference clearly. Though the relationship between the type of culture and the level of economic conditions has been found to be not very close, nevertheless it is reasonably clear and perceptible; (*b*) if the second proposition is valid, then in Ideational societies and periods we must expect to find a higher proportion of personalities of the Ideational type, and this type must be more pronounced qualitatively than in the predominantly Sensate periods. And vice versa. The proportion of the Sensate type of personality, with an unbridled desire for the satisfaction of the biological impulses, should be higher in the Sensate society than in the Ideational and Idealistic.

Thus our two major propositions mean that not only are the *forms and stimulation and inhibition* of certain actions and reactions conditioned by the type of culture, but also the activities closely related to the satisfaction of the elementary biological needs.

A complete verification of inference (2) is impossible for evident reasons: history does not record to what extent and how frequently and greedily all the members of a given society satisfied their biological needs, how strong were their lusts of the flesh, how sensual, ascetic, or balanced they were in eating, drinking, and the like.

On the other hand, a rough approximation to such verification may be attempted. Suppose we take the *totality* of the historical personalities of a given period in a given society and compare them with the *totality* of historical personalities in the same society at other periods. This totality at each period is the integrator and the bearer of the dominant culture. The very fact that the individual became a person of historical significance means that he was deeply involved in the culture of his time and place. The fact that we take the totality of the historical individuals for each period, of all who have left traces in the annals of history, no matter in which compartment of culture their activity lay — in science, philosophy, religion, art, law, ethics; in social, political, economic, or other fields — makes the group "representative." It is more representative than the group chosen from only one profession or field of cultural activity.

If we do not know just how sensual many historical figures were and whether their behavior was nearer to the Ideational or the Sensate type, in regard to many others we can be reasonably certain of their type of conduct. Nobody would contend that Alexander Borgia, or Louis XIV, or Julius Caesar, or Napoleon, or Catherine the Great were ascetic, nonsensual, or Ideational in their conduct and personality. Likewise, nobody would place in the Sensate class St. Francis of Assisi, or Pachomius the Great, or Diogenes the Cynic, or such popes as Gregory I and St. Celestine. Similarly, no historian would place Plato, or Aristotle, or Dante, or Queen Victoria in any class but the Mixed. In spite of all the uncertainties, the profile of some figures is conspicuously Sensate, of others Ideational, and of others Mixed.

If, therefore, we put all such pronounced types into the Ideational or Sensate class, and place in the Mixed class all those whose behavior does not belong conspicuously with either of the extremes; if, next, we compute the percentage of each type in the totality of the historical personalities of each period, we shall then have some very rough data as to the frequency, increase, and decrease of each type in the various cultures under comparison. Since the number of persons involved in each of the periods is rather large, the few errors of classification that may be made by investigators are not very important: a few misplaced personalities do not change appreciably the total result for each period or for all the periods compared.

I shall now present three sets of data aimed at the verification of our hypothesis of the correlation of behavior personality with cultural types.

First, the indicators of the type of personality of *all the historical figures*, for each period compared, in all fields of culture in the societies of Greece, Rome, and Western Europe, as they are mentioned in the *Encyclopaedia Britannica*. The group thus involves the totality of the personalities in the annals of each period so far as the *Encyclopaedia* represents them. This certainly embraces the overwhelming majority of the names known to history.

Second, the indicators of the type of personality of the Roman Catholic popes from the earliest to the present time. When the leaders of the same great social organization, such as the Christian Church or one of the Western empires, are compared in various periods, the fluctuation of the frequency of the Ideational and Sensate types thus disclosed may have high symptomatic value.

Third, the apportionment of the historical figures of each period among the main compartments of culture (*i.e.*, religion, science, philosophy, art, business, politics, etc.). Suppose that for a certain century in Greece 80 per cent of all the known historical persons are engaged in religious activities, and none in business; suppose further that for the following century persons in the field of religious activities compose only 25 per cent of the total, and the percentage of those in business is 30. Such a change in the course of two centuries is fairly reasonable evidence of a change in the conduct and activity of the entire body of social and cultural leaders during these times, not merely of a few individual figures.

Let us now turn to the first set of data, that is, to those which roughly show the fluctuation of the proportion of Ideational, Sensate, and Mixed (the unknown being put into the class of the Mixed) types among the totality of historical figures. I take these data from Mr. John V. Boldyreff's doctoral thesis. A few explanatory notes are necessary before Table 51 is given. First, Mr. Boldyreff recorded all the persons for each period that are mentioned in the ninth edition of the *Encyclopaedia Britannica*. Next he computed the number of the lines devoted to each person, as a rough indicator of his influence. Each was then "diagnosed" on the basis of the characterization given in the *Encyclopaedia* itself and other historical sources, and put into the Sensate, Ideational, or Mixed class of personalities, according as his Sensate needs were maximal (Sensateness) and his efforts great to satisfy them by the transformation of the external *milieu* (energy), or his needs minimal and his chief energies devoted to non-Sensate and otherworldly values, or his needs and efforts intermediate to those of the other two both quantitatively and in their nature. Then the geometric averages for the total number of persons and lines of each type, for each period, were computed. The sum of the geometric averages for all three types of personalities for each period was then taken to be 100 per cent, and from this basis the percentage of each type for each period was computed. Table 51 gives the absolute figures for the geometric averages as well as the percentages.

From these figures we may draw several important observations. First, within every fifty-year period (with five exceptions, which are undoubtedly to be explained as the result of lack of data) all the three types of personality and conduct are to be found coexisting side by side. There is only one period in the Graeco-Roman and Western societies when all the historical personalities were either Ideational, or Sensate, or Mixed. Second, all in all, when conduct and personality are considered, the Ideational type is less frequent than the Sensate or Mixed. This is comprehensible because, as has been mentioned several times in this work, the Ideational ways of behavior are more difficult to follow than the Sensate

TABLE 51. GEOMETRIC AVERAGES FOR TYPES OF HISTORICAL PERSONS FROM 950 B.C. TO A.D. 1849 INCLUDED IN ENCYCLOPAEDIA BRITANNICA

PERIOD	*Ideational*		*Mixed*		*Sensate*	
	Number	*Per Cent*	*Number*	*Per Cent*	*Number*	*Per Cent*
950–901 B.C.	0	0	0	0	17.9	100
900–851	13.7	12	0	0	102.7	88
850–801	0	0	18.0	100	0	0
800–751	21.6	53	0	0	19.2	47
750–701	53.4	76	11.8	17	5.2	7
700–651	9.8	34	11.1	38	7.9	28
650–601	21.5	22	35.6	37	38.6	41
600–551	69.6	38	61.0	34	50.7	28
550–501	120.4	40	67.5	22	114.2	38
500–451	124.6	37	107.6	33	100.9	30
450–401	68.6	11	228.9	38	306.2	51
400–351	79.6	13	326.0	56	180.7	31
350–301	43.2	7	279.9	45	290.1	48
300–251	33.1	12	192.1	70	59.7	18
250–201	12.6	5	85.3	35	148.1	60
200–151	12.5	5	96.3	39	145.1	56
150–101	0	0	43.6	45	51.8	55
100–51	16.9	4	112.4	24	333.8	72
50–1	69.4	11	224.2	35	339.1	54
0–49 A.D.	179.9	31	119.3	21	272.9	48
50–99	46.0	9	219.2	43	240.7	48
100–149	100.0	26	208.4	55	72.0	19
150–199	23.7	7	238.4	76	54.7	17
200–249	121.5	43	133.5	47	29.8	10
250–299	102.7	56	32.8	18	46.9	26
300–349	78.0	23	126.2	37	139.0	40
350–399	204.7	40	190.2	38	111.7	32
400–449	80.4	22	165.2	45	123.7	33
450–499	22.8	11	113.4	52	80.4	37
500–549	77.9	28	84.6	30	115.9	42
550–599	45.6	30	58.6	39	48.0	31
600–649	58.5	40	45.2	31	42.2	29
650–699	29.6	45	19.0	29	17.2	26
700–749	43.1	44	15.3	16	38.7	40
750–799	33.8	48	12.6	18	23.6	34
800 849	57.0	36	74.1	47	26.3	17
850–899	91.0	37	76.6	31	76.8	32
900–949	16.8	14	51.7	42	54.5	44
950–999	18.1	10	75.6	42	87.2	48
1000–1049	38.2	15	75.0	29	148.5	56
1050–1099	24.4	6	145.6	37	218.7	57
1100–1149	72.5	17	176.6	41	177.3	42
1150–1199	74.8	15	210.9	41	228.0	44
1200–1249	66.1	15	166.9	36	231.3	49
1250–1299	172.0	33	185.9	35	167.0	32
1300–1349	91.4	26	181.7	51	81.2	23
1350–1399	144.6	23	152.5	24	330.4	53
1400–1449	141.4	18	322.7	42	302.1	40
1450–1499	240.9	15	602.1	38	730.9	47
1500–1549	543.4	17	1037.5	33	1543.1	50
1550–1599	485.9	14	1429.7	41	1528.1	45
1600–1649	537.0	12	1861.5	42	2023.5	46
1650–1699	949.4	19	1641.8	34	2179.0	47
1700–1749	724.0	17	2014.4	44	1534.0	39
1750–1799	901.6	10	3566.6	41	4329.9	49
1800–1849	1460.0	9	7301.1	50	5870.5	41

or Mixed. They require an inhibition of the natural physical needs and desires of an organism, while the other ways are the path of least resistance even of the stimulation of these needs and desires. Third, looking now at the fluctuation of the percentages of each type from period to period, we notice that, notwithstanding the erratic movements, there are definite long-time waves of the relative rise and decline of each type: (1) The period 950 to 851 B.C. appears as dominated by the Sensate type of personality. Considering that the last stage of the Creto-Mycenaean culture appears to us as the overripe Sensate, we find this dominance in such a period to be in accordance with our hypothesis. (2) The period 850 to 801 B.C. appears transitional with respect to types of personality. This again is in agreement with the nature of the culture of the period. (3) The period 800 to 501 B.C. is marked by a notable rise in the percentage of the Ideational types. We have seen that the Greek culture of that period in all its main compartments showed itself to be predominantly Ideational. Thus, here again our hypothesis is well supported. (4) The period 550 to 451 B.C. appears as well balanced, the Ideational, Sensate, and Mixed types being in an even proportion, with a slight domination of the Ideational. This tallies with the Idealistic character of the culture of the times. (5) The period 450 B.C. to the beginning of our era shows a decisive change from the preceding age. The percentage of the Ideational type falls greatly, while those of the Sensate and Mixed types grow. The period is marked by a decisive domination of Sensate and Mixed personalities. We know that the culture of this particular period was Sensate. The agreement again is noteworthy. (6) Beginning with our era the data show a turn: during the first two centuries there is a sudden but unstable and intermittent spurt on the part of the Ideational type (31, 9, 26, 7, 43 per cent for the fifty-year periods from the year A.D. 1 to 249). This again seems to agree with the violently transitory character of this period which was turning away from the dominant Sensate to the coming Ideational culture. (7) Then, notwithstanding erratic fluctuations for a few fifty-year periods, the figures show a perceptible trend toward an increase of the percentage of the Ideational type of personalities, especially after A.D. 500 and throughout the subsequent centuries up to roughly A.D. 899. From 900 to 1199 there is a decline and then again a rise from 1200 to 1399, after which the curve assumes a steady downward trend in favor of either the Mixed or Sensate types. Even with the fall during the period from 900 to 1199, the percentage of the Ideational type is notably higher during these three centuries than during the periods of the domination of the Sensate culture, as, for example, 950 to 801 B.C. and 450 B.C. to the beginning of our era, and A.D. 1700 to 1849. This again is in agreement with our hypothesis. (8) The period from 1250 to 1849 is marked by an almost regular decline of the frequency of the Ideational type and a corresponding rise of that of the Sensate and Mixed types. The period 1750 to 1849 shows one of the lowest percentages for the Ideational type. This again is in agreement with the hypothesis. Even such a detail as a slight rise of the figure for the period 1650 to 1699 (from 12 to 19) for the Ideational type is perhaps not accidental. We know that this period was that of the Catholic Counter-Reformation and of a strong ascetic Protestantism, and we have noticed in many compartments of culture a sudden swing toward Ideationalism in these times.

Thus, the evidence is that historically there is an association between the type of dominant culture and the frequency of the type of conduct and personality. In the Ideational period the frequency of Ideational conduct and personality, among the figures of historical importance at least, is notably higher than in the period of the Sensate culture. To this extent our second proposition is supported by this empirical study made by another investigator, on the basis of such a source as the *Encyclopaedia Britannica*.

We have support in these data also for the first proposition of the present chapter, namely, that the relationship between the dominant type of culture and the behavior of its participants is far less close than that between the dominant type of culture and mentality. While in his mentality many a person of, say, an Ideational period appears to be an Ideationalist, in his conduct, so far as it concerns the biological needs and their satisfaction, he is far from Ideationalism, and belongs either to the Mixed or the Sensate type. Hence the figures in Table 51. Even in the dominantly Ideational periods, the Sensate type not only does not disappear but either composes the majority or is as widespread as the Ideational type. While in almost all our cultural curves, the Middle Ages show a complete or very strong domination of the Ideational *mentality* in the arts, systems of truth, social relationships, law, and ethics, there is only a *relative* increase for the same periods of the percentage of persons with Ideational *behavior*, and this rarely reaches even 50 per cent of the whole. The difference between the 100 per cent of Ideationalism in mentality and the 30, 40, 48 per cent of Ideationalism in personality and conduct is a rough measure of the much looser connection of the type of culture with behavior, as compared with the closeness of the connection between the type of culture and mentality.

Let us now consider the more detailed data concerning the Roman Catholic popes. Table 52 gives the comparative frequency of each type by two-hundred-year periods. Before turning to Table 52 one must realize that the nature of the position of the pope as the head of a predominantly Ideational institution, the Christian Church, requires an Ideational type of personality and precludes, except in periods of the decline of the Church and its corruption, the occupation of such a position by a notably Sensate type of personality. Therefore we must expect that the entire body of popes should exhibit the pre-eminence of the Ideational type over the Sensate. But the frequency and degree of Ideationalism (in respect to Sensate needs and adaptation-behavior) may possibly fluctuate from period to period. This is what is shown by Table 52: Roman popes, A.D. 42 to 1937 by two-hundred-year periods with cumulative value of the ratings of the popes whose pontificates were within the nearest two-hundred years, divided by the number of whole pontificates in this period.

TABLE 52. TYPES OF ROMAN CATHOLIC POPES

		CUMULATIVE VALUE		
Year	*Number of Popes*	*Sensateness*	*Energy*	*Adaptation*
42–235	18	II.ii	0.0	I.iii
236–440	26	I.vi	0.iv	I.ii
441–642	28	0.vii	0.5	0.0
643–844	29	I.ii	0.2	0.vii
845–1044	44	0.iv	0.0	0.ii
1045–1241	31	0.viii	0.8	0.0
1242–1447	28	0.v	0.4	0.0
1448–1644	28	0.0	1.0	0.3
1645–1846	19	0.iv	0.i	0.ii
1847–1937	5	0.0	0.4	0.0

Looking at the table we see that though the whole series is dominated by the Ideational personality, nevertheless, the conspicuously Ideational type (marked by II and then by I) is centered in the first centuries of the existence of the Christian Church, before its legalization, or in any case, in the period before 942. After that, with the exception of the century between 1045 and 1144, the conspicuously Ideational type disappears. Its place is taken mainly by the "neutral" or Mixed (all the periods marked by o) or by the very slightly Ideational type (the periods marked by o.i, o.ii, and so on). Some periods, like 1342–1549 and 942–1044, are characterized by the domination of a slightly Sensate type.

Thus Ideationality is centered in the first ten centuries of our era (just as in Table 51 of all the historical persons). After that it somewhat declines quantitatively and qualitatively. The greatest decline falls upon the fourteenth, the fifteenth, and the sixteenth centuries, when the Sensate type appeared most frequently and in its most extreme form. We know that these were centuries of the greatest corruption of the Roman Catholic Church and of the greatest crisis experienced by it. When, with the Counter-Reformation, it was cleaned of this corruption, and at the same time became almost exclusively a spiritual power — the secular power becoming divorced from it *de jure* and to a considerable extent *de facto* — the Mixed and slightly Ideational type of personality again became the norm for the position of the pope, though the Ideationalism now became much more moderate and subdued in nature than during the first centuries of the existence of the Christian Church.

Hence, even in this series, we find some definite correlation between the type of the dominant culture and the frequency of the type of personality.

In contradistinction to the pope's office, the occupation of the king by its nature cannot as a rule be successfully carried on by a conspicuously Ideational personality. An ascetic entirely divorced from this Sensate world would not be a good king. If anything, he might ruin the kingdom more completely than could a shrewd and profligate Sensualist. Therefore, the dominant type of royal personality can be expected to be Sensate or Mixed. We have already seen that this was historically so. But again the frequency of the fluctuation of the more or less Sensate type, or of the Mixed type of personality in this position, may show what our hypothesis postulates, namely, some relationship with the fluctuation in the dominant type of culture.

Table 53 deals by two-hundred-year periods with the kings of France, Russia, Austria, and England. The results are arrived at by dividing the cumulative values of the ratings of the kings for each period by the number of reigns during that time.

TABLE 53. TYPES OF MONARCHS

	CUMULATIVE VALUE			
	Year	*Sensateness*	*Energy*	*Adaptation*
French Kings	987–1180	0.6	0.5	0.5
	1180–1380	0.1	0.9	0.5
	1380–1589	1.4	0.8	1.4
	1589–1793	1.6	0.6	1.4
Russian Kings	1303–1506	0.1	0.7	0.4
	1506–1725	0.7	0.7	0.9
	1725–1917	1.0	0.7	0.8
Hapsburg Kings of Austria	1276–1458	0.ii	0.9	0.5
	1458–1657	0.i	0.3	0.1
	1657–1848	0.i	0.2	0.1
	1848–1922	1.5	1.0	1.0
English Kings	800–1016	0.1	0.3	0.4
	1016–1216	1.3	1.4	1.7
	1216–1413	0.0	0.2	0.1
	1413–1603	0.4	0.3	0.5
	1603–1820	0.0	0.0	0.0
	1820–1910	1.2	0.0	1.0

Finally, we turn to the fourth category of data: they concern the apportionment of historical figures among the various fields of activity at a given period. As we remarked earlier in the present chapter, it is neither accidental nor unimportant that at one time a large proportion of the historical persons becomes notable through, say, business activity, while at another time the leading group is engaged in the field of religion. If in a given society at a given period 75 per cent of the leading persons make their mark in business, while in another period 90 per cent become important through religion, these facts mean, among many other things, that in the first period the society was "business-minded," centered on economic concerns, oriented in a Sensate milieu, but that in the other period it was "religious-minded" and, if the religion was Ideational, oriented Ideationally both in the mentality and the behavior of its members. It means also that just because the society was Sensate and economical-minded, its leaders devoted their energy and brains — in other words their behavior — to an achievement of business or Sensate purposes; or that because the society was religious, the chief thought and efforts were directed along the channels of religious activity. These considerations explain why data of this fourth category bear closely upon our problem and compose an important body of evidence for its solution.

For these data I am indebted once again to Mr. Boldyreff. Mr. Boldyreff listed all the historical persons named in the *Encyclopaedia Britannica*, arranging them by fifty-year periods from the remotest times to the year 1849 and noting the number of lines of print devoted to each. This enumeration was done for the whole world as a unit, as well as for each country separately. To summarize the results for each period, the geometric average of the number of the persons involved and the number of lines of print for all of them together were computed. All the persons mentioned in the *Britannica*, taken by periods, were further divided into ten main occupational classes through which their historical importance was achieved: religion, statesmanship, literature, humanistic scholarship, science, philosophy, business, fine arts, music, miscellaneous. The geometric averages of the number of persons and lines of print in each of these ten fields of activity for each period were computed, for the whole world and for individual countries. Then the absolute figures for these geometric averages were turned into percentages, the total of the ten fields for each period being taken to represent 100 per cent. In this way Mr. Boldyreff obtained rough, but so far the vastest and possibly the best, numerical indicators of the fluctuation of the proportion of historical persons in each of these ten fields from period to period, for the whole world and for the separate countries. In Table 54 I give only the percentages for two fields, religion and business. The figures deal mainly with the fluctuations in Greece, Rome, and the Western World. I give only the percentages of the men that became important through religious and business activity, because these two fields are diametrically opposite, the one being nearest to the Ideational (religious activity), the other to the Sensate (business).

These explanations are sufficient for an understanding of what the figures in Table 54 mean.

TABLE 54. GEOMETRIC AVERAGES FOR HISTORICAL PERSONS ENGAGED IN RELIGIOUS AND BUSINESS ACTIVITY INCLUDED IN ENCYCLOPAEDIA BRITANNICA

EXPRESSED IN PERCENTAGES

Period	*Per Cent Religion*	*Per Cent Business*	*Period*	*Per Cent Religion*	*Per Cent Business*
900–851 B.C.	17.1		500–549 A.D.	20.2	
850–801			550–599	48.4	
800–751	26.0		600–649	65.0	
750–701	74.6		650–699	82.8	
700–651	33.7		700–749	48.1	
650–601	39.1		750–799	35.2	
600–551	38.3		800–849	46.0	
550–501	14.2		850–899	45.7	
500–451	9.1		900–949	44.3	
450–401	.6		950–999	26.2	
400–351	.5		1000–1049	33.0	
350–301		1.0	1050–1099	39.8	
300–251		5.5	1100–1149	34.1	.7
250–201			1150–1199	38.1	
200–151			1200–1249	28.7	
150–101	7.5	2.5	1250–1299	28.9	3.1
100–51	1.3		1300–1349	19.2	2.6
50–1	2.1		1350–1399	30.1	4.5
0–49 A.D.	46.2		1400–1449	20.7	5.1
50–99	7.5		1450–1499	14.8	6.4
100–149	38.1		1500–1549	26.0	2.6
150–199	30.2		1550–1599	18.7	2.1
200–249	54.6		1600–1649	12.0	1.7
250–299	74.5		1650–1699	18.9	1.4
300–349	58.3		1700–1749	15.0	1.8
350–399	61.6		1750–1799	5.2	3.1
400–449	54.0		1800–1849	6.5	4.8
450–499	18.1				

A glance at the figures shows at once the comparatively high percentage for religion and zero for business for the period 800 to 501 B.C. This agrees with the Ideational character of this period in all the main compartments of the Greek culture, as well as with the data concerning behavior given in this chapter. After 500 B.C. the percentage for religion rapidly declines and soon, beginning with the year 350 B.C., becomes zero, and remains so up to the period 150 to 101 B.C., when it rises again, though it remains low up to the beginning of our era. On the other hand, in the period 350 to 101 B.C. business activity for the first time (on the basis of the *Britannica*) becomes an avenue through which historical importance may be achieved. The results confirm the Sensate character of the Hellenistic culture and lend weight to our hypothesis. Beginning with our era the percentage for religion rapidly rises, reaches an extraordinarily high level in the sixth and seventh centuries B.C. (up to even 82 per cent of all the historical persons), and stays very high until 950, after which it subsides somewhat (though it still remains high) up to the year 1200; then slowly a declining trend creeps in. Beginning with the sixteenth century the percentage for religion rapidly declines and reaches a very low level for the latest period, 1750 to 1849. The movement of the business percentage proceeds in opposite fashion. After the beginning of our era it falls to zero and stays at zero until the period 1100 to 1149. Then it reappears and begins to grow, especially after 1250 to 1299. Subsequently, with some fluctuations, it steadily maintains itself, and beginning with 1650 to 1699 it continues to grow to the latest date, 1800 to 1849.

These figures display a notable agreement with the rise and decline of the waves of Ideational and Sensate culture from 800 B.C. to our time. In other words, this set of evidence — and it is rather important — supports the two propositions before us very well. If the detailed data for separate countries were set forth here, they would show that support to be even stronger.

The evidence given in this chapter, together with the data presented by the preceding chapter on economic fluctuations, and with other relevant materials throughout this whole work, all shows that not only logically but causally the dominant character of a culture and that of behavior are definitely integrated; that in an integrated Ideational or Sensate society, not only the dominant mentality becomes correspondingly Ideational or Sensate, but the actual *behavior* also becomes Ideational or Sensate, in whatever field it acts and, what is more important, even in the *field of activities closely related to the satisfaction of the urgent biological needs.* Though the integration of this latter part of behavior with the dominant type of culture is not so close as is the mentality, nevertheless it is quite perceptible and beyond question.

These conclusions mean that, in an integrated culture, the type of overt behavior of its bearers is correlated with it and the culture mentality; that the type of culture and mentality do not stay isolated from, or ineffective with regard to, overt actions or to their "residues," "prepotent reflexes," "biological drives," or "proclivities." On the contrary, they not only determine the "forms" and "patterns" of behavior but also the frequency and intensity of doing or leaving undone acts dictated by the biological needs. In this respect the conclusions strongly deviate from the popular assumptions of Sensate times that "mentality," "ideology," "derivations," and "derivatives" are either mere playthings in the hands of biological or material needs, or something which merely "beautifies," "rationalizes," or serves them, or something which, as "impotent illusion," stays apart from them, neither being influenced by nor influencing them. Since we find that the overt behavior is definitely integrated with the dominant type of culture, such conclusions — especially as that the ideology (culture mentality) and action behavior are independent of one another — become fallacious. In integrated cultures both behavior and mentality become parts of one integrated system. The integration is not perfect, but it is tangible.

This means, to go a step further, that human behavior in the integrated culture is not completely — even not in its greater part — illogical, or nonlogical, or alogical, as again many have asserted. The fact of its association with the culture is evidence of its logicality and its consistency with the major premises of one particular culture mentality in which it exists.

Finally, the conclusions we have reached mean that there are indeed Ideational, Sensate, Idealistic, and Mixed (including the unintegrated) forms of behavior and types of personality, and that each type occurs most often in, respectively, the Ideational, Sensate, Idealistic, or Mixed society.

This chapter completes the major task which I set for myself at the beginning of this work. Having shown that the key principles of this study do indeed apply to the field of culture mentality, bringing order and meaning to a chaos of traits, events, objects, I then demonstrated that these same principles bring similar order and significance to the welter of fragments and details in the field of human action and reaction, that is, in the field of behavior.

The groundwork is done and the frame erected. From now on in the final part of this work I can employ my chief effort and whatever materials are available to completing, strengthening, and finishing the structure the foundations of which are laid in the preceding chapters. Before passing to the final part, it is advisable to diagnose the present state of Western culture and society, on the basis of the symptomatic facts given in the above analysis of all compartments of the Western sociocultural world.

37

THE CRISIS OF OUR AGE

The organism of the Western society and culture seems to be undergoing one of the deepest and most significant crises of its life. The crisis is far greater than the ordinary; its depth is unfathomable, its end not yet in sight, and the whole of the Western society is involved in it. It is the crisis of a Sensate culture, now in its overripe stage, the culture that has dominated the Western World during the last five centuries. It is also the crisis of a contractual (capitalistic) society associated with it. In this sense we are experiencing one of the sharpest turns in the historical road, a turn as great as any of the other few made by the Graeco-Roman and Western cultures in passing from Ideational to Sensate, and from Sensate to Ideational, phases.

The diagnosis of the crisis of our age which is given in this chapter was written in 1934. Gigantic catastrophies that have occurred since that year are not included here; however, they strikingly confirm and develop the diagnosis.

We have seen during the course of the present work quite definite signs of such a turn. Not a single compartment of our culture, or of the mind of contemporary man, shows itself to be free from the unmistakable symptoms. We have observed, also, that these signs, this "handwriting on the wall," are particularly clear as we approach the end of the nineteenth and advance into the twentieth century. The curves of painting, sculpture, music, and literature; of movement of discoveries and inventions; of the "First Principles" of science, philosophy, religion, ethics, and law; up to those of wars and revolutions — all make a violent turn as we approach our time. Shall we wonder, therefore, that if many do not apprehend clearly what is happening, they have at least a vague feeling that the issue is not merely that of "prosperity," or "democracy," or "capitalism," or the like, but involves the whole contemporary (Sensate) culture, society, and man? If they do not understand it by intellectual analysis, they feel sharply the painful claws of the events, whether they be kings or housewives.

Shall we wonder, also, at the endless multitude of incessant major and minor crises that have been rolling over us, like ocean waves, during recent decades? Today in one form, tomorrow in another. Now here, now there. Crises political, agricultural, commercial, and industrial! Crises of production and distribution. Crises moral, juridical, religious, scientific, and artistic. Crises of property, of the State, of the family, of industrial enterprise, of the republic and monarchy, autocracy and democracy, dictatorship and self-government, capitalism and socialism, fascism and communism, nationalism and internationalism, pacifism and militarism, conservatism and radicalism. Crises of truth, of beauty, of justice, of righteousness. Crises of the whole system of values of our culture. Each in a rich variety of forms and with varying degrees of power, but endlessly rolling, its roar reverberating in every daily newspaper. Each of the crises has battered our nerves and minds, each has shaken the very foundations of our culture and society, and each has left behind a legion of derelicts and victims. And alas! the end is not yet in view. Each of these crises has been, as it were, a movement in a great terrifying symphony, and each has been remarkable for its magnitude and intensity. Each movement has been played, during the last three decades, by enormous human orchestras, with millions of choruses, stage performers, and actors. In 1911 the four-hundred-million-piece Chinese orchestra began one of its first festivals. This still goes on, and the mountain of its contributor victims grows higher and higher from year to year.

In 1914 a new brass band of many nations with hundreds of participants started its deadening "*Marche Militaire:* 1914–1918." The effects of this performance were appalling. The stage — the soil of this planet — was soaked with blood. Most of our values were poisoned by gas; others were blown to pieces by artillery. The very foundations of our society and culture cracked. . . .

Before this festival had ended, the Russian orchestra of some 160,000,000 virtuosi set forth its own variation entitled "Communist Revolution." The first blow of its percussion instruments overthrew the social and cultural system of the old Russia. Subsequent movements have shaken the whole human world. The performance has been so brilliant that millions of onlookers have acquired a profound distaste for the old-fashioned music of the capitalist system and gone mad with the communist modernism. In Russia millions of listeners and participants have died in the process. Other millions have sunk to the bottom of human misery, and, weary and half dead, have been longing for the end of their hopeless and joyless existence. Still other millions have been thrown into the social gutters, left moaning their desperate calls for help, and finding neither response nor assistance. The festival still continues magnificently, with ever new tricks and surprises. Having saturated the soil of Russia, the red fertilizing blood began to flow across its boundary, into the soil of the onlookers of this "marvelous experiment."

Dozens of other companies — Turkey and Hungary, Austria and Germany, Bulgaria and Rumania, Spain and Portugal, Italy and Poland, Abyssinia and Manchukuo, the Central and South American states,

Japan and Arabia, Palestine and Egypt, Syria and Afghanistan — have also been giving their crisis festivals. Some of them, like the Central and South American orchestras, have turned it into a daily entertainment; others, like Abyssinia and Manchukuo, played it to their own death. Meanwhile, the vast continent of India, too, has taken definite steps to stage its gala concert. For several years the immense India orchestra has already been rehearsing. At the first rehearsals the symphony was played *pianissimo*. Then it was replaced by the *moderato* of nonviolent resistance, more and more often intercepted by a sharp *staccato* of machine guns and drums, bombs, and the blows of police sticks. There is hardly any doubt that soon we shall hear the *fortissimo* of this thundering festival.

If we turn our ears to Europe, we can hear, without the need of any short-wave radio, as many crisis festivals as we like. One day various fascists occupy the stage; another, communists; then the Hitlerites; then the Popular Front — red shirts and black shirts and brown shirts and silver shirts, and blue shirts and green shirts. At one moment the Spanish crisis is on the front page; at another, the French or Austrian; and all accompanied by news of the shakiness of the English pound, or the American dollar, or the French franc, or the German mark. Then come "cordial co-operation and mutual understanding" between Chinese and Japanese; or blessed salvation of Abyssinia from itself; or a Soviet demonstration of "pacifism" and a plea for the "sacredness of the contracts" on the part of a government that broke all contracts; or other forms of similar "international solidarity and good will." They give for a moment excellent publicity to that otherwise forgotten homeopathic family physician, the League of Nations, or call forth one of the endless international conferences of the "shepherds of the people" to "adjust the maladjustment," after which there usually spring up a dozen new maladjustments where before there was only one.

Up to 1929 the blessed Land of the Pilgrims was free from the crisis vogue. We preferred to listen to the crisis concerts of the other countries while at home we enjoyed mainly the *andante cantabile* of "sweet prosperity." Since the end of 1929 our taste seems to have changed. Prosperity has fallen at least temporarily into disfavor. The crisis music has also captured our fancy. From any radio we hear now almost exclusively either the "classical" or "crooning" versions of the crisis of industry and agriculture, of employment and unemployment, of education and morals, of stock-market crashes, of bank failures; the *adagio lamentoso* of dissipated luxury; the *marche funèbre* and *in memoriam* of faded hopes; the *requiem* to evaporated fortunes; the *allegro non troppo* of the murmurs of dissatisfaction; the *crescendo* of the criticism of the existing order; and occasional *scherzos* of hunger marchers, "sit-down strikers," and clashes between police and radicals. With a lag of a few years we also have acquired the taste for the new music.

These are but a few of the variations on the main theme of today's symphony of history. The total number of all the variations is immense. Not only the economic and political systems, but every important aspect of the life, organization, and culture of the Western society is included in the crisis. Its body and mind are sick and there is hardly a spot on its body which is not sore, nor any nervous fiber which functions soundly.

We are seemingly between two epochs: the dying Sensate culture of our magnificent yesterday, and the coming Ideational or Idealistic culture of the creative tomorrow. We are living, thinking, acting at the end of a brilliant six-hundred-year-long Sensate day. The oblique rays of the sun still illumine the glory of the passing epoch. But the light is fading, and in the deepening shadows it becomes more and more difficult to see clearly and to orient ourselves safely in the confusions of the twilight. The night of the transitory period begins to loom before us and the coming generations, perhaps with their nightmares, frightening shadows, and heart-rending horrors. Beyond it, however, the dawn of a new great Ideational or Idealistic culture is probably waiting to greet the men of the future.

Thus history, so far, has been proceeding along the schedule of the *Dynamics*. The great crisis of Sensate culture is here in all its stark reality. Before our very eyes this culture is committing suicide. If it does not die in our lifetime, it can hardly recover from the exhaustion of its creative forces and from the wounds of self-destruction. Half-alive and half-dead, it may linger in its agony for decades; but its spring and summer are definitely over.

Under these conditions the great task of our generation and the next consists, not in a hopeless resuscitation of what is already hollow, but in a solution of two different problems: first, of making the *dies irae, dies illa* of the transition as painless as possible; second, of laying down constructive plans for the future society and culture. Any farsighted plan for a new sociocultural order must go beyond the "old regime of Sensate culture" towards the new regime of either Ideational or Idealistic culture. Without such a fundamental change no really constructive and creative society is possible in the future.

Such, it seems to me, is the position we are at on the road of history. The evidence of all the preceding chapters points in this direction. And we find our conclusion in an irreconcilable contradiction with the other current diagnoses.

First of all, it stands in sharp contradiction to all the theories of a "moderate," "sensible," and "orderly" progress. Not realizing that their progress cult is already out of date, a throng of intellectuals, humanitarians, pacifistic and progressive parlor socialists, liberal ministers, professors, politicians, and a legion of intellectual Rotarians and Kiwanians of all kinds still profess this credo. They look at the historical process as at a good little boy who steadily advances from the first grade to graduation and progressively becomes bigger and better. They depict "the next stage" as a paradise where milk rivers flow between shores of ice cream, where all arms are remade into golf clubs, radio receivers, and electric toasters, and where "international co-operation," "mutual understanding," and "good will" reign supreme. No war, no crime, no insanity, no bloodshed, no foolishness, no trouble; there the happy existence of the contented and highly progressive ladies and gentlemen (both being blessed with birth control). All the labor is performed by mechanical appliances. Everybody's dinner consists of asparagus, fried chicken, ice cream, and pie à la mode, with cocktails before and liqueurs after the meal. Everybody will have plenty of leisure for shopping, golfing, driving, bridge playing, spooning, and especially for attending conferences on sex problems or the United Nations or any of scores of other subjects. Everybody will have full opportunity to educate himself through reading every best seller and all the Book of the Month Club selections; through listening to the radio addresses of the latest "authorities"; through glancing over the "Literary" and "Readers'" and "Scientific" digests; and, finally, through movies, dance halls, and television.

Instead of this paradise, alas! my thesis offers a rather gloomy time of blood, cruelty, and misery, with "humanity uprooted," with the sweet humanitarian dreams thrown to the winds, and — what is more important — with the main and eternal values trodden down. Even the culture of tomorrow, as I see it, is in no way going to resemble this cloud-cuckoo land of the after-dinner imagination. Created in its present specific form in the second half of the nineteenth century, this utopia has been one of the fascinating soap bubbles with which contented Victorian Europe liked to amuse itself. This Europe being on the wane, its bubbles are bursting. Anybody who likes this utopia is welcome to its hearty enjoyment. On my part I hear distinctly the *requiem* that the symphony of history is playing in its memory.

My theory is no less contradictory to all the ideologies of a violent and revolutionary progress *à la sans-culotte*, *à la* Karl Marx-Lenin-Stalin, or *à l'anarchie*. After all, the difference between the theories of moderate and violent progress is small: it amounts to a mere difference in the temperament of the devotees and the technique of progress-promotion. Both parties are equally over-Sensate and both believe in a Sensate advance, but the moderates do not wish to rush its realization. They dislike bloodshed, loss of their savings, and having their parlors invaded by ruthless and crazy mobs. The extremists, on the contrary, want to hurry along progress by all means, at any cost, and regardless of whether or not others wish to enter their paradise. They have little or nothing to lose. Therefore, they are not afraid of being ruined, or of shedding blood, or of any other of the riotous occurrences of revolutionary progress making.

These revolutionary schemes are but utopias of a disintegrated mind, of demoralized man, and come as the by-product of the disintegrated culture of the transitionary period. As we have seen in the chapters on disturbances, periods of the disintegration of social and cultural systems are regularly marked by the emergence of such schemes, and by revolts of the masses of humanity with *un*integrated minds led by groups of intellectuals with a *dis*integrated mentality. The emergence and growth of the power of these unintegrated and disintegrated minds are two of the decisive characteristics of the fading day of the passing epoch. These mobs and their leaders are the vultures that appear when the social and cultural body is decomposing. Their eternal historical function is to pull it to pieces, and thus, though involuntarily, to clear the ground for a new life. Creation is not given to them. Both their "constructive" plans and they themselves are flesh of the flesh of the last phase of the disintegrating culture, with all the unpleasant traits of such a phase and without the virtues of the Sensate culture at its climax.

At the best, only a few of the traits of the coming integrated culture and society may possibly find, in distorted form, an echo in their schemes. With this exception, their utopian culture and society are as different from the society and culture to come as the familistic society differs from the compulsory, and the Ideational from a disintegrated Sensate culture.

Finally, *my thesis has little in common with the age-old theories of the life cycle of cultures and societies with its stages of childhood, maturity, senility, and decay.*

These summary remarks show that our theory and diagnosis are not a variety of any of the above conceptions, of any moderately linear, revolutionarily progressive, or cyclical-decay-and-decline ideologies. The theory developed here stands by itself, unrelated to any of the dominant social philosophies of the present. It does not need their support nor approval, because its feet are stronger than theirs and stand upon a much firmer foundation.

For the champions of the overstuffed, after-dinner utopia the theory may appear pessimistic. In a sense it is. But from a deeper standpoint it is highly optimistic. It is optimistic because it shows sociocultural forces to be infinitely richer in creative power than does the inflexible ideal of these utopians. It is richer than any theory based on the Sensate, or Ideational, or Mixed form of culture taken alone, because it embraces all these, and gives *suum cuique*. And it is also optimistic, because it does not predict either the certain death or decay of the Western culture and society. If it points to the decline of the present Sensate phase and the probability of a grim transition, at the same time it indicates the possibility of the rise of a new magnificent Ideational or Idealistic culture, society, and man. Such a standpoint raises no fear of the temporary decline, nor even regrets it. Any value at the time of its decline deserves gratitude and compassion but not admiration. Still less does it deserve the efforts to keep it alive when a new value — as great and as good, perhaps — is coming.

Mankind should be grateful to the Sensate culture for its wonderful achievements. But now when it is in agony; when its product is poison gas rather than fresh air; when through its achievements it has given into man's hands terrific power over nature and the social and cultural world, without providing himself with self-control, with power over his emotions and passions, sensate appetites and lusts — now, in the hands of such a man, with all its achievements of science and technology, it is becoming increasingly dangerous to mankind itself and to all its values.

The most urgent need of our time is the man who can control himself and his lusts, who is compassionate to all his fellow men, who can see and seek for the eternal values of culture and society, and who deeply feels his unique responsibility in this universe. If the conquest of the forces of nature is the main function of the Sensate culture, the taming of man, his "humanization," his ennoblement as the participant in the Divine Absolute, has always been the function mainly of the Ideational or Idealistic culture. The Sensate culture did its best in the way of degrading man to the level of a mere reflex mechanism, a mere organ motivated by sex, a mere semimechanical, semiphysiological organism, devoid of any divine spark, of any absolute value, of anything noble and sacred. Such a debasement now becomes increasingly dangerous for the Sensate man himself. Hence the urgency of the shift from Sensatism to Ideationalism or Idealism, from the subjugation and control of nature by man to the control of man by himself.

This control is impossible without a system of absolute or universal and perennial values. Such values are irreconcilable with the Sensate mentality and culture which by their nature are relative, utilitarian, hedonistic, and expedient only. Hence the logical necessity and practical urgency of the shift to a new Ideational or Idealistic culture. Such a man can be trusted with the power created by the Sensate culture. Even with the present power and technique, such a man could build a society and culture with less poverty and misery, free from individual and group hatred, more noble, more just, more human, and more godly, than the present phase of our Sensate society.

PART NINE

WHY AND HOW OF SOCIOCULTURAL CHANGE

38

PRINCIPLE OF IMMANENT CHANGE OF SOCIOCULTURAL SYSTEMS AND CONGERIES

> Since we never reckon that we understand a thing till we can give an account of its "how and why," it is clear that we must look into the "how and why" of things coming into existence and passing out of it.
>
> — Aristotle. *The Physics,* 194*b*.

I. Three Hypotheses on the "Why" of Sociocultural Change

We know that viewed in their empirical aspect, all sociocultural phenomena change incessantly, without any exception whatsoever. The question arises: Why do they change but do not remain unchangeable? Why this relentless becoming instead of everlasting permanency?

The general answer to this question is easy: not only sociocultural phenomena but all empirical phenomena — inorganic, organic, and sociocultural — are subject to change in the course of their empirical existence. To be in an incessant flux, as Heraclitus said, is their destiny. Therefore a mere reference to this universal uniformity of empirical reality is sufficient to answer the above question in its general form.

Granting this, the question arises: Where shall we look for the roots of change of sociocultural phenomena and how shall we interpret it? Shall we look for the "causes" of the change of a given sociocultural phenomenon in the phenomenon itself, or in some "forces" or "factors" external to it?

The question may sound "metaphysical," and yet it is not. We shall see that it is of primary methodological and scientific importance. The character of the answer to it determines the very character of almost all "causal," "factorial" and many other analyses of the social science.

Logically, three answers are possible to the question and all three have been used in social science. The first solution of it is the *"externalistic theory of change."* Such a theory looks for the reasons ("causes," "factors," or "forces") of change of any sociocultural system in some "variables" that lie outside of the sociocultural system itself. Explicitly or implicitly, this standpoint is the predominant theory at the present time.

Take almost any historical, sociological, economic or other work dealing with a study of the change of any social and cultural phenomenon. When the investigators set forth the problem of what are the "factors," "reasons," "variables" responsible for the change, they almost invariably take variables or factors *external* to the phenomenon studied, and through the change of this external factor(s) explain the change of the phenomenon under investigation. If an author sets forth a problem of why the *family* has changed during, say, the last hundred years, he turns for the explanation to such variables as the change of industrial conditions, or density of the population, or the state laws, or the biological factors, up to sun spots and climatic conditions. The family itself is assumed to be something purely passive, devoid of any capacity of change by itself, and pushed by this or that external force along the line of change. Without such a "factor" it seemingly is destined to remain changeless and "stationary." The same method is followed when an investigator deals with the factors of change of the State, of economic, political, and social institutions, of art, science, philosophy, law and ethics, and of practically any social and cultural phenomenon. The predominant mode of explanation of change is externalistic. In quantitative and statistical studies, the factor, "the independent variable," is in most cases a variable external to the dependent variable. Exceptions certainly exist, and we shall see them, but the dominant procedure is externalistic. This concerns practically all the social, and, in a considerable degree, the biological sciences. Its general manifestation is the triumph of the so-called *"environmental" theory,* especially in explanation and interpretation of human affairs.

Broadly viewed, "environmentalism" is a theory and method of externalistic explanations of any change through "environmental forces" that lie outside, but not within, the unit studied. These external — environmental — forces are assumed to be shaping, controlling, modifying, changing, pushing, pulling, creating and destroying the phenomenon studied. The unit itself is assumed to be a merely passive focal point of the application of these forces and factors. It is supposed to have no forces of change of its own. This externalistic environmentalism now pervades social sciences. Almost everything and every change is explained environmentally, from crime and religion up to the business cycle and pure genius.

Another variety of this externalism is given in widely spread *mechanistic and behavioristic interpretations of mental and sociocultural phenomena.* The very nature of the mechanistic theory of sociocultural change consists in an extreme form of the externalistic interpretation. What is curious — but typical of the contemporary mentality — is that the second part of the Descartian and Newtonian law of inertia, namely, that if a material body is in the state of motion it has to move rectilinearly and uniformly (just because it *is* in the state of motion), has been neglected: the mechanistic interpretation of sociocultural change usually assumes that any sociocultural phenomenon is in a state of rest or static equilibrium, and remains in the state of rest until some "external force" thrusts it out of its place and keeps it moving and changing. Otherwise, the phenomenon is assumed to have no *proprium motum* and must be in a state of inertia, or "being at rest." Somewhat similar is the externalism of the behavioristic theories of any psycho-sociocultural change; and not only of the behavioristic but also of the predominant psychological theories of the present time. Their fundamental principle is *"stimulus response."* Without a stimulus — and the stimulus is almost invariably something external to man or organism or any sociocultural phenomenon — man or any sociocultural system is assumed to be incapable of giving any "response," exerting any activity, or experiencing any change or transformation. Implicitly, this formula of *stimulus response* is to a considerable degree externalistic, and in the work of many a psychologist and social scientist it is such explicitly.

A further variety of this externalism is a wide current of "reform" and "reconstructive" movements, which look for the "roots of evil" and for "the patented cure" of any social and cultural phenomenon in "the environment and factors" external to the person or social institution or cultural unit under consideration. The wrongdoing and cure of a criminal are widely regarded as due to his milieu and not inherent in the criminal himself. A root of defectiveness in a social institution — be it the family, the political or economic organization — is again looked for, not in the institution itself but in its environmental forces. A modification of these conditions is expected to produce automatically the desirable change of the system itself.

This concise characterization shows the nature of the externalistic theory of change, its varieties, and its contemporary popularity. It demonstrates also that the question raised is not merely "academic." We see how the externalistic postulate determines the essential character of all the "causal and factorial" research in all the fields of the social sciences; how it shapes the "techniques and procedures" of the research; how it pervades the practical policies and activities in the field of reformistic and reconstructive social movements; how it influences the theoretical and practical mentality and activity of its partisans in their daily affairs, as well as in special sociocultural conditions.

The second solution of the problem is opposite: it may be styled the *immanent theory of sociocultural change.* In regard to any sociocultural system, it claims that it changes by virtue of its own forces and properties. *It cannot help changing, even if all its external conditions are constant.* The change is thus immanent in any sociocultural system, inherent in it, and inalienable from it. It bears in itself the seeds of its change. If the external conditions of family, State, economic organization, political party, or any social system are assumed to be constant; if the same is assumed for any integrated system of art or science, philosophy, religion, or law, each of these social and cultural systems does not remain the same, but is immanently destined to change by virtue of its own existence and functioning. Some of its properties will disappear; some new ones will emerge; certain traits will be growing; certain others decreasing. Rapidly or slowly, the system will undergo a transformation. Such, in brief, is the essential nature of this theory.

One can easily see that it is opposite to the externalistic hypothesis. Once assumed, it leads (for a consistent mind) to a series of conclusions in the study of almost all social and cultural problems quite different from those of the externalistic postulate. In a study of a transformation of any sociocultural system, the partisan of the immanent theory of change will look for the reasons or factors of the change first of all in the internal properties (actual and potential) of the system itself, and not in merely its external conditions. He will not try to find some external factor through whose "pushing," "pulling," or "pressing," he could explain the change. He may consider any such factor as subsidiary; but in most cases he will not ascribe to it the whole of the change and its essential forms. In reformistic and reconstructive schemes for the "improvement" of this or that sociocultural evil, he would not rely exclusively or even mainly upon a mere rearrangement of the external conditions. Like a doctor, he would study first of all the system itself and its immanent properties, and this study would give him a real basis for his diagnosis. If he sees that the system is, speaking figuratively, similar to the organism of an eighty-year-old man, he will declare all the attempts to turn it into an organism of a twenty-year-old youth futile, no matter what rearrangement of external conditions is made. His reason will be that, on the basis of valid experience, an eighty-year-old organism cannot be changed into a youthful system. If the immanent properties of the system have potentialities of a more cheerful nature, he will expect that, in some way, when the time comes, they will be manifested. And his prescription — which does not neglect the external conditions — will, as a rule, put an emphasis on the inner potentiality and efforts of the system itself. He would not invest much hope in a purely mechanical rearrangement of the external circumstances. To sum up, once assumed, the principle of immanent change of sociocultural systems leads to an immense amount of research and practical activity in procedures, techniques, and policies profoundly different from the principle of the externalistic theory of change. Such is the second theory in the field.

Finally, there has been the third — *intermediary or integral — answer to the problem.* It attempts to view a change of any sociocultural phenomenon as the result of the combined external and internal forces. Often it assumes an eclectic character, putting both factors side by side without any serious attempts to indicate what is the specific role of the immanent and of the external forces. In few instances, however, is the synthetic or integral character of the principle carried through and put into actual operation. In such cases — and only in these — the integral character of the principle is realized and its nature is not disfigured. Such are the three main answers to the problem put. Which of these is most valid?

My answer is in favor of the *principle of immanent change of each sociocultural system supported by the externalistic principle, within certain conditions and limits.* The main reasons for such a standpoint are as follows:

First, the principle of immanent change of a sociocultural system is supported by empirical observation. We do not know any empirical sociocultural system or phenomenon which does not change in the course of its existence or in the course of time. In the whole empirical sociocultural world there has existed hardly any system which has remained unchanged. This observation is incontestable. The objection possible is that though change is unquestionable, it remains unknown to what it is due: to purely immanent forces of the system or to an incessant influencing of it by a set of external factors. The objection is valid. Therefore, for the solution of the problem, we must turn to other empirical and logical evidences.

Such a combined — logico-empirical — evidence can be formulated in the following proposition: *Any system which is, during its existence, a going concern, which works and acts and does not remain in a state of rest, in the literary sense of the word, cannot help changing just because it performs some activity, some work, as long as it exists.* Only a system which is in an absolute vacuum at the state of rest and is not functioning can escape change under these conditions. One can take the best automobile engine, put in it the best oil, and keep other conditions constant; and yet, if it runs and works, sooner or later it will change, and after a due time it would be worn out. In our case, we agreed to keep it in the constant but best possible external milieu. Its change, therefore, is due to the fact that it runs, works, operates, acts.

The change is an immanent consequence of the system's being a going concern. Its functioning makes change inevitable. The same can be said of any other mechanical system, if it is a going concern. Still more valid is the proposition for organic systems. One of the most fundamental properties of a living organism is its activity — external or internal — its motility, its work, its dynamic nature. In other words, an organic system is a going concern by its very nature. As such, as long as it lives, it works, acts, operates. As long as it does that, it cannot help changing. "Life can never be in equilibrium." "Complete equilibrium is never attained (by an organism) and would be fatal if it were attained, as it would mean stagnation, atrophy, and death." Regardless of any milieu, man cannot help undergoing an incessant change during his existence, in passing from childhood to maturity and then to old age and death. Only perhaps freezing or putting man into semi-dead anabiotic conditions can greatly slow up the tempo of change. But such conditions mean turning the man from a living and going concern into a kind of mummy. Such a possibility corroborates and does not disprove the proposition.

Since any sociocultural system is composed of human beings as one of its components, and since any organism, so long as it exists, cannot help changing, the sociocultural system is a "going concern" and cannot help changing so long as it exists, regardless of its external conditions, even when they are absolutely constant. The very performance of any activity, any reaction or response, to a given environment A, changes the system and makes it react differently a second time, and then a third time, and subsequent times. Other components of any sociocultural system are meanings and vehicles. These also bear in themselves the seeds of their, and of the system's, change. All the meanings that contain in themselves some potential contradiction — and according to Hegel, all meanings have it (see further) — sooner or later make it explicit and germinate their own change for elimination of it. In this sense, they also change immanently, as meanings grounded in empirical reality, as thought of by empirical human beings. All the vehicles *qua* vehicles are also going concerns: functioning as vehicles they work, are used, operated with, often worn out in their functioning. Therefore, they cannot help changing too.

These logico-experiential considerations are sufficient in order to make the principle of immanent change of the sociocultural phenomena valid. If a partisan of an externalistic principle protests that any such system or organism does not exist in a vacuum, but in a certain environment to which it incessantly reacts, and through which, therefore, it is changed, the answer is that the *existence of the environment of a given system is one thing, and imputation to that environment of the whole or the main part of the change of the system is quite another thing. If of two variables — no matter what they are — one is changing while the other remains constant, no logician or statistician would ascribe the change of the first variable to the other — the constant one.* If A varies, while B remains constant (except if B is God or Prime Mover), elementary inductive logic forbids us to see in B the cause of the variation of A. If the milieu of any system that is a going concern remains constant, while the system changes, the milieu cannot be regarded as the cause or the source of the change of the system. If the simplest microörganism (for instance, *paramecium caudalum*) in Metalnikov's and Jenning's experiments reacts to a stimulus A, in a certain way for the first time, and if it reacts to the same stimulus in the same conditions differently the second time, the change evidently is due neither exclusively nor mainly to the environment nor to A, but to the immanent property of the organism to change by virtue of its very existence and therefore its activity. Even the very capacity to *react* or *respond* to the stimulus is a capacity immanent in the organism.

All this *means that the problem of why a sociocultural system changes is falsely set forth.* Its change is neither a mystery nor a problem difficult to explain. Much more difficult would it be to understand a case of unchangeableness of any sociocultural system — if such a case had ever occurred.

In view of a wide popularity of the externalistic theories nowadays, it is advisable to go deeper in the examination of their shortcomings. Their first defect is that they are useless, because, at the best, *any consistent externalistic theory of change does not solve the problem but merely postpones the solution, and then comes either to a mystery, in a bad sense of this term, or to the logical absurdity of pulling the proverbial rabbit out of mere nothing.* Suppose we assume that change is not immanent in sociocultural systems. For an example, let us take the family (A). According to the externalistic theory for an explanation of why the American family has changed during the last fifty years, we have to take some factor external to it: say, change of industrial conditions (B). When such an explanation is given, we may ask: But why have the industrial conditions changed? According to the consistent externalism, we have to take some external factor to explain the change of B. Let it be (C), say, a change in the density and mass of the population, or in the climatic conditions, or in the sun spots or what not. Being given C, we can put the same question in regard to it: why has C changed? And so on, *ad infinitum.* This is what I mean by the postponement of the solution.

Second, if a consistent externalist continues to claim that in the process of this regression he somehow can find a solution, we shall drive him into one of the four blind alleys. A. Either to the endless regression, from A to B, B to C, C to N and so on endlessly, none of which can change itself or can be a source of change for the others. The whole regression is endless and fruitless and cannot give either change or an end in this hopeless hunt for a self-starting agent in the endless regressive movement from factor to factor. Or, B, to the ultimate Prime Mover, be it God, or any other ultimate principle, itself either unmoved (as in Plato-Aristotle's theory) or self-moving (as in some other theories). If, in the search for the ultimate source of change in metaphysics, such a solution may or may not be adequate; in the study of the empirical and sociocultural phenomena such a solution does not solve the problem at all. For the externalistic theories of change do not invoke here the ultimate Prime Mover which itself is not and cannot be empirical, but take one of the empirical "variables" as the factor of change.

Or, C, to an ascription of immanent change to some of the sociocultural or generally empirical systems; for instance, to climate, to "means and modes of production" of Marxianism, to a "demographic factor," and so on. But such a solution means an abandonment of the externalistic theory and self-contradiction, for it signifies that, contrary to the externalistic thesis, some of the sociocultural or empirical systems bear in themselves the reason of their change and can be self-starters and movers of other systems or variables. Such a thesis is but a variety of an immanent principle of change. In addition, such an escape is burdened with several other sins. It has to demonstrate why some of the sociocultural systems, for instance, the family, religion, or science, cannot change themselves, while some others, for instance, means and instruments of production, density of the population, mores, art, or sun spots, can do that. Farther on, most of the externalistic factorial theories in their "explanations" of the why of change usually move from the sociocultural to the biological (demographic and other biological) factors, and from these to the inorganic (climatic, geographic, atomic, etc.) factors. They regard such a regression as particularly scientific because it "explains" sociocultural phenomena by biological, and the biological phenomena by the physicochemical. Whatever is the validity of such an assumption in the study of other problems, in this problem the procedure and respective dogma are certainly wrong. The reason is that observationally and logically, the most dynamic or changeable phenomena are exactly the sociocultural; then come the biological; then the physicochemical.

The criticized procedure thus amounts to an "explanation" of the most "self-moving" sociocultural phenomena by the less dynamic biological, and by the least "self-moving" physicochemical variables.

Finally, D, the fourth blind alley, into which such an externalist may try to run for salvation, is the logical absurdity of producing something (change) out of nothing (from the systems which are devoid of immanent change, according to the externalistic theories). If the sociocultural systems are devoid of change; if the same is true of the biological and inorganic phenomena; if neither the line of infinite regression, nor a postulating of the ultimate Prime Mover, nor an arbitrary ascription of immanent change to something is assumed, then the only source of change that is left to the externalist is "nothing." But a long time ago Melissus said: "For if it [change] comes into being, before it came into being, it must have been nothing; if, then, it was nothing, nothing could ever come out of nothing."

Such, then, are the four blind alleys into which the consistent externalistic principle leads. None of them solves or can solve the problem.

For all these reasons, the principle of an exclusive and consistent externalism is untenable. In contrast to it, the principle of immanent change of a sociocultural system is free from these logical and factual errors. Therefore, with an adequate limitation and subsidiary admission of the externalistic principle, it is much more valid than the externalistic hypothesis.

The endorsement of the immanent principle of change does not hinder a recognition of the role of the external forces in the change of the sociocultural system. Any sociocultural system lives and functions amidst other sociocultural systems. If each of these bears in itself the seeds of its own change, their interaction leads to this change still more. If a system A contains in itself the reason for its change and so do the systems B and C and N, then the interaction of A with B or C or many of these systems, facilitates the change of A and B and of each interacting system still more.

The above is sufficient to answer the problem of Dynamics: why a whole integrated culture as a constellation of many cultural subsystems changes and passes from one state to another. The answer is: it and its subsystems — be they painting, sculpture, architecture, music, science, philosophy, law, religion, mores, forms of social, political, and economic organizations — change because each of these is a going concern, and bears in itself the reason of its change.

II. Some Implications of the Principle of Immanent Change

A. *Principle of Immanent Generation of Consequences.* The first implication of the principle of immanent change may be formulated as follows: *As long as it exists and functions, any sociocultural system incessantly generates consequences which are not the results of the external factors to the system, but the consequences of the existence of the system and of its activities. As such, they must be imputed to it, regardless of whether they are good or bad, desirable or not, intended or not by the system. One of the specific forms of this immanent generation of consequences is an incessant change of the system itself, due to its existence and activity.*

B. *Principle of Immanent Self-Determination of the System's Destiny* (Existence Career). The second fundamental implication of the principle of immanent change is the principle of immanent self-determination of the potentially given course of the existence of a sociocultural system. It may be formulated as follows: *As soon as a sociocultural system emerges, its essential and "normal" course of existence, the forms, the phases, the activities of its life career or destiny are determined mainly by the system itself, by its potential nature and the totality of its properties. The totality of the external circumstances is relevant, but mainly in the way of retarding or accelerating the unfolding of the immanent destiny; weakening or reinforcing some of the traits of the system; hindering or facilitating a realization of the immanent potentialities of the system; finally, in catastrophic changes, destroying the system; but these external circumstances cannot force the system to manifest what it potentially does not have; to become what it immanently cannot become; to do what it immanently is incapable of doing. Likewise, the external conditions can crush the system or terminate an unfolding of its immanent destiny at one of the earliest phases of its development (its immanent life career), depriving it of a realization of its complete life career; but they cannot fundamentally change the character and the quality of each phase of the development; nor can they, in many cases, reverse or fundamentally change the sequence of the phases of the immanent destiny of the system.*

This proposition is a mere result of the principle of immanent change and immanent generation of the consequences. With all the traits at a given moment (T^1), the system acts in the form of A; A introduces changes in the milieu and in the system itself. Therefore, for the next moment, T^1, the system's total situation is determined by the external and internal consequences of the act A. This situation at T^1 is thus determined by the system's properties and activities at the moment T^1. The same is true for the moment T^2, T^3 . . . T^n, up to the end of the existence of the system. This means that any sociocultural system, as soon as it emerges as a system, bears in itself its future destiny. To use Aristotle's example, an acorn as soon as it emerges bears in itself its destiny, namely the unfolding destiny of an oak and of nothing else. So with the initial system of any plant or animal organism. The same is still truer of a sociocultural system: a moronic family cannot unfold itself into the Great Christian Church or develop the properties of the Royal Scientific Society; from an emerged contractual business concern one cannot expect the properties, functions, and life career of the early Christian monastery; from a Sensate "Society of Connoisseurs of Wines and Women" the characteristics and destiny of an ascetic society; from the State, the functions and destiny of a sentimental philanthropic society; from a real university, the functions, behavior and life career of a criminal gang; and so on. As soon as a sociocultural system emerges, with all its properties and *modus vivendi* and *modus agendi,* it contains in itself its "normal" future. At any moment of its existence and activity it creates it, controls it, determines it, and molds it. In this sense, to use the proverb, any sociocultural system is the molder of its own future.

This does not deny the role of the external circumstances. But as mentioned, it specifies their functions. The external agencies may crush the system and in this way prevent it from a realization of its immanent destiny. Earthquake, fire, plague, inundation, war, and other agencies external to a given system — the family, the artistic society, the religious or political sect — can kill all or a part of its members; can destroy its property and other instrumentalities of its activities; can disperse the members; and in hundreds of forms may put an end to the existence of the system. Still more frequently, the external circumstances may accelerate or retard, facilitate or hinder, reinforce or weaken a realization of the immanent potentialities of the system and therefore of its destiny. All this is granted as self-evident. And yet, all this does not determine fundamentally the "normal" career and phases of the development of the system. All this does not and cannot force the system A (oak, man, criminal gang), destined to have a life career B to have a life career fundamentally different, for which A does not have any potentiality.

C. *Immanent Self-Determinism as Synthesis of Determinism and Indeterminism.* The preceding analysis raises the question: *What is the relationship of the immanent principle to the problem of determinism-indeterminism?* Is the immanent principle of change a variety of determinism or is it that of indeterminism? *The answer is: neither or both.* So far as the immanent principle implies that the normal course and the essential traits of the system are greatly determined by the potentialities of the system at the moment of emergence, it is self-deterministic. It is also deterministic so far as the influence of external factors is concerned, when it reaches beyond the margin of the system's autonomy. Considering, however, that the determining potentialities of the system are *the system itself* and are its immanent properties, *the determinism of the system turns into self-determinism. Self-determinism is the equivalent of freedom.* When we ourselves determine something, we feel ourselves free; and especially when this self-determination flows spontaneously from us as something quite natural to us and emanating from our very nature. The self-determination of a system is exactly this: it is rooted in the system; it expresses its very nature and its most essential potentialities; it flows spontaneously from the system and cannot do otherwise. For all these reasons the principle of immanent self-determination is equivalent to the principle of *sui generis*, different from determinism and indeterminism. It is different from both also in the sense that the very notion of the potentialities of the system, as we shall see in the next paragraph, contains an element of indeterminacy on its fringes and in no way means a rigid necessity, as has been shown above. In all these aspects, the principle of immanent change of a system implies a considerable margin of autonomy from all the agencies that are external to the system ; and also some amount of indeterminacy within the system itself, so far as realization of its potentialities is concerned.

Such is the definite and precise answer to the question raised. The answer appears to be more adequate and sound than the half-truths of pure determinism and indeterminism. The stated principle organically and logically unites in itself the valid parts of either of these principles and is free from the fallacies of either. It clearly indicates in what sense and to what degree the sociocultural system is free, and in what respects it is deterministic. In application to man and man's sociocultural world it synthesizes the doctrine of "free will" with the doctrine of determinism and "predestination." The next paragraph will specify still more fully the conclusion reached.

D. *Principle of Differential Degrees of Self-Determination and Dependence for Various Sociocultural Systems.* If any sociocultural system bears in itself the reason of its change and determination of its destiny, three questions arise: 1. In the unfolding of the potentialities of the system in its life career, is there only one quite rigid and definite course for the system, or are there several possibilities or routes to be traveled? 2. Is the margin of self-determination of the system and its dependence upon the external conditions the same for all sociocultural systems or is it different for different systems? 3. If so, upon what conditions does the relative portion of self-determination and dependence upon external agencies in the systems depend?

The answer to the first question is as follows : The role of the external milieu and the nature of the immanent potentialities of any sociocultural system force us to admit a margin of indetermined possibilities in the development of the life career of the system. I say a "margin," not the complete indeterminacy. Such a margin means the rejection of a fatalistic and absolutely determined course of development of the system. Put in symbolic form, this thesis means that a given system A has an immanent potentiality B, which has to be unfolded in the course of its existence. Due to environmental factors and to potentiality containing a margin of variations at its fringes, this B in one case will actualize into Ba, in another into Bb, in the third into Bc, and so on, up to Bn. In different external milieus, the difference between the actualizations of this B will be still greater.

Turn now to the second question : *Is the margin of self-determination of the future career of the system the same for all sociocultural systems?* Are all the social and cultural systems equally dependent or independent of the external conditions in shaping their own destiny?

This destiny is shaped, as we have seen, by the immanent forces of the system itself and by the milieu in which it exists. Are the shares of both "molders" constant for any system?

The amount of self-determination of a system's destiny depends first upon *the kind of social or cultural system ;* and second, upon the *kind of milieu.*

Third, we must distinguish farther between *the total and the specific immunity* of the system from its environment, in the molding of its own destiny.

Let us assume, first, that we have social and cultural systems *of the same kind:* say, the family, or the State, or the business firm; or a philosophical school or an art system.

E. *Other conditions being equal (including the milieu), in the social and cultural systems of the same kind, the greater and better is their integration, the greater is their self-determination (and autonomy from the environment) in molding their own destiny.*

Unfolded, the proposition implies:

(1) *Other conditions being equal, of the social and cultural complexes, the least amount of self-determination is found in unorganized social groups and in cultural congeries.*

(2) Other conditions being equal, *the highest amount of self-determination belongs to those social and cultural systems which are most perfectly integrated, causally and meaningfully,* where the causal interdependence of the components and elements of the system is the greatest; and their relationship is the most solidary (among human agents) and most consistent among the components, where, neither actually nor potentially, is there any contradiction, any *Spannung,* any inner tension, antagonism or conflict.

Finally, *between these types stand the intermediate systems, which are neither congeries nor perfectly integrated systems.* Such are the social systems where only the causal interdependence is found but where relationships are not quite solidary; or the cultural systems where relationships of the elements of the system are somewhat eclectic, not quite consistent, and actually or latently conflicting between and in each of its components. In such systems there always is found what Max Weber, M. Scheler and E. Barthel style, *Spannung,* a kind of tension or latent antagonism; a hidden split or crack, which flares into an open split of the system as soon as the respective adverse interference of the external conditions takes place.

One word of caution: *integration and lack of it should not be mixed with fashionable terms like "plasticity," "capacity of adjustment to environment," "progressiveness," and the like.* These terms are not equivalent to good or poor integration.

Well-integrated systems may be both elastic and rigid in their structure and tactics, according to the conditions; the same is true of the poorly integrated systems.

Of other conditions relevant to the amount of self-direction of a system in molding its own destiny, the following ones can be mentioned:

(3) *Other conditions being equal (including the identical environment and the perfection of integration), the greater the power of the system, the greater its autonomy from the social, biological and cosmic environment, and the greater its self-control and self-direction.* The proposition seems almost axiomatic. But the weakness of the proposition consists in the indeterminacy of the term "power." Left at that, it is valid, but fairly indefinite. What is the power of a sociocultural system? How can it be measured? And measured it must be, in order that we can say which system is more powerful.

I do not know any satisfactory device for a measurement as well as for a clear definition of the power of a social or cultural system.

All that one can do is to indicate a few rough criteria which are somewhat measurable, and which can give at least a very rough, but nevertheless hardly misleading, "index" of the power of the system.

Other conditions being equal, (*a*) *the greater the membership of a social system;* (*b*) *the better their biological and mental and social qualities;* (*c*) *the greater the sum total of real knowledge, experience, and wisdom at its disposal;* (*d*) *the more efficient its organization in the sense of the distribution of rights-duties-functions among its members* (including the distribution to everybody according to his talent and ability); (*e*) *the greater the sum total of the means and instruments of influencing human conduct as well as of modifying biological and cosmic nature; and finally,* (*f*) *the better its solidary integration* (*discussed above*); *the greater is the power of the group — the more independent it is from the external conditions in the realization of its potentialities.*

With a slight modification, the same criteria are applicable to the comparative power of cultural systems. *The greater the number of the human agents of the system* (*of art, religion, philosophy, science, etc.*); *the better their biological, mental, moral, and social qualities; the greater the wisdom, knowledge, and value it incorporates* (value or system of meanings: religious, scientific, artistic, ethical, etc.); *the better it fits the social organization of its followers; the greater is its logico-causal integration* (within the system of meanings and between all its components); *the greater the sum total of means or vehicles for its unfolding, broadcasting, and maintenance at its disposal; the greater the power of the cultural system — the more independent it is from its environmental forces.*

Here, however, a greater emphasis is to be put upon the value (the system of meanings) the system incorporates and the consistency of the integration of its elements and components than in the social system.

Each of these conditions is unquestionably a basic constituent of the power of a social or cultural system. Taken separately, each condition cannot be an index of the power of the system. Taken together, they give a very approximate, but hardly misleading, indicator of that power.

This proposition then sums up, if not all, then probably the most essential uniform conditions of the comparative autonomy of the system (in building its destiny) from the external conditions, and explains the relative share of the system's self-control and self-regulation in molding its own destiny.

III. Summary

1. The reason or cause of a change of any sociocultural system is in the system itself, and need not be looked for anywhere else.

2. Additional reason for change of a system is its milieu, which is again composed mostly of the immanently changing systems.

3. Any sociocultural system changing immanently, incessantly generates a series of immanent consequences, which change not only the milieu of the system but also the system itself.

4. Bearing the seeds of its change in itself, any sociocultural system bears also in itself the power of molding its own destiny or life career. Beginning with the moment of emergence, each sociocultural system is the main factor of its own destiny. This destiny, or the system's subsequent life career, represents mainly an unfolding of the immanent potentialities of the system in the course of its existence.

5. The environmental forces are not negligible, but their role consists essentially in retardation or acceleration; facilitation or hindrance; reinforcement or weakening, of the realization of the immanent potentialities of the system. Sometimes they can crush the system and put an end to its existence; or stop the process of unfolding the immanent potentialities at one of the early phases. They cannot, however, change fundamentally the immanent potentialities of the system and its normal destiny in the sense of making the life career of an unfolding acorn that of a cow, or vice versa.

6. So far as the system, since the moment of its emergence, bears in itself its future career, it is a self-determining system. So far as the future of the system is determined mainly by the system itself, such self-determination is free, as flowing spontaneously, in accordance with nature, from the system itself. This self-determination is different from determinism and indeterminism. It is a principle *sui generis*.

7. The process of unfolding the immanent potentialities of the emerged system is somewhat predetermined by the system, but this predetermination leaves a considerable margin for variations. In this sense it is not absolutely and narrowly preconditioned. Only the main direction and the main phases of the unfolding are predetermined; the rest, including most of the details, are "free" and become an unforeseen and unpredictable matter of chance, environment, and free choice of the system.

8. Since the destiny or life career of any system is the result of the system's self-control and of the influence of the environmental forces, the relative share of each of these two factors in molding the system's career is not constant for all sociocultural systems. The share of the self-control of the system is the greater, the more perfectly the system is

integrated and the more powerful it is.

9. As a rough indicator of the elusive concept of the power of a sociocultural system, the following less elusive combination of the criteria is offered: the greater the membership of the system; the better the members biologically, mentally, morally and socially; the greater the actual wisdom, knowledge and experience the system has at its disposal; the better it is organized; the greater the total sum of means of influencing human behavior and forces of nature at its disposal; the more solidarily (or consistently) the system is integrated; the more powerful it is; the more independent from the forces of the environment, — the greater is the share of its own control in molding its destiny.

39

THE "WHY" OF SOCIOCULTURAL RHYTHMS AND SWINGS. THE PRINCIPLE OF LIMIT

The general reason why sociocultural systems change in the course of their existence has been given by the principle of immanent change which was developed in the preceding chapter. The special reason why many sociocultural systems have recurrent nonidentical rhythms and turns, instead of proceeding forever in the same direction, or undergoing ever new changes devoid of any recurrence, or running in an identical cycle, is given by the principle of limits. It is implied in the principle of immanent change but has not been unfolded. Its unfolding is now in order.

A. *Limits in Causal-Functional Relationship.* It may be safely assumed that the discovery and accurate formulation of causal or functional relationships between two or more variables is the supreme task of any generalizing science and the ambition of such a scientist or scholar. To arrive at some causal formula is the final goal beyond the great amount of arduous "spade work" which precedes it. This labor may consist of collection, tabulation, and calculation of statistical data, or experimentation, or case study, or historical exploration, or just speculation. Just because it does constitute such a highly regarded goal we are prone, perhaps, to find such causal relations where they do not exist, or to describe them in a form which is inaccurate. These scientific "sins" are quite common in the history of science, and the "graveyard" of the annals of scholarship is full of such attempts. All this is too well known to warrant further discussion.

Much less known, however, is another error committed in the search for scientific laws. This error may be described as neglect on the part of the scholars to indicate the limits within which their causal formulas are valid. Here is the essence of this mistake:

Suppose that after most careful study (statistical, experimental, or any other type), a sociologist or other scientist finds that between variables A and B there exists a definite causal connection of a certain kind, such that when the value of A is varied in a certain manner the value of B changes correspondingly. Let us grant for the moment that the formula is correct. Shall we conclude from this that the study of the relationship is complete and that the formulation is quite adequate scientifically? Explicitly or implicitly most authors answer this question positively. *But rarely,* if ever, *do such generalizations indicate the limits within which the established relationship is valid.* Since A and B happen to be causally connected within the limits of the values observed, it is concluded or assumed that the connection would remain valid for any values which might be assigned to A and B. In mathematical terminology the relationship is assumed to be of the type of continuous functional equation like

$$B = 1 + 2A^2,$$

where one can assign any value to A in full confidence that it will be continuously represented in B. Can we assume that all causal relationships are and must be of this type of continuous equation? Is this general assumption valid? Or must we state the boundaries within which the causal relationship holds and beyond which it ceases to exist, or exists only with radically changed nature?

As soon as this question is clearly stated, a series of mathematical, logical, and empirical considerations come to mind, challenging the validity of the assumption.

(1) That the premise is not the only possible one mathematically is shown by the existence of discontinuous functional equations, for example:

$$B = \frac{1}{A} \text{ or } B = \sqrt{A^2 - 1}$$

In the first instance B becomes plus or minus infinity when A takes the value of zero and passes at a jump from negative to positive infinity when A is passing through zero from a negative to a positive value. In the second formula, when A varies gradually from minus infinity to -1 and from $+1$ to plus infinity, B varies also insensibly from plus infinity to zero. But when A assumes a value between -1 and $+1$, B has no real value but instead becomes imaginary, and the function is discontinuous between these two points. Since expressions of this nature exist in the mathematical realm, it is a purely dogmatic assumption to believe that all empirical relationships are continuous. Some of them may be of this discontinuous type.

(2) We may also say that there is no logical reason whatever to assume that the observance or discovery of causal relationships for certain values of the phenomena warrants a conclusion that the same connection will necessarily exist whatever values the variables assume. This is equivalent to saying that there is a logical basis for contending that causality between two phenomena exists only within certain limits

and that outside these bounds the relationship either disappears or becomes radically altered in nature.

(3) There remains, consequently, the testimony of the empirical facts relating to the phenomena studied, and these data are the most important witnesses in the case. Putting aside for the present the problem as to whether there are some causal relationships of a continuous type ("limitless") (see later), there is no doubt that many such relationships have limit(s) in the values of the variables, beyond which the given relationship disappears or fundamentally changes. Illustrative instances may be related as follows. The more strongly I strike a piano key, the louder the resulting sound. Within a certain limit the loudness of the sound is a direct function of the force exerted in the stroke. This is certainly true, yet beyond a certain limit the result will not be an increase in the volume of the sound, but rather a broken piano, whatever be the effort expended. An adequate formula relating these two factors must not only state that the sound of the key is proportional to the intensity of the stroke, but it must add the qualification: within certain limits, and the points beyond which the formula becomes invalid must be specified. Arsenic in certain quantities is a deadly poison, but in smaller amounts it is not lethal at all. Whiskey, when taken in certain amounts, is not intoxicating, but does induce that state when absorbed in larger quantities.

Physicochemical and biological sciences are full of such phenomena and they are well summed up in the form of leading principles of these sciences, such as "stability limit" (Knorr and others), "critical temperature," "critical pressure," "critical concentration," and the like, for a designation of the limits beyond which the given equilibrium system changes or ends (either in the number of its phases, or degree of freedom, or the concentration of its components, and so on, according to Willard Gibbs's "Phase Rule") or the given relationship between the variables ceases to exist.

The same is true of the science of biology. There the principle of limit comes up at almost any proposition formulating the relationship between two or more biological, biophysical, biochemical, or biosocial variables. The simplest everyday experience shows it clearly.

Let us now turn to social variables. We have thousands of formulas which claim the existence of causal relationships but which state no bounds to their validity.

Many theories contend that there exists a positive relation or causal association of such and such a degree of correlation between:

Business depression and criminality,

Business depression and mortality,

Business revival and birth rate,
Poverty and marriage rate,
Divorce and suicide,
Resemblance and attraction in marriage,
Urbanization and mental disease,
Urbanization and irreligiosity.

Or, there exists a negative functional relationship between:

Education and suggestibility,
Population density and fertility,
Education and criminality,
A certain ecological city area and feeblemindedness,
Brachycephaly and genius,
Nutrition and low stature,
Farm income and illiteracy,
Nutrition and fertility.

Or

Irreligiosity is a factor in demoralization and decay,
Illiteracy positively influences fertility,
Order of birth and mental diseases are positively correlated,
Urbanization and marriage rates are negatively correlated,
Movie attendance favors an unsanctioned sex life,
Mental disease is the main factor of suicide.

Granting only for a moment that in all these and thousands of other formulas the evidences offered are satisfactory, shall we say that the conclusions as stated are complete and adequate, and that the positive or negative relationship found is likely to hold whatever value the variables may assume? By no means. We know that within certain limits improved nutrition tends to accelerate growth and increase stature, but beyond a certain point no additional improvement in food, quantitative or qualitative, will be followed by a further increase in stature. Poverty, below the physiological minimum, has an adverse effect on fertility, but above this line comparative poverty does not necessarily have the same result. At some point, compared with a state of relative comfort, it may serve as a stimulus or be associated with increased fertility. Similar statements may be made regarding the relations between poverty and criminality, urbanization and mental disease, marriage and suicide. Mobility within certain limits is a factor in demoralization, but in other degrees facilitates morality. We may conclude similarly as regards prosperity. Density of population within certain limits can be a positive and, within other limits, a negative factor in fertility. Likeness of a certain degree and character is a positive factor in marriage choice, but other degrees or types of resemblance hinder marriage attraction.

There is no need to multiply the instances further. With a reasonable degree of probability we can conclude that there is scarcely any causal tie between societal variables which holds for all values given to them. In other words *the hypothesis or assumption of the unlimited validity of any causal relationship which may be discovered between societal variables is faulty and conduces to still more erroneous conclusions.* It is certainly defective and most fallacious in the social sciences.

The moral of this discussion may be summarized as follows:

(*a*) The common and almost unquestioned assumption that a certain causal-functional relation discovered for variables of stated values will remain valid for any values whatever is fallacious.

(*b*) All causal, functional, or correlational formulas claiming the existence of connections between two or more variables, but not containing any indication of the limits within which the generalization is valid and beyond which it must be qualified or abandoned, are immature inferences and conclusions.

(*c*) In such incomplete and unqualified form these statements give no adequate knowledge of the interrelationships between the phenomena and often disfigure the nature of these bonds, disguise other more efficient causes or more fundamental relationships, and hinder the discovery of the true conditions existing beyond the limits which should really be imposed upon the stated conclusions.

(*d*) If such limitations are not carefully determined and stated we can hardly expect to penetrate to any real knowledge of the interactions among societal variables. We shall suffer from a multiplication of immature causal formulas, and contradictory coefficients of correlation will overwhelm us.

(*e*) The above shows that causal-functional interdependence between most diverse and numerous variables has limits within a certain value of these variables. Beyond it, it ceases to exist, or changes fundamentally.

B. *Limits in Direction of Sociocultural Change.* This principle of limits has great importance in another field of social studies, namely, the problems concerning the direction of social processes. Especially since the eighteenth century the social and, to a large extent, the biological sciences have been seduced by the theory of evolution and of progress with a perpetual linear tendency—whether unilinear, spiral, branching, or oscillatory. According to this theory Omnipotent Evolution and Providential Progress unerringly lead mankind ever nearer to some goal or toward some "bigger and better" state.

The explicit or implicit assumption of all these theories is that social or biological processes move endlessly with or without minor deviations in the same direction without limit. May we regard such a fundamental postulate as valid? For my part, I am ready to contend that in application to the majority of the sociocultural processes, it is untenable. Whether it is valid in regard to a few processes we shall see later. The general reasons for such a statement are as follows:

A perpetual tendency in social processes is a more complicated form of uniform and rectilinear motion in mechanics. Newton's law tells us under what conditions this is possible. In order for such to occur there must be absolute noninterference of any exterior forces, or absolute isolation from any environmental influence is essential. Otherwise definite movement in one direction is impossible, and friction and shocks of external forces would disturb the movement and eventually change its direction. Through gravitational forces, for instance, linear movement becomes circular or elliptical.

Do these essential conditions exist for any particular processes or for all social processes? Evidently not. Social processes, individually or in their totality, are not absolutely isolated from the outside cosmical and biological worlds nor from the "pressure" of other social processes. They permanently and ceaselessly interfere with each other. Unless we postulate a miracle or an active Providence, it is quite improbable that all these innumerable forces would act in such a way that their resultant would be negligible or constant at every moment, thus maintaining the direction of the processes unchanged. Such an assumption of a perfect and eternal balance of the numberless cosmic, biological, and social processes is equivalent to a miracle and contrary to all probability.

Even if this assumption were shown to be valid, it alone would not guarantee the indefinite trend of social processes in one direction. For this still another basic condition is needed, namely, that the social system itself — be it a small social group, mankind, a cultural system, or any social phenomenon — which is in process would retain its nature and characteristics unchanged forever. Why? Because a system of mutually equilibrated external forces acting upon the system in such a way as to maintain its direction of movement or trend would not in fact serve to assure this continuity of direction when the system itself changes. By virtue of the Principle of Immanent Change any "social system in process," just because it is in process, will inevitably be worn out, modified, or transformed. Likewise it is hardly probable that the change would occur in such a manner that all the "parts and sides" or aspects of a social system in process would become changed proportionately so as not to break the existing perpetual trend of the movement. Such an assumption also would require a miracle.

These considerations show then that for an admission of perpetual direction of social or biological processes at least two highly improbable assumptions must be made and two "miracles" expected. Consequently, in reference to all or the majority of sociocultural processes, neither assumption nor the theory resting upon it is acceptable. They are a matter of belief and cannot be propositions of science. This explains why there are turns and caesuras in the direction of the majority of sociocultural processes.

To these considerations the arguments of Aristotle and Hegel can be added. If the Aristotelian argument is not valid in application to the motion of the material body, it has some validity in reference to qualitative change.

According to Aristotle, any change can be thought of only as a passage between antithetical terms, between two contrary (like hot and cold, dry and wet) or contradictory terms (as in the case of "coming to be" and "ceasing to exist"). Without such an antithesis no change is thinkable. If then any change means a passage between the antithetical terms, it follows that no movement or change (except purely rotatory or circular) can go on forever continuously and in the same direction. "No progression other than local movement can be continuous and perpetual."

Developing this argument, Aristotle concludes that rectilinear motion (or a change) cannot be continuous (*i.e.*, uniform, uninterrupted and everlasting) because the moving or changing object sooner or later has to reach one of the antithetical poles, after which it either ceases to move or changes the direction of the movement, or reverses it. Hence the necessity of limit, of caesura, or turn, or rhythm, even of reversal, in the direction of the movement or change.

We have seen that in a modified form this argument is set forth by Hegel, in the very essence of his dialectical method. Since any concept, and the reality that corresponds to it, contains in itself its own negation — is an identity of the opposites — and in the process of its unfolding generates its antithesis, no change or movement can proceed forever continuously in the same direction and without turns and rhythms.

The totality of the above considerations is sufficient to demonstrate why many (if not all) sociocultural processes have caesuras, rhythms and turns in their directions; and why they do not proceed forever continuously and uniformly along the same trend.

C. *Principle of Limited Possibilities of Change.* The third variation of the principle of limit may be styled the *principle of limited possibilities.* It is a derivative of the principle of limit in causal and directional fields. We have seen that many processes cannot move forever in the same direction; having reached their limit, they turn in a new direction; along this new direction they also cannot move forever, and sooner or later have to turn again, and so on.

This raises a problem: is the range of these new turns and changes unlimited for all the sociocultural and other processes? Can they endlessly make new turns, new forms, new transformations, without any limit? Or is such a possibility limited, if not for all, then for many systems in the process? In other words, shall we accept the principle of limited or unlimited possibilities of "turns," forms, modifications, patterns, beats, tempi, trends, which a system in process can assume? The answer is: *if not for all, then at least for an enormous number of sociocultural systems in process, the number of fundamental possibilities as to ever new fundamental turns in direction, essentially new forms, patterns and appearances the system can assume is limited and bounded. Different concretely in number for different systems, these possibilities are not infinite but finite. Having run through all of them, the system either ends its existence, or, if it continues to live, it has to repeat again one or more of the turns and forms through which it has already passed. In that case, the process of the existence of the system would display recurrent qualitative, quantitative, spatial rhythms, turns, patterns, forms, tempi, or what not (no matter whether they are periodical or not).*

One of the main and important reasons for this was indicated above. If a given system has unlimited possibilities of change, under such conditions, the system can change so radically that it will lose all its essential characteristics and become unidentifiable. Such a change means the cessation of the existence of the system; when a system becomes unidentifiable and loses its sameness, it disappears. Hence, so long as a system lives, it has limits in its change. The selectivity of a system leads to the same result. An unlimited possibility of change for a given system means it can become anything, can ingest everything, therefore can become radically different from what it was and unidentifiable. Such a change is equivalent to the cessation of the existence of the system and to its replacement by another — quite different — system. For these almost axiomatic reasons, practically any system must have and does have limits to the range of its change. The limits transgressed, the system disappears.

Empirically, there is not the slightest doubt that an enormous number of chemical, physical, biological, and sociocultural systems follow this principle. In chemistry, for instance, a system of water can have only three phases — vapor, liquid, and solid — and no more. These phases in certain conditions can coexist all together; in other conditions, two or three coexist; in some other, there is only one; but the system of water cannot have more than three phases and its degree of freedom is also limited, according to Gibbs's formula: $P + F = C + 2$, or $F = C + 2 - P$, where P denotes the number of phases, F the degree of freedom, and C the number of components. The system with more than one component may have a greater number of phases and degrees of freedom, and yet these are finite for almost all chemical systems. There is a limit to the possibilities of transformation for each of them, and this limit is rather narrow.

The same can be said of the biological systems. Either in the duration of life of each organism, or in the size of growth, or in the variation of the anatomical and physiological traits of the organisms of the same species, or in hundreds of other traits and characteristics, the variation of the organisms of the same species, however great sometimes, is confined within certain limits. The possibilities for each organism of the same species are finite. Therefore, the variations themselves are recurrent. The same can be said of the biological processes, either within an organism, or within a species, or even a number of species. In all of these we find a set of the same processes: reproduction, alimentation, self-defence, process of growth, maturing and aging, and finally death. The details of the performance of each of these processes may vary, but the processes themselves in some form, are practically the same for all organisms. Within one species, even the "technique" of performance of these basic functions varies within very narrow limits, fixed by the *inherited reflex and instinct mechanism.* Reflex and instinct mean here very limited possibilities of variation. The same has to be said of another biological principle: heredity. It limits decisively even possibilities of variation of the individual organisms of the same species.

Quite certain limits for each species exist, further, in its *adaptation* process, *selection* process, and *survival* process. For hardly any species in all these respects does there exist an unlimited possibility of adaptation to, and survival amidst, most different milieus. For some species the possibilities may be wider, for others narrower, but for all the range is bounded. In brief, in biological processes there is an enormous number of fundamental and secondary processes that are clearly limited in the possibilities of their variation and direction. Therefore, most of these processes repeat themselves — in organisms, in species, in a conglomeration of species.

Though *homo sapiens* is considered to be a more variable creature than other species, and though sociocultural processes are probably more varying than inorganic and organic processes; yet there is hardly any doubt that the variation of individuals, of individual behavior as well as that of the sociocultural processes, has, in most cases, if not in all, a limited range of possibilities. This is perfectly clear in regard to physiological, anatomical, psychological, and sociocultural traits and behavior of individuals. Duration of life; main physio-psychological processes; the cycle of completed life, moving from childhood to senility and death; though they vary from man to man, they vary within certain limits. There has not been a *homo sapiens* who lived a thousand years; there has not been a man constructed like an elephant. The anatomical structure of the human organism and its physiological processes are essentially the same among all human beings and races. There are only two normal sexes, with the hermaphroditus sex as the third. The main psychological processes — sensation, perception, reproductive imagination, feelings, emotions, and ideas — are present in some form in all human beings, however great is the difference between an idiot and a genius. And so on.

Not so clear seems to be the situation with the sociocultural processes. And yet an enormous number of them, if not all, seem to have a clearly limited range of possibility of variation. First, we find the same basic processes among all the societies and groups: as long as they live, there is some process of getting their living and means of subsistence; there are the processes of reproduction, birth, and death; there is some kind of organization — social, economic, political, religious, or others; in some form there goes on the process of learning and its transmission from generation to generation; some sort of family and marriage, magic and religion, political and economic organization, art and science, law and mores — all these and other basic institutions are found among practically all societies. So also the phenomena of differentiation and stratification. We have hardly ever had a social system without these institutions and processes.

Turning to the variation of the processes within the same field of society and culture, we are struck again by the narrow range of the qualitative types each process has had among most different social groups. If we turn to the *types of economic organization,* classifications of the economic historians rarely go beyond five or six main economic types that have existed in history: hunters and collectors of the free produce of nature; pastoral; agricultural; industrial; or varieties of such classifications as given by Hobhouse-Ginsberg-Wheeler; by B. Hildebrandt; by K. Bücher, G. Schmoller, E. Meyer, W. Sombart, and others. If to the forms given by these classifications we add new forms to come (though all the supposedly new forms contemplated, like totalitarian, socialist, communist, anarchist economies all have occurred many times in the past), the range of possibilities remains still limited. If we take the forms of the *family and marriage* (not to mention the customs of courting and sex satisfaction) their forms, according to the historians of the family and marriage, have again been limited: the existing classifications rarely go beyond some ten or twelve main forms. The same is true of the biosocial forms of prostitution and "free sexual love."

If we turn to the forms of *political organization,* here the limited range of the forms that have existed is still narrower than in the preceding fields. Five fundamental forms of Plato and six (good and bad) forms of Aristotle and Polybius embrace practically all the main forms that have existed. In the classifications of the texts of the constitutional law, the number is often still smaller: monarchy, republic, constitutional monarchy, and some other mixed form — that is about all one finds there. Hardly different is the situation in regard to the *religious process.* No matter how various religions are classified — totemism, animism, fetishism, polytheism, monotheism, atheism, or in several different ways — the existing classifications are again few and consist of a rather small number of the main forms of religion. In *art,* no matter what is the classification, Ideational-Idealistic-Sensate; Classic-Romantic; Idealistic-Realistic; Architectural-Plastic-Malerisch; Oriental-Occidental; Paleolithic-Neolithic-Oriental-Classic-Medieval-Modern; Visual-Symbolic, and so on — all more or less serious classifications give again a limited species of the art style, of the art forms, patterns, canons.

The history of philosophical thought is but the history of an incessant variation of the same main — and few — themes, like idealism-materialism; realism-nominalism-conceptualism; empiricism-rationalism-mysticism-fideism-scepticism; determinism-indeterminism; eternalism-temporalism, and so on, which have been studied in the preceding sections of this work. All the main systems of truth fall within our three main systems: truth of faith, of reason, of the senses, plus some mixed forms.

Not very different is the situation in the *theories of ethics and law, as well as in the actual codes of ethics and law.* All the ethical systems, no matter how they are classified, incessantly "swing" between the ethics of absolute principles and that of happiness: eudemonism, utilitarianism, hedonism, and some mixture between these poles. Even the main commandments of ethical systems are practically the same in all the great religious and moral systems. Likewise, however greatly the *codes of law* differ in details, in their main principles and divisions, they give but a few types — constitutional, civil, criminal law; and again, as has been shown in the preceding chapters, the main crimes in all the codes are either identical or similar. The same is true of civil and constitutional law. Any one who is acquainted with the theories of law knows that the main classes of the theories are few, and can easily be counted on the fingers of two hands; and represent also an incessant variation of the same main themes; from the law and theory of the Code of Hammurabi, the Bible, or the Law of the Twelve Tables, with the Gaius, Ulpianus, Modestinus, Papinianus, up to the present codes and theories of law.

Even in *science,* so far as its fundamental categories and principles are concerned, the situation is not much different. As has been partly shown in the preceding chapters, — even in physics, chemistry, biology, and other natural sciences, the main principles, like atomism, vitalism-mechanism, and so on, are not very numerous, and the respective theories, however different in details, represent also a variation of the main — and essentially the same — themes.

Similarly, the *main types of society,* of *sociocultural systems and processes,* are very limited in their number. *Gemeinschaft-Gesellschaft,* society with "mechanical-organic" solidarity; religious-secular; hunters-pastoral-agricultural-industrial; clan-tribe-state-international federation; simple-compound-doubly compound-triply compound; rural-urban; savage-civilized; these and similar classifications rarely go beyond half a dozen types. So also with the more detailed classification of specified social groups, such as the family; territorial (neighborhood) group; the state; national, political party; religious group; occupational, economic, racial, sexual, age group; scientific; recreational; class; caste.

No different is the situation with regard to the main types of *cultural* systems and supersystems; in previous chapters their number has been shown to be very limited, no matter what classification we take.

So also with *sociocultural processes.* Whatever classification is taken, their main types are numerically small: isolation-contact; assimilation-conflict-adaptation; imitation-opposition-adaptation; cooperation-antagonism; differentiation-stratification-integration; war-peace; order-disorder; individualization-collectivization; organization-disorganization; progress-regress; rise-decline; prosperity-depression; production-distribution-consumption; linear-cyclical-erratically varying; and so on. The main classes rarely go beyond five or ten types.

If we take such narrower phenomena as, for instance, the patterns of dress and coiffure, and dress colors, we find there again "an eternal return" of the limited number of main patterns and colors. Sometimes striking similarity between the pattern of dress of the women of such widely removed cultures as Minoan and modern Parisian cultures can be noted.

If within each of these fundamental processes we examine more detailed subprocesses, the picture is not essentially different. From the brevity of the above examples one should not conclude that the principle of limited possibilities is something "exotic" or operative only in a few instances. Cultural anthropologists, ethnologists, historians, and sociologists have been confronted with a host of facts to which they have given the name of *cultural convergence,* meaning by it an essential similarity of cultural traits of various cultures, due neither to borrowing nor to common origin, nor to any contact of these cultures, but generated more or less independently. M. I. Rostovtzeff, A. J. Toynbee, R. Lowie, R. Thurnwald, A. Goldenweiser and many others rightly sought an explanation of the phenomena of convergence in "the principle of limited possibilities" of culture variations, as Goldenweiser and Thurnwald put it.

Dr. Lowie rightly refers to this principle in giving a series of facts of convergence. In many unrelated societies we find recurrent and limited types of descent. The reason is that generally descent may be either matrilinear or patrilinear; hence the recurrence of such systems. Likewise, the number of ways in which a skin membrane can generally be fastened to a drum is limited: therefore the modes of that are also recurrent. And so on. A. Haberlandt points out that the number of possibilities in the development and variation of arrow points is also limited; so in the case of sword handles, and many other objects. Hence the recurrence of the same forms and patterns or types. Similarly, Thurnwald indicates that the possibilities in variation of individualism-collectivism, forms of reciprocity, woman's social status, forms of inheritance, means of social control and power, production-distribution-consumption, forms of language and so on, are also objectively limited; therefore they are recurrent. A. Goldenweiser rightly says:

certain fundamental cultural forms occur again and again . . . the forms lend themselves to a classification into a fairly small number of types, which constantly recur, as one passes from culture to culture. . . . Thus one finds a social organization consists of social units (in the limited sense), or of families, or of local groups, or of various combinations of these units; that an art consists of carving, or drawing, or painting, or of a combination of these; that the form of it is realistic or semi-conventionalized, or purely geometrical . . . that a mythology comprises epics, or animal stories, or nature myths, or traditional accounts of historical happenings, or creation legends, or several of these types together; and so on through the entire series of cultural forms."

These references and remarks are sufficient to show that the principle of limit in this aspect of the limited possibilities of forms and modes of transformations is a principle applicable, if not to all sociocultural systems, then at least to their overwhelming majority.

When, farther on, we turn from such similarities to much more detailed similarities recurrent in the most different — and unrelated — cultures, for instance, to the recurrent "motive of flying gallop," the explanation seems to be again along the line of "convergence" or limited possibilities of expression of the idea "of wind's fast movement."

Still more is it so in regard to the recurrence of the main colors of dress or various objects of culture: since the number of main colors is limited to seven, they cannot help recurring again and again in space and time, in dress as well as in various cultural objects.

To sum up: from logical and factual evidences, *it is reasonably certain that an enormous number of sociocultural systems and processes have a limited range of possibilities in their variation, in the creation of new fundamental forms.* If this be so, then after a sufficiently long existence of the process given, during which it runs through all the main forms, in its further existence it cannot help repeating the forms already used, either all of them, or some of them; either in the same order as before, or in different order; but repetition and recurrence of the forms becomes inescapable under these conditions. Only the processes that end before they have exhausted all the range of the limited possibilities; or the processes whose range of possibilities is unlimited (if such processes exist) can escape this recurrence or repetition. Such is the third important aspect of the principle of limit. Having now the principle of limits at our disposal, we can turn to its use in explanation of our second and third "why's."

In order to make the problem and its difficulties clear, let us recapitulate the specific difficulties connected with it. The problem is: *How are rhythms and recurrent punctuations possible in sociocultural processes?* The specific difficulties consist in the fact that we do not postulate the changing sociocultural systems as isolated from all external forces. We know that none of the systems is isolated and that each exists and functions amidst a variety of diverse environmental forces, which themselves — and their constellations — always vary.

If the system were isolated, or the external agencies constant, the explanation would be much easier than is the actual case. Let us add that by a recurrent rhythm or punctuation, we mean not an identical reproduction, but only such a similarity between the recurrent rhythms or punctuations as justifies their subsumption under the same class or species as essentially similar, but not identical.

The above *principle of limits, especially in its second and third aspects, appears to give an answer to the problem.* If we assume that a given system has immanently limited possibilities in its transformations, a sufficient time being given during which it runs through all of these possibilities, it cannot help repeating some of the previous forms during its subsequent existence. If there are only, say, four possibilities for a given system to experience, after all four have been run through, these four — or some of them — in the same or a different order will reappear during the subsequent existence of the process. The conclusion is practically self-evident. A number of corollaries follow from it.

A. *If the immanent possibilities of various forms, or of quantitative and qualitative changes, of a system are unlimited or very large, the process of existence of the system will appear nonrhythmical, either because none of the previous forms or changes recur, or because it is exceedingly difficult to grasp their exceptionally rare recurrence amidst the ever-changing forms of the system.* Such recurrences may happen so irregularly and be separated from each other by such a large time interval, that they become practically unobservable and unnoticeable. This is the reason why I do not dogmatically ascribe rhythm to all the sociocultural processes. Some of them function without exhibiting any graspable rhythm, displaying "ever new" aspects in their existence. So far as such processes are evident in history — and they certainly are — the old motto that history is ever new and never repeats itself is justified.

B. *The less numerous are the immanent possibilities of change of a system, the more pronounced is the rhythmical character of its processes.* If a system, say, a political regime, has only six possibilities (as Plato and Aristotle thought): monarchy, aristocracy, oligarchy, democracy, mob rule, and tyranny, these regimes must recur either in the same or in different order; either all six forms or only some of them, whether in the history of the same nation, if it still exists after it has exhausted all its forms, or in that of other bodies politic, no matter where and when they exist. If, instead of our six forms, we assume only two possibilities, say, monarchy and republic, the rhythms of monarchy-republic will be still more pronounced, and, other conditions being equal, will recur more frequently and regularly. In other words, the rhythm of the sociocultural process is in reverse relationship to the number of possible forms of its change.

C. *The number of the phases of the rhythm in the sociocultural process is roughly proportional to the number of its immanent possibilities of forms of change.* If, as in the above hypothetical forms, the number of the possible political regimes is six, the number of the phases of the political rhythms will, in that case, be either six, or more or less, depending on whether all these forms recur and in what order combination. If the possible forms are only two, the rhythm will be a double-phased rhythm. However, one should not take the proportionality too rigidly and too mathematically, though roughly it is valid, and as such ties together two variables: the number of the immanent possibilities and the double, triple, quadruple or multiple character of the rhythm from the standpoint of its phases. The proposition is again almost self-evident as soon as the principle of limit itself is assumed.

Such appears to me the general principle that accounts for the recurrences and rhythms of all the sociocultural processes that are found to be rhythmical or recurrent. So far as the principle of limit itself is but a specific case of the principle of immanent constitution and change of the system, its application to this problem is also a mere derivative of this principle. The advantages of this principle here, in comparison with that of the law of action and reaction, or the principle of equilibrium, are that we are not obliged to play with mere analogies, to postulate various (unknown) forces at different angles, and all the other purely analogical reasonings criticized above. Instead, we have a principle that with an inescapable logical validity accounts for the phenomena of recurrence and rhythms. More than that, it binds together several variables, such as the number of the possibilities and the frequency or graspability of rhythms; the number of possibilities and the kind of rhythms—double, triple, quadruple or multiple. In this sense, it answers the issue not only more validly and directly, but much more precisely than the above-mentioned analogical theories.

Like any other explanatory principle, it satisfactorily explains the problem discussed, and generalizes a rather large number of singular "It is so's" into one formula applicable to a very large number of sociocultural processes, and tying together three variables, does it more precisely than the mere incidental "It is so."

Further, it has a predictive value: if I know that only three main forms of cultural supersystems are possible, say, Ideational-Idealistic-

Sensate, in integrated culture; or Realism-Nominalism-Conceptualism in the philosophical problem of the reality of the universals, I can reasonably expect first: these forms will recur in the history of culture(s), or in that of philosophical thought in this field; second: the rhythm of their succession will probably be triple, though the order of the phases may vary. If I know that in regard to sex there are only two possibilities for *homo sapiens* (barring the rare cases of hermaphroditi), I can expect only a double rhythm, male-female, in the process of birth, though not necessarily always in the same order of male-female, male-female. If I know that (let us assume with Aristotle, which assumption is roughly correct) there are only six main forms of political regimes, then I can reasonably expect a recurrence of only these six forms in any society, at all times; and the rhythm will be either six-phased or even less complex, though the order of the succession of the regimes may vary.

Thus, in all these respects, the principle answers also the second and the third "why's": namely, Why some sociocultural processes recur; and why some have double, some triple, some multiple rhythms?

D. Finally, *Why are some of the rhythms periodic, while others are not?* has already been answered above. Thus, in the sociocultural processes only those rhythms are periodic that are "social conventions" in the broad sense of the term. Social conventions are inseparably tied with "social time" and the time system of the society. Time system is one of the absolutely indispensable conditions of any social life.

So far, therefore, the social nature of the periodicity of the sociocultural rhythms is explained and the problem is answered.

40

THE PROBLEMS OF EVER–LINEAR, EVER–NEW, AND STRICTLY CIRCULAR SOCIOCULTURAL CHANGE

I. Two Important Corollaries of the Principle of Limit

The preceding chapter accounted for the "why" of sociocultural rhythmical processes and the structure of the rhythms themselves. In this chapter we shall examine whether, among the sociocultural changes, there exist processes with a linear trend throughout their existence; whether there are processes with an ever-new change, without any recurrence; and finally, if there are strictly circular processes that repeat themselves identically, with the "why" of each of these forms of change. The inquiry begins with the problem of existence and the "why" of linear processes.

A. The principle of limited possibilities of variation of a system determines clearly the conditions under which a linear process, with a permanent trend throughout its existence, as well as the ever-new process, are possible. *In a state of isolation or constant environment, the sociocultural system that has only one immanent possibility of change will be changing along one main linear trend throughout its existence.* Such an "invariant" change will be linear, in one of the four forms — unilinear, oscillating, spiral, and branching — noted above. In such case the main direction and the sense of it remain constant throughout the whole process. It would move continuously along the same line, unfolding more and more its one property, and approaching nearer and nearer its terminal point, if there is such a point at all. The result will be a process resembling many a current conception of linear evolution and progress.

B. *If, on the other hand, the possibilities of mutation of a system in process are exceedingly great or unlimited, the result will be a process that may have no recurrence, no rhythm, where each link is new, unique, unrepeated.* In that case, we shall have indeed a process which never repeats itself and is "brand-new" at each portion or fraction of its course.

The above corollaries A and B formulate with sufficient precision the essential conditions under which the process may be linear in its direction or ever new in its change. Now the question arises: Are such changes found among the sociocultural processes? Do we really have linear sociocultural processes? Do we have, likewise, perfectly "ever-new" processes? Let us turn to the discussion of the first of these problems.

II. The Problem of Linear Sociocultural Processes

Are such linear processes, with only one possibility of mutation, generally given in the inorganic and organic worlds? If we accept Carnot-Clausius's principle of entropy, such a process is certainly given in a thermodynamic system. Its essential premise is that "it is impossible to make heat pass from a cold to a warm body." In any transformation of other forms of energy into heat, or heat into other forms of energy, a part of the energy is dissipated. The result is an eternal equalization of energy in the world, with the world perpetually "running down" to a final stage where all potentials of energy are equalized and therefore universal death is the final goal. Clausius himself describes this process as follows:

> It is frequently asserted that everything in this world has a circular course. While transformations proceed in a certain direction in a certain place and time, other transformations take place in inverse direction at another place and time, in such a way that the same situations are reproduced generally and that the state of the universe remains invariable, when the phenomena are considered in their totality and in a general manner. . . . [However] the second fundamental principle of mechanical theory of heat contradicts this opinion in the most decisive [la plus formelle] manner. . . . It follows from that that the state of the universe must change more and more in a determined direction.

It tends to an end, or to death, as contemporary astrophysicists often say.

If this theory is accepted — and it is fairly generally accepted, though there are objections to it — we have here one of the most universal processes of a definitely linear type with only one possibility of direction throughout all the existence of the universe.

It goes without saying that most of the current conceptions of biological evolution are built along the linear type also — either a unilinear, oscillatory, spiral, or branching (multilinear) variety of the linear.

It is only a commonplace to say that most of the theories of social evolution and progress that have been formulated in the nineteenth and twentieth centuries have also been a variety of the linear type, with this or that perpetual trend more and more realized in the course of the existence of mankind.

We may leave the thermodynamic and biological processes, with their alleged eternal trends, without discussion. Our task is to consider the matter in application to the sociocultural processes. Are there in sociocultural reality linear processes?

The answer seemingly depends, first, upon the *duration of time* considered. *There is no slightest doubt that if the time period is not too long, there are millions of sociocultural processes with a linear trend during such period.* The reader can glance over almost all the curves and tables of the previous sections and see that during a certain period, be it one year, or a century, or sometimes even several centuries, almost all the processes considered — for instance, materialism and idealism, eternalism and temporalism, familistic-contractual-compulsory relationships, visual and ideational styles in art, and so on — each of these rival processes has been ascending or descending steadily for decades and possibly even centuries. Be it a quantitative, spatial, or qualitative direction, or the tempo of the process, there is not a doubt that during certain periods, different for different processes, most of the processes have a linear trend.

Quite different is the situation if the existence of a linear trend is asserted for an infinite time, or for a period that factually exceeds the duration of the given linear trend. It is reasonably certain that an enormous part of the sociocultural processes (for the reasons on which is based the principle of limit in its first and second form) do not have either an eternal linear trend or a trend coextensive with the duration of the existence of the system. In the preceding sections we have dealt with a number of processes. Though all of them, during a certain period, have exhibited a linear trend, when they are considered in a longer time perspective these linear trends are discovered to be finite, and are replaced by new trends either different or opposite to the previous ones. This concerns practically all the processes considered in the preceding parts: the changes of art systems with their styles, of systems of truths, philosophies, scientific principles, discoveries, inventions, systems of ethics and law, forms of social relationships, of freedom, of government, of economic well-being, of war, of revolution, and so on. For a certain period, sometimes even during several centuries, a given form appears and grows and overwhelms its rivals; then the direction of the process changes and the ascending trend is replaced by a plateau, or descending trend. And so also in regard to qualitative, spatial, and tempo directions. *In all of them there happened to be a time limit for their linear trends.*

The same can be said of thousands of other sociocultural processes not mentioned specifically in these chapters. *Thus in regard to an enormous part of the sociocultural processes it can reasonably be claimed that all of them have a time limit for their linear trends. Beyond these limits, the trends end and are replaced by different, sometimes opposite trends.* The reasons for such a "trajectory" are given in the preceding chapters: *first, the immanent principle of change; second, the principle of not only one but two or more possibilities of mutations; third, interference of the external agents which for a given process throughout its existence are neither constant, nor absent, nor changing in an equilibrium of mutual annulment.*

These reasons are quite sufficient to explain why the above proposition is valid probably for an overwhelming majority of the sociocultural processes.

But are there processes which are exempt from this rule, which have the same linear trend without any time limits, or at least within the limits of an enormous time duration? If we have to believe a legion of enthusiastic devotees of linear progress and evolution, who have formulated hundreds of "eternal historical trends and tendencies," there seems to be no doubt that such processes exist and that they are numerous. However, the slightest test of most of these "theories" and their "trends" shows their fantastic and wishful nature. If such trends exist, they can hardly be very numerous. We have already seen above that in order for such a process to exist, a miraculous and most delicate combination of circumstances is necessary. First, it is necessary that the law of immanent change be eliminated; second, that the system have only one possibility of mutation; third, that it be either absolutely isolated from the rest of the world and external agencies, or that these for an exceptionally long time be constant, or, if varying, must be continuously annulling one another so that the equilibrium of the system and of its trend is undisturbed. Such a combination of exceptionally rare and highly improbable conditions is hardly possible often. Even its rare occurrence, if given, amounts almost to a miracle.

Therefore, if such eternally linear sociocultural processes exist, they must be exceptionally few. Has their existence been proved factually? Have we indeed a process with an eternal linear trend whose reality is unquestionable and beyond any reasonable doubt? As soon as the question is put in this sharp form, the situation becomes much less clear than the partisans of linearism think. Brushing aside thousands of pseudo-linear processes claimed to be linear, the processes which seem to be more certainly linear than all the others are probably as follows: 1. *Growth of the human population on this planet in the course of time.* 2. *Growth of human knowledge and inventions in the course of time.* 3. *Growth of social differentiation and integration in the course of time, including the division of labor.*

It probably will be agreed that these processes are likely to be most linear among all the sociocultural linear processes, if there are generally such processes. Therefore, an analysis of their eternal linearity may serve as an *a posteriori* crucial test of the existence of the genuinely linear sociocultural processes which remain linear without any time limit, or as long as mankind exists.

The first argument against a claim of their unlimited linearity may be put as follows: We grant that "from the beginning of human history up to the present time the population of this planet, the knowledge of mankind, and social differentiation and integration have (with perhaps secondary and short-time fluctuations) been growing." But can we be sure that these trends will continue forever, no matter how far the future is projected in time, or as long as mankind exists? Are there any unquestionable reasons or evidences that it will be so, and that the trend will not be replaced by a different or perhaps even opposite one? So far, no convincing reason has been given why the trends will continue forever in the future, unless the hypothesis of Providence is postulated; but such a hypothesis is unacceptable to almost all the partisans of this claim. If anything, the logical reasons are against such a claim (see above). From the fact that it has always been so, it does not follow it will be so forever.

Second, this argument is reinforced by the data of the natural sciences. They assure us that the sun is the ultimate source of energy for life on this planet, including the sociocultural life also. They also assert that in the course of time the sun is cooling and therefore sooner or later the time will come when life on this planet will decline and finally die. This means, then, a decline and an end of human history. If and when human history enters this stage of the cooled sun, human population, its social differentiation and integration, and in all probability human knowledge, must also be on a declining trend, opposite to the trend that has prevailed up to the present time (according to our grant).

The natural scientists have been assuring us that such a future of the sun and life and mankind is quite certain. If this is so, then the alleged eternal trends are nothing but unusually long-time trends which, beyond a certain time limit, are bound to be ended and replaced by different, even opposite, trends. If the partisans of the perpetual trends want to avoid this conclusion, they have to disprove the above assertions of the natural sciences, which they have not done as yet. These two considerations (plus the above logical reasons) make very doubtful the theory of the eternality of the trends discussed. At the best, they appear to be unusually long-time trends, neither eternal nor coextensive with the existence of mankind.

To sum up: probably in most linear processes the linearity at best is likely to be a long-time but nevertheless limited linearity. In the perspective of still longer periods projected into the future and into the past, their linear trend is likely to be a mere part of a long-time parabola or other nonlinear curve. Even this linearity for a known part of the processes appears such only when a purely formal cumulative standpoint is taken, when the periods are large, when the whole of mankind is considered. Even so, this linearity is very uneven, intermittent, with several recessions of stagnation points. When the processes are taken more realistically, from shorter time-periods — from the standpoint of the comparative increase or decrease of the population, of discoveries and inventions, of social differentiation and integration, from each preceding to each subsequent period, and especially for separate countries — the processes appear to be not linear, even in the part known. The net result of all this is that *if there are a few indefinitely linear processes, they are such only from a half-fictitious standpoint; and their linearity is so pale and undetermined that it amounts only to a mere shadow linearity.* This means that almost all the sociocultural processes that appear to be linear are such only within the limited duration of the process in time. Beyond this time limit their direction changes, and the processes appear to be nonlinear. This excursion only confirms what should be expected from the standpoint of the reasons developed on preceding pages in connection with the principle of limit. What appeared to be improbable "deductively" — almost amounting to a miracle, or the pre-established harmony of Leibnitz — appears also improbable empirically. So much then for the linear processes.

III. The Problem of the Ever-New Processes

Turn now to the problem of the sociocultural processes with large or unlimited possibilities of forms and mutations, and therefore potentially capable of having no recurrences, no rhythms (because an unrepeated rhythm is no rhythm at all, and a very infrequent rhythm cannot be grasped as such), being a unique novelty in any link of the process.

Are such processes found among the sociocultural processes? Before an answer is given, we must distinguish between all accidental properties of a system and its essential properties (main meanings, main vehicles and agents). Any system, and anything in the world, even this table and typewriter, when taken in the totality of its accidental singularistic characteristics, is an inexhaustible and infinite microcosm, with millions and billions of traits. And any system, when taken in its essential characteristics — those whose absence makes the system non-existent or makes it radically different from what it is — has a limited number of properties, namely, those of *genus plus differentia specifica,* according to the logical definition.

If we put the question in application to a given social system, taken in the totality of all its singularistic properties, the answer is that, due to the principle of immanent change, any system changes incessantly during its existence: among all its properties something new is incessantly introduced and something old is incessantly lost from moment to moment of its existence. In this sense any sociocultural process is ever new and unrepeated. Even a change of the system along the same trend is ever new, because it moves farther, and changes at different (unique) moments of time.

We have admitted then an incessantly changing, new, and creative aspect of the sociocultural processes, without any exception whatsoever, when the totality of their properties is considered; on the other hand, it is to be noted that such an ever-new change is admitted not in regard to all the essential characteristics of the system, but only in regard to some of its accidental singularistic properties. If any system A, or its process A, were at any succeeding moment new totally, or in all its essential traits, there would be neither continuity of the same system, nor of the same process. Instead, there would be a rapidly succeeding series of perfectly different systems and processes, like the mentioned momentary cuts in movie films. If at any succeeding moment the system A (or its process) becomes brand new in all its characteristics, or in the totality of its essential properties, this means that the system A is ended at any of such moments, and is replaced by perfectly different systems B, C, D and so on. Total change of the total system or of all its essential components (meanings, vehicles, agents) means its end, and its replacement by a perfectly different system. It is not the change of the same system, because at any succeeding moment there is nothing left of A. If a given religion, law, state, man, or plant is in one moment replaced by a totally different religion, law, state, man, or plant, there is no continuity of existence or no change of these systems. There is just a replacement of them by quite different ones. In that case, we cannot talk of the process of change, transformation, modification, development, or evolution of the system at all. We can talk only of *substitution* or *replacement* of one system or process by another, totally different.

Hence the conclusion: any sociocultural process is new at any moment, and, at the same time, is old. These two seemingly opposite statements — system is ever new and ever old, ever changing and ever identical — mutually supplement one another.

If we mean just a *replacement* of one system or one set of congeries by another, in such a substitution they may "change" *in toto* at any moment. In that case, however, we have not a process of change but a *replacement* or substitution of one system or congeries by another. As soon as any given system — say, the Society for Prevention of Cruelty to Animals, or Gothic architecture, or a cow — loses its essential characteristics, the system ceases to exist *qua* Society for Prevention of Cruelty to Animals, *qua* Gothic architecture, *qua* cow, and is replaced by quite a different system.

These conclusions, translated into the terms of the range of possibilities of the system, mean that *in regard to an indefinitely large number of "accidental" traits and properties of the system, the range of the possibilities of forms and mutations is large, perhaps even unlimited. Hence the fact of the incessant change of these properties and traits in the system during its existence. But in regard to the essential properties of the system or process, the range of the possibilities is definitely limited for each system, so long as it exists. Some systems have narrow, others wider, but always limited possibilities of change, in regard to the essential traits that identify their respective sameness.* Hence the continuity of their existence; hence the coexistence of the ever new and ever old in the system, so long as it exists.

The conclusion concerning the limited possibility of essential mutations of any sociocultural system can also be reached in another way. If we imagine a sociocultural system unlimited in the possibilities of its forms and mutations, the system that can become anything and everything, cow, cathedral, university, polyphonic music, etc., such a system must be either *an infinite omnivariant God,* or absolutely indeterminate ultimate "stuff," or undefined "primary something."

Such infinite omnivariant God, or indeterminate ultimate "stuff," or undefined ultimate "something" is not a definite empirical system, because it is devoid of any empirical determination, any qualities, any quantities, any space-time properties, anything definite. It is Aristotelian formless "matter," Hegelian Pure Being, identical with Nothing, Master Eckehart's and the Mystics' "Divine Nothing," Erigena's and Nicolaus Cusanus' God, "infinitude of infinitudes," as the "*coincidentia oppositorum,*" to which none of our categories are applicable; even such as "What." Such Absolutes have nothing in common with an empirical sociocultural system, which always is finite individuality, limited, defined, and determined, with all the categories applicable to it. Such a finite system cannot be endowed with an infinite or unlimited capacity or transformation: in that case the finite would contain in itself the infinite, which is logical nonsense. Hence the conclusion of the limited possibility of its transformations, so far as its essential characteristics are concerned, with a much wider possibility of change in its accidental properties. When the limited possibility of the transformation of the system is transgressed, the system loses its identity and ends its existence.

The inexhaustibly diverse and ever-new process of culture is made up through the immanent limited change of its systems, as well as through an incessant replacement of the dying systems by newly born ones. The total history of the sociocultural world certainly displays itself as ever new, as inexhaustible in its creativeness, variations, transformations and diversity at any moment of its existence. It appears to be and probably is infinite in the possibilities of its variations. Such a result is due not only to the fact that each of the multitudes of systems of which it is made up incessantly changes, but also, and mainly, that history uses the method of incessant replacement of the systems that dissolve after reaching their terminal point by ever-new systems that take their place. Through this double method of immanent change of the systems and their replacement, it achieves inexhaustible creative variations. In any compartment of culture we see this substitution of new systems for the dead ones. A certain style in art, say, Gothic architecture, emerges, develops, reaches its full realization, and then, having exhausted its possibilities, stops, and becomes either mummified in its imitative repetitions, or dies out, giving place to a new style. The same destiny awaits this successor. A certain technological invention, say, "horse-buggy" system, emerges, unfolds itself in many varieties, and then stops in development and, sooner or later, is replaced by a new system, say, the automobile, which in no way is its further development but the start of a new system. The same is true of the specific systems in science, religion, art, law, ethics, forms of economic, political, social organization, and what not. The impressive diversity of change in all these fields is due, to a great degree, to the method of substitution. The creative forces of human history incessantly use this method; after unfolding all the possibilities of each created system, they discard it, and start a new system. Having squeezed from it all that it can give, they mold a new successor to it; and so on, *ad infinitum*. Hence, the inexhaustible creativeness of human — social and cultural — history. The same is true of the history of life. Having "experimented" with a given species in all its main possibilities, the creative forces of life discard it and give birth to a new species. So it has been, and so it is.

Each system has limited possibilities of variation, so far as its essential traits are concerned. But in variation of its accidental traits and, especially, in variation of the new types substituted for one another, when the whole process of biological and sociocultural history is considered, there seems to exist the widest, almost unlimited, range of possibilities.

IV. The Problem of Identically Cyclical or Circular Processes

In regard to this possibility we can be brief. We have seen that rhythm and recurrence are unavoidable for practically all the sociocultural processes that exist after all their possibilities are run through. But it has been indicated that the recurrence or rhythm is never identical in all its characteristics with the preceding or following recurrences. It is identical with other recurrent rhythms only in the essential traits, but not in all accidental properties. The impossibility of absolutely identical recurrences either in the same system (recurrence in time), or in different systems (recurrence in space), follows from the same principle of immanent change. By virtue of this, any system is changing by *proprio motu* and is in some degree different at any different moment. Monarchy and Republic, Gothic and Classic style, Materialism and Idealism can alternate in a sociocultural system, but each case of recurrence of Republic or Gothic style is different from the preceding case and from all the subsequent cases in a number of ways and traits. Time is different; details in the components are different: in the system of meanings, in vehicles, in agents; society and environment are different; and so on. Every one of us, from day to day, has dinner or sleep, but each dinner or sleep is not identical with the former ones: we ourselves are changed; time has elapsed irretrievably; and a number of traits of the dinner or sleep are varying.

This is quite sufficient to demonstrate the impossibility of identical recurrences and rhythms in any sociocultural system and process. In regard to them, at least, we shall abandon the old theories of "eternal return" in identical forms, surveyed above. The principle of immanent change is quite sufficient for that conclusion.

V. Summary

Thus, developing systematically the principle of immanent change and its derivative — the principle of limit — and applying it to the problem of recurrence, rhythm, linearism, and eternal novelty, we come to the conclusions already given: that the most general pattern of the sociocultural change is that of incessantly varying recurrent processes. This means:

1. Identically recurrent sociocultural processes are impossible.

2. Eternally linear sociocultural processes are also impossible. Any process that appears such is, in all probability, a long-time linear process, and when taken in its complete life, it is likely to be a non-linear process.

3. But a linear trend limited in time (whose duration is different for different systems and processes) is to be expected and is factually found in almost all sociocultural processes. In some it lasts only a few moments or hours or days or months; in others many decades and even centuries, but in all, it is limited in time and is shorter than the time of the whole existence of the system.

4. The sociocultural processes with an unlimited possibility of variation of their essential traits are also impossible — factually and logically. All such systems and processes are limited in these possibilities so far as these essential forms are concerned. Hence, "history is ever old and repeats itself."

5. As to the possibilities of variation of the "accidential" properties of the system, the range of the possibilities here is wide, in some cases, at least, theoretically, almost unbounded. Hence, an incessant change of the system in these traits as long as the system exists. Likewise, almost unlimited are the possibilities of variation of the ever-new systems through the method of substitution or replacement of the exhausted systems by new ones. Hence, history is ever new, unrepeated and inexhaustible in its creativeness.

6. Since practically all the sociocultural systems have limited possibilities of variation of their essential forms, it follows that all the systems that continue to exist after all their possible forms are exhausted, are bound to have recurrent rhythms. Hence, the inevitability of recurrence in the life process of such systems.

7. Other conditions being equal, the more limited the possibilities of variation of main forms, the more frequent, conspicuous, and graspable are the rhythms in the process of the system, and the simpler the rhythms from the standpoint of their phases. And vice versa, if in some of the processes we cannot grasp any recurrent rhythm, the reason is either that the process has comparatively large possibilities of varia-

tion that empirically prevent us from noticing the infrequent rhythm; or that it endures a shorter life span and dies earlier, before it has had a chance to run through all its forms (just as some organisms die at the prenatal stage or in childhood, before they have had a chance to run through all the main phases of human life from birth to senility). Or the inability to grasp any recurrent rhythm may be due to a co-existence and mutual "interference" of several contemporaneous and different rhythms in the same system that change them into an un-rhythmical "noise" for the listener or observer; or to the excessively long duration between the recurrences, which makes the rhythm also unobservable; or to the exceedingly complex and many-phased nature of the rhythm.

8. Thus history ever repeats itself and never repeats itself; both seemingly contradictory statements are true and are not contradictory at all, when properly understood.

9. This means that the strictly cyclical (identically recurrent) conception of the sociocultural processes; the linear, in the sense of unlimitedly linear; the unicist, in the sense of the nonexistence of any recurrent rhythms in the sociocultural processes, they being "brand-new" and unique in the totality of their traits and properties at any moment; the static conception that there is no change, and that the sociocultural world ever remains strictly identical with itself — all these conceptions are fallacious. The valid conception is that of an "incessant variation" of the main recurrent themes, which contains in itself, as a part, all these conceptions, and as such is much richer than any of them.

41

THE REASON FOR THE SUPER-RHYTHM OF IDEATIONAL-IDEALISTIC-SENSATE PHASES IN THE GRAECO-ROMAN AND WESTERN SUPERSYSTEMS OF CULTURE

I. Principles of Immanent Change and of Limited Possibilities as the First Reasons

In the light of the principles of immanent change and of limited possibilities we are prepared now to answer the problem: "Why, in the course of the historical unfolding of the Graeco-Roman and Western cultures, has its supersystem twice repeated the triple rhythm of Ideational-Idealistic-Sensate phases, from the twelfth century B.C. to the end of the Middle Ages, and after the fifteenth century for the third time entered the Sensate phase, which is seemingly declining at the present time?

However different may have been the course of these cultures during these centuries in other respects; however large, perhaps even unbounded, are the possibilities of mutation of these cultures in regard to their different aspects and traits, in their congeries and systems unrelated to the supersystem; the fact of the rhythm, and the above order of the phases of each rhythm (Sensate-Ideational-Idealistic, or, what is the same, Ideational-Idealistic-Sensate) seems to be beyond question. Moreover, in a clearly defined form, we have traced somewhat similar rhythms even in several other cultures, like the Hindu, the Chinese, the Arabian, and a few others.

What is the reason for such a rhythm? The answer is given by the principles of immanent change and of the limited possibilities of the main integrated forms of a cultural supersystem. *By virtue of the principle of immanent change, each of the three integrated forms, or phases, of the Ideational, Idealistic and Sensate supersystems cannot help changing; rising, growing, existing full-blooded for some time, and then declining.* The principle explains why each of these forms does not stay forever at its domination, and why it has to give place to the other forms of the triad. It does not explain, however, why this triple rhythm with its three phases is recurrent, and why the phases follow each other in the sequence: Sensate-Ideational-Idealistic.

The recurrence is sufficiently accounted for by the principle of the limited possibilities of the main *integrated* forms of culture. Note, I am stressing the *integrated* forms of culture (or the phases of the integrated supersystem). Only to these is the principle of the limited possibilities applicable. The number of the unintegrated forms of culture is much larger, practically unlimited, if we keep in mind all the variation of diverse congeries, accidental traits, and unrelated systems.

Even the number of unintegrated, eclectically mixed combinations of the Ideational and Sensate culture elements is enormous. In our study of the transitional periods, when one integrated form disintegrates while the other is not yet crystallized, we have seen that these transitional periods exhibited a variety of combinations of the elements of the main forms, and a dissimilarity from each other in a number of important aspects (centuries from the ninth to the eighth B.C., the sixth and the third B.C., the third and fourth A.D., the twelfth and fourteenth to the fifteenth A.D., and the present time).

Different, however, is the situation in regard to the main *integrated* forms. Their number — or possibilities — theoretically and factually, is much more limited.

In regard to the nature of the true reality — the main premise of each of these integrated forms — the number of possible answers is very limited and hardly goes beyond five fundamental solutions: first, the nature of the true reality is supersensory (Ideational premise); second, it is sensory (Sensate premise); third, it has both aspects inseparable from one another (Idealistic premise); fourth, it is entirely unknown and unknowable (premise of Scepticism); fifth, it is known only in its phenomenal aspect, while in its transcendental aspect (if it has such an aspect) it is unknowable (the premise of Hume-Kant's Criticism and Agnosticism). There exists hardly any solution of this problem essentially different from these five possibilities. There is a much larger possibility for various eclectic (unintegrated) mixtures of these five principles, but such eclectic solutions are not systems but congeries. As such they are not and cannot be a major premise of integrated forms of culture. Likewise, within each of these five fundamental forms, there is a large possibility of variation in the secondary details of the respective theories; the Idealistic philosophy of Plato differs — in a series of secondary traits — from that of Plotinus, and both from that of St. Augustine or Hegel. The materialism of Leukippos is different from that of Lucretius, and both from the materialism of Lammetrie or Holbach or Marx. However, these are secondary differences which do not concern the main characteristics of Idealistic or Materialistic premises. From the standpoint of these main characteristics, there is hardly any other main possibility of the solution of the problem, except the above five answers. If there are one or two more possibilities, they would increase the five possibilities to six or seven forms only.

Since there are only five main possibilities, two of which are negative and can hardly serve as a basis for a long-existing integrated culture, by virtue of the principle of limit and immanent change, three of these, and two others as subsystems, cannot help being repeated in the integrated cultures that continue to exist after the first run of all the three or five fundamental forms. Hence repetition of these forms; hence our super-rhythm in the history of the cultures studied. What is said of the main postulate of these three main forms of cultural supersystems can be said of all the embraced systems and rhythms of which they are composed.

Theoretically, there are and can be only five or six main integrated systems of truth: 1, the truth of faith; 2, that of reason; 3, that of the senses; 4, that of their idealistic synthesis; and 5, an integrated sceptical and agnostic, or critical system. The rest would represent merely an eclectic mixture of these systems. Since there is no other logical possibility for a fundamentally different integrated system of truth, it is but inevitable — logically and factually — that these systems should recur in any long-existing culture (in time) or in various cultures (in space). We have seen that they have indeed been recurring in their domination.

The same can be said of the main styles of art: Ideational (Symbolic), Visual (Sensate), and Idealistic (Integrated Symbolic-Visual).

There is no possibility of an additional fundamental integrated form. There is only a wide possibility of an eclectic and incoherent mixture of these elements. Hence a recurrence of these forms in the same and other cultures.

The same applies to much more detailed "patterns" of art generally, and to specific arts particularly. "Classic and romantic," "linear and malerisch," "religious and secular," "idealistic and naturalistic," "conventional" and "revolutionary," — these and hundreds of other forms so commonly used in the history and theory of art — whatever each of them means with different authors — all these detailed forms are again limited in the possibility of fundamental forms.

So also in regard to the main forms of ethics. Any integrated system of ethics may be either that of Absolute Imperative (including that of Christian Love), or the ethics of Sensate Happiness in its eudemonistic, utilitarian, and hedonistic varieties, or an organic synthesis of both.

The rest (including the extreme moral nihilism) will be an incoherent mixture of these forms. Hence the recurrence of these integrated forms in time and in space. Hence the swings of the domination of each of these main forms, which we have traced in the preceding chapters.

And so on, in regard to even such more narrow and specified principles as atomism and anti-atomism in the natural sciences, as vitalism and mechanism, as the main conceptions of time, space, and other "first principles" of science and philosophy.

Since the main forms of each of these integrated systems and subsystems have a limited range of variation, they cannot help recurring again and again in the life history of a culture whose existence exceeds the duration of the first run of all these main forms. Having occurred once, they cannot help being repeated for the second or third or more times.

So far as each of these systems of truth, of true reality, of forms of art, of ethics, of forms of social, economic, political and other relationships are but subsystems in our supersystem, and as such live and change together, their total co-ordinated recurrence gives the recurrence of the Ideational, Idealistic, and Sensate phases in the life process of our supersystem.

Thus the principles of immanent change and of the limited possibilities of the main forms give an adequate answer to the problem: Why do these phases of the supersystem, as well as the corresponding phases in all the subordinated systems of which the supersystem is made up, recur? These reasons are, however, not the only reasons for recurrence. There exists another, deeper, reason for that. Let us glance at it.

II. Inadequacy of Each of the Main Systems of Truth and Reality as a Reason for the Super-Rhythm of Ideational-Idealistic-Sensate Forms of Culture

The preceding chapters of *Dynamics* have shown that at the basis of the Ideational or Idealistic or Sensate form of integrated culture lies, as its major premise, its system of truth and reality. It is this premise that, to use W. I. Thomas' term, "defines the situation" for the rest of the related compartments of each of these forms of culture.

Art and philosophy, ethics and religion, science and forms of social organization of a Sensate supersystem are articulations of the Sensate system of truth and reality. In Ideational or Idealistic or Sensate cultures, these compartments articulate Ideational or Idealistic or

Sensate systems of truth and reality. *Now each of three main systems of truth and reality may be either entirely true, or entirely false, or partly true and partly false.*

A. If one of these systems is entirely true — is the only truth, the whole truth and nothing but the truth — then the other two systems of truth and reality are entirely or mainly false. Under such an assumption the true system of reality — and a corresponding form of culture — can exist and dominate forever, without any fear or possibility of being dislodged by the false systems. It is hardly possible that an entirely false, and inadequate, system of reality and truth can dislodge the entirely true system, or that complete ignorance can overthrow complete knowledge. Being true, it gives an adequate knowledge of the reality; through that it permits its human bearers to live a real life, to adapt themselves successfully to the adequately known environment; and, through all that, to enjoy a better social life and culture than a society and culture based exclusively upon error and ignorance. This means that under such an assumption, *a given system of true reality and knowledge can be expected to continue forever, without any rhythm of rise and decline of Ideational-Idealistic-Sensate forms.*

B. If we assume that each of these systems of truth and reality is entirely false — is nothing but an error and fallacy — none of them could dominate for any length of time, and still less could recur, because no human beings, no society, no culture can endure under the condition of complete ignorance and error. If human beings do not know what is eatable and what is not; and if they try mistakenly to eat "uneatables," and do not eat "eatables," and display similar folly in regard to other necessities and phenomena, they very quickly perish, and with them their society and culture. A minimum of true knowledge, of true reality, is absolutely necessary in order for any person or society to exist for some time; and a great deal of it is required in order to exist for decades and centuries. If each of the three main systems of truth and reality were absolutely false, none of them could have dominated millions of human beings for centuries, as they did; and after their disappearance none of them could have had any chance to recur, as they did. Even from the standpoint of the theory of selection, such an entirely false system of truth and reality would be eliminated once and for all. This means that under this assumption, no rhythm of domination of Ideational, Idealistic, and Sensate systems of truth and reality — and a corresponding form of culture — is possible. Likewise, no durable domination of such an entirely false and inadequate form of culture is thinkable. Meanwhile, as a matter of fact, each of our three main systems dominated for centuries and recurred several times in the history of the Graeco-Roman and Western cultures. And so they did also in other cultures.

C. Hence the *super-rhythm studied seems to be possible only under the condition that each of the three main systems of truth and reality — and the corresponding form of culture — is partly true and partly false, partly adequate and partly inadequate.* Only because each of them contains a vital part does it give to its human bearers the possibility of an adaptation to their milieu — cosmic, organic, and social; gives them a minimum of real experience to meet their needs; and serves as a foundation for their social life and culture. But because each of the three systems has also an invalid part — error and fallacy side by side with truth — each of these systems leads its human bearers away from the reality, gives them pseudo knowledge instead of real knowledge, and hinders their adaptation and the satisfaction of their physiological, social, and cultural needs. When such a system of truth and reality ascends, grows, and becomes more and more monopolistically dominant, its false part tends to grow, while its valid part tends to decrease. Becoming monopolistic or dominant, it tends to drive out all the othèr systems of truth and reality, and with them the valid parts they contain. At the same time, like dictatorial human beings, becoming dominant, the system is likely to lose increasingly its validities and develop its falsities. The net result of such a trend is that as the domination of the system increases, it becomes more and more inadequate. As such, it becomes less and less capable of serving as an instrument of adaptation, as an experience for real satisfaction of the needs of its bearers; and as a foundation for their social and cultural life. The society and culture built on such a premise become more and more empty, false, inexperienced, ignorant; therefore, powerless, disorderly, and base; nobody can build his or society's life and culture on error, ignorance, and pure illusion. The moment comes when the false part of the system begins to overweigh its valid part. Under such conditions, the society of its bearers is doomed either to perish, or it has to change its major premise — to "redefine the situation" — and with it, its system of culture. In this way the dominant system prepares its own downfall and paves the way for the ascendance and domination of one of the rival systems of truth and reality, which is, under the circumstances, more true and valid than the outworn and degenerated dominant system. The new dominant system undergoes again the same tragedy, and sooner or later is replaced by its rival; and so these *corsi* and *ricorsi* must go on, and have been going on. In other words, under this third assumption, the recurrence of our super-rhythm of Ideational-Idealistic-Sensate systems of truth and reality, and of corresponding systems of culture, becomes not only comprehensible but logically and factually inevitable. The only alternative to this inevitability is the perdition of the society and culture. Such is the deeper reason for the "why" of the super-rhythm studied.

The validity of this reasoning is almost axiomatic, if it can be shown that each of the three main systems of truth and reality is indeed neither wholly false, nor wholly true, but contains a part of truth and a part of error; and that with an increase of the domination of each system, its part of truth decreases while the part of error increases.

That each of the three main systems of truth — the truth of faith, of reason, and of the senses — is not the whole truth and nothing but the truth, is almost evident. If it were so, its partisans would be the possessors of the absolute truth in all its manifold infinity. They would be the Omniscient God. No error, and no further progress of either religion or philosophy or science would be possible under such an assumption: the Absolute is absolute and does not admit any addition or improvement. There is hardly any intelligent religious thinker, or philosopher, or scientist who can claim or does claim such a possession of the Absolute — complete and pure — truth. For a religious man, such a claim would mean his pretension to be the Omniscient God, which none of the great religious thinkers has ever claimed. For a scientist, such a claim is excluded by the hypothetical, relativistic nature of scientific knowledge. For a philosopher, it is excluded by the philosopher's epistemology, no matter what it is.

In addition, the assumption of the absolute truth by the representatives of any of these systems of truth would mean a presupposition that the true reality is exhaustible and finite, in all its quantitative, qualitative, and other forms and contents. Such an assumption is also impossible. No sensible man, still less a sensible thinker, can claim that he or his brand of truth is already a possessor of the whole truth. Therefore this first assumption falls down.

Can we assume that each of the three systems of truth is entirely false and does not contain anything valid in it? Such an assumption is also impossible. Empirically, as we have seen, each of these systems of truth and reality dominated in Graeco-Roman and Western (and also in other) cultures for several centuries. As has been pointed out above, an entirely false system of truth and reality cannot dominate large masses, or even a single individual for a period of even a few days: persons devoid of the instincts of animals and controlled by entirely false conceptions of truth and reality would perish physically in a very short time. Still more so would a whole society. If each of these systems of reality and truth were wholly false, it could not dominate for centuries without leading to the perdition of all its bearers. Still less could each of these systems re-emerge and become dominant again and again.

Logically, the complete falsity of all or one of the three systems of truth is also ruled out. The major premises accepted, the great theological, or philosophical, or scientific systems exhibit a creative, logical, and consistent thought; having little in common with the incoherency or absurdity of the illogical or nonlogical thinking. More than that, the great religious, philosophical, and scientific systems are the best and finest examples of human consistent thought — the standards for logic and refined thinking — and not something that needs an apology for poor logic or dialectic or illogicity. One may or may not agree with St. Augustine and St. Thomas Aquinas; with Kant or Plato; with Sir Isaac Newton or Darwin; but as soon as the major premises of these systems are admitted, one has to grant to these and to other great religious, philosophical, and scientific systems the humanly possible superlative coherency of thought.

III. The Integral Theory of Truth and Reality

In regard to scientific and philosophical systems of truth — the truth of the senses and of reason — this is hardly questioned nowadays. The systems are admitted with their sources of truth: the dialectic of human reason and the testimony of the organs of the senses. Mathematics and logic are mainly the system of truth of human reason; and the natural sciences are mainly the depository of the truth of the senses. More questionable nowadays is the truth of faith derived from such a source, which is called by diverse names as: "intuition," "inspiration," "revelation," "extra-sensory perception," "mystic experience," and so on. Does such a source, as distinct from discursive dialectics, or testimony of the organs of senses, exist?

The answer has to be positive. We may not know exactly the nature of this source of truth. We must also admit that, like observation in all its forms (experimental, statistical, clinical) and reasoning, it does not always guarantee the truth. But any careful investigator of the history of human experience, science, philosophy, religion and truly creative cultural value, can hardly deny the existence of such a source of truth and its great and positive contributions to the history of human thought, science, art, philosophy, religion, ethics, technology, and even to economic and practical creative values.

First of all, for the reason that some kind of intuition is at the very basis of the validity of the systems of truth of reason and of the senses.

Second, because intuition, as distinct from discursive dialectic and sensory experience, has been one of the most important and fruitful "starters" of an enormous number of the most important scientific, mathematical and philosophical discoveries and technological inventions. *Third,* because a variety of the religious and mystic intuition has been the main source and the main force for the creation of the greatest artistic, religious, and ethical systems of culture. *Fourth,* because there is a sufficiently large body of the testimonies of the great thinkers, creators of religion, of art values, of science, demonstrating the reality, the functioning, and the power of this source of truth. Let us elucidate these points briefly.

A. That an intuition, a direct, self-evident, axiomatic, and often momentary experience different from either perception or sensation, or still more from imagination, memory, discursive thought and ordinary observation in all its forms, lies at the foundation of the validity of the basic propositions not only of religious and philosophical, but also of mathematico-logical and empirical sciences and their truths, is nowadays well recognized by many a philosopher, scientist, thinker, and generally, investigator of this problem. Why do the basic postulates of any science, from mathematics to physics, appear to be unquestionably valid and their axioms axiomatic? Since by definition they are ultimate postulates and axioms, they cannot be based upon either logic or empirical experience; on the contrary all the subsequent logical propositions and empirical theories are based upon the postulates and axioms. The only source of the self-evident character of such postulates and axioms is intuition. In this sense, it is not a derivative of, but the condition and basis of the truth of reason and of sensory experience.

The same conclusion is reached through consideration of the fact that language, as the indispensable condition of any thought, is not created through dialectic of human reason, but represents a product of intuition. Some thinkers even go so far as to put intuition at the basis of our perception as a judge who decides whether the perception is real or illusory.

The intuition seems to be also the ultimate foundation of the beautiful, and of the ethical or moral, not to mention the religious — the sphere particularly dominated by the intuition and especially by the mystic intuition.

B. Still less questionable is the fact that intuition has been the starter of an enormous number of sensory and dialectic discoveries and inventions in all the creative fields of culture, beginning with science, from mathematics, technology and biology, to social and humanistic disciplines and philosophy, and ending with art, religion, ethics, and other cultural systems. That intuition plays an important part in mathematics and lies at the basis of the mathematical deductions, one of its most prominent representatives, G. Birkhoff, has already stated.

That a large number of mathematical discoveries have been made by intuition — and not by following F. Bacon's or the Logistics' rules — is well demonstrated by the history of mathematics. H. Poincaré's personal experiences are typical in this respect.

During fifteen days I have tried to demonstrate that no function analogous to what later on I called *les fonctions fuchsiennes* could exist. All these days I sat down at my working table, and attempted a great number of combinations and arrived at no result. One evening, contrary to my habit, I took black coffee and could not fall asleep; ideas appeared in crowds; I felt as though they were pushing one another [*se heurter*] until two of them hooked, so to speak, one another, [*s'accrochassent*] and made a stable combination. In the morning I established the existence of the class of the *fonctions fuchsiennes*. All that I had to do was to repeat the results, which took only a few hours from me.

Another time he tells that the solution of another mathematical problem came to him instantaneously as he was stepping into a bus. Having arrived at Caen, he verified it and found it correct. He cites several other instances of this kind and stresses that in all of them the solution came always "with the same character of brevity, suddenness and immediate certitude" [*avec les mêmes caractères de brièveté, de soudaineté et de certitude immédiate*].

Hardly different from this intuitional experience was Sir Isaac Newton's discovery of gravitation. "On one memorable day, an apple falls with a slight thud at his feet. It was a trifling incident which has been idly noticed thousands of times; but now like the click of some small switch which starts a great machine in operation, it proved to be the jog which awoke his mind to action. As in a vision, he saw that if the mysterious pull of the earth can act through space as far as the top of a tree . . . so it might even reach so far as the moon."

Not different is the case of Archimedes, with his famous "eureka" suddenly coming to him while he was stepping into a bath and making him forget to put on his clothes, in his excitement; of Galileo watching a swinging lamp in a church and by "short circuit" formulating the law of oscillation of the pendulum; of Robert Meyer, who, from two chance occurrences during a voyage, "with a sudden leap of thought . . . derived the law of the mechanical equivalence of heat." And a large number of great and small discoveries in mathematics and physicochemical sciences were started in a similar intuitive manner.

The same is still truer of technological inventions. "The activities of our minds concerned with innovation . . . are more closely associated with the emotions than with reason and . . . are aesthetic and intuitive in character rather than rational." "Intuitive knowledge and the works of creative imagination are more or less directly associated with delvings into levels beyond the limits of our normally conscious life." The statements of the inventors themselves make this quite clear. One says that when the need for a certain invention comes, "I immediately eject it from the objective side of my mind, that is to say, I cease to labor over it, and consign it to the 'subjective department' of my mind." There it spontaneously ripens until it "comes out."

Another says, "Ideas come when I least expect them, often when I am half asleep, or day-dreaming." Others state that they either sometimes wake with a new idea, or it comes "in a flash," or it comes in "the period of relaxation," or "in the bathtub," or suddenly, when the inventor is engaged in a different kind of work, or "quite unexpectedly," and so on.

No different is the situation in the other natural sciences. Many of their greatest representatives testify, first, that hardly any important discovery has been made there by following the *schema* of F. Bacon; second, the intuitive start or inspiration of many discoveries.

As to the discoveries in the field of philosophical, humanistic, and social science disciplines, there the role of intuition has indeed been preponderant. This is objectively testified to by the fact that almost all the great discoveries — the main philosophies, the main humanistic and social science theories — were made a long time ago, when neither laboratories, nor statistics, nor systematic data of observation, nor any other material for an empirical or even rational generalization existed. The study of the relevant facts in these fields shows that many of these creations and theories were initiated by intuition. It does not exclude the fact that in many cases the intuitional revelation comes after strenuous but fruitless work of the sensory or discursive mind. What is important is that the solution comes through intuition.

The process is well described in its extreme form, by one of the greatest philosopher-poets of the nineteenth century, F. Nietzsche. He thus describes the mental state in which he wrote *Also sprach Zarathustra:*

Has anyone at the close of the nineteenth century any clear perception of what the poets of strong ages called inspiration? If not, I will describe it.

Possessing only the smallest remnant of superstition one would hardly be able to reject the idea that one is nothing but a medium for super-mighty influences. That which happens can only be termed revelation, that is to say, that suddenly, with unutterable certainty and delicacy, something becomes visible and audible and shakes and rends one to the depths of one's being. One hears, one does not seek; one takes; one does not ask who it is that gives; like lightning a thought flashes out, of necessity, complete in form — I have never needed to choose. It is a rapture, the enormous excitement of which sometimes finds relief in a storm of tears; a state of being entirely outside oneself with the clearest consciousness of fine shivering and a rustling through one's being right down to the tips of one's toes; a depth of joy in which all that is most painful and gloomy does not act as a contrast but as a condition for it, as though demanded, as a necessary colour in such a flood of light. . . . Everything happens in the highest degree involuntarily, as in a storm of feeling of freedom, of power, of divinity.

Similarly, A. Strindberg says that poetical ecstasy was "a state of pure bliss while the writing continued."

As to arts, the creativeness there is mainly intuitional, whether it be poetry and literature, music or painting, sculpture or drama. The following self-description of the process of work by Mozart is typical. Answering the question, Mozart writes:

What, you ask, is my method in writing and elaborating my large and lumbering things? I can in fact say nothing more about it than this: I do not know myself and can never find out. When I am in particularly good condition, perhaps riding in a carriage, or on a walk after a good meal, and in a sleepless night, then the thoughts come to me in a rush, and best of all. Whence and how — that I do not know and cannot learn. Those which please me I retain in my head, and hum them perhaps also to myself — at least so others told me. . . .

Farther on, he describes how the "crumbs" spontaneously join one another into a whole, grow, and finally assume a finished form in his head.

All the finding and making only goes on in me as in a very vivid dream.

Finally, like Poincaré in the case quoted above, he puts the work on paper, and since it is practically ready in his mind, "it gets pretty quickly on to paper."

Similar is Schelling's dictum that "Just as the man of destiny does not execute what he wills or intends, but what he is obliged to execute through an incomprehensible fate under whose influence he stands, so the artist . . . seems to stand under the influence of a power which . . . compels him to declare or represent things which he himself does not completely see through, and whose import is infinite."

Finally, so far as religious and moral creations are concerned, they are overwhelmingly intuitional. They profess the revealed truth of faith; they are based almost exclusively upon the super-rational, supersensory, superempirical, Absolute Truth and Reality-God. All great religions are founded by mystics endowed with the charismatic gift of the mystic experience. Such are Buddha, Zoroaster, Lao-Tze, the Hebrew prophets, Mahavira, Mohammed, Christ, St. Paul, St. Augustine, down to the more recent mystics of Christian and other great religions. When some pseudo religion is started "scientifically," "rationally," based upon "reasonable, empirically verified truths," such pseudo religion never gets anywhere and represents at the best a third-class, vulgarized social and humanitarian philosophy or pseudo science.

All great religions explicitly declare that they are the *corpus* of the revealed, super-rational, superempirical, supersensory truth granted by grace of the Absolute to charismatically gifted persons — prophets, saints, mystics, oracles, and other instruments of the Absolute. The experience of these instruments is always super-rational or mystic. And mystic experience has little, if anything, to do with the ordinary cognition given through the organs of the senses or rational discourse. Without mystic intuition, mankind could hardly have any great religion. And any great religion means the creation of the truth of faith revealed through mystic experience. Since religion generally (and the great world religions particularly) has been one of the most important creations of human culture, this very importance testifies in favor of the most important role played by intuition generally, and mystic intuition particularly, in the history of human thought and culture. Religion, particularly, with its super-rational and supersensory intuition, puts us in touch with an aspect of the true and manifold reality which is inaccessible to us through the ordinary avenues of the truth of the senses and the truth of reason. The founders, prophets, apostles, and mystics of the great religious systems, together with the great artists, who also, are, in their own way, instruments of the mystic intuition, are the great instrumentalities of the truth of faith that puts us in touch with the superempirical and metalogical aspect of the Infinite Manifold, the *coincidentia oppositorum* of Erigena and Nicolas of Cusa.

If intuition thus plays a decisive role in any field of creativeness, it follows that it is the decisive factor in cognition, because *any genuine creation is a real cognition as any real discovery is a creation.* When Mozart or Beethoven, Phidias or Shakespeare, Buddha or St. Paul, Raphael or Dürer, Plato or Kant created their artistic or religious or philosophical systems, they actualized the hidden potentiality existing in the reality; they discovered it and brought it from the hidden state of potentiality into the actual reality. They opened out what was concealed, and disclosed to us what we did not see and did not know. In this sense, any creation is a cognition and discovery — the discovery of a new combination of the sound values (as in great music), or of the new values of architectural forms disclosed to us by a new combination of stone-marble-wood and other elements of architecture; or of new aspects of the reality opened to us by painting, literature, religion and ethics. If, for a moment, one can imagine all artistic, religious, philosophical, ethical values eliminated, and all our knowledge reduced to strictly "scientific discoveries" formulated in dry propositions, how greatly our cognition of the world and reality would be impoverished and diminished! From millionaires we would be turned into beggars.

On the other hand, any scientific discovery is also a creation, not necessarily in the sense of an imposition upon nature of what is manufactured by our mind, as Kantians and their followers say, but in the light of actualizing the hidden potentiality in nature, bringing it to the light, and thus enriching our knowledge. In this sense, Newton created his law of gravitation, R. Meyer his law of preservation of energy, Lavoisier and Lomonosoff their law of conservation of matter, and so on.

Since intuition plays such a decisive role in any creativeness, it plays this role also in any cognition and discovery.

This cursory survey explains why the thinkers of the most divergent currents of thought recognize intuition — and as its result the truth of faith — as the source and *corpus* of truth of *sui generis,* different from the source and *corpus* of knowledge given through the organs of the senses, and through dialectic of our mind. It is, likewise, the reason why they ascribe to intuition the most important role in the generation and starting of even sensory and rational cognition. After the above, the following statements of thinkers in different currents of thought will be comprehensible.

The Unconscious often guides men in their actions by hints and feelings, where they could not help themselves by conscious thought.

The Unconscious furthers the conscious process of thought by its inspiration in small as in great matters, and in mysticism guides mankind to the presentiment of higher supersensible unities.

It makes men happy through the feeling for the beautiful and artistic production.

New directions of thought arise from the flashes of intuition.

In mathematics, the positive integral numbers 1, 2, 3, . . . are found to be subject to certain simple arithmetic laws, and these laws are regarded as intuitively true. . . . There are many other abstract mathematical structures besides those just alluded to. In all cases it is found that they are made up of certain accepted intuitions (or postulates) and their logical consequences. . . . Now what I desire particularly to point out is that the mathematician goes far beyond such generally accepted clear-cut assumptions, in that he holds certain tacit beliefs and attitudes which scarcely ever find their way onto the printed page. . . . For instance, he believes in the existence of various infinite classes such as that made up of all the integers. . . . Such ideas . . . I call mathematical faith. . . . Nearly all the greatest mathematicians have been led to take points of view in this broad category and have attached the deepest significance to them. . . . The beliefs involved have been of the greatest heuristic importance as instruments of discovery.

Still more emphatic in this respect are such scientists as Eddington, Jeans, Drisch, and others.

Human spirit as "something which knows" is not quite so narrow a description as "the observer." Consciousness has other functions besides those of a rather inefficient measuring machine; and knowledge may attain to other truths besides those which correlate sensory impressions. . . . Deeper than any "form of thought" is a faith. . . . In the age of reason, faith yet remains supreme; for reason is one of the articles of faith.

Thus there is hardly any doubt that intuition is the real source of real knowledge, different from the role of the senses and reason. If so, then the truth of faith, derived from and based upon intuition, is the genuine truth as much as the truth of the senses and of reason. It is especially indispensable in the apprehension of those aspects of the true reality which are inaccessible to the senses and to reason. This explains why the truth of faith has been able to dominate for centuries, and why the super-rational religions have been eternal concomitants of the development of human culture. If the truth of faith (and intuition as its source) were entirely false, such a fact could not be. In the light of the above statement, the important and often indispensable role played by intuition in the cognition of true reality explains the perennial fact of the immortality of religion and arts, and the domination of the truth of faith over long periods; and this immortality of supersensory religion and super-rational arts and ethics and the domination of the truth of faith for long periods corroborates the important role of intuition as the source of truth, knowledge and creativeness.

For the above reasons then, the *integral truth is not identical with any of the three forms of truth, but embraces all of them.* In this three-dimensional aspect of the truth of faith, of reason, and of the senses, the integral truth is nearer to the absolute truth than any one-sided truth of one of these three forms. Likewise, the reality given by the integral three-dimensional truth, with its sources of intuition, reason and the senses, is a nearer approach to the infinite metalogical reality of the *coincidentia oppositorum* than the purely sensory, or purely rational, or purely intuitional reality, given by one of the systems of truth and reality. The *empirico-sensory aspect of it is given by the truth of the senses; the rational aspect, by the truth of reason; the super-rational aspect by the truth of faith.* The threefold integral system of truth gives us not only a more adequate knowledge of the reality, but a more valid and less erroneous experience, even within the specific field of each system of truth. *Each of these systems of truth separated from the rest becomes less valid or more fallacious, even within the specific field of its own competence.* The organs of the senses, not controlled by reason or intuition, can give us but a chaotic mass of impressions, perceptions, sensations, incapable of supplying any integrated knowledge, anything except disorderly bits of pseudo observation and pseudo impression. They can give at the best but a mass of meaningless "facts," without any coherence, relevance, and comprehension. Deprived of the co-operation of the truth of reason and of intuition, these organs of the senses are very limited instrumentalities, in the cognition of even a sensory aspect of the reality. In perception of sound, smell, sight, our organs of sense are poorer than the sense organs of a dog, as I. Pavlov's experiments show. For thousands of years such energies as radio and electricity were lying "under their nose"; and yet they were unable to see, to hear to smell, to touch these sensory forms of the reality. For thousands of years many empirical uniformities of natural phenomena were lying under "the eyes and ears" of the organs of the senses; and yet they were unable to grasp them. When they were "discovered," they were discovered only through the co-operation of other sources of cognition: logic and intuition. When these elementary verities are understood, it becomes clear how limited, poor, incoherent, and narrow would be our knowledge, if it were limited only to pure sensory cognition, and if it were dependent only upon our organs of sense in their ordinary functioning. Likewise, mere dialectic speculation cannot guarantee to us any valid knowledge of empirical phenomena. It can give us an unimpeachable syllogism or a mathematical deduction, but such a syllogism or deduction will be empirically valid only when its major and minor premises are empirically valid. And this empirical adequacy cannot be derived from and by the truth of reason. Finally, intuition uncontrolled by the truth of reason and the senses goes very easily astray, and gives us an intuitive error instead of the intuitive truth. Each of these sources and systems of truth misleads us much more easily when it is isolated from, and unchecked by, the other sources and systems of truth than when it is united into one integral whole with the others.

Hence the greater adequacy of the integral system of truth and reality compared with partial or one-sided truth and reality of each of these systems.

IV. Return to the Argument

After this all too short, and also all too long, deviation, we can return to our problem. The above explains what is meant by the inadequacy of each system of truth; and how and why, with a growing domination of one of the systems, the society, culture, and human beings are more and more carried away from the true reality and from the real knowledge of it. Suppressing the other systems of truth, and the aspects of reality they give, the dominant system of partial truth begins, under the disguise of truth, to lead the society more and more toward ignorance, error, hollowness of values, aridity in creativeness and discovery of the aspects of reality, and poverty of social and cultural life. Adaptation becomes less and less possible. And life itself becomes less and less rich in the real values and creative experience. Hence the dilemma for the respective society and culture: either to continue such a dangerous drift, and dry up and perish, or to make a great effort and restore a fuller and more genuine truth and system of values. Such a restoration means a reintroduction of the other systems of truth, reality, and value. And such a reintroduction is a new phase in the great rhythm of the system of truth, reality, value, and in the dominant form of the cultural supersystem.

Some cultures, like the Graeco-Roman and the Western, have been able to make such a shift several times; some others could not. The first cultures continued to live and to pass through the recurrent rhythm studied; the others either perished and disappeared, or were doomed to a stagnant, half-mummified existence, with their hollow and narrowed truth, reality, and value becoming a mere "survival" or "object of history," instead of being its creative subject. Such cultures and societies turn into mere material for other — more creative and alive — cultures and societies. Those who limit the reality-value by only one of the above three aspects — whether empirical, or rational, or supersensory — needlessly impoverish themselves, their reality, knowledge, and values. This applies equally to an understanding of man, society, and culture. Such an exclusive *Weltanschauung* is never adequate, and invariably falls victim to its own narrowmindedness. So also do the cultures dominated by such one-sided mentalities. The exclusively theologico-supersensory mentality of medieval culture that emerged and developed as a remedy to the hollow Sensate culture of the late Graeco-Roman period, after several centuries of domination, also dried up, failed, and buried itself in the catastrophes of the end of the Middle Ages. So also did the one-sided rationalistic mentality of the culture of the sixteenth to the eighteenth centuries (the mentality of the Renaissance and the Enlightenment). It went down in the social conflagrations at the end of the eighteenth and the beginning of the nineteenth centuries. Finally, the one-sided empirico-sensory mentality of our own culture is failing before our eyes, together with the culture dominated by it.

The theoretical failure of our predominant Sensate system of truth, reality, value and culture manifests itself in many ways, described in detail in the preceding sections of *Dynamics*. First, in a progressive obliteration of the boundary line between truth and falsehood, reality and fiction, validity and utilitarian convention. When one examines the contemporary dominant scientific and philosophical empiricism in all its variations — empiricism, positivisms, neo-positivisms, Kantian or pseudo-Kantian criticism of the *als ob* or "as if" fictions, pragmatism, operationalism, empirico-criticism, instrumentalism, and so on — one cannot fail to see how they all together tend to obliterate the difference between truth and falsity, reality and fiction, validity and mere expediency. When these dominant currents declare that scientific propositions are mere "conventions," and of several different conventions that which under the circumstances is most convenient, or most "economical," or expedient, or more useful, or more "operational," for you or me is most true (Poincaré, K. Pearson, E. Mach, W. James, and others), they obliterate the boundary between the true and the false, undermine the truth and knowledge itself. According to this criterion, all the dogmas of Stalin or Hitler or Daladier are true, because they are most convenient to them. When scientists declare they are not concerned with reality and make their schemes "as if they were corresponding to the reality," they turn reality, science, and truth into mere fiction, into a mere *als ob*, a mere expedient and arbitrary "construct." If science is not concerned with the reality, then what is it concerned with? What then is the difference, besides expediency, between the "as if" construct of the patient of an insane asylum and that of the scientist; between mere fiction and reality? What a distance have we traveled from the truth as "*adequatio rei et intellectus*" of St. Thomas!

Pragmatism leads to the same result, with its cult and criterion of the useful as equivalent to the true, as do also operationalism, instrumentalism and other similar "isms." Not different is the fruit of the current pseudo-Kantian conceptions of the laws of nature, formulated by science as mere manufactured products of our minds, imposed by us upon "nature," or upon something that we call "nature," though nobody knows what it is, or whether it exists or not. The result of such a conception is that we do not know what "mind" is, still less what it imposes upon what, in what way and why. The whole of science and truth turn into one question mark. Still truer is this of the neo-Positivist movements, of the type of the Vienna Circle, and others, which identify thought with mere language, logic with the mere syntax of language; truth with a pure tautology ("analytic proposition" of Kant); and proclaim any nontautological proposition, including all the laws of the sciences, as an uncertain arbitrary belief. Representing empiricism and scepticism in its most sterile, arid, and senile form, these currents destroy also the landmarks between knowledge and error; reality and fiction; and leave us indeed a lifeless, spiritless, thoughtless, dry and hollow world of mummified reality, reduced to a Talmudic exegesis of symbols of nobody knows what. Being the epigoni of the previous full-blooded empiricism, like any epigoni, having lost its spark of creativeness, they compensate for it by the most meticulous research of the symbolic signs, with the most precise method of scholars, of whom Lao-Tze said: "Wise men are never scholars and scholars are never wise men." The old sage exaggerated the situation, but his formula well fits these scholars.

Moving in this fatal direction, empiricism tragically narrows the realm of the reality to a mere empirical aspect of it; and in this aspect to a more and more narrow and more and more superficial "knowing more and more about less and less." Losing its creative genius and replacing it by "mechanicalness," it discovers less and less because it creates less and less, and because any real creation is discovery and any real discovery is creation.

In spite of an enormous collection of so-called facts, neither our understanding of sociocultural phenomena nor our ability to foresee their future course has increased. Amid the vast ocean of "facts" we are lost as much as ever. The empirical social theories emerge, enjoy their heyday, and after a few months or years are "gone with the wind" as failures. As to the validity of empirical forecasts of future trends of sociocultural phenomena — almost all the empirical theories of the nineteenth and twentieth centuries, from business forecasting to the theories of "progress," "sociocultural evolution," "laws of the three stages," "social and cultural trends" — all are washed out by history.

Divorcing the empirical aspect of reality from its other aspects, the contemporary dominant empiricism tragically narrowed also the world of the meaning-values and in this way enormously reduced all the infinite richness of sociocultural and cosmic reality. In this manner it has been the factor in the impoverishment of our life, of its creativeness, fullness, its infinite value, and even its Sensate happiness.

Through this divorce it separated the truth from goodness and beauty, and made empirical science indifferent to these values. It generated an amoral, even cynical science. As a result of this, empirical science has become an instrumentality ready to serve any master, Mammon as well as God, any purpose, no matter whether socially good or disastrous, constructive or destructive. Having created a world full of the most beneficial gifts, at the same time it created the most devilish means for the destruction of human life, of culture, of society. Poisonous gas, bombs, explosives are as much the children of empirical science as a refrigerator, medicine, a tractor, or similar invention. By letting loose these destructive monsters, empirical science produced the children which began to devour science itself.

On one half of this planet, the liberty of study and of scientific thought is already muzzled by those who have specialized in the control of the destructive forces created by empirical science; only what they want is permitted to be studied; what they do not want is prohibited. In this way, science itself is degraded to the role of a mere "handmaid" of the contemporary "Barbarians," who have well learned the motto of empiricism: Truth is what is convenient and useful; and of several possible conventions, that which is most convenient for me is most true. In this way, the extreme empirical science has prepared its own downfall and degradation.

The practical failure of the excessive empiricism of our culture is demonstrated by our increasing inability to control mankind and the course of sociocultural processes. Contrary to the hopeful empiricistic "*savoir pour prevoir, prevoir pour pouvoir,*" we control them as little as we did many centuries ago. Like a log in Niagara Falls, we are carried by unforeseen and uncontrolled sociocultural currents, and helplessly drift from one crisis to another, from one catastrophe to another. Neither happiness, nor safety, nor security, promised by the excessive empiricism of modern times, is realized. There were few periods of human history when so many millions of human beings were so unhappy, insecure, and miserable, hungry and destitute as they are now, from China to Western Europe. The "blackout" of culture is the sign of our time. No better evidence of its practical failure is needed.

More than that. This exclusive empiricism is responsible, to a great extent, for these catastrophies, and for the contemporary degradation of man and sociocultural values. Stripping man and values of anything absolute, superempirical, divine and sacred; reducing them to a mere "electron-proton complex," or "complex of atoms," or "reflex-mechanism," or "psychoanalytical libido," or a "sex-stomach mechanism," or mere "stimulus-response relationship," the one-sided empiricism has tragically narrowed the world of true reality-value, and degraded man and culture to the level of these "complexes," "atoms," and "mechanisms." The practical result of such a *Weltanschauung* has been the contemporary cruel treatment of man, the current catastrophes, and the current triumph of rude force in national and international human relationships. If man is a mere electron-proton complex or atom, why have any ceremony with him? If truth, justice, beauty, and other values are perfectly relativistic conventions, why hesitate at the disposal of those which are inconvenient for a given individual or group, and why not dictatorially order those which are convenient for them? In this way, the degradation of man and cultural values was begun, and progressed until, as at the present time, man and all values are relativized to such an extent that nothing absolute and sacred is left, and everything is ground into dust. Hence the contemporary triumph of rude coercion; the contemporary crisis of our society and culture; wars and revolutions; the mental, moral, and social anarchy of our time. These are the children generated by the one-sided empiricism of our culture. They now begin to devour their parent, preparing for the downfall of such a culture mentality.

Such are the consequences and such is the Nemesis of the more and more one-sided system of truth, reality, and value. And such is the suicidal way in which this one-sided system suffocates itself and opens the way for the ascendance of other systems of truth-reality-value that correct the outworn system. Such a shift becomes an absolute necessity, the condition without which the existence of creative culture becomes impossible. As such it can only be welcomed.

This reason for the succession of the phases of the supersystem of truth-reality-value–culture is the deepest and most important. It alone is sufficient to explain the super-rhythm studied. Together with the above principles of immanent change and of limited possibilities, it makes the super-rhythm perfectly comprehensible. It accounts also for the degradation of those societies and cultures which have not been able to make this shift to another system of truth-reality-value when it became necessary. For such persistence in the path of a partial and increasingly sterile system of truth, they are condemned to this degradation and to their uncreative and vegetative stagnation.

V. Why the Order of the Phases: Ideational, Idealistic, Sensate

This "why" answered, there remains another subordinated problem, namely: Why have these main forms recurred in the same order: Sensate-Ideational-Idealistic, or, what is the same, Ideational-Idealistic-Sensate? Does this mean that I claim such an order of succession as a universal uniformity to be expected *urbi et orbi,* whenever and wherever such a rhythm takes place? If so, then what are the reasons that make such an order universal, especially that the Idealistic phase comes after the decline of the Ideational, but not after that of the Sensate phase?

First of all, let me remind the reader that in the preceding sections I nowhere claimed that such an order of succession is a universal uniformity. On the contrary, in several places I stated that "the sequential order of these alternations in most of the cases is probably such as described, but it is not to be assumed that in some cases the sequence cannot be different." Or, "I do not think the sequence observed in the history of the Western society is universal or uniform for all societies and at all times." These remarks, and those in several other places make my position clear. I do not have any sufficient logical ground on which to contend that the observed order is invariable. Theoretically, it is possible, and if other cultures are studied from this standpoint more carefully, it is probable that some other order of recurrence of these main forms can be found. The more so, that some cultures never reach an integrated level from this standpoint, while some others like, for instance, the Brahmanic culture of India, have remained in the Ideational phase far longer than either the Graeco-Roman or the Western cultures. Finally, observation shows that the tempo and the sharpness of the mutations from one type to another vary from culture to culture; some shift from one type to another within narrower limits than the others, and therefore give always a less pure type of domination of one form than the others.

The only reason why the sequence of succession in domination of these forms in the Western and Graeco-Roman cultures has been such that the Idealistic stage used to come after the Ideational, but not after the Sensate, is the consideration of the empirical nature, namely: in the overripe stage of Sensate culture, man becomes so "wild" that he cannot — and does not want to — "tame himself" and, like a reckless driver, can be brought to his senses only by catastrophic tragedy and punishment, as immanent consequences of his "folly." These call for "the policeman of history," who imposes, first, a hard and purely physical coercion upon him, as the contemporary totalitarian policemen of history do; and then, gradually, after this strenuous taming, he is put into the strait-jacket of the Ideational culture for a constructive and real "re-education" and "re-orientation" in regard to himself as well as toward the world of values and the total reality. In other words, the too wild Sensate man is less able to turn spontaneously into an Idealist, and to create an Idealistic culture, after the crumbling of the over-Sensate, than is an Ideational man — say, a monk — who comes out of his cell and the supersensory world, and begins to discern the noble beauty of the magnificent world of the senses, begins to grasp it, understand it, and value it, so far as its noblest and sublimest aspects are concerned. It is easier to descend from the heights of the Ideational snow peak to the beautiful plateau of Idealistic reality than to ascend from the plane of the over-ripe Sensate culture to that Idealistic plateau. Here we have, perhaps, something reminiscent of E. Mach's principle of "the least resistance." Going down is easier than climbing up, when going down and climbing are considered as free and spontaneous, and not forced, as is the case with the passage from the Sensate to the Ideational, imposed by calamity and enforced by the rude coercion of the "policemen of history."

This consideration perhaps helps us somewhat to understand why the sequence in the cultures studied has been such as it is; and why such a sequence probably will be found — though hardly universally — in the life history of other cultures. However, the consideration is purely empirical, and as such it does not imply any necessity for such a sequence to be universal in time or space.

The above answers the question of why our super-rhythm and its numerous subordinated rhythms recur; and why there has been and will continue to be a rhythm of the Ideational-Idealistic-Sensate forms of culture.

In a profound peace of mind, we approach the end of the long and arduous pilgrimage of our analysis of the structure and change of culture. All that remains now is to cast, from the lookout attained, the last glance at the tragic scenery of the twilight of the Sensate phase of our culture. Let us do it with all the compassion of a participant in the tragedy and all the unshatterable hope of him who sees beyond the near horizon.

42

THE TWILIGHT OF OUR SENSATE CULTURE AND BEYOND

Crisis . . . Catharsis . . . Charisma . . . and Resurrection

The present status of Western culture and society gives a tragic spectrum of the beginning of the disintegration of their Sensate supersystem. Therefore, their nearest future, measured by years and even a few decades, will pass under the sign of the *dies irae, dies illa* of transition to a new Ideational or Idealistic phase, with all the satellites of such a process. In a terse delineation the following trends will prevail in this period.

Crisis. 1. Sensate values will become still more relative and atomistic until they are ground into dust devoid of any universal recognition and binding power. The boundary line between the true and false, the right and wrong, the beautiful and ugly, positive and negative values, will be obliterated increasingly until mental, moral, aesthetic and social anarchy reigns supreme.

2. These progressively atomized Sensate values, including man himself, will be made still more debased, sensual and material, stripped of anything divine, sacred, and absolute. They will sink still deeper into the muck of the sociocultural sewers. They will be progressively destructive rather than constructive, representing in their totality a museum of sociocultural pathology rather than the imperishable values of the Kingdom of God. The Sensate mentality will increasingly interpret man and all values "physicochemically," "biologically," "reflexologically," "endocrinologically," "behavioristically," "economically," "psychoanalytically," "mechanistically," "materialistically," as a universe of atoms and electron-protons with human robots enmeshed in their huge and inert web.

3. With all values atomized, any genuine, authoritative and binding "public opinion" and "world's conscience" will disappear. Their place will be taken by a multitude of opposite "opinions" of unscrupulous factions and by the "pseudo consciences" of pressure groups.

4. Contracts and covenants will lose the remnants of their binding power. The magnificent contractual sociocultural house built by Western man during the preceding centuries will collapse. With its crumbling, the contractual democracy, contractual capitalism, including the private property, contractual free society of free men, will be

swept away.

5. Rude force and cynical fraud will become the only arbiters of all values and of all interindividual and intergroup relationships. Might will become right. As a consequence, wars, revolutions, revolts, disturbances, brutality will be rampant. *Bellum omnium contra omnes* — man against man, class, nation, creed and race against class, nation, creed and race — will raise its head.

6. Freedom will become a mere myth for the majority and will be turned into an unbridled licentiousness by the dominant minority. Inalienable rights will be alienated; Declarations of Rights either abolished or used only as beautiful screens for an unadulterated coercion.

7. Governments will become more and more hoary, fraudulent, and tyrannical, giving bombs instead of bread; death instead of freedom; violence instead of law; destruction instead of creation. They will be increasingly shortlived, unstable and subject to overthrow.

8. The family as a sacred union of husband and wife, of parents and children will continue to disintegrate. Divorces and separations will increase until any profound difference between socially sanctioned marriages and illicit sex-relationship disappears. Children will be separated earlier and earlier from parents. The main sociocultural functions of the family will further decrease until the family becomes a mere incidental cohabitation of male and female while the home will become a mere overnight parking place mainly for sex-relationship.

9. The Sensate supersystem of our culture will become increasingly a shapeless "cultural dumping place," pervaded by syncretism of undigested cultural elements, devoid of any unity and individuality. Turning into such a bazaar, it will become a prey of fortuitous forces making it an "object of history" rather than its self-controlling and living subject.

10. Its creativeness will continue to wane and wither. The place of Galileos and Newtons, Leibnitzes and Darwins, Kants and Hegels, Bachs and Beethovens, Shakespeares and Dantes, Raphaels and Rembrandts will be increasingly taken by a multitude of mediocre pseudo thinkers, science-makers, picture-makers, music-makers, fiction-makers, show-makers, one group more vulgar than the other. The place of moral categoric imperatives will be occupied by progressively atomistic and hedonistic devices of egotistic expediency, bigotry, fraud, and compulsion. The great Christianity will be replaced by a multitude of the most atrocious concoctions of fragments of science, shreds of philosophy, stewed in the inchoate mass of magical beliefs and ignorant

superstitions. Constructive technological inventions will be supplanted progressively by destructive ones. More specifically:

a. Quantitative colossalism will substitute for qualitative refinement; "the biggest for the best"; a best-seller for a classic; glittering externality for inner value; technique for genius; imitation for creation; a sensational hit for a lasting value; "operational manipulation" for an enlightening intuition.

b. Thought will be replaced by "Information, please"; sages by smart Alecs; real criteria by counterfeit criteria; great leaders by frauds.

c. Even the greatest cultural values of the past will be degraded. Beethovens and Bachs will become an appendix to the eloquent rhapsodies of advertised laxatives, gums, cereals, beers and other solid enjoyments. Michelangelos and Rembrandts will be decorating soap and razor blades, washing machines and whiskey bottles. Reporters and radio babblers will once in a while condescend to honor Shakespeares and Goethes by permitting them to "make a line" in their papers and talks.

11. In the increasing moral, mental, and social anarchy and decreasing creativeness of Sensate mentality, the production of the material values will decline, depressions will grow worse, and the material standard of living will go down.

12. For the same reasons, security of life and possessions will fade. With these, peace of mind and happiness. Suicide, mental disease, and crime will grow. Weariness will spread over larger and larger numbers of the population.

13. Population will increasingly split into two types: the Sensate hedonists with their "eat, drink and love, for tomorrow we die"; and, eventually, into ascetics and stoics indifferent and antagonistic to Sensate values.

Catharsis. In this way Sensate culture and man will drift to their bankruptcy and self-destruction. With material comfort vanished, liberties gone, sufferings increasing at the cost of pleasures; Sensate security, safety, happiness turned into a myth; man's dignity and value trampled upon pitilessly; the creativeness of Sensate culture waned; the previously built magnificent Sensate house crumbling; destruction rampant everywhere; cities and kingdoms erased; human blood saturating the good earth; all Sensate values blown to pieces and all Sensate dreams vanished; in these conditions the Western population will not be able to help opening its eyes to the hollowness of the declining Sensate culture and being disillusioned by it. As a result, it will increasingly forsake it and shift its allegiance to either Ideational or Idealistic values. By tragedy, suffering, and crucifixion it will be purified and brought back to reason, and to eternal, lasting, universal, and absolute values. The atomization of values will be replaced by their universalization and absolutization. Sensate values will be supplemented and subordinated to the Ideational and Idealistic values. The major premise of Sensate culture and the Sensate supersystem will be progressively replaced by the Integralistic or Ideational premise and supersystem.

Such a shift will be led, first, by the best minds of Western society. Its best brains will increasingly become again new Saint Pauls, Saint Augustines, and great religious and ethical leaders. Their lead will be followed by the masses. When this stage of catharsis is reached, the crisis is ended.

Charisma and Resurrection. Purified by the fiery ordeal of catastrophe Western society will be granted a new charisma and, with it, resurrection and the release of new creative forces. They will usher in a constructive period of a new — more integralistic — supersystem of culture and a noble society built not upon the withered Sensate root but upon a healthier and more vigorous root of integralistic principle. In this way a new era of Western culture will open.

This uniformity — *crisis-catharsis-charisma-resurrection* — is the way in which most of the previous great crises were overcome. In ancient Egypt the crises at the end of the Old Kingdom, of the Middle Empire, of the New Empire, and twice later on, in the Saice and Graeco-Roman periods; in ancient Babylon the crisis around 1200 B.C.; several great crises in the Hindu culture, each ended by a revival of Hinduism or the emergence of Buddhism. In China the crisis of the sixth century B.C. terminated with the emergence of Taoism and Confucianism, and several later catastrophes; in the Hebrew culture, the crises of the centuries from the ninth to the third B.C. with the emergence of the prophetic religions of Elijah and Elisha, of Amos, Hosea and Isaiah, of Ezekiel and Jeremiah, up to Esdra and his successors. Finally, to mention only a few cases, in the same way the great crisis of the Sensate Graeco-Roman culture was ended through the emergence and growth of Christianity and the great Christian culture of the Middle Ages.

Ahead of us lies the thorny road of the *dies irae* of transition. But beyond it there loom the magnificent peaks of the new Ideational or Idealistic culture as great in its own way as Sensate culture at the climax of its creative genius. In this way the creative mission of Western culture and society will be continued and once more the great sociocultural mystery will be ended by a new victory. *Et incarnatus est de Spiritu sancto . . . et homo factus est . . . Crucifixus . . . Et Resurrexit . . . Amen.*

The End of the Road

In accordance with my diagnosis and prognosis in the original four-volume edition of this work published 1937-41, *the central process for the last few decades has consisted in:* a) *the progressive decay of sensate culture, society, and man;* and b) *the emergence and slow growth of the first components of the new — ideational or idealistic — sociocultural order.*

In *science* this double process has manifested itself in: a) the increasing destructiveness of the morally irresponsible, sensate scientific achievements, of invention of nuclear, bacteriological, and other Satanic means of destruction of man and of all main values; and b) a transformation of the basic theories of science in a morally responsible, ideational or idealistic direction. This change has already made today's science less materialistic, mechanistic, and deterministic — or less sensate — than it was during the preceding two centuries. For this modern science, matter has become but a condensed form of energy which dematerializes into radiation. The material atom is already dissolved into more than thirty non-material, "cryptic, arcane, perplexing, enigmatic, and inscrutable" elementary particles: the electron, and anti-electron, the proton, and the anti-proton, the photon, the meson, etc., or into "the image of waves which turn out into the waves of probability, waves of consciousness which our thought projects afar. . . . These waves, like those associated with the propagation of light quanta, need no substratum in order to propagate in space-time; they undulate neither in fluid, nor in solid, nor yet in a gas." Around a bend of quantum mechanics and at the foot of the electronic ladder the basic notions of "materialistic and mechanistic science" such as: matter, objective reality, time, space, causality are no longer applicable, and the testimony of our senses largely loses its significance. As to the deterministic causality it is already replaced in the modern science by Heisenberg's principle of uncertainty, by fanciful "quanta jumps," by a mere chance relationship or — in psycho-social phenomena — by "voluntaristic," "free-willing, law of direction" exempt from causality and chance.

Similar transformations have taken place in the new, leading theories of biological, psychological, and social sciences. In contrast to the superannuated, though still intoned, clichés of mechanistic, materialistic, and deterministic biology, psychology, and sociology, the new and significant theories in these disciplines clearly show that the phenomena of life, organism, personality, mind, and sociocultural processes are irreducible to, and cannot be understood as, purely materialistic, mechanistic, and sensory realities. According to these theories, these phenomena have, besides their empirical aspect, the far more important — mindfully-rational and even supersensory and superrational — aspects.

In these and other forms the most modern science has already become notably ideational or idealistic in comparison with what it was in the nineteenth century. This means an increasing replacement of the dying sensate elements of science by the new — idealistic or ideational — ones.

In the field of *philosophy* this double process has manifested itself in increasing sterility and decline of materialistic, mechanistic, "positivistic," and other sensate philosophies and in the emergence and growth of the "Existential," the "Intuitive," the "Neo-Thomist," the "Integral," the "Neo-Mystical," the "Neo-Vedantist," and other philosophies congenial to the basic principles of Ideationalism or Idealism.

A similar double process has been going on in all fields of *fine arts*.

In the realm of *religion* it has shown itself in the simultaneous growth of: a) militant atheism, and b) religious revival.

In *ethics* it has called forth: a) utter bestiality and horrible demoralization shown in the second World War, bloody revolutions, and increasing criminality; and b) growth of moral heroism, sublime altruism, and organized movements for abolition of war, bloody strife, and injustice.

In *politics* the double process has resulted in: a) proliferation of all kinds of tyrannical dictatorships, and b) the slowly swelling grass-roots movements for establishment of a competent, honest, and morally responsible government of the people, by the people, and for the people.

This struggle between the forces of the previously creative but now largely outworn sensate order and the emerging, creative forces of a new — ideational or idealistic — order is proceeding relentlessly in all fields of social and cultural life. The final outcome of this epochal struggle will largely depend upon whether mankind can avoid a new world war. If the forces of the decaying sensate order start such a war, then, dissipating their remaining energy, these forces can end or greatly impede the creative progress of mankind.

If this Apocalyptic catastrophe can be avoided, then the emerging creative forces will usher humanity into a new magnificent era of its history. Which of these alternative courses is going to take place depends upon everyone of us.

BIBLIOGRAPHY

This bibliography, which includes only a small fraction of the sources used and quoted in the original edition of the *Dynamics*, contains mainly works that deal with uniformities, fluctuations, rhythms, periodicities, trends, and factors in the change of either the total culture and social life or of only one specified compartment of sociocultural phenomena. These are supplemented by a few philosophical works that offer a comprehensive interpretation of historical process. For the classical works that exist in many translations and editions, like those of Plato and Aristotle, no specifications of place and date of publication are given. Other works are listed now under their original title, now under the title of their English, French, or German translations.

Abel, T., *Systematic Sociology in Germany* (New York, 1929)

Adams, B., *The Law of Civilization and Decay* (New York, 1897)

Adams, H., *The Degradation of the Democratic Dogma* (New York, 1919)

Albertus Magnus, *Methaphysica; Physica, in Opera* (Paris, 1890), Vols. III, IV

Allport, G., *Personality* (New York, 1937)

Aristotle, *De generatione et corruptione; Methaphysica; Physica; Politica; The Nichomachean Ethics*

Barnes, H., and Becker, H., *Social Thought from Lore to Science*, 2 Vols. (Boston, 1938)

Barnes, H. (ed.), *An Introduction to the History of Sociology* (U. of Chicago Press, 1938)

Barth, P., *Philosophie der Geschichte als Soziologie* (Leipzig, 1922)

Berdyaev, N., *The Meaning of History* (London, 1936); *The End of Our Time* (London, 1934); *The Fate of Man in the Modern World* (London, 1935)

Bergson, H., *L'evolution creatrice* (Paris, 1907); *De deux sources de la morale et de religion* (Paris, 1932)

Berr, H., *Civilization: le mot et l'idee* (Paris, 1930); *La synthese en l'histoire* (Paris, 1911)

Birkhoff, G. D., "Intuition, Reason and Faith in Science," in *Science*, 1938; *Aesthetic Measure* (Harvard U. Press, 1933)

Boas, F., *Primitive Art* (Oslo, 1927)

Bodin, J., *Methodus ad Facilem Historiarum Cognitionem* (Paris, 1583)

Bonald, L. de, "Essai analitique sur les lois naturelles; Du divorce; Theorie de pouvoire politique et religieux," in *Oeuvres*, Vols. I, II, III

Bossuet, J. B., *Discours sur l'histoire universelle* (Paris, 1892)

Botero, G., *Della ration di Stato* (Ferrara, 1590)

Bouglé, C., *Lecons de sociologie sur l'evolution des valeurs* (Paris, 1922)

Bovet, E., *Lyrisme, Epopee, Drame: une lois de l'histoire* (Paris, 1911)

Brunschvicg, L., *L'experience humaine* (Paris, 1922)

Brunetière, F., *Evolution de la poesie lyrique* (Paris, 1894)

Burckhardt, J., *Weltgeschichtliche Betrachtungen* (Stuttgart, 1918)

Bury, J. B., *The Idea of Progress* (London, 1920)

Campanella, T., "Aforismi politici," in *Opere di Thomaso Campanella* (Torino, 1854), Vol. II
Carlyle, R. W., and A. J., *A History of Mediaeval Political Theory in The West*, 4 Vols. (New York, 1903–1922)
Carr, H. M., *The Philosophy of Change* (New York, 1914)
Censorinus, *De die natali* (Paris, 1843)
Chambers, E. P., *Cycles of Taste* (Cambridge, 1928); *The History of Taste* (New York, 1932)
Chassel, C. E., *The Relationships Between Morality and Intellect* (New York, 1935)
Clement of Alexandria, "The Stromata," in the *Ante-Nicene Fathers* (Buffalo, 1888), Vol. II
Collingwood, R. G., *The Idea of History* (Oxford U. Press, 1946)
Combarieu, J., *Histoire de la musique*, 3 Vols. (Paris, 1913)
Comte, A., *Positive Philosophy*, tr. by Martineau, 2 Vols. (New York, 1855); *System of Positive Polity*, 2 Vols. (London, 1875)
Confucian Texts, Li-Ki, Book VII, in *The Sacred Books of the East*, edited by M. Müller, Vol. XXVII (Oxford, 1885)
Coomaraswamy, A. K., *The Transformation of Nature in Art* (Harvard U. Press, 1934)
Cornelius, F., *Die Weltgeschichte und ihre Rythmus* (München, 1925).
Coste, A., *L'experience des peoples* (Paris, 1900)
Cowell, F. R., *History, Civilization and Culture: An Introduction to the Historical and Social Philosophy of P. A. Sorokin* (London-Boston, 1954); *Cicero and the Roman Republic* (London, 1956)
Croce, B., *Aesthetics* (London, 1922)
Cusanus, Nicolaus, *De novissimis diebus; De docta ignorantia* (De la docte ignorance, Paris, 1930); *The Vision of God* (London, 1928)
Danilevsky, N., *Russland und Europa* (Berlin, 1920)
Darmststaedter, L., *Handbuch zur Geschichte der Naturwissenschaften und der Technik* (Berlin, 1908)
Dawson, Ch., *Progress and Religion* (London, 1937)
Delvaille, J., *Essai sur l'histoire de l'idee de progres* (Paris, 1910)
Deonna, W., *L'archeologie, sa valeur, ses methodes*, 3 Vols. (Paris, 1912)
Diamond, A. S., *Primitive Law* (London, 1935)
Dikmans, G., "Les types d'integration socioculturelle selon P. Sorokin," *Revue des sciences economiques*, 1939
Dilthey, W., *Einleitung in die Geisteswissenschajten* (Leipzig, 1883)
Dixon, R., *The Building of Cultures* (New York, 1928)
Draghicesco, D., *Verite et revelation* (Paris, 1934)
Dromel, J., *La loi des revolutions, les generations, les nationalites, les dynasties, les religions* (Paris, 1862)
Duhem, P., *Le system du monde*, 3 Vols. (Paris, 1914)
Dvorak, M., *Kunstgeschichte as Geistesgeschichte* (München, 1924)
Dupréel, E., *Deux essais sur le progres* (Bruxelles, 1928)
Durkheim, E., *Les formes elementaires de la vie religieuse* (Paris, 1912)
Eddington, A. S., *The Philosophy of Physical Science* (New York, 1939); *The Nature of Physical World* (New York, 1929)

Erigena, J. Scotus, "De divisione naturae," in Migne's *Patrologia latina*, Vol. 122
Ermatingen, E. (ed.), *Philosophie der Literaturwissenschaft* (Berlin, 1930)
Ewald, O., *Nitzsche's Lehre in ihren Grundbegriffen; die ewige Wiederkunft des Gleichen* (Berlin, 1903)
Ferguson, Adam, *Essay on History of Civil Society* (Edinburgh, 1767)
Ferrari, G., *Teoria dei periodi politici* (Milano-Napoli, 1874)
Fischer, E., *Passing of the European Age* (London, 1944)
Florus, Lucius Annaeus, *Epitome of Roman History* (London, 1929)
Forke, A., *The World Conception of the Chinese* (London, 1925)
Frank, S. L., *Nepostijimoye* (The Inexpressible), (Paris, 1939)
Gasset, J. O., *The Revolt of The Masses* (New York, 1937)
Gibbons, E., *The History of the Decline and Fall of The Roman Empire.* Gilgamesch-Epos (Göttingen, 1911)
Gini, C., *Teorie della populazione* (Roma, 1945); "Aree e centri culturali," in *Genus*, Vols. VI-VIII, (1943–49); *I fattori demografici dell'evoluzione delle nazioni* (Torino, 1912)
Gooch, G. P., "Some Conceptions of History," in *Sociological Review*, 1939
Granet, M., *La pensee chinoise* (Paris, 1934)
Guignebert, C., *L'evolution des dogmes* (Paris, 1910); *Christianity, Past and Present* (New York, 1927)
Gurvitch, G., *La vocation actuelle de la sociologie* (Paris, 1950); *Determinismes sociaux et liberte humaine* (Paris, 1955)
Hartmann, E. von, *Philosophy of the Unconscious* (London, 1931)
Hegel, G. W. F., *The Philosophy of History*, tr. by J. Sibree (New York, 1900); *Science of Logic*, tr. by W. H. Johnston and L. Struthers (New York, 1929); *The Philosophy of Fine Arts*, tr. by F. P. B. Osmaston (London, 1920)
Hermetica, ed. by W. Scott (Oxford, 1926)
Hesiod, *Works and Days*
Hobhouse, L., *The Material Culture and Social Institutions of The Simpler Peoples* (London, 1915)
Holwell, J., *Catastrophe Mundi* (London, 1682)
Huizinga, J., *The Waning of The Middle Ages* (London, 1927)
Hume, D., "On Populousness of Ancient Nations," in his *Essays* (London, 1870)
Huntington, E., *Mainsprings of Civilization* (New York, 1945)
Husserl, E., *Logische Untersuchungen* (Halle, 1922)
Ibn-Khaldun, "Prolégomènes historique," in *Notices et extraits des manuscripts de Bibliotheque Imperial* (Paris, 1862), Vols. XIX, XX, XXI
Irenaeus, "Against Heresies," in *The Ante-Nicene Fathers* (Buffalo, 1887), Vol. I
Iribarne, M. F., *La crisis del Estado* (Madrid, 1955); *La crisis de las clases medias* (Madrid, 1950); *La crisis del Derecho*, in *Arbor*, 1955
Jaeger, W., *Paideia*, 3 Vols. (Oxford, 1939–41)
Janet, P., *Histoire de la science politique*, 2 Vols. (Paris, 1887)
Joachim de Flore, *L'evangile eternel* (Paris, 1928)
Joël, K., *Wandlungen der Weltanschauung*, 3 Vols. (Tübingen, 1928–31)
Justin Martyr, "The Second Apology," in the *Ante-Nicene Fathers* (Buffalo, 1888), Vol. I
Kelly, D., *The Hungry Sheep* (London, 1949)

Kidd B., *Social Evolution* (New York, 1894)
Kovalevsky, M., *Costume contemporaine et loi ancienne* (Paris, 1888)
Kroeber, A. L., *Configurations of Culture Growth* (Berkeley, 1944); *The Nature of Culture* (Chicago, 1952)
Kropotkin, P., *Mutual Aid* (Boston, 1956); *Ethics* (Moscow, 1921)
Kummer, F., *Deutsche Literaturgeschichte . . . nach Generationen dargestellt* (Dresden, 1922)
Lactantius, "The Divine Institutes," in *Ante-Nicene Fathers* (Buffalo, 1888), Vol. VII
Lalo, C., *Esquisse d'une esthetique musicale scientifique* (Paris, 1908); *L'art et la vie social* (Paris, 1922)
Lantman, G., *Origin of the Inequality of Social Classes* (Chicago, 1938)
Laprade, V. de, *Le sentiment de la nature avant le Christianisme* (Paris, 1866); *Le sentiment de la nature chez les modernes* (Paris, 1868)
Leibnitz, *Monadologie* (in his *Philosophical Writings* ed. by E. Rhys (New York, 1934)
Lévy-Brühl, L., *Mentalite primitive* (Paris, 1922)
Ligeti, P., *Der Weg aus dem Chaos* (München, 1931)
Lorenz, O., *Die Geschichtswissenschaft in ihrem Hauptrichtungen und Aufgaben* (Leipzig, 1886)
Lossky, N., *Perceptional, Intellectual, and Mystic Intuition* (in Russian, Paris, 1938)
Lowes, J. L., *Convention and Revolt in Literature* (Cambridge, 1926)
Lucretius, *De rerum natura*
Lunden, W., *The Dynamics of Higher Education* (Pittsburgh, 1939)
Machiavelli, N., *Discorsi* (Discourses on the First Ten Books of Titus Livius, London, 1891)
MacIver, R., "The Historical Pattern of Social Change," in *Journal of Social Philosophy*, 1936; *Social Causation* (Boston, 1942)
Maine, H. S., *Ancient Law* (London, 1906)
Male, E., *L'art religieux du XIIe siecle en France* (Paris, 1922); *Art et artistes du Moyen Age* (Paris, 1928)
Maistre, J. de, "Considerations sur la France," "Examen de la philosophie de Bacon," in *Oeuvres* (Lyon, 1891–94), Vols. I, II, III
Mannheim, K., *Man and Society in an Age of Reconstruction* (New York, 1920); "Das Problem der Generationen," in *Kolner Vierteljahrshefte f. Soziologie,*
Maquet, J. J., *The Sociology of Knowledge* (Boston, 1951)
Mariana, J. de, *De lege et regis institutione* (Mainz, 1605)
Maritain, J., *The Degree of Knowledge* (New York, 1938)
Marx, K., *A Contribution to the Critique of Political Economy* (New York, 1904)
Mason, F. (ed), *Creation by Evolution* (New York, 1928)
Mathis, R., *La loi des trois etats* (Nancy, 1924)
Mayreder, R., *Der Typische Verlauf sozialer Bewegungen* (Wien-Leipzig, 1925)
Meinecke, F., *Die Entstehung des Historismus* (München-Berlin, 1936)
Melichar, A., *Uberwindung der modernismus* (Frankfurt, A.M., 1954)
Mentré, F., *Les generations sociales* (Paris, 1920)
Merton, R., *Social Theory and Social Structure* (Glencoe, 1949)
Meyerson, E., *Du cheminement de la pensee* (Paris, 1931); *Identite et Realite* (Paris, 1912)

Michel, A. (ed.), *Histoire de l'art*, 8 Vols. (Paris, 1926)
Mihanovich, C. S., *Social Theorists* (Milwaukee, 1953)
Montesquieux, C. L., *De l'esprit des lois; Considerations sur les causes de la grandeur et de la decadence des Romains* (Paris, 1734)
Mosca, G., *The Ruling Class* (New York, 1938)
Müller, H. von, *Zehn Generationen Deutscher Dichter und Denker* (Berlin, 1928)
Mumford, L., *Technics und Civilization* (New York, 1935)
Nevins, A., *The Gateway to History* (New York, 1938)
Newton, Isaac, *Observations upon the Prophecies of Daniel and the Apocalypse of St. John* (London, 1733); *Principia*
Nicolaus Cusanus, See Cusanus, Nicolaus
Nilsson, M. R., *Primitive Time-Reckoning* (Oxford, 1905)
Northrop, F. S. C., *The Meeting of East and West* (New York, 1946); *The Ideological Differences and World Order* (New Haven, 1949)
Novgorodzeff, P., *Ob obtschestvennom ideale* (Social Ideal) (Prague, 1921)
Nowicow, J., *Les luttes entre societes humaines* (Paris, 1896)
Noüy, L. du, *Biological Time* (London, 1936)
Núñez, L. M., y, *Las classes sociales* (Mexico); *Los Partitos Politicos* (Mexico)
Ogburn, W., *Social Change* (New York, 1921)
Olorinus, J., *Ethnographia mundi* (Magdeburg, 1641)
Oman, Charles, *On the Writing of History* (New York, 1939)
Origen, "De Principiis," in the *Ante-Nicene Fathers* (Buffalo, 1888), Vol. IV
Orosius, *Seven Books of History Against the Pagans* (New York, 1930)
Pareto, V., *Trattato di sociologia generale* (Torino, 1916); American edition of it is entitled: *Mind and Society* (New York, 1935)
Passarge, W., *Die Philosophie der Kunstgeschichte in der Gegenwart* (Berlin, 1930)
Pavlov, I. P., *Conditioned Reflexes* (London, 1930)
Petrazycki, L., *Law and Morality* (Harvard U. Press, 1955)
Petrie, F., *The Revolutions of Civilizations* (London, 1912)
Philo, Judaeus, "De eternitate mundi," in his *Opera* (Berlin, 1896–1930), Vol. VI
Pinder, W., *Das Problem des Generation in Kunstgeschichte Europas* (Berlin, 1928)
Plato, *Dialogues*, especially: Laws, Phaedrus, Republic, Statesman, Timaeus.
Plotinus, *Enneades*
Plutarch, "Why the Oracles Cease," in *Morals*, ed. by Goodwin (Boston, 1870), Vols. III, IV
Poincaré, H., *Science et methode* (Paris, 1920); *Dernieres pensees* (Paris, 1913); *Inventions mathematiques* (Paris, 1908)
Povina, A., *Sociologia*, 2 Vols. (Cordoba, 1954)
Polybius, *Histories*, tr. by W. R. Paton (London, 1923)
Radakrishnan, S., *Indian Philosophy* (London, 1929); *East and West* (New York, 1956)
Rickert, H., *Die Grenzen der naturwissenschaftlichen Begriffsbildung* (Tübingen, 1902)
Roberty, E. de, *Sociologie de l'action* (Paris, 1908); *Nouveau programme de sociologie* (Paris, 1904)
Rostovtzeff, M., *A History of the Ancient World* (Oxford, 1936); *The Social and Economic History of the Hellenistic World* (Oxford, 1942); *The Social and Economic History of the Roman Empire* (Oxford U. Press, 1920)

Saint Augustine, *De civitate Dei* (The City of God); *Confessions*

Saint-Simon, *Oeuvres de Saint-Simon et l'Enfantin* (Paris, 1877), Vol. XLI, XLII

Saint Thomas Aquinas, *Summa contra gentiles; De veritate; Summa theologica*, I, II (English translation, London, 1917)

Sarkar, B. K., *Political Institutions and Theories of the Hindu* (Leipzig, 1912)

Sarton, G., *Introduction to the History oj Science*, 2 Vols. (Baltimore, 1927–33)

Scheler, M., *Schriften zur Soziologie der Weltanschaunngslehre* (Leipzig, 1923–24); *Die Wissensformen und die Gessellschaft* (Leipzig, 1926)

Schnabel, P., *Berosos* (Leipzig, 1923)

Schneider, *Die Periodizitat des Lebens und der Kultur* (Leipzig, 1926)

Schubart, W., *Europa und die Seele des Ostens* (Lucerne, 1938)

Schüking, L., *Die Soziologie der literarischen GeschmacksBildung* (München, 1923)

Schweitzer, A., *The Philosophy of Civilization* (New York, 1923)

Smith, T. L., *Rural Sociology* (New York, 1931)

Smuts, J. C., *Holism and Evolution* (London, 1926)

Sorokin, P. A., *The American Sex Revolution* (Boston, 1957); *Contemporary Sociological Theories* (New York, 1928); *Social Mobility* (New York, 1927); *Sociology of Revolution* (Philadelphia, 1925); *Social Philosophies of An Age of Crisis* (Boston, 1950); *Crisis of Our Age* (New York, 1941); *Man and Society in Calamity* (New York, 1943); *Society, Culture and Personality* (New York, 1947); *Sociocultural Causality, Time, Space* (Duke U. Press, 1943); *Fads and Foibles in Modern Sociology and Related Sciences* (Chicago, 1956); *The Ways and Power of Love* (Boston, 1954)

Spektorsky, E., *The Problems of Social Physics in the Seventeenth Century*, 2 Vols. (In Russian, Kiev, 1910–17)

Spencer, H., *First Principles* (London, 1885); *The Principles of Sociology*, 3 Vols. (London, 1885)

Spengler, O., *Der Untergang des Abendlandes* (Munich, 1920) (English translation: *The Decline of the West* (New York, 1929); *Der Mensch und der Technik* (Münich, 1931); *Jahre der Entscheidung* (Münich, 1931)

Spranger, E., *Kulturzyklentheorie und das Problem des Kulturverfalls* (Berlin, 1926)

Steinmetz, S. R., *Soziologie des Krieges* (Leipzig, 1929)

Suarez, F., *Tractatus de legibus ac Deo Legislatore* (Naples, 1872)

Sutherland, A., *The Origin and Growth of the Moral Instinct* (London, 1908)

Suttie, J. D., *The Origin of Love and Hatred* (London, 1935)

Taine, H., *Les origines de la France contemporaine* (Paris, 1876); *Philosophie de l'art* (Paris, 1881)

Tao-Teh-King, and other Taoist texts in the *Sacred Books oj the East*, ed. by M. Müller (Oxford, 1891), Vol. XI

Tarde, G., *The Laws of Imitation* (New York, 1903); *Social Laws* (New York, 1899); *La logique sociale* (Paris, 1895); *L'opposition universelle* (Paris, 1897)

Tawney, R. H., *Religion and Rise of Capitalism* (New York, 1930)

Theophilus, Theophili Libri III de diversio artibus (London, 1847)

Tertullian, "Apology" and other works in the *Ante-Nicene Fathers* (Buffalo, 1888), Vol. III

Thucydides, *History of the Pelopponesian War* (New York, Everyman's Library)

Thurnwald, R., "The Spell of Limited Possibilities," and "Cultural Rotation" in *American Sociological Review*, 1937; *Die Menschliche Gesellschaft*, Vol. 4 (Berlin, 1935)

Timasheff, N., *Sociological Theory* (New York, 1955)

Toynbee, A. J., *A Study of History*, 10 Vols. (Oxford U. Press, 1936–1954). See also *Toynbee and History*, ed. M. F. Ashley Montagu (Boston, 1956)

Troeltsch, E., *Die Soziallehren der Christlichen Kirchen und Gruppen* (Tübingen, 1912)

Turgot, A. R. J., *Oeuvres de Turgot* (Paris, 1913), Vol. I

Unamuno, M. de, *Del sentimiento tragico de la vida* (Madrid, 1913); *Die Agonie des Christentums* (München, 1925)

Underhill, E., *Mysticism* (London, 1931)

Upanishads, The Principal Upanishads, ed. by S. Radhakrishnan (New York, 1953)

Vico, G., "Principi di una scienza nuova," *Opere*, Vol. V (Milano, 1854)

Vierkandt, A., *Die Stetigkeit in Kulturwandel* (Leipzig, 1908)

Wach, J., *Sociology of Religion* (Chicago, 1943)

Weber, A., *Ideen zur Staats-und Kultursoziologie* (Karlsrue, 1927); *Kulturgeschichte als Kultursoziologie* (Leyden, 1935)

Weber, L., *Le rhythm du progres* (Paris, 1913)

Weber, M., *Wirtschaft und Gesellschaft* (Tübingen, 1921–22); *Gesammelte Aufsatze zur Religionssoziologie* (Tübingen, 1922); *Gesammelte Aufsatze zur Wissenschaftslehre* (Tübingen, 1922)

Westermarck, E., *The Origin and Development of Moral Ideas* (London, 1906)

Wiese, L. von, *System der allgemeinen Soziologie* (München, 1933)

Wieszner, G., *Der Pulsschlag Deutscher Stilgeschichte* (Stuttgart, n.d.)

Wild, K. W., *Intuition* (Cambridge U. Press, 1938)

Williams, M. J., *Catholic Social Thought* (New York, 1950)

Wölfflin, H., *Principles of Art History* (New York, 1932)

Wright, Q., *A Study of War* (Chicago, 1942)

Xenopol, A. D., *La theorie de l'histoire* (Paris, 1908)

Ziegenfuss, W., *Versuch uber das Wesen der Gesellschaft* (Leipzig, 1935)

Zimmerman, C. C., *Family and Civilization* (New York, 1947); *Patterns of Social Change* (Washington, 1956)

Znaniecki, F., *Cultural Sciences* (U. of Illinois Press, 1952)

INDEX OF SUBJECTS

THE AUTHOR

Pitirim A. Sorokin was born and spent his childhood among the Komi, Ugri-Finnish people north of Russia. Up to his eleventh year, he had not seen a town nor learned to read or write. Orphaned at 10, and self-taught, he then became a student of a teachers college, was arrested and imprisoned for his political activities in 1906, then became "a starving and hunted revolutionary", and a student of a night school, of the Psycho-Neurological Institute, and of the University of St. Petersburg. Two more imprisonments gave him a first-hand experience in criminology, the field of his graduate study and then of his first professorship. He published his first volume, *Crime and Punishment: Service and Reward*, in 1913, and three years later received the Magister's degree in criminal law, and in 1922 the degree of Doctor of Sociology from the University of St. Petersburg.

With the explosion of the Russian Revolution, he became one of the founders of the Russian Peasant Soviet, which was dispersed by the Communists. From the beginning of the Revolution, he vigorously fought Lenin, Trotsky, Kamenev, and other communist leaders. Arrested January 3, 1918 and imprisoned for four months in the Fortress of Peter and Paul, he was then released, only to resume his struggle against the communists. In October of the same year, he was again arrested, was condemned to death, but by Lenin's order was freed and permitted to return to his academic activities at the University of St. Petersburg. There he became the founder, first professor, and chairman of the Department of Sociology; during the years 1920–1922 he published five volumes in law and sociology. In 1922, he was again arrested, this time to be banished from the Soviet Union. His good friend, President Masaryk invited him to be a guest of Czechoslovakia, where he stayed for nine months. In November, 1923, he came to this country, and the following year was offered a professorship at the University of Minnesota. After six years there, he was invited to be the first professor and chairman of the Sociology Department at Harvard. In 1930, he became a naturalized American citizen. Since that year he has remained at Harvard.

In 1948, Mr. Eli Lilly and the Lilly Endowment offered to sponsor his studies of "how to make human beings less selfish and more creative." Their generous bequest led to the establishment of the Harvard Research Center in Creative Altruism in 1949, which he is now directing.

During his years in America, many distinctions have been awarded him, including Presidency in the International Institute of Sociology, numerous honorary doctorships, and he has published besides his scientific papers, more than a score of substantial volumes.

Among the many books Professor Sorokin has written are: *Leaves from A Russian Diary (1924); Sociology of Revolution (1925); Social Mobility (1926); Contemporary Sociological Theories (1928); Social and Cultural Dynamics (4 vols., 1937–41); Crisis of Our Age (1941); Man and Society in Calamity (1942); Russia and the United States (1944); Society, Culture, and Personality (1947); Reconstruction of Humanity (1948); Social Philosophies of An Age of Crisis (1950); The Ways and Power of Love (1954); Fads and Foibles in Modern Sociology (1956); The American Sex Revolution (1957).*

SOCIAL AND CULTURAL DYNAMICS

The full force of Sorokin's findings in his Dynamics *must not be missed. They reveal that a scientific study of any culture leads one to a connected set of basic predominant premises from which all the different factors of that culture follow, exactly in the manner in which a scientific study of nature by the mathematical physicist leads to a connected set of theoretical principles.* F. S. C. NORTHROP

Sorokin had experienced immense history and brought to sociology the historical perspective so widely neglected by the surveyors of contemporary scenes. CHARLES A. and MARY R. BEARD

Professor Sorokin's large and encyclopedic volume will certainly repay the reader for the efforts involved in studying these pages crammed with the results of years of patient and thoughtful research. He writes a very readable and graceful style. Even those who disagree with his evaluations and prognostics will be profoundly impressed by the depth and earnestness of his searching, by the range of his scholarship, and by the brilliance of many of his illuminating sentences. HANS KOHN

The comparative historical study of the various stages in Western civilization in Professor Sorokin's hands turns out to be the most brilliant tool any sociologist has employed. CHARLES E. ELLWOOD

Sociology in the grand manner; perhaps its grandest so far. The title might have been 'What the educated man should know about civilization' or 'Civilization — its ups and downs'. FRANK KNIGHT

Dynamics *gives new and striking theories about historical change and the development and decay of human societies. Sorokin's great and solid achievements provide more than a new approach to the explanation and understanding of past days and vanished civilization. His work also offers a new basis for the study of sociology.* F. R. COWELL

St. Augustine, St. Thomas Aquinas, or John Wesley did not write more lucidly than Sorokin, since his thinking is in every way as provocative and pivotal as theirs. While more inclusive, it cannot be said that he has written less significantly. A titan, Sorokin has not yet reached the average man, or even the average college professor. DAVID W. SOPER

It is impossible to oppose prevalent theories of a generation without calling forth a vivid reaction. However, even the critics cannot fail to grant an enormous erudition of Sorokin's stupendous explanation of his preparatory researches, brilliant logic of his deductions, frank sincerity, independence and originality of his mind and finally, ardent good will of his enthusiastic soul. L. DECHESNE

Unlike many 'philosophies of history' that have been evolved from the inner consciousness by processes of deduction, this survey is constructed by induction from the facts. Apparently, it is as free as possible from the influence of prejudice or predilection. It would be difficult to avoid the conclusion that the findings of this great work do help us to understand more clearly the historic position and characteristic coloring of our time.
KARL T. COMPTON

Sorokin's magnum opus is a new philosophy of history. Rare indeed are the contributions that equal his in scope and importance, and for years to come it will serve the student of the philosophy of history as a source and a guide. THEODORE ABEL

As yet the only thorough and consistent effort to integrate all *special cultural science into a general theory of culture is that of Sorokin. It is certainly superior to all philosophies of culture developed by his predecessors, including Hegel, Comte, Spencer, Pareto, Toynbee and others.*
F. ZNANIECKI

In comparison with Sorokin's great work, the works of Comte, Spencer, Pareto, and Spengler appear to be arbitrary and fanciful. L. von WIESE

Publication of the monumental Dynamics *marks a great turning point in the history of social thought.* G. DYKMAN